Headgear of Hitler's Germany

Vol. 3: Hitler · NSDAP · Political Leaders · NS-Frauenschaft · DAF · SA

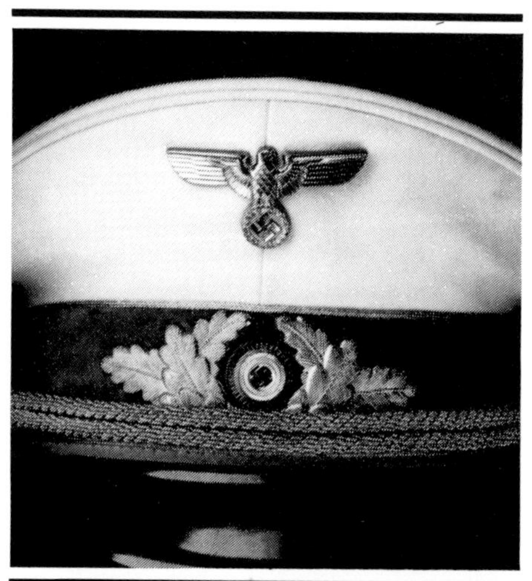

Wilhelm P.B.R. Saris
and Jill Halcomb Smith
with Otto Spronk

1st Edition

Published by R. James Bender Publishing,
P.O. Box 23456, San Jose, California 95153
Phone: (408) 225-5777
Fax: (408) 225-4739

Designed by Roger James Bender
Cover photo by Jack Christiansen, cap
courtesy of Richard Horton Collection

Printed in the United States of America

ISBN No. 0-912138-72-6

Contents

Acknowledgements

The continuation of this series on headgear was delayed because of the availability of masses of new information found in various archives throughout Germany. Thousands of pages had to be read and translated, which proved to be difficult in cases, because of the technical aspects of the material, plus the understanding of the political functions and systems.

In 1992 the text of this volume was close to completion, but due to the above-mentioned material, it was necessary to rewrite almost all of the chapters to avoid a later, large addendum. It was also felt by the authors that this had to be done as a service to you, the collector and historian. And even as this new re-write was close to completion, much new information was discovered on the Reichsautozug "Deutschland" which we felt had to be included. We hope that the results of our work, which you now find in your hands, will meet with your satisfaction.

Another problem which arose was the lack of illustrative photo material to support the newly expanded chapters. In some chapters we wanted photographic evidence to back up some of our new textual finds...in some cases we succeeded, and in others we did not. Those of you who have done your own research know that it can be very difficult to find hundreds of photos of organizations whose existence was hardly known. But in this close-knit collectors' community many individuals came forward with excellent and rare photographic material, thus, resolving many of the problems we had. We have to especially thank Otto Spronk from Rosmalen, who was of immense help by opening his vast photo files, and Renske Smits (from the Netherlands), who guided the authors towards the finished product you have in hand. We are particularly thankful to Klaus D. Patzwall, Frau Spencker, Frau Bertram, and their employees in Germany. The material in their archives was of great help in filling our needs. We would also like to thank Frau Hilde Steppe and Frau Margarete Winter, both from Germany, as well as Michael C. Shaner from St. Louis, Missouri, for providing the detailed information on the NS-Schwesternschaft and the other nurses leagues. Ed Stadnicki was invaluable with his assistance in various fields, especially the SA. The reader will probably understand the difficulties the authors had with both the SA and the DAF when reading the complex footnotes related to these two chapters.

Additionally, we would like to thank "Ulric of England" for his photographic assistance, Peter Klubert of Germany, Rolf Halfen from Düsseldorf in Germany, and a Dutch SA collector, Hans van Diggelen, who supplied us with new, unknown collector contacts. We wish to express our gratitude to Peter Coleman of Australia who gave us access to his beautiful photos, published in this volume and future ones in the series. One person who we cannot forget is Frau Stockinger from the Munich city library "Monacensia." Through her assistance we were able to locate the wonderful photos on the Reichsautozug. A. Stam was also most generous with his photo files and they are used profusely thoughout this volume.

Our deepest regards and thanks, however, go to Stan Cook, who did such a tremendous job of editing and rewriting where needed. He worked on the project for many months, and without his assistance Volume 3 would have had an even longer delay. Our special recognition and heartfelt thanks are extended for his unselfish efforts.

There are, of course, many individuals who assisted this project in many ways and our thanks and gratitude also goes to them. They are listed alphabetically. These collectors and historians helped us with subject matter for all the organizations covered, and it is their combined efforts which have made this volume a "feast for the eye" with all its uniqe illustrations and in-depth information. Hopefully, the coming years will give us and Mr. Roger James Bender, our most patient publisher, the health to continue this massive project. We have hundreds and hundreds of never-before-published photos which are awaiting their appearance in future volumes.

For the first time in this series, the authors have added pertinent documents and portions of regulations which, normally, the readers and collectors do not have access to. This is done as an added learning tool and as evidence of some of the statements made. These inclusions will be a part of each of the future volumes in the series.

W.P.B.R. Saris
Jill Halcomb Smith

Individuals and Institutions:

L. van Aerle
Amann & Söhne, Germany
E. Angermair
Tim Alexander
J.R. Angolia
Army Museum, Brussels
E. John Bagale
Bayerisches Hauptstaatsarchiv, München
Bayerische Staatsbibliothek, München
Klaus D. Benseler
Robert Bernard
Bibliothek für Zeitgeschichte, München
Markus Bodeux
J.G. Bornebroek
James J. Boulton
E. Bouwmeester
Dr. Braun
Chris Bruner
Bundesarchiv Koblenz and Potsdam
Heinz Buntenbach
Peter Bürkner
Francis Catella
Len Champion
Jean-Pierre Chantrain
Derek Chapman
Josef Charita
C. Cornelissen
Nigel Cox
John Coy
Adolf de Crousaz
Gregory Currie
Brian L. Davis
Clyde R. Davis
Richard Deeter
David Delich
D. Deuster
Deutsche Bücherei/Bibliothek, Frankfurt

Deutsche Lufthansa,
Köln
W. Deutschmann
B. Diroll
Rudie Dolfin
Jerry Drake
Mrs. Eichel
Alfred Ex
Richard de Filippi
J. Floch
Hartwig Friedrich
Carl Fromann
Paul Geers
Philippe Gillain
G. Gregoire
Jeff Hansen
W. Hartmann
Herman Heikamp
Arie Hendrikx
Mr. Heyne
Mr. Hoover
Dr. R. Horn
Iveco-Magirus AG, Ulm
G. Innes
Jay Jeandron
Edwin Johnson
Thomas M. Johnson
Jan de Jonge
Richard Kindel
Jim King
T. Knight
Mrs. Kuhl
Dr. J.H. Kumpf
Ron Kwan
Library of Congress,
Washington D.C.
R. LaRue Curren
Dr. Lauchs
David Littlejohn
Mr. Loop
Luftfahrt Museum Köln-
Butzweiler Hof e.V.
Jess Lukens
Niall Malcolm
Ron Manion
Mrs. Maerten
Robert McCarthy
Wayne Milburn
Hermann Miller
Museum Dec. '44, La Gleize
National Archives,
Washington, DC
Navorsingsinstituut, Brussels
Bendt Nielsen
A. Obermeier
Warren Odegard
P. Pauwels
George Petersen
Martijn Pot
Dr. H-P. Rasp
Mrs. Rastenhofer
Bill Rentz
Pieter Roelse
Mr. Roeske
Gerhard Rudloff
Rijksinstituut vor
Oorlogsdokumentatie
(RIOD), Amsterdam
Joe Salas
Dr. Saupe
Dr. E. Schipper
Oskar Schönweitz
Arie Schouten
Carlton Schwab
Mr. Schwarz
Frans Sellenslagh
Helga Sichermann-Spielhagen
René Smeets
Andy Southard
Staatsarchiv, München
Staatsbibliothek zu Berlin,
Preuss. Kulturbesitz
O. Stengel
Stadtarchiv, Mönchengladbach
Stadtarchiv, München
Roger S. Steffen
Joe Stone
Art Sylvie
Alain Taugourdeau
Robert J. Theige
Bob Treend
C. Gary Triggs

Richard Valdez
Robert Velsir
W. Walker
Bernd Wedeking
Mrs. Wehmeyer
Helmut Weitze
B. Weyerer
S. Wisniewski
Steve Wolfe/Neil Hardin

The authors and publisher wish to express their deep sympathy to the family of Ed Stadnicki. Ed was a leading force in our hobby and he will be missed by all.

CHAPTER

1

Adolf Hitler

FÜHRER UND KANZLER DES DEUTSCHEN REICHES
LEADER AND CHANCELLOR OF THE GERMAN REICH

In January 1919 the "Deutsche Arbeiterpartei," originally known as the "Deutscher Arbeiterverein," was created. It was a nationalistic, right–wing organization. Adolf Hitler joined the Party in September 1919 quickly becoming its chief spokesman and later the propaganda leader. So started the history of this Nazi organization.[1]

In 1920 this political organization was renamed the "Nationalsozialistische Deutsche Arbeiterpartei" (NSDAP) and in 1921 Hitler became the president of the Party after an internal election.

At the beginning of his political career, Hitler did not want to be photographed: It was his idea that, if he was not portrayed in newspapers and periodicals, then the press would concentrate on his political ideas and the public would become more curious. "Who was this Hitler and what did he look like?"

Heinrich Hoffmann (the Matthew Brady of his time) received a request for a photo of the rather obscure Austrian–turned–Bavarian politician from the Associated Press. Hoffmann would be paid $1,000.00 for this photograph. Several attempts to get a shot of this "Hitler" failed, due to his guards, who knocked the camera from Hoffman's hands. Hoffmann was finally able to get a photo without the guards seeing him. Hitler had seen him, however, and he went to Hoffmann who spontaneously destroyed the photo. Conversly, this meeting marked the beginning of a long friendship between the two men. Heinrich Hoffmann became the sole proprietor of official Hitler photographs and a millionaire in the process.

During the years 1920 through 1945 Hitler wore various forms of headdress, beginning with a civilian, wide–brimmed fedora. It was not until early 1926 that he began wearing what was later known as the "Hitlermütze." This cap resembled a ski cap without a leather chin strap, but with a cloth covered visor. In the same year he started wearing this cap with a chin strap. A colored button secured the center of the cap flaps. (It must be noted that this form of headdress was not a specific item for the Nazis only: Members and leaders in

[1] *"Daten und Geschichte der NSDAP." Berlin: 11.Auflage 1943. Section II: Die Vorgeschichte der NSDAP, p.4 and section III: Die NSDAP von 1919 bis 1923, pp.5–6.*

Above: Hitler holds a fedora during German Day in Nuremberg (September 1/2, 1923).

the districts Braunschweig and Hannover from the Stahlhelm–organization also wore light brown caps in this form earlier than 1924).[2]

Hitler during a cross-country propaganda trip in 1923.

[2] *"Stahlhelm, Erinnerungen und Bilder," 1932. Chapter: "Symbole und Tracht des Bundes," p. 171 also "Fünfzehn Jahre Stahlhelm in Niedersachsen," 1936: Gau Braunschweig, their leaders in 1924, p. 10 and Gau Süd–Hannover, consecrating flags at Ostenrode in 1924, p. 89.*

In 1926 Hitler was first seen wearing the SA style coffee can cap made of tan material, as was used in making the SA brown shirt. A brown leather chin strap was worn above the cloth covered visor; the flap was secured with what appeared to be a dark brown, leather button. The edge of the flap, as well as the crown, seem to have been piped (probably in gold). At the end of the 1920's Hitler was wearing this form of headdress without any insignia or piping. Photographs show that he preferred to wear several forms of the leather "flight cap" during airplane and car trips.

Otto Spronk

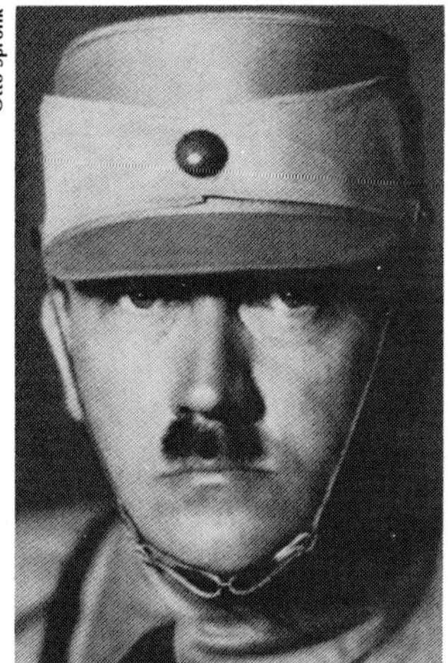

Hitler wears a SA kepi in the style of late 1926-1927. This version had a leather button and chin strap.

Hitler holds his modified "coffee can" cap during the 1929 Parteitage.

Otto Spronk

Hitler wears a SA kepi in 1926. Note this so-called "Hitlermütze" is without a chin strap.

Otto Spronk

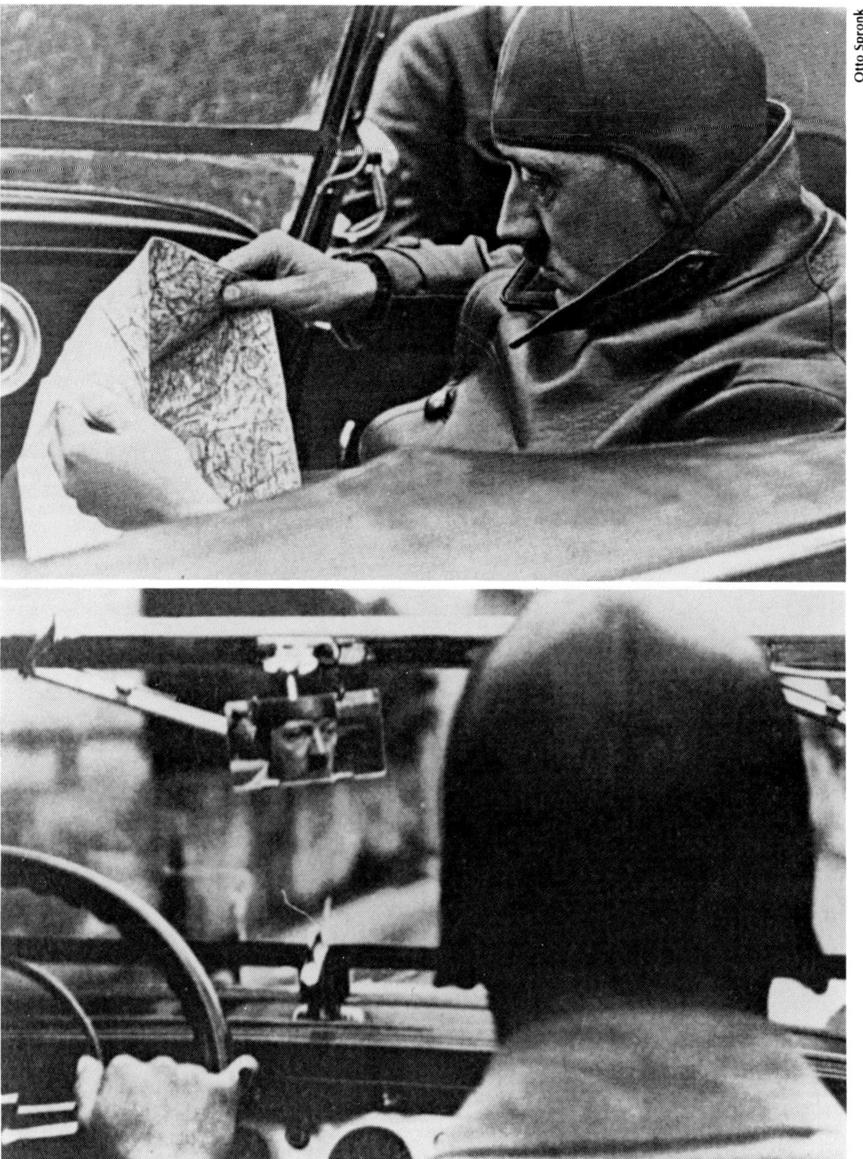

Two occasions when Hitler wore the "flying cap" during an auto trip. Note the bottom photo which shows the cut of the helmet on his forehead in the mirror.

Hitler began wearing a visored cap sometime in 1933. One of the earliest had a tan cloth top, like that worn by political leaders, with a medium brown velvet cap band. The dark brown leather visor had no outer raised edge. Gold cap cords with a center knot were worn above this. The reason for the center knot is not known, but possibly reflected the cap cords as worn by the Party's political leaders at that time. The top of Hitler's cap was piped in heavy gold cord; the cap band was piped in white at the upper and lower edge. It should be noted that at this time Hitler was the only person within the Party system al-

Hitler wears a visored cap of the 1934 style with the small political eagle. Note he does not wear a cockade on the cap band and that the cap cord has one knot in the center.

Jill Halcomb Smith

Otto Spronk

Here, Hitler wears the same form of visored cap but with a cap cord without knot and a hand-embroidered national emblem.

lowed to wear a national emblem in gold. Political leaders were not allowed to wear a golden eagle earlier than spring 1939 (see also chapter: Politische Leiter der NSDAP).[3] Most of the early metal eagles have a black painted swastika. It has not been established if Hitler actually wore the eagle in gold, his position would assume that he did. Between 1932 and the fall of 1934 he denied others the right to wear the national emblem in gold. Viktor Lutze received permission to wear the gold national emblem in September 1934.[4]

Hitler wore this form of visored cap until at least early 1938, but with the addition of golden cap cords without the center knot. The early style national emblem was replaced by another version (a metal form has been observed). This style national emblem was hand–embroidered in silver directly to the top front

---

3 "Die Uniformen der Braunhemden." Freiherr von Eelking. Berlin; March 1934, p. 38: describes it as being in gold. It literally says in German: "In Gold trägt das Hoheitszeichen nur Adolf Hitler."

4 "Verordnungsblatt der Obersten SA–Führung," Nr. 33. München: September 10, 1934, p. 2: Nr. 6: National Emblem "Stabschef." It is especially noted that all others of the SA had to wear silver.

Hitler, while at Neuschwanstein in 1934, hold his cap as described at left. Note that it is soft-bodied and crushable.

Upper right: Hitler is shown in 1935 wearing the 1934 style cap, still with a metal national emblem and without the knot on the cap cord. This cap is unique in that the leather visor appears to be a light brown.

An early Hitler visored cap with heavy gold cord piping around the crown and white piping on the top and bottom of the cap band. The national emblem is silver wire, hand-embroidered on tan. The top is tan, the cap band is medium brown and the visor is dark brown. The manufacturer was Holters of Berlin.

of Hitler's cap. Photographs often do show a later gilt bullion wire version, but period photographs seem also to show at times the silver form. The gilt cap cords were held in place by silver pebbled buttons.

During his visit to Italy in May 1938 Hitler wore a specially designed uniform which had a visored cap in the style worn by army generals, but brown in color. The visor of this cap was Havana–brown leather without the raised rim. The cap band was somewhat wider than normal, and of rust–brown velvet.[5] A metal national cockade was secured to the band's center, surrounded by a thin, gilt army–style wreath. This wreath was probably of metal at first and shortly thereafter replaced by a hand–embroidered version. The hand–embroidered na-

Hitler during the state visit to Italy in May 1938.

Mussolini, von Ribbentrop, Hitler, Ciano, Goebbels and King Victor Emanuel in Italy, May 1938.

tional emblem was of the form worn since approximately 1936. The cap band was piped in white as earlier; the crown was piped with an approx. 4mm wide golden cord.

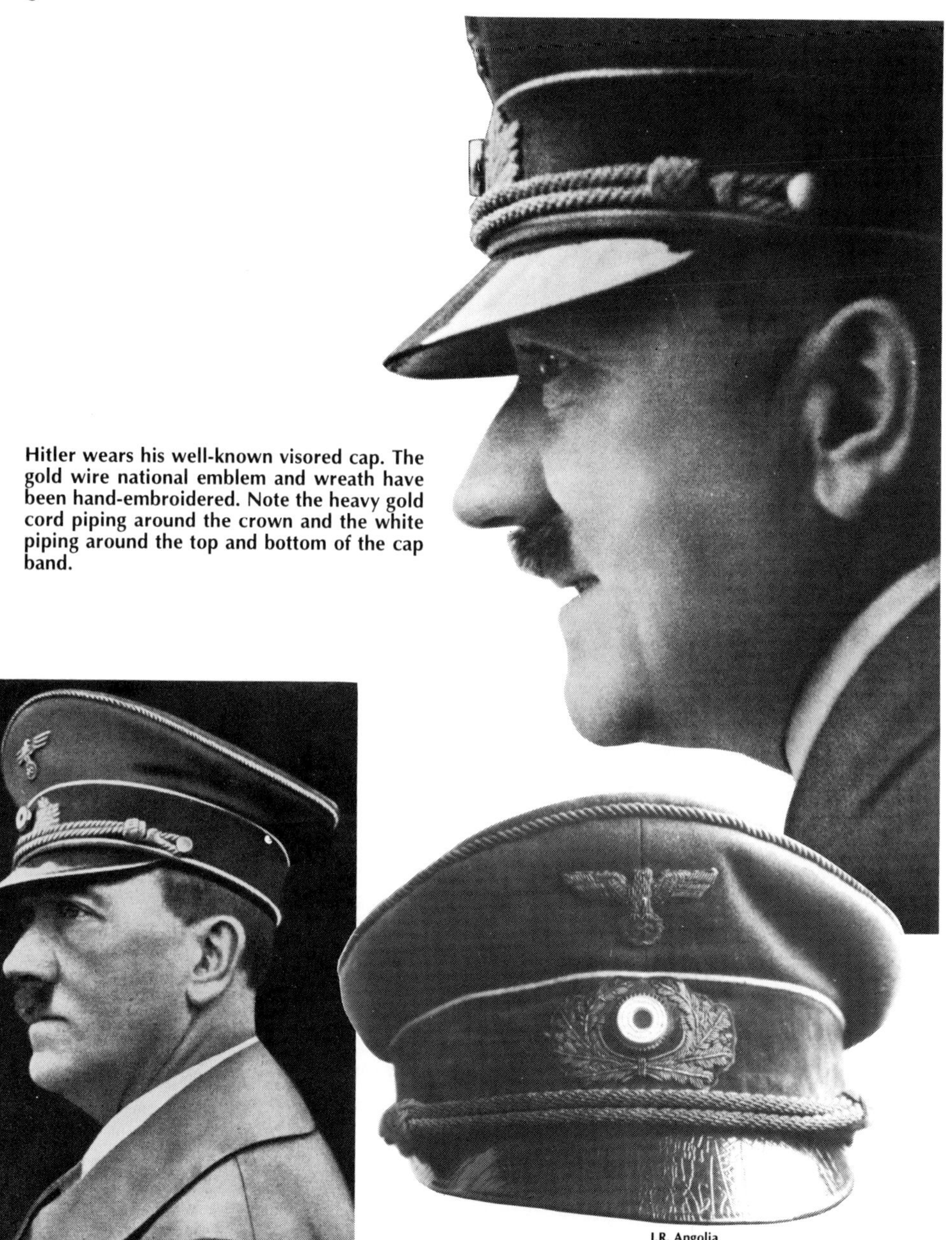

Hitler wears his well-known visored cap. The gold wire national emblem and wreath have been hand-embroidered. Note the heavy gold cord piping around the crown and the white piping around the top and bottom of the cap band.

J.R. Angolia

In the summer of 1939 the color of Hitler's "saddle" form visored cap was changed to a darker greenish field–grey and the pebbled cap cord buttons were

[5] *"Uniformen–Markt," Nr. 10. May 15, 1938, p. 151.*

in gold. The color of the cap band was somewhat darker than the version worn earlier. The metal cockade was surrounded by a hand–embroidered gilt wreath in a modified form.[6]

Otto Spronk

Deutsche Luftha

Left: Hitler's visored cap on the phone table in his private quarters of the Reich Chancellery. Right: The Führer wears his visored cap with gold cap cord and lighter (silver) side buttons. Note the thick, gold crown piping and the two white pipings on the cap band. The oakleaf wreath is the hand-embroidered form.

Other visored caps in "Teller" or "Sattel" form were also worn by Adolf Hitler, varying in several shades. The exact number of caps owned by him is not known, but could be small in number due to his "style" or because he hated to wear the coffee can cap or visored cap (he disliked the marks caused by the pinching of the inner band on his forehead). Sometimes he wore a cap to suit the occasion, such as the DAF–Walter (DAF official) cap he wore while he was aboard cruise ships of the "Kraft durch Freude" movement. He also occasionally wore a white topped visored cap in his special design.

A series of photographs shown, illustrates the various known forms of headdress as worn by Hitler, beginning in 1916 while he served at the front during World War I. We also have proof that he did wear the SA–style coffee can cap on

---

[6] *Ibid, Nr. 18, September 15, 1939, p. 279.*

Left: Hitler aboard the KdF ship *Robert Ley* wearing the visored cap as used by DAF funtionaries with the addition of the 1936 national emblem. Right: On another occasion he wears a similar cap but with a wide-winged national emblem.

National Archives

Right: Hitler is shown wearing a white-topped visored cap. The crown is piped with gold cord. The fate of this unique piece is currently unknown.

The famous Holters logo on the sweat diamond in Hitler's visored cap is clearly evident in this photo.

James J. Boulton

Count Ciano and Hitler, wearing his white-topped visored cap, at the Berghof.

more than one occasion. The fate of Hitler's caps, with the exception of some in collections in the United States, remains a "mystery." One can only speculate, for example, about the fate of the early coffee can or the late war field–grey visored cap. Were they destroyed during the last days of the war? Or were they "liberated" and still exist in an unknown collection or even "stored" in some attic in Europe or the States.

Otto Spronk

Hitler during the presentation of a Grand Admiral's baton. Note he wears the brown-topped visored cap.

Otto Spronk

Otto Spronk

Left: Hitler wears the "Krätschen" in 1916. Note the cockade on the upper part of the cap and the Imperial insigne on the lowest cap edge. Right: This photo from Hitler's weapons permit shows him wearing the enlisted man's style visored cap in 1919.

Note the form of headdress worn by Hitler at Bayreuth in 1926.

Otto Spronk

Otto Spronk

Hitler wears a visored cap in the approximate 1934 style with a small political eagle. Note he does not have a cockade on his cap band and that his cap cord has one knot in the center.

Otto Spronk

Hitler and Göring use their cap cords to prevent their caps from being blown off. The occasion is an air show on the coast of Vor-Pommern.

Otto Spronk

Robert Ley, Hitler and von Ribbentrop during a 1939 event. Note that Hitler is wearing the "Tellerform" visored cap, and that Ley is already wearing the new style eagle and oakleaf wreath. The other political leaders are still wearing the cockade on the cap band and the 1936 style eagle.

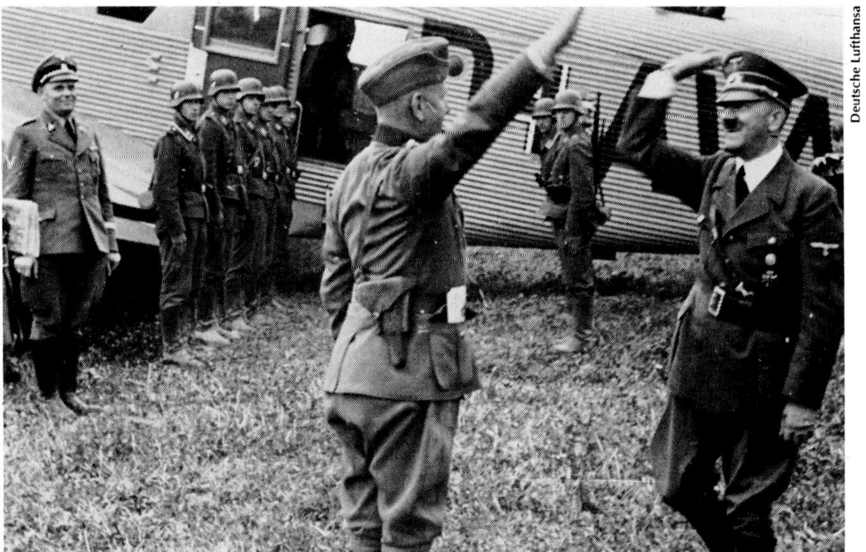
Deutsche Lufthansa

Hitler visits the German front wearing one of the last versions of his visored cap. At far left is Hans Bauer, Hitler's personal pilot, who wears his SS uniform.

Otto Spronk

Otto Spronk

Left: Hitler wears the visored cap with a darker field-grey top. Note the difference of color of the cap band and visor. Right: Hitler wears another form of visored cap. Note the gold color of the crown piping and insignia (eagle, wreath and cap cords), the regular national cockade, and the white piping of the cap band. Also note the reddish-brown of the cap band and the Havanna-brown visor.

CHAPTER

2

Nationalsozialistische Deutsche Arbeiterpartei (NSDAP)

Founded in 1919 as the "Deutsche Arbeiterpartei," and after March 4, 1920, known as the "Nat.Soz.Deutsche Arbeiterpartei," there was created for this political organization and her associated groups diverse uniforms that would through the following years, vary in so many styles and types up to the wars end in 1945 that it would be safe to say that the world will probably never again see its equal.

In the first years of the parties existence, the most fanatic and militaristic members of the Nazi Party adopted various forms of headdress that were being

National Archives

Early NSDAP members wearing various forms of headgear. Note the wearing of the swastika on the cap band in the foreground. The individual next to him wears the Edelweiss on the traditional, mountain-climber's hat.

worn during that period in Germany. These many forms of headdress included visored caps in the regular military styles, skiing caps in various shades and colors, as well as the German steel helmet. Often a unique insigne was attached or painted on the headdress, consisting of death's heads, swastikas or old military devices. The swastika and death head were not used exclusively by the national socialists in the early years after World War I.

Otto Spronk

A gathering of the first Nazis, in Unterfranken in 1920, wearing various forms of headgear. Note that several members are already wearing a cap which later became known as the "Hitlermütze."

The alliance with the SA (officially instituted August 2, 1921) and other right–wing organizations (often later absorbed within the SA) was so close that it is sometimes very difficult to distinguish between friend or foe, or even be-

Otto Spronk

During the preparations for the 1923 "Putsch" several styles of headgear are worn by these right-wing, national socialists. Note the diamond-shaped insigne on the left side of the black ski caps, probably with an Edelweiss design. The individuals photographed are Bund-Oberland members.

tween various members of the NSDAP (having leadership functions, but not having membership in the SA) or the SA. In the late 1920's dress regulations were separated from those of the SA but for those persons within the Party–system having leadership functions or in high positions the old SA form of uniform were simply adopted.

This confusing situation would come an end in 1932/33 when special uniform and insignia were created for political leaders of the NSDAP. Before this it was usually not possible to tell with 100% certainty (when Party insignia, often un-officially, was worn for example with the headdress) if a person was a member of the NSDAP or SA. It is certain that during the years 1921 through 1925 almost anything was worn and in fact hardly any regulations were in effect; the years 1925/1926 would bring about the true beginning of some permanent changes.

Otto Spronk

This photograph, dated March 1924, was taken during the Sudetendeutschen March festivities in Vienna, Austria. Note the early style caps worn by these members of the Austrian Nazi Party with cockades and Party insignia.

In cases where presumed authentic photographs are not supplied with reliable documentation (even such documentation must be carefully checked and verified as it can many times itself not be reliable at all) or the photographs are acquired from a source that is possibly not reliable, it is very difficult to give an accurate estimate of their true nature or accuracy.

It should be noted that NSDAP members, when wearing the SA type cap during 1926, were not allowed to wear the silvered buttons on the front of the flap. These buttons were only allowed for wear by members of the SA. This rule was not changed until the early 1930s[1] . (for more information see the chapters: Der Pol.Leiter der NSDAP, as well as Sturmabteilungen der NSDAP – both

---

[1] SA-Befehl (SABE) Nr. 10 Sturmf. (OSAF), dated November 14, 1926, Nr. 1; Also GRUSA V.OSAF, dated July 30, 1930.

within this volume). From then on, the wearing of a uniform for political leaders, the SA (as well as SS, NSKK or HJ) was allowed for NSDAP members, if this person was a member of any of the above mentioned formations. If not a member he was only allowed to wear the Party badge with civilian cloths or after two years of membership a brown shirt with his civilian dress[2].

Uniform for Wearer's of the Blood Order (Uniform der Blutordenträger)

In 1937 another confusing situation was created when the special uniform for holders of the Blood Order (Blutordenträger) was authorized. A special office (Amt für den 8./9. November 1923) had to supply all wearers of the Blood Order (with the exception of uniformed members from the Armed Forces, the German police and some unknown others) with this special uniform. This actually means that this uniform was in fact worn only by early SA members, members of the earlier "Reichskriegsflagge" and "Bund Oberland": in total a very limited number of persons, probably not over 250.

A sample of the early "Hitlermütze" (Model 1923). The flaps have two small buttons and a national cockade is positioned on the front top.

Ulric of England

Otto Spronk

Josef Goebbels at a NSDAP meeting in 1926. Note the earliest type of uniforms and so-called "Hitlermütze" being worn. At left the cockade is on the cap top. This individual also wears his "old army" brocade belt and buckle.

---

[2] *Organisationsbuch der NSDAP. München, 1936. Section 1: Der Parteigenosse, p. 9.*

This special uniform was only allowed to be worn for the first time in 1937 at events held during the commemoration of 8 and 9 November. It consisted of a windbreaker (the form as worn during the early period of struggle "Die Kampfjahre") and the grey "SA–Mütze," known as the Model–1923[3]. With the outbreak of war in 1939 this special uniform was no longer worn during the November activities. No evidence has been found showing its wear during the later years of the war.

Navorsingsinstituut Brussel

Members of the NSDAP during the memorial service at the Feldherrnhalle in Munich on November 9, 1937. Note the wind-jacket and early form "Hitlermütze" with the earliest form of political eagle, as authorized for the "wearers of the Blood Order."

Otto Spronk

Victims of the failed bomb attempt by Georg Elsner, laying in state before the Feldherrnhalle in Munich (November 1939). Note the wind-jacket uniform authorized for "wearers of the Blood Order." This type of photograph, when not properly dated, could cause confusion and be put into the wrong time period.

[3] *Uniformen-Markt, Nr. 22. November 16, 1937, p. 338.*

CHAPTER

3

Politische Leiter der NSDAP

POLITICAL LEADERS OF THE NSDAP

The development of the uniform for political leaders of the NSDAP began in 1929 after a further organization and expansion of the Party and its establishment in all of Germany. In addition to Department I (Organisationsabteilung I), Hitler created during 1929 Department II, which was meant to organize the political Party for the coming national socialist state in Germany.[1] On January 1, 1929 the so–called "Zeugmeistereien" (sections that managed the issuing of materials and uniforms) were first created to govern the supplies of the SA and SS.[2] In July 1931 six of these departments existed, including the Austrian section, known as "Vaterländischer Schutzbund"; by 1932, eleven had been established.[3]

The final development of Party uniforms was delayed by internal, as well as external problems such as the "Uniformverbot," the government ban placed on the wearing of uniforms during the years 1930–1932. The prohibition of the SA and SS in 1932 caused a delay in the design and procurement of a final, official, unique uniform for NSDAP officials (Amtsleiter or persons having duties in a department) which was not introduced until late summer of 1932. In June of that year the political organization of the NSDAP was unified and on July 15th, initial dress–regulations for the PO (Politische Organisation, an abbreviation which was abolished by Rudolf Hess in July 1935[4]) were first published, during an "Uniformverbot" in effect April 17 through July 24, when the ranking system was also announced.[5]

---

1 *"Das Dritte Reich: Die Kampfjahre 1918–1933." Berlin: 1936, p. 159.*

2 *"Uniformen–Markt," Nr. 13. July 1, 1937, p. 199.*

3 *"Verordnungsblatt der Reichsleitung der Nationalsozialistischen Deutschen Arbeiterpartei" (further referred as Vbl.d.RL.d.NSDAP), Nr. 4. München: July 26, 1931. Announcement from the Reichsschatzmeister Schwarz, dated July 10, 1931, p. 9. (April 1, 1933 the Zeugmeistereien were disbanded, and the Reichszeugmeisterei was created in their place).*

4 *"Daten der Geschichte der NSDAP," 11. Auflage. Section V: Die NSDAP von 1925 bis 1933. Berlin/Leipzig: 1943, p. 45.*

5 *"Entwurf–Dienstvorschrift für die PO der NSDAP," authorized July 15, 1932. The numbers 160 through 180 give exact descriptions, pp.51–55. Section: Dienstanzug der Amtswalter der NSDAP.*

Otto Spronk

A very early photograph of an NSDAP–Party member, wearing the so–called "Hitler-mütze" having the Party badge on the center of the top front.

Otto Spronk

A photograph dated 1927 showing members of the NSDAP (in the middle are Daluege and Goebbels), wearing various forms of headdress. The original caption reads: "The leaders from Berlin." It is obvious that in those days uniforms were seldom worn and hardly any difference existed between NSDAP organizations, other than the SS wearing the black kepi.

Eventualy, corrections for this 1932 regulation came from the "Landes– und Reichsinspektionen" (National Inspections) prior to October 1, 1932.[6] (Some smaller corrections relating to the uniforms, etc. had already been made). The wearing of this transitional uniform by the PO had started, its "final" form was authorized by Hitler on January 20, 1934.[7]

Upon the appointment of Dr. Robert Ley as "Stabsleiter der PO" (staff leader of the political organization), December 15, 1932, he made it official that political leaders were to be easily recognized by their uniforms.

National Emblem (Hoheitszeichen) 1931 – 1945

The first designs for the eagle came from Hitler himself, assisted by Otto Gahr, a Munich goldsmith. Gahr worked out Hitler's sketches and produced the first eagles in his house on the Mariannestrasse.

The first national emblem (known as the "Adler–Kokarde," the symbol of the Party[8] worn by political leaders in 1931 was the silver Model 1927 eagle, with wings outstretched, the head facing to its left. The eagle clutched an oak leaf wreath in its talons. A canted, embossed black painted swastika was within the wreath. This eagle was also worn by members of the SA and SS. The wingspan of the national emblem varied from 37 to 39mm, its height being approximately 28mm. Various early forms do exist (Assmann Nr.20469, but in addition, the smaller versions Nr.20640 and Nr.33983 were used until 1933). This insigne was manufactured in silvered "neusilber," a nickel alloy, silvered brass or tombak (an alloy, used to imitate gold). It must be noted that specimens of this eagle having vaulted wings, as well as those with straight wings exist.

James Boulton

Left: The earliest style national emblem (with recessed swastika) as worn in the center of the top of the political SA–style cap, also worn with the first versions of the visored cap. Right: The 1934 introduced political eagle emblem as worn with the visored caps until late 1936 and even later.

With the official introduction of the new uniforms in January 1934, a new and larger political eagle was introduced. It resembled the old form, but the ends of the wings were now pointed. The always straight wingspan was approximately 49mm, its height being approximately 33–35mm. The field behind the swastika itself being silver (Assmann Nr.22347). The manufacturing procedures were as for the first model. This eagle was positioned on the front of the visored cap, partly upon the band and partly on the top. The part with the swastika was positioned on the band, the lowest part of the wings resting upon the upper band

---

6 *"Vbl.d.RL.d.NSDAP," Nr. 32. September 1932. Decree Nr. 7, signed by Strasser and dated September 17, pp. 73–74.*

7 *Ibid, Nr.64. January 31, 1934. Announcement from the Oberste Leitung der PO 1/34 and decree from Hitler January 20, 1934, pp. 141–142.*

8 *Befehl Nr.2, Schutzstaffel–Oberleitung. München: November 4, 1927. Par. 4.*

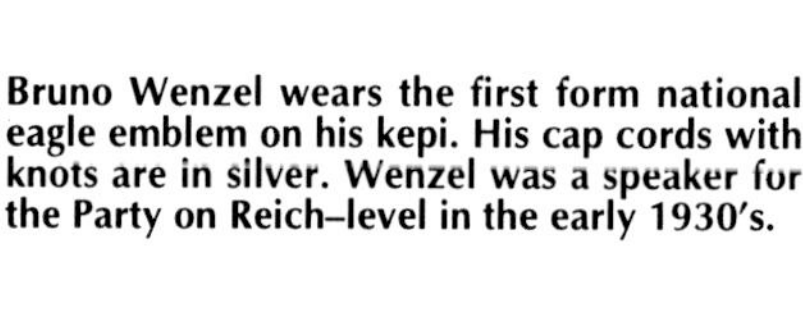
Bruno Wenzel wears the first form national eagle emblem on his kepi. His cap cords with knots are in silver. Wenzel was a speaker for the Party on Reich–level in the early 1930's.

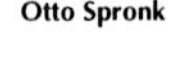
Otto Spronk

A political leader on Kreis–level, indicated by the black top piping, is wearing his visored cap in the 1934 form, in accordance with the new regulations placing the eagle emblem partly upon the cap band. From May 5, 1934, the eagle had to be positioned 10mm above the upper band piping.

piping. The outstretched wings were positioned upon the lowest part of the top.[9] An order from Ley on May 5, 1934 changed the eagle's position to: 10mm above the upper cap band piping (so that it rested entirely upon the lower portion of the top).[10]

W.P.B.R. Saris

P.O.-Hoheitsabzeichen für Mütze

Drawing from the "Mitteilungsblatt der Reichszeugmeisterei" of the 1934 form national eagle emblem.

A. Stam

Political leaders and Allgemeine–SS members are waiting for the Leibstandarte Adolf Hitler, visiting Mönchengladbach, July 13, 1934. The person in the foreground is a Kreisleiter. Note the wearing of his national emblem. Officially he should have already worn this emblem 10 mm above the cap band. The political leaders standing in the background do wear the eagle as ordered.

SA–Stabschef Viktor Lutze and "Stellvertretender Gauleiter" Görlitzer, photographed in late 1934. Note that Görlitzer is wearing the 1934–eagle emblem in the front center of the top. The political leader behind him is still wearing his emblem partly on the cap band. Very interesting in this photograph is that Lutze is wearing his first form collar tab, devoid of the ribbon at the base. A form that he would wear for many years.

Bundesarchiv

---

[9] *"Die Uniformen der Braunhemden" by Freiherr von Eelking. München, March 1, 1934. pp. 60–63.*

[10] *"Vbl.d.RL.d.NSDAP,"Nr.72. München: May 1934, p. 166*

The wearing of the 1934 version eagle and swastika cockade by an Ortsgruppenleiter. This photograph gives an excellent view of the "Teller" form shaped cap with low top and the cap–band in the same color as the top.

In early 1936 a new version political eagle was introduced. This modified form had wings which were no longer pointed, but resembled the 1937 pattern national emblem worn by SA members, but with a shorter wingspan. This wingspan was approximately 56mm, the height being 34mm (Assmann Nr.24430).[11] The eagle was made of aluminum or other light weight metals. The eagle's head faced its right.[12] The reverse had three pins.

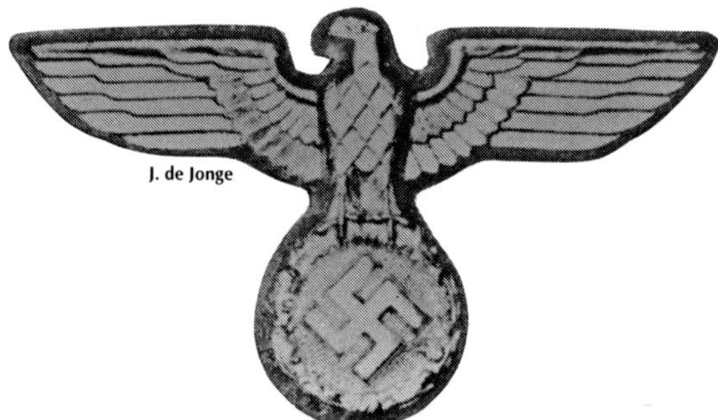

The national eagle emblem introduced in 1936 for political leaders, photographed from the Assmann–catalogue. Note the eagle's head looking to its right: Wingspan 56mm.

In a 1936 issue of the "Reichsgesetzblatt," a decree of March 7th stated that the eagle's head faced its right.[13] Manufacturer's began to make the 1936 model with eagle's heads facing both to the left and to the right, caused by con-

[11] *F.W. Assmann & Söhne, Lüdenscheid. Katalog, 1937: NSDAP–articles, p. 27 (text and picture pages).*

[12] *"Organisationsbuch der NSDAP. " München: 1936. (the picture page – Tafel 5); Ibid, 1937 (with this publication the picture page – Tafel 5 shows the eagle facing its left wing).*

Otto Spronk

Dr. Robert Ley during the "laying of the first stone" for the KdF–Seebad Rügen, May 2, 1936. All political leaders are still wearing the 1927 or 1934 model national eagle emblem. The man at the bald headed man's left is still wearing his national emblem, partly on the cap band, a position that officially had been forbidden since 1934. Note also the top hats worn by the bricklayers, their official traditional headdress during those years.

Gauleiter Carl Röver from Weser–Ems shown wearing the 1936 introduced to its right looking eagle, and the newly introduced swastika/cockade.

---

[13] *"Reichsgesetzblatt," Nr. 21. March 11, 1936, pp. 145–146.*

Otto Spronk

Reichsparteitag 1936. All political leaders are wearing the 1934–model national eagle emblem, in spite of the fact that a new form had been introduced. The wearing of the old version was a favorite during 1936, due to the squabbling about the position of the eagle's head; left or right.

Otto Spronk

Political leaders wearing their national emblem according to both the old and new regulations.

W. P.B.R. Saris

An early form army eagle from 1936 and 1937, often used as political eagle.

The 1937 form national emblem as published in the RZM.

Hoheitsabzeichen für die Mützen der Politischen Leiter

Die Herstellung von Hoheitsabzeichen für die Mützen der Politischen Leiter in goldfarbener Legierung ist verboten. Von sämtlichen Politischen Leitern wird das Hoheitsabzeichen nur in Silber-Ausführung getragen.

In the *Mbl.* from the RZM, dated February 1936, it was announced that the wear of a golden national emblem with the visored cap of the political leader was forbidden and silver was the only correct color.

fusion with the heraldic definition. (It should be noted that prior to April 1939 *all* political eagles had a silver finish. A gold finish was not allowed.[14])

The problem of the correct form of national emblem still existed in 1937 when Hitler's deputy, Rudolf Hess, officially decreed that the eagle which faced its right wing was allowed for wear.[15] From period photographs it is observed that the first model of national emblem was favored in 1936. In the spring of 1937 Hitler finally decided that, for the official national emblem of the Party and its organizations, the eagle's head must face its left wing, which is the opposite direction than the heads of national emblems worn by state organizations.[16]

The final form eagle was introduced in April 1939,[17] and was gilt in color (in fact the same national emblem as worn by the SA). The wingspan varied officially from 65–66mm, the height being approximately 32–33mm, and the size of the swastika being 7mm. Metal, as well as embroidered forms were permitted.

---

14 *"Mbl.d.RZM," Nr. 5. February 29, 1936. p. 72; Ibid, Nr. 15. July 15, 1936, p. 307.*

15 *"Rundschau–Deutsches Schneiderfachblatt," Nr. 46. München: November 13, 1937, p. 1657; "Mbl.d.RZM," Nr. 18. August 8, 1937, p. 227.*

16 *"Uniformen–Markt," Nr. 11. June 1, 1937, p. 170.*

17 *Ausführungsbestimmungen zur Verfügung des Führers. April 2, 1939. "Vbl.d.RL.d. NSDAP," Nr. 194. Mid–June 1939. Section VIII: given specific announcements of the regulations Nr. 20/39; Nr. 22/39 and Nr. 23/39.*

Wreath (Mützenkranz)
1939 – 1945

Simultaneously with the new 1939 eagle, a gold anodized oakleaf wreath was introduced and manufactured in several variations, some having a center plate to which the political cockade was fastened, while others were made without the plate. (It must be noted that manufacturing specifications for a wreath were available in late 1938, this was the DAF–form.[18]) Most of these wreaths were vaulted to fit the curvature of the cap band.

1939 national emblem and political leaders wreath, which was always gold in color.

Reverse of the wreath worn on the final pattern visored cap, showing the RZM control label.

The wreaths were mainly made of Cupal, an aluminum and brass sheet which was heated to 560° and rolled out by a machine. But they also existed in five different qualities, being stamped of aluminum or other light–weight materials.[19] The thickness of the wreath measured 1.2 to 1.4mm. The wreath had a pair of clips or prongs on the reverse of each side which were pushed through the cap band and flattened on the inside.

The total length according the RZM specifications was 115mm. (including its vaulting), the height approximately 44mm. Variations were also manufactured, being 108/110mm in length. The design for this wreath consisted of four leaves, joined by a cord design within its middle four upraised "beads." Thc leaf pattern has a stripe pebbling to simulate embroidery. The Assmann variation, for examplc, had the round plate in the middle between the leaves, with two small and one bigger vertical slot (11 x 4mm) for positioning the cockade. (F.W. Assmann Nr.27130[20]).

A wreath with a lacquered surface was also manufactured. This lacquer "mittelgold" W.L.8016 came from the Herbig–Haarhaus A.G. company of Köln–Bickendorf.[21]

The "Cupal" version, vaulted, wreath as manufactured by Matthias Salcher & Söhne at Wagstadt (Sudetenland). Shown are the front and reverse, as well as the "vaulting".

---

18 *"RZM–Herstellungsvorschriften, 1938." p. 41; "Mbl.d.RZM," Nr. 13, July 1, 1939 specified the PL. wreath procedures were available now.*

19 *Procedure from "Vereinigte Silberhammerwerke" Hetzel & Co., a Cupal manufacturer from Nürnberg.*

20 *F.W. Assmann & Söhne, Lüdenscheid. Katalog, 1939, p. 26a.*

21 *"RZM–Herstellungsvorschriften, 1938," p. 41.*

On the reverse of most wreaths, three metal (aluminum or brass) flat or round prongs (0.5 x 1.5mm) having a length of 22mm were affixed. The RZM marking should be on the reverse of the wreath. Versions having two prongs are also known. The Dr. Franke company of Lüdenscheid for example, manufactured this form, but without the inner–plate for the cockade (Nr.2/3947). Its length was 110mm.[22] The form without the inner–plate was forbidden in July 1941.[23]

Jill Halcomb Smith

Jill Halcomb Smith

The assembled cockade.

Reverse of inner wreath and swastika.

White woven twill background for swastika.

---

[22] *Dr. Franke & Co. K.G., Lüdenscheid. Katalog, 1939, p. 9.*

[23] *"Mbl.d.RZM," Nr. 10, July 12, 1941, p. 54.*

Above: Reverse of wreath showing "RZM M1/16" marking: Dr. Franke & Co. K.G.

Far left: Wreath and cockade.

Middle: Reverse of wreath showing cockade assembly and plate which is part of wreath.

Left: Backing plate for cockade.

Note:

At the time of introduction, only five firms were permitted to manufacture the new wreath for political leaders:

M1/52 Deschler & Sohn,
M1/47 C. Th. Dicke,
M1/16 Dr. Franke & Co.,
M1/45 Fr. Linden
M1/111 Gebr. Gloerfeld

*At this time in August 1939 the Assmann firm had not yet been included.

Obverse and reverse of cockade base plate.

The cockade is marked M1/34: the concern Karl Wurster from Markneukirchen.

George Petersen

Franz Ritter von Epp, Reichsleiter, is wearing a visored cap with unauthorized insignia. This photograph is dated later than the summer of 1939, as he is wearing the final pattern collar patches. In 1938, the saddle–form visored cap was introduced, but von Epp is still wearing an approximately 1936 national emblem, as used by the navy and army. Instead of the regular wreath for political leaders, von Epp is apparently wearing the DAF style wreath.

Cockade (Kokarde)
1934 – 1945

Due to the wearing of a cockade or button with the SA–style headdress[24], political leaders also positioned a button or a cockade with the newly introduced visored cap. This was against regulations, and on May 5, 1934 it was ordered that buttons or cockades had to be removed from the cap.[25]

Most likely this order of Ley's caused problems within the PO–organization. On July 27, 1935 Rudolf Hess forbade the abbreviation "PO" at the time that the political organization was reorganized. A few weeks later, on August 12, 1935 the cockade was re–introduced by Ley.[26] This order was sanctioned by Hitler. It was especially noted where cockades had to be positioned (somewhat higher than the middle of the band; while the eagle remained in its place – 10mm above the band's piping) by the start of the 1935 Reichsparteitag.

Prior to May 1934, the standard black/white/red cockade as worn by the army, or the black/white/red form, with a swastika in its center, upon a red field, were worn.

---

[24] *Ruhl/Starke. "Adolf Hitler's Braunhemden" Leipzig: 1933, p. 25. Section PO describes the cockade being the black/white/red version with a silvered swastika upon a red field.*

[25] *"Vbl.d.RL.d.NSDAP," Nr. 72, End–May 1934, p. 166.*

[26] *"Dienstanzug und Dienstrang des Politischen Leiters (NSDAP Gau Schwaben)." Schwaben: 1936. Addendum concerning the cockade, August 1935, p. 11; "Mbl.d.RZM," Nr. 24, August 31, 1935, p. 241.*

Otto Spronk

B. Rust, J. Goebbels and W. Darré, photographed on September 30, 1934 during the harvest-home celebration on the Bückeberg near Hameln. Note that Rust is wearing a cockade. The political leader behind Goebbels is not wearing any, nor does Goebbels

Otto Spronk

Martin Bormann and Rudolf Hess wearing the early style political leaders visored caps. Bormann's cap is devoid of the cockade. Hess is wearing a cockade as officially ordered in June 1935.

A group of cockades, devoid of a swastika, as also used by political leaders.

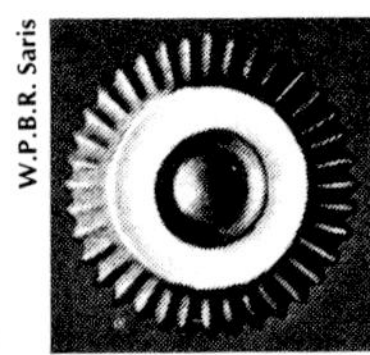
W.P.B.R. Saris

Version with the red, glass, "eye."

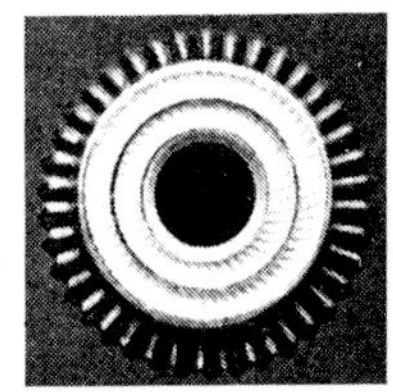
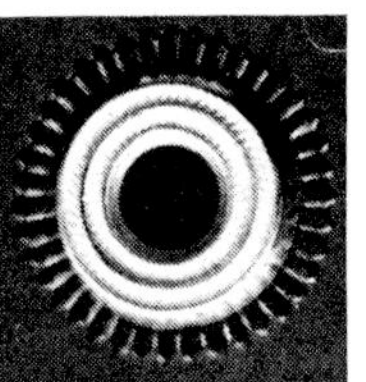

Two regular versions with the black fluted back.

W. P.B.R. Saris

The swastika version cockade as manufactured by Ad. Baumeister at Lüdenscheid. Note that this type does not have the thick backplate, but a fluted, black fiber backing.

L. van Aerle

The 1935 political leaders cockade. See disassembled three pages back.

Joe Stone

A political leader wearing the "Teller" form visored cap with the 1934–form eagle and the large, round, swastika cockade.

Several types of cockades without a swastika, often used by political leaders.

A political leader during the festivities of the Saar return, March 1935, wearing his visored cap devoid of a cockade, according to the regulations.

The model 1935 was 23mm in diameter and contained a back plate, 1.5mm thick, edged in silver. The surface of the plate was red enamel with stripes, which gave a ribbed impression. There were four small holes (later, only two) on the reverse of the back plate, which were used to fasten the regular white aluminum upper cockade section (approximately 17mm in diameter). This portion contained the black painted or black enameled canted swastika in its center. Between the back plate and the upper cockade was a small, round piece of red felt or white cloth, cotton or linen, which gave the swastika its backing. On the reverse of the upper portion of the cockade were two long and two short pins or clips which fastened to the back plate. The total height for the completed cockade was approximately 9mm. (Assmann Nr.27610).[27]

The form of this cockade remained unchanged until 1942. In November 1942, a decree was issued which ordered that the model 1935 had to be replaced

[27] *F.W. Assmann & Söhne, Lüdenscheid. Katalog, 1939. p. 26a.*

W.P.B.R. Saris

Mütze für Politische Leiter

An der obengenannten Mütze wird an Stelle der bisherigen Hakenkreuzkokarde die Wehrmachtskokarde verwendet. Lagerbestände werden aufgebraucht.

A very short note, published in November 1942, announcing the introduction of the cheaper national cockade, worn by the Armed Forces.

with the regular national cockade as used by the Armed Forces, which had no swastika.[28] Old stocks were first to be used up. (For more details on the regular national cockade, see Volume 1 of this series, Chapter 1: p.16; Chapter 4: p.130). It should be noted that none of the cockade forms for political leaders existed in gold.

1931 – 1933

The first forms of headdress worn by political leaders of the NSDAP were in fact a transitional form, being the regular kepi, or "coffee can" as worn by the SA.[29] This cap became official in July 1932, but had already been used for some time with a brown leather chin strap for all NSDAP officials in high positions. A national emblem was not worn until approximately 1931. This form of headdress was short–lived.

The oval top (20cm long with a size 56 and approximately 17cm wide) was approximately 9.4cm high at the front, including a 1.5mm piping in the same color and fabric as the top, and was supported by a 1 x 0.3mm iron wire. The back of the cap was often a few millimeters shorter than the front.

The top of the cap interior was lined in light brown, waterproof oil cloth moiré. Outside, the flaps measured approximately 6 or 7cm high and approximately 4.5cm at the front and center. A smooth, metal button secured the center

Otto Spronk

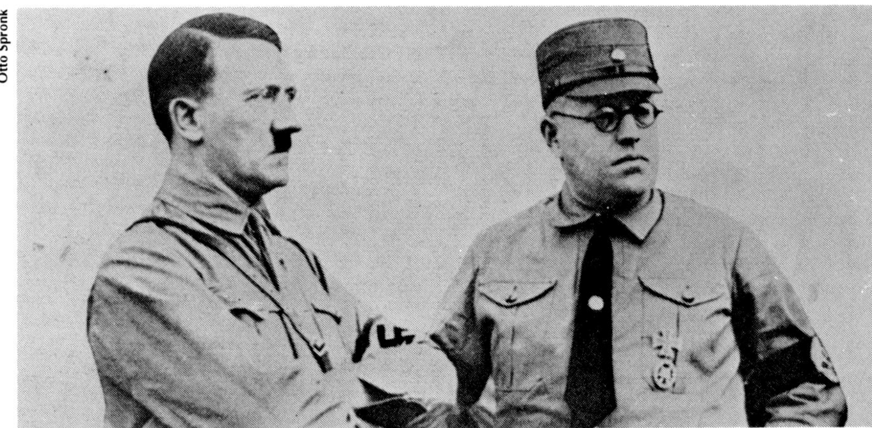

Adolf Hitler and the NS–Minister of Braunschweig Franzen in March 1931. Note Franzen is wearing the SA style cap with the leather chin strap and devoid of the first form eagle emblem. The wear of these caps was instituted in the early thirty's for "political leaders."

[28] *"Uniformen–Markt," Nr. 23, December 1, 1942, p. 178; Schwert u. Spaten, Nr. 11. November 30, 1942, p. 121; "Mbl.d.RZM," Nr. 15, November 14, 1942, p. 80.*

[29] *"NSDAP, Aufbau und Abzeichen." Leipzig: 1933, Section PO, p. 17.*

of the flaps (in the late 1920's and early 1930's a brown leather button was commonly used. From 1932 the silver or gilt pebbled button embossed with the political eagle and static swastika was used. Its diameter was 20.5mm). The vaulting of the flaps began at the side of the visor. It must be noted that these flaps (the turn–up) were sewn directly to the body of the cap for political leaders and were non–removable. Often these samples came from SA stocks, so that caps with loose flaps are to be found. Two light brown enameled ventilation holes (4mm in diameter) were positioned approximately 5mm from the crown seam (or later, the piping) on each side. A silver, first model national emblem or the small "Hoheitszeichen" of the Party was worn just above the turn–up of the flaps in the front center of the kepi.

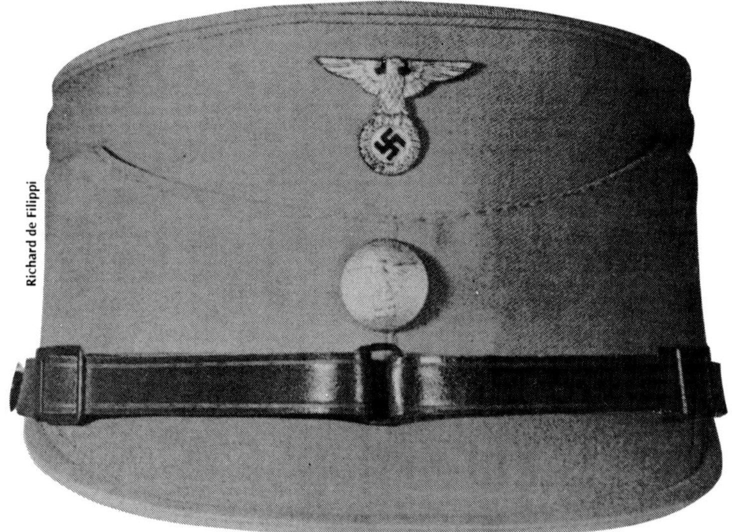

Richard de Filippi

An example of a political leaders cap in the SA–style, as worn in mid 1932 by the ranks Blockwart and Zellenwart. Note that the construction is exactly as for the regular SA, but the top is in the same type of fabric as the flaps and visor and that instead of the smooth button, the embossed political leaders button is positioned.

The cloth covered visor was approximately 24cm long, 5cm in the front and installed at a 32° angle. The visor was stitched through twice, 6mm from the edge, with light brown thread The interior of the visor was often made of black (or natural) colored waterproof, impregnated cardboard, but cannot be seen as it is under the material. These caps were stiffened on the inside at the seams with rigid linen material. The sweatband was made of Havana–brown leather measuring approximately 3cm in width. The two–part leather chin strap was made of dark brown leather, approximately 12mm wide. A brown, rectangular metal buckle with rounded edges (thickness of 1.52mm) connected the two straps at the center of the front of the cap. The strap was positioned above the visor and secured at each end by a brown metal button, 14mm in diameter. It could be extended for wear under the wearer's chin by two brown metal buckles, which measured 18 x 21cm. The early buttons snapped together on the inside (so–called "Junggesellen" buttons, being in fact snap fasteners that clicked together) and did not have flat pins or prongs.

Otto Spronk

National Archivees

Above: During a meeting in the period of struggle. The SA–style cap of Rust is laying in front of him. Note that a "tinny" is positioned at the left side. Officially these were never allowed for wear by the SA, or political leaders.

Left: The wearing of the early form SA–style cap by a political leader in the rank of Zellenwart. His cap has the crown piping, silvered front button and silvered strap–buttons, but with the leather brown chin strap. Probably this was worn for a short time during a transitional period: the crown piping was introduced in late 1932 and the leather chin strap abolished in July 1932.

W.P.B.R. Saris

A person with the rank of Blockwart is holding his kepi with a leather chin strap at his wedding.

Otto Spronk

Political leader holding the kepi in his hand giving a good view of the leather chin strap and the ventilation grommets in the top. He is wearing the 1933 form Gauleiter brassard. By regulation, his kepi should at least have the cords.

NSDAP officials were authorized cap cords in silver or gold. Different regulations for cap cords or chin straps are known: A system worn before July 1932 and another system, worn from July 1932 until the introduction of the new

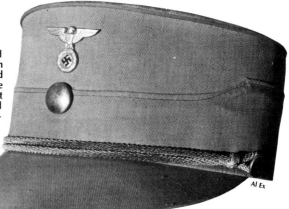

The earliest form cap for political leaders in the regular SA–style as worn since July 1932 by the Blockwart and Zellenwart ranks, indicated by the silver cap cords. Note the single vent hole; this example was manufactured by Otto Baader of Spalt in Mittelfranken.

Al Ex

uniform for political leaders.[30] It must be noted that these thin cords were often worn with the new type visored cap, probably due to stock shortages. The old form had to be officially replaced, however, according to an announcement of May 1934.[31]

OFFICIALS OF THE NSDAP (AMTSWALTER)
System before July 1932

Rank/Function:	Strap/Cord	Button:
Blockwart:	brown chin strap	brown;
Zellenwart:	ibid	ibid;
Ortsgruppenleiter:	silver cord with one knot in the middle	silver;
Kreisleiter:	silver cord with two knots	ibid;
Gauleiter:	golden cord with one knot in the middle	gold;
Reichsleitung:	golden cord with two knots	ibid.

Otto Spronk

Alfred Proksch, one of the joint founders of the NSDAP in Austria. He is wearing in this early photograph a cap with no piping, but with a golden cap cord with two knots due to his position on Reich–level. Proksch was the Landesleiter for the NSDAP in Austria.

[30] *Ibid, pp. 16–19; Die Uniformen und Abzeichen der SA, SS, HJ, usw. Berlin, 1933. p. 20.*

[31] *"Vbl.d.RL.d.NSDAP," Nr. 72. End–May 1934. p. 166.*

OFFICIALS OF THE NSDAP (AMTSWALTER)
System according to the July 15, 1932 regulation, until introduction of new uniforms:

Rank/Function:	Strap/Cord	Button:
Blockwart: (Block Warder) Zellenwart: Cell Warder) resp.	silver, no knot	silver, matte;
Stützpunktleiter: (Point of support Leader)	ibid	ibid;
Ortsgruppenleiter: (Local Group–Leader)	ibid, one knot	ibid:
Kreisleiter: (District Leader)	ibid, two knots	ibid;
Gauleiter: (Province Leader)	Gold, one knot (from May 1933 two knots were worn)	gold, matte;
Landesinspekteur: (State Inspector)	ibid	ibid;
Reichsinspekteur: (Inspector on Reich–level)	ibid, two knots	ibid;
Reichsorganisationsleiter: (Reich–Organization Leader)	ibid	ibid.

STAFF OFFICIALS FOR THE POLITICAL ORGANIZATION (Stabswalter der PO):

Staff Officials for Zelle–or Stützpunkt:	as Blockwart;
Ibid for Ortsgruppe:	as Zellenwart or Stützpunktleiter;
Ibid for Kreis:	as Ortsgruppenleiter;
Department Chiefs for Kreis: (Abteilungsleiter)	as Zellenwart or Stützpunktleiter;
Staff Officials for Gau:	as Kreisleiter;
Department Chiefs for Gau:	as Ortsgruppenleiter;
Staff Officials for State Inspections; (Stabswalter der Landes–Inspektion)	as Gauleiter;

STAFF OFFICIALS FOR THE REICHSORGANISATIONSLEITUNG (Stabswalter der Reichsorganisationsleitung):

Main Department Leaders for the departments III, IV, V, VI: (Haupt–Abteilungsleiter)	as Reichsinspekteur;
Department Chiefs: (Abteilungsleiter)	as Gauleiter;
Sub–Department Chiefs: (Unter-Abteilungsleiter)	as Kreisleiter;

OFFICIALS IN THE REICHSLEITUNG (Amtsleiter der Reichsleitung):

(such a person was allowed to establish rank and uniform for his subordinated officials)	as Reichsorganisationsleiter;

FRACTION LEADERS AND DEPUTIES ON STATE LEVEL
(Fraktionsführer und Abgeordnete)

Fraction Leader: (Fraktions führer)	as Landesinspekteur;
Deputy: (Abgeordnete)	regular NSDAP officials uniform according to function.

FRACTION LEADERS FOR CITY OR PROVINCE LEVEL AND MUNICIPAL REPRESENTATIVES
(Fraktionsführer und Gemeindevertreter):

Fraction Leader:	as Kreisleiter;
Municipal-representative: (Gemeindevertreter)	regular NSDAP officials uniform according to function;

Deutsche Lufthansa

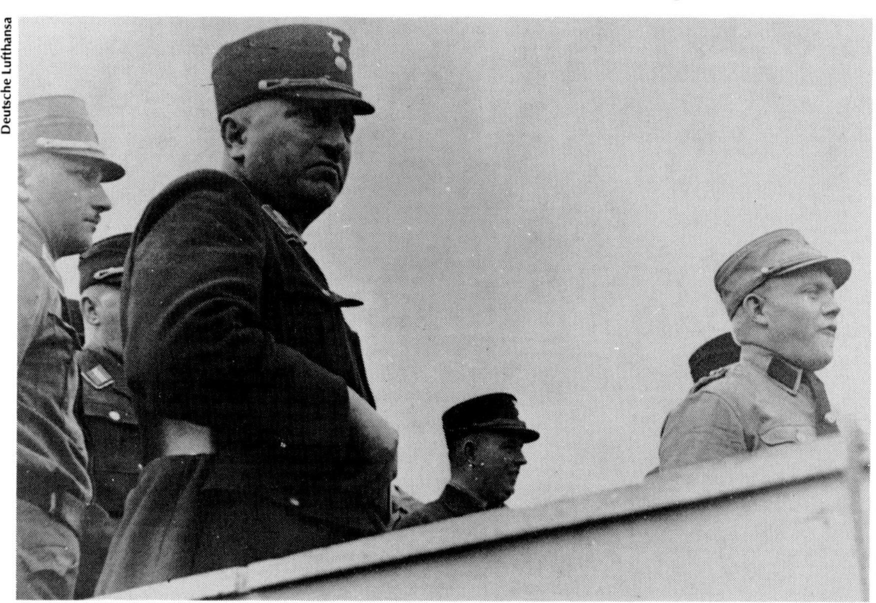

Dr. Robert Ley is wearing the earliest form political cap, according to his Reichsleitung–rank in 1933. Note that Ley is wearing golden cap cords with the two knots in the middle and that this form of cap was then devoid of any top piping. This was introduced in late 1932. Dr. Reesen at left is wearing the silver cap cords with two knots, according his rank as Kreisleiter. The first version eagle emblem is worn by Ley.

(It is very interesting to note that it was announced in August 1932 that the rank "Reichsorganisationsleiter" should wear a kepi with a colored top in crimson with a 10mm gold lace[32] It was even intended to enlarge the group of wearer's. Another interesting fact is that a lace system was not introduced within the SA before July 1933. No photo was found showing this).

The introduction date for the piping system to be used on the cap crown is unknown, but it is believed that it was not earlier than late 1932. Photographs show that most of the political functionaries never wore them, due to the fact that it was known that a new uniform was being developed. Sketched for the new uniform were already published by mid 1933.[33]

W.P.B.R. Saris

The Prime Minister of Baden, Walter Köhler is wearing the kepi with golden crown piping and the very thin golden cap cords. He is wearing Gauleiter collar patches, in the earliest form.

A. Stam

"Sieg Heil." The mayor of Gladbach–Rheydt, Kreisleiter Pelzer, saluting during a meeting on July 11, 1933. Note he is not wearing the brassard, nor does the person at his right (who is wearing below the eagle emblem upon the arm the badge for "Fraktionsführer und Gemeindevertreter" with state symbol). Pelzer is wearing a dark kepi with silver cords due to his Kreisleiter rank.

---

32 *"Vbl.d.RL.d.NSDAP," Nr.29, August 15, 1932, p.65. An announcement by Ley, dated August 2, says literally: "Im Dienstbuch Seite 53, Abschnitt 167 und auf Seite 55, Abschnitt 178, sind zwei Fehler unterlaufen – two mistakes were made. Seite 53 Abschnitt 167 muss heissen: Reichsor ganisationsleiter: Dienstanzug wie vor. An der Mütze ein 10 millimeter breites Goldband auf karmesinrotem Grund, etc.".*

33 *"Uniformfibel," Knötel. Berlin: December 1933, p.36, Section 3: Die Politischen Organisation.*

Peter Whamond

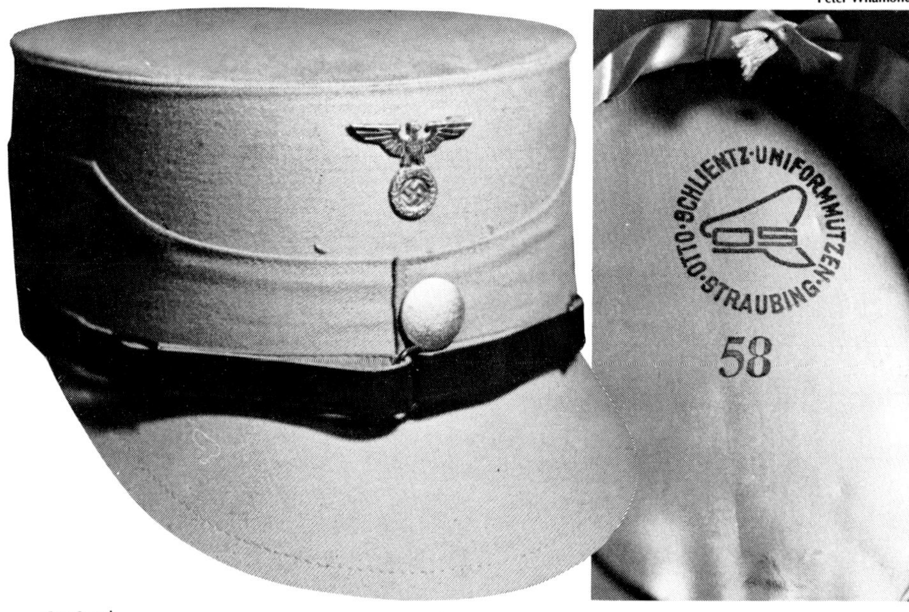

Otto Spronk

Above left: Kepi intended for use by political leaders and manufactured by Otto Schlientz-Uniformenmützen at Straubing (RZM permission A 1/26). Because of the introduction of the new political leader's cap, this kepi was tranformed into a regular SA kepi.

Above Right: The Schlientz logo on the inside of the kepi.

Erich Koch is wearing the early form cap for political leaders in the heavier cloth fabric. Note the wearing of the cap cord with one knot and his cap is devoid of crown piping. The heavier cloth caps were mainly worn with the tunic. The twill version was meant for wearing with the brown–shirt.

LATE 1932 PIPING:

Rank/Function:	Piping:
Blockwart:	silver crown piping;
Zellenwart:	ibid;
Ortsgruppenleiter:	ibid;
Kreisleiter:	ibid;
Gauleiter:	golden crown piping;
Landesinspekteur:	ibid;
Reichsinspekteur:	ibid;
Reichsorganisationsleiter:	ibid.[34]

Designs for a completely new uniform for political leaders were developed in early 1933. On May 12, Robert Ley had a meeting with professor Paul Ludwig Troost. It was expected that his designs would be finished in June as Hitler himself had ordered that this new uniform had to be completed (endgültig). Those holding the rank of Gauleiter from then on had to wear the uniform like that worn by those in the rank of "Reichsinspekteur." Persons who had been granted the right to wear the political uniform were ordered to wear this when performing service.[35] Available lists from the Reichszeugmeisterei from May and June 1933 (published in August) did not yet include an official form of headdress for political leaders .[36]

Political leaders (Amtswalter, Amtsleiter, etc). who were honorary SA–Führer were authorized to wear the kepi with a silver–grey velvet top. The color of the flap button was silver or gilt, according to the color worn by the SA

5/33

Anordnung Nr. 21/33.

Nach einer heutigen Rücksprache mit Herrn Professor Trost wird der Entwurf der neuen Uniform erst in einigen Wochen fertiggestellt sein, da er nach Wunsch des Führers endgültig sein soll. Bis dahin bleibt die alte Uniform in Kraft. Die Gauleiter tragen grundsätzlich die Uniformen der ehemaligen Reichsinspekteure.

In diesem Zusammenhang möchte ich bitten, im Dienst ver Politischen Organisation nur die Uniform der Politischen Leiter zu tragen.

München, den 12. Mai 1933. Dr. Ley.

„Freiheit und Brot!"

Verordnungsblatt

der Reichsleitung der Nationalsozialistischen Deutschen Arbeiter-Partei

Das Verordnungsblatt der Reichsleitung der NSDAP. erscheint monatlich zweimal und kann nur durch die Post bezogen werden; Bestellungen nehmen alle Postanstalten in Deutschland zum Preise von 40 Rpf. pro Vierteljahr entgegen. Das Verordnungsblatt kann auch im 2. und 3. Monat des Vierteljahrs zum Preise von 25 Rpf. und für den 3. Monat zu 15 Rpf. bestellt werden

Folge 47, 2. Jahrgang — München, den 15. Mai 1933

W.P.B.R. Saris

The order, dated May 12, 1933, as published in the *Verordnungsblatt der Reichsleitung der NSDAP* and mentions that Ley had that day had a meeting with Troost, the designer of the new uniform. Professor Troost had not yet finished this and it was expected that he needed a few weeks more to finish. Hitler wished the designs finalized. Interesting is that it is said that the Gauleiter fundamentally had to wear the uniform, as worn by the "Reichsinspekteur." Goebbels already wore a sort of uniform with a visored cap beginning in 1932. This type of uniform resembles the later worn political leaders style headdress. Note Vbl. "masthead."

34 *"Die Uniformen und Abzeichen der SA, SS, HJ usw." Berlin: 1933. Pictures–list 20.*

35 *Vbl.d. Kl.d. NSDAP, Nr. 47, May 15, 1933, p.100. Decree Nr. 21/33, dated May 12, 1933 and signed by Ley.*

36 *Ibid, Nr. 53, August 16, 1933, p.113. This announcement gave directives for what were official Party–uniforms and insignia.*

Otto Spronk

Goebbels is wearing a visored cap during sport festivities at Stuttgart in 1933. Note the light brown cap band, the brown leather chin strap and that his cap was devoid of any piping. The visor of the cap was chocolate–brown. It is observed that during this day all other political leaders wore the SA–style cap.

Larry W. Smith

Dr. Robert Ley is wearing the early political light brown SA–style cap in his rank as Gauleiter: one knot in the middle of his golden cap cords. Note that the edge of the flap is also piped. Officially this was only allowed around the crown of the cap. Probably this signifies his SA–honor rank, but this would also indicate that Ley is wearing the grey top with this cap.

Butzweiler Hof Museum

Hitler and Blomberg at Berlin airport congratulating the winner of the "Deutschlandflug" on August 27, 1933. At Hitler's left is Reichsstatthalter Jacob Sprenger, wearing the political kepi with the cords and two knots, due to his rank of inspector.

Adolf Hitler during the "first spade" for the Frankfurt–Darmstadt Autobahn on September 23, 1933. Note that the political leaders are wearing both versions of headdress. Robert Ley in the background wears the SA–style cap and the man standing next to Hitler wears the new style cap for political leaders introduced in the fall of 1933.

National Archivees

Early Party officials with the Italian aviator Italo Balbo. This photograph gives an excellent view of a wide range of worn political leaders caps with leather chin strap, or cords with knots in silver or gold, along with the heavier fabric cap forms or light brown .

W.P.B.R. Saris

An NSDAP orator speaks to an attentive audience sometime around 1933. The political leaders are wearing the light brown kepi with the dark tunics. The political leader on the tail gate of the truck is wearing a leather chin strap. He is probably a member of the NSBO.

Political leaders wearing the kepi and visored cap. Note the smooth button worn with the kepi and the extremely dark shade of the visored cap.

J. Bornel

Butzweiler Hof Museum

Hermann Göring signing a dispatch during his visit to Köln on June 17, 1934. Göring was at the city for his receiving the "Ehrenbürger" (Freeman) Honor title. Standing at far right is Gauleiter Florian from Düsseldorf, wearing his kepi. Normally he should have already been wearing the new visored cap. Note the SA–Sturmführer in the background wearing the Fliegersturm collar patch.

"Gruppe."[37] (After the official introduction of the visored cap, the use of the kepi with the above mentioned colored top was discontinued from early summer of 1934).

With an announcement dated September 28, 1933 (being after the Reichsparteitag 1933) it was said: "The new uniform for Amtswalter der PO is ready. Its ranking system and its pictures will be available shortly. The wearing of this uniform and rank system is only allowed when the person in question owns the identification paper allowing officially the wearing of the uniform." (This order mentioned the positions up to Kreis–level, granted by the Reichsleitung; all others were granted by the "Gauleiter"; those not having a function within the Party were not allowed to wear a uniform as ordered for political leaders).[38] It is known that during the Reich Party Days the new uniform was shown to Hitler. Some groups experimentally wore this uniform at that time. During the last months of 1933, the uniform was worn quite often. Requirements for the identification papers were first published on December 15, 1933.

Der neue Dienstanzug für die Amtswalter der PO. ist fertiggestellt. Rangabzeichen und Abbildungen werden in Kürze den Dienststellen zugehen. Die Rangabzeichen des Dienstanzuges sind auf vorher angeführter Rangstufung aufgebaut. Jeder Amtswalter bis zur Kreisleitung einschließlich erhält einen abgestempelten Ausweis der Reichsleitung (vorgedruckte Muster gehen den Gauen zu). Alle übrigen Amtswalter erhalten nach gleichem Muster abgestempelte Ausweise durch den Gauleiter.

Nur diejenigen Amtswalter, die einen solchen Ausweis besitzen, dürfen den Dienstanzug tragen. Außerdem muß der Dienstanzug durch den jeweiligen Hoheitsträger noch besonders verliehen werden. Nur der ein Amt in der Partei hat, darf den entsprechenden Dienstanzug tragen. Ich werde rücksichtslos jeden der Bestrafung zuführen, der den Dienstanzug mißbraucht. Es ist auch verboten, den Dienstanzug der PO. in Schnitt und Farbe ohne Rangabzeichen von einem Parteimitglied, welches nicht Amtswalter ist, zu tragen. Der Dienstanzug ist eine Auszeichnung für geleistete Pflicht und muß als solche gewertet werden.

Amtswaltern, die ohne Verschulden aus dem Dienst ausscheiden, kann der Dienstanzug auf Antrag von dem nächsthöheren Hoheitsträger bewilligt werden.

München, den 28. September 1933. Dr. Ley.

W. P.B.R. Saris

Ley's notice of September 28, 1933 in which is stated that a new political leaders uniform was available. Its designs and ranking system would become available within a short time. In fact this new uniform had already been worn experimentally during the 1933 party days.

1934 – 1936

On January 20, 1934 Adolf Hitler officially granted the new uniforms for political leaders, including the visored cap form of headdress (known as Form 1). Descriptions of cap band color, piping, cord system and buttons (varying in

---

[37] *Erlass, Nr. 2. "Der Oberste SA–Führer." München: July 7, 1933. Addendum 1: "Neugliederung der SA." (it was not specifically said that this velvet was to be worn with the headdress for political leaders, but as also crimson was ordered for the Reichsorganisationsleiter it is surely a possibility).*

[38] *"Vbl.d.RL.d.NSDAP," Nr. 57, October 15, 1933. p. 124: a decree from the PO High Command, signed by Ley on September 28, 1933.*

W.P.B.R. Saris

Die Oberste Leitung der PO.

1/34

Anordnung.

Durch nachstehende Verfügung hat der Führer endgültig den Dienstanzug der PO. genehmigt und damit zum Ausdruck gebracht, daß es sein Wille ist, daß der durch den Kampf herausgebildete Typ des politischen Leiters der NSDAP. nichts mit den zivilen Politikern früherer Parteien und Staaten zu tun hat, sondern, daß in dem politischen Leiter der NSDAP. dem Deutschen Volke endlich jene politische Führung entstanden ist, um die es zweitausend Jahre gerungen hat.

Wir sind Prediger und Soldaten zugleich. Das ist unser Stolz. Dem soll der Dienstanzug der PO. weithin sichtbaren Ausdruck verleihen.

Politische Leiter!

Bedenkt, welche gewaltige Mission ihr damit übernommen habt und dankt dem Führer für seine großmütige Tat dadurch, daß ihr eueren Pflichteifer, eueren Opfermut, eueren Fleiß verdoppelt und zeigt dem Führer, daß ihr durch eine unerhörte Disziplin seine gehorsamsten Soldaten sein wollt!

20. Januar 1934. Dr. Robert Ley.

Der Führer

Verfügung.

Der Dienstanzug der PO.-Leiter.

Der Dienstanzug wird besonders verliehen. Nur PO.-Leiter, denen der Dienstanzug verliehen wurde, sind berechtigt, denselben zu tragen.

Der Gesellschaftsanzug der PO.-Leiter.

Dienstrock, schwarze Hosen mit schwarzen Bisen, schwarze Halbschuhe, schwarze Strümpfe, braunes Hemd, schwarzer Binder.

München, den 20. Januar 1934. Adolf Hitler.

A part of the January 1934 orders for the new political leaders uniform. The upper part from Ley states that this uniform was now definitive, for the time being. The last part states that every PL uniform must have permission to be worn (otherwise its wearing was prohibited).

Otto Spronk

Political leaders waiting and resting on one of the fields near to the main field of the "Reichsparteitaggelände" at Nürnberg in 1933. These political leaders are experimentally wearing the new form visored cap.

color depending on rank or NSDAP office held by the wearer – see list January 20, 1934) were published. Hitler probably pushed things forward, to honor its designer, Troost, who was ill, and, in fact, died one day after Hitler's decree.[39]

The top of the cap was officially made of light brown material, the same color as the uniform tunic, but often was in a dark brown shade until early 1935. The light brown was a different shade from that worn by SA members. The visored cap shape (Tellermütze, having a low crown) was like those worn by army officers, and became the generally worn form of headdress after its approval. Periodicals in those days often described wrong insignia or wrong colors of the cloth for the cap.[40] The leather or fiber visor was brown, varying in shades from light to dark.

POLITICAL ORGANIZATION LEADERS
(Leiter der Politische Organisation: system January 20, 1934)

	Cords:	Buttons:	Piping:	Band:
Reichsleitung				
Reichsleiter:	gold	gold	golden/ yellow	dark brown velvet;
Amtsleiter:	ibid	ibid	ibid	ibid;
Abteilungsleiter:	silver	silver	ibid	ibid;
Unterabteilungs–leiter:	ibid	ibid	ibid	ibid;
Gauleitung				
Gauleiter:	gold	gold	red	ibid;
Stellvertretender–Gauleiter:	ibid	ibid	ibid	ibid;
Amtsleiter:	silver	silver	ibid	ibid;
Abteilungsleiter:	ibid	ibid	ibid	ibid;
Unterabteilungs–leiter:	ibid	ibid	ibid	ibid;
Kreisleitung				
Kreisleiter:	gold	gold	black	ibid;
Amtsleiter:	silver	silver	ibid	ibid;
Abteilungsleiter:	ibid	ibid	ibid	ibid;
Unterabteilungs–leiter:	ibid	ibid	ibid	ibid;
Ortsgruppenleitung				
Ortsgruppenleiter:	gold	gold	light blue	light brown cloth;
Amtsleiter:	silver	silver	ibid	ibid;
Stützpunktleiter:	ibid	ibid	ibid	ibid;
Zellenwart:	ibid	ibid	ibid	ibid;
Blockwart:	ibid	ibid	ibid	ibid.[41]

[39] *Ibid, Nr. 64, January 31, 1933, pp. 141–142. Hitler's decree was signed January 20, 1933 and agreed to by Ley the same day.*

[40] *"Mbl.d.RZM," Nr.1. June 1, 1934, pp.1–3.*

[41] *"Vbl.d.RL.d.NSDAP," Nr.64, January 31, 1934, pp.141–142; "Mbl.d.RZM," Nr .1, June 1, 1934, pp.1–2. (Other framed lists were often published. We will not enclose these to avoid misunderstandings and much confusion. These lists however give a much better guide to the systems for ranks in relation to offices on all levels. NSDAP Gau Schwaben in 1936 published such a list with directives for the political leaders uniforms and ranking/function system).*

Otto Spronk

Hans Schemm, Gauleiter of the Bayern-Ostmark district, chats and drinks beer during the 1933 Reichsparteitag. This photograph shows that, probably experimentally, political leaders were already issued with the visored cap. Later in the fall of that year this new uniform was often worn, although officially introduced on January 20, 1934.

In April 1934 directives were published giving details regarding out–of–date insignia (veraltete Rangabzeichen). Corrections had to be made immediately. This was specifically noted for the headdress with new piping (as the old uniform was still allowed to be worn, including the dark brown cap). The cords for the cap had to be changed into the new style (without the knots).[42] On May 5th, Ley ordered that when a political leader wore golden cords, golden buttons also had to be worn, replacing the formerly worn silver buttons (and noted that no cockade or button, was allowed on the front of the cap band).[43] Twelve days later Ley announced the Reichsparteitag uniform: all political leaders had to wear the new style uniform, insigne and visored cap.

All new introductions and proposed introductions of uniforms and insignia were supervised by the "Prüfungs–und Bewachungsamt" (Office for Experiments and Supervision), later termed under Hauptstelle III.3c as "Stellenplanung und Überwachung." Purchasing had to be approved by the Reichsorganisationsleiter, in agreement with the Reichszeugmeisterei.[44] A special office, the Hauptstelle Graphik (VII–I), designed uniforms and insignia.[45]

The introduction of the new style visored cap in early 1934 and the enormous growth of the political organization caused stock shortages. Visored caps

42 *"Vbl.d.RL.d.NSDAP," Nr. 70, End–April 1934, p. 159. Order by Ley dated April 13, 1934; Ibid, Nr. 78, Mid–August 1934, p. 184: Order Nr. 10/34, dated July 30, 1934. (the cords were allowed in cheaper materials instead of the heavier gold or silver wire).*

43 *Ibid, Nr. 72. End–May 1934. p. 166. This order was especially meant for members of the NSBO.*

44 *"Organisationsbuch der NSDAP. " München: 1936, pp. 166–168.*

45 *Ibid, 1943, pp. 161–170.*

P.O.-Mütze

Auf dem Seitenteil, 10 mm über dem Mützenrand, ist ein besonderes Hoheitsabzeichen anzubringen, zu beziehen nur durch die R.Z.M.

Es ist besonders darauf zu achten, daß die Mütze möglichst leicht scharfkantig und griffig weich ist.

Mützenkordeln und Paspelierungen

	Rand	Kordel	Knopf	Paspelierung
Reichsleitung:				
Reichsleiter	hellbraun Samt	gold	gold	goldgelb
Amtsleiter	"	"	"	"
Hauptstellenleiter	"	silber	silber	"
Stellenleiter	"	"	"	"
Gauleitung:				
Gauleiter	"	gold	gold	rot
Gauleiterstellvertreter	"	"	"	"
Amtsleiter	"	silber	silber	"
Abteilungsleiter	"	"	"	"
Unterabteilungsleiter	"	"	"	"
Kreisleitung:				
Kreisleiter	"	gold	gold	schwarz
Amtsleiter	"	silber	silber	"
Abteilungsleiter	"	"	"	"
Unterabteilungsleiter	"	"	"	"
Ortsgruppenleitung:				
Ortsgruppenleiter	Grundstoff	gold	gold	hellblau
Amtsleiter und Stützpunktleiter	"	silber	silber	"
Zellenwart	"	"	"	"
Blockwart	"	"	"	"

In late September 1934, the *"Mbl.d.RZM"* published the political leaders cord and piping systems for the visored cap. In this publication some other rank and function indications were given, as for example published in the *"Vbl.d.Reichsleitung der NSDAP."* Instead of Abteilungs– and Unterabteilungsleiter in this one the words Hauptstellenleiter and Stellenleiter (on Reich–level were used. These were the names that later were almost always used. Note that in this publication the words Zellen– and Blockwart were used. Both names were officially changed in May 1934 to Zellen– and Blockleiter.

manufactured for the Hitler Youth were adapted to political leaders standards. Some manufactures also produced visored caps of wrong materials. Instead of the color ordered for the cap band a very dark brown (shading to black) one was used. Caps were also supplied with black visors.[46] This explains why at present, some political leaders visored caps are found with black leather visors or other colored bands (for political leaders the black visor was never officially sanctioned).

Due to all these mistakes, new manufacturing regulations and a list with color schedules were published in the Mitteilungsblatt der Reichszeugmeisterei, dated September 29, 1934. It specified that this visored cap form was also to be worn by political functionaries of NSBO and NS–Hago. The included RZM–list was practically the same as the January 1934 list. Some ranks on Reich–level were renamed and added. For that purpose the system for the section

46 *"Mbl.d.RZM," Nr. 2, June 9, 1934, p. 6; Ibid, Nr. 13, August 25, 1934, p. 1.*

Otto Spronk

An Unterabteilungsleiter on Reichs–level is wearing his properly piped visored cap with dark brown cap band, the swastika cockade and earliest form national eagle emblem. Note the red piping on the collar of his tunic.

Alfred Rosenberg shown wearing his Reichsleiter uniform and visored cap in September 1934. Note that Rosenberg is wearing the 1934 type eagle emblem on the front center of the top and his cap still has the old style cap cords (in gold) with the two knots. The cap band is dark brown velvet, piped in golden–yellow.

W.P.B.R. Saris

Karl Weinreich, the Gauleiter of Kurhessen, is wearing the political leaders visored cap with the red top piping and golden cords. Note the knots–system with the cords on this 1934–model cap. The cockade is devoid of the swastika.

Otto Spronk

Gauleiterstellvertreter Kurt Schmalz is wearing the gold version cap cords. It is very remarkable that the cap band piping is very light. Normally this should be in red (so it would not stand out against the cap band so brightly). Note that he is still wearing the political leaders sleeve insigne and stripe with entry year. He is also wearing the Gau-München commemorative insigne. This photograph could easily confuse someone, as it was published in fall 1937 in a book for the Kreistag at Braunschweig.

L. van Aerle

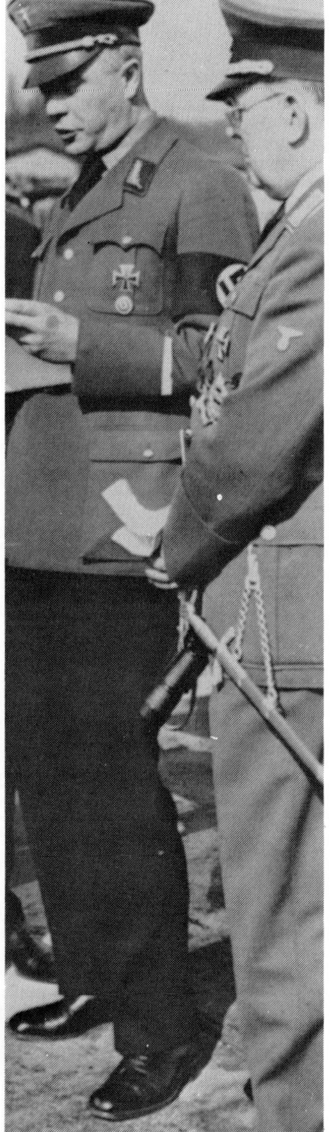

L. van Aerle

Kreisamtsleiter (z.b.V. = zur besonderen Verwendung) Grave of the city Braunschweig–Stadt is wearing the "Teller" form visored cap with black piping around the crown and cap band in rust-brown. Note that he is wearing in 1935 the first form of national emblem. Above the visor rests a silver cap cord.

A"Stellvertretender Gauleiter" (Deputy Province Leader) is wearing his visored cap with red piping: the cap band is devoid of the cockade.

National Archives

The man in center obviously wears an Ortsgruppe-level visored cap because the cap band is of the same material as the rest of the cap (see chart) Note, however that he is wearing a leather chin strap. This was not allowed after July 1932.

W.P.B.R. Saris

Ortsgruppen-Zellenleiter Bruno is wearing his visored cap with a rust-brown cap band, devoid of a cockade. The photograph is dated July 15, 1934.

W.P.B.R. Saris

Political leaders visiting the Zugspitze in 1934. This photograph probably shows us the entire leadership of a local level. Standing at right is the Ortsgruppenleiter, followed by a Zellenleiter, an Amts- or Stützpunktleiter, a Blockleiter and at the far left another Zellenleiter.

5/34

Anordnung.

Betreff: **Veraltete Rangabzeichen.**

Ab sofort müssen sämtliche früher geltende Rangabzeichen der PO. einschließlich der Silber- und Goldschnüre am Kragen abgelegt werden.

Das Tragen des Dienstanzuges ist nur in folgender Art genehmigt:

1. Bis auf weiteres kann die alte PO.-Uniform aufgegetragen werden;
   a) ohne Abzeichen (vorläufig, sofern neue Abzeichen noch nicht zu beschaffen sind),
   b) mit neuen Abzeichen (Bisen müssen jedoch in der Farbe des Hoheitsgebietes sein, das gleiche gilt für die Mütze).
2. Neuer Dienstanzug der PO. ohne Abzeichen, (vorläufig, sofern neue Abzeichen noch nicht zu beschaffen sind).
3. Neuer Dienstanzug der PO. mit neuen Abzeichen.

In jedem Falle ist Voraussetzung, daß ein Dienstrang vom zuständigen Hoheitsträger genehmigt ist. Das Tragen der PO.-Uniform ohne genehmigten Dienstrang, auch ohne Abzeichen, ist verboten.

Betreff: **Mützenkordel.**

Die Mützenkordel muß nach Vorschrift der Reichszeugmeisterei verstellbar sein.

Betreff: Tragen der Pistole.

Die Pistole wird am Koppel auf der rechten Seite getragen. Mit Mantel wird Koppel mit Pistole übergeschnallt. Wird lange Hose getragen, kommt die Pistole in Fortfall. Bei langer Hose mit Mantel wird untergeschnallt.

Betreff: **Koppel.**

Das Koppel wird von rechts nach links geschnallt.

Betreff: Kragenpassepoilierung.

Die Kragenpassepoilierung muß in der Ausführung analog der Spiegelpassepoilierung sein.

München den 13. April 1934. Dr. Ley.

The order dated April 13, 1934, stating with b. that the visored cap should have the correct piping colors for the levels (Reich, Gau, Kreis or Ortsgruppenleitung). Simultaneously it was said that it was allowed to wear a new form of cap and insignia with the "old" form uniform (often being in the darker color). The new form adjustable cords had to be installed. The old form cords with knots were abolished, as they were not adjustable.

10/34

Bekanntgabe.

Betrifft: Vereidigung der Politischen Leiter.

Die Vereidigung der Politischen Leiter findet einmal in jedem Jahre statt.

Der Termin wird durch den Stellvertreter des Führers festgelegt und zeitig genug vorher bekanntgegeben.

Betrifft: Stabsleiter.

Stabsleiter beim Gau und Kreis sind nicht zulässig. Das Aufgabengebiet eines Stabsleiters wird in jedem Fall vom Stellvertreter des Hoheitsträgers bearbeitet.

Betrifft: Dienstbezeichnungen der Partei.

Die für die Bearbeitung eines Blocks, bzw. einer Zelle verantwortlichen Politischen Leiter der Partei heißen ab sofort:

Blockleiter, bzw.
Zellenleiter.

Die mit der Führung eines Blocks, bzw. einer Zelle betrauten Parteigenossen bei der NSBO. und NS-Hago heißen:

Blockobmann, bzw.
Zellenobmann.

München, den 5. Mai 1934.

Betrifft: Dienstbezeichnungen der betreuten Organisationen Deutsche Arbeitsfront und „Kraft durch Freude".

Die in der Deutschen Arbeitsfront stehenden und mit der Führung eines Amtes betrauten Partei- bzw. Volksgenossen führen, sofern sie nicht in Personalunion einen Dienstrang als Politischer Leiter innehaben, für die in der Partei übliche Bezeichnung „Leiter" die Bezeichnung:

„Walter" (Zellenwalter, Propagandawalter).

Mit Bezug auf die Organisation „Kraft durch Freude" wird die Bezeichnung

„Warte (Zellenwarte, Propagandawarte)

gebraucht.

Betrifft: Uniform.

Die Uniform der nunmehr als Block, bzw. Zellenleiter benannten Parteigenossen ist die Uniform der bisherigen Block-, bzw. Zellenwarte der Partei.

Die Uniform der Zellen-Obmänner der NSBO., bzw. NS-Hago ist die Uniform eines Blockleiters der Partei.

Block-Obmänner der NSBO. und NS-Hago sind vorläufig ohne Dienstrang.

Betrifft: Knöpfe (Ausführung: Mit Hoheitszeichen, Hakenkreuz ohne Kranz).

Politische Leiter, bei denen goldgewirkte Litzen, bzw. goldgewirkte Mützenschnur zum Dienstanzug gehören, tragen statt der silberfarbigen goldfarbige Knöpfe.

Dasselbe gilt für Koppelschnalle und Haken.

Betrifft: Hoheitszeichen.

Das Hoheitszeichen für den Zivilrock darf nur der Parteigenosse tragen, der ein Amt in der Partei als Politischer Leiter innehat.

Betrifft: Dienstmütze:

Die Dienstmütze der PO. wird ab sofort ohne Kokarde oder Knopf getragen.

Das Hoheitszeichen wird in großer Ausführung 10 mm über dem mittleren Mützenrand am oberen (schrägen) Teil der Mütze angebracht.

München, den 5. Mai 1934.

Dr. Ley.

Two orders by Ley dated May 1934. The first one introduces the names Blockleiter and Zellenleiter. The second abolishes the cockade at its end. The position for the larger national emblem is stated as 10 mm above the upper cap band edge.

W.P.B.R. Saris

W.P.B.R. Saris

P.O.-Mützen

Verschiedentlich werden noch falsche P.O.-Mützen angefertigt und getragen. Die richtige Mütze sieht folgendermaßen aus:

Sie ist aus hellbraunem *Gabardine* angefertigt und trägt *weder Kokarde noch Amtswalterknopf* auf dem Randstreifen. Die Mütze hat lediglich ein besonderes Hoheitsabzeichen, das so angebracht sein muß, daß es 10 mm über dem Randstreifen sitzt. Der Randstreifen selbst ist aus braunem Samt, der nicht zu dunkel sein darf. Man sieht sehr häufig politische Leiter mit einer Mütze, die einen fast schwarzen Samtstreifen trägt. Die richtige Farbe des Samtes entspricht ungefähr dem S.A.-Braun, alles andere ist falsch. Der Mützenschirm ist aus braunem Lackleder hergestellt. Die Paspelierung der Mütze

goldgelb für Reichsleitung
hochrot für Gauleitung
schwarz für Kreisleitung
hellblau für Ortsgruppenleitung

besteht aus je einem Paspel am Mützenboden und an beiden Seiten des Randstreifens.

Die *Verwendung von braunem Tuch oder Trikot* zur Herstellung von P.O.-Mützen ist *untersagt*. Derartige Mützen sind von allen Verkaufsstellen und Käufern zurückzuweisen. Jede Mütze muß außerdem als Gewähr dafür, daß sie den Vorschriften der R.Z.M. entspricht, eine *Erkennungsmarke* haben.

Apparently the correct visored cap was often not worn. The "*Mbl.d.RZM*" pointed in spring 1934 to various specific details in relation to these new caps, being the abolishing of the earlier worn cockade or button with PL device; the color for the cap band (often being nearly as dark as black) and the correct piping colors and their position.

Otto Spronk

Political leaders shown during Hitler's visit to the Reichsführerschule at Bernau in late 1933. Note the various forms of headdress in light through very dark shades.

Above: Early political leader's visored cap with no piping. The national emblem is the only insignia. This form was often used by leaders from the HJ during the years 1931–1932. Goebbels wore this form in 1933.

Unidentified political visored cap.

"Reichsleitung" is included and adjusted. Another interesting detail is that the color for the cap band was changed from dark brown to a lighter brown.

	Cords:	Buttons:	Piping:	Band:
Reichsleitung				
Reichsleiter:	gold	gold	golden/ yellow	light brown velvet;
Hauptdienstleiter:	ibid	ibid	ibid	ibid;
Hauptamtsleiter:	ibid	ibid	ibid	ibid;
Amtsleiter:	ibid	ibid	ibid	ibid;
Hauptstellenleiter:	silver	silver	ibid	ibid;
Stellenleiter:	ibid	ibid	ibid	ibid.[47]

Description Model–1934 Visored Cap

The cap was a "Klappmütze" (Form 1), in the style known as the "old army officers" visored field cap. It must be noted that this style cap had no ventilation grommets on the underside of the cap top. The top was made of khaki colored, light brown, gabardine material (the earlier used tricot was forbidden) and had four panels. It measured in front approximately 5.7cm, 4.3cm on both sides and

[47] *"Vbl.d.RL.d.NSDAP," Nr. 79, End–August 1934, p. 189; "Mbl.d.RZM," Nr. 21, October 20, 1934, p. 5. (The renaming of the two ranks Abteilungs– and Unterabteilungsleiter into Hauptstellen– and Stellenleiter on Reich–level took place with these orders, but became official in 1936).*

Otto Spronk

Reichsstatthalter Jacob Sprenger, the Gauleiter from Hessen–Nassau, is wearing his visored cap with the cap cords with knots. Note the wear of the Party–Province Commemorative Badge. Photographs show that the highest ranked political leaders often adopted the wearing of the cockade in 1933/34 with the introduction of the new form of headdress.

The Gauleiter from Düsseldorf, Friedrich Karl Florian, shown wearing his visored cap in the approximate 1935 style. Excellent details are given in this photograph of the silk cap cords, as well as the silk top and cap band piping in the earliest manufacturing form, being cords. His cockade is devoid of the swastika.

4.9cm at the rear (these measurements are for a size 56 cap). The cap top length was 26cm, being approximately 24.5cm wide. The crown of the cap was piped in 2mm thick material. A 2mm, loose iron wire – 1.5 x 0.6mm – retained the shape of the crown (photos show this wire was often removed).

The cap band was supported by a 0.4mm thick, black lacquered piece of cardboard, which measured approximately 5cm high, including the 2mm upper and lower cap band piping, and the lowest edge of the band, under the bottom piping. The good quality, inside lining was in a color which complimented the color of the cap top. In between the lining and the cap top was a light, gummed waterproof layer. The front of the cap was supported by a metal stiffener, covered with linen and a 6cm wide piece of wadding.

A celluloid sweat shield diamond, measuring 13.5 x 10cm was sewn onto the top lining. A 4.5cm light brown sheepskin sweatband was sewn on the inside of the cap band. An RZM tag was positioned 10mm above the cap band on the inside. The visor was made of dark brown lacquered leather, 4.6cm wide in the center and approximately 24cm long.[48] (For details on cords etc. consult the January 1934 regulations and the interim adaptation. The RZM label for the cap

48 *"Mbl.d.RZM," Nr. 18, September 29, 1934, p. 3. (It was noted that the national emblem was still 10 mm above the cap band).*

National Archives

Bernhard Rust, the Gauleiter from Hannover–Süd, is wearing his slides positioned as for the two knots, corresponding with those worn on his shoulder strap. Note that Dr. Goebbels wears a rather nondescript visored cap.

cord was executed with violet overprint. Note that the cap band for local level Ortsgruppenleitung was of light brown worsted material).

W.P.B.R. Saris

A mark as often positioned on the lining of the best qualities, published in the 1935 RZM. "Sonderausführung" means special finish; "Höchstleistung" means maximum performance.

The piping was made of artificial silk, quality Ia. It was spooled over a white cord inlay. The golden/yellow color for Reichsleitung was the color as worn by the SA Gruppe Schlesien (Schwefelgelb); the official designation was "Indanthrengelb 4GK" or "Indanthrengoldorange 3G." The color designation for the Amann cotton thread company was A/606;

The color red worn by Gauleitung was the red as used by SA Gruppenstäbe. It is known as "Indanthrenscharlach GG" or "Indanthrenrot CLG;"

The black for Kreisleitung was the black as worn by the SA Gruppen Niederrhein and Berlin–Brandenburg and is known in the industry as "Indocarbon CLG;"

The light blue color worn by the Ortsgruppenleitung was the light blue as worn by the SA Gruppe Hochland–Bayern, and is known as "Indanthrenblau

GCD" or "Indanthrenbrillantgrün B" (this so–called "brilliant green" is blue shaded). The color code for the Amann Company was A/1342.[49]

In 1935 Hess agreed to the introduction of a "new" rank level: Stützpunktleiter. This was caused by the enormous growth of the Party. By May 1935, approximately 8,566 of these "points of support" (being smaller than the local level) existed all over Germany. It was said that this rank was put on an equal level as the local "Amtsleiter" (wearing silver cords), but was in fact authorized to wear the golden cap cord and buttons. The wear of silver cords was used before May for leaders of such a support.[50] In July 1935 other new ranks were announced: "Mitarbeiter" (co–worker) for the levels Reich, Gau, Kreis and Ortsgruppe; and "Hilfsstellenleiter" on the Reich–level only (its position was between the rank Stellenleiter and Mitarbeiter).[51]

Joe Stone

This Ortsgruppenleiter wears his visored cap according to local level standards at the 1935 Reichsparteitag at Nürnberg.

W.P.B.R. Saris

Vertriebsstelle Nr.:

Herstellerfirma Nr.:

Mitgliedsnummer des Trägers:

Unbefugter Besitz parteiamtlicher Kleidungsstücke wird laut Verordnung des Reichspräsidenten vom 21. 3. 1933 mit Gefängnis bis zu 2 Jahren bestraft.

N. S. D. A. P. Reichszeugmeisterei Nr.:

RZM

Für S.A.-, P.O.- und H.J.-Dienstmützen

The early form tag for the visored cap of political leaders.

---

49 Ibid, Nr. 17. May 25, 1935. p. 168; "RZM–Herstellungsvorschriften" (manufacturing procedures), 1936, pp. 161–162.

50 "Vbl.d.RL.d.NSDAP," Nr. 96, Mid–May 1935, p. 271; "Mbl.d.RZM," Nr. 17, May 25, 1935, p. 165. One must note that the rank of Stützpunktleiter was classified equally as Zellenleiter from 1932–1935.

51 "Mbl.d.RZM," Nr. 20, July 6, 1935, p. 202, announcing Ley's orders Nr. 8/35, dated April 4, 1935 and Nr. 12/35, dated June 17; "Vbl.d.RL.d.NSDAP," Nr. 100, Mid–July 1935, p. 292.

Jakob Sprenger, the Gauleiter of Hessen–Nassau, is wearing the 1934–model political leaders visored cap with the cords/knots system and piped in red.

Otto Spronk

Joseph Wagner, the Gauleiter of Westfalen–Süd, wearing the 1934 form political leaders visored cap with light piping, instead of red. He is wearing the light piping due to his appointment (in December 1932) as Ley's deputy.

Otto Spronk

Otto Spronk

Rudolf Jordan, later Gauleiter from Halle–Merseburg, shown wearing his visored cap with light colored piping, indicating Reich–level. In 1933 Jordan was a Privy Councilor. Note that he is wearing a "button" instead of a cockade.

W.P.B.R. Saris

Ortsgruppenleiter shown at his marriage is wearing the 1936 form visored cap with 1934 national eagle emblem and a cockade devoid of the swastika, upon the cap band which is in the same color as the top.

Otto Spronk

A group of political leaders during the Reichsparteitag 1934. Note the light–brown cap band, indicating Ortsgruppen–level.

John Coy

Early 1934 form visored cap for a political leader on Ortsgruppe–level. Note that the top and cap–band are manufactured in the same color material according to regulations. The 1934–form eagle is used, as well as the introduced in 1935 cockade with swastika and back–plate.

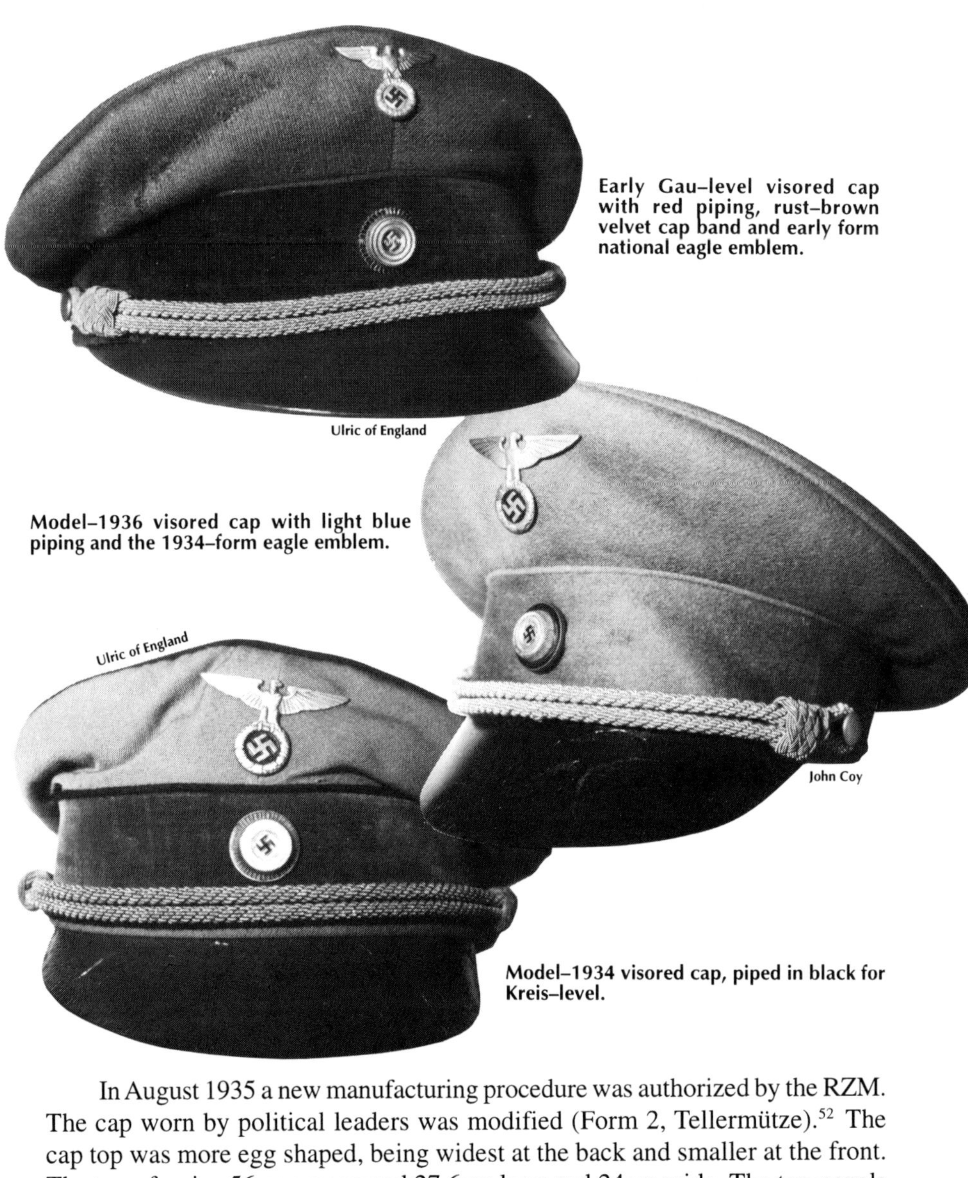

Early Gau–level visored cap with red piping, rust–brown velvet cap band and early form national eagle emblem.

Ulric of England

Model–1936 visored cap with light blue piping and the 1934–form eagle emblem.

Ulric of England

John Coy

Model–1934 visored cap, piped in black for Kreis–level.

In August 1935 a new manufacturing procedure was authorized by the RZM. The cap worn by political leaders was modified (Form 2, Tellermütze).[52] The cap top was more egg shaped, being widest at the back and smaller at the front. The top of a size 56 cap measured 27.6cm long and 24cm wide. The top panels were: in the front 6.6cm, at the sides 4.5cm and at the back 5.2cm. A rustproof wire (0.2 x 4mm) was sewn within the top lining and another 10mm wide piece of cloth was added for additional shaping. A 13mm wide inlay was sewn into the side of the under panels of the cap top. To further support and enhance the shape of the front of the cap, a 7cm long stiffener (8cm wide at the top, and 2.5cm wide at the bottom), was sewn into the top, along with a 10cm long piece of rustproof metal and a metal spring. The entire cap top was supported on the inside by double wadding and gauze. The sweatband was now allowed to be made of imitation leather, and was then always stamped with the letters "RZ." It is inter-

52 *"Mbl.d.RZM," Nr. 23, August 17, 1935, p. 234.*

esting to note that the RZM publication of the time stated that the national emblem was still worn 10mm above the upper cap band piping (at that period of time freely worn by most political leaders much closer to the top. This was officially ordered February 1938). No cockade was yet authorized.

Rumors made the rounds that new uniforms were expected. This was denied in September 1935, but a modified visored cap was introduced in 1936.[53] (For better understanding a 1936 system is included in the coming 1936–1939 section).

Joe Stone

A mixture of the Model 1934 and Model 1936 (known as the "Tellermütze") visored cap in wear.

1936 – 1939

With an order, dated January 6, 1936, the ranks for Abteilungsleiter and Unterabteilungsleiter on the levels for Gau–, Kreis–, Ortsgruppe and Stützpunkt were officially renamed Hauptstellenleiter and Stellenleiter.[54] It should be noted that, in fact, the renaming had started as early as the fall of 1934.

SYSTEM ACCORDING TO ORGANIZATION BOOK – 1936

	Cords:	Buttons:	Piping:	Band:
Reichsleitung				
Reichsleiter: (Reich Leader)	gold	gold	yellow or golden/ yellow	rust or light brown velvet;
Hauptdienstleiter: (Senior Service Leader)	ibid	ibid	ibid	ibid;
Hauptamtsleiter: (Main Office Leader)	ibid	ibid	ibid	ibid;
Amtsleiter: (Office Leader)	ibid	ibid	ibid	ibid;

---

53 Ibid, Nr. 25, September 14, 1935, p. 256.

54 "Vbl.d.RL.d.NSDAP," Nr. 114, Mid–February, 1936, p. 377: Announcement by Ley, number 1/36.

H. Friedrich

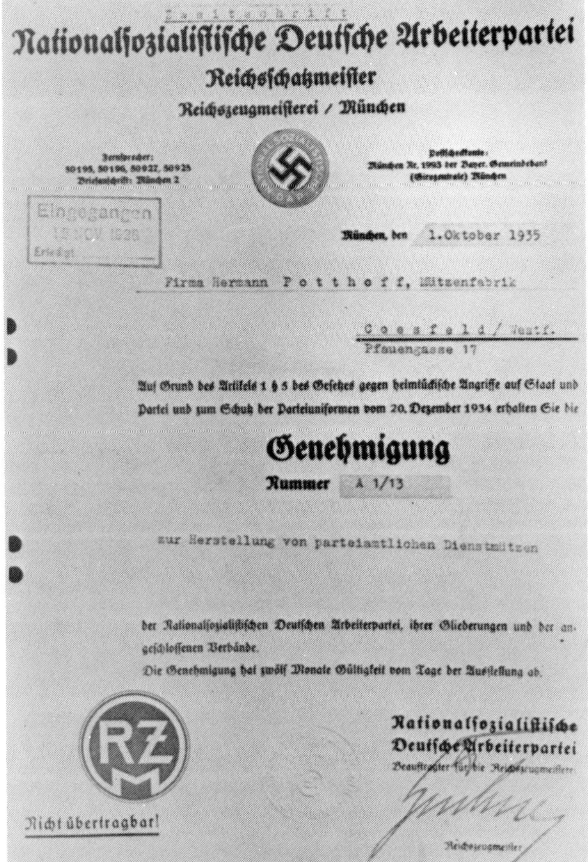

Zweitschrift

Nationalsozialistische Deutsche Arbeiterpartei
Reichsschatzmeister
Reichszeugmeisterei / München

Fernsprecher: 50195, 50196, 50927, 50925
Briefanschrift: München 2

Postscheckkonto: München Nr. 1993 der Bayer. Gemeindebank (Girozentrale) München

Eingegangen 18 NOV 1938 Erledigt

München, den 1.Oktober 1935

Firma Hermann P o t t h o f f, Mützenfabrik

C o e s f e l d / Westf.
Pfauengasse 17

Auf Grund des Artikels 1 § 5 des Gesetzes gegen heimtückische Angriffe auf Staat und Partei und zum Schutz der Parteiuniformen vom 20. Dezember 1934 erhalten Sie die

Genehmigung

Nummer A 1/13

zur Herstellung von parteiamtlichen Dienstmützen

der Nationalsozialistischen Deutschen Arbeiterpartei, ihrer Gliederungen und der angeschlossenen Verbände.

Die Genehmigung hat zwölf Monate Gültigkeit vom Tage der Ausstellung ab.

Nationalsozialistische Deutsche Arbeiterpartei
Beauftragter für die Reichszeugmeisterei

Reichszeugmeister

Nicht übertragbar!

A permit to manufacture caps for the NSDAP, issued October 1, 1935 for the concern Hermann Poffhoff from Coesfeld in Westfalen with license–number A 1/13. Note that above the license–masthead is typed "Zweitschrift": this means duplicate, distributed November 1938.

W.P.B.R. Saris

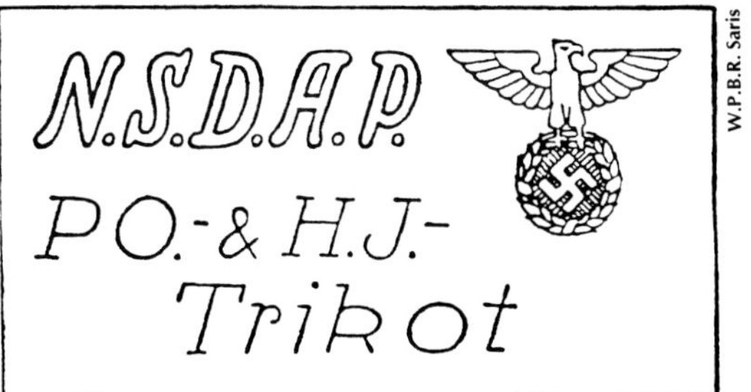

Examples of the stamps for the tricot and gabardine cloth for political leaders. These stamps were placed in white paint on the roll at regular distances, according the RZM–specifications. Often these stamps had also the word "Mützen" placed on them.

Reichszeugmeisterei
der
Nationalsozialistischen Deutschen
Arbeiterpartei

Herstellungsvorschriften

für
parteiamtliche Bekleidungsstücke und
Ausrüstungsgegenstände

1936

Alle früher erschienenen Vorschriften werden mit dieser Ausgabe für ungültig erklärt.

The front page of the 1936 RZM manufacturing regulations for the political organizations uniforms, its insignia and equipment. The phrase at the foot of the page says literally that all earlier published regulations were certified as invalid with the appearance of this issue.

Page 117 of the aforementioned 1936–issue. It gives full detailed information in relation to the visored cap for political leaders. The first part gives its form and sizes. The other parts are the sections: Visored cap top, cap band, lining, visor, cords and sweat band. The last part gives the position for the eagle and cockade .

Mütze der Politischen Leiter

Die Mütze für die Politischen Leiter ist eine Tellermütze in Sattelform mit braunem Lacklederfeldschirm. Der Grundstoff ist Gabardine, welcher nach Vorschrift der Reichszeugmeisterei angefertigt und gestempelt ist.

Maße bei Größe 56, an der fertigen Mütze gemessen:

a) Boden: eiförmig, nach vorne sich verjüngend (s. Schnittmuster)

Durchmesser von vorn nach hinten gemessen 27,6 cm
Durchmesser von einer Seite zur anderen 24 cm

b) 4 Seitenteile, zwischen den Biesen gemessen:
vorn 6,3 cm Höhe
seitlich 4,4 cm Höhe
hinten 5,2 cm Höhe.

Der Mützenboden ist mit einer 2 mm starken farbigen Biese eingefaßt. In der Deckelbiese wird zur Versteifung des Bodens ein 4×0,20 mm starker rostfreier Stahlbügel fest hinternäht. Zur Erzielung einer schönen abgerundeten Bodenkante wird ein 10 mm breiter, dem Zweck entsprechender Einlagefilz im Boden vor dem Paspelieren eingenäht. Im Seitenteil wird zum gleichen Zweck eine etwa 13 mm breite entsprechende Einlage ebenfalls eingenäht.

Der Randstreifen ist einschließlich Biesen zirka 5 cm hoch und oben und unten von je einer 2 mm starken Biese eingefaßt. Der Mützenrand wird als 3 mm breiter Vorstoß aus Grundstoff abgeschlossen. Als Randeinlage ist eine 0,5 mm starke Friedensrandpappe eingearbeitet.

Der Futterboden besteht aus feinstem Futtersatin, in der Farbe [illegible]

Zwischen Mützenboden und Futterdeckel ist eine leicht gummierte wasserdichte Einlage eingearbeitet.

Als Versteifung ist vorn eine Stütze dauerhaft eingenäht. Diese besteht aus einem 7 cm langen Leinenstück, das oben 8 cm breit ist und sich nach unten auf nur 2,5 cm verjüngt. Auf dieses Leinenstück ist eine Wellenfeder und eine rostfreie 0,6 mm starke Bandfeder von 10 cm Länge aufgenäht. Die Bandfeder ist zwischen die Wellenfeder und das Steifleinenstück fest einzuschieben.

Außerdem ist in den Vorderteilen ein 20 cm langer und 6,5 cm breiter Watteſtreifen und darüber Mützengaze einzunähen.

Im Mützenfutter, genau in der Mitte des Bodens, ist ein Celluloidspiegel in Parallelogramm-Form mit einer Länge von 13,5 cm und einer Breite von 10 cm einzunähen. Unter dem Celluloidspiegel auf dem Futterdeckel ist die Kopfweite mit säurefreier Tusche gut leserlich aufzustempeln.

Der Schirm besteht aus dunkelbraunem Spalt-Lackleder in Feldschirmform mit leicht eingepreßter Rille. Dieser ist an der breitesten Stelle 4,6 cm breit und 24 cm lang, an der fertigen Mütze gemessen.

Die Mützenkordel, ganze Länge höchstens 29 cm, von Schlaufenbogen zu Schlaufenbogen gemessen, wird auf die 1 cm hinter dem Mützenschirmrand angenähten Mützenkordelknöpfe geknöpft. Die Kordelknöpfe sind mattgekörnt und haben einen Durchmesser von 12 mm. Sie sind unmittelbar oberhalb der unteren Randbiese mit weißem Zwirn fest anzunähen. Die Verwendung von Splintknöpfen ist nicht gestattet. Für die Mützenbiesen ist das den Hoheitsgebieten entsprechende Spiegeltuch gemäß untenstehender Aufstellung zu verwenden

Ortsgruppe	hellblau	= für SA. —	Hochland
Kreisleitung	schwarz	= für SA. —	Berlin-Brandenburg
Gauleitung	hochrot	= für SA. —	Gruppenstäbe
Reichsleitung	gelb	= für SA. —	Schlesien

Als Schweißleder ist ein 22½" (= 5,2 cm) breites, ungestücktes, echtes Schafleder einzunähen, hellhavanna eingefärbt, das zur Vermeidung jedes Stirndruckes über den Schirm auf der Fleischseite mit Gummischwamm unterklebt ist. Ferner erhält das Schweißleder auf der Stirnseite eine Perforation. Außer Schafleder kann auch Kunstschweißleder mit dem aufgeprägten Stempel „RZ" verwendet werden. Das Schweißleder ist gestürzt einzunähen. Die beiden Enden werden genau über der hinteren Seitenteil- und Randnaht liegend mit einem Seidenfaden-Kreuzstich geschlossen. Splintverschluß ist verboten.

Auf der vorderen Seitenteilnaht, 10 mm über der oberen Randbiese, ist das Mützen-Hoheitsabzeichen für Politische Leiter anzubringen, das nur durch die Reichszeugmeisterei zu beziehen ist. Etwa 3 mm über der Randstreifenmitte wird die weißrote Kokarde für Politische Leiter angebracht. Es ist bei dem Aufstecken der Abzeichen darauf zu achten, daß die Achsen der Abzeichen genau in der Richtung der vorderen Seitenteilnaht liegen. Es sind nur Abzeichen zu verwenden, die den RZM.-Stempel tragen. Die durchgestochenen Splinte sind gut umzubiegen.

W.P.B.R. Saris

W.P.B.R. Saris

Bei dem Bügeln der Mütze ist darauf zu achten, daß die Bodenkante schön abgerundet gebildet wird.

Die Erkennungsmarke wird am Rand des Seitenteilfutters mit der Schrift nach dem Mützenboden weisend auf der linken Seite der Mütze über der Seitenteilnaht angebracht.

Die Bezeichnungen links und rechts beziehen sich auf d Betrachtung der Mütze von vorne.

Abweichungen: Ausführung ± 5%
Farbe ± 10%

Mützenkordel und Paspelierung

	Rand		Kordel	Knopf	Paspelierung
Reichsleitung:					
Reichsleiter	hellbrauner	Samt	Gold	Gold	Gelb
Hauptdienstleiter	"	"	Silber	Silber	Gelb
Hauptamtsleiter	"	"	Gold	Gold	Gelb
Amtsleiter	"	"	Gold	Gold	Gelb
Hauptstellenleiter bis Mitarbeiter	"	"	Silber	Silber	Gelb
Gauleitung:					
Gauleiter	"	"	Gold	Gold	Rot
Gauleiterstellvertreter	"	"	Gold	Gold	Rot
Amtsleiter bis Mitarbeiter	"	"	Silber	Silber	Rot
Kreisleitung:					
Kreisleiter	"	"	Gold	Gold	Schwarz
Amtsleiter bis Mitarbeiter	"	"	Silber	Silber	Schwarz
Ortsgruppenleitung:					
Ortsgruppenleiter	Grundstoff		Gold	Gold	Hellblau
Stützpunktleiter	"		Gold	Gold	Hellblau
Amtsleiter bis Mitarbeiter	"		Silber	Silber	Hellblau

Schnittmuster sowie Farbproben des vorgeschriebenen Samtes sind bei der Reichszeugmeisterei, Abtlg. Ausrüstun anzufordern.

Mützen für die Mitglieder der Parteigerichte

Oberstes Parteigericht:

Der Vorsitzende und die Vorsitzenden der Spruchkammer sowie die Beisitzer beim Obersten Parteigericht tragen die vorschriftsmäßige Mütze der Politischen Leiter mit hellbraunem Mützenband aus Samt, goldgelber Paspelierung und goldener Mützenkordel.

Gau- und Kreisgericht:

Der Vorsitzende und die Kammervorsitzenden tragen die Mütze wie vor, jedoch mit blauer Paspelierung aus Tuch.

Die Mütze für die Beisitzer dieser Gerichte unterscheidet sich nur durch die Anbringung einer silbernen Mützenkordel.

Ortsgericht:

Der Vorsitzende trägt dieselbe Mütze wie der Vorsitzende und die Kammervorsitzenden im Gau- und Kreisgericht. Die Mütze für den Beisitzer ist in der Ausführung gleich, jedoch mit silberner Mützenkordel.

Page 118 giving detailed information about the 1936 system for the four levels in relations to the colors used on the cap band, cords, buttons and piping. The last part gives color details for the visored cap as worn by the various Party court levels.

Hauptstellenleiter: (Main Department Leader)	silver	silver	ibid	ibid;
Stellenleiter: (Department Leader)	ibid	ibid	ibid	ibid;
Hilfsstellenleiter: (Assistant Depart–ment Leader)	ibid	ibid	ibid	ibid;
Mitarbeiter: (co–worker)	ibid	ibid	ibid	ibid;

Gauleitung

Gauleiter: (Province Leader)	gold	gold	red	ibid;
Stellvertretender Gauleiter: (Deputy)	ibid	ibid	ibid	ibid;
Hauptamtsleiter:	silver	silver	ibid	ibid;
Amtsleiter:	ibid	ibid	ibid	ibid;
Hauptstellenleiter:	ibid	ibid	ibid	ibid;

Stellenleiter:	ibid	ibid	ibid	ibid;
Mitarbeiter:	ibid	ibid	ibid	ibid;
Kreisleitung				
Kreisleiter: (District Leader)	gold	gold	black	ibid;
Hauptamtsleiter:	silver	silver	ibid	ibid;
Amtsleiter:	ibid	ibid	ibid	ibid;
Hauptstellenleiter:	ibid	ibid	ibid	ibid;
Stellenleiter:	ibid	ibid	ibid	ibid;
Mitarbeiter:	ibid	ibid	ibid	ibid;
Ortsgruppenleitung/ Stützpunktleitung				
Ortsgruppenleiter: (Local Group Leader)	gold	gold	light blue gaberdine;	light brown
Stützpunktleiter: (Support Leader)	ibid	ibid	ibid	ibid;
Amtsleiter:	silver	silver	ibid	ibid;
Zellenleiter: (Cell Leader)	gold	gold	ibid	ibid;
Blockleiter: (Block Leader)	ibid	ibid	ibid	ibid;
Hauptstellenleiter:	silver	silver	ibid	ibid;
Stellenleiter:	ibid	ibid	ibid	ibid;
Mitarbeiter:	ibid	ibid	ibid	ibid.[55]

Otto Spronk

Political leaders marching in March 1936 during festivities during the German re-militarization of the Rhine district

---

55 *"Organisationsbuch der NSDAP. " München, 1936, pp. 27–28; "RZM–Herstellungsvorschriften," 1936, p. 118; NSDAP Gau Schwaben: "Dienstanzug und Dienstrang des Politischen Leiters," 1936, pp. 20–23; "Mbl.d.RZM," Nr. 12, June 6, 1936. p. 244 introduces the gold cords for "Zellen– und Blockleiter" also Nr. 15. July 18, 1936, p. 307. (This was the most extended list at the moment, since the renaming and adding of some new ranks in the course of 1935 and early 1936).*

The form for the political leader's visored cap was constantly modified during the years 1934 through 1936. To avoid misunderstandings regarding manufacturing procedures, the companies were ordered to obtain a cap from the RZM called a "Standardmuster." This RZM model was then to be used as an example of correct specifications. Caps, known as "Standardmuster" (a pattern sample of the actual item, which the firms had to use as a design guide after which to pattern their final product) were clearly identified as pattern pieces by means of a special attached seal . This seal (first made of wax and from 1936 in lead, was approximately 11.5cm in diameter) always had the RZM emblem (Schutszeichen) on its obverse and the letters "MPA" (Materialprüfungsamt – Materials Inspection Office) on the reverse and was attached to the item by a twisted cord.[56]

The model–1936 was known as "Form 3" (Wehrmachtschnitt). In April a new manufacturing procedure was introduced.[57] The size of the egg shaped top, being a "Tellermütze" in "Sattelform," remained the same, but the size of the side panels was changed slightly: in the front to 6.3cm, the sides to 4.4cm and the rear portion remaining 5.2cm. Also the other manufacturing procedures remained, the cap band being approximately 5cm high. The light brown or rust–brown velvet cap band was approximately 4.3cm and was piped in 2mm material at the upper and lower edge. A 3mm bottom edge in the same color as the cap top was visible below the bottom piping. The cap band color for local groups was in light brown gabardine.

National archives

Gauleiter Rust wears the Model–1936 visored cap. Foreign Minister von Ribbentrop is shown wearing the uniform of an honorary SS member.

---

[56] *"Mbl.d.RZM," Nr. 3, February 3, 1936, p. 26. (it noted that so–called "Wiederverkäufer – salesman – were also allowed to obtain these special samples); Ibid, Nr. 25, December 3, 1938, p. 249 with drawings of the seal.*

[57] *Ibid, Nr. 9. April 25, 1936, p. 161; "RZM–Herstellungsvorschriften" (further referred to as "HV"), 1936. Section equipment, pp. 117–118.*

An example of the Model–1936 (Form III) visored cap for Gauleitung (note the silver cap cords and national emblem as worn by "Mitarbeiter" rank through "Hauptstellenleiter."

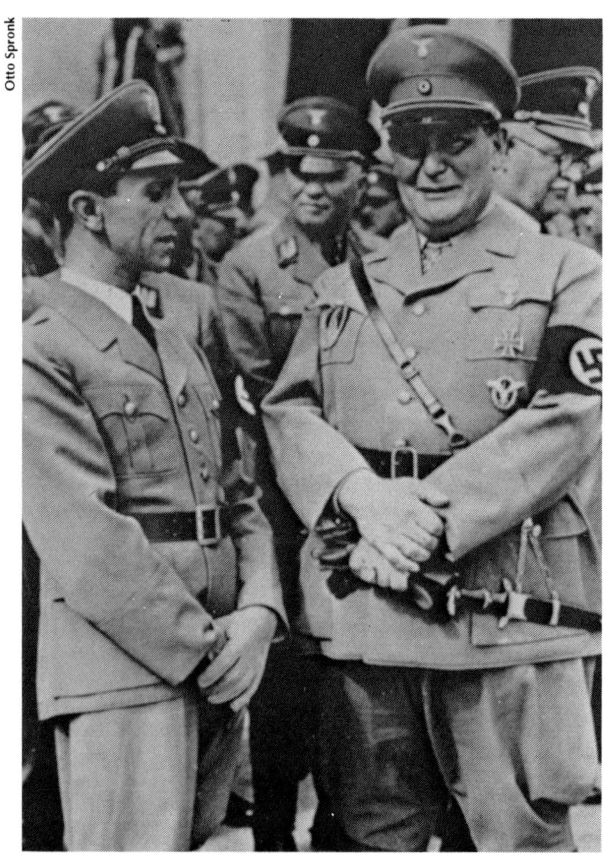

Dr. Goebbels and Hermann Göring during the Reichsparteitag in 1936. Note Göring's cap, having a very light colored cap band and an extremely good view of the golden piping. It is very clear that he also wore the regular type army cockade devoid of the swastika, and the first form of eagle.

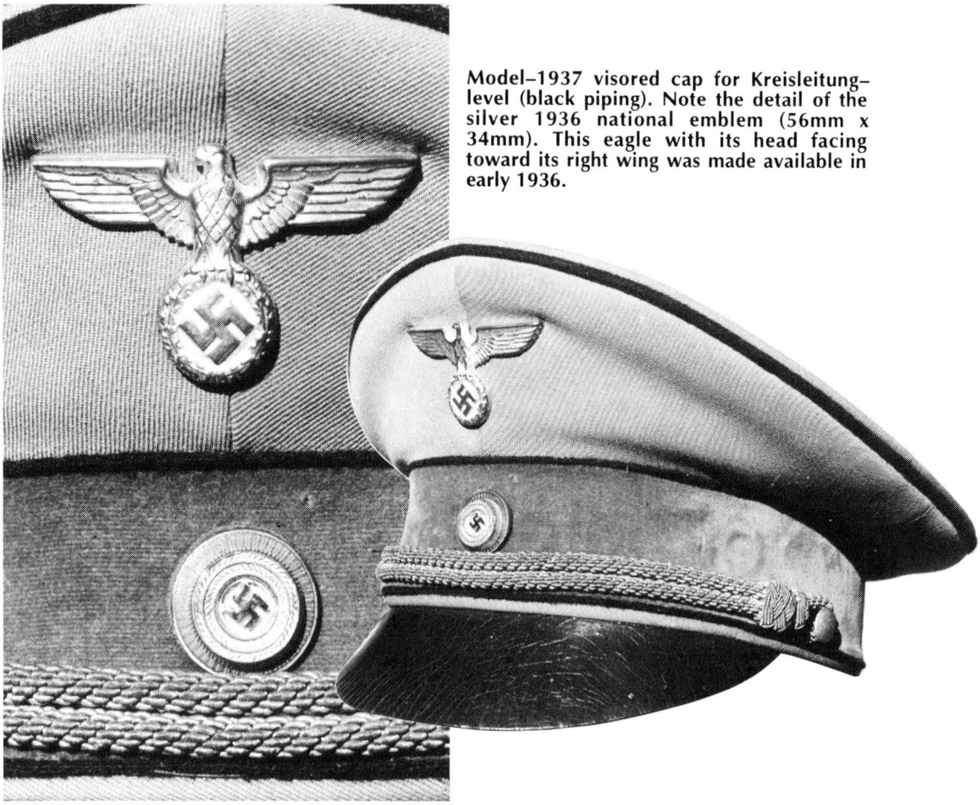

Model–1937 visored cap for Kreisleitung–level (black piping). Note the detail of the silver 1936 national emblem (56mm x 34mm). This eagle with its head facing toward its right wing was made available in early 1936.

Visored cap as worn by political leaders on Reichsleitung–level. Note the brown velvet cap band and the silver cap cords. An army national emblem is worn instead of the political leader's eagle. Silver cords were worn by the ranks "Mitarbeiter" through "Hauptstellenleiter"

With these regulations the visor was still dark brown lacquered leather, with a light or Havana–brown underside, but the visor now featured a raised leading edge. It was also specified that the 12mm diameter cap cord buttons with an eyelet on their reverse had to have a matte finish and were sewn to the cap band with thick, white thread only. Buttons with clip systems were not permitted, but were probably re–introduced during the war.

The sweatband was 5.2cm wide and made of light Havana–brown sheepskin or imitation leather and was closed at the back of the cap by a small, silk ribbon bow. The use of split pins on the sweatband closure was forbidden at this time. The position of the national emblem was still officially 10mm above the upper piping of the band; the cockade was secured 3mm above the center line of the band.[58]

A black RZM tag was sewn in at the left side of the lining at the edge of the side panel with the script to the top's inside.[59] In early 1937 the RZM complained that manufactures still were producing the "Form 2" and drew attention to the new "Form 3."

Klaus D. Patzwall

A political leader wearing a black piped visored cap.

Gauleiter Koch during the presentation on June 16, 1938 of the "Gauehrenzeichen der NSDAP Ostpreussen" at the castle of Königsberg. Note that the political leader on the left is wearing the 1936 version eagle, the person standing at his left is wearing the 1934 eagle.

[58] *"RZM–HV," 1936, p. 117; page 164 notes the black printed tag (earlier this was violet).*

[59] *Ibid, p. 118.*

A. Stam

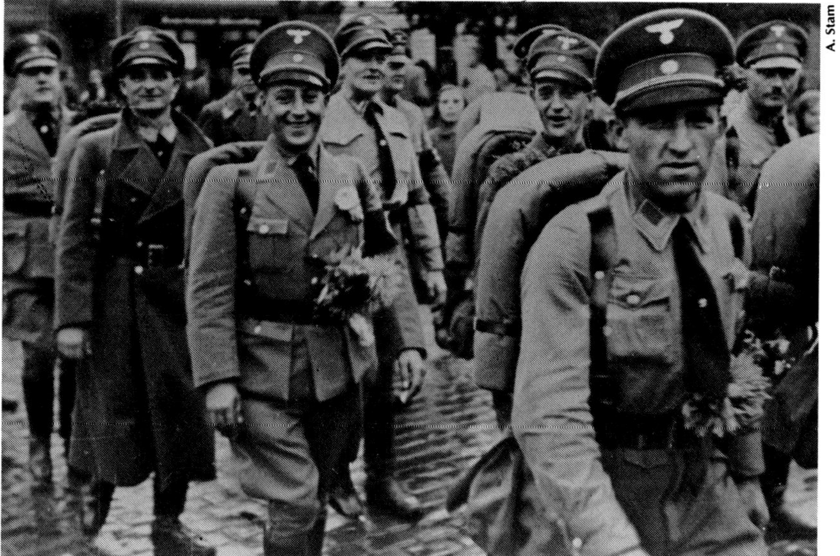

Political leaders from Mönchengladbach returning from the Reichsparteitag at Nürnberg in September 1937. Note the wear of the light brown cap bands and the various forms of visored caps and national emblems.

The drawings from the "Mitteilungsblatt der RZM" of the seal for the pattern samples. The obverse with the lettering RZM, the reverse the lettering MPA.

W.P.B.R. Saris

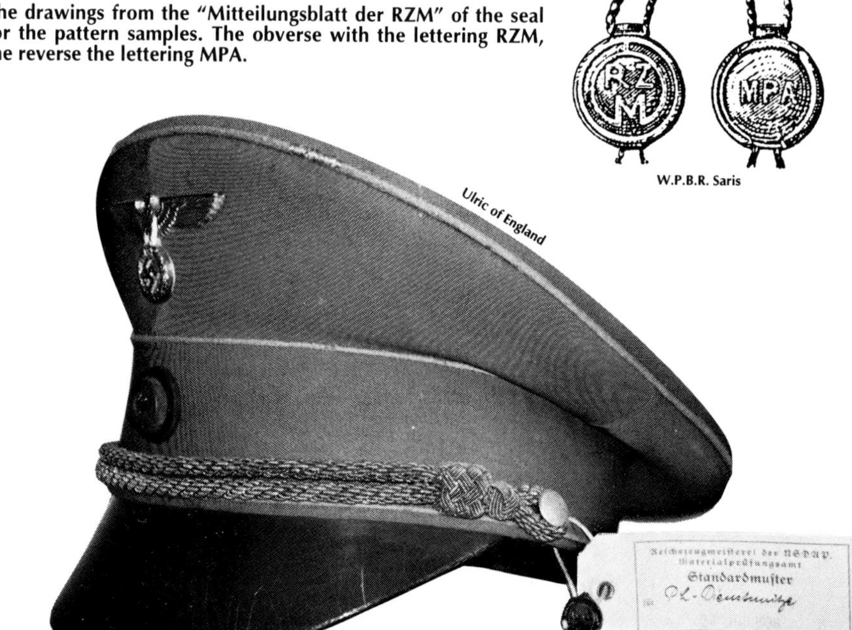

Ulric of England

A fine example visored cap referred to as the "Standardmuster" from the RZM for Local–level. The seal is properly attached to the cord with its specific label, confirming it as the pattern sample for political leaders from the Materials Inspection Office. The tag is dated July 24, 1936. It is interesting that with this sample the national emblem is the form with a to its right looking eagle. At mid–1936 this form was correct, as well as the to its left looking type. The last became the only official form in the spring of 1937.

Visored cap as worn by Kreisleitung in the Form 3 with black piping of the crown and cap–band. Note that the later form national emblem is being used.

Political leaders during a funeral. Note the various forms of visored caps. Some even wear the visored caps with the very low top; the person at the right of the flag bearer, as well as the persons directly after him in the middle. The 1934 and 1936 eagle forms are being worn.

Political leaders from Ortsgruppe Riederwald (a part of the town Frankfurt am Main) during a funeral in 1937, wearing the 1936 type eagle emblem and the 1936–model visored cap. The man in the background, wearing a dark visored cap with cockade and eagle emblem is an employee of an undertaker (discussed in a later volume).

Reichsleitung–level visored cap with 1936 national emblem.

A. Stam

A political leader during a Kreis–level animal show on June 21, 1939. The person speaking is "Kreisbauernführer" Oerding, who held an Amtsleiter rank. He is wearing the proper silver cords and black piped cap. On his left pocket he is wearing the Deutsches Reiterabzeichen in gilt.

In early 1936 the manufacturing procedures for the cap cords were published.

Cord construction:

Golden cords: Three thin nickeled silver brass wires with a gold content of 392 (3 grams per kilo), were twisted together to the left, four of such threads, twisted to the right, formed two main cords, 5mm thick. The runner/slides (approximately 15 x 15mm) consisted of a cardboard cylinder, covered by 5 nickeled gold threads, plaited together. The loops (with a 25mm inner opening) held together by two smaller knots (approximately 8 x 12mm). The length of a pair of cords was approximately 29cm.

Silver cords: Same as above, but the wire was made of nickeled silver brass with no gold content.[60] The color of the RZM tag, tied to cords, was printed in violet . The Gothic script on these tags changed during the war to Roman script.

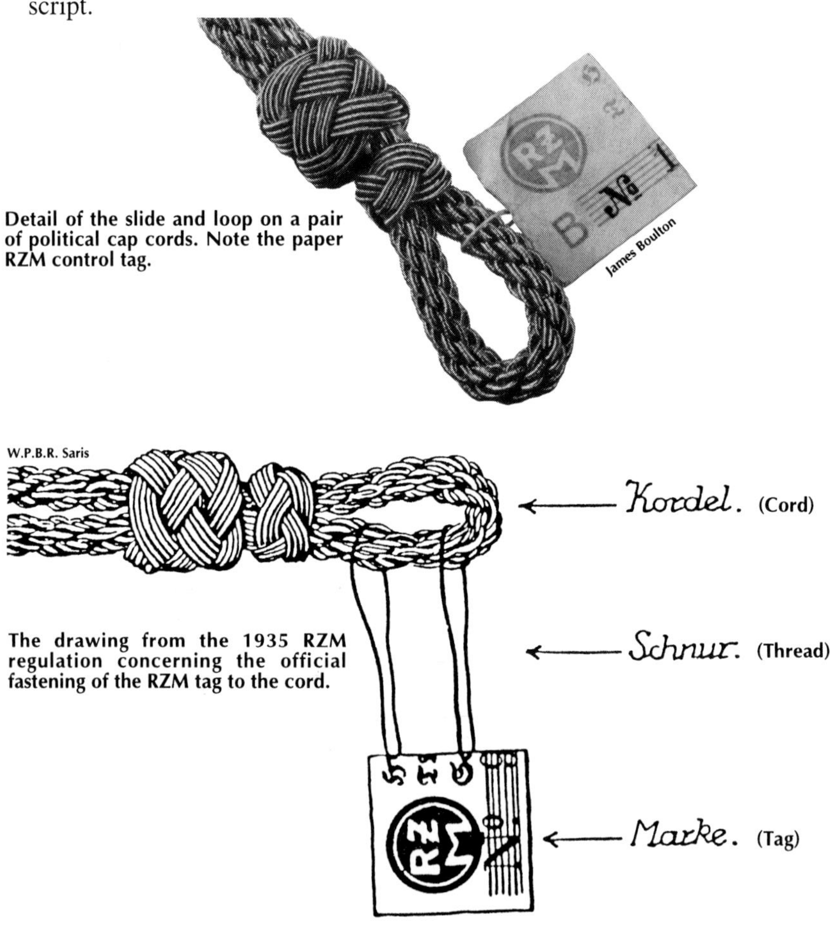

Detail of the slide and loop on a pair of political cap cords. Note the paper RZM control tag.

The drawing from the 1935 RZM regulation concerning the official fastening of the RZM tag to the cord.

The cylinders of the cords were also manufactured in aluminum or light weight metal and had four small holes on the front surface (Friedrich Linden,

[60] *"Mbl.d.RZM," Nr. 5, February 29, 1936, p. 71; "RZM–HV," 1936, pp. 166–169.*

Nr.5917).[61] The metal was 2mm thick, and the cylinder was 15 x 16mm.[62] (It must be noted that the small knots and runner/slides often vary in size, this because of procedures other than those sanctioned by the RZM).

In July 1937 the manufacturing procedure for cap cords was modified. Less expensive gold plated aluminum wire was allowed to be used to make the cords, and instead of five threads being used in the plait, four were now used for the small knot and the runner/slides.[63] The further use of the 1936 manufacturing procedures were prohibited in July 1937.[64] The cap cord button was positioned 1cm behind the visor on the cap band.

Button construction:

White buttons: The upper portion, pebbled and made of 0.3mm light weight metal in DIN 1713, anodized and lacquered with a transparent varnish, or in thin sheet iron, matte lacquered. The inner metal portion was of 0.4mm white sheet metal with an inlay of another thin piece of metal or cardboard, 0.4mm thick. The eyelet was of light weight, 1.75mm thick, wire, raising approximately 5mm out of the reverse of the button. The RZM markings were stamped into the back plate of the button.

Yellow buttons: The upper portion was of pebbled brass plated steel with a lacquered surface.[65] Other procedures were as with the white buttons.

(It must be noted that in 1938 the procedures were changed and cheaper buttons were manufactured now).

There were repeated efforts from all sides to change the color of the political leader's uniform during 1936–1938. Changes were blocked by Dr. Robert Ley. It was, in fact, Ley who planned a new style and new insignia. Preparations of the new design began in early 1938. The motive behind the new uniform was to enhance and modernize the appearance of Party officials. On February 11, 1938 Ley ordered the "Fest–Dienstanzug" (uniform meant to be worn during very special festivities only) and the "Ausgehanzug" (walking out dress). Simultaneously, he ordered a new visored cap for these forms of dress and the center front of the top as the position for the *silvered* national emblem. This, in fact definitive type cap, was known as "Form 4" (Wehrmachtschnitt IV) and would become the standard form of headdress from 1939 and later.[66] With 1938 Reichparteitag orders for "Gau–Wettkämpfe" (competitions) this new headdress was on the list of uniform orders.[67] Apparently this plan was canceled.

In the course of 1938 the rank of "Stützpunktleiter" was put on a level with "Ortsgruppenleiter" and the name disappeared totally.

---

[61] *Friedrich Linden, Lüdenscheid. Katalog, May 15, 1939, p. 6a.*

[62] *"RZM–HV," 1936, p. 95.*

[63] *"Uniformen–Markt," Nr. 15, August 1, 1937, p. 233; Mbl.d.RZM, Nr. 22, October 23, 1937, p. 257. notes this new form in aluminum. In the issue Nr. 3, dated January 29, 1938, p. 14, the new form in gold is first mentioned.*

[64] *"Mbl.d.RZM," Nr. 15, July 17, 1937, p. 196.*

[65] *"RZM–HV," 1936, p. 95.*

[66] *"Vbl.d.RL.d.NSDAP," Nr. 165, End–March, 1938. Section VIII: Order Nr. 4/38.*

[67] *Ibid, Nr. 172, Mid–July 1938 Announcement Nr. 15.*

Otto Spronk

Left: Dr. Joseph Goebbels during the Reichsparteitag at Nürnberg in September 1937. Note that he is still wearing the first eagle emblem.

Below: The Gauleiterstellvertreter Ostpreussen presents the first honor badge Ostpreussen in June 1938 to his superior, Gauleiter Koch. Note the dark (red) piping around the crown.

Klaus D. Patzwall

In November new manufacturing procedures for this cap were authorized. This form was then only worn by members of the "Werkscharen" from the DAF. (For exact detailed manufacturing procedures, see the chapter: "Die Deutsche Arbeitsfront," section "Werkscharen" within this series).

The plans for the new uniform were implemented during 1938. Due to the knowledge (caused by press releases) firms and manufacturers began manufacturing these uniforms. This was prohibited by the RZM.[68] One must note that the new uniform was officially introduced by orders dated April 4, 1939.

1939 – 1945

New uniforms were urgently needed, when on April 20, 1938 approximately 600,000 new political leaders were sworn in at Munich during a meeting celebrating Hitler's birthday.[69]

The "Mitteilungsblatt der RZM" announced in March 1939 that changes for the uniform – model 1939 – for political leaders were ready to be published, and specified that the visored cap and insigne were changed (the color of the cloth remained the same).[70]

During a speech however, at the opening in Frankfurt/Main on the day for "Volksgesundheit und Genussgifte" (public health and enjoyment), Dr. Ley

68 *"Mbl.d.RZM," Nr. 7, April 8, 1939, p. 101. (June 17, 1939 the RZM announced that a new manufacturing procedure would be published in July).*

69 *"Daten der Geschichte der NSDAP," 11.Auflage, Berlin/Leipzig: 1943. Section VI: "Das Deutsche Reich und die NSDAP seit 1933," pp. 77–78.*

70 *"Mbl.d.RZM," Nr. 5, March 11, 193,. pp. 77–78; Ibid, Nr. 7, April 8, 1939, p. 101.*

NSKK–Korpsführer Hühnlein is saluted by Oberführer Stift during the opening of the new motorsport school in Mönchengladbach–Rheindahlen on March 9, 1938. Standing at right are Gauleiter Grohé from Köln–Aachen and Florian from Düsseldorf. Note the difference in the forms of the tops with these visored caps. Grohé is wearing the eagle form of the Allgemeine–SS or similar form.

Gauleiter Florian chats with a young girl from the "Jungmädel" at Mönchengladbach on June 18, 1938. Note the fine form of his saddle visored cap.

A. Stam

Political leaders from Gau– and Kreis level during the celebrations of the delivery of a building to the Kreisleitung at Mönchengladbach on June 18, 1938. In the foreground at left a Gau–piped cap; at right a Kreis–piped visored cap. Both persons have golden cords.

W.P.B.R. Saris

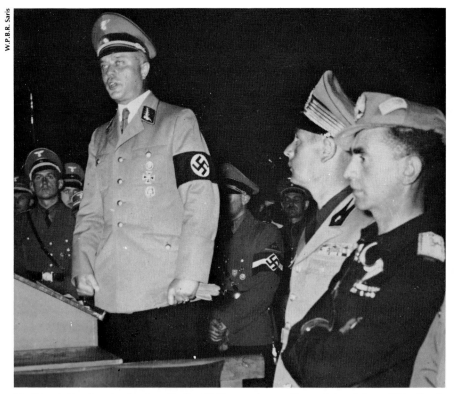

The Deputy Province Leader from Berlin, Görlitzer welcomes the participants from Hitler Youth and Italian cyclists in August 1938. At right positioned is the Generalkonsul Renzetti and the leader of the Italian youth Sandro Bonamici. Görlitzer is wearing the visored cap with red piping in the definitive form, known as Wehrmachtschnitt IV, with golden cap cords.

proudly announced that in February Hitler had approved the final design for the new uniform and insigne.[71] It is often said that Ley inspected this new uniform in May 1939, but it must be noted that they had already been shown to him during a congress of province and district leaders at Sonthofen in March. A special exhibition had been set up to introduce the new uniforms and to show the political leaders there.[72]

In mid–June 1939 the "Verordnungsblatt der Reichsleitung der NSDAP," as well as the "Mitteilungsblatt der RZM" finally published details of the service–, parade– and walking–out dress. Wear was allowed from June 1st. The old form of uniform was still allowed to be worn, but only with correct insignia.

The main, most striking alterations for the political leader's visored cap were: the national emblem and the wreath introduced in gold for all ranks and levels (silver had to be replaced by June 1). The wreath was the PO–form, the latter often being embroidered directly to the cap band. This embroidered form was only authorized for those who were also allowed to wear embroidered rank insigne, so being officials in the rank of Abschnittleiter and above:[73]

W.P.B.R. Saris

D. Politische-Leiter-Dienstmütze

Die Ausführung der Mütze für Politische Leiter wird wie folgt festgelegt:

a) Mütze in hellbraun (Gabardine):
Wehrmachtsschnitt. Rostbraunes Samtband und brauner Lackleder-schirm. Goldkordel, goldfarbenes Hoheitszeichen, goldfarbenes Eichen-laub, gestickt oder Metall, mit Hakenkreuzkokarde.
Paspel entsprechend der Paspelfarbe des Hoheitsgebietes.

b) Mütze mit weißem Oberteil.
Wehrmachtsschnitt. Weißes Oberteil ohne Paspel, Rostbraunes Samtband und brauner Lacklederschirm. Goldkordel, goldfarbenes Hoheitszeichen, goldfarbenes Eichenlaub, gestickt oder Metall, mit Hakenkreuzkokarde.
Paspel am Samtband, entsprechend der Paspelfarbe des Hoheits-gebietes.

Die Mütze mit weißem Oberteil kann zu folgenden Dienstanzügen getragen werden:
1. Dienstuniform mit weißem Rock;
2. Große Dienstuniform mit weißem Rock;
3. Ausgehuniform in weiß.

Herstellungsvorschrift erläßt mit meinem Einvernehmen die Reichs-zeugmeisterei der NSDAP.

In 1939 the new political leaders uniforms were extensively discussed and information was published in almost every periodical or newspaper. In practically every district the new regulations were also being published and appeared immediately. The descriptions shown are short parts from two of these regulations: "*Die Uniformen der Politischen Leiter der NSDAP*" from Gau Franken, 1939 and "*Uniform–Vorschrift für die Politischen Leiter der NSDAP*" from Gau Saarpfalz, 1939. The given details with D are the brown and white visored cap and in the last when to be worn. With A1 the official date of introduction of June 1, 1939 is given; with A2 the wearing of a metal or embroidered wreath and the abolishing of the silver national emblem, cords and cap cords buttons were specified. With A4 the form was noted and with A5 the piping for Kreisleitung was announced as from then on to be white instead of the earlier worn black.

---

71 *"Uniformen–Markt," Nr. 6, March 15, 1939, p. 82.*

72 *"Ibid," Nr. 7, April 1, 1939, p98.*

73 *"Mbl.d.RZM," Nr. 15, July 29, 1939. Addendum in relation of manufacturing procedures as published July 13, 1939.*

A

Einführung der neuen Uniformen, Mützen, Pistolengehänge, Feldbinden und Fangschnüre der Politischen Leiter der NSDAP.

1. Einführung der neuen Uniformen.

a) Die in der Anordnung Nr. 9/39 bekanntgegebenen neuen **Dienstuniformen, Paradeuniformen** und Ausgehuniformen können von den im Einzelnen [illegible] der Anordnung bestimmten Politischen Leitern zu [illegible] ebenfalls bekannten Anlässen **ab 1. Juni 1939** getragen werden.

2. Mützen:

a) Laut Anordnung Nr. 9/39 wird ab 1. Juni 1939 an der Mütze das **metallene oder gestickte Eichenlaub** (goldfarben) angelegt.

b) Gleichzeitig sind an der Mütze das **silberfarbene Hoheitszeichen, die Mützenkordel und Knöpfe durch goldfarbene zu ersetzen.**

4. Dienstmütze der Politischen Leiter:

Die Dienstmütze der Politischen Leiter wird seitens der Reichszeugmeisterei der NSDAP. **ausschließlich im Wehrmachtsschnitt, Form 4,** geliefert.

Beim Erwerb der Mützen in Verkaufsstellen der Reichszeugmeisterei der NSDAP. ist ausdrücklich darauf hinzuweisen.

Dies gilt für Mützen mit hellbraunem und mit weißem Oberteil.

5. Paspel an Kragen und Mü[illegible] der Politischen Leiter der Kreisleitung der N[illegible]DAP.:

a) **Ab 1. Juni 1939** werden die **Mützen der Politischen Leiter der Kreisleitung** (Wehrmachtsschnitt Form 4) **mit weißer Paspel** getragen.

b) Gleichzeitig ist am **Kragenrand**, anstelle des bisherigen, **weißer Paspel** anzubringen.

c) Die **schwarzen Paspel an den bisherigen Rangabzeichen verbleiben vorläufig; die weißen Paspel an den Spiegeln werden erst bei den neuen Dienstrangabzeichen eingeführt.**

d) Die Mützen sind sofort zu bestellen. Minderbemittelte Politische Leiter im Stabe der Kreisleitung der NSDAP. erhalten über die Beschaffungskasse (Dienststelle Hauptorganisationsamt) auf besonderen Antrag des Kreisleiters (auf dem Dienstwege) Mützen gestellt.

Durchführungsbestimmungen über Beschaffung und Lieferung vorschriftsmäßiger Einzelteile, Bestellung der Mützen und Paspel usw. erläßt das Hauptorganisationsamt der NSDAP.

Heil Hitler!

F. d. R.: Mehnert. gez.: Dr. R. Ley.

Dr. Ley visiting Mönchengladbach on February 4, 1939. He is welcomed by Gauamtsleiter Kinkelin at the cycling track in the "Volksgarten." Kinkelin is wearing the silver cords of his rank.

Ley inspecting a formation of political leaders from the Mönchengladbach area. The visored cap of the person he is inspecting has the two ventilation grommets. These should not be installed. The photograph is dated February 4, 1939.

On Orts–level these were the ranks Oberabschnitt– and Abschnittleiter;

On Kreis–level: Dienstleiter, Haupt–Bereichsleiter, Ober–Bereichsleiter, Bereichsleiter, Haupt–Abschnittleiter, Ober–Abschnittleiter and Abschnittleiter;

On Gau–level: Gauleiter, Ober–Befehlsleiter, Befehlsleiter, Haupt–Dienstleiter, Ober–Dienstleiter, Dienstleiter down to Abschnittleiter;

On Reich–level: Reichsleiter, Haupt–Befehlsleiter, Ober–Befehlsleiter down to Abschnittleiter.[74]

All other ranks from political leaders candidates (Pol. Leiter–Anwärter) up to Hauptgemeinschaftsleiter were only allowed to wear metal insignia.

From mid–June 1939 on, all cords and buttons were gold in color; a new piping system was introduced and the cap band for the local level authorities was light or rust brown velvet.[75] Simultaneously a white top visored cap was introduced for wear during the summer season.

---

[74] *"Organisationsbuch der NSDAP." München: 1943. Picture–pages: 18, 20, 22 and 24.*

[75] *Ibid, München: 1938 and 1940, p. 28; "Uniformen–Markt," Nr. 6, March 15, 1939, p. 81; Ibid, Nr. 7, April 1, 1939, p. 98; "Vbl.d.RL.d.NSDAP," Nr. 194, Mid–June, 1939. Section VIII: decrees Nr. 23/39 A and B.*

On July 1, 1939 new specifications for the visored cap were authorized.

Brief Description 1939 Form Visored Cap

Piping schedule:

Reichsleitung:	Goldgelb or Schwefelgelb;
Gauleitung:	Dunkelweinrot (instead of bright red: other shades of red were abolished);
Kreisleitung:	Weiss (instead of black);
Ortsgruppe:	Hellblau.

This "Sattelform" shaped visored cap had a brown fiber visor (officially introduced at this time) with a brown velvet band (so–called Linden). The crown and cap band were piped 2.5mm (SA–Spiegeltuch); upon the band a golden embroidered or metal wreath; the cockade in the exact front center of the band. On the top front a golden national emblem was positioned, 15mm above the upper cap band piping. Above the visor rested the gold colored cords (wide 31cm in the sizes 53–55; 32cm wide in the sizes 56–58 and 33cm wide in the size 59 and higher, mainly manufactured from early 1940 in a material known as "Cellophan"[76] (celleon – for more information on celleon, see Volume 1 this series, chapter Reichsheer/Heer), held by 12mm pebbled buttons with eyelet's (no pins were allowed).

The lining is in golden/yellow artificial silk. A celluloid sweat shield diamond (measuring 13.5 x 10mm) is positioned inside; the sweat–band is of light brown sheepskin or artificial materials, known as "Alkor" in Havana–brown or beige, from August 1939.[77]

The model 1939 visored cap with red piping and metal wreath.

[76] *"Mbl.d.RZM," Nr. 1, January 27, 1940, p. 2: new introduction.*

[77] *Ibid, Nr. 17, August 26, 1939, p. 226.*

Visored cap for Reichsleitung in the form known as Wehrmachtschnitt IV. Note the wreath directly embroidered upon the band.

1939 form visored cap for Gau–level. The wreath is hand embroidered; the golden eagle is the metal form.

Sizes with a size 56:

Top, equable oval:	length	27cm;
	width	24cm;
Side panels, between crown and upper band piping:	in front	7.5cm;
	sides	4.4cm;
	back	5.3cm;

Cap band, between the pipings: 4.5cm.[78]

The old form visored cap, with new insignia and piping, was allowed to be worn until December 31, 1941. The "Form 4" remained unchanged until the end of the war. It must be noted that many visored caps survived the war having the old form piping, black instead of white, but having the new form gilt national emblem. In many instances, the oakleaf wreath was never worn on the cap band. This was caused by material shortages resulting from the war. Various rank–levels (lower cadre) never were supplied with the 1939 introduced rank insignia.[79] The wreath and the golden national emblem for example were no longer delivered after November 1943.[80]

The 1939 model visored cap with white top was never officially piped at the top and was made of white wool gabardine or white navy cloth. The form for this summer cap was also "Form 4"; the cap band was rust brown velvet with piping. The visor was light brown with a raised rim.[81]

A. Stam

Gauleiter Florian welcomes the youngest member of the Motor–HJ from Mönchengladbach in September 1940. Note the wear of his rank insigne.

Below: Form IV visored cap having the wreath embroidered directly onto the cap band (Gauleitung level).

John Coy

78 Ibid, Nr. 13, July 1, 1939. Addendum department Equipment; "Die Uniformen der Pol.Leiter der NSDAP. " Anordnung Nr. 9/39, p. 40; "Uniformen–Vorschrift für Pol.Leiter der NSDAP," April 2, 1939, pp. 1–2, etc.

79 "Mbl.d.RZM," Nr. 4, May 22, 1943, p. 26.

80 Ibid, Nr. 7. November 20, 1943. p. 56.

81 "Die Uniformen der Pol.Leiter der NSDAP," 1939, pp. 8, 36–37.

Ulric of England

Model 1939 Kreisleitung–level visored cap with the gold wire wreath embroidered onto a separate piece of velvet backing and then sewn to the cap band.

Otto Spronk

A political leader, probably Reichsleitung–level, with the rank Haupt–Dienstleiter is wearing the model 1939 visored cap.

Politische Leiter

	Preisänderungen	RM.
7571	**Dienstmütze,** mit Eichenlaubkranz, Metall, und Goldkordel	7.45
7571a	**Dienstmütze,** mit Eichenlaubkranz, gestickt, und Goldkordel	11.75
7604	**Eichenlaubkranz,** gestickt	4.60
7609	**Dienstmütze,** weiß, mit Eichenlaubkranz, Metall, und Goldkordel	9.70
7608	**Dienstmütze,** weiß, mit Eichenlaubkranz, gestickt, und Goldkordel	14 —

W. P.B.R. Saris

The prices for the caps were constantly corrected. This is a correction for the brown and white caps with metal or embroidered forms of wreaths, published in May 1941.

King

Baldur von Schirach, head of the HJ, was also a political leader of the NSDAP on Reichsleitung–level and wears his golden–yellow piped visored cap in the form "Wehrmachtschnitt IV." Note the beautiful embroidered brassard.

Ron Kwan

Reichsleitung–level visored cap with golden–yellow piping.

Reichsstatthalter Baldur von Schirach wears the visored cap with metallic gold piping, representative of his rank.

Model 1939 Reichsleitung–level official's visored cap.

John Coy

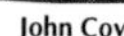

Ron Manion

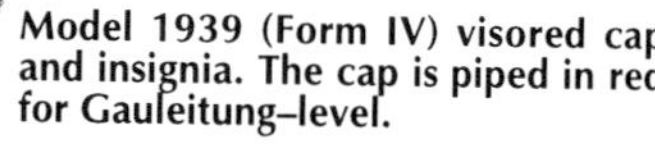

Model 1939 (Form IV) visored cap and insignia. The cap is piped in red for Gauleitung–level.

Dress regulations authorized five forms of dress in 1939:

I. Dienstuniform (Service Dress):

With the brown shirt or light brown four pocket tunic for wear by all political leaders.

The white visored cap and white tunic were allowed to be worn by:

a. Ortsgruppenleiter;

b. Pol.Leiter eines Amtes aufwärts (leaders from a department and upwards), Kreisleitung (political leaders of a Kreis–level department) in the upwards ranks, being:

Amtsleiter (Department Leader);
Hauptamtsleiter (Main Department Leader);

c. Pol.Leiter einer Hauptstelle aufwärts, Gauleitung (political leaders of a main Gau–level department) in the ranks upwards, being:

Amtsleiter;
Hauptamtsleiter;
Stellv.Gauleiter (Deputy);
Gauleiter (Province Leader);

d. Pol.Leiter einer Stelle aufwärts, Reichsleitung (political leaders with a position or function on Reich level) in the ranks upwards, being:

Stellenleiter;
Hauptstellenleiter;
Amtsleiter;
Hauptamtsleiter;
Hauptdienstleiter;
Reichsleiter.[82]

National Archives

Hitler's personal physician Dr. Theo Morrell, wears a political leader's visored cap. The piping and insignia color are unknown but probably gold.

---

[82] *Ibid, Gau–Saarpfalz: April 2, 1939, p. 12; "Uniform–Vorschrift für Pol.Leiter der NSDAP," April 2, 1939. Gauorganisationsamt, Gau Saarpfalz.*

Otto Spronk

A photograph taken of political leaders wearing the visored caps "Wehrmachtschnitt IV" with 1939 insignia, during a meeting in the Netherlands. At left a "Haupt–Gemeinschaftsleiter" on Kreis–level, as a leader of a main department; his cap is piped in white. At right an "Ober–Bereichsleiter" on Gau–level, as a leader of a department; his cap is piped in bright red, instead of the darker red.

Above: Reichsleiter Franz Xaver Schwarz wears the visored cap with wreath embroidered directly onto the cap–band.

Jill Halcomb Smith

Right: Oberbereichsleiter Mende wears the final pattern political leader's visored cap, 4 August 1941.

II. Grosse Dienstuniform (Ceremonial Dress):

With the light brown tunic to be worn by all, or with the white tunic by those, see I a. up to including d, during all official, ceremonial occasions and meetings involving the Party, its organizations and associated groups, the Armed Forces, the State, etc., or upon any function when the political leader was a guest of honor.

It must be noted that the white uniform was only allowed to be worn during suitable weather conditions. Often it is said that the white cap was worn by only those with high positions, but research has shown that the white uniform was also worn by lower ranked political officials. The light brown visored cap was never allowed to be worn with the white uniform, the only official exception being when the white tunic was worn beneath the greatcoat.[83] The "Organisationsbuch, 1940" mentioned the wear of the light brown visored cap with the white tunic. This was never officially sanctioned or mentioned in regulations. Probably it was intended to allow this, but the order may have been delayed due to war circumstances.

III. Parade–Uniform (Parade Dress):

With the light brown or white tunic, worn by:
Kreisleiter;
Pol.Leiter eines Amtes aufwärts (for ranks, see I c, on Gau–level);
Pol.Leiter einer Hauptstelle aufwärts (for ranks, see I d, on Reich–level);
This dress was only worn during special ceremonial occasions and only when ordered.[84]

Josef Charita

This photograph shows the wear of a visored cap with brown top with a white tunic. The visored cap has the 1939 national emblem, but is missing the wreath. The white tunic has collar patches for an SA Gruppenführer.

---

[83] *Ibid, Decree Nr. 9/39, p. 11; "Mbl.d.RZM," Nr. 8, May 31 1941, p. 46 mentions the white visored cap with metal, as well as embroidered insignia (RZM article numbers 7608 and 7609).*

[84] *"Die Uniformen der Politischen Leiter der NSDAP." Anordnung Nr.9/39. Gauorganisationsamt Gau–Saarpfalz. pp.20–22.*

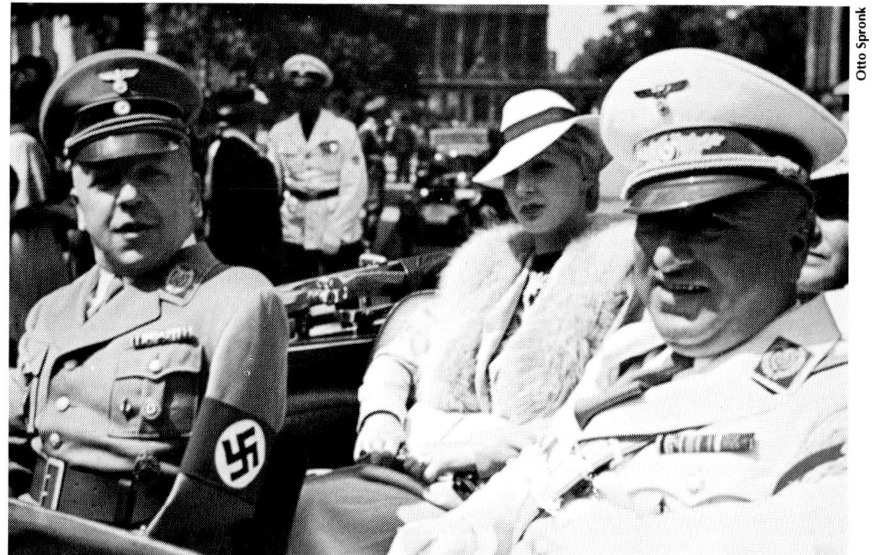

Otto Spronk

Robert Ley and his wife Inga during a parade in 1939. Note that Ley is wearing a white top visored cap with gold piping with the newly introduced insignia. The top has the regular white material "piping." Reichsleiter Amann at left is wearing his visored cap with the old–form insignia.

Ulric of England

The white top visored cap for Reich–level. The band is piped properly with the golden piping, the top is correctly piped in white.

Otto Spronk

Hamburg, July 1939. Probably one of the earliest photographs showing the white political leaders uniforms being worn, along with the new insignia.

Ulric of England

Golden–yellow piped, visored cap with non-detachable white top.

Dr. Goebbels, the German Propaganda Minister, in a gondola on the Grand Canal in Venice (with Signor Alfieri, the Italian Minister for Culture) on August 8, 1939. Note the wear of the white top visored cap in the 1939 style.

Otto Spronk

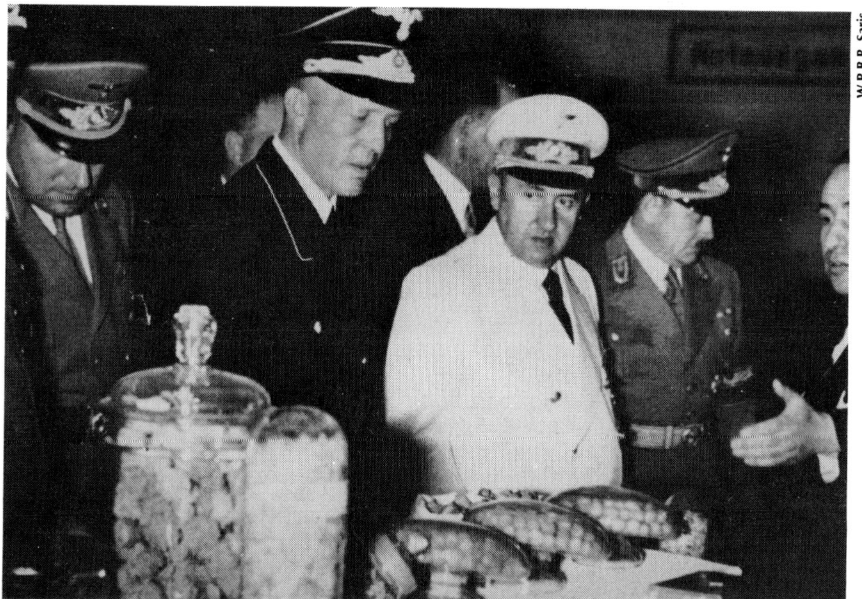

W.P.B.R. Saris

High ranked political leaders and officials from State agencies during the opening of a fair at Königsberg on August 11, 1940. From left to right: Reichsminister und Generalgouverneur Dr. Frank, Reichsfinanzminister Graf Schwerin von Krosigk, Reichswirtschaftsminister und Präsident der Deutschen Reichsbank Funk and Gauleiter Erich Koch. Frank is wearing a Reichsleitung piped cap; Funk is wearing the white cap with what seems to be a piped top; Koch is wearing a dark red piped visored cap.

Model–1939 white top visored cap with cap band piped in black, indicating Kreis–level. Due to the new regulations however this had to be in white.

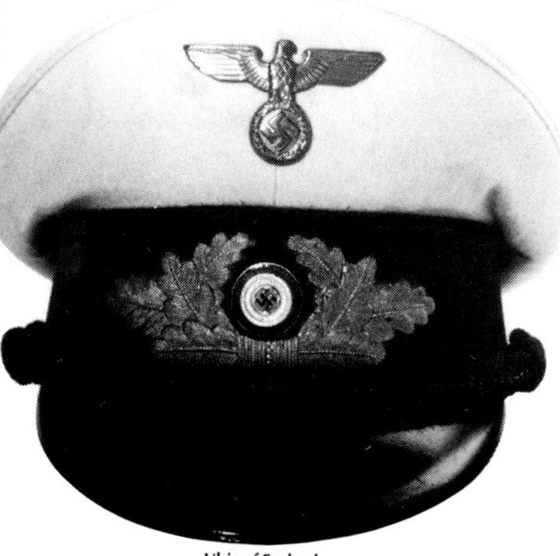

Ulric of England

Jill Halcomb Smith

Gauleiter Josef Wagner, delivers an address in Rome, 1939. His white top visored cap rests on the desk before him. Note that the cap has no cap cords.

IV. Ausgeh–Uniform (Walking–Out Dress):

With the light brown, single–breasted tunic, allowed to be worn by all political leaders, or with the single–breasted white tunic, by those, see I a, up to including d. The last officials were also allowed to wear the double–breasted, light brown tunic.[85]

V. Büro–Dienstanzug (Office Dress):

The visored cap was not permitted to be worn with the office dress, worn indoors. Occasionally, the garrison cap (Hausmütze) was worn instead.

Political Leader Candidates (Pol.Leiter Anwärter) were allowed to wear only the numbers I, IV (single–breasted) and V.[86]

The actual implementation of the newly introduced regulations went slowly, due to stock shortages and the RZM manufacturing procedures which were often too precise .

RZM regulations insisted that an RZM tag was always to be sewn into the visored cap, but it has been observed that caps manufactured outside Germany (for example, in the Netherlands) were seldom provided with the tags. Examples from a company at Breda were manufactured in complete disregard for the RZM specifications. Those produced before 1940 had no tag at all. In Germany, as well, items manufactured were not always according to specifications (productions from 1934 through 1945). With orders of March 1941 tags were not longer attached to metal insignia (such as national emblems and the political leaders wreaths).[87]

The permission to wear the political leader's uniform was also granted to, for example members of the NSD–Dozentenbund (NS Teachers Union), the NSD–Studentenbund (NS Students Union), Reichsrechtsamt (Reich Office for Justice) and Deutsche Arbeitsfront.[88]

The Gauinspektor (Inspectors on Gau level) was a plenipotentiary of the "Gauleiter" and was allowed to wear the uniform according to his rank. Officials who resigned their office or position, were allowed to wear the uniform only when permission was specially granted, and after a long term of service as a political leader. Otherwise, the uniform had to be re–dyed and the insignia removed.[89]

Vorderseite: W.P.B

Nationalsozialistische Deutsche Arbeiterparte

Ausweis für Politische Leite

Gültig für die Amtsdauer

als:

Name:

Vorname:

Unterschrift und Stempel der Dienststellen

Eigenhänd. Unterschrift

Reichsleitung Gau Kreis O. Gr

den

Mitgl.-Nr. der Partei

Unterschrift der Dienststelle

A sample of a political leaders I.D.–card, specifying the validity for a specific person. The reverse (sample is Gau Schwaben) specified which uniform the person was allowed to wear. For persons "off duty" a similar I.D. card was issued.

Nachstehenden Parteigenossen erteile ich die Genehmigung zum Tragen der Uniform eines Politischen Leiters mit den für Ausgeschiedene vorgeschriebenen Abzeichen:

A. Die Uniform mit den Abzeichen eines ehemaligen Gauleiters

von Corswant, Walter

B. Die Uniform mit den Abzeichen eines ehemaligen stellvertretenden Gauleiters

Frank, Karl Hermann

C. Die Uniform mit den Abzeichen eines ehemaligen Gauamtsleiters

1. Gau Berlin	Dr. Kiehl, Erhard
2. Gau Düsseldorf	Henjes, Paul Schmalhorst, Leopold
3. Gau Franken	Glück, Richard Maas, Ernst
4. Gau Hessen-Nassau	Dr. Savelkouls, Hermann
5. Gau Kurhessen	Brinkmann, Otto
6. Gau Magdeburg-Anhalt	Klau, Bruno
7. Gau Mainfranken	Fedler, Alfons
8. Gau Mark Brandenburg	Pardun, Arno
9. Gau München-Oberbayern	Dr. Leitmeyer, Karl
10. Gau Ostpreußen	Fuchs, Erich
11. Gau Pommern	Schweig, Helmut
12. Gau Saarpfalz	Deyerling, Otto
13. Gau Schlesien	Franzius, Georg Gunzer, Karl
14. Gau Schleswig-Holstein	Fründt, Theodor
15. Gau Thüringen	Demme, Otto Schwartze, Oskar
16. Gau Westfalen-Nord	Barthel, Herbert Böhmer, Karl Budde, Fritz Gerdes, Josef Hartmann, Erich Heidemann, Karl Klemm, Kurt von Oeynhausen, Adolf Dr. Wiegand, Eduard
17. Gau Westfalen-Süd	Bornemann, Heinrich Flach, Gottfried am Wege, Rudolf
18. Gau Auslandsorganisation	Langmann, Otto Schleler, Rudolf Witte, Reinhold Zuchristan, Walter

D. Die Uniform mit den Abzeichen eines ehemaligen Kreisleiters

1. Gau Baden	Frank, Karl
2. Gau Bayerische Ostmark	Förtsch, Burkard
3. Gau Hamburg	Petersen, Arnold
4. Gau Hessen-Nassau	Dr. Barth, Robert Hinterwälder, Georg
5. Gau Köln-Aachen	Ebel, Willi Loevenich, Heinrich
6. Gau Magdeburg-Anhalt	Fiedler, Karl
7. Gau Mainfranken	Memmel, Theo
8. Gau Ostpreußen	Lemke, Arthur Ratzki, Erich Uschdraweit, Paul
9. Gau Pommern	Mildebrath, Paul
10. Gau Süd-Hannover-Braunschweig	Lehmann, Herbert
11. Gau Schlesien	Fülbier, Georg
12. Gau Westfalen-Süd	Weber, Fritz
13. Gau Württemberg-Hohenzollern	Hörmann, Josef Anton Maigler, Franz
14. Gau Auslandsorganisation	Ender, Gerhard Schinke, Otto

München, den 25. November 1939.

Adolf Hitler

The permission to wear a political leaders uniform had to be granted. Political leaders while "on duty" had to receive authorization to wear a specific uniform. Shown here is an order from Hitler, dated November 25, 1939, in which specifications are given. With A the allowance to wear the former uniform of a Gauleiter was given; with B the former uniform of a Gauleiter deputy; with C the former uniform of a Gauamtsleiter and with D the former uniform of a Kreisleiter. If such an official permission had not been received, the wear of the uniform was *never* allowed.

---

85 *Ibid, pp. 22–32*

86 *Ibid, p. 32.*

87 *"Mbl.d.RZM," Nr. 3, March 27, 1941, p. 13.*

88 *"Organisationsbuch der NSDAP." München 1936, p. 75.*

Rückseite:

Gau Schwaben

eis:

tsgruppe:

rechtigt zum Tragen der Uniform eines

89 *Specific directives were published in the "Vbl.d.RL.d.NSDAP" during 1936, 1938 and in 1942. It was precisely specified through the years to whom a uniform was granted with what rank. The last list is dated, February, 1940 (the "Vbl.d.RL.d.NSDAP" was available for this research up till November 1942); the last found announcement on resigning–ranking was published in Nr. 238, dated November 1942 (Decree V 20/42).*

TRAINING COURSES (SCHULUNGSKURSEN):

Training courses for political leaders did not become a necessity until the NSDAP became a de facto power. In the summer of 1933 the Reichsführerschule der NSDAP (Reich Leadership School) at Bernau was officially opened by Adolf Hitler. The educational system was directed by Alfred Rosenberg through the Hauptschulungsamt. The system involved instruction on provincial, as well as in district schools (Gau–und Kreisschulen), later renamed Gau–und Kreisschulungsburgen. Also professional training for political leaders on the highest instructional level at Ordensburgen (Order Castles) was provided. These last were instituted in early 1936, followed by other NS–education systems, such as the Adolf Hitler Schulen and the Nat.Pol.Erziehungs–Anstalten or the NS–(Deutsche) Oberschule "Starnbergersee" (for further detailed information see coming chapter, "NS–Schulung" within this series).

In this section we will discuss only the headdress worn during these training courses or during the instruction of higher–ranking functionaries. In spite of the fact that thousands of pages of regulations were available for this research, hardly any stated the official introduction or forms for the field–caps. It is known that a form of headdress was also worn during marches and target practice *(Vorschrift für Einzel–u. Marschausbildung der Pol.Leiter, as well as Ausbildungsvorschrift Pistole).*

Sports activities were often lead by trainers of the NS–Gemeinschaft "Kraft durch Freude" (Strength through Joy) from May 1936. It is known that a special dress form was authorized and ordered for wear by the Auslands–Organisation sports groups (see section in this chapter).

FIELD CAP (LAGERMÜTZE):

A brown field cap was apparently introduced for wear by participants of courses, probably not earlier than spring 1934 (During the Party Rallies of 1934 the field cap was already being worn with the Model 1934 metal eagle on the left front side of the cap. During the Party Rallies of 1935, this form of headdress was favored by various Political Leader Bands). The form for the cap was like that generally later worn by a "Stamm–Mannschaft" of the NSD–Studentenbund.[90]

These early caps were devoid of piping, later examples with a crown piping (or for the flap only) were also manufactured. The majority being made of light brown material, and later medium brown.

The piping was:

Reichsschule: yellow;
Gauschule: bright red;
Kreisschule: black.[91]

(Schools on local level probably never existed).

The piped turn–up vaulted slightly, and a swastika cockade or embossed button was positioned in its lower front center. A small white (or silvered) wo-

---

90 "Uniformen–Markt," Nr. 5, April 16, 1936, p. 78.

91 Letter, Stellvertreter des Führers. München: November 18, 1935.

J.R. Angolia

The field cap as worn during courses at an Ordensburg. In the center of the flap's front is positioned an embossed silvered eagle button; the eagle faces to its left.

W.P.B.R. Saris

RZM VORSCHRIFTSMÄSSIGE
20,5 mm
PO-METALLKNÖPFE
Herst. Nr. ______ Lauf. Nr. * 016449

A paper tag as ordered by the RZM, for the wrapping up the buttons, as used for the field cap for political leader's.

Ed Stadnicki

Detail of the silver–colored button.

John Coy

A roll of political leader national emblems for the side of the field cap, machine–woven aluminum wire on dark brown. Note direction eagle's head is turned, correctly in its final form.

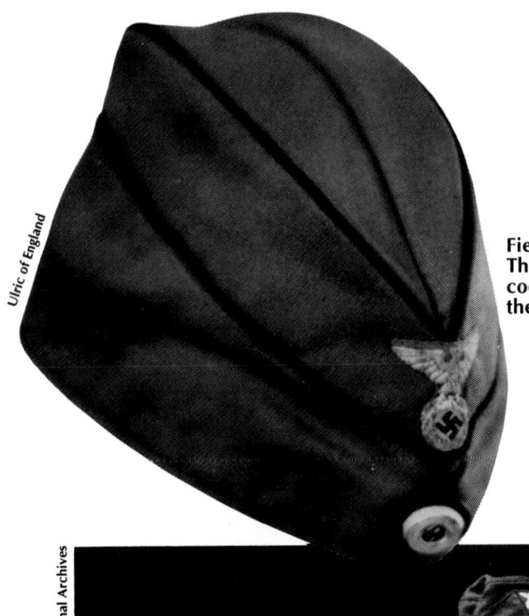

Field cap for political leader's on Gau–level. The flap and crown are piped. The swastika cockade is positioned on the front center of the flaps.

Party officials wearing the field cap as illustrated earlier, but with the early style national emblem on the left flap.

ven political national emblem was worn either at the left side upon the flap, or on the front center of the top. These caps were the property of the school. During courses at an Order Castle, caps from these schools were supplied.

In addition to the aforementioned cap, a dark blue or black un–piped field cap, in the SS–Feldmütze style with scalloped, functional flap, was worn during school courses by members of NSDAP organizations. An embossed button with the national emblem was secured to the front center of the turn–up. The exact date of introduction is not known, but is estimated to have been late 1935 or early 1936.[92]

92 *"Organisationsbuch der NSDAP." München: 1936. Picture–page 24.*

Ulric of England

The field cap is shown being worn by a young fellow, but with a metal M36 national emblem mounted on the front. Note the man far right wearing the M39 visored cap.

Josef Charita

A political leader candidate, wearing the garrison cap (Hausmütze). The cockade with swastika is in the embroidered form. The eagle is machine embroidered. It is very rare seeing this cap worn.

GARRISON CAP (HAUSMÜTZE):

This cap was probably introduced in 1940 and meant to be used during indoor activities only, and was allowed to be worn by all ranks. It resembled the field–cap, as worn by the AO sports groups. The cap color and material was light or medium brown gabardine (later, tricot was used as well). The flaps were slightly curved and not sewn to the body. These caps were piped. Observed are caps with a flap piping only. Other caps had crown, as well as flap piping. The golden–yellow woven cotton national emblem was sewn to the front center of the cap top, just above the flap.

SPECIAL NSDAP FUNCTIONARIES (SONDERBEAUFTRAGTE DER NSDAP):

These functionaries on Reich, Gau or Kreis–level wore the regular visored cap with proper piping.[93]

PATROL SERVICE (STREIFENDIENST):

A number of regulations were authorized to insure the dignified behavior of political leaders in public. These regulations were enforced by NSDAP patrol services (Streifendienst), who wore the regular visored cap with proper piping.[94]

POLITICAL LEADERS IN EASTERN TERRITORIES (OSTEINSATZ DER NSDAP):

Political leaders from Germany were assigned to duties in the Eastern countries (NSDAP im Generalgouvernement) from May, 1940, often being a "Sonderbeauftragte der NSDAP." As mentioned above they wore the regular visored cap with proper piping. Also Germans (Volksdeutsche), assigned to Party functions, were allowed by Hess in May 1940 to wear political uniforms with the visored cap with proper piping (these persons were mainly Pol.Leiter Anwärter).[95] Shortly thereafter this was also ordered for the area of Böhmen und Mähren (Reichsprotektor).

In late 1944 a new uniform for political leaders, assigned to "Osteinsatz," was introduced. The color was described as "brown" (this color resembles the brown as worn by SA–Wehrmannschaften, varying to the shade used for NSKK uniforms); manufacturing procedures were available in December. It was especially noted that a "PL–Mütze für Osteinsatz" was manufactured.[96] The form, insignia and piping were as for the regular visored cap for political leaders.

PARTY COURT OF JUSTICE (PARTEIGERICHTE) 1934 – 1945 :

Before November 1934 functionaries assigned to a Party Court wore the regular headdress with no special marks of recognition. Plans were developed

---

93 *Ibid. München: 1940 and 1943. p. 28*

94 *Ibid, 1936. pp. 55–56.*

95 *"Vbl.d.RL.d.NSDAP," Nr. 208, May 1940, Order Nr. 6/40; Ibid, Nr. 210. July 1940; Decree V3/40 and announcement B31/40; "Mbl.d.RZM," Nr. 5, April 20, 1940, p. 33.*

96 *"Mbl.d.RZM," Nr. 5, December 27, 1940, p. 40. Section: Dienstkleidung states the "Einsatzuniform für Pol.Leiter", another section the visored cap.*

by Chief Judge Walter Buch in early 1934 for different identification for the Parteigerichte.[97]

In October 1934 the "Mitteilungsblatt der RZM" published regulations regarding the visored cap for members of the Party Court.[98] On November 27th, Rudolf Hess ordered that members of these courts wear a special sign of recognition on their visored caps.[99] (see color schedule, November 1934 for Party Court officials).

Otto Spronk

Goebbels, the Nazi Minister of Propaganda with Reichsleiter Martin Bormann at his left and Max Amann, the Reichsleiter who was in charge of the Nazi Press. At far left is Reichsleiter Walter Buch, the Chief Judge of the Nazi Party Court (and the father–in–law of Martin Bormann). All are wearing the 1934–model political leaders emblem, only Buch is wearing the cockade (devoid of the swastika). It seems that shortly before this picture was taken, Amann and Goebbels removed their cockade. The position where the cockade should be positioned, is visible.

PARTY COURTS (POLITISCHER LEITER DER GERICHTSBARKEIT), BY ORDER HESS, NOVEMBER 27, 1934 :

	Cords:	Buttons:	Piping:	Band:
Oberstes Partei–gericht (Supreme Party Court)				
Vorsitzender: (President, as well as the President of the Judgement–Court, Vorsitzender der Spruchkammern)	gold	gold	golden/ yellow	dark brown velvet;

[97] *"Vbl.d.RL.d.NSDAP," Nr. 65, Mid–February 1934, p. 144. (Buch, the "Oberster Richter der Partei" was appointed by Hitler as "Reichsleiter" on September 5, 1935: Ibid, Nr. 104, dated mid–September 1935: addendum)*

[98] *"Mbl.d.RZM," Nr. 20, October 13, 1934, p. 3.*

[99] *Letter: Stellvertreter des Führers. München, November 27, 1934: "Dienstanzug für Träger der Gerichtsbarkeit", pp. 1–2.*

Beisitzer: (Assessor)	ibid	ibid	ibid	ibid;
Gau–Gericht (Province Court)				
Vorsitzender:	ibid	ibid	blue	ibid;
Kammervorsitzender: (President of this Court)	ibid	ibid	ibid	ibid;
Beisitzer:	silver	silver	ibid	ibid;
Kreis–u. Ortsgericht (District–and Local Courts)				
Vorsitzender:	gold	gold	blue	ibid;
Beisitzer::	silver	silver	ibid	ibid.

It must be noted that in place of dark brown, the RZM–specification mentioned light brown and for courts on Gau–level no red color was introduced in 1934. The blue introduced was in fact a darker color blue. The color for the national emblem was always silver. With the evening–dress (Gesellschaftsanzug) no headdress was ordered. Permission to wear the uniform was granted by Hitler or Hess only.[100]

In early 1935 members of a Party Court on local–level were ordered to use the light brown velvet cap band[101] (these courts were dissolved during early 1936).

In August 1935, the German press announced a new uniform for members of the Party Courts. The Reichsleitung noted that this was not final; a decision had not yet been made.[102] It must be noted that the colors of the cords and piping varied in 1936, as published in the "Organisationsbuch der NSDAP, 1936" and the "Mitteilungsblatt der RZM." The reason for this was not researched. Introduction was delayed until spring 1938 probably due to internal problems concerning the organizational structure of all Party Courts.[103] We have to consider that the Organisationsbuch information was sometimes very inaccurate.

	Piping Org.Buch:	**Piping Mbl.d.RZM:**
Oberstes Parteigericht:	golden–yellow	golden–yellow;
Gaugericht:	red	blue;
Kreisgericht:	black	blue;
Ortsgericht:	not included	blue.

(note that the RZM continued to use the blue piping).

---

100 *Ibid, p. 2; "Mbl.d.RZM," Nr. 20, October 13, 1934, p. 2.*

101 *"Mbl.d.RZM," Nr. 4, January 26, 1935, p. 31.*

102 *"Vbl.d.RL.d.NSDAP," Nr. 104, Mid–September, 1935, p. 315. Announcement by Hess, dated September 5.*

103 *"Mbl.d.RZM," Nr. 12, June 4, 1938, p. 93. The included price–list announces the abolishing of old forms of collar patches and simultaneously the introduction for the new forms, as were published already in the Org.Book. 1936. In the Org.Book issued in 1937 pp. 345–356 contain with Nr. 25 erasures (Streichungen), while decisions were not final.*

The local courts were not included in the Org.Buch and with all courts–levels more ranks and positions were announced, see 1936 list.

PARTY COURTS (PARTEIGERICHTSBARKEIT), ACCORDING TO ORGANISATIONSBUCH, 1936:

	Cords:	Buttons:	Piping:	Band:
Oberstes Partei–gericht:				
Oberster Richter der Partei, Reichsleiter: (Supreme Party Judge, Reich Leader)	gold	gold	golden–yellow	rust–brown velvet;
Kammervorsitzender: (Chamber President, when nominated by Hitler)	ibid	ibid	ibid	ibid;
Richter: (Judge with a long–term service or on special selection)	ibid	ibid	ibid	ibid;
Richter: (with basic duties & fundamental rank)	silver	silver	ibid	ibid;
Hilfrichter: (Assistant–Judge)	ibid	ibid	ibid	ibid;
Leiter der Geschäfts–stelle: (Leader of a Court Office)	gold	gold	ibid	ibid;
Mitarbeiter: (co–worker)	ibid	ibid	ibid	ibid;
Gaugericht:				
Vorsitzender: (President)	silver	silver	red	ibid;
Kammervorsitzender:	ibid	ibid	ibid	ibid;
Richter:	ibid	ibid	ibid	ibid;
Leiter der Geschäfts–stelle:	ibid	ibid	ibid	ibid;
Mitarbeiter:	ibid	ibid	ibid	ibid;
Kreisgericht:				
Vorsitzender:	ibid	ibid	black	ibid;
Kammervorsitzender:	ibid	ibid	ibid	ibid;
Richter:	ibid	ibid	ibid	ibid;
Leiter der Geschäfts–stelle: (position existed when on Kreis–level more than one	ibid	ibid	ibid	ibid;

Chamber–Presidents were on duty)				
Leiter der Geschäfts–stelle: (based on rank)	ibid	ibid	ibid	ibid;
Mitarbeiter:	ibid	ibid	ibid	ibid.[104]

Otto Spronk

An unknown judge of the Supreme Party Court shown wearing his visored cap with golden piping. On the front center of the top he is wearing the 1934–form eagle emblem; on the center of the dark brown cap band he is wearing the 1935 introduced swastika cockade with the enameled back-plate.

Ulric of England

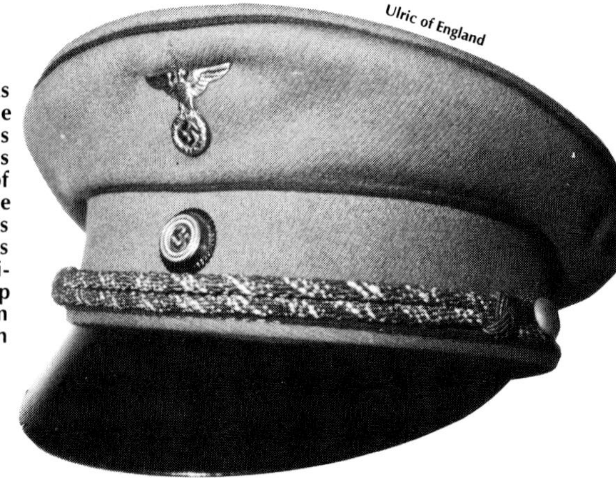

A rare example of a visored cap, as probably worn by officials of the Ortsgericht (Local Court). The cap is piped in dark blue and the cap cords are woven in alternating shades of light and dark. No regulations have been found that mention this alternating color. The regulations said "prescribed as for other political leaders." Normally the cap band was in light brown velvet from the summer of 1935, but was then also worn by other court members.

A close up photo showing the 1935 swastika cockade, the 1934 national eagle, the blue pipings and the rust-brown velvet cap band.

Below: Extremely rare visored cap which easily could be identified as an Orts-level visored cap. This cap, however, was worn by an Assessor from a Gau-, Kreis- or Orts-level court during early 1935 until 1936. The blue piping differs from the regular Orts-level light blue, as it is darker. The cap band is in velvet. An Orts-level visored cap should have a cap band in the same color as for the top.

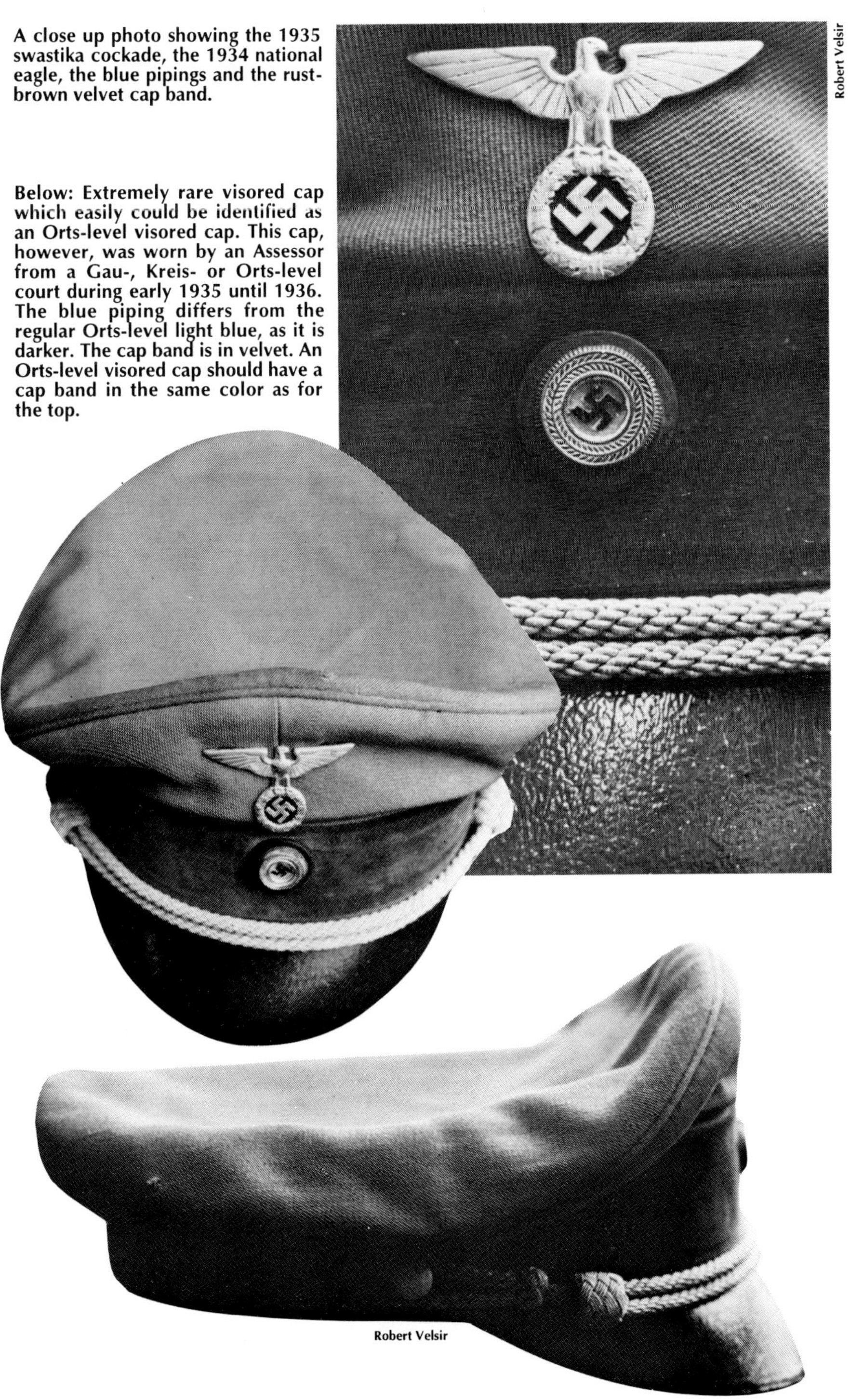

Robert Velsir

Robert Velsir

---

104 "Organisationsbuch der NSDAP." München, 1936, section 3: pp. 354–356 and picture–pages 29a and 29b.

Robert Velsir

The courts visored cap and the inside RZM label. The cap was manufactured by Georg Bornschein of Düsseldorf (RZM permission Nr. 207). Note the sweat shield with the lion emblem.

OBERSTES PARTEIGERICHT, GAU–UND KREISGERICHT:

Richter were earlier known as "Beisitzer." In fact not a new rank, but a renaming of the former. When not officially appointed the wear of only the service–, or walking–out dress in regular form for political leaders was allowed.[105]

It must be noted that the colors red and black were not used before June 1938. It is very likely that the new insignia was hardly ever worn, as was also the case of the visored cap for court officials. With the introduction of the new 1939 regulations, no different headdress was worn. The only distinguishing feature worn was the cuff–title, sewn to the left sleeve.[106]

---

105 Ibid, p. 354.

106 Ibid, 1940 and 1943 Issues. p. 28.

Courts were re–organized and existed on Kreis–, Gau– and Reich–level, as well as the level "Ortsgruppe Braunes Haus."[107] It is certain that the golden–yellow, dark red and white piping was worn from 1939 by court members. The name for the court known as "Ortsgruppe Braunes Haus" is confusing and one could assume that the light blue piping also was worn. Nevertheless it was structured as being on Gau–level and for this reason the dark red was worn by those serving on this court.

BANDSMEN (MUSIK–UND SPIELMANSZÜGE):

A band became an official NSDAP–band when it was considered by a Gau– or Kreisleiter that a particular band was good enough to be one. The best band in a province is a "Gaukapelle;" the best for a district a "Kreiskapelle," all bands on local level were known as "Ortsgruppenkapelle."

On May 18, 1934 the Reichsorganisationsleiter Dr. Ley published an announcement outlining the uniforms and insigne for these bands.[108] It was especially noted that tinnies, such as a lyre, were *not* allowed for wear, with the uniform *or* the visored cap.

Members of bands, and drum and trumpet corps, wore the regular visored cap.[109] The highest rank that a "Musikzugführer" (Leader of a music formation) could hold was Hauptstellenleiter of a Gau, Kreis or Ortsgruppe, indicating that before 1939 golden cap cords and buttons could not have been officially worn by these persons.

Bandmasters, musicians and drummers wore the following till 1939:

Gauleitung:	red cap piping, silver cords and buttons and light– or rust–brown velvet cap band;
Kreisleitung:	black piping, remainder as above;
Ortsgruppenleitung:	light–blue piping, remainder as above; but cap band in the same color as the top.[110]

Probably no bands existed on Reich–level prior to 1939, with the exception of the "Ordensburg" bands. Such bands are first mentioned in the Organisationsbuch, 1940 issue. However, if such a band existed before the introduction of the new uniforms in 1939, a visored cap was worn with golden–yellow piping and silver cords. At no time were the golden–yellow cords allowed to be worn by members of these Ordensburg bands, before June 1939.

Bandmasters, musicians and drummers wore the following from 1939–1945:

Reichsleitung: (Ordensburgen)	golden–yellow piping, golden cords and buttons and rust–brown velvet cap band;
Gauleitung:	dark red, remainder as above;
Kreisleitung:	white, remainder as above;

[107] *Ibid, issue 1940–1943. pp. 342–345.*

[108] *"Mbl.d.RZM," Nr. 2, January 12, 1935, p. 9; NSDAP Gau Schwaben. "Dienstanzug und Dienstrang des Pol.Leiter," 1936, Section 7, section 48, pp. 29–30.*

[109] *"Mbl.d.RZM," Nr. 4, January 26, 1935, p. 31. During the Party Rallies the field cap was worn by bandmembers.*

[110] *"Organisationsbuch der NSDAP. " München: 1936, p. 32; NSDAP Gau Schwaben. "Dienstanzug und Dienstrang des Politischen leiter," 1936, Section 7: Partei–Musikzug und Uniformierung, pp. 29–31.*

W.P.B.R. Saris

Members of a political leaders band, wearing the 1936–form of headdress and insignia during festivities during the opening of the fair "der DOM" at Hamburg in November 1937. The wear of a dark cap band, as well as piping indicates that the band is of a Gau– or Kreis–level.

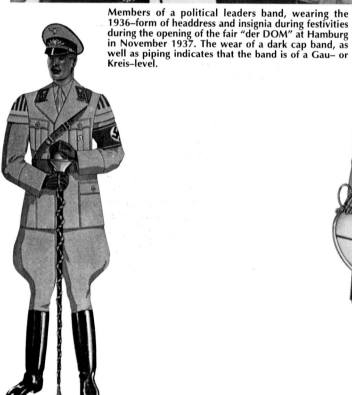

National Archives

A band, probably a Kreiskapelle, performing in brown shirts. Note the "Jingling Johnny," as well as the xylophone with red/white/black hair bushes.

Ortsgruppenleitung: light blue, remainder as above;
Betrieb: as for Ortsgruppenleitung (within factories and concerns bands existed, organized as bands on local level, wearing regular PL–uniform).[111]

FOREIGN DEPARTMENT (AUSLANDS–ORGANISATION DER NSDAP):

A foreign department (Ausland–Abteilung) was created May 1, 1931 on orders from Strasser and led by Hans Nieland. Assigned to it were all NSDAP individuals and local groups living abroad with the exception of Deutsch–Österreich, Danzig and the Saar–area.[112] One year later a department "Seefahrt" (for NSDAP members that were sailors with the German merchant navy) was raised, led by Kurt Thiele. In November 1932 both departments were renamed by order of Strasser into "Gau Ausland" and "Gau Seefahrt." By order of Ley in March 1933, the department "Gau Seefahrt" was abolished and "Gau Ausland" was renamed "Abteilung für Deutsche im Ausland" (this included the sailors, as well as the so–called "Landesgruppe" Italy and Switzerland) and was assigned to the NSDAP High Command, led by Ernst Wilhelm Bohle. Strasser had exceeded his powers.[113]

---

[111] *"Organisationsbuch der NSDAP. " München: issue 1940 and 1943, Section IV, pp. 31–31a. The band, known as "Betrieb" are discussed in Org.Book on page 31a.*

[112] *"Vbl.d.RL.d.NSDAP," Nr. 2, June 27, 1931, p. 6. In late 1933 the Saar–area was not listed anymore, instead came Memel (Nr. 57, dated October 15, 1933), p. 122.*

[113] *Ibid, Nr. 43, March 15, 1933, pp. 91–92; Ibid, Nr. 49, June 15, 1933, p. 106.*

In 1933 it was officially forbidden that Germans in the Reich wear the brown shirt (or uniform) when abroad. In the fall of 1933, only groups on local level existed abroad or on ships. This was extended up to Kreis level approximately in 1935; in Germany the department was organized on Gau–level.

By an order of Rudolf Hess, dated October 3, 1933 the department was renamed into "Auslands–Organisation der NSDAP,"[114] having an office "Seefahrt." The Netherlands would become a "Status apart" (an exception) as with the date October 15, 1940 the Netherlands was separated from the AO–organization and renamed as, "Arbeitsbereich der NSDAP in den Niederlanden" (Operations–area of the NSDAP for the Netherlands), assigned to Reichskommissar Seyss–Inquart and led by "Dienstleiter Generalkommissar z.b.V.," Schmidt–Münster.[115] (Consult the special section within this AO–section for further information).

Otto Spronk.

E.W. Bohle of the Auslandsorganisation in the rank of a Gauleiter at left, carrying the model–1939 visored cap "at rest." At his left is an Adjutant of the SS also wearing the Auslandsorganisation sleeve diamond.

[114] Ibid, Nr. 66, End–February 1933, p. 145. (Order Nr. 10/34, simultaneously Bohle was promoted to Gauleiter); Ibid, Nr. 74, dated end–June 1934, p. 175.

[115] Ibid, Nr. 213. October, 1940. Decree V 9/40, dated October 9, 1940.

RANKING SYSTEM 1936:

Germany

Leader with the rank of Gauleiter;

His deputy with the rank Stellvertretender Gauleiter;

All officials of the AO (Amtsleiter in der Leitung der AO) and the governors abroad (Auslandskommissare; to these officials various smaller "Landesgruppe" and "Landeskreise" were assigned. On some occasions even being an entire continent) were ranked as Gauamtsleiter (or later also as Gauhauptamtsleiter).

It must be noted that in later years the position of governor largely disapp–eared and its function was taken over by the Landesgruppenleiter (as by then the AO existed in most countries of the world).[116]

Abroad:

Landesgruppenleiter with the rank of Gauamtsleiter (in later years this function was identified by a cuff–title);

Landeskreisleiter with the rank of Kreisleiter;

There further existed Kreisleiter, Ortgruppen–and Stützpunktleiter, (for explanation on color for cords, buttons, piping and cap band, consult the 1936 list and the later changes).

AO SPORTS GROUPS (AO–SPORTGRUPPEN):

The introduction date for the uniforms to be worn by members of the sports groups "AO" is unknown, but believed to have been approximately 1940 (it isn't contained in the 1940 issue for the Org.Book). It was ordered for wear during meetings, inspections, border service, or whenever so ordered. Two kinds of dress regulations are known:

Grosser Dienstanzug (Ceremonial dress);

Dienstanzug für Sportausbildung (Service Dress for sports education and training).

A field cap of blended brown (melange–brown), gabardine, tricot or khaki tropical cloth was worn with both forms of dress. The flap and crown were piped in light blue or white. A swastika cockade was worn on the front center of the flap or turn–up. A woven golden political eagle emblem (a smaller version of the regular national emblem for political leaders) had officially to be worn on the upper left forward portion of the flap,[117] but photographs show its wear mainly on the front center of the top.

It must be noted that the forms of headdress worn by members of the AO in foreign countries were manufactured to German design and standards.

NSDAP OPERATIONS–AREA NETHERLANDS (ARBEITSBEREICH DER NSDAP IN DEN NIEDERLANDEN):

By order of October 15, 1941 Bormann promoted Schmidt to the rank of Oberdienstleiter (on Reich–level) and ordered that the ranks also be official at

116 "Organisationsbuch der NSDAP. " München, issues 1936, 1937, 1938, 1940 and 1943, pp. 143–144.

117 Ibid, 1943. Section VI: "Dienstanzüge und Sportanzug der Sportgruppen der AO," A and B, pp. 33a–33b.

Alain Taugourdeau

The Landesgruppenleiter from Italy is wearing the white tunic and visored cap. Note the wear of the cuff title. It is difficult to observe, but the top of the cap is piped in white; the cap band is piped in red according to his Gau–level rank. Officially he should have the Gauamtsleiter rank. This person is holding the rank Unterabteilungsleiter.

W.P.B.R. Saris

VI.

Dienstanzüge und Sportanzug der Sportgruppen der AO.

A. Großer Dienstanzug der AO.-Sportgruppen

Tragevorschrift:

Dieser Dienstanzug wird nur zum Dienst getragen: er ist einheitlich und ohne Rangabzeichen.

Der Dienstanzug ist anzulegen bei Aufmärschen, Absperrdienst, Großveranstaltungen, Besichtigungen und auf besonderen Befehl.

Beim Auftreten in geschlossener Formation wird der Mantel hochgeschlossen getragen.

1. Mütze:

In Schiffchenform aus melangebraunem Trikot oder Tropenstoff. Hellblaue Paspelierung. An der Stirnseite Hakenkreuzkokarde, an der linken Seite goldfarbener gewebter Hoheitsadler.

B. Dienstanzug für Sportausbildung der AO.

Tragevorschrift:

Dieser Dienstanzug für die Sportausbildung ist zum Exerzierdienst, Geländedienst, Schießausbildung und auf besonderen Befehl beim Einsatzdienst zu tragen.

1. Mütze:

Wie unter A. beschrieben.

A note from the original organization book from 1943 specifying the headdress with light blue piping (no other colors were mentioned) for the so–called sports groups from abroad. The swastika cockade was ordered worn on the front lower center . The left side had the gold woven national eagle emblem.

A political leader's field–cap, piped in light blue as ordered for the sports groups of the Auslands–organisation der NSDAP.

A meeting to celebrate the existence of the "Arbeitsbereich" at Arnhem (Netherlands), October 31, 1941. Note the piping around the crown of the field cap worn by the political leader standing in the middle.

the Kreis–and Orts–levels.[118] The order from Bormann meant in fact that the wear of visored caps, by lower ranked political leaders (piped either in white or light blue, other colors did not exist) was allowed. (Political leaders from Germany who were assigned duty in the Netherlands wore the piping colors ordered for Germany).

It has been established that visored caps manufactured by Dutch companies varied in sizes: for example the sweatband often measured 40mm, the top

118 *"Vbl.d.RL.d.NSDAP," Nr. 225, October, 1941. Decree V 3/41, dated October 15, 1941 and signed by Bormann in the Führerhauptquartier.*

Otto Spronk

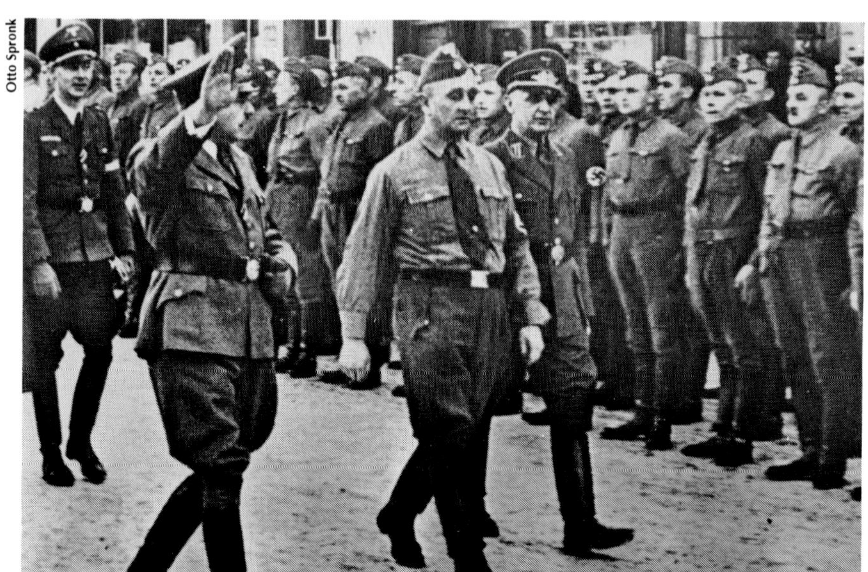

Political leaders of the NSDAP along with members of the AO in the Netherlands; note the wear of the model–1939 visored caps (person in the middle is wearing the old style collar patches). None of the other members is wearing collar patches, with the blouse.

Otto Spronk

The wearing of various piped visored caps for political leaders in the Netherlands. At left standing, Fritz Schmidt in a raincoat. In the middle a dark red piped cap, at right a white piped cap.

piping 3mm, the upper cap band piping 1.5mm, and the lower cap band piping 2.5mm. The top measured 64mm, the back 45mm and the width of the visor at its center was approximately 43mm. Hardly any of these caps had an RZM tag and were marked instead with a company stamp on the inside of the sweatband leather, at the right side as seen from the front .

Fritz Schmidt in his rank Ober–Dienstleiter during a meeting in the Netherlands. Note that the political leader at far left is still wearing the old form of collar patches, as also does the man behind Schmidt's right shoulder. Schmidt was the "Generalkommissar zur besonderen Verwendung der NSDAP" for the occupied Netherlands from June 1940. He died under mysterious causes three years later at Chartres in France. It is fairly certain that he was murdered by the SS.

GERMAN PEOPLES LEAGUES (DEUTSCHE VOLKSBÜNDE):

Organizations, such as the VDA (Volksbund für das Deutschtum im Ausland) and other pure German alliances existed abroad, not being part of the Auslands–Organisation der NSDAP, but directly led by the NSDAP command in Berlin.

To avoid confusion we will not discuss these groups, but out of necessity, and in the interest of this series, a few photos of the headdress forms (look–a–likes) or even completely diverging forms worn by those organizations are shown. Occasionally, headdress forms worn by National Socialist groups in other countries are shown. For more detailed information, see the series, "Foreign Legions of the Third Reich, Volumes I–IV, David Littlejohn and published by R. James Bender Publishing.

To close this chapter we would like to give a quick idea of the enormous numbers of political leaders headdresses that were needed. Once a year on Hitler's birthday, April 20, political leaders of the NSDAP and its sub–organizations were given their oath by Hitler's deputy Rudolf Hess on the "Königsplatz" at Munich by radio transmission. In 1936 he swore in approximately 1,250,000 officials and in 1937 approximately 734,000 while in 1938 approximately 600,000 persons were inducted.

In 1939 Hess gave the oaths from the "Sportpalast" in Berlin, because of the celebrations connected with Hitler's 50th birthday. Approximately 1,000,000 persons were sworn in, giving a total of 3,584,000 in four years. The largest part of these were political leaders of the political organization.[119] With the authorization of more gold ranking insigne in 1939 these political leaders were scornfully described by the German public as "Goldfasanen" (Gold Pheasants).

Otto Spronk

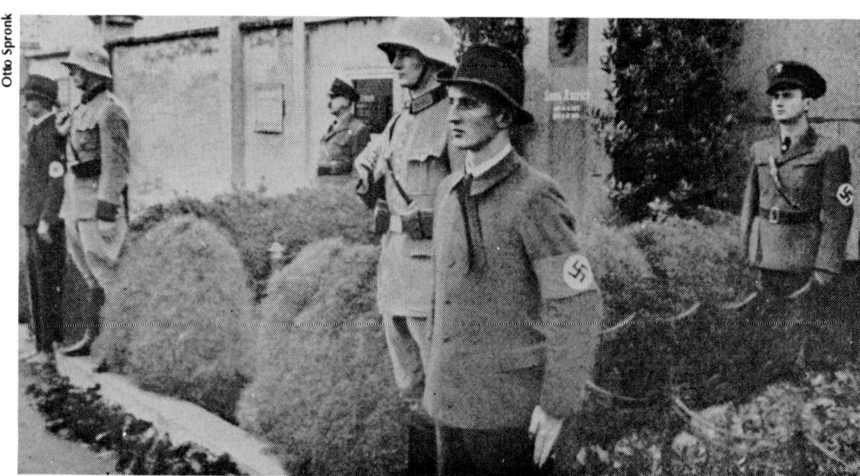

Police personnel and members of the Sudetendeutsche party at the grave of Hans Knirsch in 1938. Note the wearing of the rare form visored cap with a small political eagle by the person on the right.

National Archives

National Socialists, probably of Swedish origin, wearing various forms of dark top visored caps. The person at right could possibly be a member of a guard corps resembling the "SS."

30. De stormleiders dragen om den bovenkant der pet het tweekleuren koord in de kleuren van de standaard waartoe zij behooren. (Zie afb. 31a).

Vanaf stormbanleider wordt het gouden of zilveren koord gedragen. (Zie afb. 32).

Standaard en brigadecommandanten dragen behalve het gouden of zilveren koord, boven rond de zwarte petrand het tweekleuren koord van de standaard waartoe zij behooren. (Zie afb. 33).

Zijn zij belast met het **commando** over een standaard, dan dragen zij onder het tweeleuren koord een gouden liskoord van ½ c.M. reedte. (Zie afb. 34).

18

De chef van den staf draagt een gouden lisoord van 1 c.M. breedte.

31. Het dragen van insignes of dergelijke ›p de pet anders dan de voorgeschrevene (S.A. ienstteeken enz.) is verboden.

Verder wordt nog op diensthemd of dienst-.is door S.A.-mannen, schaarleiders en troep-.eiders, behoorende tot het roode kruispersoneel, iet roode kruis op wit veld op rechter boven :rm gedragen. (Zie afb. 35).

32. Alle formatieleiders dragen een fluit-:oord in de kleuren van de standaard van de echter borstzak naar de tweede knoop van ›oven in de middelste knoopenrij. (Zie afb. 36).

19

W.P.B.R. Saris

Pages from the SA section of the NSNAP 1933 regulation. Note the visored cap form worn by the Dutch SA, closely resembling the 1934 form for German political leaders.

Rijksinstituut voor Oorlogsdokumentatie

Adalbert Smit, the founder of the Nat.Soc.-Nederlandsche Arbeiders Partij, is wearing a visored cap with a light brown top, black cap band, as well as black visor and leather chin strap. In the center for the band the regular NSNAP insigne is worn.

Rijksinstituut voor Oorlogsdokumentatie

The wearing of the uniform, which resembles that of the NSDAP, by members of the NSNAP-Kruyt in the Netherlands. Note that the visored cap has the light top, dark cap band and that cap cords are resting above a brown visor. At the right a member of the SA der NSNAP.

119 *"Daten der Geschichte der NSDAP" by Volz. 11.Auflage. Berlin/Leipzig: 1943. section III, pp. 69,73,77–78,86.*

CHAPTER

4

NS–Frauenschaft/Deutsches Frauenwerk

NATIONAL SOCIALIST WOMEN'S GROUP/GERMAN WOMEN'S ENTERPRISE

In the early 1920's right–wing women's organizations were created in various districts of Germany. A woman by the name of Elsbeth Zander created in 1924 the "Völkische Frauenorden."[1] From this organization would grow the NS–Frauenschaft, but females joined the NSDAP as early as 1920 and organized branches, known as "Frauengruppen." In 1923 the "Frauengruppe der NSDAP" was officially founded. The alliance of Zander was renamed on January 2, 1928 as the "Deutscher Frauenorden (Rotes Hakenkreuz)" and was simultaneously incorporated into the NSDAP Party system as the league for all National Socialist females.[2]

On July 6, 1931 Gregor Strasser announced that a new NS–Frauenschaft (NSF) was to supersede the existing Nazi women's groups (Deutscher Frauenorden, as well as Frauenarbeitsgemeinschaften) and on October 1, 1931 the Nat.Soz.–Frauenschaft (Deutscher Frauenorden), a Party organization, was officially instituted.[3] Due to both internal and other problems, Ley tried to create an umbrella organization in May 1933, the "Deutsche Frauenfront," intended to be analogous to his new Labor Front.[4] A counter–measure was taken by Frick leading to another women's organization. (By 1934 it can be said that most of the problems were solved). Since August 1, 1933 a sub–organization was raised for overseas membership, named "Arbeitsgemeinschaft der Deutschen Frau im Ausland," led by Wera Behr.[5]

---

1 "Daten der Geschichte der NSDAP," 11.Auflage. Berlin: 1943. Section: Die NSDAP von 1925 bis 1933, p. 24. (in various references this organization was named as "Deutscher Frauenorden", being created in 1923, as well as "Völkischer Frauenbund." This is Zanders' organization addressed at Nürnberg in 1924).

2 "Das Dritte Reich. Die Kampfjahre 1918 – 1933." Berlin: 1936, p. 136.

3 "Verordnungsblatt der Reichsleitung der NSDAP" (further referred as Vbl.d.RL.d.NSDAP), Nr. 3, München, July 13, 1931, p. 7; Ibid, Nr. 11, November 16, 1931, pp. 27–28 with organization definitions.

4 Ibid, Nr. 54. August 31, 1934, p. 116. (Ley's announcement stated that he was taking over the department NS–Frauenschaft. It is obvious he did not succeed).

Until April 26, 1933 the NSF was led by Zander, who was succeeded first by BDM leader Lydia Gottschewski[6], then Dr. Gottfried Krummacher, and finally on February 24, 1934[7] by the leading woman of the Frauen–Arbeitsdienst (Women's Labor Service), the well–known Gertrud Scholtz–Klink. She was the Reichsfrauenfühererin (Reich Female Leader) until the end of the war.

M. Shaner

The Reichsfrauenführerin Gertrud Scholtz–Klink in her younger days. She was seldom seen wearing any form of headdress.

The name NS–Frauenschaft (Deutscher Frauenorden) [the subtitle in brackets later was discontinued and no longer used] was created along traditional lines. The purpose of this organization was to supply the Party and others with women able to assume leadership positions for their various sections or departments and formations, but also for the later Deutsches Frauenwerk or a planned nursing organization.

The Deutsches Frauenwerk (DFW) resulted, because of the 1933/1934 problems, which came to a head in 1934 and was a part of the NSF. Its main objective dealt with the state and domestic economies and for a while leading the

---

5 *"Nachrichtendienst der Reichsfrauenführerin," Nr. 20, München: November 15, 1935, p. 430 – 433. (in this announcement it was especially noted that it was named as "Arbeitsgemeinschaft" and not as "NS–Frauenschaft A–O").*

6 *"Vbl.d.RL.d.NSDAP," Nr. 45/46, München: April 30, 1933, p. 97.*

7 *"Nachrichtendienst der Reichsfrauenführung" Nr. 1, Berlin: January 1939, p. 50: 5 Jahre Reichsfrauenführung.*

Reichsmütterdienst (National Mother's Service, later largely led by the NSV). The DFW was also led by Scholtz–Klink.

It may confuse the reader somewhat, but the NSF and DFW worked together where the cooperation of women was required, such as with the female section of the labor service (NS–Arbeitsdienst, as well as the later RADwJ), the female bureau of the DAF (Frauenamt der DAF), BDM, Deutsches Rotes Kreuz (Reichsfrauenbund, an umbrella organization of "Rotkreuzfrauenvereine,"and since May 1934 a part of the DFW[8]) or nursing organizations, but also the Reichsnährstand, the females from the Reichs–Kolonial–Bund, NS female students (NS–Studentenbund), Reichsbund Dt.Akademikerinnen, the Reichsluftschutzbund and may others. (It must be noted that the NSF and DFW were also closely linked with the NSV – it is a misunderstanding to think the NSV existed within the NSF/DFW, see separate chapter within this volume)[9].

In April 1938 Scholtz–Klink announced the "Frauenhilfsdienst (für Wohlfahrts–und Krankcnpflcgc),"a nursing section that in fact came from the "Hilfsdienst," formed in the summer of 1936 very closely linked to the NSV but also active with DAF.[10]

M. Shaner

A female from the Frauenhilfsdienst is wearing a white cowl without an emblem during her service at a NSV "Kindergarten."

During the years 1933 through 1935 many members of these NSDAP female organizations, especially the Deutsches Frauenwerk, came from the Neulandbund, Schutz–und Trutzbund, Bund Königin Luise (regarded at first as

8 "Nachrichtendienst der NS–Frauenschaft," Nr. 3, München: February 1, 1935, p. 58.

9 Various issues and volumes of the "Amtswalterinnenblatt der NSF"; "Nachrichtendienst der NSF/DFW" and "Nachrichtendienst der Reichsfrauenführerin" (later Reichsfrauenführung) between 1933 and 1942 were used for this information (especially the year 1935 that often gave many specific directives). It is known that even more organizations had to be mentioned.

10 "Nationalsozialistische Frauenschaft, Schrift der Deutschen Hochschule für Politik." Berlin: 1937, p. 29; "Nachrichtendienst der Reichsfrauenführung," Nr. 6, München: June 1938, p. 206.

a hostile organization, but from 1933 cooperating with NS–organizations and then dissolved in April 1934) and the Stahlhelm–Frauenbund (officially dissolved in the autumn of 1935). The growth of the female leagues was so enormous that by February 1, 1936, its ranks were closed to further members (membership was again opened later).

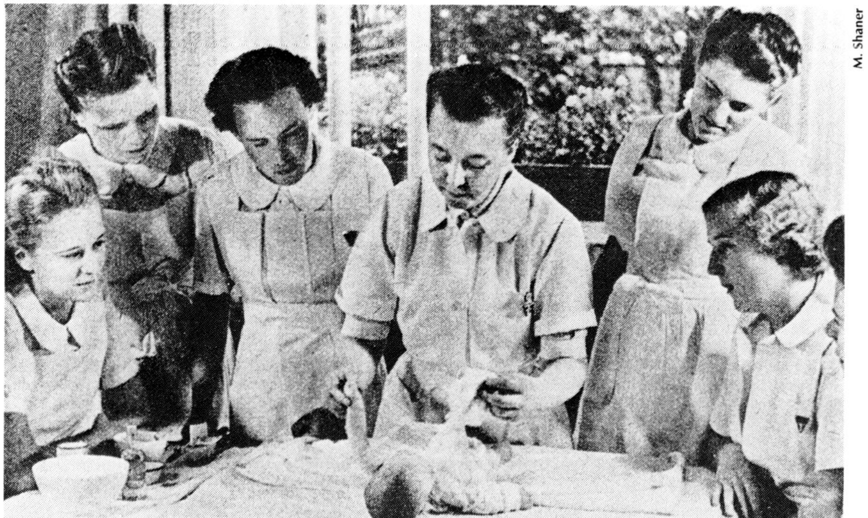

M. Shaner

Females wearing a nurse–like dress during a course for infant care at Amsterdam at a so–called "Mütterschule." No hood or cowl was worn.

The forms of headdress worn by females of the RAD, BDM, DRK, etc. will be discussed in their respective chapters in this series. This chapter will deal only with the NSF/DFW and their youth groups.

NS–Frauenschaft

It was during the years 1931/1934, under the leadership of Zander, that various attempts were made to standardize the dress, but the Reichsleitung der NSDAP (section Frauenschaft) refused and it was pointed out that any standardization was strictly forbidden until October 1933.[11] Members of the female Nazi groups had adopted the color brown as with other branches of the Party and the wearing of berets (Baskenmütze) was not uncommon. From every direction the females pushed for a standard uniform

Shortly thereafter, in December 1933, Dr. Krummacher, yielded and proposed to introduce a dress (Ehrenkleid), based on traditional German lines in dark brown. No headdress was included.[12]. The only firm allowed to produce the

---

11 "Informationsdienst der NS–Frauenschaft" (Deutscher Frauenorden), Nr. 13, München: May 7, 1933, p. 26; Ibid, Nr. 14, May 21, 1933, p. 45 and "Amtswalterinnenblatt der NS–Frauenschaft" (Deutscher Frauenorden), Nr. 23, München: October 1, 1933, p. 180.

12 "Amtswalterinnenblatt der NS–Frauenschaft" (Deutscher Frauenorden), Nr. 28/1, München: December 15, 1933/January 1, 1934, pp. 284–285.

W.P.B.R. Saris

Anordnung betreffend Tracht der N.S.-Frauenschaft.

Die Uniformierung Deutscher Frauen wird mit Recht von allen Frauen wie Männern abgelehnt, — die Freimachung von ausländischen Moden ist nicht dadurch möglich, daß man sie nur ablehnt, sondern dadurch, daß man eine

deutsche Tracht

schafft. Volkstrachten gibt es leider nur noch in engbegrenzten Bezirken. So sehr wir diese bejahen, sind sie doch nicht der Ausdruck des gemeinsamen Willens aller deutschen Frauen zu Volk, Rasse und Staat.

Diejenigen Frauen, die sich durch das Bekenntnis zur N.S.-Frauenschaft der Volksarbeit im Staate Adolf Hitlers zur Verfügung stellen, haben das Recht,

ein Ehrenkleid

zu tragen. In Anlehnung an bisher vielfach geübte Bräuche habe ich nunmehr eine Klubjacke aus dunkelbraunem Tuch herstellen lassen, die ein Bestandteil der Tracht der N.S.-Frauenschaft werden soll. Zu dieser Klubjacke wird ein einheitlicher Gürtl aus Kalbleder geliefert, der elegant und geschmackvoll gearbeitet ist. Klubjacke und Gürtel können zu jedem Kleid getragen werden. Zur Ergänzung der Klubjacke wird, um unsere Frauen vor Erkältung zu schützen eine hellbraune Strickjacke mit Aermeln eingeführt, die in Tönung und Gestaltung der Klubjacke angepaßt ist. Da im kommenden Frühjahr mit der sportlichen Tätigkeit systematisch begonnen werden soll, wird die Strickjacke als Sportkleidung dienen.

Einheitliche Kleider und gleiche Kopfbedeckung ist grundsätzlich verboten zu tragen.

Dr. Krummacher's article in the "Amtswalterinnenblatt der NS–Frauenschaft" of December 1933, in which he suggested a dress for females of the NSF. In April 1934, this plan was torpedoed by the new NSF leader Scholtz–Klink.

dress was Karl Böcker at Waldbröl in the Rhine area. Krummacher's plans however were torpedoed April 1934 by the new NSF leader Scholtz–Klink.[13]

It took until 1939 for the Reichsfrauenführerin Scholtz–Klink to address the idea of an official dress. With a letter, dated April 25, she announced a costume for females of NSF/DFW occupying leadership positions (those officials holding the position of Abteilungsleiterin of a department or higher) in blue.[14] This very dark blue had unofficially been in use for some years. It had the same, but modified, form as had been earlier worn by other female organizations (see Volume 2, chapter Der Stahlhelm, section Stahlhelm–Frauenbund, pages 255 and 256).

In spite of extensive research, documentation concerning headdress worn by the women of the NS–Frauenschaft is meager, and we have to conclude that the wearing of a hat by these females was merely a privilege for those serving within the Reichsfrauenführung and in the highest positions at Gau level, in the summer of 1939 as below:

Reichsfrauenführung (Reich Level):

Reichsfrauenführerin (it is known that Scholtz–Klink seldom wore a hat);
Reichskassenwalter (Reich Treasurer—most often being a man);

---

13 *Ibid, Nr. 6, München: April 15, 1934, p. 100. It was stated that: "Hitler's official point of view in relation with a unified dress is once again announced."*

14 *"Nachrichtendienst der Reichsfrauenführung," Nr. 6, Berlin: June 1939, p. 261. (The precise text of this letter is not known, but it is located in a known archive; if further information becomes available this will be mentioned in a later addendum). "Uniformen–Markt," Nr. 13, Berlin: July 1, 1939, p. 193 (an article in relation with uniforms and dresses for females for various organizations).*

Amtswalterinnenblatt

der N. S. Frauenschaft (Deutscher Frauenorden)

Verantwortlich für den Gesamtinhalt: Oberste Leitung der P.O. N. S. Frauenschaft (Deutscher Frauenorden)

Amt für Frauenaufgaben Stellv. Hildegard Passow. Mtl. 20 Pfg. d. die Gau-Frauenschaftsleiterinnen z. überweisen

Postscheckkonto: Nat.Soz. Deutsche Arbeiter-Partei Reichsführung Frauenschaft München 5980

München, Folge 6
15. April 1934

Bekanntmachungen.

Die offizielle Stellungnahme des Führers gegen jegliche gleichmäßige Tracht oder Uniformierung der N.S.-Frauenschaft wird hiermit noch einmal nachdrücklich zur allgemeinen Kenntnis gebracht.

Darunter fällt auch die Braune Jacke, die ebenso wie das Braune Kleid aufgetragen, aber nicht neu beschafft werden darf. Die Neuherstellung der Braunen Jacke ist eingestellt worden, es werden nur noch die vorhandenen Bestände verkauft.

Es ist eine selbstverständliche Aufgabe aller Amtswalterinnen, in den Frauenschaftsabenden und gemeinsamen Veranstaltungen für eine schlichte Kleidung aller Teilnehmerinnen Sorge zu tragen und darin selbst vorbildlich zu wirken.

Die Gau- und Kreiskulturwartinnen bleiben bestehen, aber nur die berufenen Frauen. Es ist sehr viel Wert auf gute Zusammenarbeit mit den entsprechenden Gliederungen der P.O. zu legen, damit auch bei deren Veranstaltungen unsere Bedürfnisse und Wünsche berücksichtigt werden.

gez. Frau Scholtz-Klink.

The April 1934 announcement of Scholtz–Klink where in the first paragraph is mentioned Hitler's negative view regarding a unified dress for females. The second paragraph states that the manufacturing of the brown jacket had begun, but was to be stopped immediately. Note the "Caption" of the periodical, which during this period was referred to as "Amtswalterinnenblatt."

Hauptabteilungsleiterin (Main Department);
Abteilungsleiterin, but also

Gaufrauenschaftsleitung (Gau Level):
Gaufrauenschaftsleiterin;
Gaukassenwalterin;
Gauabteilungsleiterin.
(those females heading an office or department on Reich and Gau levels only).

Whether the ranks Kreisfrauenschaftsleiterin or Ortsgruppenleiterin were ever officially permitted is not known, but it is certain that the ranks of Zellenfrauenschafts– or Blockfrauenschaftsleiterin never were. The number of wearers was in fact very limited: an available list of persons in high leadership positions in departments on the Reich level shows that only approximately 50 women (including the women in high official positions of the so–called Reichsschulen)

The Reichsfrauenführerin Scholtz–Klink seldom wore any type of headdress. In this photograph she is wearing a beret–like head-dress in the spring of 1939.

might have worn a hat, in addition to approximately 50 females with the rank of Gaufrauenschaftsleiterin.[15]

During the war females of the staffs, belonging to the "enger" or "erweiterter Stab" (small and extended staffs) of the Gaufrauenschaftsleiterin probably started wearing the NSF hat. From available documents, it is known that by 1939, females often wore brown berets during political courses.

The hat was very dark blue (close to black) material. It was wide brimmed and had a black silk, ribbed hat band around the lowest part of the hat. A small bow or knot was worn either on the wearer's left side, or at the back, resting on the brim. The somewhat creased top was approximately 12 cm high, the brim in the front approximately 9 cm and 6 cm at the back. The brim was raised at the left side (it has been observed that hats with both sides of the brim upraised were also worn). These hats were in fact nothing more than copies of the hats in the typical style worn by the civilians of the period.

It has been said that a gold national emblem was worn on the front of the hat, but no evidence has been found to support this. It stated in a dress directive that "...the wearing of *one* national emblem on the left sleeve was enough (for females)."

Research has revealed that this form of dress or similar forms were also worn, for example, in Belgium by the higher ranking females of the Vlaams Nat.Vrouwen Verbond (VNVV) and "Les Femmes Rexistes," members of the Nat.Soc.Vrouwen Organisatie (NSVO) of the Netherlands or the Vrouwenschap

---

[15] "Sonderdruck zum Nachrichtendienst der Reichsfrauenführung." Berlin: July 1938, section 2: Aufteilung der Arbeitsgebiete der Reichsfrauenführung, pp. 2–4.

der NSDAP, and certainly by those of the (NS–Frauenschaft) Arbeitsbereich in den Niederlanden.

These hats were manufactured within the clothing industry (Fachgruppe 6, Kopfbekleidungs–Industrie) by companies who made hats for women. Others, (Fachgruppe 7, Bekleidungsbehör–Industrie) manufactured accessories.[16]

Navorsingsinstituut Brussel

NS–Frauenschaft female leader wearing the wide brimmed hat during a visit of the Finnish Lotta–Svard president Fanni Luukkonen at Berlin May 14, 1943. The wearing of these hats was optional but mandatory on special occasions

Otto Spronk

During a visit of German officials of the Party in the Netherlands during an early period of the war. The NS–Frauenschaft female member is wearing a white wide brimmed hat in the style worn by females of the Deutsche Lufthansa.

16 *"Uniformen–Markt," Nr. 20, October 15, 1937, p. 303.*

Robert McCarthy

Females in Germany wearing typical hats of the period.

Robert Bernard

An example of the hat type in very dark blue with black silk hat band (approximately 1 cm wide) as worn by the females in the highest positions of the NS–Frauenschaft.

Deutsches Frauenwerk

A few women holding high positions in the Deutsches Frauenwerk also wore a dark blue dress, but were never allowed to wear the official "costume,"nor was a hat ever sanctioned for these females for wear during special activities. The Deutsches Frauenwerk was under the control of the NS–Frauenschaft.

The NS–Frauenschaft or Deutsches Frauenwerk members who were training in the field of public health were under the control of, and were auxiliaries of the German Red Cross (DRK) and sometimes the NSV.[17] They wore the regular DRK or NSV nurses' dress. The headdress was a white, triangular piece of cloth, usually linen or a white, starched hood with a small woven red cross on the front[18] (for more information see the chapter NS–Volkswohlfahrt within this volume, as well as the chapter "Deutsches Rotes Kreuz," in a future volume). It must be noted that females of the DFW working in welfare (Frauenhilfsdienst) or other nursing situations adopted a nurse–like dress. With this the small white hood was worn. Most often no forms of headdress were worn at all.

During a meeting of Party and the armed forces in the Netherlands, a female of the NSVO is shown wearing a dark hat with a light colored hat band.

Females from the NS–Frauenschaft and Deutsches Frauenwerk during a meeting where membership badges are being presented.

17 *Ibid, Nr. 1, December 1934, p. 5.*

18 *"Diensttracht der Helferin des DRK," 1935.*

A woman from the NS–Frauenschaft helping care for German soldiers during a trip to the front lines. No official headdress was ever worn in this service.

(Deutsche) Kinderschar (Kindergruppen der NSF)

There existed within the NS–Frauenschaft a section for small children (probably first raised in 1932, for those too young to join the Hitler Youth).[19] Again and again the introduction of unified clothing for these youngsters was attempted in several districts.[20] In late 1933 this was left to the direction of the Gaufrauenschaftsleiterin.[21] The attempts to introduce a unified dress came to a halt in May 1936, when the Reichsfrauenführerin ordered that clothing already in use had to be worn out.[22]

This section for children was officially incorporated into the Hitler–Jugend in May 1936,[23] but it should be noted that even in later years these youth groups were still being mentioned in the NSF official sources.

Not much information has been found, but it is known that brown or black berets were sometimes worn.

---

19 *Letter from the NS–Frauenschaft, Gauleitung at Schleswig–Holstein. Altona: April 26, 1932. This letter included directives for raising the NSF on local level, "Jungmädchengruppen", as well as Kindergruppen der NSF (Deutscher Frauenorden).*

20 *"Mitteilungsblatt der RZM," Nr. 1, München: January 4, 1936, p. 1.*

21 *"Amtswalterinnenblatt der NS–Frauenschaft" (Deutscher Frauenorden), Nr. 23, München: October 1, 1933, p. 181, section "Kleidung."*

22 *"Nachrichtendienst der Reichsfrauenführerin," Nr. 6, mid–June 1936, p. 227, concerning a letter from Scholtz–Klink, Nr. F.58/36, May 20, 1936.*

23 *"Verordnungsblatt der HJ," Nr. IV/12, May 1936, p. 146.*

M. Shaner

A youth group from Berlin visiting wounded soldiers in a hospital. This form of standard dress was often seen in photographs, but no photographs have been found showing the wearing of a headdress of any kind.

Jungmädchenschaft

What has been noted about the "Kinderschar" was also applicable for the young girls within the NSF (first known as NS–Mädchengruppen, and later renamed the Jugendgruppen der NSF/DFW) in all aspects. During the first years, the age for these girls was from 18 through 22 (later from 21 through 30).[24]

In 1936 these girls were absorbed into the BDM. Nevertheless in July 1937 new importance was given to this section (from these girls it was expected that the new leaders for the NSF and DFW would come). An order of June 1 announced the incorporation of girls, not having a leadership position within the BDM and above the age of 21, into the Jugendgruppen der NSF/DFW.[25]

In the spring of 1937 the girls were given a "Festkleid,"a dress to be worn during special celebrations (before September 1936 a standardization of their clothing was not sanctioned by the NSDAP High Command).[26] The color and form for this "Festkleid" were left up to each Gau's desire.[27]

Final preparations for a standard dress came in the summer of 1938, when in August new complete directives for the girls were published by the NSF High

---

[24] *Letter from NSF, Gauleitung Schleswig–Holstein. Altona: April 26, 1932. Section V: Ortsgruppe.*

[25] *"Nachrichtendienst der Reichsfrauenführerin," Nr. 7, München , July 1937, p. 178 (order of Scholtz–Klink).*

[26] *"Mitteilungsblatt der RZM," Nr. 1, January 1, 1936, p. 1.*

[27] *Nachrichtendienst der Reichsfrauenführerin," Nr. 5, München: May 1937, p. 129. (here a letter was published from Scholtz–Klink – Nr. F.64/37, dated April 12, 1937).*

M. Shaner

A girl from a youth group of the NSF Berlin wearing the kind of standard dress as authorized, but without any headdress. This dress form for the most part resembles the BDM dress.

W.P.B.R. Saris

Übersicht ü. .r die Rundschreiben der Reichsfrauenführung
vom 10. April bis 9. Mai 1939

Anordnung der Reichsfrauenführerin

1 vom 25. 4.	Einheitliches Kostüm der Frauenschaftsleiterinnen, Beurteilung über Lehrkräfte der Abteilung Mütterdienst und Volkswirtschaft-Hauswirtschaft

Übersicht über die Rundschreiben der Reichsfrauenführung
vom 10. Mai bis 9. Juni 1939

F 95 vom 6. 6.	Werbung für Erntelager der Jugendgruppen
F 97 vom 7. 6.	Dienstbluse, Armstreifen, Diensthut
FW 75 vom 6. 6.	Kursus der Gaujugendgruppenführerinnen in Coburg vom 29. 6. bis 3. 7. 39

Two notes from the "Nachrichtendienst der Reichsfrauenführung" in which is noted the order from Scholtz-Klink, dated April 25, 1939 regarding the costume for female leaders and a circular letter F 97, dated June 7, 1939 which mentions the hat for female youth.

Command.[28] Girls with this costume were first seen during the Reichsparteitag in 1938.[29] These dresses were so new that neither the German public, or the press knew to what organization these young females belonged to. In the fall of 1938 it was specifically announced that this costume was to be worn only when on duty in groups or special occasions .

No headdress was worn officially, but it is known that in this youth group the berets from the BDM were also worn. On June 6, 1939 (probably even earlier) a hat for special occasions was announced. The form was the same as that of the NSF, but always in black. Above the brim rested a wide band, its color is unknown, but is believed to have been lighter brown.[30]

M Shaner

Females from the youth group NSF Gau München–Oberbayern wearing the hat with band during the funeral of Maria Hinle, November 11, 1939. Hinle was one of the victims of the bombing of the "Bürgerbräukeller" in Munich on November 8th.

Kraftfahrer

Females were not officially allowed to drive cars for the NSF/DFW. Driving duties were performed by members of political organizations such as the SA, SS, NSKK, DAF or HJ.

---

28 "Sonderdruck zum Nachrichtendienst der Reichsfrauenführung." Berlin: August 1938. Section IV notes that a black costume was allowed.

29 "Uniformen–Markt," Nr. 20, October 15, 1938, p. 319, and Ibid, Nr. 21, November 12, 1938, p. 332.

30 Letter for "Jugendgruppen," Nr. F.97, dated June 7, 1939 announcing cufftitles and a hat. ("Nachrichtendienst der Reichsfrauenführung," Nr. 7, Berlin: July 1939, p. 311 – this note does not give specific detail). In an earlier announcement of October 15, 1938, for the first time, a headdress is mentioned; "NS. Frauen–Warte," Nr. 13, January 1940, p. 294.

CHAPTER

5

NS–Volkswohlfahrt e.V.

NAT.SOZ.STATE WELFARE FEDERATION

In addition to the NS–Frauenschaft and Deutsches Frauenwerk an aid service existed: the NS–Volkswohlfahrt e.V. (NSV). This federation was instituted in Berlin during April 1932 and in October of that year, assigned to the Gau Gross–Berlin of the NSDAP. By a decree of Hitler, dated May 3, 1933 this NSV, led by Erich Hilgenfeldt, joined the Party system and was designated as the organization concerned with welfare work, charity, national prosperity, help to the youth and public health.[1] Its incorporation into the NSDAP took place officially on March 29, 1935.[2]

The NSV was very closely linked to the DRK (Deutsches Rotes Kreuz), the RLB (Reichsluftschutzbund), the WHW (Winterhilfswerk) and sisters in the field of nursing. As noted in the earlier chapter NSF/DFW and also for the NSV many of its members came from the organizations mentioned in that chapter.[3] The NSV was also responsible for the phenomenon of "Kinderlandverschickung" (sending of children to the country), Hilfswerk "Mutter und Kind" (aid service for mothers and children), the management of soup kitchens for the poor and assisting the unions of welfare and health that were assigned (approximately 18 leagues and unions).[4]

In May 1933 an umbrella organization for social and health services was instituted: Reichsarbeitsgemeinschaft der Berufe im sozialen und ärztlichen Dienste e.V. (RAG). This RAG was assigned to the Ministry of the Interior and also was led by Hilgenfeldt, and from June 1934 by Dr. Walter. (Within this RAG the "Reichsfachschaft Deutscher Schwestern und Pflegerinnen" and the "Reichsfachschaft für Krankenpfleger" were organized in 1933 with approxi-

---

[1] *"Daten der Geschichte der NSDAP," 11.Auflage. Berlin: 1943. Section IV: Das Deutsche Reich und die NSDAP seit 1933, p. 54; "Vbl.d.Rl.d.NSDAP," Nr. 49. München: June 15, 1933, p. 106.*

[2] *"Organisationsbuch der NSDAP. " Berlin: 1936. Section 3: Das Hauptamt für Volkswohlfahrt (NSV), p. 224.*

[3] *"Der Stahlhelm" (Süddeutsche Ausgabe, Beilage: Die Junge Front), Nr. 42, October 15, 1933.*

[4] *"Organisationsbuch der NSDAP. " München: 1937, p. 270 – 282b.*

mately five different nursing sections, including those from the NSV, Red Cross and Catholic churches).

On January 5, 1934 the Hauptamt für Volkswohlfahrt of the NSDAP was ordered by Hess from the Reichsleitung der NSDAP to unify the so–called "Schwesternschaften." The existing sections, "Braune Schwestern" and "Rote Hakenkreuzschwestern," (NS nurses) had to be disbanded ten days later. This order did not include females from the NSF serving in the field of welfare. The new section was re–named into "Schwesternschaft der NSV." On May 17, 1934 a new organization was officially instituted under the name of the NS–Schwesternschaft,[5] led by Käthe Böttger. In October 1935 Hilgenfeldt announced that those nurses not as yet organized had to join the Schwesternschaften der NSV. This reflected another new organization: Reichsbund der Freien (Deutscher) Schwestern und Pflegerinnen e.V. (a uniting of all nurses not members of a trade union), led by Generaloberin Rancke. By April 1937 all NS–nurses automatically had to be a member of the NS–Frauenschaft. In May 1938 Reichsorganisationsleiter Ley ordered that all members of the NS–Schwesternschaft, the "Reichsbund," as well as DRK–Schwesternschaft had to also be members of the DAF.

From March 11, 1936 the NSV and DRK worked together closely as the DRK assigned females as auxiliaries for the NSV. In 1937 there were still "free" nurses and some (not belonging to the NS) formed new unions. In 1938 the Caritas–Union, as well as the "Innere Mission" assigned nurses to NSV positions on the local level.

The war caused the transfer of DRK or NSV nurses to branches of the Armed Forces. NS nurses served from 1941 within the BDM–Gesundheitsdienst and Bormann ordered the combining of the NS–Schwesternschaft and the Reichsbund mentioned earlier. From this combination grew in July 1941 the NS–Reichsbund Deutscher Schwestern (NSRDS.e.V)., led by Generaloberin Moser. Nurses from occupied countries volunteered, due to the lack of enough qualified German personnel. In January 1944 the SS–Führungshauptamt ordered the beginning of nurse training for these Germanic volunteers. It was pointedly noted that these females were not to be classified as "Ausländer" (foreigners).[6]

This chapter will deal with the forms of headdress used by the male and female members of the NS–Volkswohlfahrt, the NS–Schwesternschaft and the Reichsbund der Freien Schwestern und Pflegerinnen e.V. The DRK or the "Schwesternschaft des Deutschen Roten Kreuzes e.V., as well as the WHW will be discussed in a future volume. (We will mention the above as required in this volume. In any event other nursing or similar services will be discussed in the future volume, for example the "Reichsgemeinschaft freier Caritasschwestern," "Schwesternschaft der Reichssektion Gesundheitswesen" or "Dakoniegemeinschaft").

---

5 *"Vbl.d.Rl.d.NSDAP," N.63, January 15, 1934, Order 7/34, p. 137; "Richtlinien der NS–Schwesternschaft. Gliederung und Aufgaben." Berlin/München: June 21, 1934, pp. 3–4.*

6 *Data, information and dress regulations were supplied to W.P. B.R. Saris by Mrs. Hilde Steppe, author of "Krankenpflege im Nationalsozialismus," published in Frankfurt/M., 1989. Mrs. Steppe has a function within the "Berufsfortbildungswerk" of the Deutschen Gewerkschaftsbundes GmbH (a trade–union)*

NS–Volkswohlfahrt

It should be noted that it is very difficult to identify in photographs whether the nurse is from the NSV, the NS–Schwesternschaft in particular (brown) or the Reichsbund and her precursor "Freie Schwesternschaft" (blue). With the last two, it is even more difficult. Only the brooches if worn can give a final answer and for this reason these are shown to give the reader a better help with the identification of photographs.

W.P.B.R. Saris

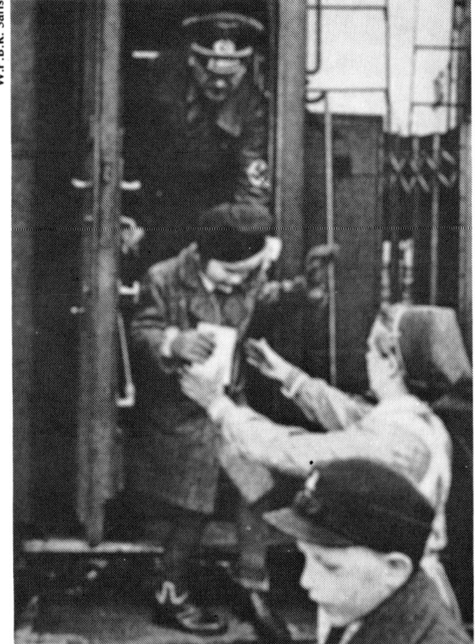

An NS-nurse helping youngsters from the train as part of the "Kinderland-verschickung." Note the wearing of the short nurse cap without the cap band, indicating that she had not yet completed her examinations. Note also the visored cap with regular army type insignia. This could indicate that the person was from the NSKK-Transporteinsatz.

Navorsingsinstituut Brussel

A nurse of the NS-Schwesternschaft assisting at a "mothers and childrens home." Note the wearing of the white hood and band.

An unsuccessful drive to standardize the dress worn by NSV members occurred in the early years of it's existence.[7] The regular dress as worn by females of the Deutsches Frauenwerk was worn during activities, since most of the females were members of this league also. Soon however, females serving as nurses aids started wearing white hoods, copied after regular nursing forms or from the Red Cross. This form remained practically unchanged until the end of the war. Most often however civilian cloths were worn.

Members of the NSV, known as "Volkspflegerinnen," a nursing type section, received a standard dress in the summer of 1939.[8] This dress was of dark brown material and patterned after the style worn by members of the NS–Schwesternschaft. Two styles of hoods are known: one short, the other long. Both were of dark brown material, often linen (but also known are wool forms, probably indicating the season). A small brown band with white lettering was sometimes worn above the cap edge, just above the wearer's forehead. The band probably had the letters "NSV" alternating with the NSV symbol in the style as worn on the bands used by the NS–Schwesternschaft. A white band with lettering and NSV symbol was worn on the white caps.

The brooches for NSV nurses, from left to right:
(Drawings by W.P.B.R. Saris)

NS–Volkswohlfahrt

NS–Schwesternschaft (brown nurse)

Freie Schwesternschaft (blue nurse)
precursor of the Reichsbund

Reichsbund der Freien Schwestern u. Pflegerinnen (blue nurse)

In early 1940 two hundred nurses and attendants of the "Kindergarten" (classes for infants) from the Gau Mark Brandenburg received a standard dress

[7] *"Uniformen–Markt," Nr. 1, December 1934, p. 3.*

[8] *Ibid, Nr. 15, August 1, 1939, p. 229: "Diensttracht der Volkspflegerinnen der NSV."*

W.P.B.R. Saris

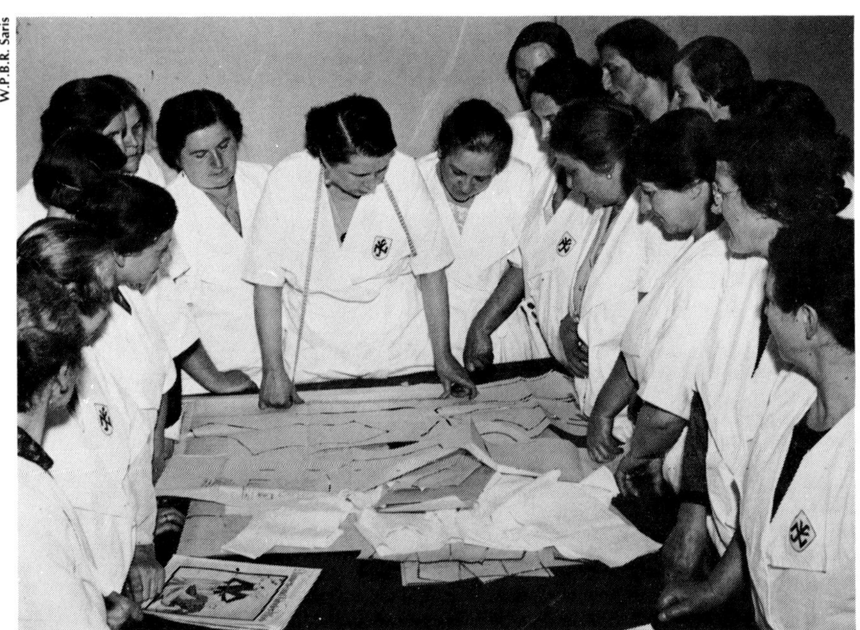

NSV females during a tailoring course in April 1942. They wear white aprons with the NSV symbol upon the left lapel. A hood or cowl was never authorized for wear with this kind of dress.

Navorsingsinstituut Brussel

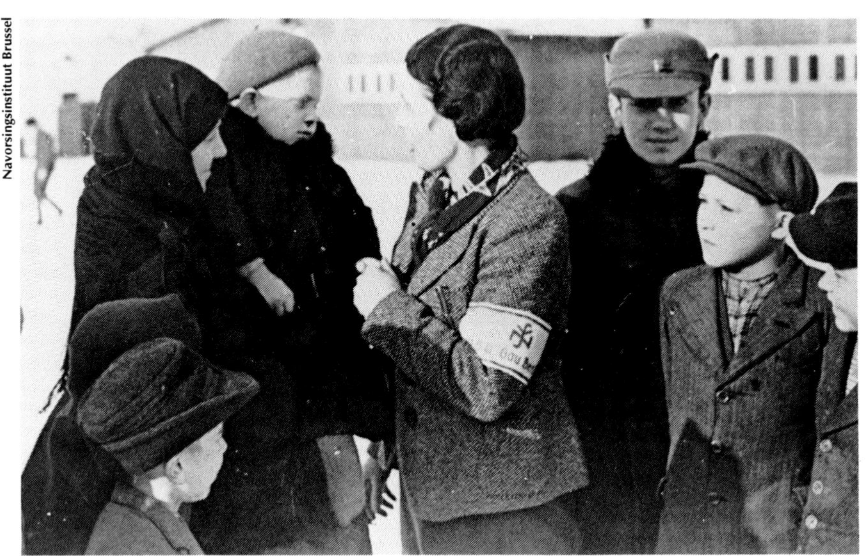

A female of the NSV from "Gau Berlin" is wearing regular civilian clothes in January 1940. The wear of the special dress was never authorized for non-professionally educated aids.

styled after that worn by the regular DRK.[9] Exact details or designs aren't known. Completely white caps with white linen bands without lettering are documented. Often these hoods were provided with a white round piece of cloth with the

[9] *Ibid, Nr. 4, February 15, 1940, p. 28: "Diensttracht für Kindergärtnerinnen und Pflegerinnen."*

NSV symbol or a red cross. It must be noted that only true nurses, and never student nurses, were permitted to wear a hood band.

NSV Officials (Amtswalter)

Male officials serving in the NSV office for State Welfare (Amt für Volkswohlfahrt) did not wear a special uniform in the first years of the existence of this organization.[10] This was changed during 1934 as persons serving as Amtsleiter on Orts–, Kreis– or Gau– level were political leaders.

In October 1934 Hilgenfeldt and Ley came to terms with an agreement and enlarged this group with persons serving as department or sub–department leaders of the NSV office on all levels including "Stützpunkt" (point of support, not large enough to be an "Ortsgruppe") or honorary rank. These persons were allowed to wear the regular form uniform, insignia and headdress forms for political leaders, when officially being granted,[11] (see for detailed information for the headdress for political leaders its respective chapter within this volume; the years 1934–1945).

A. Stam

Erich Hilgenfeldt, "Oberbefehlsleiter" of the NSV, at Mönchengladbach at the opening of a new home for his organization, April 29, 1942. Hilgenfeldt is in civilian cloths. The political leaders from his department are still wearing the old form insignia with part of the new form on the visored cap. The political leader at his right is still wearing the model 1927 form of eagle.

---

[10] *Ibid, Nr. 1, December 1934, p. 3. : "Amtswalter des Amtes für Volkswohlfahrt."*

[11] *"Vbl.d.Rl.d.NSDAP," Nr. 84, mid–November 1934, p. 209: "Oberste Leitung der PO – der Stabsleiter"; Letter Nr. 38/34, dated October 29, 1934.*

A nurse serving in the NSV, photographed in 1942, wearing a white cap or hood with the round NSV symbol

NS–Nursing Forces (NS–Schwesternschaft)

In May 1934 Rudolf Hess declared the Schwesternschaft of the NSV to be an organization of the NSDAP and gave it its designation "NS–Schwesternschaft." Preparations for a unified dress started immediately. The official introduction would take until early 1936.

On June 21, 1934 regulations were authorized for this group of NS nurses (subordinated to the Amtsleiter der Obersten leitung der Pol. Organisation/NSV Ärztebund). Simultaneously a unified dress was then described:[12] the groups authorized for wear were classified as "Vollschwester" (professional educated persons), also known as NS–Schwester. Candidates, known as NS–Schwester-anwärterinnen or students, were known as "Lehrschwestern." The highest rank for this nursing organization was the Generaloberin (General Prioress); offices were led by a nurse on Gau level position (Gauvertrauensschwester).[13]

The NS–Schwester was authorized to wear the brown dress with a long brown linen hood (length 65 cm) or cowl known as "Haubentuch" and the band (Haubenstreifen). The candidates and students weren't allowed to wear the cap band. This brown woven band with white lettering alternating with the NSV symbol and the letters "NS" was worn with hood and cowl. The symbol and the letters were separated by a square on its point and was bordered at each edge by thin white stripes.

On some occasions nurses wore white hoods with a round cloth insigne with the NSV symbol, thought to be in red. Probably the authorized females started wearing various patterns unofficially. In December 1935 Hilgenfeldt

---

[12] *"Richtlinien der NS–Schwesternschaft: Gliederung und Aufgaben." Berlin/München: June 21, 1934. Section VI: "Diensttracht", pp. 8–9.*

[13] *"Organisationsbuch der NSDAP. " München: 1937 and 1943, p. 282b and picture plate 23 (resp 29c).*

announced (to avoid problems) that from January 1, 1936 the NS–Schwesternschaft was to be supplied with the dress through the Main–Office of the Volkswohlfahrt.[14] All females would receive four hoods and one cowl.[15] When leaving the service the dress and other equipment had to be returned.

Only five concerns were allowed manufacturing rights on orders of Hilgenfeldt, being:

Erich Thamm from Berlin;
Gerhard u. Heinrich Kohnen from Berlin;
Simon & Wente from Hannover;
Gotthard Völkel from Breslau;
A. Hausburg from Stuttgart.

With the exception of Kohnen, these concerns were in production until the end of the war. For some reason Kohnen was eliminated in the autumn 1937. It must be noted that manufacturing only was allowed with RZM permission.[16]

Nationalsozialistische Deutsche Arbeiterpartei
Reichsleitung

Reichsgeschäftsstelle:
München: Briennerstraße 45
Briefanschrift: München 43, Briefsach 80
Telefon-Nummern: 54901, 58344 u. 56081
Postscheckkonto: München 23319

Kampfztg. d. Partei: „Völkischer Beobachter"
Geschäftsstelle der Zeitung: Thierschstraße 11
Telefon-Nummer 20647
Schriftleitung: Schellingstraße 39
Telefon-Nr. 20801 / Postscheckkonto 11346

N. S. D. A. P. Reichsleitung
Hauptamt für Volkswohlfahrt

Fernsprecher: F 2 Neukölln 3001, 3011
Postscheckkonto: Erich Hilgenfeldt
Kto. N.S.D.A.P. Reichsleitung, Hauptamt
für Volkswohlfahrt, Berlin Nr. 30768
Bank-Konto: Berliner Stadtbank,
Berlin C 2, Alexanderplatz 2
Erich Hilgenfeldt
Kto. N.S.D.A.P. Reichsleitung
Hauptamt für Volkswohlfahrt, Nr. 1001

NS-Schwesternschaft

Berlin SO 36, den 19. Dezember 1 1935
Maybach-Ufer 48-51

An alle Gauleiter der N.S.D.A.P.
" " Gauamtsleiter des Amtes für Volkswohlfahrt
" " Gauamtsleiter des Amtes für Volksgesundheit

A n o r d n u n g Nr. V 9/35

Betrifft: NS-Schwesterntracht.

Um eine einheitliche Einkleidung der NS-Schwestern gemäss Anordnung Nr. V 3/35 zu gewährleisten, wird die Beschaffung der Schwesterntracht ab 1. Januar 1936 zentral durch das Hauptamt für Volkswohlfahrt geregelt.

The letter from Hauptamtsleiter Hilgenfeldt (of the NSV), dated December 19, 1935 with order V 9/35 which mentions the five manufacturers of the NS–nurses dress. Page 2, number 5 lists the five different forms of headdress. (Letter continued on next page.)

14 *Letter NSDAP Reichsleitung, Hauptamt für Volkswohlfahrt. Berlin: December 19, 1935. Order Nr. V 9/35, concerning NS–Schwesternschaft.*

15 *Ibid, signed by Hilgenfeldt. Berlin, April 25, 1935. Order Nr. V/35: "Dienstbezüge für NS–Schwestern."*

16 *"Mbl.d.RZM," Nr. 13, München: June 19, 1937, p. 174.*

Zur Lieferung der NS-Schwesterntracht sind nachstehende Fi
men zugelassen:

Erich Thamm, Berlin W 35, Potsdamer Str. 49
Gerhar und Heinrich Kohnen, Berlin NW 21, Turmstr. 3(
Simon & Wente, Hannover, Grupenstr. 16/17
Gotthard Völkel, Breslau, Albrechtstr. 56
A. Hansburg, Stuttgart-S, Eberhardstr. 69

Mit diesen Lieferfirmen sind Stoffqualitäten mit folgenden Preisen für die Dienstkleidung der NS-Schwestern vereinbar

1)	Dienst- oder Waschkleid ohne Pelerine (Konfektionsgrössen)	RM 12,
	Pelerine	RM 2,
2)	Wollkleid (Sonntags- oder Festkleid) aus Wollgeorgette für das nach Mass angefertigte Kleid (Massarbeit)	RM 41,
3)	Gabardine-Mantel, der Mantel halb gefüttert nach Mass angefertigt	RM 40,

Höflichkeitsformeln fallen bei parteiamtlichen Schreiben fort.

- 2 -

4)	Garnitur	
	a) Garnitur zum Wollkleid aus reiner Georgetteseide und Manschettenpaspel	RM 1,10
	b) Garnitur zum Waschkleid Feinrips	RM 0,80
5)	Haube ungestärkt	RM 0,90
	Haube gestärkt und gebügelt	RM 1,—
	Haube mit Band	RM 1,15
	Haube mit verstärkter Stirn und Band	RM 1,25
	Haubentuch aus imprägnierter Regenseide mit Schwesternband	RM 3,65
6)	Weisse Schürzen	RM 2,90

Die Vereinbarung gilt für das gesamte Reichsgebiet.
Die NS-Schwestern beziehen ihre Tracht nur bei den zur Lieferung zugelassenen Firmen zu den vereinbarten Preisen. Mehrkosten, die durch Sonderwünsche der Schwestern bei Anfertigung der Tracht entstehen, sind von diesen selbst zu tragen.

Die durch die NS-Schwestern bezahlten Rechnungen der Lieferfirmen sind dem Hauptamt für Volkswohlfahrt zur Rückerstattung der verauslagten Beträge einzureichen.

Die Gauamtsleitungen melden dem Hauptamt bis zum 15. Januar 1936 namentlich unter Angabe der Mitgliedsnummern die Schwestern, welche bisher durch die Gauamtsleitung eingekleidet worden sind. Diese Meldung muss ausserdem den Tag der Lieferung der Tracht enthalten.

Von dieser Anordnung ist den NS-Schwestern umgehend Mitteilung zu machen.

Heil Hitler

Hilgenfeldt

Hauptamtsleiter

H. Heikamp

A "Vollschwester" of the NS–Schwesternschaft is wearing the brown long coat and the long brown hood with cap band.

Navorsingsinstituut Brussel

Two nurses serving in the NS–Schwesternschaft, photographed during the ten years celebration of the founding of the NSV at Berlin in 1942. The person at left is wearing the long brown hood–cowl (Haubentuch) with "Haubenstreifen;" on the right shows the wear of the short brown "Dreieckhaubentuch," also with the cap band. Both are "Vollschwester." Candidates were not allowed to wear the lettered cap band.

Chantrain/Smeets

The brown, machine woven band for the hood of nurses belonging to the NS–Schwesternschaft. The lettering and edges are in white.

The white hoods were available in various forms: soft, consolidated or ironed types, as well as the hood with the band or one with a consolidated forehead or consolidated band.[17] Later the long hood–cowl was also manufactured in waterproof material. With the white hood the white band with brown lettering was worn.

In January 1936 at last the NS–Schwesternschaft received this long expected official "uniform"; the "NS–Lehrschwestern" each received six hoods, but without the band.[18]

W.P.B.R. Saris

Nationalsozialistische Deutsche Arbeiterpartei

Reichsleitung

Reichsgeschäftsstelle:
München: Briennerstraße 45
Briefanschrift: München 43, Brieffach 80
Telefon-Nummern: 54901, 58344 u. 58081
Postscheckkonto: München 23319

Kampfztg. d. Partei: „Völkischer Beobachter"
Geschäftsstelle der Zeitung: Thierschstraße 11
Telefon-Nummer 20647
Schriftleitung: Schellingstraße 39
Telefon-Nr. 20801 / Postscheckkonto 11346

N.S.D.A.P. Reichsleitung
Hauptamt für Volkswohlfahrt

Fernsprecher: F 2 Neukölln 8001, 8011
Postscheckkonto: Berlin Nr. 30768
NS Volkswohlfahrt e. V. Reichsführung
Bank-Kto.: Bank der Deutschen Arbeit AG., Berlin, Konto Nr. 6705
NS Volkswohlfahrt e. V. Reichsführung

NS.-Schwesternschaft

Berlin SO 36, den 18. Sept. 1937
Maybach-Ufer 48-51

An die Gauleiter der N.S.D.A.P.
" " Gauamtsleiter der N.S.D.A.P. Leiter der Ämter für Volkswohlfahrt
" " Gauamtskassenverwalter der N.S.D.A.P. im Amt für Volkswohlfahrt
" " Gauamtsleiter der N.S.D.A.P. Leiter der Ämter für Volksgesundheit

A n o r d n u n g Nr. V 7/37

Betrifft: NS.-Schwesterntracht

Mit Wirkung ab 1. Oktober 1937 wird den Vollschwestern und Lernschwestern der NS.-Schwesternschaft die Tracht von der jeweils zuständigen Gauamtsleitung zur Verfügung gestellt.

Die Bezahlung der beschafften Trachten ist ab 1. Oktober 1937 Aufgabe der Gaue aus Mitteln der NS. Schwesternschaft.

Zur Lieferung der NS.-Schwesterntracht sind nachstehende Firmen zugelassen:

A part of a letter, dated September 18, 1937 with order V 7/37, in which is stated that the so–called "Vollschwestern" and "Lernschwestern" of the NS–Schwesternschaft will receive their dress at no cost. The costs were paid from funds of the NS–Schwesternschaft.

In October 1937 a new type of hood was introduced for those serving as NS–Gemeindeschwester (municipal nurses), a so–called "Dreieckhaubentuch" (a triangular formed hood). With this hood the nurse (Vollschwester) was also allowed to wear the band.[19] It must be noted that this form of hood was not allowed for wearing by students. Females serving as "Gauvertrauensschwester" (a governing nurse on the Gau–level) occasionally wore the brown hood or cowl: in fact they weren't authorized any form of headdress. This order, however, was disobeyed.

No important changes or additions took place in later years, or during the war, as by then the white hoods or cowls were mainly worn as the favorite headdress.

Navorsingsinstituut Brussel

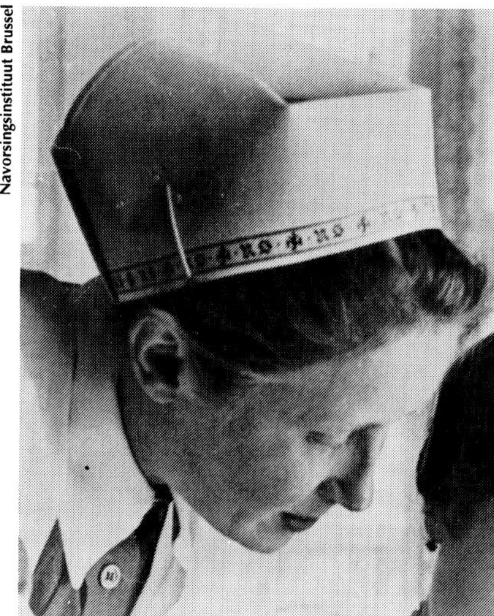

A nurse of the NS–Schwesternschaft from Berlin in March 1944, wearing the white hood with the white band and brown lettering with symbol. This photograph gives an excellent view of the folding and positioning by use of a hair pin.

Josef Charita

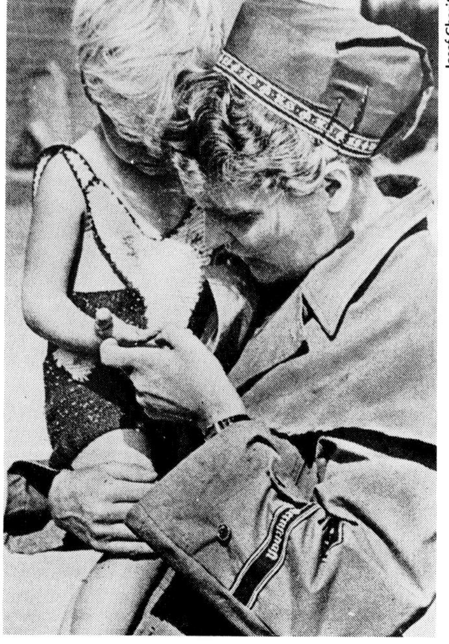

A nurse of the NS–Schwesternschaft wearing the short brown "Dreieckhaubentuch" with cap band. Note her cuff title on the lower left arm.

---

[17] *Letter NSDAP Reichsleitung, Hauptamt für Volkswohlfahrt. Berlin: December 19, 1935. Order Nr. V 9/35. p. 2.*

[18] *Ibid, December 4, 1936. Order Nr. V 6/36.*

[19] *Ibid, September 18, 1937. Order Nr. V 7/37. Concerning: NS–Schwesterntracht, p. 3*

Navorsingsinstituut Brussel

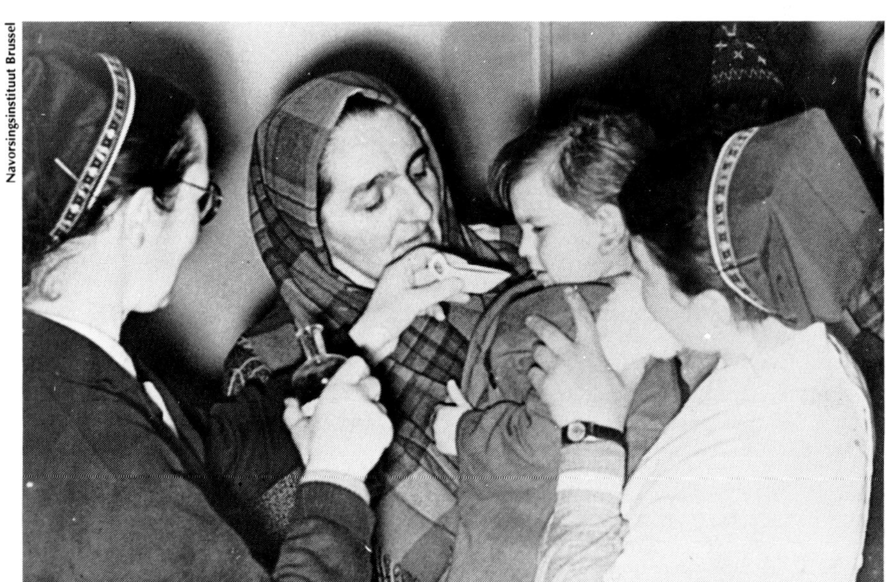

At a health station in Berlin–Köpenick. NS–nurses are taking care of women and children during the winter of 1940. These "NS–Gemeindeschwestern" are wearing the short, brown hood with the cap band: the "Dreieckhaubentuch". Note the positioning and wrapping of the cap by the use of a hair pin.

H. Heikamp

An "NS–Gemeindeschwester" on skis in the mountains of southern Germany wearing a dark hood with cap band. Due to the cold weather it seems that this hood is of a heavier, possibly knitted, material.

REICHSBUND DER FREIEN SCHWESTERN UND PFLEGERINNEN e.V. (LEAGUE FOR FREE SISTERHOOD AND NURSES)

Raised from "free" nurse leagues in the fall of 1936. This sub–organization existed along with the NS–Schwesternschaft.[20]

The females serving with this league practically wore the same dress as ordered for the NS–Schwesternschaft. In October 1936 regulations for the dress were authorized. The color being blue not brown.

The white hood with white band was worn with the working dress (note that the NS–Schwesternschaft also officially wore the white hood with the working or service dress). The walking out dress was supplied with the dark navy blue "Haubentuch" with the band, piped in white.[21] It was noted that the hood for the walking out dress was 65 cm long. The background for the lettering is blue instead of the brown for the NS–Schwesternschaft. The exact lettering is

M. Winter

Nurse from the Reichsbund in work dress with short white hood and white band.

---

[20] *"Uniformen–Markt," Nr. 21, December 15, 1936.*

[21] *"Schwesterntracht–Ordnung des Reichsbundes der Freien Schwestern und Pflegerinnen e.V.," 1936. Pages not numbered, sections: Arbeitskleidung and Strassenkleidung.*

FS (Freie Schwestern) alternating with the NSV symbol. It was thought that during the war the lettering RFS (for the Reichsbund) was used, but advertisements found used the lettering FS.

Nurse from the Reichsbund wearing the dark blue walking out dress with coat and long hood with the band. Photos are taken from the original regulations.

Long hood with dark band. Note the lettering as FS (Freie Schwester) and the NSV symbol.

In June 1941 the NS–Schwesternschaft and the Reichsbund der Freien Schwestern und Pflegerinnen e.V. were combined.[22] No new forms of dress were authorized. Plans may have existed to introduce a new uniform, but due to the war and lack of material a new "uniform" was not introduced.

22 "Vb.d.Rl.d.NSDAP," Nr. 22, August 1941. Parteikanzlei: Order A 31/41, dated July 19, 1941 signed by Bormann at the "Führerhauptquartier."

Die Schwesternschaften in der NS.-Volkswohlfahrt

M. Shaner

Die Nationalsozialistische Schwesternschaft

bildet in allen Teilen des Großdeutschen Reiches in staatlich anerkannten Kranken- und Säuglingspflegeschulen junge Mädchen im Alter von 18 bis 28 Jahren für den Schwesternberuf aus. Die kostenlose Ausbildung schließt nach 1½ Jahren mit einer staatlichen Prüfung ab. Die Schwestern werden anschließend 1 Jahr im Krankenhaus und später auf den für sie geeigneten Arbeitsplätzen in den verschiedensten Aufgabengebieten eingesetzt, z. B. in Gemeinden, Krankenhäusern, Kinderkliniken, ϟϟ-Lazaretten, ϟϟ-Mütter- und Säuglingsheimen, Schulen der NSDAP. und Ordensburgen.

Als Aufnahmebedingung gelten neben gesundheitlicher, charakterlicher und politischer Eignung eine abgeschlossene Schulbildung, der Nachweis des Reichsarbeitsdienstes und des hauswirtschaftlichen Jahres, das in Einrichtungen der NSV. abgeleistet werden kann.

Nähere Auskunft ist bei den Dienststellen der NS.-Schwesternschaft in den Gauamtsleitungen der NS.-Volkswohlfahrt zu erhalten. Die Anschrift gibt jede Ortsgruppe der NSV. bekannt.

Der Reichsbund der Freien Schwestern und Pflegerinnen e. V.

Der Reichsbund der Freien Schwestern und Pflegerinnen e. V. gibt jungen Mädchen im Alter von 18 bis 35 Jahren Gelegenheit zur kostenlosen Ausbildung in der Kranken- und Säuglings- und Kinderpflege. Die Ausbildung dauert 1½ Jahre, der sich ein praktisches Jahr anschließt. Ausbildungsstätten in allen Gegenden Deutschlands.

Haushaltsjahr und Arbeitsdienst gehen der Ausbildung voraus. Das Haushaltsjahr kann auch als Vorschülerin in Arbeitsfeldern des Reichsbundes und in Einrichtungen der NSV. abgeleistet werden. Vorschülerinnen erhalten neben freier Station ein Taschengeld.

Nach abgeschlossener Ausbildung können die Schwestern des Reichsbundes in Operationssälen, Krankenhäusern, Kinderkliniken, Sahatorien, Heimen, Milchküchen, Kinderkrippen, in der Wohlfahrts- und der Privatpflege, nachgehenden Säuglings- und Kinderfürsorge in den ländlichen Notstandsgebieten, in der krankenpflegerischen Tätigkeit im Ausland, im Büro und als Sprechstundenhilfe nach eigener Wahl arbeiten.

Die Anmeldung erfolgt bei den Gaugeschäftsstellen des Reichsbundes in der Gauamtsleitung der NSV. Die Anschrift gibt jede Ortsgruppe oder Dienststelle der NSV. bekannt.

Advertisement from the NS–Frauen Warte 1940 used for recruiting the NS–Schwesternschaft and the Reichsbund. Pictures from the so–called Haubenstreifen were used. Note that with the FS band the NSV symbol is somewhat smaller.

M. Shaner

Two "blue" nurses from the Reichsbund shown wearing white hoods devoid of the band. Note the fastening using hair pins.

CHAPTER

6

Deutsche Arbeitsfront (DAF)

(GERMAN LABOR FRONT)

Included in the general title, "Die Deutsche Arbeitsfront," the organization for NS–laborers, we will discuss in this chapter the organizations that were involved in Germany with the laborers of the Party, with the exception of the "Reichsarbeitsdienst" (National Labor Service); this organization will be discussed in a separate chapter, probably in volume 4 of this series.

Among these organizations, some are well known. For example, the "Nat.Soz.Betriebszellen–Organisation" (Nat.Soz.Industrial Cells Organization), the "NS–Hago"– Nat.Soz.Handwerks–, Handels–und Gewerbe–Organisation: (NS.Trade–, Commercial–and Industrial Organization,) the "DAF–Werkscharen" (DAF Labor Troops), the "NS–Gemeinschaft Kraft durch Freude" (NS.Community Strength through Joy, with various sub–organizations as for example, "Schönheit der Arbeit" or "KdF–Schiffe"), and the "Werkscharen der Abteilung

Otto Spronk

Hermann Göring during an address of the Deutsche Arbeitsfront.

Luftfahrt u.Wehrmacht" (Labor Troops for the Department of Aviation and Armed Forces) and organizations abroad.[1]

We shall give a historical summary of these organizations and their relative relationship to each other, since they overlap and their uniforms are *often* similar (as is the case with other NSDAP organizations.) It is sometimes difficult to distinguish between them. In many cases it may cause enormous confusion, due to the complicated structures, especially for positions of political leaders of NSBO/NS–Hago and DAF, being Party members or not. We have tried to put some light into "the darkness," but still the DAF chapter must be considered as one of the most difficult chapters within this series.

Although the "Reichskulturkammer" (National Chamber of Culture), the "Reichsnährstand" (National Peasantry), the "NS–Rechtswahrer–Bund" (NS–Justice Advise League), the "Reichsbund Deutscher Beamten" (League of German Employees), the "NS–Lehrerbund" (NS–Teachers League) and some others were in cooperation with the DAF or its sub–organizations, they will be discussed in a later volume if required. This is also the case with regard to the "Gewerkschaften" (Trade Unions) and the "Reichsinnungsverbände" (German Guild Societies), as far as they are of importance for this series in relation to certain forms of headdress or insignia, worn by their members.

POLITISCHE LEITER DER NSBO; NS–HAGO UND DAF (NSBO; NS–Hago and DAF Political Leaders)

To begin, we will survey the political leaders "functions" from the political organization (leading a level) in relation to NSBO, NS–Hago, DAF/KdF (approximately 1934 through 1938) along with a short explanation. From these it is possible to see a connection regarding the piping worn and the color of the cords as worn by NSDAP political leaders on their headdress (for detailed information see the chapter: Pol.Leiter der NSDAP the years 1933–1938 and the associated lists).

PO:	NSBO:	NS–Hago:	DAF:	KdF :
Reichsleitung				
Stabsleiter der PO			Führer der DAF;	
Reichsleiter				
	Reichsobmann		Stabsleiter d.DAF	
	Landesobmann		Bezirks–walter der DAF	Bezirks–wart KdF

The "Stabsleiter der PO" (NSDAP/PO–Staff Leader) was the "Führer der DAF" (Both these positions being held by DAF leader Robert Ley). Assigned to the "Stab der Obersten Leitung der PO, Amt NSBO" (Staff of the PO High Command, Department NSBO) were thirteen persons with the rank "Landes-

[1] *"Organisationsbuch der NSDAP." München: 1936, pp. 472–478.*

obmann der NSBO." These foremen for a larger area, were simultaneously "Bezirkswalter der DAF," but also "Bezirkswart der KdF"–District Warder. (Each of these persons had three functions). Their deputies were known as "Bezirksbeauftragter der NS–Hago" (District Plenipotentiaries.)

Otto Spronk

Johannes Engel, Landesobmann for NSBO district Brandenburg, held the position of Bezirkswalter der DAF. He is wearing a visored cap with gold pipings and cords in this circa 1934 photograph. Note his cap is without a cockade.

Otto Spronk

Landesobmann Becker from the Hessen/Hessen-Nassau Süd district wears the visored cap for the NSBO. The photograph clearly shows the light pipings around the crown and the cap band, as well as the knots being in gold, because of his rank of Amtsleiter on Reich-level.

The "Reichsobmann der NSBO" (National Foreman: from 1934 Claus Selzner, an NSDAP Hauptamtsleiter) was simultaneously the "Stabsleiter der DAF." To his staff were assigned sixteen persons known as "Reichsbetriebsgemeinschaftsleiter" (RBGL–persons leading a branch of trade and ranked as "Abteilungsleiter der NSBO" (Division Leader). (Consult also the section DAF members, being Party members. Here are details given showing that in July 1935 these RBGL officials were *not* authorized to wear the political leaders uniform). Also the same thirteen persons as mentioned above plus one manager were assigned to the Selzner Staff. To the "Stab des Amtsleiters der NS–Hago" (the staff for the Office Leader) were assigned the NS–Hago staff leader, two "Reichsbetriebsgemeinschaftsleiter" as "Abteilungsleiter" and thirteen persons known as "Bezirkswalter Stellvertreter" (Deputy District Wardens.)

In 1935 the designation "Bezirkswalter/wart" was renamed to Reichsleiter. This was *not* in any way at the same level as the Reichsleiter of the NSDAP political organization.

Gauleitung

Gauleiter	Gaubetriebs–zellenobmann	Gauamtsleiter	Gau–walter	Gauwart

The Gauwalter in function was always Ley's deputy for the Gau he was assigned to.

Kreisleitung

Kreisleiter	Kreisbetriebs–zellenobmann	Kreisamts–leiter	Kreis–walter	Kreis–wart

Ortsgruppenleitung

Ortsgruppen–leiter	Ortsgruppen–betriebsobmann	Ortsgruppen–amtsleiter	Ortsgr.–walter	Ortsgr.–wart
	Betriebszellen–obmann		Bebriebs–walter	Betriebs–wart
Zellenleiter (Zellenwart)	Zellenobmann	Zellenobmann	Zellen–walter	Zellen–wart
Blockleiter (Blockwart)	Blockobmann	Blockobmann	Block–walter	Block–wart[2]

Otto Spronk

Left: Members of the NSBO. The original caption reads, "S-Strassenbahner Betriebszelle Bahnhof." The NSBO political leader in the foreground wears his cap with a leather chin strap. Note the NSBO diamond on the upper left arm, just above the brassard. The other persons are wearing their regular tramway visored caps with cockade and proper insignia.

Otto Spronk

Above right: NSBO political leaders during a march are wearing the political leaders' (SA-style) caps with cords or chin strap. Note the wear of the NSBO diamond on the upper left arm and the so-called "Studentenmütze" by the person in the background. The individual at far right wears a leather chin strap.

---

2 *"Organisation der Deutschen Arbeitsfront und der NS–Gemeinschaft Kraft durch Freude," 1934. Sections: Vorwort; Der Aufbau und die Aufgaben der DAF; Gebietseinteilung; Dienststellen der PO; Dienstellen der DAF usw., pp. 5–14; Vbl.d.Rl.d.NSDAP, Nr. 27. End–May 1934, p. 166; Mbl.d.RZM, Nr. 3. June 16, 1934, p. 1.*

In fall 1936, the Gau–, Kreis– and Ortswalter were generally known as Gau–, Kreis– and Orts– Obmann der DAF. They also held command of the KdF.[3] In May 1937 the designation "Betriebswalter" was renamed "Betriebsobmann". Other changes of name are left out, due to the 1937–1939 Werkschar– and DAF reorganizations and renaming of ranks or functions, (consult the section: Werkscharen der DAF). Two exceptions however are mentioned. In early 1938, the "Reichsbetriebsgemeinschaften" were renamed "Fachämter" (Trades Branch) and the DAF Block– and Zellenwalter, as well as the same ranks in a company were renamed into "Strassen–Blockobmann" or "Strassen–Zellenobmann" and "Betriebs–Blockobmann der DAF" or "Betriebs–Zellenobmann der DAF."[4]

Headdress

The political leaders serving in the NSBO and NS–Hago were allowed to wear the political leaders uniform when permission was granted or when ordered to do so by the High Command, in conjunction with the regular forms of headdress, being the coffee–can cap or the visored cap. In the earliest years, the visored cap for NSBO officials was often made of a darker brown material, the cap band also being dark–brown cloth or velvet. (In photographs this gives the impression that a black or dark–blue cap is worn, resembling the DAF visored cap called the "Festmütze.")

The crown, as well as the cap band were piped according to the level the person was performing duty with i.e., Reich–, Gau–, Kreis– or Orts–. Occasionally a black visor and during the first years a (probably black) chin strap were worn. The chin strap ceased to be worn approximately in spring of 1933. The cords with knot or knots, worn according to the rank or position of the person were in the same form as worn by political leaders.

Some puzzles and question marks remain. Various visored caps having white piping (without any doubt NSBO) survived the war. No regulations have been found that authorizes the white piping. Also in many 1933/34 photographs, it is obvious that a light piping was worn. It is unknown if this is possibly the gold for Reich level or light blue for Orts level. A possibility of course would be that it was intended to introduce a visored cap for the NSBO political leaders in contravention to the regular form for political leaders. Decisions for the new political leaders cap were in fact not finalized by early 1933. Perhaps a combination was made regarding the NSBO between the political leaders and the visored cap for the Allgemeine–SS (which in fact was introduced in 1933 and had white piping.)

Most of the original uniform references dating from approximately 1933 do not discuss the NSBO, other than the NSBO diamond worn upon the arm. In the reference by von Eelking he indicates information regarding the NSBO in the index, but the book doesn't contain any information regarding the organization, it is simply left out. Could von Eelking also have been confused by the intricate systems in use? Why isn't anything included in his March 1, 1934 addendum?

---

[3] *"Amtl.Nbl.d.DAF," Nr. 20. August 24, 1935, p. 249.*

[4] *Ibid, addendum for Nr. 1, January 31, 1938, pp. 6–7.*

Otto Spronk

Political leaders of the NSDAP and NSBO during the first trip of the "Kraft durch Freude" from Wiesbaden. Note the various early forms of headdress: At left with the NSBO insigne and cockade; and next to him the early NSBO visored cap with political eagle and cockade. The two individuals in the foreground are NSDAP political leaders.

Ulric of England

A 1934 version worn by NSBO functionaries. The cap is constructed of medium brown material with a black leather visor. The top and cap band are piped in white, and the cap cords are gold. An early eagle and swastika embossed button is worn in the center of the band.

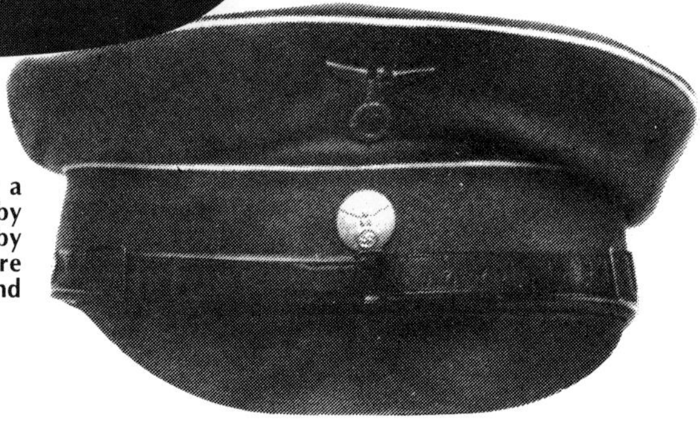

A brown-topped visored cap with a dark brown felt cap band as used by the NSBO approximately in 1934 by functionaries. The cap and band are piped in white and the chin strap and visor are black.

The first patterns of the national emblem as ordered for political leaders were also worn. An early embossed eagle button or cockade was often worn in the front center of the band. On orders from Ley, both were forbidden to be worn starting in early May 1934.[5] It was explicitly stated that NSBO or NS–Hago

5 *"Vbl.d..RL.d.NSDAP," Nr. 2. End–May 1934, p. 166.*

P. Coleman

A political leader, ranked as Zellenwart, assigned to the DAF is wearing a dark-blue, early form, visored cap with leather chin strap, cockade and early form national eagle emblem.

officials wearing golden insignia of rank had to wear golden cords with golden instead of silvered buttons.

With regards to the NSBO, the Organization Books of 1937 and 1938 should be taken with a grain of salt. NSBO officials within the DAF had already held leading positions for some time. It must be noted that in 1931 through 1933, there was hardly any distinction between NSBO or NS–Hago officials and the NSDAP political leaders.

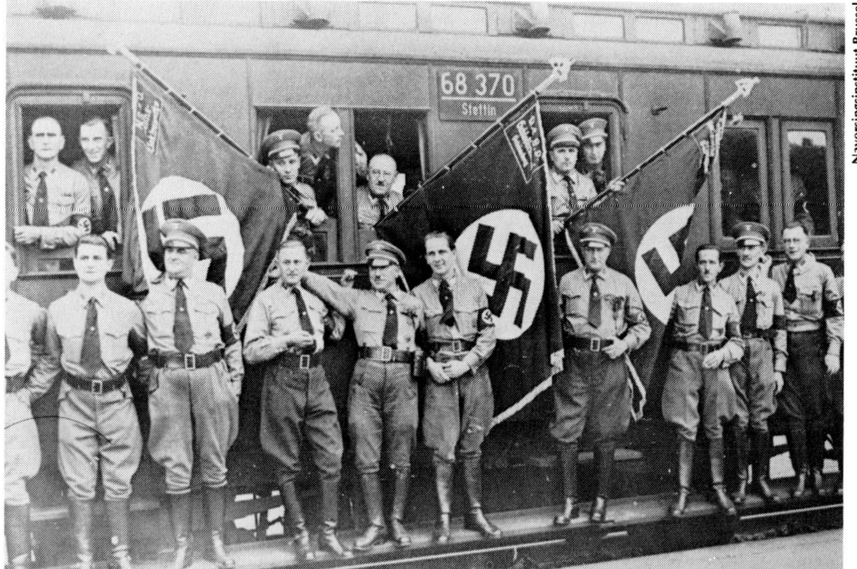

Navorsingsinstituut Brussel

Members of several NSBO cells head for the Reichsparteitag at Nürnberg. Note that the left flag reads "N.S.B.O. Reichs Electrowerke," and the middle flag reads "N.S.B.O. Schlossbräuerei Schöneberg." The third flag is unreadable. Note the wear of political leaders' visored caps without cockades.

Nat.Soz.Handwerks–, Handels–und Gewerbe–Organisation (NS–Hago) (N.S. Trade–, Commercial– and Industrial Organization)

During the years 1932 and 1933 industrial and commercial alliances were created by the National Socialists. An artisans union for the industrial middle class was formed on December 15, 1932, called "Kampfbund des Gewerblichen Mittelstandes,"[6] and on May 3/4, 1933 the "Reichsstand des deutschen Handwerks und des deutschen Handels" was created.[7] Both were led by Dr. Theodor A. von Renteln (an NSDAP Hauptamtsleiter). In August 1933 both organizations were renamed and divided into the "Nat.Soz. Handwerks–, Handels–und Gewerbe–Organisation" (better known as NS–Hago) and the "Gesamtverband Deutscher Handwerks–und Gewerbetreibender" (GHG).[8]

With the official institution of the DAF in 1933, its reorganization in January 1934 and by the decrees of Hitler in February and October 1934, the NS–Hago was led by NSDAP political leaders, assisted by "Amtswalter." It was their task to take care of and look after the DAF organization and the two "Reichsbetriebsgemeinschaften.[9]

In early 1935 it was ordered that NSBO members (with skills in the trades and [handy]–crafts) had to become NS–Hago members. Simultaneously, it was ordered that those not being in the trade or crafts had to move from NS–Hago to

---

6 *"Das Dritte Reich. Die Kampfjahre 1918–1933." Berlin: 1936, p. 236.*

7 *"Daten der Geschichte der NSDAP. " 11.Auflage. Berlin/Leipzig: 1943, p. 54. Section VI: Das Deutsche Reich und die NSDAP seit 1933.*

8 *Newspaper: "Hannoverscher Anzeiger," Nr. 250. Hannover: Tuesday, October 24, 1933, front–page.*

9 *"Vbl.d.RL.d.NSDAP," Nr. 72. End–May, 1934, p. 165.*

the NSBO organization.[10] Offices of the NS–Hago (and GHG) existed within the DAF organization (with some exceptions of minor importance) and continued to exist in name only.[11] NS–Hago directives were largely as ordered for the NSBO.

Extensive research has confirmed that the specific NS–Hago insigne was never worn with any form of headdress. NS–Hago members wearing the dark–blue visored DAF cap wore the insigne according to NSBO orders.

W.P.B.R. Saris

Members of the N.S. Hago carry the symbol of their union during a meeting of the "laborers of the trade unions" at Hannover on October 23, 1933. Note that these political leaders wear their regular headdress which is the SA-style kepi.

Nat.Soz.Betriebszellen–Organisation (NSBO) (NS. Industrial Cells Organization)

In Berlin during 1927/28, Party member Johannes Engel[12] formed the precursor of what would become the NSBO, called the "NS–Wählerschaft bei der Knorrbremse," an election committee of National Socialist employees of the Knorrbremse AG firm.[13] Shortly thereafter some other factory "cells" were formed, and in November, Party member Rheinhold Muchow launched the idea to establish a similar organization on the province level. From all directions an attempt was made to institute a National Socialist trade union, but in August 1928 the NSDAP High Command rejected its creation. It then took until May 1930 until the first provincial level factory cells were officially instituted in Berlin. During 1931, this idea swept throughout Germany.

---

10 *"Amtliches Nachrichtenblatt der DAF und der NSG 'Kraft durch Freude'" (simply referred as Amtl.Nbl.d.DAF), Nr. 2. February 2, 1935, p. 10.*

11 *Ibid, Nr. 3. February 9, 1935, front–page.*

12 *"Das Dritte Reich. Die Kampfjahre 1918–1933." Berlin: 1936, p. 189.*

13 *Starke, Gerhard."Die Deutsche Arbeitsfront." Berlin: 1940, p. 28.*

Johannes Engel, founder of the NSBO, wears a dark brown visored cap with probably gold piping and cords with knots, because of his position as foreman on the Reich-level.

Otto Spronk

Walther Schumann, the NSBO leader (Amtsleiter) from 1931-1932, wears his political leader uniform and the kepi with gold cords with two knots...a symbol of his function on Reich level.

With the creation of the "Reichsbetriebszellenabteilung" (RBA – National factory Cells Department) on January 15, 1931, it could be said that a force for the National Socialist Party laborers (a sham or covert trade union) existed in the struggle against the Marxist–Communist and other trade unions. On March 5th of the same year, the RBA was officially renamed the "NSBO," and was led by Reichs–Betriebszellenleiter Walther Schumann. In 1932 the NSBO leader became Reinhard Muchow while constant reorganization took place. It is noted that it was possible to hold membership as a sympathizer, and not be a member of the NSDAP.[14]

---

14 *"Daten der Geschichte der NSDAP. " 11.Auflage.Berlin/Leipzig: 1943, p. 32. Section V: Die NSDAP von 1925 bis 1933; "Vbl.d.RL.d.NSDAP," Nr. 4, July 27, 1931, p. 10; Ibid, Nr. 5, August 19, 1931, p. 13; Ibid, Nr. 27, July 15, 1932, p. 61.*

It was on May 2, 1933 that this NSBO, under the command of Dr. Ley, along with the SA and SS, by orders of Hitler, took over control of all free trade unions in Germany. During the same period of time, the DAF was officially instituted by Ley on May 10th, as the sole labor organization permitted in Germany.[15]

Even earlier than the institution of the DAF and its reorganization, the NSBO was led by NSDAP political leaders. Their task was to lead and look after the DAF, the sixteen "Reichsbetriebsgemeinschaften" and "Kraft durch Freude" (this last mentioned was led by lower level NSDAP cadre, known as "Amtswarte").[16] The NSBO was since 1934, the main center of political leaders within the DAF. In March 1937 the "old" NSBO became the core of the Werkscharen, due to the political duties of these labor troops.[17] Most members of the "old" NSBO were ordered to wear the Werkschar uniform.

For clarity the section relating to NSBO headdresses is divided into the following parts:

NSBO (Party members, not being political leaders);

NSBO (not being Party members).

(this is the same regarding the NS–Hago also)

NSBO (Party Members, not being Political Leader)

In 1935 NSBO members who were also Party members (but not yet selected as a political leader) and who were managing a DAF or KdF office, were in February granted the position of NSDAP political leaders, to be constituted as the NSBO staff (Stab der NSBO). Simultaneously they were allowed to wear the political leaders uniform when authorized or ordered for wear.[18]

It is known that prior to 1935 (probably since around 1933) these officials wore a dark–blue visored cap with the first pattern national emblem. No colored piping was mentioned. In 1934 the first pattern eagle was often replaced by the model–1934 version. No cockade was worn. Above the black visor rested a

Otto Spronk

Members of the Deutsche Bank during a NSBO march on May 1, 1934. Note that the political leaders in the front rows wear the visored caps as well as the SA-style caps. All regular members wear the DAF visored cap with the oval DAF insigne.

black leather chin strap. This cap was the same form as was worn by NSBO members, not being a Party member.[19]

The cap band used in 1933 was a black, ribbed and shiny moiré band, in place of dark cloth. It should be noted that at times factory foremen sometimes adopted silver cords with a knot, fastened by silver buttons, like those worn by political leaders.[20]

For officials who were not appointed as a political leader, the wearing of the above cap later then 1935 at the latest, replaced the earlier worn band by a black, oak leaf pattern cap band (see also section NSBO below). This cap was in fact the regulation DAF visored cap form, ordered as the "DAF–Mütze für Festanzug."[21]

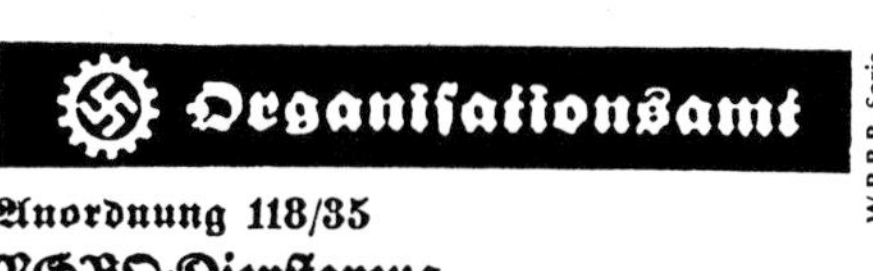

Organisationsamt

Anordnung 118/35

NSBO-Dienstanzug

Zum NSBO-Dienstanzug ist ausnahmslos die vorschriftsmäßige DAF-Mütze zu tragen.

gez.: Claus Selzner,
Leiter des Organisationsamtes.

The November 1935 order from Selzner, the leader for department organization, which ordered that with the NSBO uniform, the regular DAF visored cap was to be worn without exception.

A festivity march on May 1, 1934 at Bochum-Linden-Dahlhausen. The NSBO members and officials wear various forms of headdress and insignia. In the front row are the Ortsgruppenleiter-ranked Berggräf and Rechel, at right is NSBO leader Altmiks. Note that there is only a minor difference in the shades of the visored caps for the political leaders and the dark blue cap worn by Altmiks. The NSBO members in the background all wear the NSBO insigne with a cockade.

---

15 *"Daten der Geschichte der NSDAP. " 11.Auflage. Berlin/Leipzig: 1943, p. 54.*

16 *"Vbl.d.RL.d.NSDAP," Nr. 72, München: End–May, 1934, p. 165.*

17 *"Amtl.Nbl.d.DAF," Nr. 4, March 5, 1937, pp. 42–44.*

18 *"Mbl.d.RZM," Nr. 7, München: 16 February, 1935, p. 53.*

19 *"Uniformen u.Abzeichen der SA,SS,HJ, usw." Berlin: 1933, picture–page 20.*

20 *"Uniformen–Markt," Nr. 9, September 1, 1935, p. 7. (this was observed for example by an "Ortsfachleiter", but also with other low ranked individuals).*

21 *"Mbl.d.RZM," Nr. 31, December 7, 1935, p. 329; in the "Amtl.Nbl.d.DAF," dated November 16, 1935 it was said : "With the NSBO dress the DAF cap according to regulations has to be worn without exceptions." The order was signed by Claus Selzner.*

An NSBO (NSDAP Party) member wears his visored cap with the eagle emblem on the cap top and the NSBO cogwheel on the cap band in 1934. This occasion was during a visit of Hitler to the ship building yard of Blohm & Voss at Hamburg.

A reconstruction of a NSBO visored cap in the style known as "Zivilmütze." The cap band is black, and the top is dark blue without piping. The national eagle emblem and the NSBO hand/cogwheel insigne are properly positioned.

NSBO (not a Party Member)

An order by Hess, dated April 27, 1935, granted to the NSBO and NS–Hago members (not being Party members, but being a member of NSBO or NS–Hago prior to May 9, 1933) the right to wear the dark–blue DAF visored cap with oval insigne and black leather chin strap for wear with the brown shirt. It was stated in this order that Hess had closely watched their devotion to the NS system and had decided to change his order, dated June 1933.

In the June 1933 order, Hess permitted the above mentioned persons *solely* to wear the NSBO insigne (fist/cogwheel). One must note that between February and December 1935, NSBO or NS–Hago members were not allowed to use the oval DAF insigne if they had joined the NSBO or HS–Hago after May 9, 1933.[22]

Otto Spronk

Members of an industrial gymnastic group wear the so-called "Zivilmütze" in dark blue with a shield insigne on the top's center. Above the cloth-covered visor is positioned a black silk cap cord. The man at far right wears a NSBO cap insigne. Note the wear of the round cloth patch on the left arm with the four "Fs," symbolizing Fresh, Happy, Pious and Free.

Apparently Ley had "conned" Hess. This order had already been published in the "Mitteilungsblatt der RZM" in February 1935 and announced for those who were a NSBO member before the "Machtübernahme" (the assumption of power by Hitler).[23] Since December 1935 all were ordered to wear the DAF visored cap with oval DAF insigne so that the ability to distinguish (the fist/cogwheel emblem) between those who were NSBO members prior to or after the assumption of power disappeared.[24]

---

22 *Ibid, Nr. 96, Mid–May 1935, p. 272. Letter Nr. 28/35, dated April 27, 1935.*

23 *"Mbl.d.RZM," Nr. 7, February 16, 1935, p. 53. (The order from Hess as mentioned in the preceding note was published in the "Mbl.d.RZM," May 1935).*

24 *Ibid, Nr. 31. December 7, 1935, p. 329.*

The May 1, 1935 festivities at Mönchengladbach-Rheydt. NSBO and DAF members are shown with their flags. Note the wear of both the DAF oval and NSBO insignia.

With the orders of February 1936, the oval DAF insigne had to be replaced by the national emblem.[25] Before Ley's order in February 1935, NSBO members (not being a Party member, nor NSBO or NS–Hago member) wore a dark–blue visored cap, known as "Zivilmütze". The metal insigne worn was the NSBO emblem upon the front center of the top.[26]

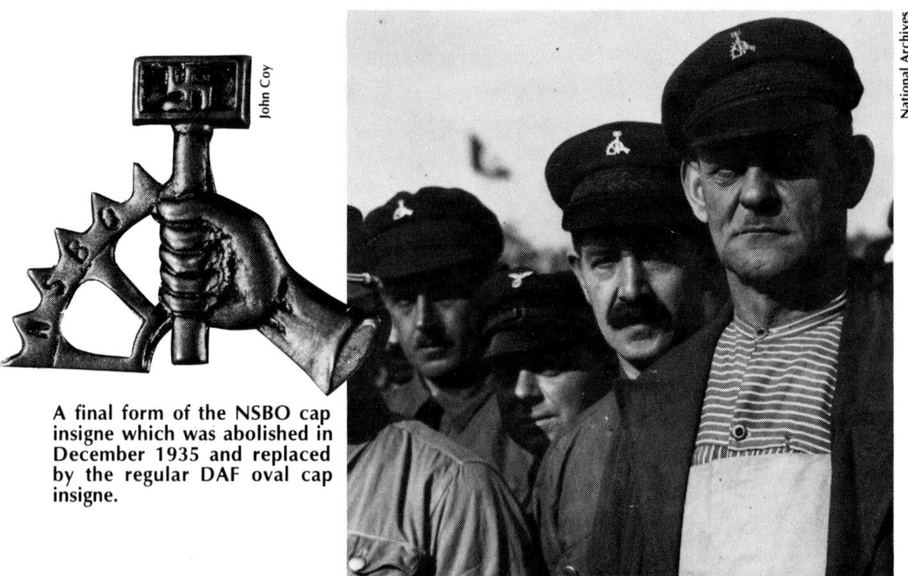

A final form of the NSBO cap insigne which was abolished in December 1935 and replaced by the regular DAF oval cap insigne.

An NSBO cap in wear. Note that the NSBO Party member in the back wears the eagle insigne.

---

[25] *"Amtl.Nbl.d.DAF," Nr. 8, February 29, 1936, p. 54.*

[26] *"NSDAP, Aufbau und Abzeichen." Leipzig: 1933, p. 22. "Uniformen u. Abzeichen der SA, SS, HJ, usw." Berlin: 1933, picture–plate 20.*

It is known that before 1935, the earliest visored cap was supplied with an unofficial pattern oakleaf band. Instead of the black leather chin strap, black, silk cords were sometimes worn attached to the cap by two black, silk covered buttons. In fact this was the civilian form of cap, known as "Zivilmütze." The official NSBO pattern cap had at first a cap band without any oakleaf pattern. The chin strap was always black leather.

In the summer of 1934, the DAF visored cap (standard form) for the "Festanzug" was introduced. Its wear was not official for NSBO or NS–Hago members, as noted earlier in the beginning of this section dealing with the NSBO (not being a Party member). February 1935 (Consult the section DAF for the DAF visored cap and oval insigne.)

NSBO emblem

The NSBO insigne, as worn by those not being a Party member, consisted of a right hand clutching a hammer, embossed with an immobile swastika on a black background. The hand and hammer were superimposed upon a quarter section of a cogwheel, upon which were displayed the initials, "N.S.B.O." on the outer rim. This insigne existed in silver (or natural color,) and was made of stamped, silvered brass or "Neusilber." This insigne was most often marked "ges.gesch." (gesetzlich geschützt – protected by law). It was permitted for wear with the headdress, known as the "Zivilmütze" or the "DAF–Mütze" during normal work periods. Aluminum versions of this insigne appeared during 1936, but were not used as a cap badge, as its use for this was already abolished by earlier orders.

The NSBO cap insigne in the 1933 form.

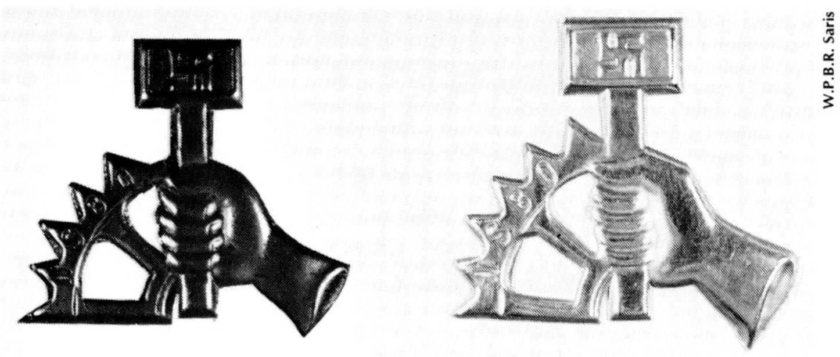

The semi-official authorized NSBO cap insigne in its final form which was worn until December 1935.

W.P.B.R. Saris

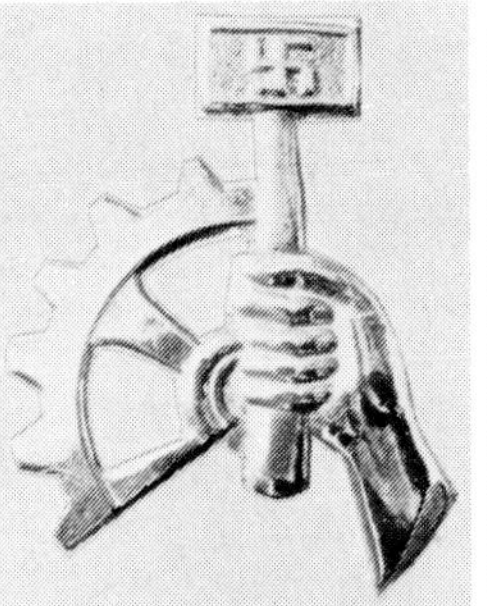

Variations of the NSBO cap insigne manufactured and worn between 1932 and 1934. Note that some of the examples have a period after the NSBO letters, the variations of the quarter of the cogwheel, and the position of the hand.

L. van Aerle

Another variation with blackened letters and swastika background.

It must be noted that due to varying manufacturing designs, many versions of the hand/cogwheel insigne, were produced prior to late 1934, when a final form was adopted.[27] The variations usually measured approximately 29mm wide by 27mm high. This NSBO emblem ceased to be worn on the headdress in December 1935 and disappeared almost immediately.

NS–Jugendbetriebszellen (NS. Youth Factory Cells)

A youth section of the NSBO was established in September 1932 for National Socialist youth who were not members of the "Hitler–Jugend." HJ members, however, were not excluded. After the assumption of power in 1933, this youth organization became superfluous and was incorporated within the HJ in October of the same year.[28]

No information concerning a uniform for this youth organization has been found. Due to its short existence and unimportance, plans for uniforms may never have existed, other than an insigne for its members.

Within the DAF there existed the "Jugendamt der DAF," closely cooperating with the "Ausbildungswesen" of the DAF organization. In 1935 both departments were deeply involved in the creation of the well known "Werkscharen."

27 *"Mbl.d.RZM," Nr. 29, December 15, 1934, p. 7.*

28 *"Verordnungsblatt der Hitler–Jugend," Nr. 53, October 20, 1933.*

Youths (being pupils in the DAF) were from 1943 ordered to wear the regular form HJ ski–cap with HJ diamond.[29]

Deutsche Arbeitsfront (DAF) (German Labor Front)

From 1933 this organization, in fact the sole organization for all German laborers, was led by Dr. Robert Ley, as its fanatic force. The DAF was known as the "Stirn und Faust" (Forehead and Fist). Its purpose was to ensure political stability and a trouble free operation of German industry and commerce and to educate German laborers. The DAF was devised to parallel the NSDAP structure and was responsible for maintaining morale, job satisfaction (by the Kraft durch Freude organization), social care and utilization of spare time (also through the KdF).[30]

Ley obtained the cooperation of the DAF treasury and Reichsschatzmeister Schwarz (Reich Treasurer) in July 1934, probably to secure the developing plans for "his" DAF.[31] With orders dated October 24, 1934 the DAF officially became an organization of the NSDAP, but not to be considered of the same importance as the SA, SS, or HJ then.[32]

Otto Spronk

Hitler shakes hands with DAF members. They are wearing various forms of caps with the oval DAF insigne as worn by the DAF (not being Party members). At far left is a DAF-Warden wearing the 1936 version eagle on the center of the top.

Due to its enormous membership and wealth (created from the treasuries of former Trade Unions, taken over by the National Socialists in 1933) the DAF

29 *"Amtl.Nbl.d.DAF," Nr. 1, February 15, 1943, p. 8. (Signed order from Marrenbach the DAF Chief, formerly Ley's personal adjutant, dated January 1, 1943).*

30 *"Organisationsbuch der NSDAP. " München: Issues 1936, 1937, 1938, 1940 and 1943, pp. 185–232.*

31 *"Vbl.d.RL.d.NSDAP," Nr. 77, early–August 1934, p. 179.*

32 *"Amtl.Nbl.d.DAF," Nr. 7, March 9, 1935, front–page.*

became more and more a problem for the NSDAP, to whom it was subordinated. In 1937 the DAF was once more reorganized and the "Werkschar der DAF" (Labor Troops) became an important factor. (These Labor Troops are discussed in a separate section, due to their importance and uniforms). On January 1, 1939 the "Danziger Arbeitsfront" was incorporated within the DAF system.[33]

During the war the Deutsche Arbeitsfront cooperated closely with those organizations that were employed in construction tasks such as the "Organisation Todt".

For clarity the DAF section is divided into the parts:

DAF (officials, not being Party members, but having positions in offices);

DAF members (Party members or not being Party members).

A. Stam

DAF and NSBO members carry a coffin on June 25, 1936. The individuals wear the regular dark blue "Zivilmütze" with the 1934 form national emblem.

A. Stam

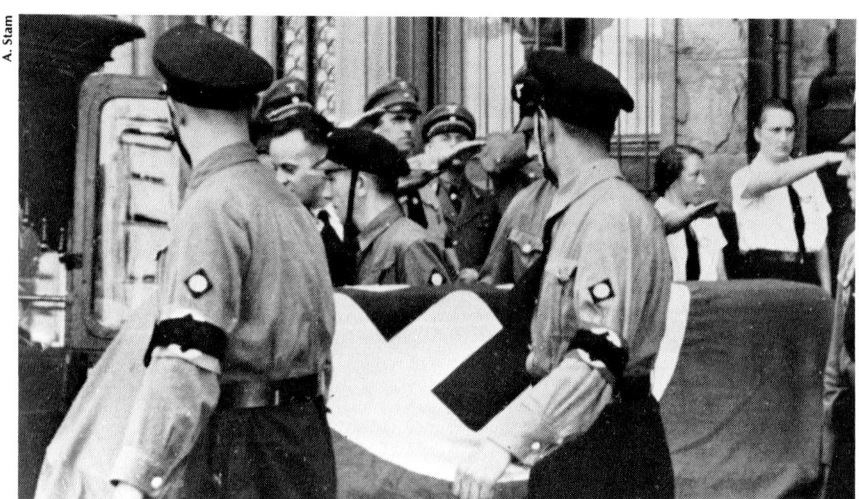

DAF (Officials, not being Party Members, but having Positions in Offices.)

DAF officials leading an office (not being members of the NSBO or NS–Hago, but being a Party member) were given the title in orders of May 5, 1934 as "Walter" (translated as warden but in fact being a manager) and within the section "Kraft durch Freude" as "Wart" (Warder or a supporting person).

Due to their enormous growth in the first year, the DAF and KdF urgently needed officials. Employees (National Socialist minded persons) from the outside were recruited for jobs in offices. These persons were appointed as unofficial DAF–Walter or KdF–Wart and were in fact neither members of the NSBO, or Party members. In early 1935, after a one year probation, they were ordered to wear the dark–blue DAF visored cap with DAF oval insigne. Instead of a brown shirt these persons had to wear a white shirt as a distinction. With photographs this is difficult to identify as such. (Political–) Training of these "DAF–Walter" and "KdF–Warte" took place during PO courses given by the Ausbildungswesen der Pol.Organisation.[34]

All appointed DAF–Walter and KdF–Warte were confirmed with an oath by Hess on February 24, 1935.[35]

National Emblem (Hoheitszeichen)

With an order from Ley, dated February 1936 the above mentioned officials were ordered to wear the national eagle emblem. (Consult also the section NSBO – not being Party members).[36] The wear was only allowed when these

Amtliches
Nachrichtenblatt
der Deutschen Arbeitsfront und der
NSG „Kraft durch Freude"

2. Jahrg. · Folge 8 · Erscheint wöchentlich
Sonnabend, den 29. Februar 1936

Nachdruck, auch auszugsweise, verboten. Das Verordnungsblatt ist nur für den inneren Dienstverkehr der Deutschen Arbeitsfront bestimmt

Anordnung 16/36

Mützen-Hoheitszeichen
für DAF-Walter und -Warte

Der Stellvertreter des Führers hat den DAF-Waltern und -Warten in Anerkennung ihrer Verdienste das Recht zum Tragen des Hoheitszeichens der NSDAP an der DAF-Dienstmütze verliehen.

gez.: Dr. R. Ley, Reichsleiter der DAF.

W.P.B.R. Saris

The early 1936 Ley order with the authorization to wear the national emblem by DAF officials known as DAF-Walter and DAF-Warte. Note the masthead of the periodical.

DAF-Walter wear the dark blue visored cap with the chin strap worn under the chin, during the funeral of the poet Heinrich Lersch at Mönchengladbach on June 25, 1936.

---

33 *Ibid, Nr. 9. November 14, 1938, p. 125.*

34 *"Mbl.d.RZM," Nr. 7, February 16, 1935, p. 53; "Vbl.d.RL.d.NSDAP," Nr. 19, mid–February 1935, p. 240.*

35 *"Amtl.Nbl.d.DAF," Nr. 9, March 23, 1935, p. 73.*

36 *"Mbl.d.RZM," Nr. 6, March 14, 1936, p. 101; "Amtl.Nbl.d.DAF," Nr. 8, February 29, 1936, front–page.*

officials were in the possession of an identity card. The 1936 version silvered eagle had a 4.9cm wingspan, its height being 3.3cm and was to be positioned on the upper top center of the cap. The wear of a cockade or any other form insigne upon the oakleaf cap band was strictly forbidden.[37]

Beginning with the introduction of the larger SA national emblem, this (silvered or aluminum) form was also worn, having the regular 65mm wingspan. Upon the reorganization of the DAF–Werkscharen in 1938 they also wore the regular Werkschar field cap and the visored cap (Form 4), when permission was granted, with the DAF pattern oakleaf wreath upon the cap band.[38]

W.P.B.R. Saris

Organisationsamt

Anordnung 12/36

Mützen-Hoheitszeichen für DAF-Walter und -Warte

Ausführungsbestimmungen:

Das Hoheitszeichen darf nur von den Waltern und Warten an der DAF-Mütze getragen werden, die sich im Besitze eines vorschriftsmäßigen Personalausweises befinden.

Das silberne Hoheitszeichen in Flügelspannweite 49 Millimeter, Höhe 33 Millimeter, wird in der Mitte des oberen Mützenteiles getragen.

Die Anbringung sonstiger Abzeichen und Kokarden, insbesondere am unteren Mützenteil (Kopfband mit schwarzer Eichenlaubverzierung) ist untersagt.

Die DAF-Mütze wird seitens der DAF-Walter und -Warte ohne Ausnahme mit Lacklederriemen getragen.

Das Hoheitszeichen ist von der Reichszeugmeisterei bzw. deren zugelassenen Verkaufsstellen zu beziehen.

In Abänderung der Anordnung des Reichsorganisationsleiters 2/35 vom 19. Januar 1935 wird zur NSBO-Uniform die DAF-Mütze mit Hoheitszeichen, wie vorstehend aufgeführt, getragen.

gez.: Claus Selzner,
Leiter des Organisationsamtes.

Anordnung 33/36

Mützen-Hoheitszeichen für DAF-Walter und KdF-Warte

In Ergänzung der Anordnung 12/36 vom 29. Februar 1936 des Organisationsamtes wird nunmehr folgendes angeordnet: Sämtliche DAF-Walter und KdF-Warte haben bis zum 1. August 1936 ausnahmslos an ihren DAF-Mützen den vorschriftsmäßigen Mützen-Hoheitsadler zu befestigen. Die Mützen-Hoheitsadler sind durch die Reichszeugmeisterei und deren angeschlossene Verkaufsstellen zu beziehen.

gez.: Claus Selzner, Leiter des Organisationsamtes

Two 1936 orders from Selzner relating to the national emblem for DAF officials. The February order 12/36 discusses the DAF visored cap (with oakleaf pattern cap band) and the eagle's size and its positioning. At this time a cockade was not permitted. The NSBO visored cap was also to have an eagle emblem. The July order 33/36 is an additional order referring also to the national emblem and abolishes the oval or NSBO insigne worn by DAF or KdF officials.

May 1, 1936 festivities at Mönchengladbach-West by Waldhausen. Ortsgruppenleiter Rainaü is shown speaking. In the front are DAF members wearing the dark blue "Zivilmütze" with insigne.

A standard DAF visored cap, with the earliest type of national emblem, as worn by DAF-Wardens.

[37] *"Amtl.Nbl.d.DAF," Nr. 8, February 29, 1936, p. 54. (It must be noted that also other, early, pattern eagle emblems were worn).*

[38] *Ibid, Nr. 22, October 22, 1938, p. 215.*

Richard Kindel

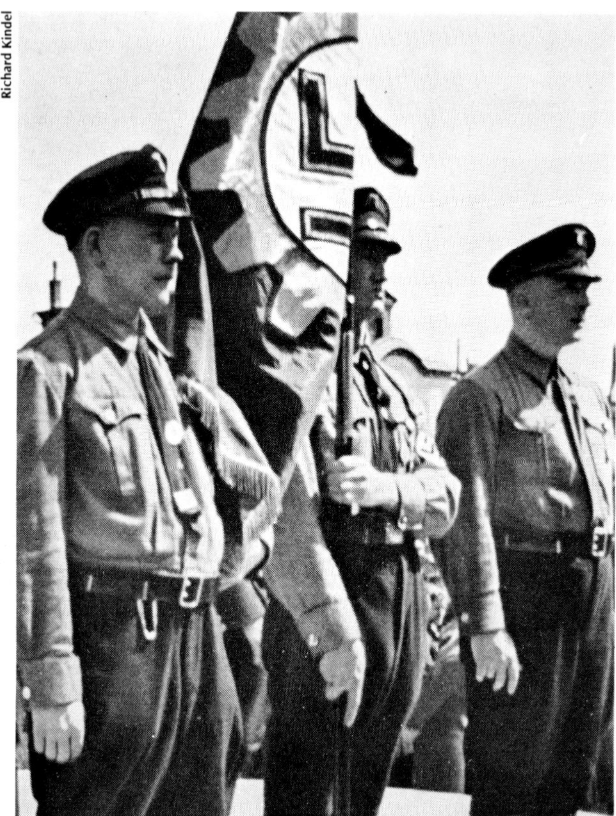

The authorization of the gold DAF flag on May 1, 1937 to the firm of BSW (Berlin-Suhler Waffen u. Fahrzeugwerke GmbH at Weimar). Note that during the presentation the DAF wardens are wearing the visored cap with the small national emblem.

Robert Bernard

The DAF visored cap as worn by DAF wardens with the 1937 version national emblem.

DAF members (being Party Members)

Just how intricate the systems were can be seen by the appointment of sixteen persons to the positions of "Amtsleiter der DAF" in the eighteen Reichsbetriebsgemeinschaften in June 1935. None of these persons were allowed to wear a political leaders uniform.[39]

One week later, another announcement published by Rudolf Schmeer (Ley's DAF deputy) said literally: "The appointment for "Amtsleiter der DAF" does not mean the granting of the rank "Amtsleiter der NSDAP."[40] These DAF persons for the most part wore the regular DAF cap and uniform, occasionally following the DAF–Walter orders.

J. Bornebroek

This individual wears a totally unknown form of visored cap and a mix of insignia. Apparently the cap is piped in white and the cords appear to be aluminum. On the top he is wearing a SS eagle. His DAF cogwheel is positioned within a regular army wreath. It is possible that he was a guard at a factory.

DAF Insigne (Mützenabzeichen)

The insigne worn by DAF members was introduced in early spring 1934 and permitted its manufacturing by weaving mills. The cap manufactures were

39 *"Amtl.Nbl.d.DAF," Nr. 20, June 20, 1935, p. 181. (The wearing of a political leaders uniform for the 18 persons was denied by Ley).*

40 *Ibid, Nr. 21, June 29, 1935, p. 194.*

not allowed to deliver the DAF cap without insigne. This order was changed in July 1934 allowing members to replace insigne if their old one was lost. The insigne consisted of a metal back plate, an oval cardboard backing, wide metal clips (of one piece), cloth inlay and outer ring.[41]

The oval outer ring was made of aluminum or light weight metal, gold anodized with a rope decoration (53.5mm high by 40mm wide). At the reverse were six clamps or prongs. The black cloth inlay had a woven (BeVo) cogwheel (approximately 26.5mm in diameter) and within this a canted swastika (12.5mm). In the lower section of the insigne were oakleaf twigs. The cloth was glued to a piece of cardboard for support.

A nickeled back plate (with raised suppliers number and RZM logo) had two brass prongs attached through a slot, was vaulted so that, when fixed together, the cloth inlay bulged.[42] From December 20, 1934 this insigne was protected by law.

L. van Aerle

A disassembled DAF cap insigne for the visored cap worn with the festival dress. Left: the light-weight, gold anodized outer ring; in center the woven cloth swastika/cogwheel and oakleaf branches; and at right the nickel-silver backplate with RZM marking and supplier code (Lieferant) No. 391.

41 *"Mbl.d.RZM," Nr. 2, June 9, 1934. p. 6.*

42 *Ad.Baumeister, Lüdenscheid. Katalog; photo page item Nr. 5518.*

The 1937 form cogwheel with somewhat angular cogs. Earlier forms often had either straight or rounded cogs.

James J. Boulton

Left: "Festival Cap" insigne. Right: Gold wire, hand-embroidered version of same.

Otto Spronk

Peter Klubert

Wilhelm Potthoff wears the standard visored cap with oval insigne for the Deutsche Arbeitsfront (May 1, 1935). This photograph clearly shows the oakleaf cap band and insigne as well as its positioning: Three-quarters of it on the top and the rest partially on the cap band.

Totally embroidered insigne was introduced in 1934. It is very interesting to know that this form was *only* allowed for wear as an experiment in the Gau Sachsen (Saxony.)[43]

D.A.F.-Mützen-Abzeichen

D.A.F.-Mützen-Abzeichen dürfen nur von den für die Anfertigung von Abzeichen textiler Art zugelassenen Herstellerfirmen gewebt werden und nur an zugelassene Mützenhersteller, zugelassene Großhändler und eigens für den Vertrieb der D.A.F.-Mützen zugelassene Verkaufsstellen geliefert werden. Es ist den Fabrikanten des D.A.F.-Mützen-Abzeichens ausdrücklich und strengstens verboten, unmittelbar an Belegschaften D.A.F.-Mützen-Abzeichen zu liefern, ebenso wie es den Mützenherstellern verboten ist, die D.A.F.-Mütze ohne Abzeichen zu liefern.

Für den Gau Sachsen ist die Verwendung eines gestickten D.A.F.-Mützenabzeichens sowie einer Mützenkordel an Stelle des Ledersturmriemens freigestellt worden. Die vorschriftsmäßige D.A.F.-Mütze mit gewebtem Mützenabzeichen und Ledersturmriemen behält auch in Sachsen ihre Gültigkeit. Alle anders lautenden Bekanntmachungen sind falsch.

Die Erfahrung hat gezeigt, daß teilweise und sogar in sehr ansehnlichen Mengen irgendeine minderwertige blaue Zivilmütze, die natürlich in keiner Weise der vorgeschriebenen Qualität entsprach, als D.A.F.-Mütze angeboten und verkauft, dem Arbeiter also in unverantwortlichster Weise das Geld aus der Tasche gestohlen wurde. Der Verkauf des D.A.F.-Mützen-Abzeichens ohne Mütze wurde nur deshalb freigegeben, um seinen etwaigen Verlust ersetzen zu können, ohne daß eine neue Mütze gekauft werden muß; nicht aber deshalb, um dem Schwarzhändler Tür und Tor zu öffnen.

The DAF oval's center was to be manufactured only by those who were authorized. This publication also states that the experimentally worn embroidered version of this oval were worn by members from Saxony. For a short time they were also permitted to wear on an experimental basis cords instead of the regular chin strap. The last paragraph states that some inferior quality visored caps had been sold and that this was irresponsible and was "stealing" from the laborers who had purchased them.

Abzeichen für die Mütze der Deutschen Arbeitsfront

Die Herstellung von gewebten Abzeichen für die Mütze der **Deutschen Arbeitsfront** wird mit sofortiger Wirkung verboten.

Abzeichen für die Mütze der Deutschen Arbeitsfront

Die weitere Herstellung von gestickten Abzeichen für die Mütze der Deutschen Arbeitsfront wird hiermit untersagt, da diese Abzeichen voraussichtlich geändert werden.

Two separate messages in the *Mbl. d. RZM* abolishing the embroidered DAF oval in the spring of 1937.

Rumors in the press noted that this insigne was not an official item. The RZM affirmed the use of the insigne only in Saxony. Manufacturing of the embroidered form was forbidden by the RZM as of August 28, 1937.[44] This prohibition was repeated in October 1937 for the simple reason: a new form had been developed and planned for introduction.[45] As far as research can determine, this

[43] *"Mbl.d.RZM," Nr. 6, June 9, 1934, p. 6. (It was noted in this order that with the visored cap the Saxony area was allowed to wear cords [no color was mentioned] instead of the leather chin strap. The cords were prohibited the same month).*

[44] *Ibid, Nr. 18, August 18, 1937 p. 226.*

[45] *Ibid, Nr. 22, October 23, 1937, p. 258. The new form was announced on this page .*

new insigne was a round shaped emblem with the cogwheel and a canted swastika in heavy gold embroidery. Later, this emblem was worn by females on the breast.

Most likely, the plan to introduce this new form of insigne must not have been carried through. The old oval insigne was still being manufactured even later than the summer of 1941.[46] Variations in the size of the insigne varied depending on the manufacturer.

Otto Spronk

A beautiful hand-embroidered gold swastika and cogwheel on a round background. This insigne was probably intended as the new form to be worn with the DAF "Festival Cap."

DAF symbol for German Streetcar and Private Railway Concerns (DAF–Mützenabzeichen deutscher Strassenbahnen, Klein–und Privatbahnen)

In November 1936 a special emblem was introduced with Ley's agreement by Körner of the branch of trade for Traffic and Public Works to be used by employees of streetcar and private railway companies. It exists in two forms and consists of the DAF cogwheel, wings and a train wheel for railway companies. The insigne for electric streetcars had "lightning bolts" on both sides of the train wheel.[47] These insignia will be discussed in detail in a forthcoming volume of

This special cap insigne was worn by members of public streetcar firms whose personnel all belonged to the DAF. It was introduced in November 1936. The insigne is pressed from sheet metal and silvered (30mm high and 68mm wide). It was also permitted to be worn by personnel, with the above mentioned conditions, of so-called "Klein- und Privatbahnen" (privately owned railways), but without the lightning bolts.

---

[46] *Ibid, Nr. 10, July 12, 1941, p. 54. (The DAF oval insigne was not classified here with the organization DAF, but as Political Leader).*

[47] *"Amtl.Nbl.d.DAF," Nr. 28, November 24, 1936, pp. 199–200; Ibid, Nr. 4, August 30, 1939, p. 65; "Mbl.d.RZM," Nr. 26, December 19, 1936, p. 603.*

this series in the chapter relating to streetcars and railways which were as far as can be determined, the only ones that were given documented permission .

DAF Headdress (DAF–Mütze): 1934–1945

In early 1934, a visored cap for the DAF–"Festanzug" (Festival Dress) was introduced as the official headdress to be worn by DAF members, DAF–Walter and KdF–Warte. This dress was usually worn during any ceremonies of the DAF organization, but mainly during May 1st ceremonies and on Hitler's birthday.

This cap in many respects resembled the so called "Zivil–Mütze." Manufacturing methods remained unchanged. Its manufacturing was preceded by those who already manufactured the "Zivil–Mütze" prior to July 1, 1933.[48] (consult also Volume 2, chapter Sports Pilots p.150 the so called "Form Tetje"). The wearing of sub–standard quality caps was forbidden. It is known that many types of inferior caps were offered for sale during the period and passed off as the official DAF cap or "Festmütze."

This visored cap was of dark–blue material and had a black cap band. The piping was of the same color and material as the cap top. The black oakleaf pattern cap band was from 1934 also protected by law (ges.gesch.). The black visor is of leather (later fiber). From 1935 on, the inside top lining of the cap had a celluloid diamond with the DAF emblem positioned on it.[49] The use of the celluloid sweat diamond with imprinted DAF symbol was forbidden in October 1937.[50]

Mütze der Deutschen Arbeitsfront

Die Herstellung und Verwendung von Celluloidspiegeln mit aufgedrucktem oder geprägtem DAF.-Abzeichen für die Mütze der Deutschen Arbeitsfront ist verboten.

An October 1937 order that states that the printed DAF symbol on the celluloid diamond was officially forbidden.

In April 1936, new manufacturing procedures were introduced for this visored cap . It was ordered to be produced in the form of the well known "Tellermütze," its style modified and developed from the earlier worn "Zivilmütze."

Description: Model 1936

The material was navy blue, nearly black DAF wool. The oval top measured approximately 26.3cm in length. The width was approximately 25cm (measurements taken from a size 56 visored cap). In front, the top was low, being 5.1cm high, the sides being 4.5cm and the top at the rear measured 4.6cm. The crown piping was 2.3mm thick and of the same color and material as the top.

The interior of the front was stiffened by two rust proof metal bars (0.6mm wide), sewn to a 3cm wide stout piece of linen. The cap band body was strengthened by a 0.4–0.5mm thick piece of natural colored, or blue cloth covered card-

---

[48] *Ibid, Nr. 2, June 9, 1934, p. 6.*

[49] *Ibid, Nr. 13, March 30, 1935, p. 118.*

[50] *Ibid, Nr. 22, October 23, 1937, p. 257.*

This drawing, published in 1936, is from the RZM regulations for manufacturing specifications for the DAF festivities dress. Note that the insigne on the visored cap is round instead of oval. This was either the artist's misconception or he was made aware of plans for a new, round form of insigne.

Don Frailey

The DAF "Festival Cap" in wear.

DAF "Festival Cap."

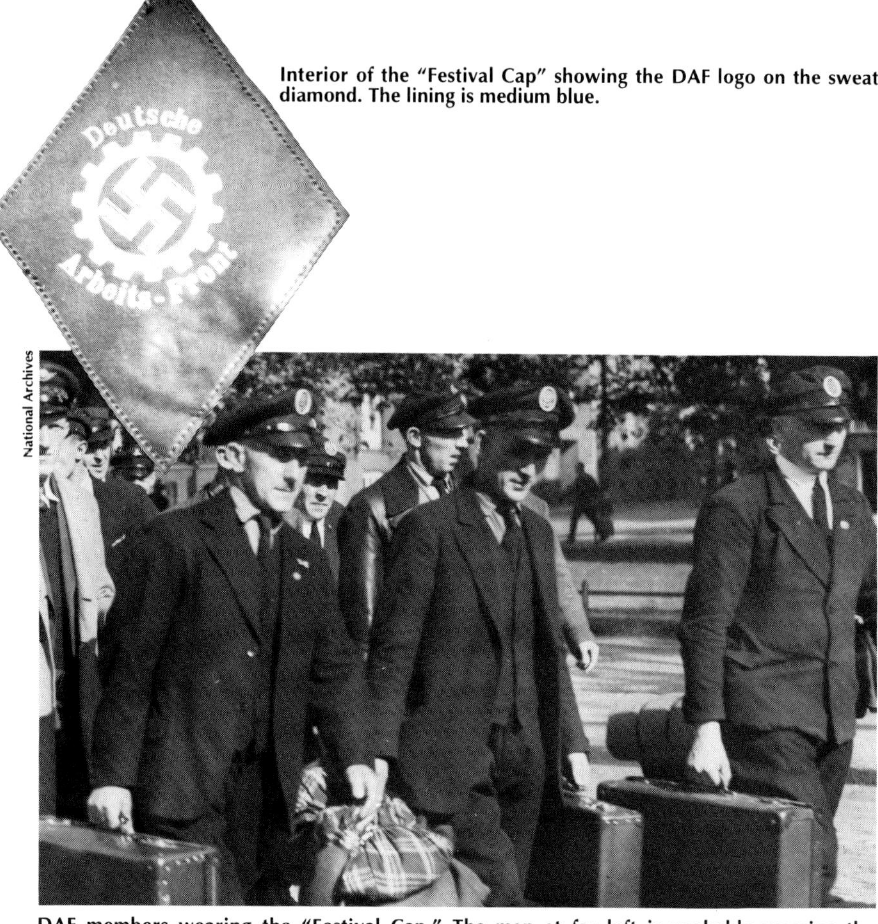

Interior of the "Festival Cap" showing the DAF logo on the sweat diamond. The lining is medium blue.

National Archives

DAF members wearing the "Festival Cap." The man at far left is probably wearing the "Werkschar-Luftfahrt" insigne.

board, 3cm wide. The lining of the cap was always of medium blue cotton satin. A celluloid, diamond oil shield, measuring 13.5 x 10cm was sewn on the top inside lining.

The completely black visor, smooth and glossy on the outside, matte on the underside, was made of fiber with a 0.5cm black lacquered muslin edging. The width of the visor in the center was approximately 4.6cm and sewn to the cap body at a 32° angle. Above this rested the two part black sheepskin chin strap (1.5mm thick and 13mm wide). Both parts of the chin strap were 29cm long with a black, 18mm high rectangular buckle with rounded edges. The strap could be extended by two black metal buckles (18 x 21mm) and was fastened by two black, ribbed cloth covered buttons (12 or 12.5mm in diameter). These buttons were sewn to the band. Later, buttons with prongs were used.

The sweatband (approximately 40mm wide) was beige colored, and of substitute materials. The latter was always stamped with an "RZ" marking. The (blue) RZM tag was positioned on the viewer's left interior, just beneath the sweatband, upon the inside cap body lining, with the tag's lettering to the inside

John Coy

John Coy

Two examples of a DAF-related sweat diamond. The cap lining is medium blue.

Deutsche Arbeitsfront Mütze
Herstellerfirma Nr:
RZM
N.S.D.A.P.
Reichszeugmeisterei.
Serie I

Marke
für DAF.-Mütze.

W.P.B.R. Saris

The DAF/RZM tag as published in the 1936 regulations. Note the tag indicates Series 1. The tag from an obversed visored cap indicates Series II.

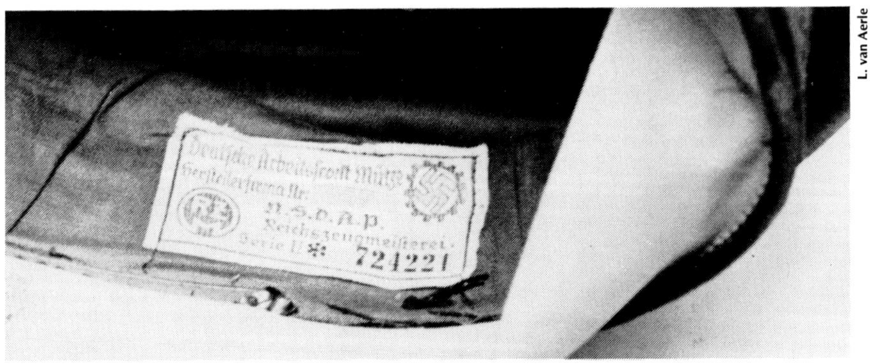

L. van Aerle

The inside of a "Festival Cap." Note the RZM label sewn beneath the sweat band.

L. van Aerle

The sweat diamond with the swastika/cogwheel but without lettering. Normally, the lettering "Lodenfrey, München," "Die D.A.F. Mütze nach Vorschrift" or "Deutsche Arbeits-Front" is also on the diamond.

of the top. The loose stiffening wire was often removed as it was only used to retain the cap's shape.[51]

Officially, the oval DAF insigne was positioned with half of it extending down onto the cap band, the other half on the cap top. Later, in 1937, the insigne was positioned somewhat higher on the top and from fall 1938 it was worn entirely on the cap's front, with the lowest edge touching the upper cap band piping.[52]

Two black, rust proof ventilation grommets were positioned on the surface of the side panels, approximately 15mm beneath the piping around the crown.

The 1936 manufacturing procedures were officially withdrawn in March 1938.[53] The "Form 4," as ordered for political leaders, was intended to be used as the regular DAF form. The old form however remained in use authorized by a new order, dated April 9, 1938 as by then the March order was already withdrawn.[54] In October 1938, the subject was returned to. The procedures for the "Form 4" were also authorized for the DAF visored cap. The style was as used for the new form to be used by political officials. DAF officials were ordered to use a better quality saddle form visored cap.[55] The black fiber visor always had a glossy finish with the underside of Havana–brown in color. The black muslin

---

51 *"RZM–Herstellungsvorschriften," 1936, p. 122.*

52 *"Mbl.d.RZM," Nr. 21, October 8, 1938, p. 209.*

53 *Ibid, Nr. 7, March 26, 1938, p. 51.*

54 *Ibid, Nr. 8, April 9, 1938, p. 54.*

55 *Ibid, Nr. 21, October 21, 1938, p. 209.*

edging was no longer used (for more detailed information consult the section "Werkschar" within this chapter).

Substitute materials were allowed to be used. For example, "Alkor," a product of the Karl Lissmann concern at Solnn near Munich, was cheaper and was used in the manufacturing of the chin strap.[56] Sometime in early 1942, this concern developed another much cheaper material for the chin strap, "Texokor."[57] Sweat bands were, during the war manufactured from a substitute material, known as "Monakor."[58] (These substitute materials must be considered for any visored cap manufactured during the war. It was not specifically meant for the DAF only).

Also, occasionally the visorless field cap with appropriate insigne was worn by officials in later years. The DAF visored cap continued to be worn in the known forms until 1945 with regular insigne.

Cap Band Decoration (DAF–Mützenband)

The use of the black cap band decoration (known as the "DAF Mützenband") was not limited to the DAF only, but was also worn on the visored cap for Werkschar leaders, the NSKOV visored cap (for more information consult, Volume 2 of this series, chapter: Veterans' Organizations. p.296.) and the commonly worn "Zivilmütze."

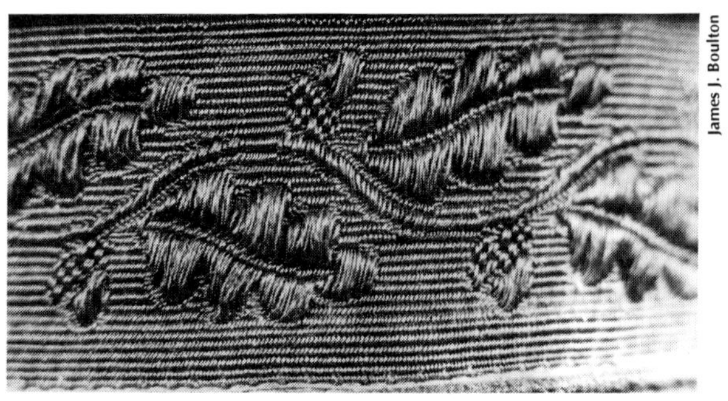

James J. Boulton

A detailed photograph of the cap band with oak leaf pattern.

This black silk, ribbed band is approximately 40mm wide, with a rib every 1mm. The waving stem of the leaves is 1.5mm thick. The acorn is 9mm long and 7mm wide and each leaf is 39mm in length and 14mm wide. Every 6.0cm was one acorn with one leaf positioned above the stem and one beneath (see detail of design). Normally, twelve or thirteen leaves are visible above and below the stem when the band is sewn to the cap body.

DAF Members (not being Party Members)

In 1934 these members were not allowed to use the DAF visored cap with insigne, but in fact, were allowed to simply wear the cogwheel with swastika insigne (Abzeichen der DAF) only with civilian dress .[59] Wear of this emblem

[56] *Ibid, Nr. 12, June 12, 1937, p. 153.*

[57] *Ibid, Nr. 3, February 14, 1942, p. 13.*

[58] *Ibid, Nr. 3, April 10, 1943, p. 13.*

[59] *Ibid, Nr. 7, July 14, 1934, p. 1.*

was propagated with the orders of December 12, 1934.[60] Probably incorrect emblems must have been produced as on April 13, 1935 an announcement was made. "The cogwheel must always have fourteen teeth."[61] (see details in the section "Werkscharen").

L. van Aerle

A variation of the Werkschar cogwheel. Note that the inside of the swastika is checkered.

After the reorganizations, the wear of the regular form DAF visored cap with oval insignia was allowed.

Labor Front Abroad (DAF–Auslands–Organisation)

This department was probably created in October 1934, led by Gauleiter Bohle from the "Auslands–Organisation der NSDAP" and structured as such. In July 1935 the "DAF–AO" was reorganized.[62] No uniform regulations were announced, but must have been largely as those worn in Germany. Special DAF schools were formed later at London, Paris and Barcelona. In October 1941 a DAF section AO for future colonies was formed, led by Gauobmann Karl Nahrat.

In 1940, under direction of the "Arbeitsbereich Nederland," Germans in the Netherlands were required to join the DAF. Later the Dutch Labor Front was established on May 1, 1942 as the NAF (Nederlands Arbeitsfront, descended from the Nederlands Verbond van Vakverenigingen – trade unions).[63] It was officially instituted by a decree of Arthur Seyss–Inquart and led by H.H. Woudenberg.

It is known that Germans residing in the Netherlands occasionally wore regular DAF uniforms. The uniform worn by the Dutch in the NAF does not fall within the sphere of this series.

Female Members of the DAF (Weibliche Mitglieder der DAF)

Women who worked in factories were assimilated into the "Frauenamt der DAF" (Females DAF Department), led by Gertrud Scholtz–Klink of the NS–Frauenschaft and later, during the war, by Rilke. No Labor Troops (Werkscharen) for females existed, but instead, groups were formed known as "Werkfrauengruppe" for females above the age of 21 in 1935.[64]

---

60 *"Amtl.Nbl.d.DAF," Nr. 5, February 23, 1935, p. 36.*

61 *Ibid, Nr. 11, April 13, 1935, p. 94.*

62 *Ibid, Nr. 25, July 27, 1935, pp. 221–222.*

63 *"Documentatie" (a reference for justice purposes after the war). Bijzonder Gerechtshof t.b.v. bijzondere rechtspleging. Amsterdam, 1946/47, p. 62.*

64 *"Amtl.Nbl.d.DAF," Nr. 41, December 7, 1935, p. 347.*

W.P.B.R. Saris

NSG „Kraft durch Freude"

Abt. Werkscharen

Anordnung 5/35

Werkscharen

Um Mißverständnissen vorzubeugen, stelle ich hiermit fest, daß es **weibliche Werkscharen nicht gibt.** Statt dessen ist für weibliche Gefolgschaftsmitglieder über 21 Jahren mit dem Frauenamt eine Regelung getroffen worden, nach der nach Bedarf Frauenwerkgruppen aufgezogen werden können.

Für weibliche Gefolgschaftsmitglieder unter 21 Jahren ist die Frage der Zusammenarbeit durch Vereinbarung mit dem Jugendamt, Folge 3 vom 9. Februar 1935, geregelt worden.

gez.: Dressler-Andress,
Leiter der NSG „Kraft durch Freude".

This December 1935 order states that *no* "Werkscharen" for females existed, but the related "Frauenwerkgruppen" were established.

Females having official positions were regularly known as "Frauenwalterinnen der DAF" (Female DAF Wardens). They were assigned to the staff of a department manager, but also simultaneously to the staff of an office leader of the NS–Frauenschaft.[65]

During the years 1933 and 1934, requests were presented to the "Oberste Leitung der PO" (the High Command of the political organization) for the introduction of a dress or uniform for the women serving within the DAF.[66] Several requests were rejected, but the wear of a dark–blue "Kletterjacke" (a climbing jacket in the standard BDM style) was introduced. In the summer of 1935 it was pointed out that neither an official dress, nor a special form of headdress, existed.[67] In fact the wearing of any headdress was forbidden,[68] and was not desirable even while marching. To the National Socialists this did not show a refined taste and was improper for females .[69]

It is remarkable that in early April 1934 the German press proudly announced the "Festanzug" (a dress for ceremonial purposes) as the new dress for DAF females. They wore a very dark–blue, BDM style, beret without insignia.[70] Special insigne for females in leadership positions was introduced as early as November 1937.[71] These females often wore the dress as worn by females of the NS–Frauenschaft, but as far as is known did not include a hat.

---

65 *Ibid, Nr. 28, August 17, 1935, p. 246.*

66 *"Mbl.d.RZM," Nr. 13, August 25, 1934, p. 3.*

67 *"Amtl.Nbl.d.DAF," Nr. 28, August 17, 1935, p. 246.*

68 *"Mbl.d.RZM," Nr. 28, October 26, 1935, p. 289.*

69 *"Amtl.Nbl.d.DAF," Nr. 3, February 9, 1935, p. 22.*

70 *"Leipziger Illustrierte Zeitung," Nr. 4644, March 3, 1934.*

71 *"Amtl.Nbl.d.DAF," Nr. 16, November 20, 1937, pp. 187–188. This insigne was not worn with any headdress.*

P. Roelse

This photograph published on March 3, 1934 in the *Leipziger Illustrierte Zeitung* announced the "Festanzug" for females serving within the DAF. Note the beret without insignia.

A. Hendriks

This photograph shows the work clothing for females. Gertrud Lampei wears a field cap with two buttons and the cogwheel insigne in 1939. During the war she served within the postal system as a "postman."

Many organizational regulations were available for this research. None of these pointed towards any unified dress and such was probably never officially implemented, although some period photographs show women wearing DAF style field caps, complete with insigne. It is also known that approximately forty girls in Vienna from the DAF Department Armed Forces were uniformed in 1940. It is said that they were dressed in a uniform, due to the 2.Reichsstrassen-sammlung (2nd. National Street Collection). Exact details are not known, nor has a photograph been found.[72]

Female Industrial Labor–Groups (Werkfrauengruppen)

A civil, but unified, dress was worn by women in many of the larger factories and companies, usually voluntarily provided by the management. These dresses bore no resemblance to any Party dress.[73] It is observed that these female laborers, "Werkfrauen," often wore aprons of different styles with an insigne of their company. For example, the firm of Peek & Cloppenburg (at Berlin). Most of the time, the women wore cowls or scarves. Photos also show berets being worn. During the war, many women had special duties in factories or volunteered for state jobs, as postal services and rail and streetcar concerns.

W.P.B.R. Saris

Women from a Werkfrauengruppe are lined up during a presentation of an award. They wear no form of headdress.

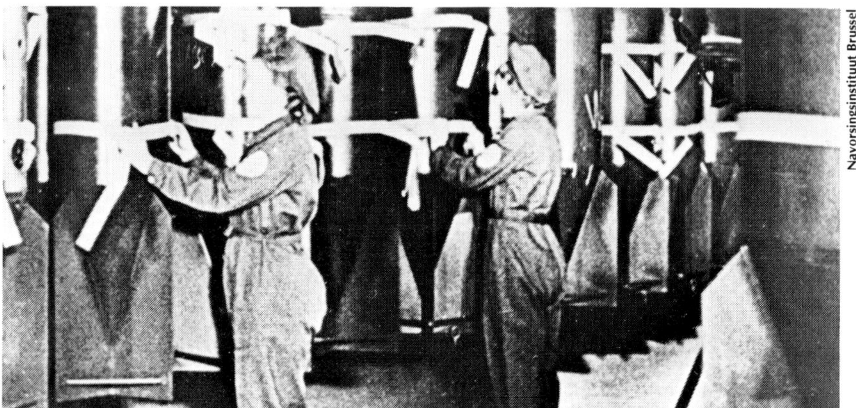

Navorsingsinstituut Brussel

Females at work in a wartime weapons factory. They wear a beret-style headdress which was often supplied by many industrial managements.

72 *"Uniformen–Markt," Nr. 21, November 1, 1940, p. 164.*

73 *"Rundschau–Deutsches Schneiderfachblatt," Nr. 37, September 11, 1937, p. 1343.*

Werkscharen der DAF
(DAF Labor Troops)

Another well known group was created within the DAF in early 1935. The name "Werkschar" is first found in February, in connection with the sections "Ausbildungswesen" and "Jugendamt der DAF."[74] Males from a factory (in the ages 18 through 25 years) formed in such a concern a "Werkschar" (Labor Troop), usually led by an SA leader and having a minimum of fifteen members.[75]

It was more of a para–military group, trying to convey National Socialist ideals to industrial communities. In reality it proved to be a watchdog for the Party, and began the competitions in both achievement and skills within the Reich. It became a very important force.[76] June 1, 1935 the department Werkschar became an independent section within the KdF on orders of Gohdes.[77]

Otto Spronk

Members of the Werkscharen present the golden honor flags of the DAF.

---

[74] *"Amtl.Nbl.d.DAF," Nr. 3, February 9, 1935, p. 21.*

[75] *Ibid, Nr. 2, January 18, 1936. (agreement between Ley and Lutze); Nr. 4, February 1, 1936, p. 32.*

[76] *Starke, Gerhard . "Die Deutsche Arbeitsfront" Berlin: 1940, p. 99.*

[77] *"Amtl.Nbl.d.DAF," Nr. 13, May 14, 1935, p. 111.*

This group was organized so quickly that internal problems arose within the DAF (Hitler compared the Werkscharen in their uniforms to Soviet shop stewards). Practically all its members were simultaneously DAF members, but others (not being Party members, but having National Socialist ideas) were allowed to join the Werkschar with the agreement of the "Betriebswalter" (Company Warden).

In March 1937 the department Werkschar became independent of the KdF. From now on all were members of the NSDAP or one of its sub–organizations. The Werkschar became the DAF spearhead within companies to fulfill political "goals" for the NSDAP. The "new form" Labor Troops were led by Ley, as the "Reichswerkscharführer."

The "Werkschar" from a concern was now composed of:

1) The "old" NSBO, Wardens and Warders from the DAF and members of a "Werkschar" ages 30 through 45, formed the core: "Stammannschaft;"

2) Werkschar members, who had completed their Armed Forces obligation up through the age of 30, formed the shock troops: "Stosstrupp";

3) Werkschar members from 18 through entry into the Armed Forces, formed the juniors: "Jungmannschaft."[78]

Otto Spronk

Members of the "Betriebszelle Reichsversorgung, Betriebsgemeinschaft 10" (traffic and public services) are lined up during a meeting on May 1, 1938. At a glance this photograph can be confusing: At left are political leaders wearing the 1934 national emblem; at the far left this leader still wears his dark uniform. The SA leader at the podium wears the earliest form of national emblem. For political leaders, as well as for the SA, the new forms of national emblems were introduced in 1936 and 1937. The Werkschar members wear field caps which are properly piped (these pipings were introduced in April 1937).

Specific directives were published according functions and systems. During 1937, the new form Werkschar was constantly planned and reshaped, particularly in August and December.[79] Duties were: vocational training, activities on

[78] *Ibid, Nr. 4, March 5, 1937, pp. 42–44.*

[79] *Ibid, Nr. 12, August 26, 1937, pp. 143–144; Ibid, Nr. 17, December 18, 1937, p. 205.*

behalf of health (Werkschar–Gesundheitstruppen) and assignment with the department KdF. The Werkschar areas of responsibility were extended in March 1938 with regard to training. All training within the DAF was organized through these Labor Troops.

One of the last important steps occurred in May 1939 as Ley and Hess agreed to a transformation of the company–system into the NSDAP local–level system. The Werkschar was now composed as a "Stosstrupp" (Shock Troop; and existed with names such as "Stosstrupp für KdF," "Stosstrupp für Berufserziehung," and others) and "Werktrupp" (Labor Troop). Duties were purely political within industry.[80]

A new and intricate system regarding uniforms was begun in July 1939 and was related to: DAF–Walter (Party members) who were from then on, NSDAP lower level political leaders; Werkschar–members (being Party members, but not simultaneously having a DAF function as DAF–Walter) were political leader candidates and Werkschar members (not being a Party member) were also political leader candidates (the collar tabs had no eagle insignia.) Those not being a Party member, but serving a Werkschar, could join the NSDAP. Officially the word "Werkschar" disappeared and was replaced by "DAF."[81]

Most of the plans intended to be implemented with were not executed, due to the beginning of the war. In those areas where Labor Troops did not exist prior to the end of 1939, their formation was ordered before December 31, 1939.[82] This DAF–force remained practically unchanged until the end of the war and was used for various purposes. Through the years this force was led by different leaders, the last was probably Ponath, and they cooperated very closely with the Organisation Todt from 1944. Even with the changes, the German public continued using the old expression "die Werkscharen."

Cogwheel (DAF–Abzeichen)

The cogwheel insigne used on the field cap was first manufactured in silvered brass and "neusilber," existing in several variations. The earliest type had

Anordnung 3/35.

Das Abzeichen der Deutschen Arbeitsfront.

An dieser Stelle mache ich noch einmal darauf aufmerksam, daß das Abzeichen der Deutschen Arbeitsfront ein Hakenkreuz in einem Zahnrad mit **vierzehn** Zähnen ist und andere Entwürfe nicht statthaft sind.

W.P.B.R. Saris

A 1935 order stating that the cogwheel should always have fourteen teeth. It also stated that other designs were not permitted.

---

80 *Ibid, Nr. 2, May 31, 1939, p. 23; "Mbl.d.RZM," Nr. 13, July 1, 1939, p. 181.*

81 *"Vbl.d.RL.d.NSDAP," Nr. 196, mid–July, 1939. Section VIII: Einbau der Werkschar in die Ortsgruppe der NSDAP; DAF, Gauwaltung Franken, Rundschreiben Nr. 14, dated July 15, 1939.*

82 *Ibid, Nr. 6, December 23, 1939, p. 92.*

an approximate diameter of 18.5mm and was slightly vaulted, its material being approximately 1mm thick. As already noted it must always have fourteen teeth.

The cogwheel manufactured in early 1936 was made of aluminum or light weight metals and was larger than the first type. This insigne had a diameter of approximately 30mm and a swastika which measured approximately 13.5mm (RZM price list Nr. 8199). Two prongs were fastened on the reverse.[83] This larger cogwheel insigne was short lived within the Werkschar. It was worn for one year only, and was replaced by the national emblem.

Jill Halcomb Smith

Detailed photo of the Werkschar cogwheel insigne.

A Werkscharmann, circa 1936, wearing the field cap with scalloped flaps and white metal DAF cogwheel insigne with a 18.5mm diameter.

National Emblem (Hoheitszeichen)

The silver woven or embroidered national emblem (which always had an eagle looking to its left) introduced in April 1937 for the Werkschar field cap, had a wingspan of 48mm and a height of 36mm. It was sewn by hand to the cap top center approximately 2mm above the piping along the edge of the flap.[84] From 1938, instead of silver the term aluminum was used. It is observed that on some occasions a metal eagle was positioned in a vaulted form to conform to the bend of the field cap's front.

With an order of June 1937 the woven and embroidered forms of insignia were specified: hand embroidered insigne was allowed for wear by "Werkscharführer"; a woven national emblem was worn by Werkscharmeister, Truppführer

---

83 *F.W. Assmann, Lüdenscheid. Katalog, 1936, p. 25; RZM price list, 1936, p. 7.*

84 *"Organisationsbuch der NSDAP." München: 1937, p. 231.*

and Rottenführer.[85] In July and late October it was noted that Werkschar leaders with golden rank insigne had to wear the silvered eagle. Gold was not allowed until 1938.[86]

W.P.B.R. Saris

Hoheitsabzeichen für Werkscharführermütze

Das Hoheitszeichen für Werkscharführermützen ist auch bei goldener Mützenpaspelierung silberfarbig.

Hoheitsabzeichen für Werkschar-Führermütze

Das Hoheitszeichen an den Werkschar-Führermützen ist silberfarben.

Diese Abzeichen sind einheitlich und werden auch dann in silberner Ausführung getragen, wenn die Mützenpaspelierung goldfarben ist.

Two special announcements published in the Mbl.d.RZM. Both indicated that a silver national emblem was to always be worn (this is 1937), and also by those who wore gold piping.

W.P.B.R. Saris

A Werkschar member wearing the Model 1937 field cap with proper piping. Note that the eagle looks to its left. This is, in fact, the only official authorized form.

Due to the repeated reorganizations, a new rank system was badly needed. In March 1938 this was addressed when Ley introduced the golden national emblem for wear with the headdress by high ranking Werkschar leaders.[87] This golden eagle was also manufactured in a woven or embroidered form.[88] The golden form of insigne was always worn by persons holding honorary rank.

With the Werkschar visored cap, the regular form was worn as ordered for political leaders and the SA (consult for sizes, etc., the particular chapters).

---

85 *"Mbl.d.RZM," Nr. 13, June 19, 1937, p. 173.*

86 *Ibid, Nr. 14, July 3, 1937, p. 182; Ibid, Nr. 22, October 23, 1937, p. 258.*

87 *"Amtl.Nbl.d.DAF," Nr. 3, March 28, 1937, pp. 50–51.*

88 *"Mbl.d.RZM," Nr. 18, August 27, 1938, p. 169; new entry: insigne in gold.*

Otto Spronk

A Werkschar member proudly poses with some friends during the 1937 Reichsparteitag at Nürnberg. His cap is piped and has two silvered buttons and a national emblem as ordered in June 1937. The caps are in the new, second form (Luftwaffe-style).

	Neuzugänge	Paar	—.45
7566	Hoheitszeichen für Mannschaftsmütze, goldgewebt		—.05
7576	Hoheitszeichen für Führermütze, goldgestickt		2.40
8160	Stern für Armabzeichen des Hauptstoßtruppführers		—.10

W.P.B.R. Saris

RZM price list, dated August 27, 1938, for the gold embroidered and woven eagle emblems for Werkschar leaders and enlisted ranks.

1936 – 1938

Plans for a standard service dress were begun in early 1935. Its introduction was repeatedly delayed for unknown reasons in spite of the fact that details had already been published in May and July 1935.[89] One month later, on August 8, 1935, Ley finally authorized (agreed to by Rudolf Hess) the "Werkschar–Uniform."[90] This uniform did *not* include a headdress. The wearing of such was in fact forbidden.

89 *Ibid, Nr. 17, May 25, 1935, p. 167; Ibid, Nr. 20, July 6, 1935, p. 204.*

90 *"Amtl.Nbl.d.DAF," Nr. 29, August 24, 1935, p. 263; "Mbl.d.RZM," Nr. 24, August 31, 1935, p. 241. (most of the designs for new uniforms for the DAF and related sections were created by the graphics department of the DAF).*

W.P.B.R. Saris

Werkschar-Uniform

Die für die Werkscharen in der DAF. vorgesehenen Uniformen werden zunächst nicht eingeführt.

Die teilweise veröffentlichten Angebote und Abbildungen einzelner Firmen sind dadurch ungültig.

Mit dieser Veröffentlichung gelten alle von den zugelassenen Verkaufsstellen, Kleiderhandlungen und Herstellerbetrieben eingegangenen Anfragen wegen dieser Werkschar-Uniform als beantwortet.

The July 1935 announcement relating to the delay of the Werkschar uniform. The previously published and illustrated designs were now invalid.

W.P.B.R. Saris

Abteilung Werkschar

Anordnung 31/35

Jeglicher Kauf von Ausrüstungsgegenständen, wie Tornister, Zeltbahnen, Decken, Kochgeschirre usw. wird für die Werkscharen verboten.

Die Gaue versehen lediglich diejenigen Werkscharen, die zum Reichsparteitag nach Nürnberg vorgesehen sind, mit vollständiger Ausrüstung.

gez.: Gohdes,
Hauptamtsleiter.

Anordnung 32/35

Der Reichsorganisationsleiter hat unter dem 8. August 1935 nachstehende Anordnung erlassen:

Im Einvernehmen mit dem Stellvertreter des Führers wird folgendes bekanntgegeben.

Betrifft: Anzug der Werkscharen in der DAF.

Der Anzug der Werkscharen wird wie folgt getragen:

Bluse: Dunkelblau Zwirn-Moleskin oder Tuch, Blusenschnitt offen und geschlossen zu tragen. Zwei aufgesetzte Faltentaschen mit Patte, Knopf und Knopfloch. Sechs mattsilbergehämmerte Koppelhaken, mattsilberne Knöpfe. Hakenkreuzarmbinde am linken Oberarm (kurz über dem Ellenbogen).

Hose: Dunkelblaues Tuch, Stiefelhose, zwei schräge Beuteltaschen mit Patte, Knopf und Knopfloch.

Stiefel: Schwarze Marschstiefel oder schwarze Motorradstiefel oder schwarze Stiefel mit schwarzen Ledergamaschen.

Koppel: Schwarzes Lederkoppel mit Arbeitsfrontschloß.

Hemd: Hellblaues Hemd mit hellblauem Kragen und schwarzem Binder.

Sämtliche Anzugsteile sind durch die Reichszeugmeisterei und deren zugelassene Verkaufsstellen zu beziehen.

gez.: Dr. R. Ley.

Ich gebe vorstehende Anordnung zur Kenntnis. Sämtliche Anfragen über Uniform der Werkscharen finden hiermit ihre Erledigung.

In vorstehender Anordnung nicht aufgeführte Bekleidungsstücke bzw. Abzeichen dürfen nicht getragen werden.

gez.: Gohdes,
Hauptamtsleiter.

The August 24, 1935 order (32/35) by Gohdes. Note that the words "Mütze" or "Schiffchen" are not included at this time. The first Werkschar uniforms were worn without any form of headdress.

A few months later a headdress was designed. It was first mentioned in November 1935 and its form was tentative.[91] Manufacturing procedures were announced, but a final agreement had to be awaited. It was not earlier than February 1936 that a cap was officially introduced by order 3/36, signed by Schneider from the Department Werkscharen.[92] The RZM had already published the manufacturing procedures with the date January 18, 1936.

This headdress, a field cap (Schiffchen), resembled the SS–field cap, but was dark–blue in color as was the uniform for this group. The insigne worn was

[91] *"Mbl.d.RZM," Nr. 30, November 23, 1935, p. 316.*

[92] *"Amtl.Nbl.d.DAF," Nr. 4, February 1, 1936, p. 32.*

W.P.B.R. Saris

An illustration from the July 29, 1937 issue of *Rundschau-Deutsches Schneiderfachblatt,* a tailor's magazine. It shows a Hauptwerkscharführer from a firm. The field cap still carries the cogwheel emblem. The national emblem had just been introduced.

Mütze für die Werkscharen der Deutschen Arbeitsfront

Für die Werkscharen wird eine Mütze festgelegt. Die Vorschriften werden nach endgültiger Genehmigung bekanntgegeben.

W.P.B.R. Saris

The first announcement indicating that a Werkschar headdress would soon be introduced.

Anordnung 3/36

Kopfbedeckung der Werkscharen

Die Mütze für die Werkscharen der Deutschen Arbeitsfront erhält genau die Form und Ausführung der SS-Feldmütze, in Farbe des dunkelblauen Tuches für den Werkscharanzug. Am oberen Teil der Mützenstirnseite wird das DAF-Abzeichen angebracht.

Die Mütze wird nur als Schutz bei schlechtem Wetter getragen.

gez.: H. Schneider.

W.P.B.R. Saris

The February 1936 order announcing the introduction of a field cap in the style worn by the SS. The intended insigne was a cogwheel and not the national emblem. The last paragraph indicates that it should only be worn in bad weather.

Otto Spronk

Werkschar members writing home during the Party days at Nürnberg, 1936. It is almost certain that they are from the Hochland region because of the Edelweiss being worn of the left side of the field cap, a practice which was never sanctioned within the DAF. Also note the cuff title. The first word could either be "Nürnberg" or "Starnberg" (a small town in the München area), and the second word is "Werkschar," flanked by a cogwheel at right. If the first word is "Nürnberg" it is a cuff title manufactured specifically for the Party days since that is when the Werkschar first appeared. Regulations do not mention the wearing of any cuff title by Werkschar units.

Otto Spronk

A Werkscharmann with his flag during one of the Party days at Nürnberg in 1936. Note that the field cap, introduced seven months earlier, is worn with its first style insigne...the cogwheel.

the DAF cogwheel on the upper front. It was especially noted that in 1936 this headdress was meant for wear during bad weather conditions only. Later, orders regarding when the cap could be worn were modified to allow other uses.

Description: Model 1936

The material the cap was made of was a very dark–blue, nearly black, DJ cloth (as used for the blouse, but SA or HJ navy cloth was used as well). This cap was egg–shaped, tapering to the back. Its length was approximately 26cm (with a size 56). The side panels sloped gently. The front of the cap was approxi-

W.P.B.R. Saris

An example of the RZM stamp as positioned in white on rolls of cloth designated as "DJ-Blusenstoff," the material from which the Werkscharen field caps were made.

Zum 1. Mai: Die Arbeitsfrontmütze

Aufnahmen (5): Danke

Zum dritten Male kann am 1. Mai 1936 der „Nationale Feiertag des deutschen Volkes" festlich begangen werden. Der Befehl des Führers zu Beginn der Arbeitsschlacht am 21. März 1934 an die gesamte schaffende Nation:

„Deutsche Arbeiter, fanget an!"

hat tausendfältige Frucht gebracht.

Von 100 arbeitslosen Bekleidungsarbeitern am 30. Januar 1933 stehen heute schon 60 wieder schaffensfroh am Werk. Für 300 000 Heimarbeiter in der Bekleidungsindustrie ist, abgesehen von einigen kleineren Gruppen, für die die Regelung folgt, der bezahlte Urlaub eine in Tarifordnungen gesetzlich verankerte Tatsache geworden. 123 000 RM. von Fabrikanten falsch berechneter Heimarbeiter-Entgelte mußten allein in Berlin an Heimarbeiter nachgezahlt werden. Was sonst noch zu diesem Thema zu sagen ist, bringen die vordersten Seiten dieser Ausgabe in Zeichnung und Bild klar und eindringlich zum Verständnis des Lesers.

Die Bilanz, die wir ziehen, zeigt uns eine umfassende Neuordnung aller sozialen, wirtschaftlichen und kulturellen Dinge nicht nur im Bekleidungsgewerbe, sondern auf allen Lebensgebieten der Nation, und die Ablösung einseitig gerichteter kapitalistischer Gedankengänge durch völlig neue, die wahrhaft nationalsozialistischen Geist atmen.

Kann es bei der Fülle dieser Erfolge in so kurzer Zeit verwunderlich erscheinen, daß das deutsche Volk den Dank für die unerhörten Leistungen des Nationalsozialismus in gewaltigen Massenaufmärschen bekunden und abstatten will?

Der Weg zur Kameradschaft den die unermüdliche Arbeit der Partei und der Deutschen Arbeitsfront weist, hat all diese Erfolge leichter und schneller wachsen lassen. Und so wie die Kameradschaft der Armee, der S.A., der S.S. und der Partei einen Ausdruck in gleicher, schlichter und einheitlicher Kleidung äußerlich sucht, so legt auch der selbstbewußte deutsche Arbeitsmensch die Schieber- und Proletenmütze weg und greift zur Mütze der Deutschen Arbeitsfront. Damit legt er endgültig die ihm im verflossenen System künstlich eingeimpften Minderwertigkeitsgefühle ab und gibt nach außen hin mit dieser kleidsamen, sauberen Kopfbedeckung Kunde vom Wiedererstarken und Wachsen einer inneren Haltung, wie sie nur den deutschen Arbeiter auszeichnen kann. Immer hat die Deutsche Arbeitsfront in ihren Aufrufen die Mitglieder aufgefordert, diese innere Geschlossenheit auch äußerlich durch das Tragen der Arbeitsfrontmütze zu zeigen. So ließ der Gau Schlesien folgenden Anschlag in den Betrieben anbringen:

„Am 1. Mai jährt sich wieder der Tag, wo das schaffende deutsche Volk in einer geschlossenen Einheit unter dem Banner des neuen Deutschland marschiert. Auch in diesem Jahre werden Betriebsführer und Gefolgschaftsmänner in einem einzigartigen Aufmarsch aller schaffenden Deutschen ihre Treue zu Adolf Hitler bekunden. Es ist gut, wenn die Einheitlichkeit des Willens auch äußerlich zum Ausdruck kommt. Eine Maßnahme ist wirtschaftlich durchaus durchführbar:

Die einheitliche Kopfbedeckung.

An sämtliche Männer ergeht der Ruf zur Anschaffung der „Arbeitsfrontmütze". Die Betriebsführer werden gebeten, ihrer Gefolgschaft bei der Anschaffung der Arbeitsfrontmützen behilflich zu sein."

Wo etwas verkauft wird, finden sich auch schnell die Juden ein. Im vergangenen Jahr versuchten verschiedene Hersteller und Vertriebsfirmen, die von der Reichszeugmeisterei nicht zugelassen waren, minderwertige „Jakobsware" statt der vorschriftsmäßigen D.A.F.-Mütze an den Mann zu bringen. Jedes Gefolgschaftsmitglied sollte deshalb beim Kauf auf die Kontrollzeichen achten. Das

„Gesetz gegen heimtückische Angriffe auf Staat und Partei und zum Schutz der Parteiuniformen"

vom 20. Dezember 1934 gibt die Möglichkeit, alle unbefugten, gewissenlosen Elemente schnell dem Richter vorzuführen, falls sie versuchen sollten, ein D.A.F.-Mitglied durch Anbieten oder Verkauf von unvorschriftsmäßiger Schundware zu betrügen. Der Paragraph 5 des Gesetzes lautet:

„(1) Wer parteiamtliche Uniformen, Uniformteile, Gewebe, Fahnen oder Abzeichen der N.S.D.A.P., ihrer Gliederungen oder der ihr angeschlossenen Verbände ohne Erlaubnis des Reichsschatzmeisters der N.S.D.A.P. gewerbsmäßig herstellt, vorrätig hält, feilhält, oder sonst in Verkehr bringt, wird mit Gefängnis bis zu zwei Jahren bestraft. Für welche Uniformteile und Gewebe es der Erlaubnis bedarf, bestimmt der Reichsschatzmeister der N.S.D.A.P. im Einvernehmen mit dem Reichswirtschaftsminister durch eine im Reichsgesetzblatt zu veröffentlichende Bekanntmachung."

In der Bekanntmachung vom 16. Januar 1935 gemäß Artikel 1 § 5 des Gesetzes sind die Mützen der Deutschen Arbeitsfront, und in der dritten Verordnung vom 16. März 1935 zur Durchführung des Gesetzes sind das Hoheitsabzeichen und die Abzeichen der Deutschen Arbeitsfront als durch dieses Gesetz geschützt angeführt.

Die Reichszeugmeisterei teilte nun folgende Anordnung, die den Verkauf der Arbeitsfrontmütze betrifft, mit:

„An der vorschriftsmäßigen D.A.F.-Mütze ist außer den durch Reichsgesetz vom 20. Dezember 1934 geschützten beiden Abzeichen das Mützenband als Flächenmuster gerichtlich deponiert.

Die vorschriftsmäßige D.A.F.-Mütze ist also kenntlich durch das gesetzlich geschützte Eichenlaubband und durch das eingeprägte D.A.F.-Abzeichen auf dem Deckelfutter unter einem Zelluloidspiegel.

Unvorschriftsmäßige blaue Mützen, die als D.A.F.-Mützen, Festmützen oder mit irgendeinem irreführenden Namen bezeichnet werden, verfallen der Einziehung, und der Hersteller hat Strafverfolgung zu gewärtigen.

Die Ausgabe der D.A.F.-Mützenabzeichen darf nur gegen Vorlage einer vorschriftsmäßigen Mütze und eines besonderen Ausweises der zuständigen Dienststelle erfolgen. Falls Ersatz eines defekten Mützenabzeichens verlangt wird, ist das defekte Mützenabzeichen der Verkaufsstelle vorzulegen.

Von der Verkaufsstelle ist bei Abgabe eines neuen Abzeichens der besondere Dienststellenausweis oder das alte bzw. defekte Abzeichen einzuziehen. Alle Verkaufsstellen machen wir darauf aufmerksam, daß wir die Durchführung dieser Bekanntmachung durch unsere Kontrollbeamten besonders überwachen lassen.

Vielfach haben billige „Ramschjuden" versucht, aus irgendwelchen minderwertigen, blauen Schirmmützen durch Anbringen des Arbeitsfrontabzeichens „vorschriftsmäßige" D.A.F.-Mützen zu machen. Damit keiner der Käufer aus den Gefolgschaften der Betriebe wegen Unkenntnis der Vorschriften Schaden erleidet und außerdem für teures Geld eine schlechte Mütze ersteht, zeigen die Bilder dieser Seite die wichtigsten Merkmale der nach den Vorschriften hergestellten D.A.F.-Mützen:

An der Stirnseite der Mütze befindet sich das D.A.F.-Abzeichen. Das Zahnrad der Deutschen Arbeitsfront ist fest in den Mützenboden eingestempelt und wird durch ein durchsichtiges Zellophanschild geschützt. Unter dem Schweißleder ist ein Lizenzetikett der Reichszeugmeisterei München eingenäht, aus dem die Zulassungsnummer der Herstellerfirma und die Qualitätsbezeichnung hervorgehen.

Bei der Arbeitsfrontmütze für D.A.F.-Walter und -Warte wird das silberne Hoheitsabzeichen in der Mitte des oberen Mützenteils getragen. Außer dem Hoheitsabzeichen dürfen andere Abzeichen und Kokarden auch am unteren Mützenteil nicht angebracht werden. Außerdem wird diese Arbeitsfrontmütze von den D.A.F.-Waltern und -Warten (ebenso auch zur N.S.B.O.-Uniform) ohne Ausnahme mit Lackledernriemen getragen.

Die Werkscharmütze der D.A.F. entspricht in Ausführung und Form der S.S.-Feldmütze. Sie wird jedoch im blauen Tuch der Uniform hergestellt. Das D.A.F.-Abzeichen wird dabei am oberen Teil der Mützenstirnseite angebracht. Die Werkscharmütze ist nur in dem engeren Kreis von Geschäften erhältlich, die die braune Lizenz der Reichszeugmeisterei haben. Die D.A.F.-Mütze wird in allen Hutgeschäften angeboten, die die D.A.F.-Lizenz besitzen. K. D.

1. Das D.A.F.-Mützenabzeichen darf nur gegen Vorlage eines Ausweises abgegeben werden.
2. Das Abzeichen der D.A.F. ist in den Mützenboden eingestempelt.
3. Das Cellophanschild ist zum Schutz darübergenäht.
4. Das Lizenzetikett der Reichszeugmeisterei (RZM), München, ist unter dem Schweißleder eingenäht.

5. Das Hoheitszeichen aus Silber, in Flügelspannweite 49 mm, Höhe 33 mm, wird nur von zugelassenen Verkaufsstellen der RZM, München, abgegeben.

6. Das Mützenband ist als Flächenmuster gerichtlich deponiert und als Eichenlaubband gesetzlich geschützt.

7. Der Lackledergürtel ist ausnahmslos von allen D.A.F.-Waltern und Warten an der D.A.F. Mütze zu tragen

Die Werkscharmütze trägt an der oberen Stirnseite das D.A.F.-Abzeichen.

Die Werkscharmütze trägt auf dem Mützenboden das Lizenzetikett der Reichszeugmeisterei

W.P.B.R. Saris

Page 40 taken from the DAF periodical *Die Bekleidungsarbeit,* dated March 18, 1936. For the headgear industry in Germany a special addendum was provided (Ausgabe C - Kopfbekleidung der Fachgruppe Kopfbekleidungsindustrie). This page illustrates the various forms of headdress to be worn during the May 1, 1936 festivities for the "National Feiertag des deutschen Volkes" (May Day), as well as information on RZM laws and insignia positioning.

mately 9.5cm high, being approximately 8cm in the middle, and approximately 7cm at the back seam.

The non–functional flap (sharp edged in the front) was sewn to the body 0.3cm from the lower edge. It measured approximately 4.5cm in front, and vaulted to 7.5cm (over an 8cm distance). It vaulted again slightly to the rear to approximately 5.5cm. The lining was grey or blue–grey material (dark blue was used also), and was sewn to the top and lower edge seams. An RZM tag was positioned on the inside of the bottom at the front of the cap.

On the front center of the front of the top, the cogwheel insigne was positioned. The flaps were secured by two white, matte pebbled buttons, 12mm in diameter. They were the type used to secure the cap cords on the visored cap of political leaders. These buttons were sewn to the flap approximately 15mm from the upper and lower flap margins.[93] It must be noted that *no* piping was worn yet.

Richard Kindel

Werkschar members of the BSW firm wear the cogwheel emblem and two silvered buttons on unpiped field caps. The event, on October 27, 1936, was during an address by Fritz Sauckel to the firm's workers.

Richard Kindel

Werkschar members of the BSW firm during a speech by Robert Ley on July 3, 1937. They are wearing both the scalloped and Luftwaffe-style unpiped field caps with the cogwheel insigne. Production of the new version field caps started in the fall of 1936, with official introduction to take place in June 1937. It is obvious from this photo that the new regulations for piped field caps to be worn were not carried out at this time, as four weeks since their announcement was too short a time for implementation.

With the early 1937 Werkschar reorganization new field caps were badly needed, due to the new rank system. In April 1937 Ley and Mehnert, the Leader of the Department Organization agreed this "new uniform" for the Labor Troops. The field cap for the most part resembled the earlier type. Instead of the cog-wheel insigne the national emblem was utilized.[94] Leaders of the labor troops (Werkscharführer) had to wear silver piping around the different shaped edge of the flap, as well as the crown and silvered buttons when silver insigne was worn; a golden crown and flap piping and golden buttons were worn when golden insigne was worn. This meant:

Reich (Zentralbüro): (Reich Central Office)	piping:
Reichsorganisationsleiter der NSDAP und Leiter der DAF; Reichswerkscharführer: (Reich Organization Leader of the NSDAP; Supreme Leader of the DAF; Reich Labor Troop Leader. All functions are in Ley's possession)	gold;
Oberstwerkscharführer: (Chief Labor Troop leader)	silver;
Gauwaltung:	
Gauobman (Gauwerkscharstammführer); (Province Foreman/Province Labor Troop Tribe Leader)	gold;
Gauwerkscharführer (Oberwerkscharführer): (Province Labor Troop Leader/Chief Labor Troop Leader)	silver;
Kreiswaltung:	
Kreisobmann (Kreiswerkscharstammführer): (District Foreman/District Labor Troop Tribe Leader)	gold;
Kreiswerkscharführer (Werkscharbannführer):	silver;
Ortswaltung:	
Ortsobmann (Ortswerkscharstammführer): (Local Foreman/Local Labor Troop Tribe Leader)	gold;
Ortswerkscharführer:	silver;
Betrieb:	
Betriebsobman (Betriebswerkscharstammführer): (Company or Factory–level Foreman/Company or Factory Labor Troop Tribe Leader)	gold;

93 *"Mbl.d.RZM," Nr. 2, January 18, 1936, p. 14.*

94 *"Amtl.Nbl.d.DAF," Nr. 6, April 21, 1937, pp. 63–66.*

Hauptwerkscharführer: silver;
(Squad Labor Troop Leader)

Werkscharführer: silver;

Werkscharmeister: no piping;
(Foreman)

Truppführer: no piping;
(Group Leader)

Rottenführer: no piping;
(Leader for a smaller group) [95]

In the April order above, no colored piping identifying Reich–, Gau–, Kreis– or Orts– level were introduced. These were introduced not earlier than mid–June 1937.

Deutsche Lufthansa

Reichswerkscharführer Dr. Robert Ley at the Munich airport in February 1937. He is shown welcoming Cianetti, the president of the Italian Laborers League. Ley is holding the piped field cap at this time. Officially, the piping was introduced with April 1937 orders and Ley obviously was given his cap in advance.

During the summer of 1937, Ley granted the use of a service dress for Labor Troops also to be worn by factory managers, who were not members of the NSDAP nor DAF, but who had shown merit in the care of Ley's subordinate laborers.[96]

The manufacturing procedures for the modified 1937 field cap were already published in the fall of 1936, and were far ahead for its final introduction in April 1937. Production was not allowed before the new procedures were pub-

---

[95] *"Mbl.d.RZM," Nr. 12, June 5, 1937, pp. 149–150; Ibid, Nr. 13, June 19, 1937, p. 173. "Rundschau–Deutsches Schneiderfachblatt"(RDS), Nr. 46, November 13, 1937, p. 1631.*

[96] *"Uniformen–Markt," Nr. 15, August 1, 1937, p. 233.*

lished by the RZM.[97] In June, 1937 Ley's order for the new uniform and insigne was announced officially in the Mitteilungsblatt der RZM.[98]

Mitteilungsblatt der Reichszeugmeisterei

der Nationalsozialistischen Deutschen Arbeiterpartei

Herausgeber: Reichszeugmeister Richard Büchner; verantwortlich I. A.: Josef Müller. Druck: Münchner Buchgewerbehaus M. Müller & Sohn KG., sämtliche in München. Bezug nur durch die Reichspost. Unmittelbare Bestellungen bei der RZM. können nicht angenommen werden. Erscheint 14tägig. Preis vierteljährl. RM. 1.—. Nachdruck, auch auszugsweise, verboten.

Ausgabe 13 | München, 19. Juni 1937 | Jahrgang 4

Inhalt: Nachtrag zur Anordnung 8/37 über die Dienstbekleidung der Werkscharen der DAF.

Reichsorganisationsleiter

Hauptorganisationsamt

Nachtrag

zur Anordnung 8/37 über die **Dienstbekleidung der Werkscharen der DAF.**

Mütze. Werkscharform mit silberfarbigem Hoheitszeichen.

a) **Werkscharführer** mit silberfarbigem Dienststellenabzeichen tragen:

Silberfarbige Biese um den oberen und mittleren Mützenrand.
Silberfarbige Knöpfe an der Stirnseite der Werkscharmütze.

Werkscharführer mit goldfarbigem Dienststellenabzeichen tragen:

Goldfarbige Biese um den oberen und mittleren Mützenrand.
Goldfarbige Knöpfe an der Stirnseite der Werkscharmütze.

Das Hoheitszeichen ist handgestickt.

b) **Werkscharmeister,** Truppführer und Rottenführer sowie sämtliche Werkscharmänner tragen:

Paspel um den oberen und mittleren Mützenrand in der Farbe des zuständigen Hoheitsgebietes:

Reich . . . . gelb
Gau . . . . hochrot
Kreis . . . . schwarz
Ortswaltung und Betrieb . . . . . . hellblau

Silberfarbige Knöpfe an der Stirnseite der Werkscharmütze.

Das Hoheitszeichen ist in gewebter Ausführung.

NB.! Sämtliche Uniformteile, Ausrüstungsgegenstände und Abzeichen für die Dienstbekleidung der Werkscharen der DAF. sind durch die Reichszeugmeisterei oder deren zugelassenen Einzelhandelsgeschäfte zu beziehen.

W.P.B.R. Saris

This June 1937 order by Dr. Ley refers to the field cap for the "Werkscharen der DAF" with a silver national emblem. Section *a* mentions the embroidered form for Werkschar leaders and a woven form for the ranks of Werkscharmeister, Trupp- und Rottenführer. Also, the specific pipings for crown and flap are described with silver or gold buttons. Section *b* gives the colors for the crown and flap pipings for lower ranks. With these the buttons were always silver.

---

97 *"Mbl.d.RZM," Nr. 8, April 10, 1937, p. 102.*

98 *Ibid, Nr. 12, June 5, 1937, pp. 149–150.*

Otto Spronk

Dr. Robert Ley is dressed in a Werkschar uniform. Note that the cap in his hand is piped in gold according to his rank of Reichswerkscharführer.

W.P.B.R. Saris

Die neuen Dienstgradabzeichen der Werkscharen

DAF 125 Zeichnung: Eckensberger

Die am rechten Ärmel getragenen silber-blauen Winkel bedeuten:

1. Werkscharführer, 2. Hauptwerkscharführer, 3. Werkschar-Bannführer, 4. Oberwerkscharführer, 5. Oberst-Werkscharführer.

An illustration from the *Schwert u. Spaten* magazine dated May 1937. The field cap carries the national emblem.

Description: Model 1937

The cap shape was now more oblong and tapered to the back, comparable to the shape of the Luftwaffe field cap. It was usually made from DJ blouse cloth in dark–blue wool, referred to as "Tirtey."

This cap was supported on the inside by a piece of dark–blue cloth, glued to a rubberized, wadded inlay. A 2cm wide piece of wadding was sewn into the top seam. A strong, rust–proof iron wire (1.5mm thick), whale bone, celluloid or small horn bar was sewn in for more support.

The sweat proof, dark–blue, blue–grey or black lining was sewn directly to the top and lower cap edge. The front of this cap was approximately 10cm high, 12cm in the middle at the highest point and 10cm at the back. The flap was not functional and measured in front/center approximately 5.5cm, 8.2cm in the middle and 8.2cm at the back. This flap was stiffened on the inside with a 2.5cm wide piece of oil–cloth. The sweatband was Havana–brown leather, 37mm wide and sewn between the margins of the cap.[99]

[99] *"RZM–HV," 1936, p. 18 and p. 233.*

The length for a size 56 cap was approximately 26cm, the width being 6.2cm at the most. Sizes with a width of 5.5cm were allowed starting in June 1937.[100] The two buttons remained on the cap as previously, but later they had to be sewn directly to the cloth *before* the parts of the cap and lining were sewn together, in accordance with SA manufacturing procedures. The buttons were silver in color for Werkscharführer or gilt, for use by persons with the rank insigne in gold. The woven or embroidered national emblem was positioned on the front center of the cap top.

The "Mitteilungsblatt der RZM" described a crown and upper flap edge piping in the colors as used for the "Hoheitsgebiet" (levels) with the manufacturing procedures of late 1936. This was literally said and means that the Reich–, Gau–, Kreis– or Orts– level colors for lower ranks were introduced in April 1937. However in Ley's April order the colors for the field cap apparently *were forgotten.* This mistake was corrected in June. Simultaneously the authorized persons were mentioned, being: Werkscharmeister, Truppführer, Rottenführer and Werkscharmänner;

light blue	(Ortswaltung & Betrieb – local or concern):
black	(Kreis – district):
bright red	(Gau – province):
golden–yellow	(Reich – national):[101]

Richard Kindel

A Werkscharführer wearing the model 1937 field cap with proper pipings and insigne.

100 *"Mbl.d.RZM," Nr. 15, July 17, 1937, p. 196.*

101 *"RZM–HV," 1936, p. 233; "Mbl.d.RZM," Nr. 13, June 13, 1937, p. 173.*

Werkschar field cap (model 1937) with gilt piping and buttons, plus a silver national emblem.

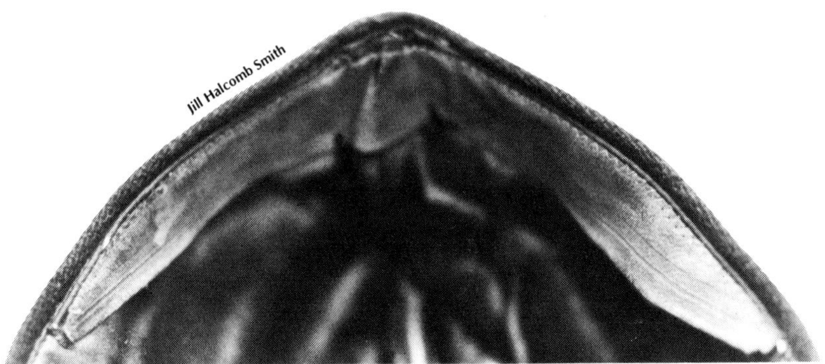

Interior of above cap showing the leather half sweatband.

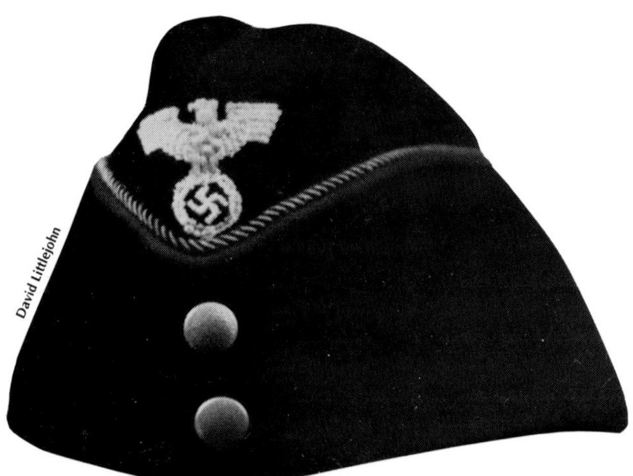

A field cap of the 1937 form with improper piping and national emblem. The combination red and silver piping was never authorized, and especially with just crown piping. The national emblem is also incorrect, as this version looks to its right. Werkschar field caps should have, officially, only a left-looking national emblem.

Two photographs of Werkschar members wearing the field cap according to the 1937 regulations, which carried crown and flap piping plus the two buttons at the front of the flap.

The 3mm wide, silk piping, filled on the inside with white cotton, was attached to a 4.5mm wide black lace and was sewn into the crown seam of the cap and around the leading edge of the flap. An RZM tag with brown lettering was sewn on the cap's left interior.[102]

For leaders the piping was 3mm gold or 3mm aluminum (instead of silvered material) from early summer 1937. This piping was a 1.3cm lace with an inlay of "Mulegarn" (gauze) in the same color as the cap cloth and rolled.[103] For a short period the vertical front, as well as the back seam for the top were piped also. This was discontinued probably sometime during late summer of 1937. Photographs show the caps worn during the war (simultaneously showing that the old forms were still also being worn).

It must be noted that although the specifications were authorized in late 1936, they were not fully implemented until April 1937, when the new pattern field cap was officially introduced. The piping colors yellow, bright red, black and light blue were in use for a very short time: June 1937 until March 1938 (approximately only nine months). The field cap was worn by low and high

---

102 *"Mbl.d.RZM," Nr. 13, June 19, 1937, p. 176.*

103 *Ibid, Nr. 15, July 17, 1937, p. 196; Ibid, Nr. 17, August 14, 1937, p. 214.*

Otto Spronk

This 1937 field cap has the piping around the crown and flap, the national emblem and the two buttons. This cap is the second form which does not have the scalloped flaps. Note the piping at the vertical front seam, just above the national emblem.

ranking personnel, and was issued in enormous quantities. It was a very comfortable form of headdress, and could be easily folded flat and stored.

1938 – 1939

Due to the new and enhanced capacity of the Werkschar, Ley announced in March 1938 plans for a new rank system. Some ranks were renamed while other ranks were abolished (Gauwerkscharführer, Oberstwerkscharführer and even Reichswerkscharführer). In fact the complete level system for "Reich", "Gau", "Kreis" and "Ort" disappeared and with this the use of colored piping for these levels. The level "Betrieb" remained, but here a gold or silver piping was ordered, according to rank or position.

The most striking change was the introduction of the golden national emblem.[104] Simultaneously an honorary rank (Ehrenwerkscharmann) was also introduced. In fact these were all the former "Werkscharführer" from Reich–, Gau– and Kreis– levels, who no longer fit into the new rank/position system.[105] Honorary ranks were also authorized the use of the golden national emblem (and

---

104 *"Amtl.Nbl.d.DAF," Nr. 3, March 28, 1938, pp. 50–51; "Mbl.d.RZM," Nr. 18, August 27,1938, pp. 169–170.*

105 *"Mbl.d.RZM," Nr. 18, August 27, 1938, p. 170.*

W.P.B.R. Saris

Rangabzeichen für die Werkschar

Der Reichsorganisationsleiter hat mit Anordnung 107/38 den Aufgabenbereich der Werkscharen neuerdings festgelegt. Gleichzeitig wurden die Dienstrangbezeichnungen geändert, die Rangabzeichen jedoch in der bisherigen Ausführung, mit wenig Ausnahmen, belassen. Wir verweisen dieserhalb auf die im heutigen Mitteilungsblatt erschienenen Preislisten-änderungen.

Die Bekleidungs- und Ausrüstungsstücke sowie die sonstigen Abzeichen der Werkscharmänner bleiben wie bisher bestehen.

Alle bisherigen Werkscharführer im Reich, Gau und Kreis wurden laut Anordnung 29/38 zum

Ehrenwerkscharmann

ernannt und tragen zusammen mit allen jenen, denen ehrenhalber die Werkscharuniform verliehen wurde, folgende Abzeichen:

Goldenes Hoheitszeichen an der Mütze, goldene DAF.-Abzeichen auf den Achselstücken, goldene Paspeln an Mütze und Achselstücken.

One of the first orders referring to the ranking insigne for honorary members of the Werkscharen. For them the color gold was ordered. In the last paragraph, the words, "gold piping" means the piping for the field cap with gold national emblem. Later, an allowance was received for the visored cap which never had pipings.

W.P.B.R. Saris

Werkschar members marching during a Kreis meeting on May 22, 1938. This photo shows the pipings on the crown and flap from behind. At right stand officials from the political party at Kreis-level, the HJ, DJ and Luftwaffe.

piping). Active DAF members were granted permission to wear the Werkschar uniform.

The piping system was finally developed and changed as follows:

Betriebsobmann (Werkscharführer):	gold
Werkscharmeister:	silver (instead of light blue)
Betriebszellenobmann:	gold
Truppführer:	silver (instead of light blue)
Betriebsblockobmann: (the Hauptwerkscharführer)	gold (instead of silver)
Rottenführer:	silver (instead of light blue)
Werkscharmänner:	silver (instead of light blue)[106]

106 *"Organisationsbuch der NSDAP." München: 1938, p. 231.*

P. Coleman

Werkschar members from an aviation department and Lufthansa pilots during a visit of Ley and Cianetti. In this early war photo both forms of field cap are worn. The Model 1936 is without piping in the rows of men behind Ley. Only the three Werkschar leaders at front are wearing the Model 1937 cap. Note the wear of an unknown pattern cuff title. At far left is the leader of an office on Kreis-level (Bereichsleiter und Leiter eines Amtes).

Otto Spronk

A group of Werkschar members lined up for the May 1, 1939 festivities. Shortly thereafter the Werkscharen were reorganized. Note the NSBO flag which was the traditional flag for Werkschar units.

Above: Field caps with the national emblem and two metal buttons on the flap front are worn. Note the vaulting of the flap on some of the caps. These are the first form of cap with piping added later. The man in the left foreground wears the second form of cap with slightly vaulted panels (Luftwaffe-style). The photo is dated December 31, 1939.

A Werkschar field cap with gold pipings, buttons and national emblem.

A Werkschar fife and drum corps. The members wear the field cap introduced in June 1937 piped in the appropriate color. The photo is dated April 20, 1939.

Visored Cap (Werkscharmütze)

In October 1938 manufacturing procedures for a Werkschar visored cap were published. The DAF wreath was introduced. Wear was authorized for all Werkschar members (including "Ehrenwerkscharmann") outside the concern and was in fact meant as a walking–out dress (Ausgehmütze). The order simultaneously said that the field cap had to be worn during all activities within the concern and in close formation.[107] The publication contained a color chart for the national emblem, the wreath and the chin strap or cords, according to ranking system.

Uniform Facings, Fall 1938:	Eagle Emblem:	DAF–Wreath	Chin Strap	Cords
Stosstrupp: (Shock Troop)				
Werkscharmann up to and incl. Rottenführer:	silver metal	silver metal	black leather	
Werkscharführer in the ranks Werkscharmeister and below:	silver embroidery	silver embroidery		aluminum
Werktrupp: (Labor troop)				
Werkscharmann up to and incl. Rottenführer:	matte golden metal	matte golden metal	black lacquered leather	
Werkscharführer as Betriebsobmann, Betriebszellenobmann, Betriebsblockobmann, Walter und Warte der DAF:	matte golden embroidery	matte golden embroidery		gold
Ehrenwerkscharmann: (Honorary Labor Trooper)	matte golden embroidery	matte golden embroidery		gold

Description Visored Cap:

The style of this cap was known as "Form 4" (Wehrmachtschnitt): the same form also worn by political leaders. The oval cap top was of navy–blue DAF wool.[108] It had four underpanels for the top and measured approximately 7.5cm

107 *"Mbl.d.RZM," Nr. 21, October 8, 1938, pp. 211–212.*

108 *Ibid.*

W.P.B.R. Saris

Trage-Vorschrift

Die Werkscharschirmmütze wird zusätzlich zum Werkschardienstanzug eingeführt.

Die Schirmmütze kann von den Angehörigen der Werkschar nur außerhalb des Dienstbetriebes getragen werden. Im Dienst und in geschlossenen Abteilungen wird einheitlich die Schiffchenmütze getragen.

a) **Für Werkscharmänner bis einschl. Rottenführer, die dem Stoßtrupp angehören,** mit silberfarbigem Metall-Hoheitsabzeichen, silberfarbigem Metall-**DAF.**-Abzeichen mit Eichenlaubkranz und Lackledderriemen.

b) **Für Werkscharmänner bis einschl. Rottenführer, die dem Werktrupp angehören,** mit mattgoldfarbigem Metall-Hoheitsabzeichen, mattgoldfarbigem Metall-**DAF.**-Abzeichen mit Eichenlaubkranz und Lackkunstlederriemen.

c) **Für Werkscharführer vom Werkscharmeister ab, die dem Stoßtrupp angehören,** mit **gesticktem** silberfarbigem Hoheitsabzeichen, gesticktem silberfarbigem **DAF.**-Abzeichen mit Eichenlaubkranz und Alu-Kordel.

d) **Für Werkscharführer, die dem Werktrupp angehören** (Betriebsobmann, Betriebszellenobmann, Betriebsblockobmann, Walter und Warte der **DAF.**), mit gesticktem mattgoldfarbigem Hoheitsabzeichen, gesticktem mattgoldfarbigem **DAF.**-Abzeichen mit Eichenlaubkranz und Goldkordel.

e) **Für Ehrenwerkscharmänner** mit gesticktem mattgoldfarbigem Hoheitsabzeichen, gesticktem mattgoldfarbigem **DAF.**-Abzeichen mit Eichenlaubkranz und Goldkordel.

This October 1938 publication introduces the visored cap and related insignia. The field cap was still ordered during regular service. With *a*), a silver metal insigne and lacquered leather chin strap were ordered for "Stosstrupp" enlisted ranks; with *b*), a matte gold insigne and lacquered artificial leather chin strap were ordered for "Werktrupp" enlisted ranks; with *c*), a silver embroidered insigne and cords were ordered for "Stosstrupp" leaders; with *d*), a matte gold embroidered insigne and cords were ordered for "Werktrupp" leaders; and with *e*), honorary members who are referred to as "Ehrenwerkschar" should be as *d*).

Josef Charita

A Werkschar leader wearing the model 1938 visored cap with cords.

in front, 4.4cm on both sides, and 5.5cm at the back (with a size 56). The length of the top was approximately 27cm and the width was 24cm.

The crown was piped in dark blue material, the same material as used for the top. A small, thin wire was installed within the piping and a loose, rustproof iron wire (1.5 x 0.6mm) retained the shape of the top. The dark–blue cap band (reinforced by a 0.6 – 0.8mm thick, black lacquered piece of cardboard) was approximately 5.2cm high. This included the 2mm upper and lower cap band piping (dark–blue wool) and the lower 3mm edge.

Between the top and bottom cap band piping was the 40mm oakleaf pattern band (DAF Mützenband of shiny silk, according to RZM specifications). The seam of this cap band was always in the center of the back of the cap. The good quality lining was medium–blue cotton–satin for lower ranks and golden yellow artificial silk for higher ranks. It was sewn to the inside of the body with thick, white, thread. Gauze and a 13mm wide piece of felt were sewn in between thc lining and the dark blue material as a stiffener.

Model 1938 visored cap worn by a Werkscharführer of a Werktrupp (gold hand-embroidered insignia and gold cap cords), as well as honorary ranked persons.

To support the inside of the top, a stout linen stiffener (4cm wide at the top, 2cm at the bottom) and a small piece of metal were fastened in the front. Inside, the peak of the front was further supported with wadding and white gauze. The rear of the cap top was stiffened with a 2.5cm piece of wadding.

A celluloid sweat shield, 13.5 x 15.5cm, was sewn into the top lining. Its shape was like those found in other caps, being round at the end and forming a point at the other. A portion of the shield was sewn in a manner to form a 2cm slot to hold a piece of paper with the owner's name. No factory markings were permitted to be stamped or printed on the shield.

A 4.5cm wide Havana–brown sheepskin sweatband was sewn into the cap. The ends of the band were fastened at the rear of the cap with an "X" stitch. The size of the sweatband varied. Those made of artificial leather and marked with the "RZ" designation were forbidden in November 1938.[109] A gummed pad was

[109] *Ibid, Nr. 23, November 5, 1938, p. 229.*

Dr. Ley wears the style visored cap but with a variant cap wreath.

glued to the inner side of the sweatband, and was perforated in four rows. The RZM tag was positioned beneath the band on the viewer's left side, with its lettering facing the inside of the cap.

The black, rimmed fiber visor was Havana–brown on the underside. Leather visors were not officially allowed.[110] A black, lacquered leather chin strap was worn above this, secured by two 14mm black lacquered buttons for lower ranks, (buttons with pin backs were permitted for the lower ranks) or 12mm nickel plated or gilded brass pebbled buttons for higher ranked officials. Buttons with pin backs were not permitted to be used for the higher ranks.

The silver (in most occasions aluminum) or gold cap cords were either 31cm long for cap sizes 53 through 55, 32cm long for cap sizes 56 through 58, or 33cm long for cap sizes 59 or larger. The insigne consisted of a national emblem and a DAF–pattern oakleaf wreath with the cogwheel emblem. This wreath was positioned 13mm above the lower cap band piping. The wreath and swastika of the national emblem was positioned 15mm above the upper cap band piping. The embroidered form had to be carefully sewn by hand to the cap

---

110 *"Uniformen–Markt," Nr. 24, December 15, 1938, p. 378.*

A. Stam

Dr. Ley visiting Mönchengladbach on February 4, 1939. At right are Werkschar members wearing the visored cap and the field cap.

band and/or cap top. Sometimes the wreath was embroidered directly upon the cap band.

It must be noted that this visored cap was *never* piped around the crown and cap band edges with aluminum (or silver), gold or any other colored piping.

The intention to supply all members with this form of headdress failed, due to the war. In fact, it was never worn in great quantities and the supplies in stock were hardly used. This indicates why most of these caps in collections are in mint condition. It was even believed that none of the caps were ever supplied with the leather chin strap, indicating that the introduction for lower ranks had also not been implemented. This assertion is pure nonsense and probably caused by a decree from Ley in March 1939 which noted that the visored cap (Schirm-

Josef Charita

A Werkschar Musikzug. The "Musikzugführer" is the only person wearing a visored cap.

mütze für Werkscharen) was suspended. This was only by name as from now on this cap was known as the DAF–Schirmmütze (not to be confused with the one with the oval insigne).[111] The wearing of the regular field caps was continued, (consult also the section 1939–1945).

P. Coleman

A portrait of a young Werkschar member wearing the Model 1938 visored cap with proper insignia. Note the matte leather chin strap indicating that he is a member of a Stosstrupp.

Oak Leaf Wreath (DAF Mützenkranz)

The DAF pattern oakleaf wreath was officially introduced in October 1938, having an approximate length of 116mm and was approximately 39mm high. This insigne was manufactured of either Cupal or light weight metals, and existed in aluminum (white or silvered) or gilt finish. The wreath consisted of four oakleaves on each side, with a small band decoration in the middle of the two lowest leaves. The edge of the leaves, as well as the leaf veins, were slightly upraised. The inner field of the leaves was pebbled.

Gilt metal national emblem and wreath for wear by Werkscharmänner through Rottenführer serving in a Werktrupp.

111 *"Mbl.d.RZM," Nr. 13, July 1, 1939, p. 181.*

The swastika/cogwheel and oakleaf part were for the most part manufactured in one piece. It must be noted however that the swastika/cogwheel insigne existed in various sizes, some which touched the lowest edge of the highest leaves of the wreath. The embroidered versions had a black or very dark–blue cloth backing (this wreath form varies from the political leaders pattern).

National emblem and wreath hand-embroidered in silver wire for wear by Werkscharführer serving in a Stosstrupp.

Model 1938 visored cap with silver metal insignia (instead of embroidered) and silver cap cords. Officially, with metal insignia, a leather chin strap should be worn.

As above, but with a leather visor. This cap was probably used during a transition period, as leather visors were not permitted.

Otto Spronk

This Betriebsobmann from a "Stosstrupp im Betrieb" is wearing his visored cap with embroidered wreath, cog wheel and national emblem.

1939 – 1945

With the May 1939 reorganizations, the time was ripe for the "final Werkschar–uniform." The order noted that the old form of uniforms had to be worn out. It was not required to purchase new uniforms due to the expected changes.[112] Regulations regarding the new "form" Werkscharen were published in the "Amtliches Nachrichtenblatt der DAF." The forms of headdress remained for a transitional period. One must note that the planned system of rank was intricate. In photographs it is seen that this system was hardly worn in later years. The old forms generally remained in use. The July 1939 ordered headdress was:

DAF–Walter (Party member) and Werkschar–members with a political leaders rank (not owning a NSDAP political leaders uniform): DAF or Werkschar visored cap with national emblem, cords, oakleaf wreath with cockade, identical to the 1939 political leaders insigne in gold. *No* piping. If the above mentioned persons possessed a political leaders uniform they were from this time on authorized to wear this uniform, even when they were leading the Labor Troops.[113]

W.P.B.R. Saris

Werkschar members collecting donations during the 6th national street collection of 1940 in Berlin. Note the individuals playing Churchill and Chamberlain.

112 *"Amtl.Nbl.d.DAF," Nr. 2, May 31, 1939, p. 23.*

113 *Ibid, Nr. 3, July 25, 1939, p. 41; "Vbl.d.RL.d.NSDAP," Nr. 196, mid–July, 1939. Section VIII: Nr. 6.*

P. Coleman

Werkschar members from unit 228, the "Köningsmühle" papermill at Merseburg near Leipzig. All are wearing the final form, Luftwaffe-style field cap with proper insigne and pipings. Note the difference in color of the arm chevrons worn by the two persons standing behind the drums, and also the leather equipment for the drummers with drum-hook (front row at left).

Josef Charita

This Werkschar-Spielmannszug, wearing field caps, is ready for departure. Note the wearing of swallow's nests, and that the leader of the band wears fringe on his. Note also the trumpet banners with the DAF cogwheel.

W.P.B.R. Saris

A Werkschar group during the war with their political leader officials. The political leader in the right foreground is a "Leiter einer Hilfsstelle/Blockobmann." At his left is a Briebsobmann from the firm. Many of the individuals in this photo are elderly and their tunics are without shoulder

Bundesarchiv

The presentation of DAF flags in 1942. The DAF functionary (political leader) is wearing the final form of insignia.

straps. Some are obviously honorary members as their national emblems appear to be darker, i.e., the gold version. For example: In the second row the man at far left and the second man from right.

The war and the resulting economy stopped Ley's plans. Even the use of the regular form headdress with political leaders facings as planned was certainly not widespread among DAF leaders or officials. In November 1939 it was planned to sell the existing stocks from lower and higher ranks Werkschar field caps for civilian purposes.[114] These plans were never implemented as the existing stocks were handed over to the Amt für Arbeitseinsatz (a department for relief workers) during the mid–war period. Between 1939 and mid–1943, the word "Werkschar" was seldom used in official announcements or documents.

In July 1943 Ley ordered the creation of an aid–force to be utilized in the most threatened areas during air raids, known as "Werkschareinsatz, Rhein und Ruhr." Members from this force were ordered, when in service, to wear the regular blue Werkschar–uniform with the piped field cap.[115] Due to successes, achieved by the group "Rhein und Ruhr," more of these special forces were created in other areas from September 1943.

114 *"Mbl.d.RZM," Nr. 21, November 4, 1939, p. 258.*

115 *DAF–decree 27/43. Berlin: dated July 19, 1943 and signed by Reichsleiter Ley.*

W.P.B.R. Saris

Anordnung 25/39

Einbau der Werkschar in die Ortsgruppen der NSDAP.

In Ausführung meiner Anordnung 19/39 — Amtliches Nachrichtenblatt 1939, Seite 23 — erlasse ich nachstehende Durchführungsbestimmungen:

1. Die in den Betrieben tätigen DAF.-Walter sind als Parteigenossen Politische Leiter der NSDAP.

   Sie tragen (einschließlich der Werkschar, Rottenführer usw.) Spiegel mit Hoheitszeichen und dem Dienstrang der ersten Stufe, der ihnen auf Grund der Anordnung infolge ihrer Dienststellung als Politischer Leiter zusteht.

2. Die Angehörigen der Werkschar sind, sofern sie nicht gleichzeitig eine DAF.-Dienststellung einnehmen, als Parteigenossen Politische-Leiter-Anwärter.

3. Die Mitglieder der Werkschar, die Nichtparteigenossen sind, erhalten dieselben Spiegel wie zu 2. ohne Hoheitszeichen.
   Nachdem die Mitgliedssperre der NSDAP. aufgehoben ist, haben Werkscharangehörige und DAF.-Walter, die noch nicht Parteigenossen sind, die Möglichkeit, ihre Aufnahme in die NSDAP. zu beantragen.
   Sie melden sich dieserhalb bei ihrer Wohnortsgruppe.

4. Die bisherige blaue Uniform ist aufzutragen. Die Winkelabzeichen werden bei der blauen Uniform bis zur Verleihung eines Politischen-Leiter-Dienstranges beibehalten. Zur blauen Uniform sind ab sofort die neuen Rangabzeichen der NSDAP. mit Hoheitszeichen für Parteigenossen und ohne Hoheitszeichen für Partei-Anwärter zu tragen.

5. Sofern dem einzelnen DAF.-Walter bzw. Werkscharführer und -unterführer Dienstrang als Politischer Leiter verliehen wird und er die blaue Uniform aufträgt, wird der Politische-Leiter-Dienstrang mit Spiegeln und Armbinden ebenfalls zur blauen Uniform getragen.

6. Sofern der einzelne DAF.-Walter und Werkscharangehörige Politischen-Leiter-Dienstrang besitzt und er die blaue Uniform aufträgt, hat er zu dieser die blaue Schildmütze zu tragen. Auf dieser sind Hoheitszeichen, Mützenkordel, Eichenlaub und Kokarde analog der Politischen-Leiter-Dienstmütze anzubringen.

7. Sofern die DAF.-Walter bzw. Werkscharführer bereits Uniform als Politische Leiter haben bzw. sich erst eine Uniform anschaffen müssen und sich demzufolge nicht mehr eine blaue, sondern sofort die Politische-Leiter-Uniform beschaffen, können sie als Politische Leiter die Werkschar, auch wenn diese noch in blauer Uniform gekleidet ist, führen.

A portion of the July 1939 order relating to the reorganization. Of interest is the explanation of what type of collar patches are to be worn. Also of note is number 6 which discusses the Werkschar visored cap, but now to be worn with the national emblem, cords, wreath and cockade as worn by political leaders.

Stadtarchiv Mönchengladbach

A. Stam

Werkschar members from the "Werkschareinsatz Rhein und Ruhr," plus civilians and political leaders repairing a road. The Werkschar men are wearing their regular uniforms.

Drivers (Kraftfahrwesen der DAF)

This section existed for some years before it was reorganized in February 1937 as the "Werkschar Kraftfahrwesen der DAF." On every Gau– level a drivers Labor Troop existed, including mechanics. In this period Schneider, the leader of the Department Werkscharen ordered the regular Werkschar uniform and headdress, that being the field cap.[116]

From July 1, 1937 this section cooperated with the NSKK. In July 1939, Ley's adjutant, Marrenbach acted under orders from Ley when he announced that all drivers were ordered to wear the uniform when in official service, and civilian clothing was no longer allowed. If the driver was not an NSDAP member, or a member of one of the sub–organizations (so in fact not allowed to wear a uniform) he was ordered to join for example the SA, NSKK or SS. After joining, he was allowed to wear the regular Werkschar uniform.[117]

Department Armed Forces (Werkscharen Abt.Wehrmacht)

It is known that the Deutsche Arbeitsfront was divided into the so–called "kleine" or "zweite" (second) Arbeitsfront. It was the task of the Department Armed Forces within the DAF (Abteilung Wehrmacht der DAF) to take care of concerns, working for the Armed Forces. (In the earliest years of the National Socialist regime its members were not allowed to belong to the NSDAP or any sub–organization while serving in the Armed Forces).[118]

◀ The funeral of dead DAF members at Viersen on December 31, 1939. Note the crown and flap pipings on the caps worn by DAF/Werkschar men. In the center is Gauleiter Florian and at far left is Kreisleiter Riem who is still wearing his old insignia.

116 *"Amtl.Nbl.d.DAF," Nr. 3, February 23, 1937, p. 39.*

117 *Ibid, Nr. 3, July 23, 1939, p. 47.*

118 *"Uniformen–Markt," Nr. 7, May 15, 1936, p. 105.*

Shortly after the institution of the Labor Troops in early 1935, offices and concerns attempted to persuade the highest DAF management to introduce for that particular branch a special DAF insigne, to be worn on the visored cap and other forms of headdress. Wild rumors were published approximately in 1936, especially in the tailoring industry magazines. No special emblem was ever permitted to be worn with a headdress.

On July 11, 1940 Ley and Keitel, the Chief of the Armed Forces High Command (Chef Oberkommando der Wehrmacht), agreed that the Highest Commander (Oberbefehlshaber) for the OKW, army, navy and air force were to be identified as "Betriebsführer" (acting manager) in relation to works, assigned to the DAF.[119] The Department Armed Forces was then led by Schulte. A system was published regarding DAF relations and the above mentioned Armed Forces and special rank/function identifications were given (for example Wehrkreisobmann, Obmann der Marinestation or Luftgauobmann). These names reflect the coupling to the (Werkschar) DAF. Persons holding leading positions in one of these sections wore the regular Werkschar–uniforms and rank insignia according to their duties.

Department Aviation (Werkscharen Abt. Luftfahrt)

The DAF, Abteilung Luftfahrt (in 1936 led by Walitschek and during the war by Braun) was in fact a sub–department of the Abt.Wehrmacht, and may be considered as a twin organization.[120] With the institution of the NSFK in 1937, the Labor Troops from the Department Aviation worked closely together with this new organization. In fact it was ordered that the Labor Troops were to join the NSFK.

W.P.B.R. Saris

This employee of an aviation company wears the dark blue visored cap with an eagle insigne. Often this form of insigne was worn with the work dress, and varied in patterns. They had no association with the authorized Werkschar insigne for the aviation department.

119 *"Amtl.Nbl.d.DAF," Nr. 4, August 15, 1940, pp. 29–30.*

120 *"Uniformen-Markt," Nr. 7, May 15, 1936, p. 105.*

An employee, probably from an aviation firm, wears a swastika within a winged wreath on his cap at the "Jagdausstellung" at Berlin in the fall of 1937. This unofficial badge was probably worn with the expectation that a special insigne would be soon authorized for aviation firms.

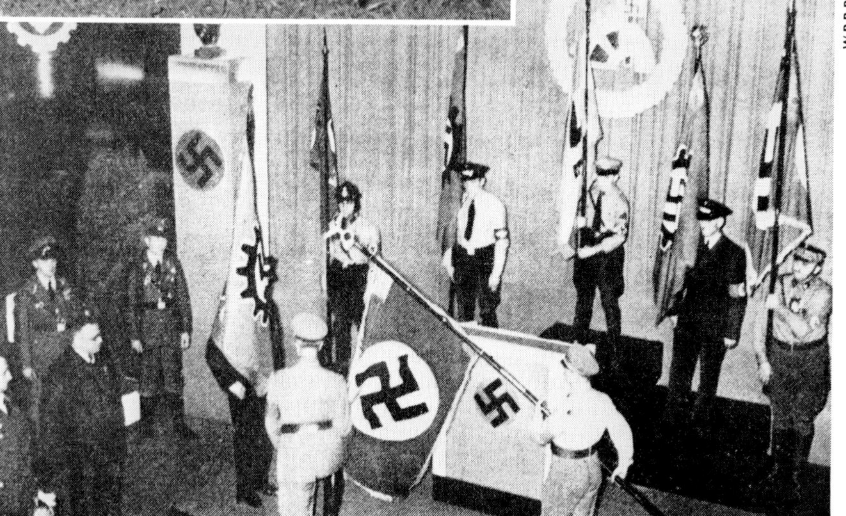

The deputy Gauleiter of Berlin, Görlitzer, during a consecration of flags on November 17, 1936. To Görlitzer's right is a Betriebszellenobmann of the DAF who was with the staff of the Reichsluftsportführer. In the background are two men holding the DAF and NSBO flags, and wearing the dark blue visored cap with a large insigne on the band (probably a wing as shown in volume 2, page 339). The person behind the podium also wears this same insigne on an armband.

An agreement as noted above between Ley and Keitel, (July 11, 1940) also existed between Ley and Göring regarding the Luftfahrt with the date April 20, 1940 and largely resembles what was noted above. It is interesting that Göring was ranked as a "Hauptbetriebsobmann."[121] Other ranks/functions were for example: Luftgaubetriebsobmann, Standortbetriebsobmann, Betriebsobmann.

---

[121] *"Amtl.Nbl.d.DAF," Nr. 3, July 1, 1940, pp. 18–20.*

In late 1935 members of aviation factories and concerns (Luftfahrtbetriebe, along with the Luftfahrt–Arbeitsgemeinschaft) unofficially started wearing a silvered insigne which consisted of a swastika flanked by small wings.[122] This insigne also was worn from 1936 by civil air force employees. Often regular factory insigne was worn.

Probably the influence of this department was stronger than the Department Armed Forces. In the spring of 1937, a special form of insigne was introduced only for wear with the DAF visored cap. It consisted of a DAF cogwheel with four stylized wing–parts on each side. Two propellers were probably placed behind the cogwheel. Exact details are not known, but it was a combination of the cap insigne as worn by air force fire brigade members and the insigne as worn by airport managers. It was expected that the above mentioned form would disappear soon and a new one would be authorized instead. It is known that manufacturers started producing all kinds of diverging emblems; in fact most of them being in an incorrect form.

The new form being described is smaller than that above and consisted of the DAF cogwheel with three wing–parts and probably no propellers. Further negotiations still took place and a final decision was delayed. It was literally said that manufacturing of the first form of insigne had to end immediately because of a large existing stock.[123]

In November 1937 the Reichsluftfahrtministerium authorized an insigne for wear by civil personnel of the Aviation Government Administration (Luftfahrtverwaltung) for use on the DAF visored cap. The insigne consisted of an oakleaf wreath (open at the upper part) with two wings, holding together a swastika. This emblem was manufactured by only one concern in aluminum or gold. The last exists for those having longer service.[124]

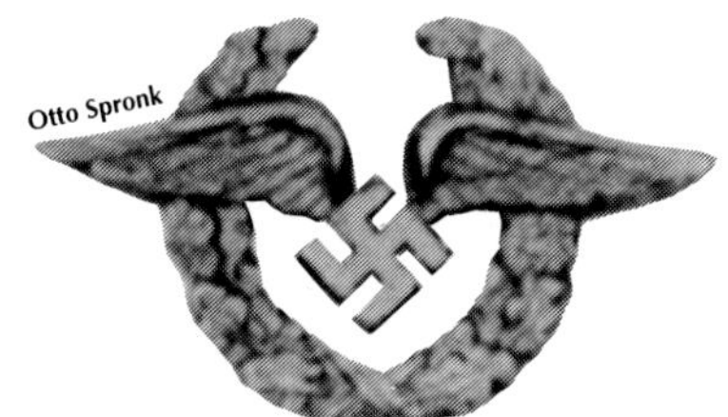

The metal insigne for Werkschar der Luftfahrt which was introduced in November 1937 and abolished for wear with headdress in January 1938. This photo is from the 1939 Friedrich Linden catalog. It is probable that this was the only firm authorized to produce this emblem.

The fall 1937 order was very short lived. In February 1938 it was published in the German press that all above mentioned insigne, whether being introduced or intended for authorization were abolished for wear with any form of head-

---

122 *Ibid, Nr. 12. December 1, 1935, p. 9.*

123 *Ibid, Nr. 9, May 1, 1937, pp. 130–131.*

124 *Ibid, Nr. 23, December 1, 1937, pp. 360–364.*

125 *Ibid, Nr. 5, March 1, 1938, p. 78.*

126 *Ibid, Nr. 24, December 15, 1937, p. 377.*

dress. From that point on, the regular DAF or Werkschar headdress forms with insigne were ordered.[125] In fact this order had already been issued in December 1937 when Labor Troop members (as well as the NSFK members) were ordered by Ley to wear the regular Werkschar uniform and headdress. The only difference was an NSFK arm badge. When not being in service within the company, the regular NSFK uniforms were worn.[126]

Prior to the completion of this research, no visored cap was found having the aforementioned insigne, even though it was described in various magazines. Therefore, such an insigne would be considered as rare.

Foreign Workers (Werkscharen der Ausländer)

Foreigners, employed in Germany before the war were joined together to form labor troops, but were never allowed to wear the regular form of headdress and certainly not the insigne of their German counterparts. Several offices were opened for these laborers.

The Dutch, for example, were assimilated under the "Reichsverbindungsstelle für Niederländer beim Amt für Arbeitseinsatz der Deutschen Arbeitsfront" (Reich Communication Institute for Dutch, the Office for Employment of the DAF).[127]

NS–Gemeinschaft "Kraft durch Freude" (KdF) (NS.Community "Strength through Joy")

On November 27, 1933 a system was instituted to coordinate the use of the spare time of (NS) laborers, to be known as the KdF. It was supervised by the DAF[128] and a cooperative from March 1935. This organization was created to mold all German laborers to NS standards and ideals. For this purpose about six special departments were formed, taking care of workers during illness and hardship, starting an education program through the "Werkscharen" (as these Labor Troops existed at first within the KdF), travel, hiking, sports, concerts, theater (the first theater opened January 18, 1934 in Berlin and was known as the "Theater des Volkes" or Peoples' Theater), sea baths and health spas.[129] In the early years this program was funded from the treasuries of the disbanded trade unions.

The KdF cooperated closely with other organizations to implement all of the above, for example the "Reichsbund für Leibesübungen" (an umbrella sports–organization), "Reichsbund der deutschen Schwerhörigen (Alliance for the Hard of Hearing), "Reichsnährstand" (Reich or National Peasantry), "Reichsautobahnen" (especially taking care of shelter for the laborers constructing the highways) and "Wehrmachtheime" (homes for soldiers).

Well known is the German car "Volkswagen" (People's Car), designated by Hitler in May 1938 as the "Kraft–durch–Freude–Wagen." Another very important phenomenon was the transportation as holiday makers of thousands of laborers by ships (KdF–Schiffe) between March 1935 and approximately June 1939. These voyages to Madeira, the Mediterranean, North Africa (Tripoli) and

---

[127] *Documentatie. Bijzondere Gerechtshof t.b.v. bijzondere rechtspleging. Amsterdam 1946/47, p. 71.*

[128] *"Daten der Geschichte der NSDAP" by Volz. 11.Auflage. Berlin/Leipzig: 1943. Section VI. p. 59.*

[129] *"Das Gesicht der Partei," 1940, p. 40; "Organisationsbuch der NSDAP," issues 1936–1940, pp. 209–211.*

other sunny destinations, are very well known. In May 1939 five of these ships transported the members of the "Legion Condor" from Spain to Hamburg. During the war several ships served as hospital ships.[130] At the war's end these ships evacuated Germans living in "threatened" areas around the Baltic, back to Germany.

Approximately twelve ships served the KdF, some being (DAF–KdF) property, for example the "Wilhelm Gustloff" and "Robert Ley." Other ships were also owned by the KdF, but managed by other companies. For Example, "Der Deutsche" or "Sierra Cordoba," earlier owned by the NDL (Norddeutscher Lloyd) and then sold to the DAF/KdF but still managed by the NDL. Other ships were chartered from merchant navy companies (for example, "Oceana," "St. Louis," "Monte Olivia" and "Monte Sarmiento").

Otto Spronk

Hitler is shown wearing the visored cap authorized for wardens of the DAF and KdF. The photograph was taken during his cruise on the North Sea.

For all sections functions as warders (KdF–Warte) or chiefs (Referenten) existed. Most of them being political leaders and authorized for a lower ranked political leaders uniform. We will not go into the most extravagant designations they had, but some we will mention:

A "Gaureferent," (for example, he was responsible for decent uniforms and dress); "Gausportreferent" (supervising the Gausportwart and the utilization of sports and games in coordination with the so–called "Betriebssport-

[130] *Volz, "Daten der Geschichte der NSDAP," 11.Auflage. Berlin/Leipzig: 1943. Section VI. pp. 66–87.*

gemeinschaften"); Wart für "Schönheit der Arbeit" (the warder who supervised the section "Beauty of Labor") or Wart für "Reisen, Wandern und Urlaub" (the warder who managed the section journey, hiking and holiday); "Feierabend-wart." (warder for spare time arrangements) or KdF–Wagenwart.

A "KdF–Wart" when holding a political rank was almost always a "Stellen-leiter"; a "KdF–Wagenwart", a "Hilfsstellenleiter."[131] This goes for practically all other functions and means that with a political leaders uniform the cords were always in silver. When not a political leader the warders always wore the dark–blue DAF (or earlier the NSBO) visored cap in the regular form with the various patterns of national eagle emblem. (For detailed information consult the section DAF officials, not being Party members or DAF Party members within this chapter).[132]

W.P.B.R. Saris

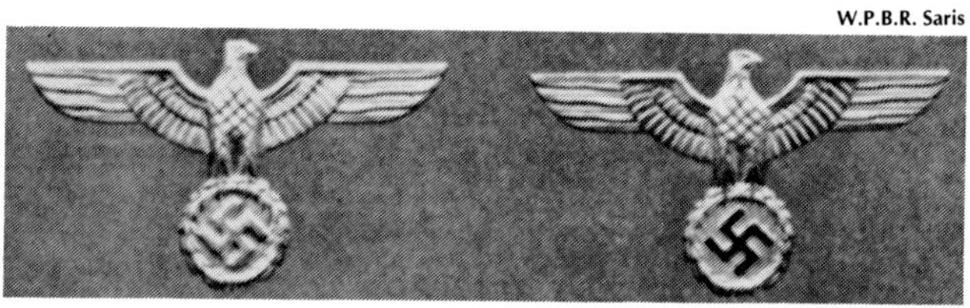

The style of eagles often worn with the KdF visored caps in 1936 and 1937 were the regular army types.

W.P.B.R. Saris

The eagle style worn from 1938.

Several period photographs show insigne variations worn on the DAF form visored cap. For example a KdF symbol embroidered directly to the front center of the cap. Above this the full title "Kraft durch Freude" is embroidered in a half

131 *"Amtl.Nbl.d.DAF." The years 1935 through 1939 gave much specific ranking information in relation to political leaders and do mention, also, all those different disignations for KdF.*

132 *"Kraft durch Freude." Jahresprogrammheft, Gau Koblenz–Trier: 1938, p. 3.*

circle in white or aluminum. In the center of the cap band the word Führungsdienst (guides for excursions etc.) was embroidered and above the visor aluminum cords were worn. This headdress was authorized from the summer of 1936.[133]

Navorsingsinstituut Brussel

A member of the "KdF-Führungsdienst" from Berlin wears a visored cap with cords and embroidered lettering on the cap band and top. He also wears a "Führungsdienst" cuff title on his left lower arm.

These professionally trained personnel accompanied the holiday–makers on their KdF journeys and were often assisted by regular KdF–Warders. (One must note that these journeys were in fact not meant for members of the SA, SS or one of the NSDAP organizations, if not also being a DAF member . Families of DAF members were also authorized travel).[134] It is believed that other rare forms may have existed due to the many different functions utilized. No indications whatsoever were given in official sources, nor are photographs found that show any. This assertion is based on behalf of the above mentioned "Führungsdienst." It would not be uncommon for the Germans to have also used names such as: KdF–Bühne (theater groups) or KdF–Ausbildungsdienst.

---

133 *"Uniformen–Markt," Nr. 12, August 1, 1936, p. 191.*

134 *"Kraft durch Freude." Jahresprogrammheft, Gau Koblenz–Trier: 1938, p. 48.*

This insigne is believed to have been worn by crew members of KdF ships. It is manufactured in light-weight metal.

Nurses of the DRK or the NS–Schwesternschaft etc. who accompanied the travels and cruses wore the regular authorized uniform or outfit.[135]

As stated in the introduction we will return to subjects if required. We intend to certainly cover the tallies worn by crew members of merchant navy ships and company insignia. As a preview we will show some of the tallies worn by crew members of the KdF ships (however, these were mainly used as souvenir items in those days and bought by holiday–makers).

A KdF-Wart wears the regular visored cap with the national emblem on the center of the top, during an excursion.

135 *"Uniformen–Markt," Nr. 11, June 1, 1939, p. 173.*

Marcus Bodeux

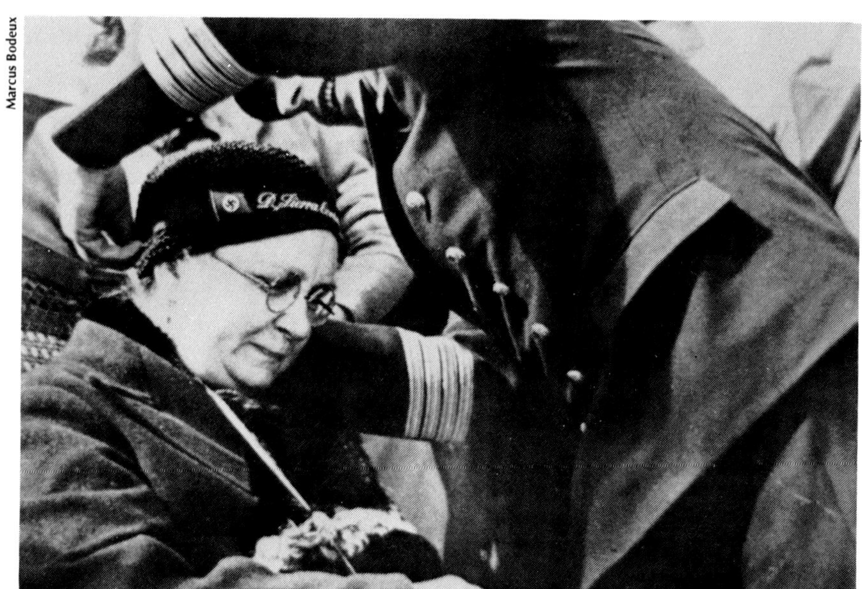

The captain of the KdF ship *Sierra Cordoba* authorizes an elderly lady aboard the ship to wear the "Erinnerungsband." Note this tally is of the white style discussed. It also has the abbreviation "D," and the left flag is flying to the right.

Marcus Bodeux

On March 23, 1938 the crew of the KdF ship *Wilhelm Gustloff* is gathered on the sundeck of the ship. On this occasion they were taking over the ship from its builder, Blohm & Voss from Hamburg. The crew wears various forms of insignia, as well as with and without the Party national emblem.

Otto Spronk

Kapitän Falkenbach, the commanding officer of the DAF/KdF-ship "Robert Ley," wears a higher-styled oakleaf wreath. In the center of this wreath is the HAPAG-concern flag.

Bodeux/Wedeking

The tally for *Der Deutsche.* The words are flanked by a swastika flag and the firm flag of the Nord-deutscher Lloyd from Bremen. Both flags are waving to the right. The words are in yellow; the "D" stands for "Dampfer," which means steamer. This ship was the first ship of the KdF-fleet. In May 1938, upon completing its 100th KdF trip since March 1935, it returned to Bremerhaven and was welcomed by congratulatory telegrams from Adolf Hitler and Robert Ley.

Clyde Davis

An "Erinnerungsband" (souvenir tally) for *Der Deutsche.* The yellow words are flanked by the words D.A.F. N.S. Gemeinschaft "Kraft durch Freude" in light grey and the DAF flag, which waves to the left, and the words Gau Düsseldorf in light grey and the KdF flag, which waves to the right.

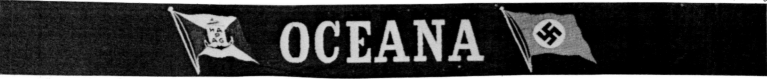

Bodeux/Wedeking

The tally for the *Oceana*. The word is flanked by a white/blue firm flag of the Hamburg-Amerika-Linie from Hamburg, and the swastika flag at right. Both flags are waving to the right. The *Oceana* was one of three ships which started in March 1935 with travels for the KdF.

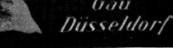

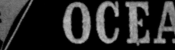

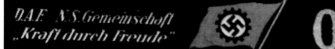

Bodeux/Wedeking

A "souvenir" tally for the *Oceana* in the same form as *Der Deutsche,* with DAF and KdF flags.

Bodeux/Wedeking

A tally for the *St. Louis.* The words are flanked by a swastika flag and the firm flag of the H.A.P.A.G. Both flags are waving to the right. The words are in yellow; the abbreviation M.-S. stands for "Motorschiff," which means motorship. The *St. Louis* was not a ship from the KdF-fleet, but was chartered since March 1935.

Bodeux/Wedeking

A regular merchant-navy form tally for the *Sierra Cordoba.* The Norddeutscher Lloyd firm flag, in white with light-blue symbol, is waving to the right. The lettering is in yellow. The capital letters are 11mm high, and the lower case letters 5mm high. A tally such as this was worn by the firm's crew members from 1923 through 1945. The same form tally was also used by the steamer *Berlin,* which was also chartered from the Norddeutscher Lloyd occasionally for KdF purposes. From the same firm the *Dresden* and the *Columbus,* a so-called Turbinen-Schnelldampfer, were also chartered. The *Berlin, Columbus,* and *Dresden* were, as far as can be researched, not chartered before 1939.

Richard Kindel

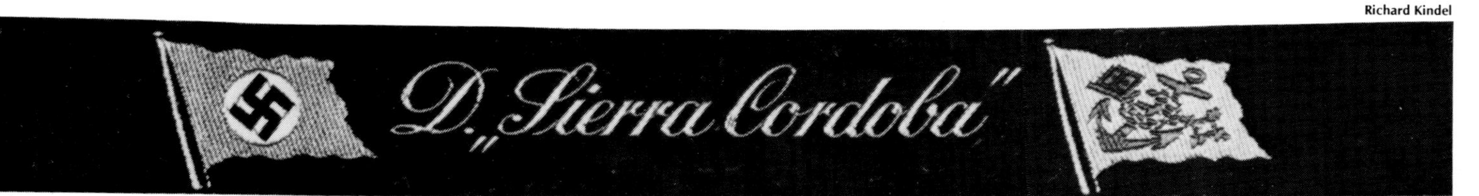

A variation tally for the *Sierra Cordoba* and the first form to be used when serving for the KdF. The words are flanked by a swastika flag and the Nord-deutscher Lloyd firm flag of Bremen. Both flags are waving to the right. The words are in yellow; the D stands for "Dampfer." The *Sierra Cordoba* was the third ship for the KdF fleet, and served since early 1936.

Bodeux/Wedeking

The same form tally, but in white for the *Sierra Cordoba.* The width of the tally is 32mm, the capital letters are 15mm high, and lower case letters are 7.5mm high, and the flag staffs are 30mm long.

Bodeux/Wedeking

Another variation tally for the *Sierra Cordoba* in black silk with the DAF flag and KdF flags, one waving to the left and one to the right. The sizes on this tally are: 32mm in width; the capital letters are 11mm high; the lower case letters are 6mm high; the flag staffs are 33mm long and the flags are 32mm high and 35mm long.

Bodeux/Wedeking

An "old form" *Monte Olivia* tally with two Hamburg-Südamerikanische Dampfschiffahrtsgesellschaft firm flags. Note the left one waves to the left and the right one waves to the right. Note also that the flag staffs are positioned differently from some of the other illustrated tallies (other tallies for the merchant-navy will be discussed in a later volume).

Bodeux/Wedeking

The *Monte Olivia* tally as used during cruises for the KdF. At left is the firm flag, waving to the right, and at right a swastika flag, waving also to the right. The lettering is 19mm high. Note that for the *Monte Olivia,* a form also exists as for the *Gau Düsseldorf.* It is not known if other tallies were manufactured with Gau-names for this or other ships. This ship was not a ship from the official KdF fleet, but since 1936 was always chartered from the HSDG firm.

Bodeux/Wedeking

A regular merchant-navy form of tally for the steamer *Stuttgart* from the Norddeutscher Lloyd firm (in the same form as for the *Sierra Cordoba*). Note the difference of the letters N and L on the *Sierra Cordoba* tally. Also, the sizes of the letters vary. The capital letters are 16mm high, the lower case letters are 9mm high. The *Stuttgart* was the fourth ship of the official KdF fleet and served since 1936. From early 1937 this fleet existed with four KdF ships. With the launching of the *Wilhelm Gustloff* on May 5, 1937 at the yard of Blohm & Voss at Hamburg, a ship parade was held. From the *Aviso Grille* Hitler watched the show of the six steamers who served for the KdF: *Der Deutsche, Oceana, Sierra Cordoba, Stuttgart, St. Louis,* and the *Monte Olivia.*

Bodeux/Wedeking

The cap tally for the *Wilhelm Gustloff,* the flagship of the KdF-fleet, in black with red/white edge stripes, each being 2mm. Note that both the swastika and the DAF flag wave to the right. The abbreviation M.S. stands for "Motorschiff." This ship was the fifth large ship from the German merchant-navy fleet. Its first trip was made in April 1938. During this trip its captain, Carl Lübbe, died of a heart-attack.

Clyde Davis

Same form tally, but in white with blue lettering. This tally's edging is black/white/red. It is interesting to note that a tally also exists with a black/white/red backing.

Richard Kindel

A variation tally for the *Wilhelm Gustloff.* With this form no colored edging is present. The lettering varies slightly from the tally with edging.

Bodeux/Wedeking

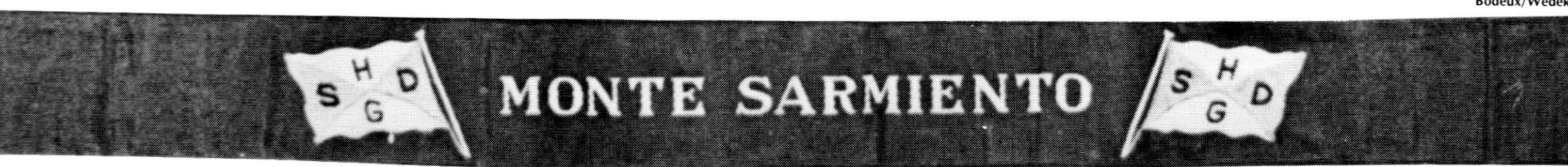

An "old form" *Monte Sarmiento* tally with two Hamburg-Südamerikanische Dampfschiffahrtsgesellschaft firm flags in the same style as for the *Monte Olivia.* Note the smaller lettering used, due to the larger word Sarmiento. It is known that a tally also exists with the firm flag at left and a swastika flag a right. This ship was not mentioned earlier than 1939 and was chartered.

Bodeux/Wedeking

The *Monte Sarmiento* tally, but with the DAF flag at left, waving to the left and the KdF flag at right, waving to the right.

Clyde Davis

A black tally for the *Robert Ley* with white/silver-grey lettering. This form does not have edging. The position of the flags is different from the *Wilhelm Gustloff,* and instead of the earlier used DAF flag, the KdF flag was used. The swastika flag at left is waving to the left and the white KdF flag at right is waving to the right. The abbreviation E.S. stands for Elecktro-Turbinenschiff, which means "electric turbine-ship." The launching of this ship took place on March 29, 1938 at the Howaldt-Werke yard at Hamburg. It became the new flag-ship of the KdF fleet. The first try-out trip took place one year later on March 24, 1939. In April 1939 it took off for its first cruise.

Clyde Davis

The same form tally, but with a white backing and silver-grey lettering. It is known that *Robert Ley* tallies also exist with blue and yellow lettering. It is possible that the one with blue lettering has the black/white/red edgings.

CHAPTER

7

Sturmabteilungen der NSDAP

STORM DETACHMENTS OF THE NSDAP

The official date of the SA's founding was August 3, 1921, and due to a government ban on paramilitary organizations, it was called a "Turn–und Sportabteilung," a gymnastic and sport detachment. It was also known as the "Schutz–und Propagandatruppe der NSDAP," a protection and propaganda unit. This early SA was led by a retired navy lieutenant, Hans Ulrich Klintzsch, until March 1923. He had been placed at Hitler's disposal by Ehrhardt of the free corps "Marinebrigade Ehrhardt" which had been created in 1919. Klintzsch had to organize the SA, but left this unit in May 1923.[1]

Throughout its existence, the SA was led by the following persons: Hermann Göring, Walter Buch, Franz Felix von Pfeffer von Salomon, Adolf Hitler, Adolf Wagener, Ernst Röhm, Viktor Lutze and finally by Wilhelm Schepmann.

On September 17, 1921 this "sports group" became known as the "Sturmabteilung" or storm detachment, a term officially sanctioned by Hitler after the meeting of November 4, 1921 at the Hofbräuhaus in Munich. Hitler bestowed this name in honor and admiration in recognition of their baptism in fire and also considered this title which had already been used as fitting well for his propaganda.[2] The further history in regards to the SA is well–known and is outlined in several references .

There initially was no standard dress during the early stage of the development of the SA, but soon, a form of dress was introduced and called by the German public, "Räuberzivil," or "highwaymen clothing." The first serious attempts regarding the creation of a distinctive headdress for the SA were made shortly after the "Battle of Coburg" in October 1922. The precursor of the later SA kepi was a grey ski cap (designed after the form worn in Austria), which was not universally worn in the SA.[3]

The first unit to wear the ski cap was the 11.Hundertschaft from Munich, commanded by Rudolf Hess. This headdress was worn during the first Party

[1] *Volz."Daten der Geschichte der NSDAP," 11.Auflage, Berlin/Leipzig: 1943, Section VIII: Die SA und SS und das NSKK (1921–1942), pp. 119–120.*

[2] *Ibid; also "Dokumente der Zeitgeschichte," München: 1936, p. 129.*

[3] *Ibid, p. 131.*

Otto Spronk

An extreme enlargement of a well-known photo of Hans Ulrich Klintzsch, the commander of the SA, photographed in 1922. This photo clearly shows the wear of the chinless death's head with the swastika insigne above on the black cap which was later adopted by the SS.

Otto Spronk

Members of the SA during a trip to Tölz on September 12, 1922 wearing the so-called "Räuberzivil." This photo clearly shows that there was no uniformity during the earliest days of the SA.

Day (Reichsparteitag), held at Munich from January 27 until 29, 1923.[4] Slowly but surely the grey ski cap became the official SA headdress, until it was replaced in 1924 by the well known brown kepi. This occurred during the reorganization of the SA and the re–establishment of the NSDAP, then called the "Frontbann," created by Röhm as a substitute for the forbidden NSDAP.[5]

Due to the intricacy of this organization, especially during the years 1931–1934, the reader is provided with a number of summaries of the color lists for SA Groups. The number of lists may seem somewhat exaggerated, but are necessary due to the constant changes of districts within the SA. At times a subject will be repeated due to its importance.

---

4 *"Das Dritte Reich." Die Kampfjahre 1918–1933, München: 1936, p. 252.*

5 *"Uniformen–Markt," Nr. 13, July 1, 1937, p. 199.*

Otto Spronk

The SA uniform in the style as worn at the end of 1922. The NSDAP badge is worn in the center of the top of this style of ski cap. The wear of badges of any form with an SA headdress was forbidden in November 1926.

During the late 1920's and early 1930's, various right winged groups were incorporated within the SA. Often these groups wore headdress look–a–likes of the SA cap. Members of the Rossbach group within the Frontbann with a Rossbach flag are wearing uniforms that are like the SA.

Otto Spronk

Otto Spronk

The SA, during a period when the uniform was prohibited, wearing white shirts. The man in the middle is wearing his regular SA style cap with the two buttons on the flap.

In addition, a difference is made between enlisted ranks and SA leaders. The piping or Tresse (tresse) lists are to be found in the section for SA leaders, and also for the lowest ranked leaders (Unterführer), to avoid misunderstanding. Note that the colors for the top are discussed in the section for SA leaders until 1933. Until 1933 the colored tops were solely worn by SA leaders. The schedules which describe the cap top color for enlisted ranks begins in July 1933.

During the periods that the government banned the wearing of uniforms by NSDAP formations (and other groups as well) the dark blue civilian visored cap without insignia was the highly favored headdress.[6] This "Zivilmütze" is described fully within the chapter, Deutsche Arbeitsfront, or in Volume 2, chapter 3: Air Organizations of Germany, pp.150–151.

Youth League (Jugendbund der NSDAP) :

On March 8, 1922 Hitler founded a youth section named the "Jugendbund der NSDAP," which was led by Adolf Lenk. During the second Party Day at Weimar in July 1926 the Hitlerjugend was officially founded by Hitler and he appointed Kurt Gruber as its first Reichsführer (National Leader).

About sixteen weeks later, on October 27, 1926 this Hitlerjugend (HJ) was subordinated to the SA and on April 27, 1931 placed totally under the SA High Command (Oberste SA–Führung).

---

[6] *Ibid, Nr. 11, June 1, 1940, p. 86.*

Otto Spronk

An early photograph of young Horst Wessel as a member of the "Jugendbund der NSDAP." Note the wearing of the early style headdress with the Party badge on the top.

From April 27, 1931 through May 31, 1932 the Hitler Youth was subordinated and placed under SA high command. The original caption for this photograph reads: "SA im Jahre 1932." It is obvious that HJ leaders wore their regular form headdress, on this occasion the light brown cap with cloth covered visor.

On May 13, 1932 Baldur von Schirach was appointed "Reichsführer der Hitlerjugend."[7] He then reorganized the HJ as an independent organization.

In spite of the HJ's early affiliation with the SA, its headdresses will be discussed in the Hitlerjugend chapter, in Volume 4 of this series.

National Emblem (Hoheitszeichen) 1931 – 1945

During the early years the only insigne worn on any SA headdress was a smooth, silver–white button (or at times even brown leather types). In November 1926, a new change ordered that some SA districts would instead be authorized to wear a golden colored button.[8] The Party badge or other forms of insignia were often worn, contrary to regulations.

The standard form NSDAP Party badge was often worn on the front center of the SA cap during the "period of struggle." In November 1926 its wear was forbidden.

Otto Spronk

Hermann Göring commander of the SA is wearing the NSDAP Party badge as a cap insigne on his cap in 1923, during a meeting of the "Arbeitsgemeinschaft der vaterländische Kampfverbände" (known as the "Kampfbund" from Bavaria). Note the wearing of a death's head in the background at left.

---

[7] *Volz."Daten der Geschichte der NSDAP," 11.Auflage, Berlin/Leipzig: 1943, pp. 133–135.*

[8] *Der Oberste SA–Führer. November 13, 1926. SABE (SA–Befehl = SA–Order) 13 Gauführung: Einteilung des Gausturmes, section 5.*

Confusion arose in February 1931 when Hitler ordered the wearing of the national eagle emblem on the tie by political leaders and members of the SA and SS.[9] Two weeks later, intending to show his power and influence, SA Stabschef (Chief of Staff) Ernst Röhm ordered that the NSDAP party badge was to be worn as a "cockade" above the cap button on the front center of the cap top.[10] Apparently Röhm had not understood Hitler's orders and chaos ensued for a short time.

Otto Spronk

SA bandmaster wearing his cap with the single smooth button and without a national emblem according to pre April 1931 orders.

W.P.B.R. Saris

The first pattern national emblem worn according to the April 1931 orders. The cap was manufactured of light brown twill, to be worn with the brown shirt.

Therefore, on April 9, 1931 during a meeting of SA group leaders, Hitler ordered that the NSDAP eagle would from that time on be allowed to be worn on the caps of all SA members.[11] This order was officially published April 20, 1931. It literally said: "The national emblem in the small form has to be worn with the civil dress; with the headdress the larger form (as authorized for the SS) has to be worn." So it must be carefully noted that the SA did not wear an eagle

---

[9] *Ibid. February 27, 1931, Erlass (further indicated as order) 3, signed by Adolf Hitler. Nr. 387/31.*

[10] *Ibid. München: March 12, 1931, Verordnung (further also indicated as order): Nr. II.b. Nr. 779/31.*

[11] *Ibid. München: April 22, 1931, Verfügung (further indicated as decree) I.a.Nr. 1679/31: Dienststellungsabzeichen; Verordnungsblatt der Obersten SA–Führung (further indicated as Vbl.d.OSAF), Nr. 1, München: April 20, 1931, Nr. 2: Hoheitsabzeichen, p. 4.*

earlier than early April 1931. This stylized, looking to its left, silver eagle (Model 1927) had a wingspan of 37–39mm. Its height is approximately 28mm. (consult also the chapter: Political leaders of the NSDAP).

24. Betrifft: **Hoheitsabzeichen.**

Das Hoheitsabzeichen in der bisherigen (kleinen) Ausführung ist lediglich als Abzeichen am bürgerlichen Anzug bestimmt; an der Mütze ist das große (wie bei SS eingeführt) anzubringen.

I a

München, den 20. April 1931.

W.P.B.R. Saris

The April 1931 order, as published in the *Vbl.d.OSAF*, introducing the early pattern eagle emblem which was then already worn for quite some years by the SS.

Otto Spronk

SA during a demonstration at Braunschweig in October 1931. The caps are without the colored top, as this was introduced not earlier than July 1933. Some SA members do not wear the national emblem, allowed since April 1931.

With an order issued in September 1934 by Hitler, a golden national emblem was authorized for wear by SA Stabschef Lutze.[12] Prior to this date Hitler was the only person allowed to wear the golden national emblem. Sometime in 1933 a manufacturer took matters into his own hands and started producing

6. Betrifft: Hoheitsabzeichen.

In SA-Anzugsordnung Teil I, Abschnitt IX, Ziffer a, Seite 47 ist unter „Stabschef" in Spalte 3 hinzuzufügen:

„Hoheitsabzeichen an der Dienstmütze in Gold".

Alle übrigen Angehörigen der SA tragen wie bisher das Hoheitsabzeichen an der Dienstmütze in Silber. F.

W.P.B.R. Saris

The September 1934 order authorizing the wear of a golden eagle emblem by the chief of staff Lutze, which was a supplement to the March 1934 authorized dress regulations of Röhm. All others had to wear the silver version of the national emblem.

[12] *Ibid, Nr. 33, September 10, 1934, p. 2. Nr. 6: Hoheitszeichen Stabschef.*

national emblems for the SA kepi in the golden form, probably thinking that with the golden button a golden eagle also had to be worn. A publication in the "Verordnungsblatt der OSAF" noted that SA members had been seen wearing this golden form. This was strictly forbidden.[13]

W.P.B.R. Saris

16.) Betrifft: Hoheitsabzeichen.

Eine Firma hat eigenmächtig das auf der Dienstmütze anzubringende Hoheitsabzeichen statt aus Silber in Gold hergestellt und verkauft. Angehörige von SA-Einheiten haben dieses vorschriftswidrige Abzeichen gekauft und getragen. Die Firma hat sich zu Unrecht als anerkannte Lieferfirma ausgegeben.

Ich mache erneut darauf aufmerksam, daß alle Änderungen oder Neueinführungen von Abzeichen, Bekleidung und Ausrüstung ausnahmslos von mir angeordnet werden. Eigenmächtighandelnde Lieferfirmen oder im Auftrage untergeordneter SA-Dienststellen arbeitende Erzeugerfirmen oder Verkäufer werden in Zukunft zur Verantwortung gezogen.

Angehörige der SA dürfen nur bei Firmen, denen ein Verkauf durch die Oberste SA-Führung genehmigt ist oder die von der Reichszeugmeisterei anerkannt sind, kaufen; dadurch schützen sie sich vor unnützen Ausgaben und strafbarem Tragen unvorschriftsmäßiger Bekleidungs- und Ausrüstungsstücke.

The message as published in the *Verordnungsblatt der OSAF*, dated December 1, 1933. The first paragraph gave manufacturing specifications regarding the golden eagle emblems and that these were not authorized to be sold to SA units.

Hans v. Diggelen

Rottenführer Alfred Spiller of signals brigade 29 from Berlin–Brandenburg, wearing the first pattern national emblem in spring 1937. Spiller had just received his "Nachrichtenschein der SA" with number 843. Note the fine detail of the eagle emblem, the nice shape of his cap and collar patch. He is wearing the pebbled button with this heavier fabric SA kepi.

[13] *Ibid, Nr. 16, December 1, 1933, p. 4. Nr. 16: Hoheitszeichen.*

Until approximately 1933 the only firm to manufacture the eagle for the cap was F.W. Assmann & Söhne of Lüdenscheid. Officially the Assmann samples had to be marked with the concern marking, an "A" and "ges.gesch." (protected by law).[14] In later years this eagle was produced by various manufactures, having three prongs and polished sides or two or three prongs without polished sides.[15]

W.P.B.R. Saris

The first pattern national emblem worn according to the April 1931 orders. The cap was manufactured of light brown twill, to be worn with the brown shirt.

Otto Spronk

SA Gruppenführer Heinrich Schoene shown wearing his SA cap piped around the crown and flap. On the top he is wearing the first pattern national emblem; upon the flap the smooth button as ordered for the twill or tricot cap. Schoene was appointed in 1934 to the rank of SA–Obergruppenführer and from 1943 was the inspector of the Marine–SA.

SA candidates (SA–Anwärter, not being a Party member) were not allowed to wear the national emblem for the first two months.[16] SA candidates, being a Party member on the contrary were authorized to wear the national emblem with no probationary period.

[14] *"Vbl.d.RL.d.NSDAP," Nr. 14, München: December 31, 1931, p. 35. (Announcement by Büchner from the Reichszeugmeisterei at Munich. He noted that other markings or national eagle emblems without any marking on the reverse were not allowed to be manufactured. But most often the early national emblems are devoid of any markings).*

[15] *SA price list late 1936, p. 7. (RZM article numbers 6307 (yellow), 6306a, 6286a and 6287 (white).*

[16] *"NSDAP, Aufbau und Abzeichen." Leipzig: 1933, p. 34.*

P. Coleman

A SA-Anwärter, not being a Party member, was not permitted to wear the national emblem for the first two months. A SA-Anwärter who was a Party member could, however, wear the national emblem with no probationary period.

P. Coleman

The early form of national emblem in wear.

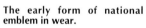

P. Coleman

This SA member from Jägerstandarte 19 "Merseburg" (SA-Group "Mitte") wears an emerald-green cap top instead of the official orange-yellow top, because a part of his district was located in the Saxony area.

Hans v. Diggelen

The 1937 pattern, SA national emblem is positioned on a grey-blue cap top (Sudetenland).

Otto Spronk

The final form of the SA national emblem in wear.

Otto Spronk

Members of the Sudetendeutsche SA in 1939 wearing the SA kepi with the colored top. Note that *NO* eagle is on the caps. This could indicate that all pictured were SA candidates, not being members of the NSDAP or they were just issued uniforms and the insignia was not yet available.

The eagle forms, as introduced for political leaders in 1934 (wingspan 49mm with the pointed, straight wings) and the Models 1936 and 1937 (wingspan 56mm; to its right and to its left looking), were hardly worn by the SA because preparations for a new national emblem for the entire SA were being made. It, however, took until mid–1937 before the new form was worn.

The earliest form SA national emblem, the standard Party eagle as allowed for wear beginning in April 1931.

The final form SA national emblem introduced in June 1937.

This eagle was introduced by Lutze on June 28, 1937 and was to be worn beginning July 1. The old form was officially allowed to be worn until December 12, 1938.[17] This new, to its left looking, national emblem was of silvered

W.P.B.R. Saris

176. Betrifft: Neues Hoheitsabzeichen für die SA.-Dienstmütze. F 2 b 13736.

Für die SA.-Dienstmütze wird ein neues Hoheitsabzeichen eingeführt. Dasselbe ist ab 1. 7. 1937 bei der Reichszeugmeisterei und deren Verkaufsstellen erhältlich und nur von diesen zu beziehen. Das alte Hoheitsabzeichen kann bis zum 31. 12. 1938 aufgetragen werden.

The order, as published in the *Vbl.d.OSAF* from June 1937, stating the introduction of the new form national emblem and the authorization to use the former insigne till December 12, 1938.

metal. being aluminum or light weight metals. Its wingspan was approximately 65mm; its height approximately 33mm. "Neusilber" was no longer allowed. (During the war, pot metal or zinc was also used).[18] Officially there were three pins on the reverse and the sides and highlights were polished.[19] (In the fall of 1938 versions with snap or press buttons were introduced).

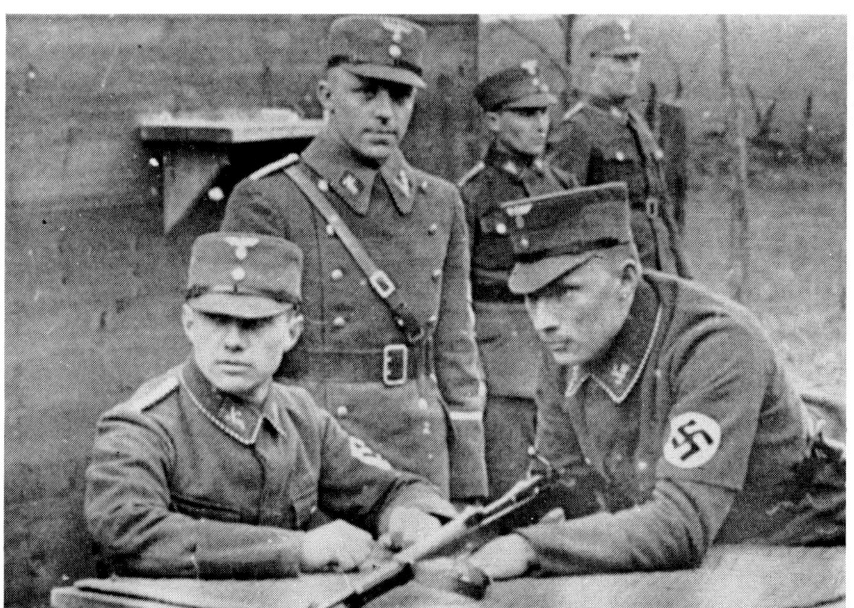

National Archives

Members of the Nordmark district wearing various forms of the national emblem with their emerald green cap tops. The person in the background at right is wearing the first pattern; the person sitting at left is wearing the 1936 form national emblem as introduced for political leaders. Note the black/white piping around the crown of the cap worn by the SA–Obersturmführer.

[17] *"Vbl.d.OSAF," Nr. 9, June 28, 1937, p. 64. Nr. 176: Neues Hoheitszeichen für die SA–Dienstmütze (F 2b 13736).*

[18] *F.W. Assmann & Söhne, Lüdenscheid. Katalog 1937/1938, pp. 27 and 27a (article Nr. 25321).*

[19] *"Mitteilungsblatt der Reichszeugmeisterei" (further indicated as Mbl.d.RZM), Nr. 15, München: July 17, 1937, p. 193: new entry Nr. 6285. Simultaneously the model 1927 form was abolished. In September SA members were asked to collect and return the old eagles for recycling.*

A. Stam

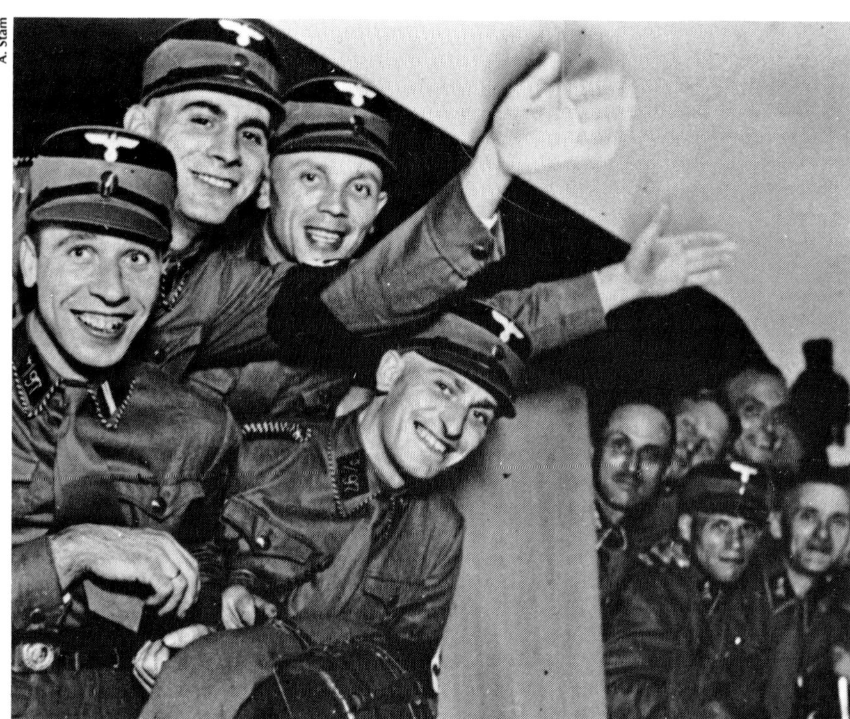

Members of the SA from Mönchengladbach on September 7, 1937, ready for departure to Nürnberg, to join in the annual Party Days. Note the wear of the final pattern national emblem. Standarte 97 shown, was located in the Niederrhein district and the color of the cap top should be black.

Clyde Davis

Members of the SA wearing two various eagle forms: the first pattern and the final form.

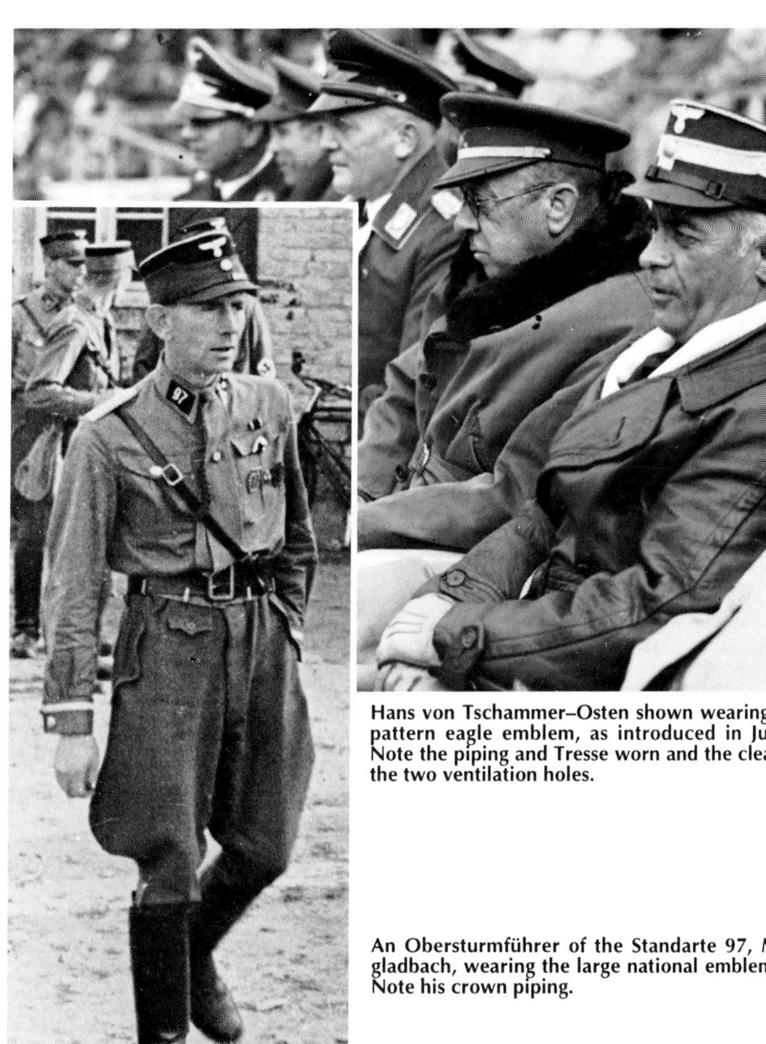

W.P.B.R. Saris

A. Stam

Hans von Tschammer–Osten shown wearing the final pattern eagle emblem, as introduced in June 1937. Note the piping and Tresse worn and the clear view of the two ventilation holes.

An Obersturmführer of the Standarte 97, Mönchen-gladbach, wearing the large national emblem in 1939. Note his crown piping.

In August 31, 1937 this Model 1937 eagle was also introduced for wear by Marine–SA units. It must be noted that no gold version was yet allowed to be worn, even by the Marine–SA.[20] The golden version was authorized on May 23, 1938 (in fact the later model national emblem as worn by political leaders was used starting in 1939).[21] The 1937 pattern continued to be worn until the end of the war.

The national emblems for Marine–SA, the garrison cap (Lagermütze) and other various forms will be discussed extensively in their related sections.

---

[20] *"Vbl.d.OSAF," Nr. 11, München: August 31, 1937, p. 83. Nr. 240: Hoheitszeichen für Marine–SA Dienstmütze.*

[21] *Ibid, Nr. 5, May 23, 1938, p. 41. Nr. 91: Abzeichen für Marine–SA–Dienstmützen.*

SA Enlisted Ranks (SA–Mannschaften) 1922 – 1924

Visored caps of an undetermined color (probably field–grey as used by the army) are pictured in the earliest photographs, bearing as their insigne a metal cockade on the center of the front top and a metal swastika, either canted or static, on the front center of the cap band. This form of swastika was also worn on civilian caps (see also this volume, chapter: NSDAP).

National Archives

Early photograph of the 4th Company of the SA regiment Munich. Note the wearing of various forms of headdress with swastika insigne or other forms of insignia.

During the fighting that erupted at Coburg in 1922 it was almost impossible to quickly distinguish between friend and foe. Because of this, a short visored, mountain ski cap was adopted for wear, being worn in varying shades of grey and patterned after the form worn in Austria. These caps were purchased in mass quantities and at low cost from unissued stocks found in Austria. This cap closely resembled the cap later worn by various branches of the Armed Forces, having a cloth visor with functional side panels and that sloped forward to the front center of the cap. The flaps were joined by two small horn or smooth

Early form "Hitlermütze," model 1923. Note the positioning of the two small buttons and the cockade on the top front.

An SA delegation wearing light colored caps in 1923 during the consecration of flags for the Bund Oberland, which was part of the 5 Komp. des Regiments "München."

metal buttons, the wearing of which was for the most part discontinued by 1929. An Imperial state cockade was often worn affixed to the cap front. Many units wore unofficial badges in front, as well as on the left side of the cap. The NSDAP Party insigne was often used in place of the cockade,[22] the use of which was officially forbidden in 1926.[23] Photographs show it still being worn into the late 1920's.

---

[22] *Eelking, Freiherr von. "Die Uniformen der Braunhemden." München: March 1, 1934, p. 2.*

[23] *Der Oberste SA–Führer. November 14, 1926. SA–Order: 10 Sturmf., signed by v.Pfeffer: Dienst–Anzug, section 2.*

A brown cap with a single button was developed from the form worn earlier and the civil sports skiing cap in the summer of 1924 and was mostly worn by members of the Frontbann at Munich.[24] This form of headdress soon became known as the "Hitlermütze." The design for this brown SA cap was kept very simple so that all members would be able to obtain a headdress for the uniform. This new cap, with a cloth covered visor, was formed in a more round, slightly oval shape according to new regulations. The official term for this cap was simply "Mütze" and less often the term "Kappe" was used. The last term was used by civilians who saw similarities in the cap with the French kepi.

National Archives

Members of the Frontbann wearing the early form cap without the leather chin strap and featuring the single button and cockade. The Frontbann was formed May 30, 1924 during a period of prohibition (from November 1923 to February 1925), it was nothing more than a substitute SA.

John Coy

An early form of soft styled cap with a gilt button and with the earliest form of national emblem. This style was a favorite of the SA as well as the NSDAP during the period of struggle. Note the non-regulation chin strap.

John Coy

Early SA members wearing the early mountain–style cap, 1924. Note that they also wear the double–breasted windbreaker, the first form of SA uniform.

It is often said that brown was Hitler's favorite color, as a pact with the German soil. A better explanation would be that this brown was purchased in the spring of 1924 by the SA–Wirtschaftsstelle (SA economic department) at a very low price from existing stocks used by boy scouts and other early youth related organizations supplies. The SA economic department and the Sportverband Schill[25] were the main suppliers in those days for SA goods. It is often thought that this "Sportverband" was the forerunner of the SA–Wirtschaftsstelle, but both in fact existed side–by–side. The economic department bought the brown cloth and ordered several cap manufactures to produce the SA caps.

The claim that this "brown" came from tropical stocks of Imperial Germany is most likely incorrect or possibly that with these stocks, shortages for the SA were completed to meet their needs. Probably an announcement regarding the new brown items has been misunderstood. In this announcement it was literally said: "the new shirt is in brown (so the "brownshirt") and designed in the style of the "Lettow–Hemd" (the officers quality shirt as worn by the Imperial Colonial Troops).[26]

1925 – 1933

On February 26, 1925 Hitler ordered the renewal of the SA as a Party organization. After February 1925, (in fact, its official creation date) the brown SA cap became the regular form of headdress since it had a better appearance when worn with the brownshirt. The expression "Braunhemden" ("Brown Shirts") was born when in Germany, the public began to become accustomed to the ever

24 *"Uniformen–Markt," Nr. 11, July 15, 1936, p. 163.*

25 *Ibid, Nr. 13, July 1, 1937, p. 200.*

26 *Richtlinien für die Neuorganisation der SA der NSDAP. May 24, 1924: Order in relation to the new uniforms.*

Otto Spronk

Members of the SA wearing dark visored caps during a meeting in 1925. At right is their commander Lutze, later the Stabschef. He is wearing the early pattern "Hitlermütze."

Otto Spronk

The SA of Vienna, Austria in late 1925 during a meeting held in the Weigls Dreherpark. Note the wearing of various forms of headdress. Second from left in the front row is Oberleutnant Hermann Reschny, who was the Oberführer of the Austrian SA.

present SA. This occurred in large numbers for the first time in 1926 at Weimar when 6,000 SA members marched before Hitler[27]

A modified form of cap was later introduced in 1929, having since been labeled by the collecting community as the "coffee can." Except for some minor modifications, this form would largely remain in use until the end of the war. There was no special indication for enlisted SA ranks other than the color of the cap button. In fact, all variations were authorized for higher ranking SA members only.

Jeff Hanson

Gautag Essen, 1926. Note the dark color visored caps in wear.

Otto Spronk

The SA in 1926 during the Reichsparteitag at Weimar: note the wearing of the so–called "Hitlermütze," as well as visored caps.

We should not deny the reader an amusing anecdote from 1929: In the SA order of July regarding the Reichsparteitag of August to be held at Nürnberg it was said that during the retreat of the "Festmarsch" (festivity march) from the Luitpoldplatz a pastry issuing point was placed every 75 meters. All participants of the march had to remove their caps and pastries were tossed into them. It then was immediately to be taken out of the cap and consumed or stowed in the

[27] *Volz."Daten der Geschichte der NSDAP," 11.Auflage, Berlin/Leipzig: 1943, p. 122.*

Otto Spronk

SA men from Pommern (Pomerania) wearing in 1927 the light brown SA–style caps with the two buttons on the flap. Several caps are without the chin strap and in fact these men are wearing their "old form" SA caps.

Otto Spronk

Otto Spronk

Members from the SA wearing the early style SA caps with two buttons. Note the person in the foreground at right: he is not wearing his flaps correctly, but lifted upwards. This photograph is dated March 7, 1929 and taken at Wörden in Holstein.

A photograph, taken from the book "Dokumente der Zeitgeschichte," showing the official SA uniform, as introduced by an order of November 14, 1926. The cap has the button in the front of the flap and above the visor, rests a leather chin strap.

pocket or bread bag. Halting during the distribution of the pastries was not permitted.[28]

The most important change that occurred during the years 1929 through 1931 was the introduction of the first pattern national eagle emblem, granted by Hitler on April 9, 1931.[29] All SA members were to utilize this eagle by June 1 of that year.[30]

A draft regulation for the SA was published May 31, 1931,[31] and was simultaneously implemented. All earlier SA orders were abolished. On October 1, 1932 a renewed publication was available and a special uniform regulation was in preparation.

Otto Spronk

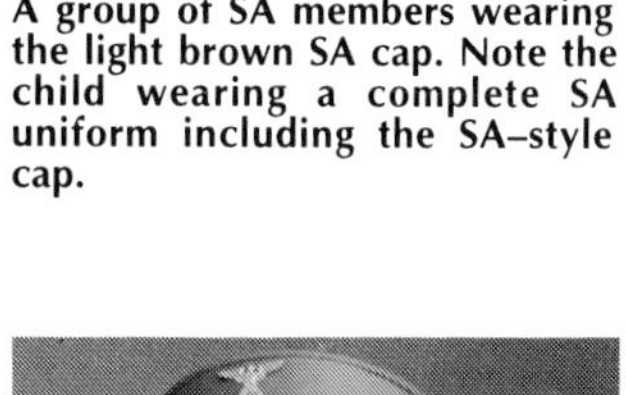

A group of SA members wearing the light brown SA cap. Note the child wearing a complete SA uniform including the SA-style cap.

W.P.B.R. Saris

SA candidate Dörnte of Dinkelhausen-Langenthal in the SA district Niedersachsen is wearing the SA cap as ordered for wear with the "brownshirt." Note the beautiful stiff construction and the very high top with the early national emblem. The flaps are closed by a smooth golden button, as ordered for this type of cap.

---

28 *Der Oberste SA-Führer, July 13, 1929. Allgemeiner SABE (original SA-Order): Reichsparteitag Nürnberg 1.-4. August, 1929 (für jeden Gruf.) Section: Festmarch; number 24 gave specific orders.*

29 *"Vbl.d.OSAF," Nr. 1, April 20, 1931, p. 4. Nr. 24. (This is a different issue as the earlier noted issue. In this instance it is: NSDAP, Verordnungsblatt der Obersten SA-Führung, but instead of the SA emblem this issue shows the political eagle emblem on top of the page. The Vbl. with the SA symbol is a May 1934 reprint).*

30 *Der Oberste SA-Führer. München: April 22, 1931, Ia.Nr. 1679/31, decree: Dienststellungsabzeichen. In the opening of this decree, signed by Röhm, the wearing of the national emblem was also recorded.*

31 *Volz."Daten der Geschichte der NSDAP. " 11.Auflage, Berlin/Leipzig: 1943, pp. 124-128; Entwurf Dienstvorschrift für die SA der NSDAP. Diessen, 1931,*

Otto Spronk

This SA man from the Sturm 21/L (Leibstandarte Munich) is wearing a soft fabric SA cap in approximately 1932.

The SA kepi proved impractical, the biggest disadvantage being that it could not be folded. In the spring of 1932 attempts were made to develop an entirely new style of cap. The regular civil form of hat ("Stumpen," – a felt hat with a crease over the length of the top, also known as a homburg) was rejected.[32] This rejection resulted in two forms of visorless field or garrison caps (experimentally being worn by some smaller units of the SA groups of Schlesien and Berlin–Brandenburg); a ski cap (experimentally worn by units from the SA groups Hochland and in Austria) and a visored cap in the regular army style (experimentally worn by the SA group West, but also by NSKK–members).[33] Another form of visored cap was also experimentally worn by some units of the Berlin–Brandenburg district during 1933. In the end, however, the kepi remained in use. This decision was based on tradition.[34] The ski cap and the garrison caps were later authorized for wear (consult the related sections).

Due to the 1933 reorganization of the SA, new regulations were badly needed to make a distinction between groups, leaders and enlisted ranks. The systems were simplified. The colored top for the kepi was introduced for wear by the enlisted ranks July 7, 1933.[35]

---

32 "Uniformen–Markt," Nr. 10, May 15, 1937, p. 146.

33 Der Oberste SA–Führer. München: July 7, 1932. Qu.Nr. 1543/32: Bekleidung. Section 2 of this order describes the experimental forms. The wear of the visored cap by the group West was abolished in 1933, With the introduction of the visored cap SA members obtained such visored caps for wear with the "walking–out" dress. This was strictly forbidden by the SA High Command. The visored cap as worn by Berlin–Brandenburg was officially abolished in July 1934 (Mbl.d.RZM, Nr. 6, July 7, 1934, p. 5).

34 "Mbl.d.RZM," Nr. 26, September 28, 1935, p. 269.

35 Der Oberste SA–Führer. München: July 7, 1933, Ch.Nr. 1350/33: Neugliederung der SA. Decree Nr. 2 settles with section D the introduction for the colored top for the enlisted ranks. (Until July 1933 SA leaders, mainly having duty positions, were exclusively allowed to wear the colored top).

Der Oberste SA-Führer.
Qu. Nr. 1543/32.

München, den 7. Juli 1932.

Betrifft: Bekleidung.

Verteiler: IVb, jedoch Reichsführer SS nur 100.

Die nat.-soz. Bewegung steht im Endkampf um die politische Macht. Die SA – als ihr Kern und ihre Vorhut – bringt täglich Opfer von unerhörtem Ausmaße. Unser Blick ist auf den politischen Feind gerichtet. Innere Organisationsarbeit darf uns jetzt nur insoweit fesseln, als es gilt, Gliederungen und Führungsverhältnisse dem Tempo des Wachstums der SA anzupassen und unseren Befehlsorganismus zu straffen.

In dieser Lage und besonders mit Rücksicht auf die wirtschaftlichen Verhältnisse der überwiegenden Mehrzahl der SA-Männer hat der Führer entschieden, von Bekleidungsänderungen für die gesamte SA, die an sich wünschenswert wären, abzusehen.

Der Dienstanzug der SA bleibt daher bis auf Weiteres nach wie vor das bisher eingeführte Braunhemd. Der Nachteil, daß dieses den klimatischen Verhältnissen in Deutschland zu wenig Rechnung trägt, muß in Kauf genommen werden.

Um aber schon jetzt eine für spätere Zeit in Aussicht genommene Verbesserung des Dienstanzuges der SA entsprechend vorzubereiten, habe ich die Durchführung von Versuchen befohlen.

1. **Der neue Dienstrock,** dessen Modell in der Anlage 2 beschrieben ist, darf von SA-Führern und SA-Männern zunächst nur außer Dienst oder zum kleinen Dienst getragen werden. Besonders mache ich darauf aufmerksam, daß kein Führer seinen Untergebenen finanzielle Lasten auferlegen darf. Ueberdies sind die Vorarbeiten für die Herstellung eines in Farbton und Güte entsprechenden Stoffes noch nicht abgeschlossen, sodaß bei schon jetzt erfolgender Beschaffung unter Umständen spätere Abänderungen erforderlich werden können. Ein Befehl zur Anschaffung des neuen Rockes darf auch neu in die SA Eintretenden nicht gegeben werden; vielmehr haben sich auch diese in erster Linie das Braunhemd zu beschaffen. Im übrigen empfehle ich allen SA-Führern und -Männern, die in der Lage sind, sich den neuen Rock zu beschaffen, Rücksicht zu nehmen auf ihre ärmeren Kameraden, die oft nicht das Nötigste zum Leben haben.

2. **Die bisherige Dienstmütze** ist kein Ideal. Ihr haftet vor allem der große Nachteil an, daß sie nicht zusammengefaltet und bequem in Tasche oder Tornister untergebracht werden kann. Diese Forderung ist für unsere sport- und wanderlustige SA wichtig. Die Gruppen Schlesien und Berlin-Brandenburg beauftrage ich, die schirmlose Dienstmütze nach den beiden ausgegebenen Mustern bei einigen unterstellten Einheiten auszuproben und mir bald über Bewährung und Beliebtheit zu berichten. Auch den Generalinspekteur und die einschlägigen Inspekteure ersuche ich um Bericht.

   Die Gruppen Hochland und Oesterreich erwägen, ob ihrer Sonderbekleidung nicht eine Dienstmütze nach Art der weichen Skifahrermütze anzupassen wäre. Ueber Versuche ist alsbald zu berichten.

   Gruppe West u. NSKK erproben eine Dienstmütze nach Art der Armeemütze. Muster wird übersandt.

   Bis zur Bekanntgabe der endgültigen Bestimmungen bleibt allgemein mit Ausnahme der von den genannten Gruppen bestimmten Einheiten die bisherige Dienstmütze.

3. **Die Hose** soll von gleicher oder wenigstens ähnlicher Farbe sein wie das Braunhemd. Wird der neue Dienstrock getragen, so muß die Hose die gleiche braune Farbe besitzen wie dieser. Die Untergruppe München-Oberbayern und die Standarte 20 der Untergruppe Schwaben tragen im Sommer die kurze Lederhose, dazu weiße oder hellgraue Strümpfe und braune oder schwarze Halbschuhe. Jedoch soll bei Aufmärschen ein einheitlicher Anzug gewährleistet sein.

   Die Motor-SA trägt schwarze Hose.

4. **Mantel.** Die bisherigen feldgrauen Mäntel werden aufgetragen. Das Modell eines braunen Mantels wird später bekannt gegeben.

5. **Als Fußbekleidung** können hohe braune oder schwarze Stiefel bezw. braune oder schwarze Schnürstiefel mit dazupassenden Leder- oder Wickelgamaschen, im Notfalle auch Halbschuhe und zur Farbe der Hose passende lange Sportstrümpfe getragen werden. Auf gute Fußbekleidung haben sämtliche SA-Führer ihr besonderes Augenmerk zu richten und hier soweit nur möglich helfend einzugreifen.

A part of a copy of the July 7, 1932 OSAF order relating to the SA uniform. Paragraph 2 describes the experimentally worn, headdress by the groups, Schlesien, Berlin–Brandenburg, Hochland, Österreich, Gruppe West and in addition, the NSKK, as this was still under the command of the SA.

Note: German cap makers succeeded in manufacturing SA and SS kepis from felt (Hutstumpenmaterial), from one piece, to include the visor and flaps. This form of manufacture, however, was too expensive. ("Die Bekleidungsarbeit," Ausgabe C, Kopfbekleidung, Nr. 4 from April 21, 1937, p. 55.)

W.P.B.R. Saris

Members of the SA are wearing the semi–stiff SA cap in twill as ordered for wear with the brownshirt. No colored top was worn.

National Archives

C. Schwab

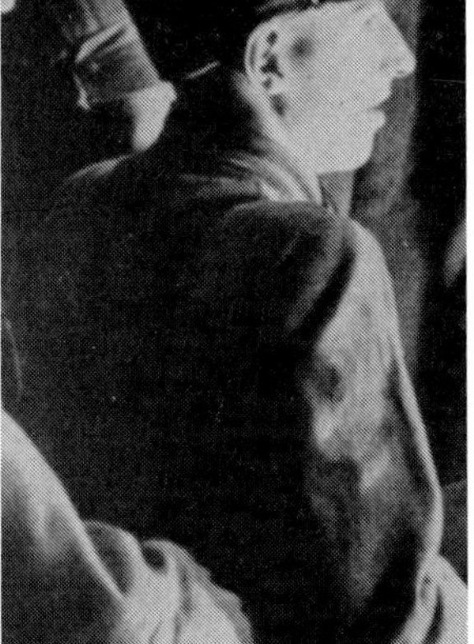

SA–Mann wearing the soft form of early SA cap.

SA band members wearing the soft fabric SA cap, without a colored top. This top was introduced in July 1933. Note that there are no ventilation holes on these caps.

National Archives

A member of the Leibstandarte Munich is wearing an early form of SA cap, without a colored top. Note the goggles, and the L (for Leibstandarte) upon the light blue collar patch. He is wearing the semi–stiff form of cap.

W.P.B.R. Saris

Karl Siebert from Wiensen in Niedersachsen is wearing the standard SA cap in twill, matching the color of his brown shirt.

Otto Spronk

A very rare moment showing the visored cap being experimentally worn with the early pattern NSDAP national emblem version on the top. This is the form of cap that was also worn by NSKK members, starting in July 1932. Its wear was officially ended in July 1934.

List: July 7, 1933

GROUP OR DISTRICT:	TOP COLOR:	PIPING (WHEN ALLOWED):	BUTTON:
Ostland: (province Ostpreussen and the city of Danzig until 1939)	dark wine–red	black/white	gold;
Westfalen:	ibid	ibid	silver;
Niederrhein: (a part of the Rhine province and Ruhr area)	black	ibid	gold;
Berlin–Brandenburg: (province Mark Brandenburg and the city Gross–Berlin)	ibid	ibid	silver:
Ostmark: (province Grenzmark)	pinkish–red	ibid	gold;
Pommern: (province Pommern and parts of Grenzmark)	apple–green	ibid	ibid;
Thüringen: (free state of Thüringen)	ibid	white/bright red	silver;
Westmark: (a part of the Rhine province and a part of the province Hessen–Nassau. From the beginning of the war also Luxembourg)	dark–brown	black/white	silver;
Niedersachsen: (free state of Braunschweig and a part of the Hannover province)	ibid	ibid	gold;
Sachsen: (free state of Sachsen)	emerald–green	white/emerald–green	silver;
Nordmark: (province of Schleswig–Holstein and later the free city of Lübeck)	ibid	black/white	gold;
Mitte: (province of Sachsen and free state of Anhalt)	orange-yellow	ibid	ibid;

Otto Spronk

SA members of the Sturm 1/14, during festivities in Berlin. The top color is dark wine–red, as Standarte 14 was from Danzig and during this period was located in the Ostland district.

Südwest: (free state of Baden and Württemberg)	ibid	black/orange–yellow	silver;
Schlesien: (provinces Ober– and Niederschlesien)	sulfur–yellow	black/white	ibid;
Franken: (districts Mittel– and Unterfranken)	ibid	white/blue	gold;
Hochland: (districts Oberbayern and Schwaben)	light blue	white/light blue	silver;
Bayerische Ostmark: (districts Niederbayern, Oberpfalz and Oberfranken)	ibid	ibid	gold;

Österreich: (Austria)	steel–green	red/white	silver;
Nordsee: (free–state of Oldenburg and parts of the Hannover province and the free–city of Bremen)	ibid	black/white	gold;
Hansa: (free city of Hamburg and the province Mecklenburg)	navy blue	light blue/ sulfur–yellow	ibid;
Hessen: (province Hessen–Oberhessen and parts of the province Hessen–Nassau[36]	ibid	light blue/ bright red	silver.

Students

In mid–July 1933 the wearing of a colored top (in the color of the SA–district) with the regular form headdress for students, was permitted with the SA dress by the SA High Command (for detailed information on the Studentenmütze, see Volume 4, the chapter: NS–Schulung, education). Its wear was only allowed during student meetings indoors. With an order dated late July 1935, the above order was withdrawn.[37]

Bob Treend

The first pattern national emblem being worn with the SA kepi.

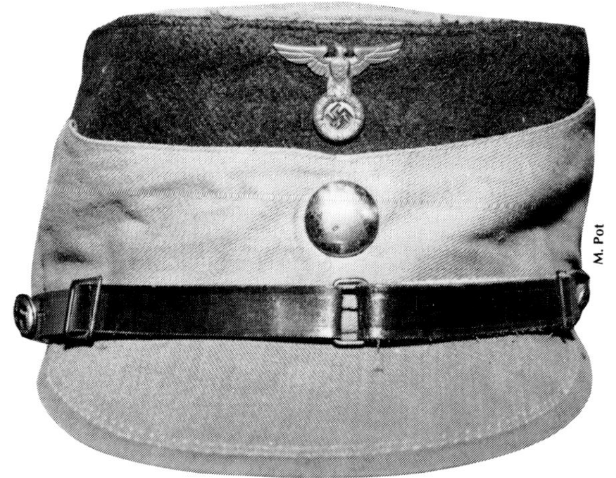

SA cap in the semi–stiff form for the district Niederrhein, having a black top and golden button. Note the chin strap button is the version with the embossed swastika. This was forbidden in spring of 1934.

An SA–Sturmmann from Niederumelsdorf, near Straubing, is wearing a light blue top. His collar patch is for the reserve Jägerstandarte 15, located in Bayer. Ostmark. Note the wearing of the insigne for "Jäger," being two green balls, as ordered for those units that were formed in Bavaria.

---

36 *Ibid. München: July 7, 1933, Ch.Nr. 1350/33: Neugliederung der SA. (One must note that on this list specified areas are those from approximately 1936, Prior to and after shifts were made to parts of the provinces from one to another. It would be very complicated to enclose all of these changes to districts and would only cause more confusion).*

37 *"Vbl.d.OSAF," Nr. 24, July 29, 1935, p. 111. Nr. 269: SA–Dienstanzug mit Couleurband.*

Deutsche Lufthansa

Two SA members boarding an aircraft. Note the dark and light colored tops on the SA coffee can style caps. The man at right is 82-year-old Mr. Paradies who was an old SA member, and invited to Munich.

Richard Kindel

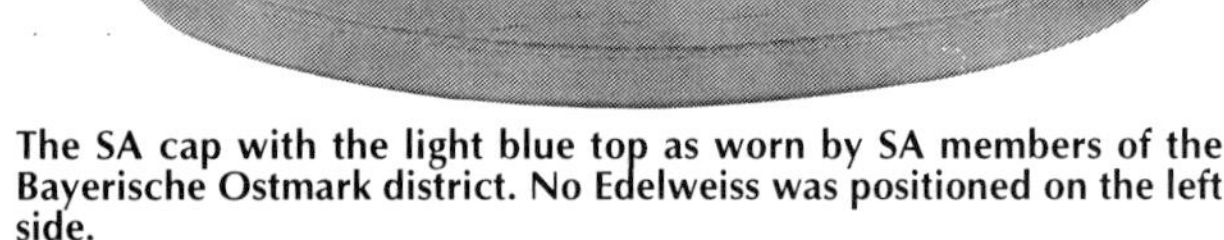

The SA cap with the light blue top as worn by SA members of the Bayerische Ostmark district. No Edelweiss was positioned on the left side.

Niall Malcolm

SA kepi from the group Hochland with light blue top and silvered button. The body is light brown khaki. Note the curvature of the flap.

1934 – 1936

Between the summer of 1933 and March 1934 one group was added, being Kurpfalz (changed again in May of the same year). Austria's color was also changed:

GROUP OR DISTRICT:	TOP COLOR:	PIPING (WHEN ALLOWED):	BUTTON:
(up until late May) Kurpfalz: (districts Rheinpfalz, Saar area and Rhein–Hessen. Since early war also Lothringen)	pinkish–red	black/white	silver:
(from late May) Kurpfalz:	steel–green	ibid	ibid;
Österreich:	red brown	bright–red/white	silver.[38]

During the 1930's the material for the top was made by:

1) Zittauer Militärtuchfabrik, Julius & Rudolf Hübner, from Zittau. They manufactured the colors sulfur–yellow, orange–yellow, light blue and dark wine–red;

2) C.F. Dürr from Reichenbach and made the colors steel–green, apple–green, emerald–green and navy blue;

3) Müller & Schöner from Görlitz. This company manufactured the colors dark–brown, black, pinkish–red, crimson and bright red. In 1936 white was also added to their program.[39]

(In early 1935 two large companies started manufacturing all the known colors, at the request of the RZM. These were the firms of Bernard Voigt of Esslingen and Johannes Forster from Friedrichshaven).[40]

Two kinds of dress regulations were officially authorized with the new March 1934 regulations:

1) "Grosser Dienstanzug" (Greater Service Dress): to be worn with the brown shirt during festivities, parades (in front of the "Führer"), at the consecration of flags and banners and at funerals etc., or when ordered by the staff. (It must be noted that high ranking leaders always had to wear the colored top when the service dress with brown shirt was ordered. In the early thirties the wearing of the colored top was in fact not allowed when the smaller service dress was worn by these leaders).

2) "Kleiner Dienstanzug" (Smaller Service Dress – the everyday dress: to be worn with all other occasions.

---

[38] *"Anzugs–Ordnung für die SA" (Teil 1, part 1). Der Oberste SA–Führer. München: March 1, 1934, Section VIII. pp. 42–45. (It must be noted that part 2 was never published. In the 1939 SA handbook a complete list of SA regulations was published on page 62. It even specified which regulations were rewritten); "Vbl.d.OSAF," Nr. 23, May 28, 1934, p. 1. Nr. 6: Abzeichen für Kurpfalz.*

[39] *"Mbl.d.RZM," Nr. 3, München: June 16, 1934, pp. 4–5.*

[40] *Ibid, Nr. 4, January 26, 1935, p. 31.*

Johann Steidl, a member of the Bayer. Ostmark district, wearing the early pattern national emblem with his light blue topped kepi.

Hans v. Diggelen

Otto Spronk

An SA member wearing his tunic for the smaller service dress and his kepi for the greater service dress. Officially this was not allowed.

Below: Members of the SA during a wedding, wearing the SA cap manufactured in the heavier cloth with the "kleiner Dienstanzug." At right, the person is wearing his greater service dress. The Sturmführer is wearing a two–colored crown piping.

Bernd Wedeking

With the introduction of the olive–brown tunic in tricot or heavier SA cloth the SA kepi was also manufactured from this material from mid–1933. This brown was officially known as "SA–braun" and shades varied to a brownish–green.[41] Shortly thereafter the "Abendanzug" (evening dress), worn at events when not being in service or ordered for the greater service dress, was introduced.

Extensive manufacturing regulations were published during 1934: The "SA–Dienstmütze," the SA cap worn for example during parades etc., was mainly made of light brown, near khaki colored twill and existed in both the semi–stiff or soft bodied SA caps. Some variations were stiffened. This material was delivered by the concern Atlas–Ago from Mölkau near Leipzig.[42] This cap always had a smooth button.

W.P.B.R. Saris

Wilhelm Diedrich from the Niedersachsen district wearing the semi–stiff form SA cap with a dark brown top and the first pattern national emblem.

The SA cap for the smaller service dress was manufactured in tricot or heavier cloth for regular service. This cap exists in the semi–stiff form only.[43] In March it was ordered that this cap should always have a pebbled button with a diameter of 22.5mm.[44] Apparently this size must have been incorrect, as in May it was noted that the size had to be 20.5mm.[45] It must be noted that in those days

---

41 *Der Oberste SA–Führer, München: November 3, 1933, I. Nr. 1648.*

42 *"Mbl.d.RZM," Nr. 16, September 15, 1934, p. 7.*

43 *"Ausrüstung und Bekleidung für den SA–Mann." Leaflet from "Der Stahlhof." Magdeburg: April 1934.*

44 *"Mbl.d.RZM," Nr. 9, March 3, 1935, p. 71.*

45 *Ibid, Nr. 16, May 11, 1935, p. 86.*

all caps were delivered without the colored top. This was sold separately to the members of the SA to avoid problems, due to the many geographic shifts of SA groups. Often the SA members were not in easy circumstances and could not afford buying an entire new cap.[46]

Otto Spronk

This SA-Mann wears his kepi in the second part of 1933. Apparently he has improperly removed his old dark top color with remnants being visible just below the crown. Note he is not wearing a shoulder strap which was introduced for wear on May 26, 1933. The colored cap top was introduced on July 7, 1933 for enlisted ranks.

In early August 1934 "Österreich" was renamed "Hilfswerk Nordwest" due to the prohibition of the SA in Austria. The staffs and offices had already been transferred to Munich in June 1934. After Röhm's "removal" the "Stabswache" (staff guards) were renamed in September 1934 "Wachdienst" (guards service) and again changed to "Wachstandarte" (guards unit) in late October 1934. The colors were:

GROUP OR DISTRICT:	TOP COLOR:	PIPING (WHEN ALLOWED):	BUTTON:
Hilfswerk Nordwest:	red brown	bright red/white	silver;
Wachstandarte:	crimson	crimson/white	silver.[47]

[46] *Ibid, Nr. 1, June 1, 1934, p. 7.*

[47] *"Organisationsbuch der NSDAP. " München: 1936, pp. 388–389.*

In December 1934 a full description was published regarding the semi-stiff and soft bodied SA caps in the "Mitteilungsblatt der Reichszeugmeisterei."

Ed Stadnicki

SA.-Bekleidung und -Ausrüstung

SA.-Diensthemd, mit Binder, ohne Knöpfe, Gr. 44—54	RM.	5.25
Langes Braunhemd, m. Binder	„	4.90
Uniformhemd m. 2 Kragen	„	5.60
Tuchhosen, m. Nierenschutz, SA.-braun, 44-54	„	24.—
Tuchhosen, m. Nierenschutz, blau f. Marine, 44-54	„	19.75
Trikothosen, mit Nierenschutz, SA.-braun, 44-54	„	27.—
SA.-Mäntel, Qualität III	„	48.25
Cordhosen, mit Nierenschutz, SA.-braun, 44-54	„	9.25
Dienstmütze, Köper halbsteif (ohne Band)	„	2.60
Dienstmütze, Köper weich (ohne Band)	„	2.05
Dienstmütze, Tuch (ohne Band)	„	4.—
Dienstmütze, Trikot (ohne Band)	„	4.40
Gruppenstreifen für SA.-Mütze	„	—.30
SA.-Leibriemen, m. Zweidornschn., weiß, 4,5 cm	„	2.80
SA.-Leibriemen, m. Zweidornschn., gelb, 4,5 cm	„	2.90
SA.-Schulterriemen, m. weiß. Beschlag	„	2.—
SA.-Schulterriemen, m. gelb. Beschlag	„	2.10

Versand nur gegen Nachnahme od. Vorauszahlung; Sendungen von RM. 50.— an porto- u. verpackungsfrei.
Lieferung in bester Beschaffenheit nach Vorschrift der Obersten S.A.-Führung

Reichszeugmeisterei der NSDAP., München 2, Schwanthalerstraße 53/55

Fernsprecher 50195/96 u. 50927/28

Ed Stadnicki

Two advertisements published in the SA periodical "Der SA-Mann" in January 1935. Note that four grades of kepi were available, and that the colored top was sold separately (indicated as "Gruppenstreifen für SA-Mütze," and priced at RM.30).

Description SA Cap 1934, Semi–Stiff Form (halbsteife SA–Mütze)

The material used was light brown, impregnated twill, cloth or tricot in the lighter color (phrased as "alte Farbe," [old color]) and a darker color (phrased as "neue Farbe," [new color]). This is often referred to as "olivbraun." The slightly oval top (20cm long with the size 56 and approximately 17cm wide) was 9cm in front, including a 1.5mm piping or seam in the same color and fabric as the top and body. The top was stiffened by a rustproof iron wire, 1.0 x 0.3mm thick, which was installed into the cap piping. An extra wire (1.0 x 0.6mm) was inserted to retain the cap's shape.

On the inside of the cap top a waterproof oilcloth moiré liner, in light or Havana–brown color, was sewn in along with the cloth for the top. The upstanding body was stiffened by unshrinkable and impregnated material (Plasma or Dermatoid), consisting of cotton and horsehair (50% cell wool and 50% cotton – "Mützenrosshaar"). The latter was available mainly through the Atlas–Ago firm.[48]

The cap flaps were approximately 6.5 – 7cm high at the rear and approximately 4.5 – 5.0cm at the front. The right flap closed 0.5cm over the left one. The vaulting of the flaps began 3cm before the side edges of the visor. These flaps were sewn to the lower body edge and could be unfolded. Two brown ventilation holes, with a 0.4cm diameter, were positioned approximately 5mm beneath the crown piping (or seam). These brown grommets were mainly installed by machine after 1936, since grommets installed by hand looked too untidy .

The cloth covered visor was approximately 24cm long and 5cm wide in the front and was sewn to the cap body at a 32° angle. The visor was stitched through along the leading edge, another seam being 2.5mm from the cap body. The interior visor material was black 1mm thick waterproof, impregnated cardboard. A

National Archives

Navorsingsinstituut Brussel

Members of the SA waiting at the court of Altona in connection with a trial. Regulations specified that wearing the SA uniform was not allowed in front of the court of justice. Note the wearing of the "Zivilmütze," as well as the "DAF" style visored caps. Some men are wearing a round insigne on the front center of the cap top.

A sample of the stamp that was positioned at the beginning and at the end of a bolt of Mützenroszhaarstoff, material often used to reinforce SA caps.

W.P.B.R. Saris

M.R.20

two part chin strap (quality Ia) rested above the visor. It was of 13mm dark–brown leather and not thicker than 1.5mm. A brown rectangular metal buckle (thickness 1.5 – 2.0mm) with rounded edges kept the two parts together. This strap could be extended by two brown metal buckles (18 x 21mm) and was fastened to the cap by two flat brown metal buttons with a 14mm diameter. The earliest buttons were the type that snapped together and did not have flat pins or prongs, which were officially forbidden in 1934.

The cap was reinforced at the seams on the inside by stiff linen material. The 3cm sweatband was Havana–brown in color. The plated button, which secured the flaps at the cap front, was 20.5mm in diameter (also see information on button above this description). The RZM article numbers were: 4063a for the twill; 4064 for the cloth and 4065 for the tricot cap.

◀ This photograph shows the variations in the width of the flaps on the cap front.

---

48 *"Mbl.d.RZM," Nr. 16, September 15, 1934, p. 7.*

A national emblem of "neusilber" was fastened to the cap top above the flaps and button upon the loose colored top. In the earliest years this top was mainly fastened by two small press studs. Only those who could afford it bought a cap with a permanent sewn on colored top.

W.P.B.R. Saris

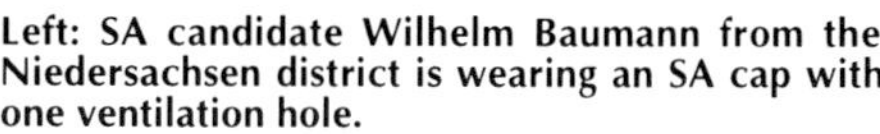

Left: SA candidate Wilhelm Baumann from the Niedersachsen district is wearing an SA cap with one ventilation hole.

Otto Spronk

Right: SA–Mann from the Mitte district is wearing his cap with a orange–yellow top with his greater service dress. The original photograph clearly shows that this person is wearing a loose cover for the colored top.

Hans v. Diggelen

SA band members wearing the chin strap under the chin.

W.P.B.R. Saris

Above: SA members of the SA Leibstandarte from Munich during a memorial service on November 9, 1934. Note the wearing of a cap at left with a light top, without any ventilation holes. Pay special attention to the flap patch and the top of the flag: Sturm 1 of the Leibstandarte with the honor name of Max–Erwin von Scheubner–Richter.

Otto Spronk

This SA-Scharführer, who was photographed at the time of his wedding on June 8, 1935, wears the "Grosser Dienstanzug."

Soft SA–Cap (weiche SA–Mütze)

In general it can be said that the manufacturing procedures for this cap were like the aforementioned semi–stiff cap, but the horsehair stiffener and wire were not present. The inside moiré was replaced by a cotton lining in the top. This cap was manufactured according to the regulations only in twill and was not to be made of any other cloth or tricot material. The colored cap top was in this case *not* loose or detachable but was sewn directly to the body, to hold it in place on this soft cap.[49] The RZM article number of this cap was 4062.

During the summer of 1935 it was once more requested that the SA kepi and the garrison cap (Lagermütze) styles be changed. The OSAF refused this because of the tradition of the caps having been worn by the SA for years.[50] Jägerstandarten (rifle regiments) with the numbers 1 and 3 from the Hochland district were allowed to wear the mountain or ski cap, but not with the greater service dress. No headdress was worn with the sport outfit (however, the kepi was worn with the "Wehrsport" uniform).

With types which were made in 1936, the cloth and tricot caps had a button hole in the flap, while the flaps of the twill caps were sewn together. The buttons were either in white, nickeled or "gold" plated material with prongs on the reverse or the earlier pebbled form button types often had the "Öse," or eyelet, on their reverse. It was strictly forbidden to close the prongs on the interior of the cap (this had to be done in the space between the top color material and the cloth of the top, or between the material for reinforcement. It must be noted that this

Otto Spronk

A member of the SA salutes his comrad. Note the soft style SA cap in his hands.

regulation was largely disobeyed because one did not normally have the patience to comply with it). The size of the button was as earlier ordered.

The inside material of the visor was natural colored cardboard 1mm thick (the black cardboard was discontinued). Above the visor rested the chin strap with its two small impressed borders (earlier types often do not have this). It was secured to the flaps by dark–brown buttons, which were sewn through a hole 2cm behind the visor. From the fall of 1936, the use of substitute ("Ersatz") leather was authorized.

An RZM tag was positioned on the inner left side of the cap, partly behind the sweatband. This sweatband was also allowed to be manufactured in substitute leather, then stamped "RZ." Note that the RZM tag for the twill cap was in brown lettering while in black for the cloth or tricot cap. According to regulations the ventilation grommets (distance of 3cm) were to be lacquered in the same color as the cap top. It has been observed that this was largely ignored and the grommets often were brown.[51] The manufacturing procedures for the soft version SA kepi were not changed.

Herstellerfirma Nr.:

Mitgliedsnummer des Trägers:

RZM Serie 1

Verkaufsstelle Nr.:

N.S.D.A.P. R.Z.M. № 091342

Schwarze Marke
für SA.- u. NSKK.-Dienstmütze (Tuch, Trikot),
für SA.-Marinemütze,

W.P.B.R. Saris

A sample of the label in black, as published in the *Mitteilungsblatt der RZM* in 1936, to be used for the SA cap in tricot or twill or for the SA naval visored cap.

DIENSTMÜTZE

Herstellerfirma Nr.

Verkaufsstelle Nr.

RZM

Reichszeugmeisterei der N.S.D.A.P. Nr. E

Braune Marke
für SA.-Dienstmütze (Köper),
für SA.-Lagermütze,

W.P.B.R. Saris

A sample of the label in brown, also published in 1936 in the *Mitteilungsblatt der Reichszeugmeisterei*, to be used for the SA cap in the heavier cloth or the regular form of SA forage cap.

49 *Ibid, Nr. 28, December 8, 1934, p. 4.*

50 *Ibid, Nr. 26, September 28, 1935, p. 269.*

51 *"RZM–Herstellungsvorschriften," 1936, pp. 114–115; "Mbl.d.RZM," Nr. 10, May 9, 1936, p. 187.*

1936 – 1945

From the summer of 1937 the new pattern national emblem was worn. A "new" SA cap was announced in October 1937. The main difference from the previous caps was that the order specifically stated that the side panels were to be sewn directly to the cap body.[52] The sizes also changed:

SA district Berlin–Brandenburg cap with the earliest form of national emblem. The top is black, the button is silver. The chin strap is fastened by silver buttons: officially these were always in brown. Niederrhein had a black top with a gold button.

Len Champion

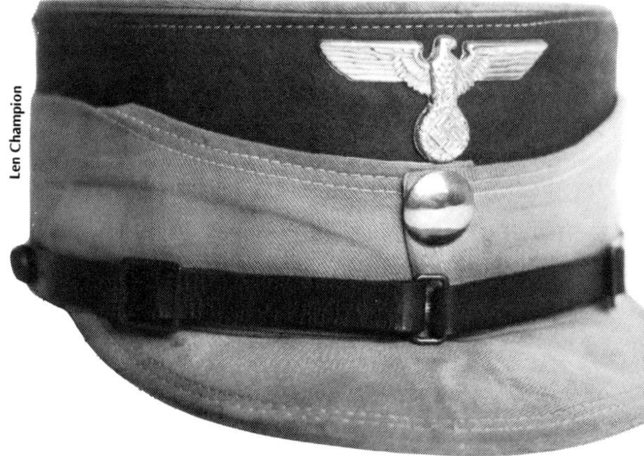

Len Champion

Enlisted ranks SA cap for the Nordmark district with the emerald–green top and a gilt button. Note the wearing of the final form national emblem, as introduced July 1937. Caps with the same colored top, but with a silver button were worn in the Sachsen district.

Brief Description of a Size 56 Kepi

The oval top was now 21cm in length and 17.2cm wide. The back was 8.6cm high and 8.2cm in the front. The size of the flap at the back was 6.6cm, at the front it was 4.2cm. Other variations in sizes were not officially allowed. Another remarkable fact is that the diameter of the buttons changed to 18mm and the ventilation grommets, approximately 5mm in diameter, were installed 1cm from the top edge.

The sewn on colored top was only 2cm wide. The visor was still 5cm wide, again with a black stiffener. Other procedures remained largely as before. Specifications for the smaller buttons were published in late October.

---

52 *"Mbl.d.RZM," Nr. 21, October 9, 1937, p. 250.*

SA cap for the Westfalen district with dark wine–red top and silver button. The final form national emblem is worn on the cap. Ostland had a wine-red top with a gold button.

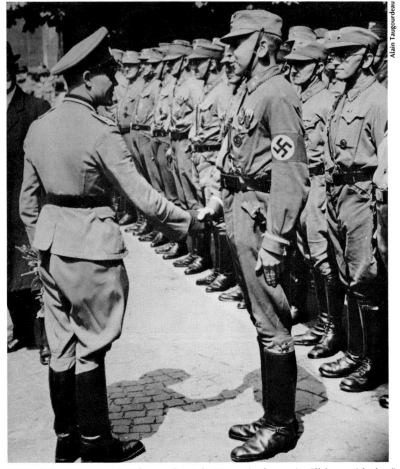

Alain Taugourdeau

Members of the SA are wearing the regular style SA cap in the semi–stiff form with the final form national emblem. During this demonstration the highest in rank is an SA–Obertruppführer. He was not allowed to wear piping.

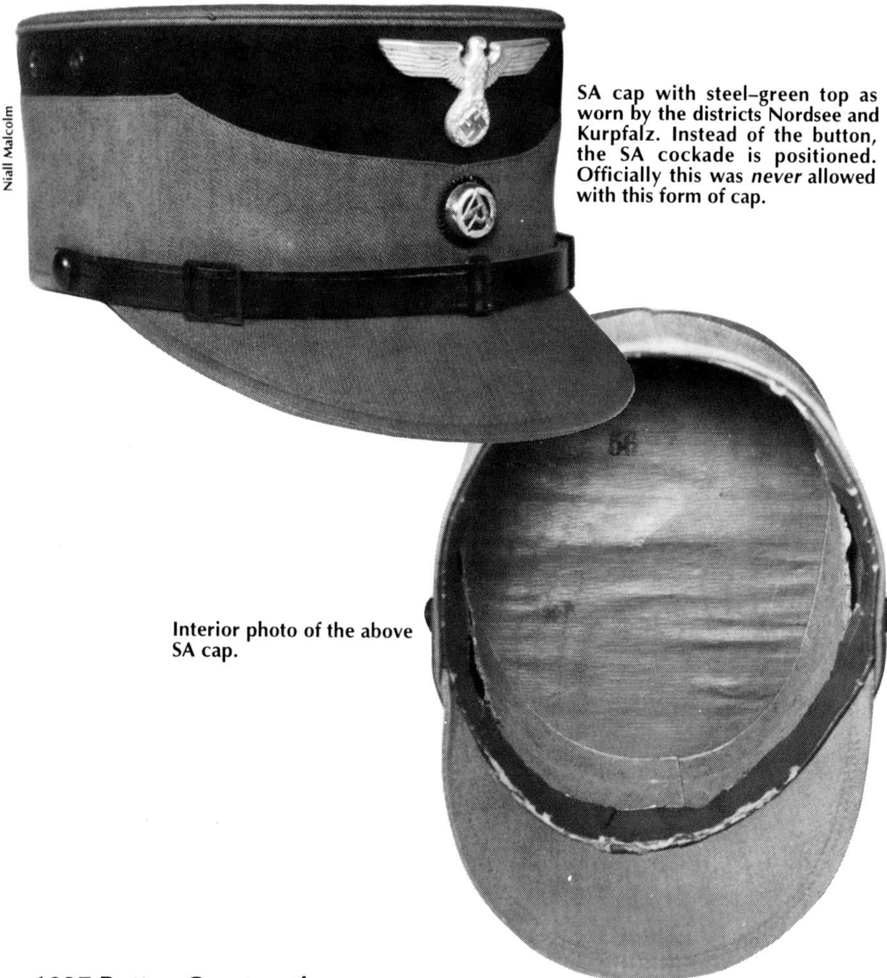
Niall Malcolm

SA cap with steel-green top as worn by the districts Nordsee and Kurpfalz. Instead of the button, the SA cockade is positioned. Officially this was *never* allowed with this form of cap.

Interior photo of the above SA cap.

1937 Button Construction

white/yellow smooth: The upper portion was made of 0.3mm nickeled or "tombak" plated steel and polished. The inner metal portion was of 0.4mm white sheet with a slot to push through the prongs (nickeled iron 0.6 – 1.6mm wide, with an 18mm length). The inlay is of 0.4mm steel. The size of the button could vary 0.3mm. The reverse had the RZM logo, manufactures code number and year stamped on it.

white/yellow pebbled: Largely as above with a "wildmatt" pebbling (which has an irregular pebbling; the old pebbling having a regularity in the pebbling pattern is referred to as "punktmatt").[53]

The most striking modifications during the years 1938 through 1945 are listed below:

[53] *Ibid, Nr. 22, October 23, 1937, pp. 258–259.*

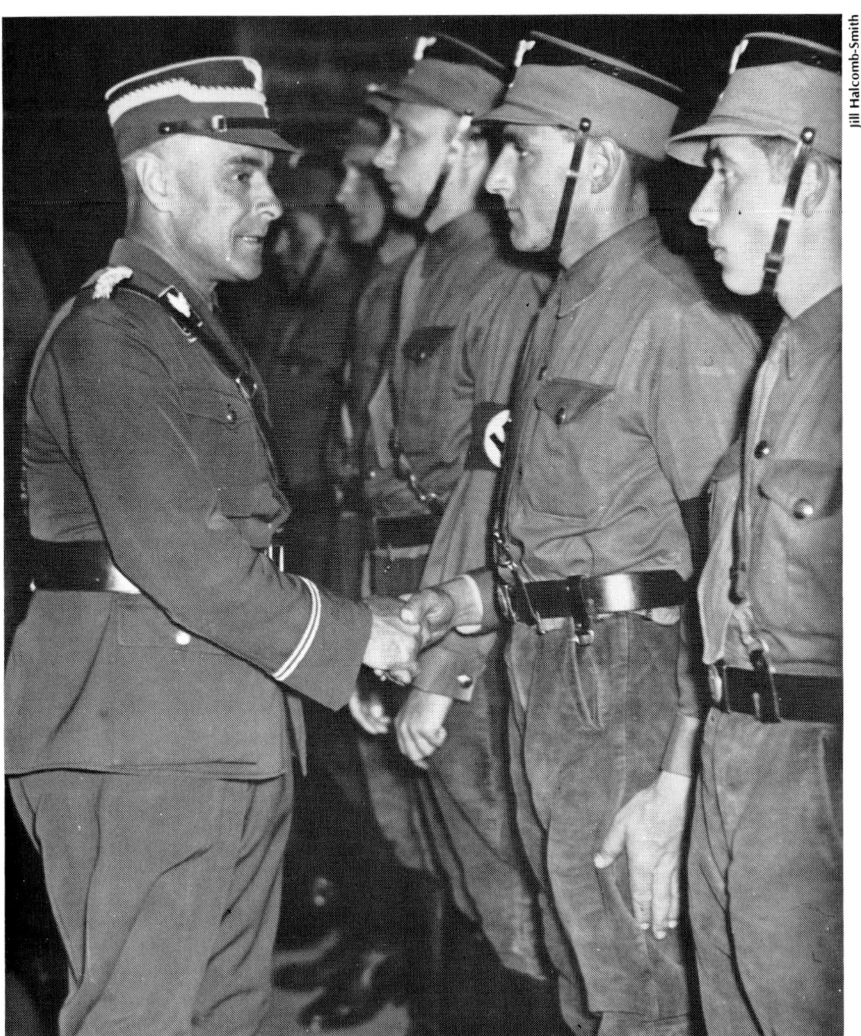

Oberführer Künemund, the deputy from Berlin–Brandenburg, says farewell to Austrian SA comrades. Shortly before this photograph was taken on May 29, 1938, these Austrian members received their new uniforms for their return to their homeland. The top is red–brown. Künemund wears a silver crown piping, a black–white flap piping and the Tresse per regulations.

October 1938: Substitute materials were used instead of leather for the manufacturing of the chin strap (Alkor and later Texokor, consult also the chapter: DAF). The color remained brown. The stamps on the reverse were:
L10/........../38 and the RZM symbol.[54]

May 1941: To cut down stocks and simultaneously as a simplification the use of gold was terminated. Thereafter, all cap buttons (with the exception of the Marine–SA) were made of sil-

[54] *Ibid, Nr. 21, October 8, 1938, p. 201.*

Otto Spronk

An Obersturmführer from the staff of the Niederrhein district. His cap top color is black and the crown piping is black/white. The white summer tunic was introduced for the ranks of Sturmführer and above on May 25, 1939. This tunic was permitted for wear while attending horse and auto meetings, but not actual races. The collar piping was abolished in mid-1940.

vered or white pebbled metal.[55] The gold buttons had to be replaced as soon as possible. Aluminum buttons were mainly used after 1942. Also, during the war pot metal and zinc were used.

September 1943: The manufacturing of caps in twill was forbidden; tricot had not been used since early in the war. The heavier SA cloth was the only material now used.[56]

Late 1944: The manufacturing of the felt–like material (as used for the top) was largely discontinued. The remaining stocks were to be used in the uniform industry only and probably not for the headgear production. It must be noted that this industry met with many problems due to war circumstances and manufacturing was on many occasions very difficult.[57]

The color lists were not changed between September 1934 and September 1938. In this month three new districts were added. Some others followed up until September 1942. In 1941 and 1942 six districts were renamed. All changes

---

55 "Vbl.d.OSAF," Nr. 2, May 20, 1941, p. 5. Nr. 11: "Vereinheitlichung des SA–Dienstanzuges."

56 "Deutsche Uniformen–Zeitschrift," Nr. 7, October 15, 1943, p. 9:"Mbl.d.RZM," Nr. 6, September 9, 1943, p. 43.

57 "Mbl.d.RZM," Nr. 12, December 1944, p. 4.

C. Cornelissen

A rare photograph showing a hodge–podge of uniforms from political organizations. This photograph was probably taken just as the war ended. Note that practically no rank insignia or brassards are being worn. All forms of headdress are visible still with the national emblems: the regular SA kepi, the forage cap for the SA–Wehrmannschaften, an SA garrison cap with the eagle in the center of the lowest part (mid–photo) and so on.

or added districts are listed below. The used dates were as published in the "Verordnungsblatt der Obersten SA–Führung," being:

GROUP OR DISTRICT:	TOP COLOR:	PIPING (WHEN ALLOWED):	BUTTON:
September 19, 1938 Alpenland: (districts Oberdonau, Salzburg and Tirol–Vorarlberg)	red–brown	bright red/white	silver;
Donau: (district Niederdonau and the city of Vienna)	ibid	ibid	gold;
Südmark: (districts Steiermark and Kärnten)[58]	pinkish–red	ibid	silver.
November 26, 1938 Sudeten: (Sudetenland)[59]	blue–grey	yellow/bright red	gold.

[58] *"Vbl.d.OSAF," Nr. 9, September 19, 1938, pp. 63–64. Nr. 149: Farbe für die Gruppen Donau, Alpenland und Südmark.*

[59] *Ibid, Nr. 12, November 24, 1938, p. 81. Nr. 196.*

March 9, 1940 Weichsel: (the city of Danzig and the Westpreussen district)	ibid	silver/brown	silver;
Warthe: (the district Wartheland)[60]	cornflower–blue	ibid	ibid.
March 31, 1941 Oberrhein: (parts of the free–state Baden and Elsass)[61]	ibid	ibid	ibid
September 1, 1942 Generalgouvcrnement: (Poland)[62]	bright grey	ibid	ibid.

The old stocks kept by some companies for SA–reserves, now became very useful to the Generalgouvernement.

Otto Spronk

The wearing of a bright grey top was introduced in September 1942 for the district Generalgouvernement in Poland. This SA member was assigned to the Einsatzstab Reichsleiter Rosenberg. The photograph was taken at Krakow in 1943.

A SA higher leader's cap worn by the ranks of Oberführer and Brigadeführer. This rare example has a bright grey colored top which was used by the unit from the Generalgouvernent (Poland: the area between Warsaw, Cracow, and Lemberg). Bright grey was introduced on September 1, 1942 and worn for about two years. The Tresse is an unofficial form. Its useage is not unique because of stock shortages during the war.

Renamed July 1, 1941

The group Ostmark was renamed Oder and Westmark to Mittelrhein.[63]

Renamed August 1942

The group Bayer. Ostmark was renamed Bayernwald, Mitte to Elbe, Südwest to Neckar and Ostland to Tannenberg.[64] (The color of the top remained unchanged with these changes).

Edelweiss for Hochland

From 1931, all members of the Hochland district were allowed to wear the metal Edelweiss flower insigne on the left side of the flap, just above the chin strap button.[65] No evidence mentioned any official wear of this insigne for the district of Bayerische Ostmark (formed due to the separation from the Hochland district during the July 1933 SA reorganization). It is known that this form of flower was also worn in this region from mid–1933. With the 1934 SA dress regulations this insigne was restricted to the Hochland district only.[66]

The stemless flower insigne with nine large petals (one is a double petal), and five smaller petals in between, was approximately 3.8cm wide and approx-

---

[60] *Ibid, Nr. 1, March 9, 1940, p. 2. Nr. 3; "Mbl.d.RZM," Nr. 3, March 9, 1940, Color addendum for Sudeten, Warthe and Weichsel.*

[61] *Ibid, Nr. 2, May 20, 1941, p. 6. Nr. 14;"Mbl.d.RZM," Nr. 7, May 10, 1941, p. 41.*

[62] *Ibid, Nr. 3, September 1, 1942, p. 17. Nr. 84: Farben und Dienstgradabzeichen SA–Einheit Generalgouvernement (Ch/F.Nr. 13708); Mbl.d.RZM, Nr. 12. August 22, 1942. p. 55.*

[63] *"Vbl.d.OSAF," Nr. 2, May 20, 1941, p. 5. Nr. 10: Umbenennung von SA–Gruppen (Ch.Nr. 11210).*

[64] *"Mbl.d.RZM," Nr. 12, August 22, 1942, p. 55.*

[65] *"Entwurf Dienstvorschrift für die SA der NSDAP. " Diessen near Munich: 1931, p. 145. In 1932 it was also worn by members of the Austrian SA.*

[66] *"Anzugs–Ordnung für die SA," Teil 1. Der Oberste SA–Führer. München: May 1, 1934, Section II: Anzugsarten; sub–section 22: Sonderabzeichen der Gruppe Hochland, p. 27.*

R. LaRue Curren/O. Spronk

A member of the SA district Hochland wearing an Edelweiss flower insigne on the left side of his cap as ordered. Note that the center of the insigne is without the swastika.

imately 4.0cm high, and mainly made of stamped brass. It was finished with silver paint, but examples in plain brass have also been observed. The first versions occasionally were made of "neusilber." This insigne was often altered. The swastika, 9mm in diameter, was superimposed in black with brass (or yellow edges) and rested upon ten yellow stamens. This version for the Hochland district was never positioned upon an extra piece of (light blue) cloth. Early versions often lack the swastika.

A smaller version of this insigne existed, being approximately 2.8cm wide and 2.9cm high. The swastika with this example was 6mm in size. This form of Edelweiss insigne was never officially adopted by the SA, but photographs show this emblem often being worn.

Probably the members of the "Hilfswerk Nordwest" during their stay in Germany wore this form of insigne (in 1934/35) upon a red–brown diamond, prior to being replaced by the second form.[67]

Ulric of England

Two forms of Edelweiss insigne. At right the regular size; at left the smaller version, having the swastika symbol. On the reverse the RZM markings were positioned.

[67] This diamond was on the SA price list from the RZM in 1936 with article number 4078 and placed in the section for headdresses. A second version Edelweiss was not listed in this price list, so it is almost certain that the Hochland version was worn.

SA–Gruppe Hochland SA cap: note the position of the Edelweiss: it is positioned much too high. According to regulations, it had to be attached on the flap. The top color is light blue.

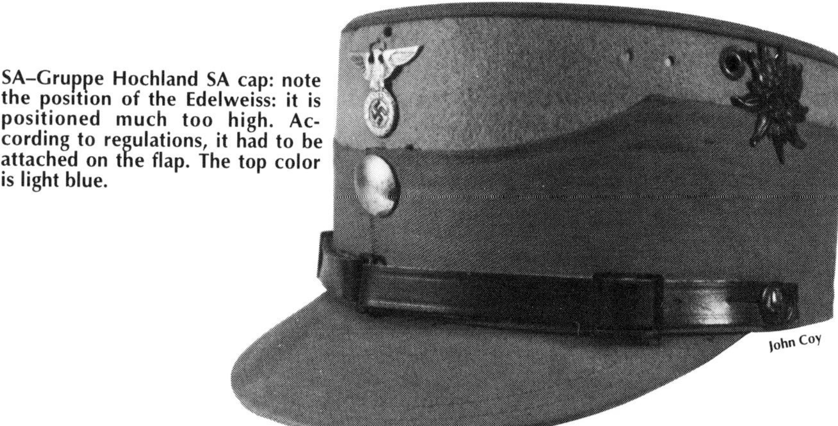

John Coy

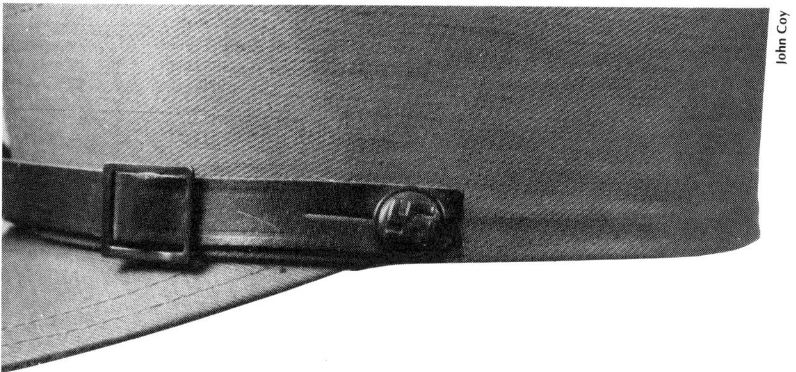

John Coy

Detail of the non–regulation chin strap button: note the embossed swastika in a horizontal position.

Clyde Davis

The Edelweiss flower, positioned on the left side above the chin strap button, as officially authorized to be worn by members of the Hochland district .

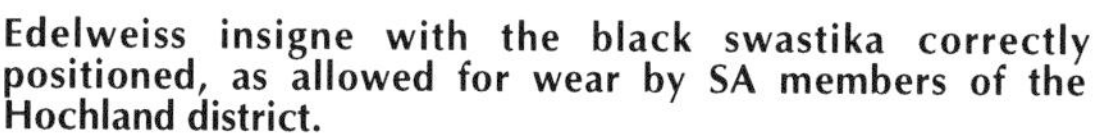

Edelweiss insigne with the black swastika correctly positioned, as allowed for wear by SA members of the Hochland district.

National Archives

W.P.B.R. Saris

During ski competition at Garmisch–Partenkirchen in February 1941, the Edelweiss flower is worn by a member of the SA district Hochland. Note the wearing of a silver crown piping and that the cap is without the ventilation holes.

Edelweiss for Austrian Units

Another variation of Edelweiss existed. No exact introduction date has been found, but it is believed to be 1935 as it was seen worn during the RPT at Nürnberg. This form with a stem, known as the "Edelweiss für Österreich," was mainly manufactured in light weight metals, such as aluminum and measured approximately 2.5cm wide by 5.1cm high. A swastika is never found on this badge, which was not included in the 1936 RZM price list..

The star shaped flower had twelve petals with six yellow, pebbled stamen. The stem was curved and had four "S" shaped long leaves, two being positioned next to the flower, the smaller leaves tipped the longer ones. This form was officially worn from November 1938 by the members of the SA groups Donau, Alpenland and Südmark. From June 1939, this insigne was referred to as "Edelweiss–Abzeichen für österreichische Gruppen" or "Ostmark–Edelweiss" and was in the same form as the Edelweiss introduced in 1941, known as "Form II," which was used by, for example, the inspection of the Ordnungspolizei at Salzburg.

This emblem was always worn on the left side of the flap upon a colored cloth diamond: red–brown for the districts Alpenland, Donau, and the regions of Oberdonau, Salzburg and Tirol–Vorarlberg, Niederdonau and Wien (Vienna). A pinkish red cloth diamond was worn by the Südmark district and the regions of Steiermark and Kärnten.[68] The colors for this diamond were the same as used for the cap top color. For staff and OSAF crimson and bright red diamonds were introduced in the spring 1942.

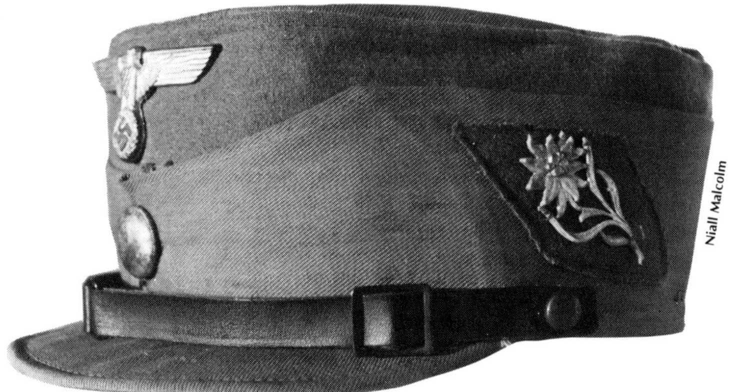

Südmark district SA cap with the pinkish–red top color. Note the Edelweiss upon the diamond in the same color. Note the rare short visor.

Detail of the Edelweiss, known as Form II, on a pinkish–red colored diamond.

No other colors were authorized for wear, but it is thought that in some regions in the Generalgouvernement of Poland a light grey diamond was worn from the fall of 1942.

The length of the diamonds were approximately 8.3cm and 4.3cm wide. An embroidered or woven version of the Edelweiss insigne was never sanctioned for wear with the SA headdress.

---

68 "Handbuch der SA." Berlin: 1939, p. 31. In the "Vbl.d.OSAF" the second form Edelweiss was firstly mentioned with the introduction for the colors for Alpenland, Donau and Südmark in September 1938, In the order it was literally said: the Edelweiss insigne with stem, as described until now for the Austrian group (die Gruppe Österreich).

Note the Edelweiss upon the backing: its position is not correct as the lowest tip of the flower's stem had to point downwards. The diamonds one side had to run parallel with the lower cap edge.

Jill Halcomb Smith

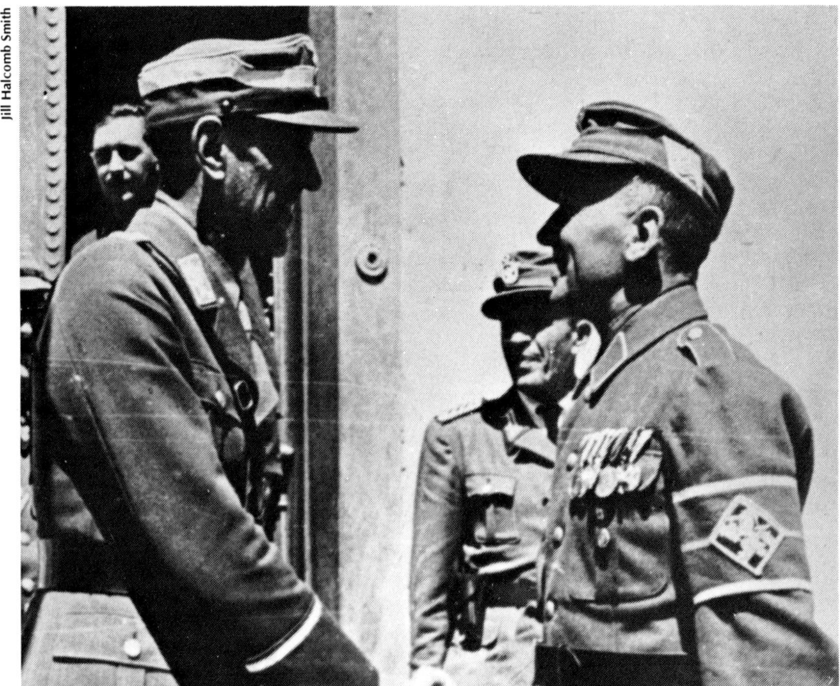

A member of the Styrian SA is wearing his mountain style SA cap with on the left side, the diamond with the Edelweiss flower for Austrian units.

Otto Spronk

Members of the SA district Alpenland are wearing the SA cap with the red–brown top during the Reichsparteitag in 1938. The "Kornett der Sturmfahne," in the middle, is bearing the SA flag of Salzburg: on the left side of his cap the Edelweiss insigne upon the diamond is positioned. Note also the wearing of the ski pants and ski boots with leggings.

W.P.B.R. Saris

A member from the Alpenland district is holding his SA kepi in his hand. Upon the left flap the Edelweiss for the Austrian area is positioned.

Ed Stadnicki

This cap was designated as "Dienstmütze der Jägereinheiten" for the Südmark district. It has the pinkish-red top and diamond for the Edelweiss flower. This style of cap is often incorrectly referred to as the "Einheitsfeldmütze '43."

Ed Stadnicki

SA cap for wear by a middle–class ranked leader according to the 1940 regulations for the staff of the Südmark district and the regions Steiermark and Kärnten. Probably due to a promotion, the flap piping was installed by hand using the aluminum form. The ventilation holes are in a contrasting color, being light–pink. With this form Edelweiss, the final form national emblem had to be worn at all times.

SA Garrison Cap (SA–Lagermütze)

Since the SA "coffee can" was considered among many to be impractical, a visorless garrison cap (in the regular field cap style) was developed in the spring of 1932. Groups in Schlesien and Berlin–Brandenburg were the first to wear this new form of headdress on an experimental basis. Röhm already wore such a cap prior to his announcement.

E.J. Bagale

A rare photograph showing Stabschef Röhm wearing the SA–Lagermütze with piping. The photograph is dated July 2, 1932.

Members of the SA wearing the SA garrison cap: the cap of the man left shows clearly the curvature of the flap portion. Note also that his cap is without the button.

Otto Spronk

This cap was meant to be worn during marches and exercises.[69] A second form was also developed, but not authorized. Its introduction was delayed until 1939 and it is believed that this was the form as introduced for wear by members of the SA–Wehrmannschaften (for more information, see this chapter, section: SA–Wehrmannschaften).

Officially, the SA garrison cap was introduced in February 1934 and described as "Lagermütze" or "Käppi" (simply "cap"), and was meant to be worn by leaders, as well as enlisted ranks.[70] This form was permitted during all occasions, except when the greater service dress was worn. This cap was not stiffened, and the curvature of the flap was similar to that of the "coffee can" cap.

SA–Lagermütze: Prior to the introduction of the woven silver wire national emblem, the metal national emblem in the early form was worn upon a colored felt triangle. This example has a brown backing, indicating the SA district Niedersachsen, as the button is in gilt. If the button was silver, the district would be Westmark.

Len Champion

[69] *Der Oberste SA–Führer. München: July 7, 1932. Qu.Nr. 1543/32: Bekleidung, section 2.*

[70] *"Vbl.d.OSAF,"·Nr. 17, February 1, 1934, p. 7. Nr. 19: Lagermütze (Kappi).*

The flap was closed by one small button. Color and material were as for the regular SA headdress.

An early style national emblem, half the size as the regular form (wingspan approximately 22 – 25mm, its height approximately 13mm: Assmann nrs. 23983 and 20640) was worn. This insigne had to be positioned in the front center above the flap. No piping, colored band or Tresse were allowed.[71] In fall 1934 new instructions for the manufacturing of this cap were authorized, and the regular form national eagle emblem was moved from the front to the left side of the cap.

Description 1934 Garrison Cap

This garrison cap was raindrop shaped terminating into a point at the back, (Reichsheer field cap style) and manufactured in heavier brown SA cloth (wool with a rough finish). The regular length of the cap (measured inside the top) was approximately 25cm for a size 56 cap. The height of thc body was 16cm at the most.

The front and back showed an overall, stitched–through seam. The flap could not be turned down, although it was loose. The curve of the flap, measuring 5cm high at the front center, vaulted to a 9.6cm height, and decreased in the back to approximately 7.2cm. The curve was 7.5cm long, and measured from the front center to the sharp edge, just below the ventilation grommet, which was positioned in the middle of the top and the upper edge of the flap. The inside lining was a field–grey cotton material and was sewn together with the cap material. A 3.5cm wide piece of cloth sweatband (Wachstuchstreifen) was sewn between this lining and the cloth, at its lowest edge.

Hans v. Diggelen

SA garrison cap with a black triangle and gilt button as used by the SA district Niederrhein.

The ordered insigne was positioned on the left side of the cap touching the sharp edge of the flap. It consisted of an equilateral triangle (sides 5cm) in felt in the color of the SA district. The early pattern SA eagle in regular size, in sil-

[71] *Illustrierter Beobachter. 7.Jahrgang. Samstag, July 2, 1932: front page photo; Deutsche Kraftfahrt, July 1934 issue, p. 9: an NSKK member of the Motorbrigade Leipzig wore an old SA style field cap.*

SA garrison cap for the Hochland district. The blue triangle is very small. Officially the eagle emblem had to fit completely inside the edges. Note the position of the ventilation hole.

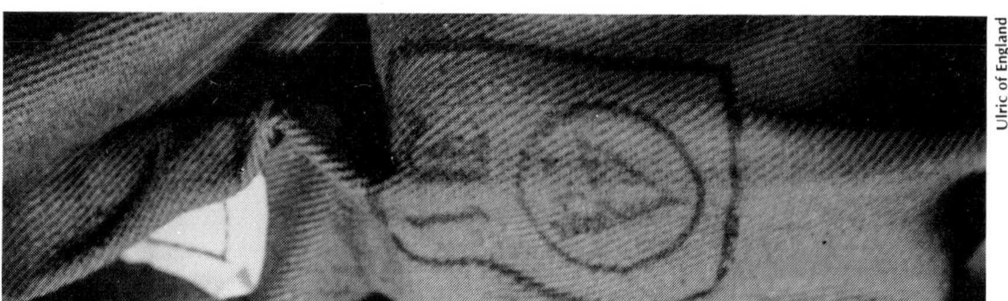

Inside stamp for the above SA garrison cap for the Hochland district, Jägerstandarte 1 ("Oberland" from Hochland).

vered metal, was positioned upon the center of the triangle.[72] Further, a button with a diameter of 18mm was worn on the front center of the cap flap. This button had a pebbled finish, and was in silver or gold, depending on the color for the SA district. The brown RZM tag was positioned on the inside of the cap front.

Note the SA–man at left. He is wearing his cap slanted. The front button is above his right eye.

72 *"Mbl.d.RZM," Nr. 15, September 8, 1934, pp. 3–4.*

W.P.B.R. Saris

The wearing of an SA garrison cap by an Obertruppführer. Note the ventilation hole and the position of the triangle. Photograph is dated 1936, Reichsparteitag.

Ed Stadnicki

Two SA garrison caps with the colored felt triangle and early pattern national emblem in metal, as allowed for wear from the fall of 1934 until September 1937.

The style of this cap remained, but in September 1937 a new style insigne was introduced. This national emblem was a silver woven eagle, facing its left, upon a colored field. The button with prongs was pulled through a metal grommet, which was installed in the front.[73] The old form triangle with metal insigne was abolished. (This garrison cap was occasionally worn by SA leaders through

[73] *RZM–Herstellungsvorschriften," 1936, 3.Nachtrag (addendum), p. 235; "Mbl.d.RZM, Nr. 19, München: September 11, 1937, p. 234.*

the years. The crown and flap edge were piped in silver or gold, according to the SA system for these higher ranking officials. The use of this piping was *never* officially permitted).

An SA–Lagermütze in the SA brown fabric with a silver wire, machine–woven national emblem on a black triangle and a matte, silver, pebbled front button, indicating the Berlin–Brandenburg district.

W.P.B.R. Saris

Apple-green (Thüringen and Pommern).

The woven SA national emblem for the garrison cap which was introduced in 1937. The triangle is 60mm wide and in the color of the SA district. Thüringen with silver button: Pommern with gold button.

A member of a signals unit from the district Berlin-Brandenburg wearing his garrison cap during the "Reichswettkämpfe der SA" on July 18, 1939. Note the manner of wear and the creases in the crown.

White on wine-red triangle for the districts of Ostland and Westfalen. The background is khaki colored. Ostland–gold button; Westfalen–silver button.

Jill Halcomb Smith

Edwin Johnson

Unique SA-Lagermütze with unofficial light blue/white piping around the crown of the cap. Note the white on light blue triangle and metal Edelweiss badge.

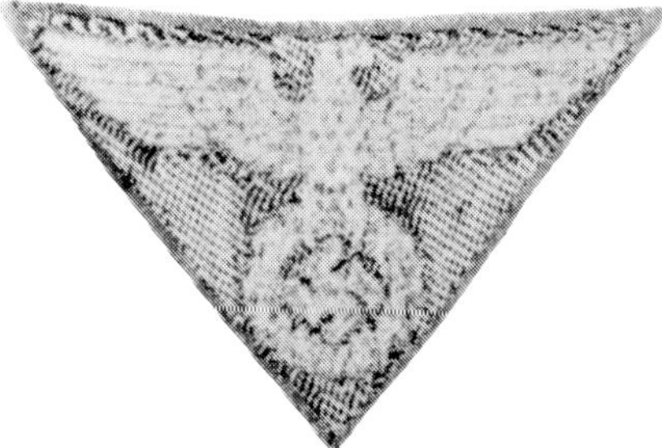

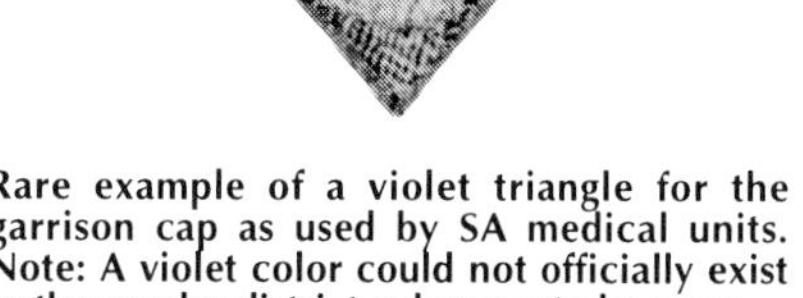

Rare example of a violet triangle for the garrison cap as used by SA medical units. Note: A violet color could not officially exist as the regular district color was to be worn.

An emerald-green triangle for Sachsen (with silver button); for Nordmark with gilt button.

Garrison Cap for SA leaders (SA–Führer Lagermütze)

Perhaps due to the aforementioned reasons, a new style garrison cap was authorized in December 1936. Beginning on January 2, 1937, this form was available from RZM stocks and for wear by the ranks Sturmführer and upwards. This cap was to be worn instead of the visorless garrison cap.[74] Its style had nothing in common with regular field or garrison cap styles.

This new cap was similar to the SA "coffee can" cap and made in SA gabardine with a cloth covered visor. The cap body was not stiffened. All regulation piping or Tresse were worn with this cap. An aluminum or white woven national emblem upon a district colored backing was positioned in the center of the cap front, with a golden or silver button on the flap. The structure of this cap resembled the regular form cap and therefore, period photographs do not prove

SA cap with a woven white national emblem upon a bright red top. This cap is not the standard SA kepi, but an SA garrison cap for leaders as introduced in early 1937. The bright red top indicates group staff members. It is often difficult to identify a cap in this style in photographs.

---

[74] *"Vbl.d.OSAF," Nr. 18, December 14, 1936, p. 132. Nr. 346: Lagermütze für SA–Führer.*

that this cap was actually worn. One period cap observed and attributed to Hitler's adjutant, Wilhelm Brückner, was described as a "Dienstmütze." This is probably not correct as in this case, the cap was an example of the visored SA leaders garrison cap. This particular example did not have a colored band, but did have embroidered insigne.

A September 1937 price list states that these caps were delivered with the colored top.[75] Regulations for wear:

a) to be allowed in–and outside service with the smaller service dress;
b) with the greater service dress when staying in a camp;
c) during sports or exercises;
d) during marches.
(c and d were only allowed when the enlisted ranks also wore a field cap).

Otto Spronk

SA members from the Nordsee district lined up during a training course. Note the wearing of a smaller version national emblem. Close observation of this photograph show that instead of a metal insigne, the triangular form was worn. This could indicate that all are wearing the so-called garrison cap for SA leaders.

---

[75] *Ibid, Nr. 12, September 3, 1937, p. 101. Nr. 274: Änderungsanzeigen der RZM; article number 4069, "Lagermütze für Führer mit Schild und Kinnriemen, sowie Gruppenstreifen"; "Mbl.d.RZM," Nr. 3, January 30, 1937, p. 29.*

Ski Cap and Mountain Cap (Skimütze u. Bergmütze)

In April 1932, an experimental ski cap was considered for wear by groups in the Hochland district, as well as by Austrian groups. An official ski cap and mountain cap were first mentioned in the March 1934 SA dress regulations, but were probably introduced in 1933. These caps were authorized for wear by the Jägerstandarten (hunter and rifle regiments) 1 and 3 from Hochland, as well as by mountain groups from Tirol, (Standarte 1), Salzburg (Standarte 59) and Oberösterreich (Standarte 2) in the Austrian areas.[76] Both forms were worn with the smaller service dress. With the greater service dress the regular SA kepi was ordered (for a color definition see further on in this section).

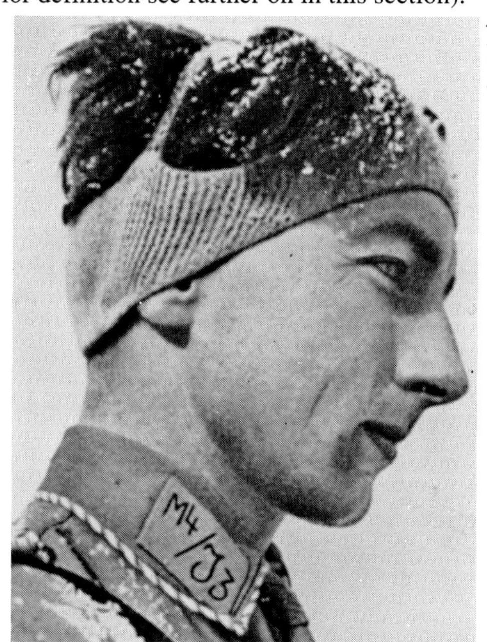

L. van Aerle

SA–Skiläufer of the Hochland district (from Motor–Sturm 4 of Jäger–Standarte 3) wearing the light brown (or sometimes grey) knitted head band. The Standarte 1 and 3 were for a long period of time the only groups that were allowed to wear the ski and mountain cap. In 1938, this changed, as by then other mountain units were also authorized, and the official ski uniform was introduced.

Previously an SA brown, knitted headband had been worn with the ski dress. The ski cap and the mountain cap, resembled for the most part the later lines of the "Einheitsfeldmütze 43" (which was introduced for the Armed Forces), being more of a longer oval, and having a large cloth covered visor. The flaps for the ski cap are usually closed by one, the mountain cap by two buttons. Both forms were worn together during skiing or mountain activities. In later years during skiing events, the ski cap was allowed to be worn by all other districts. It is not stated in orders if the Edelweiss flower was worn between 1934 and 1938 with the ski cap or the mountain cap, but those areas who were allowed this flower insigne surely would have utilized it. The wear of this emblem was officially not allowed for SA members of other regions.

---

76 *"Anzugs–Ordnung für die SA," Teil.1, München: March 1, 1934, Section II: Anzugsarten. p. 13.*

Otto Spronk

Members of a SA "Jäger-und Schützenstandarte" wear the cap with a light blue top as well as the dark green balls and cord attached to the right breast pocket (insigne for Jäger-und Schützen). The ski or mountain cap was to be worn during skiing activities, and the regular SA cap for parades. The SA coffee can cap was to be worn with the service dress.

Navorsingsinstituut Brussel

Members of the SA district Hochland at the Party Day Rally at Nürnberg in 1934. This photograph is interesting because of the excellent view of the insignia for "Jäger–und Schützen–Standarten," the so–called "Bolle," worn by the person standing in the middle. With the greater service dress, the standard SA kepi had to be worn.

In November 1938 an official uniform for skiing competition was authorized. A slightly modified gabardine ski cap with larger visor was ordered with a colored top. A woven national emblem was worn in the front center of the top.[77] It is surprising that a ski cap was first introduced by the RZM in early 1939, in spite of the fact that it had already been mentioned in the 1934 and the 1938 regulations.[78]

W.P.B.R. Saris

199. Betrifft: Bekleidung für Schi-Wettkämpfe.
FD 2 b Nr. 13704.

Für die NS.-Winterkampfspiele wird folgende Bekleidung festgelegt, die gleichfalls bei Gruppen- und Standartenwettkämpfen, sowie bei Teilnahme SA.-Angehöriger an sonstigen wintersportlichen Veranstaltungen getragen werden kann:

1. Schirock

   aus SA.-Gabardin mit 2 aufgesetzten Brust- und 2 eingelegten Seitentaschen. In Hüfthöhe ist eine Futtermanschette mit Gummizug eingearbeitet, ebenfalls befinden sich in den Ärmeln Futtermanschetten, die durch Gummizug fest am Handgelenk abschließen (Wind- und Schneeschutz).

   Dienstgradabzeichen und Armbinde werden am Schirock getragen, nicht dagegen die Ärmelstreifen.

2. Schihose

   aus SA.-Gabardin in Keilform mit Stegen; dazu kurze Gummi-Gamaschen.

3. Laufbluse

   aus Mazepo, SA.-braun, mit Reißverschluß am Kragen, 2 Brusttaschen und Hüftbund mit Gummizug. Sie ist hemdartig geschnitten und wird über oder in der Hose getragen. Auf der linken Brusttasche ist das SA.-Abzeichen, 9 cm Durchmesser, in schwarz auf weißem Grund, aufgenäht.

4. Schi-Pullover

   aus Trockenwolle, braun, mit Ärmel, hochgeschlossen, auf der linken Brustseite SA.-Abzeichen wie vor.

5. Schimütze

   aus SA.-Gabardin mit Gruppenstreifen, gewebtem Hoheitsabzeichen und langem Schild.

6. Fingerhandschuhe

   aus Trockenwolle, braun.

7. Rucksack

   mit Gewehrtasche und Anschnallriemen für Gewehr, grau.

Die Schibekleidung ist bei der Reichszeugmeisterei erhältlich.

In November 1938, a special ski uniform was ordered. Paragraph 5 states that the ski cap be made from gabardine with a colored top, a woven national emblem and a long visor. The claim that such a cap was the "Einheitsfeldmütze 43" is, therefore, not true.

---

[77] *"Vbl.d.OSAF," Nr. 12, München: November 24, 1938, p. 81. Nr. 199: Bekleidung für Schi–Wettkämpfe.*

[78] *Ibid, Nr. 5, April 1, 1939, p. 36. Nr. 35: Preisänderungsanzeige der RZM Nr. 1/39, section new entry Nr. 4419: Schi–Mütze.*

Hoover

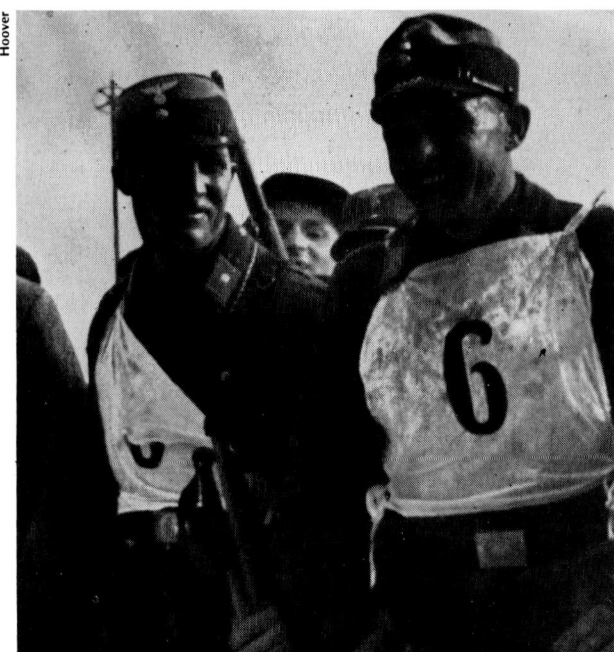

Members of the SA during ski matches. Note the wear of the soft bodied cap at right.

Otto Spronk

Members of the SA during ski activities are wearing their SA cap with the colored top.

The mountain cap was modified in the summer of 1938, having a somewhat larger visor and a colored top. Another modified form was introduced in the spring of 1942. The top of this mountain cap was higher and more oblong. Through the years it was manufactured in the heavier brown cloth (SA–Manteltuch, oliv–meliert). No colored top was mentioned, but it is known it was included. (The crown of the ski and also the mountain cap were probably piped for a short while according to district colors, since specimens exist with various

John Coy

The SA ski cap with a red top piping. The button and national emblem are in white metal. Officially, a woven national emblem was ordered for wear with the ski headdress.

A Standartenführer from the Hochland district. Note that his cap has two buttons. On the front center is positioned the new form national emblem.

colored piping. It is thought this practice was done because no colored top was worn earlier. No manufacturing or other regulation, however, mentions a piping for either the ski or mountain cap).

The flaps were closed by two olive (or brown) colored buttons and with a 12mm diameter "eyelet."[79] In late 1942 two forms mountain cap were available: one having a colored top, the other without. Both were sold having either the reddish–brown or pinkish–red diamond with the Edelweiss flower (for the districts Alpenland, Donau and Südmark) on the left side and from December 1942 both forms were also used by the Hochland district with the specific Edelweiss for that area.[80]

During the war this headdress was regularly worn by members of the SA–Wehrmannschaften stationed in previously mentioned areas. The mountain cap was officially identified as "Dienstmütze für Jägereinheiten." (It must be noted that, at this time, this cap was in fact not a new style. After the war the "Dienstmütze für Jägereinheiten" was incorrectly referred to as "Einheitsfeldmütze 43." One must note that this form surely existed in late 1938, as it was mentioned in the Mbl.d.RZM, as well as the Vbl.d.OSAF). The crown was piped in silver or gold, according to SA custom (from May 1941 only silver, or aluminum was allowed). If two colored piping was ever worn it was not mentioned in any regulation. In addition, no period photograph has been found showing it being worn.

One of the most well–known active units within the SA–Wehrmannschaften was the "Steierischer Heimatbund" (Styrian Home League), formed from al-

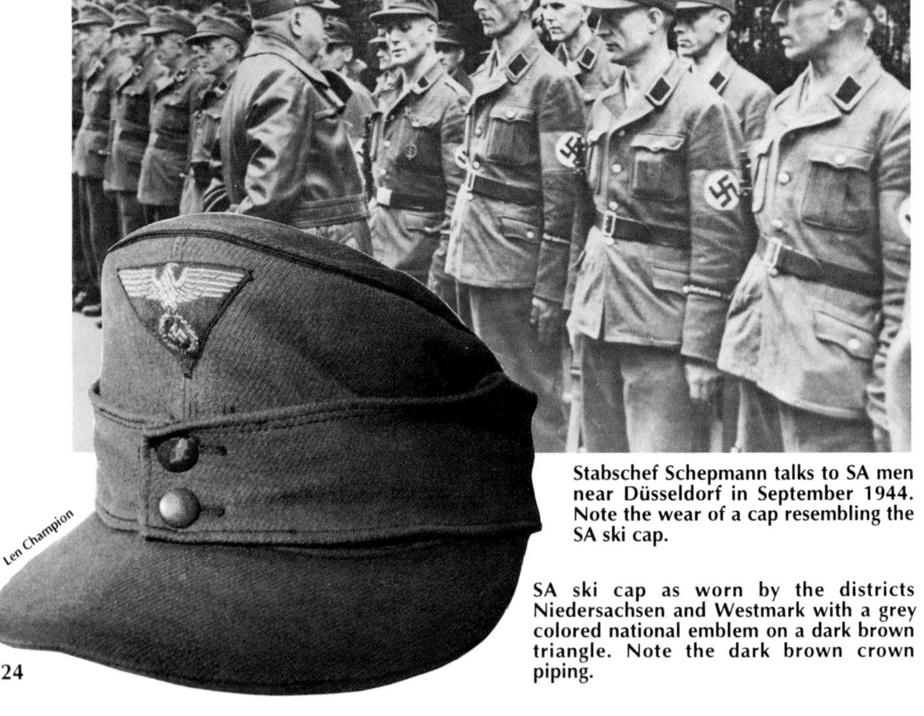

Stabschef Schepmann talks to SA men near Düsseldorf in September 1944. Note the wear of a cap resembling the SA ski cap.

SA ski cap as worn by the districts Niedersachsen and Westmark with a grey colored national emblem on a dark brown triangle. Note the dark brown crown piping.

ready existing mountain units (Jägereinheiten) in the Südmark district to protect their borders. The members of this unit were not supplied with the regular form of garrison cap and regularly wore the SA mountain cap with the Edelweiss insigne with stem, positioned upon a pinkish red cloth diamond on the left side of the flap. The stem officially had to point downwards. The top color was pinkish red (the Italian style forage cap, as introduced for the SA–Wehrmannschaften, was also worn by Styrian units).

One must note that the description in regulations of the SA color brown is sometimes quite confusing. In the March 1934 regulations, it literally says: ...with the definition SA brown is meant the, with order I.Nr.1648, dated November 11, 1933, newly introduced "brown–green" color." The greatcoat was of the varying color olive–green. This color was changed in the spring of 1934 to olive–brown and later referred to as "oliv–meliert," a brownish–green shade. (In the reference book "Die Uniformen der Braunhemden" by von Eelking, March 1934, the tunic was defined as a middle olive–brown (mittleren Oliv–braun); the greatcoat as olive colored). We note this as through the years the color for the ski and mountain uniform (including the forms of headdress ordered) resembled the color of the greatcoat. It was, in fact almost always a color with an greenish–olive shade; the same color as, in later years, also worn by the SA–Wehrmannschaften, and also at SA schools and training camps or at SA motor schools (for details consult the section within this chapter).

A sample of a stamp which was positioned in white paint, usually upon the cloth identified as "SA–Manteltuch" and as published in the Mitteilungsblatt der RZM.

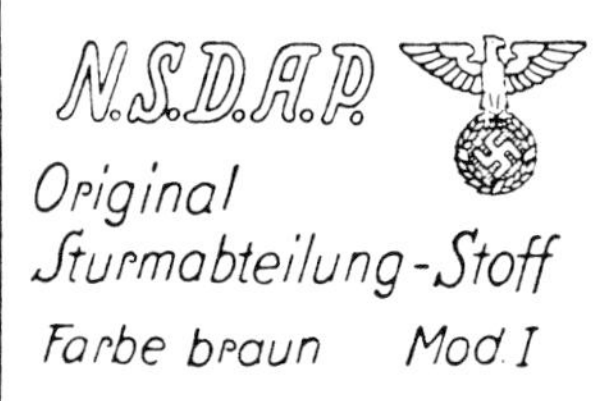

Other forms of stamps as usually found on cloth rolls. These stamps were not always found on the inside of caps, as they were further apart on the manufactured material.

---

[79] *Ibid, Nr. 1, April 10, 1942, p. 6; Ibid, Nr. 4, December 5, 1942, p. 24; "Mbl.d.RZM," Nr. 8, May 31, 1942, p. 36.*

[80] *"Vbl.d.OSAF," Nr. 4, December 5, 1942, p. 24.*

W.P.B.R. Saris

68. Betrifft: Änderungsanzeige der R.Z.M.
Nr. 7/41 und 1/42.
VB 1 a — 444 00/42.

Änderungsanzeige Nr. 7/41.

Preisänderungen:

Nr.	Artikel	RM.
1 123	Socken, Wolle, grau	1.80
1 133 (neue Nummer)	Übergangsanzug, braun-oliv	9.70

Neuzugänge:

Nr.	Artikel	RM.
1 083/10	Bergmütze, Tuch ohne Gruppenstreifen, mit Hoheitsabzeichen, 2 Knöpfen u. Ostmark-Edelweiß auf rosa oder rotbrauner Raute	3.50
1 083/11	dto. mit Gruppenstreifen	3.55

109. Betrifft: Änderungsanzeige der R.Z.M. Nr. 3/42, 4/42, 5/42 u. 7/42.
VB. 1a — 444 00/42.

Änderungsanzeige Nr. 7/42.

Preisänderungen:

Nr.	Artikel	RM.
1 081/11	Dienstmütze, Tuch, mit Gruppenstreifen u. Hoheitsabzeichen	3.25
1 083/10	Bergmütze, Tuch, ohne Gruppenstreifen, mit Hoheitsabzeichen und Ostmark-Edelweiß	3.65
1 083/11	Bergmütze, Tuch, mit Gruppenstreifen, Hoheitsabzeichen und Ostmark-Edelweiß	3.70
1 430/1	Kragenspiegel, blank, in allen Gruppenfarben	--.19
1 430/3	Kragenspiegel, bestickt, in allen Gruppenfarben	--.35

Neuzugänge:

Nr.	Artikel	RM.
1 083/13	Bergmütze, Tuch, ohne Gruppenstreifen mit Hoheitsabzeichen und Hochland-Edelweiß	3.65
1 471	Ärmelstreifen „Carl Röver", silbergrau bestickt	—.40

Der Stabschef:

Lutze.

The SA price lists were constantly corrected and new items were added. Here shown, are two parts of such corrections and additions from late 1941 and 1942. It is interesting to read that a new entry, Nr. 1083/10, was available, being a mountain cap without a colored top, but with the national emblem, two buttons and the Ostmark form of Edelweiss, upon either a pink or red-brown diamond. Nr. 1083/11 was the same but with a colored top. Nr. 1083/13 was as for the earlier mentioned Nr. 1083/10 but with the Hochland Edelweiss. This cap was available from mid-1942.

Südmark SA leaders' mountain cap with two flap buttons and pinkish–red top color. Note the Austrian version Edelweiss flower upon a diamond, as per regulations. Members of the Styrian and Kärnten Wehrmannschaften often wore this form of headdress. It was normally known as the Dienstmütze für Jägereinheiten, a cap most often worn in mountain areas. Often this cap is referred to as a "Einheitsmütze '43.'"

Ed Stadnicki

Styrian Wehrmannschaften in action.

Museum Dec. '44 – La Gleize, Belgium

SA mountain cap with a cloth triangular eagle emblem. The eagle is in woven grey upon red–brown backing. The cap is without the colored top; the buttons are painted SA brown.

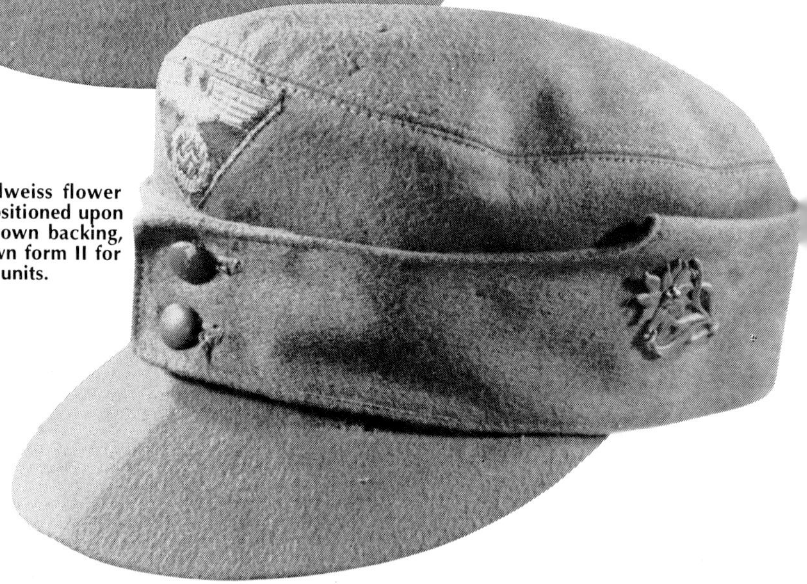

The Edelweiss flower is not positioned upon a red–brown backing, the known form II for Austrian units.

The RZM tag for the Mountain cap. The sweat band is in light brown; the tag is also in brown, reading "Tuchmütze." The manufacturer number 18 indicates Theodor Dittrich from Chemnitz in Saxony.

SA Leaders (SA–Führer)

B. Diroll/Klaus D. Patzwall

Various SA leaders in 1934. At left is a Standartenführer-ranked man with no leadership function; at right is a Standartenführer who was leading a Standarte. The Obersturmbannführer in the center possibly had an advisory function, and for this reason he would be permitted to wear the cap Tresse.

1926 – 1928

In early fall 1926, shortly after the Party Day at Weimar, the SA cap for leaders was modified. The flap of this cap was higher than for enlisted ranks. At the back and the sides the flap was 1cm below the crown, so that any authorized colored top for SA leaders was visible.[81] It must be noted that this colored top, made of a felt–like material, was intended for wear by the ranks of Sturmführer and Standartenführer only. The group of wearers was very restricted and may not have exceeded a total of twenty–five throughout the entire membership of the SA during 1926. The order was extended at the last moment to the highest SA ranks, being Brigadeführer and Oberführer from a province staff (Gaustab). The color of this top matched the color of the collar tabs. The leather chin strap became a standard item. In the same decree it was stated that the wearing of any other form of insigne, i.e. death's head's, etc. was forbidden.

Piping for the ranks Standartenführer, adjutants and ranks upwards were first introduced November 11, 1926. This officially 3mm piping was worn at the crown only in gold or silver, depending on the color of the ordered cap button.[82] This button color system was officially authorized two days later by another decree.[83]

A list was published November 13, 1926. The button color was officially ordered for all ranks. (Note: The two color piping system was not introduced earlier than 1929, but to avoid another complete list, this system is included with this 1926 list).

---

81 *SA–Befehl der OSAF. November 12, 1926. 12.Sturmführer, section II: Mütze, number 15.*

82 *Ibid. November 11, 1926. 11.Sturmführer.*

83 *Ibid. November 13, 1926. 13.Gauführung: "Einteilung des Gaust.."*

GAU COLOR: (PROVINCE–LEVEL)	COLLAR TAB COLOR, ALSO USED FOR THE TOP:	PIPING OR BUTTON:	TWO COLOR PIPING:
München, Oberbayern, Schwaben and Nieder–bayern:	light blue	silver	light blue/ white;
Franken and Nordbayern:	white	ibid	ibid;
Württemberg:	black	ibid	black/red;
Baden:	yellow	gold	yellow/red;
Hessen:	light blue	silver	light blue/red;
Thüringen:	green	gold	green/black;
Sachsen:	ibid	silver	green/white;
Böhmen:	dark red	ibid	dark red/white;
Österreich:	black	gold	black/yellow;
Schlesien:	yellow	silver	yellow/white;
Berlin, Brandenburg, Ostmark and Pommern:	black	ibid	black/white;
Ostpreussen and Balten–land (also known as Ostland):	white	gold	ibid;
Mecklenburg:	yellow	ibid	yellow/black;
Halle, Merseburg, Magdeburg and Anhalt:	white	silver	white/green;
Hannover:	ibid	gold	white/yellow;
Schleswig–Holstein, Hamburg, Lübeck (also known as Nordmark or Waterkant):	ibid	silver	white/red;
Friesland, Oldenburg and Bremen:	dark blue	ibid	dark blue/red;
Ruhr:	black	ibid	black/green;
Rhein:	light blue	gold	light blue/black;
Pfalz, Saar, Elsass–Lothringen:	black	ibid	black/blue.[84]

[84] *Ibid.*

E.J. Bagale

Members of the SA in Munich wear the single button type cap. It appears in this photograph dated April 15, 1925 that a colored top has been added. This was not officially introduced for wear until late 1926 and then exclusively ordered for wear by a limited group of higher ranked persons. Note that no leather chin strap is being worn, and the unique shape of the collar patches.

Otto Spronk

Kurt Daluege, later a police general, shown as leader of an SA Gau, with his adjutant, photographed wearing the earliest style SA caps in the mid–twenties.

W.P.B.R. Saris

CSAF. **SABE 11 Sturmf.** 11. 11. 26.

Verantwortlich für die Aufbewahrung ist nicht nur der bezeichnete F sondern auch dessen Vorgesetzter. Letzterer hat sich von Zeit zu Zeit nicht nur von dem Vorhandensein zu überzeugen, sondern auch von der Art der Aufbewahrung.

Abzeichen (im Einzeln).

1. Das Haupt-Zeichen ist der Spiegel. An ihm erkennt man die einzelnen Verbände. An seinen Sternen erkennt man die unteren Führer. Spiegel mit Rändern bezeichnet stets einen höheren Führer.

2. Bis zum Sturm einschließlich trägt alles die Sturm Nr. auf dem rechten Spiegel.

3. Der Gruf 1 Stern auf linkem Spiegel.

4. Der Trf 2 Sterne auf linkem Spiegel.

5. Der Sturmf 3 Sterne auf linkem Spiegel.
   Die Spiegel gerändert.
   Halstuch gerändert.

6. Der Staf 4 Sterne auf linkem Spiegel, Sta Nr. auf rechtem Spiegel.
   Die Spiegel mit einer Schnüre gerändert.
   Halstuch mit Schnüre gerändert.
   Mützendeckel mit Schnure gerändert.
   Ärmel mit Schnüre gerändert.

7. Der Sta-Adj beide Spiegel mit Sta Nr.
   Halstuch, Mützendeckel, Ärmel und Schnüre gerändert.

Sonstiger Stab: nur auf rechtem Spiegel Sta Nr.

Spielmannszug: außerdem Schwalbennester, Führer wie 3 oder 4.

Sanitäter: weiße Binde mit rotem Kreuz.

gez.: v. Pfeffer

One of the first SA orders. This one is dated November 11, 1926 and gives specific information about rank insignia for use with the collar patch. It is interesting to note that the Standartenführer was then the highest rank in command. In paragraph 6, this rank is described as having the cap crown piped. Paragraph 7 is for the adjutant of the Standartenführer, which also had crown piping.

OSAF. 5. 6. 27.

GRUSA V

Grundsätzliche Anordnungen der SA.
Streng vertraulich! Nur für den Dienstgebrauch innerhalb der NSDAP!

(Neudruck v. 30. 7. 30.)

Dienst-Anzug. — Abzeichen.

1.) Der Dienstanzug ist ein Ehrenkleid. Sein Träger ist der öffentliche Repräsentant unserer Bewegung. Niemand darf das auch nur einen Augenblick vergessen.

2.) Der Dienstanzug ist das Braunhemd (Halstuch und Mütze) mit Abzeichen. SA-Abzeichen sind: Spiegel, Nummern, Sterne, Schnüren, blanke Metallknöpfe an Mütze und Brusttaschen, Armbinde. All dieses darf nur von SA-Männern getragen werden, die selbst darauf sehen müssen, daß nicht eines dieser Abzeichen von Unberechtigten getragen wird. Braunhemd (Halstuch und Mütze) ohne Abzeichen sind kein Dienstanzug und dürfen von jedem Pg getragen werden.

3.) Verboten sind alle nicht ausdrücklich vorgeschriebenen Abzeichen zum Dienstanzug, insbesondere: Kokarden, Totenköpfe, Schwerter, Kronen, Pfeile, Edelweiß, Federn, Litzen, Schleifen, Bänder, Sterne, Broschen, Plaketten usw.

4.) Zum Dienstanzug sind kurze Hosen, möglichst braune, zu tragen. Windjacken gestattet, ohne Abzeichen. Gegen Kälte ist jedoch besser, Wollzeug unterzuziehen. Gegen Regen ist umgehängte Zeltbahn besser, die auch gerollt besser zu tragen ist. Immer aber muß der Anzug innerhalb des Sturmes einheitlich sein.

5.) Der Dienstanzug darf nur im Dienst getragen werden. Wer den Dienstanzug trägt, befindet sich im Dienst und untersteht den SA-Vorschriften und der Kommandogewalt seines Vorgesetzten. Wer zur Arbeit oder im täglichen Leben ein Braunhemd tragen will, darf seinen Dienstanzug nur dann dazu verwenden, wenn er ihn ausrangiert und alle Abzeichen entfernt hat.

6.) Die Abzeichen sind Dienststellen-Abzeichen, nicht Rangabzeichen. Es gibt bei uns keinen Rang, alle SA-Männer haben denselben Rang. Also gibt es niemanden, der Rang und Abzeichen eines Staf trägt, aber keine Sta führt, ebenso gibt es niemanden, der eine Sta führt, dem aber nur Rang und Abzeichen eines Tf zuständen. Die (Dienststellen-) Abzeichen sind vielmehr mit dem Wechseln der Stelle an- und abzulegen. Wechsel und Rücktritt sind also keine Schande und keine Degradierung.

7.) Der SA-Mann trägt in beiden Kragenecken einen Spiegel, dessen Farbe bei den einzelnen Verbänden verschieden ist. Auf dem rechten Spiegel wird die Sturm-Nr. getragen.

8.) Überholt durch Sabe „Abzeichen im Einzelnen (zu Grusa V") v. 25. 5. 29

9.) „

10.) „

11.) „

12.) „

gez.: v. Pfeffer

Für diese grundsätzlichen Anordnungen übernimmt die Parteileitung die Verantwortung.

Der Vorsitzende der NSDAP:
gez.: Adolf Hitler

Another early order. This one is officially dated June 5, 1927, but was repeated on July 30, 1930. Paragraph one orders the use of a the smooth cap button. Paragraph 3 forbids the wearing of cockades, death heads, the Edelweiss and other insignia. Note that this order was signed by Hitler as chairman of the NSDAP.

Franz von Pfeffer von Salomon, wearing an early cap without a chinstrap. Note the two buttons on the flap.

Otto Spronk

Hitler and Franz Pfeffer von Salomon during the third Party Day Rally in 1927 at Nürnberg. Pfeffer von Salomon is wearing the "Hitlermütze" without the colored top. Note the wear of two buttons. The member of the Allgemeine-SS, at right, wears his black style SS cap with the death's head as the only insigne, shortly before the introduction of the eagle national emblem in the fall of the same year.

Otto Spronk

The SA marches in November 1926.

1929 – 1930

The development of the SA accelerated during the late twenty's and steps had to be taken for a better system of identification. For this reason, the 1926 piping system was introduced for wear on the collar with the date March 25, 1929. Simultaneously, this system was also implemented for wear on the cap by middle and higher ranked SA leaders. The cap top color for the highest SA leaders within the OSAF was changed to red.[85] (For more information consult the March 25, 1929 list with colors for top, piping and buttons for the highest SA ranks and functions. This list is composed from details given in various orders from spring 1929 and includes the ranks up to Gruppenführer).

New classifications were given to SA districts. The 1926 color schedule was changed and adapted for various districts and had to be in force by the Party Day Rallies at Nürnberg in August:

Franken:	from white to yellow;
Hessen:	from light blue to dark blue;
Österreich:	from black to brown;
Brandenburg and Ostmark:	from black to white;
Pommern:	from black to blue;
Mecklenburg:	from yellow to blue;
Halle, Merseburg, Magdeburg and Anhalt:	from white to yellow;
Hannover:	from white to brown;
Schleswig–Holstein and Hamburg;	from white to green;
Friesland:	from dark blue to brown;
Rhein:	from light blue to dark blue;

[85] *SA–Befehl der OSAF zu GRUSA V. München: March 25, 1929.*

Some districts were incorporated into others: Nordbayern, Baltenland, Lübeck, Oldenburg and Bremen. Some new districts were added:

Danzig:	white;
Lüneburg:	green;
Dithmarschen:	ibid;
Nassau:	blue;
Oberpfalz:	ibid.

(No information concerning the color for the district Elsass–Lothringen was given; Böhmen was now referred as "Ausland").

The colored top was mainly the removable type, since they were in fact nothing more than a loose cover. Only those who could afford it, obtained caps with a colored top directly sewn around the body of the cap.

March 25, 1929 :

RANK:	TOP COLOR:	CROWN PIPING:	FLAP PIPING:	BUTTON:
Chef des Stabes, der Oberste SA–Führer: (Chief of Staff and Highest SA Leader)	red	gold	gold	gold;
OSAF–Stellvertreter: (Deputy OSAF: this was most often a person holding the rank of Oberführer)	ibid	silver	silver	silver;
Stab und Adjutant der OSAF: (Staff and Adjutant for the OSAF)	ibid	ibid	ibid	ibid;
Stab und Adjutant OSAF–Stellvertreter:	no colored top	gold or silver according to button color from 1926 list	no piping	color per 1926 list;
Oberführer:[86]	ibid	ibid	ibid	ibid;
Adjutant–Oberführer:	no colored top	ibid	no piping	ibid;
Oberführer Stab:	ibid	no piping	ibid	ibid;
Brigadeführer:	as Ober–führer	as Ober–führer	ibid	ibid;
Adjutant–Brigadeführer:	no colored top	ibid	ibid	ibid;

Brigadeführer Stab:	ibid	no piping	ibid	ibid;
Standartenführer:	ibid	as for Ober–führer	ibid	ibid;
Adjutant–Standartenführer:	ibid	two color piping per 1926 list	ibid	ibid;
Standartenführer Stab: (Staff for the Standarten–führer)	ibid	no piping	ibid	ibid;

Otto Spronk

A photograph from the "Oberste SA–Führer" of Franz von Pfeffer von Salomon during the Party Day Rally in 1929. This photograph clearly shows the colored top and crown, as well as the flap piping. No eagle emblem was yet permitted. Von Pfeffer wore a red colored top, golden piping and a gold–colored button.

86 The rank Oberführer did not wear a colored top, but when more than two units in the size of a "Standarte" were in service or action he was allowed to wear a cover in the color of the collar tab, worn according to his district assignment.

Sturmführer:	ibid	two color piping	ibid	ibid;
Truppführer:	ibid	no piping	ibid	ibid;
Gruppenführer: (this lower rank should not be confused with the later high leaders rank, introduced in April 1931)	ibid	ibid	ibid	ibid;
Musikzug: (members of a band)	ibid	ibid	ibid	ibid;
Musikzugführer: (leader of a band)	ibid	two color piping	ibid	ibid;
Spielmannszug:	ibid	no piping	ibid	ibid.[87]

It is interesting to note the colors for the cap top as prescribed and ordered for the march during the Party Day at Nürnberg on Sunday August 4, 1929. This survey gives the exact number of wearers during this day. Only twenty–two persons were permitted to wear a colored top. Another interesting fact with this order is, that some of the ranks given for the persons assigned to the OSAF wore their old Armed Forces ranks and not their SA rank:

Der Oberste SA–Führer (OSAF)	
Hauptmann Franz von Pfeffer von Salomon:	red
His adjutant Hallermann:	no colored top
Der OSAF–Stellvertreter/Ost	
Hauptmann Walter Stennes from Berlin:	red
Under his command were the groups Ostpreussen, Danzig, Pommern, Schlesien, Mecklenburg and Magdeburg/Anhalt led by:	
Brigadeführer (II) Stucken:	yellow
and Brandenburg/Ostmark and Berlin led by:	
Oberführer Jahn from Berlin/Brandenburg:	black
Der OSAF–Stellvertreter/Nord	
Major Paul Dincklage from Hannover:	red
His adjutant Korsemann:	no colored top
Dincklage commanded the groups Hannover, Lüneburg, Friesland (Weser–Ems) and Nord–mark led by:	
Oberführer Schoene from Nordmark:	green
Dincklage also commanded Schleswig and Holstein led by:	
Brigadeführer (III) Böhmcker:	ibid

Otto Spronk

Goebbels, as Gauleiter of Berlin, speaks in front of the SA in 1929. Note the SA leader in front of the car who is obviously wearing no crown piping. His flap however has piping clearly visible.

and Dithmarschen led by:	
Brigadeführer (V) Grantz:	ibid
and Hamburg led by:	
Brigadeführer (I) Ellerhusen:	ibid
Der Oberführer Ruhr	
Oberleutnant Viktor Lutze from Elberfeld:	black
His adjutant Pelz:	no colored top
Lutze commanded the group from Westfalen.	
Der OSAF–Stellvertreter/Nord	
Oberleutnant Kurt von Ulrich from Kassel:	red
His adjutant von Fichte:	no colored top
Von Ullrich commanded Rheinland, Pfalz, Hessen and Nassau led by:	
Brigadeführer (II) Vosshagen:	blue
Der OSAF–Stellvertreter/Mitte	
Kapitänleutnant Manfred von Killinger from Dresden:	red
His adjutant Spindler:	no colored top
Von Killinger commanded Thüringen led by:	
Oberführer Zunkel from Thüringen:	green

[87] *SA–Befehl der OSAF zu GRUSA V. München: March 25, 1929.*

and Halle–Merseburg led by: Brigadeführer (I) Weinreich:	yellow
and Sachsen led by: Oberführer Schlegel from Sachsen:	green
Der OSAF–Stellvertreter/Süd Major August Scheidhuber from München:	red
Scheidhuber commanded Baden led by: Oberführer Windhagen from Baden:	yellow
and Württemberg led by: Brigadeführer (III) von Jagow:	black
Scheidhuber also commanded Bayern, Oberpfalz, Niederbayern, Schwaben and München–Oberbayern led by: Brigadeführer (I) Helfer:	blue
as well as Unter–Franken, Mittel–Franken and Oberfranken led by: Brigadeführer (V) Mehl:	yellow
Der Oberführer Österreich Oberleutnant Hermann Reschny from Wien:	brown
His adjutant Türk:	no colored top

Reschny commanded the group from Österreich, but also the foreign groups from Böhmen, Paraguay, Chicago, Barcelona, Süd–West–Afrika and Schweden.[88]

Otto Spronk

Viktor Lutze, the Oberführer Ruhr and commander of the Westfalen group, during the Party Day Rally1929 at Nürnberg. Lutze was allowed to wear the colored top in black. Only leaders with special functions were allowed to wear the colored top at this time.

[88] *Spezial–Verfügung zum "Festzug der SA." Nürnberg, Sunday August 4, 1929.*

Festzug der SA

Nürnberg / Sonntag, den 4. August 1929

Alle SA-Männer tragen in beiden Kragen-Ecken farbige Spiegel. An den verschiedenen Farben sind die SA-Verbände zu erkennen. Abteilungen ohne Spiegel sind Reserve-Abteilungen (SAR) des unmittelbar vorhermarschierenden SA-Verbandes. Reihenfolge des Festzuges:

Der Oberste SA-Führer (Osaf), Hauptmann Franz v. Pfeffer
Adj. Hallermann (rote Spiegel)
nur von der Fleischbrücke bis zum Hauptmarkt, wo er mit Adolf Hitler den Vorbeimarsch abnimmt.

Der Osaf-Stellv/Ost, Hauptmann Walter Stennes-Berlin, (roter Mützenrand)

Ostpreußen: . . . . weiße Spiegel
Danzig: . . . . weiße Spiegel
Pommern: . . . . blaue Spiegel
Schlesien: . . . . gelbe Spiegel
Mecklenburg: . . . . . . blaue Spiegel
Magdeburg/Anhalt: . . . . gelbe Spiegel
unter Brif II Stucken, (gelber Mützenrand)
Brandenburg/Ostmark: . . weiße Spiegel
Berlin: . . . . schwarze Spiegel
unter Obf BB Jahn, (schwarzer Mützenrand)
Staffettenläufer Berlin-Nürnberg tragen grüne Kränze
Neue SA-Küchen, auf dem Marsche ohne Wartung kochend

Der Osaf-Stellv/Nord, Major Paul Dincklage-Hannover, (roter Mützenrand)
Adj. Korzemann (rote Spiegel)

Hannover: . . . . braune Spiegel
Lüneburg: . . . . grüne Spiegel
Friesland (Weser-Ems): . . braune Spiegel
Nordmark: . . . . grüne Spiegel
unter Obf NM Schoene (grüner Mützenrand)
Schleswig
Holstein
unter Brif III Böhmker (grüner Mützenrand)
Dithmarschen
unter Brif V Granz (grüner Mützenrand)
Hamburg
unter Brif I Ellerhusen (grüner Mützenrand)

Der Oberführer Ruhr, Oberleutnant Viktor Lutze-Elberfeld, (schwarzer Mützenrand)
Adj. Pelz

Ruhr: . . . . schwarze Spiegel
Westfalen

A part of the march order for Sunday August 4, 1929, at Nürnberg. Note the use of army ranks for v. Pfeffer, the Oberste SA–Führer; Stennes, the OSAF deputy "East"; Dincklage, the OSAF deputy "North" and for Lutze as the Oberführer for the Ruhr district. This order gave specific instructions as to who was allowed to wear a colored cap top.

Otto Spronk

Oberführer Paul Dincklage of Hannover wears a silver crown and flap piping, due to his position as OSAF deputy for group "Nord." Officially, he was allowed to wear a red colored top by special order. No eagle is worn, as this was introduced in April 1931 and this photograph is dated around 1929. Dincklage was known by the nickname "der Rucksackmajor" and was assigned to the OSAF Nord as a Party speaker. Until 1933, he visited thousands of meetings, all by means of a bicycle.

Otto Spronk

Oberführer Kurt von Ulrich of Kassel wears a red colored top in late 1929, as well as crown and flap piping because of his position as OSAF deputy for group "Nord." Officially, a person with the rank of Oberführer was not allowed to wear flap piping, but a person in the position of deputy was authorized to wear the piping. Note the absence of a national emblem. On May 28, 1930, von Ulrich was appointed as the inspector-general of the SA and SS.

Otto Spronk

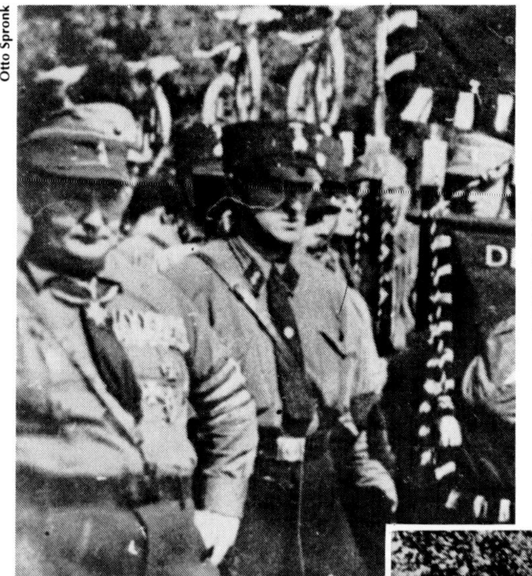

Hermann Göring photographed during the 1929 Party Day Rally at Nürnberg. He wears his cap piped around the flap and crown. Göring was not allowed to wear the colored top, as he had no special duties on that day, nor was he commanding a group.

Otto Spronk

The SA leader corps during the 1929 Reichsparteitag. In the foreground Franz von Pfeffer von Salomon, the Oberste SA–Führer. He is wearing the red top according to regulations for this day. He also wears the crown and flap piping. The Standartenführer at left, is wearing crown piping, but no colored top. This because he did not command a group. The Oberführer behind him is also wearing crown piping, but due to the fact that more than two "Standarte" sized units were marching he was permitted to wear a colored top.

The order especially noted that during this Party Day Rally, the Hitler Youth members wore no headdress and that the Reichsführer–SS Heinrich Himmler and his Schutsstaffeln wore the black kepi. The order also indicates that the March orders were changed for this occasion. For example Hallermann, the adjutant of von Pfeffer, did not wear the red top ordered earlier. An attentive reader will have noticed that in fact only six colors were in use for the 1929 Party Day. No important changes took place between August 1929 and early 1931. The rank Oberführer was abolished (in fact this rank was renamed) with an unknown date, but would be re–introduced in the fall of 1931.

Otto Spronk

Reichsparteitag 1929 at Nürnberg: Ritter von Epp, at right, is wearing a steel helmet. In the middle of this photograph is Ulrich Graf wearing the SS cap with the skull and eagle emblem. The SA leaders are wearing a colored top and piping authorized for their rank and positions.

Jahn, Hitler, and Lutze in Oldenburg in late 1930.

1931

The relentless growth of the SA resulted in new regulations and classifications in 1931. New ranks were added, the piping system was expanded and the top color was adjusted. Other signs of recognition or leadership identification were introduced in April 1931. (For detailed information consult the April 22 list. For doctors or administrative leaders consult the respective sections within this chapter).

April 22, 1931

RANK:	TOP COLOR:	CROWN PIPING:	FLAP PIPING:	BUTTON:
1) Chef des Stabes:	bright red	gold	gold	gold;
2a) Gruppenführer: (division leader)	ibid	silver	silver	silver;
b) Generalinspekteur:	ibid	ibid	ibid	ibid;
c) Chef des Personalamtes: (chief of the personal office)	no colored top	ibid	ibid	ibid;
d) Quartiermeister: (paymaster)	ibid	ibid	ibid	ibid;
e) Chef des SA–Führungs-stabes:(chief of the SA leaders staff)	ibid	ibid	ibid	ibid;
f) Führer der Reichs-führerschule: (highest leader of the Reich SA leaders school)	as for Gruppenführer	ibid	ibid	ibid;
g) Stellv.Führer des NSKK: (deputy leader of the NSKK)	no colored top	ibid	ibid	ibid;
3a) Untergruppenführer: (the rank below Gruppenführer)	color according to district color for the collar patch	gold or silver same as button	no piping	color as for dis-trict;
b) Leiter des Nachrichten-stabes der OSAF: (leader for the signal staff of the OSAF)	no colored top	gold	ibid	gold;
c) Stabsleiter der Gruppe: (division staff leader)	ibid	silver	silver	silver;

4a) Standartenführer (regimental leader)	as for Untergruppenführer	as for Untergruppenführer	no piping	color as for district;
b) Referenten der OSAF: (OSAF functionaries)	no colored top	gold	ibid	gold;
c) Adjutant des Führers: (adjutant to the leader, Adolf Hitler)	ibid	ibid	gold	ibid;
d) Adjutant des Obersten SA–Führers: (adjutant to the chief of staff)	ibid	ibid	no piping	ibid;
5a) Sturmbannführer: (battalion leader)	ibid	gold or silver, same as button	ibid	color as for district
b) Referenten und Adjutanten der Gruppe: (functionaries and division adjutants)	ibid ibid	silver silver	ibid ibid	silver; silver;
c) Adjutanten der Untergruppe und Standarte:	ibid same as button	gold or silver	ibid	color for district;
6a) Sturmführer: (company leader)	ibid	two color piping	ibid	ibid;
b) Adjutant des Sturmbanns: (battalion adjutant)	ibid	ibid	ibid	ibid;
7) Truppführer: (platoon leader)	ibid	no piping	ibid	ibid;
8) Scharführer: (section leader)[89]	ibid	ibid	ibid	ibid.

[89] *Der Oberste SA–Führer. München: April 22, 1931, Decree, I.a.Nr. 1679/31. The colored top was to be worn by special order only, when more than one group of the size of a "Standarte" was marching or in action. (This order was changed slightly in 1932). It must be noted that only lower ranked members assigned to the OSAF or a group staff wore the two colored piping around the crown of the kepi. By order of March 1932, instead of the above mentioned piping those personnel had to wear the crimson or bright red piping. (Vbl.d.OSAF, Nr. 7. March 22, 1932). Piping was generally approximately 2.5 – 3.0mm wide.*

National Archives

Hess and von Pfeffer von Salomon in conversation during a Reichsparteitag at Nürnberg. Often this photograph is described as von Pfeffer being the Chief of Staff, but this is incorrect. Von Pfeffer is already wearing the first pattern national emblem. This emblem was introduced by Röhm on April 20, 1931. Röhm was the Chief of Staff from January 1931. Note the button securing the chin strap, not being brown, and the clear view of the ventilation holes.

The Chief of Staff, Röhm, wearing the heavier fabric SA cap with golden piping. He is probably not wearing a colored top, as the color for this would match the color of the collar patch.

Bibliothek für Zeitgeschichte.

Otto Spronk

A photograph, taken during the "Tag der Nationale Opposition" festivities at Bad Harzburg, dated November 11, 1931, which requires some explanation: Several persons with the rank of Oberführer are lined up in front of Hitler's auto, for example Lutze and Röhm. All SA leaders are wearing the golden or silver crown piping, as well as the colored top. For Lutze this was black for the Ruhr district. His piping was in silver. The top for Röhm was bright red with gold piping. It must be noted that in those days, the wearing of a colored top was only permitted when more than one "Standarte" was marching, or when ordered during celebrations.

Clyde Davis

SA Gruppenführer Ernst wears the early national emblem. His cap is piped in silver around the crown and the edge of the flap and does not extend down the flap front center.

National Archives

A Standartenführer wearing a light colored top, crown piping and early pattern national emblem. Note the wearing of the early form of collar patch, and both the Pfeifen as well as the Adjutanten schnur.

W.P.B.R. Saris

Graf Hellendorf and the commissioner of police for Potsdam, von Levetzow, photographed during sport festivities at the Berlin "Sportpalast." Von Hellendorf with Gruppenführer rank, is wearing his piping as ordered in April 1931. His cap top is bright red, piping in silver as is the button color.

Lists were constantly changed or added to. With an order dated August 15, 1931 the rank "Zeugmeister" and the employees of such a department supplying goods were ordered to wear the SA dress during duty. With the entry of October 1, the rank of "Reichsmusikinspizient" was introduced:

RANK:	TOP COLOR:	CROWN PIPING:	FLAP PIPING:	BUTTON:
Zeugmeister: (Leader of a goods supply office)	no colored top	gold	no piping	gold;
Vorstände: (management)	ibid	ibid	ibid	ibid;
Angestellte: (employcc)[90]	ibid	crimson	ibid	ibid.
Reichsmusikinspizient: (National music inspector)[91]	ibid	gold	ibid	ibid

In April 1931 it was decided to rename the rank of Oberführer to Untergruppenführer (therefore this last rank–name is used in the April list). This plan was not carried out, as in an order dated November 28 the rank name Oberführer was used again. The function Gruppenstabsführer, often being a person with Oberführer rank, was ordered to wear a flap piping, even if this person actually held the rank of Oberführer (who in fact was not allowed to wear this flap piping). The SA leadership corps was divided now into lower, middle and highest SA leaders. This also affected the previously discussed systems.[92]

In November 1931 the cap top color was changed from bright red to crimson for members of the Oberste SA–Führung, Reichführerschule and Generalinspekteur. The button color was golden. Also, shortly thereafter, the rank Gruppenführer was required to wear the crimson top, but had to wear the earlier ordered silver button. The NSKK Deputy Leader started wearing a black top, as did the Inspector of Motor–SA units.

November 28, 1931 additional and renamed ranks :

RANK:	TOP COLOR:	CROWN PIPING:	FLAP PIPING:	BUTTON:
Obergruppenführer: (higher division leader)	crimson	gold	gold	gold;

---

90 "Vbl.d.OSAF," Nr. 3, August 15, 1931, Nr. 5: Abzeichen der Zeugmeister, usw.

91 Ibid, Nr. 4, October 12, 1931, p. 2.: Reichsmusikinspizient. From 1933 the systems governing rank or rank function were maintained for those mentioned in the earlier notes. It is quite certain that the diverging systems were abolished. No special notice were found stating otherwise.

92 Der Oberste SA–Führer. München: November 28, 1931. Decree 4/5, appendix 2. I/II, Nr. 7162/31: Dienstgrad–und Dienststellungsverhältnisse.

National Archives

In spite of the fact that this photograph has been used in several references, it must be included here. From October 1931 a position of Reichsmusikinspizient was created. Obermusikmeister a.D. Krümmel was appointed to this position. He was allowed to wear the golden crown piping, a golden lyre and the oakleaf on his collar, also in gold. In this photograph, taken shortly after the appointment of Krümmel, his cap does not have a colored top. No regulation ordered the wear of the colored top, but as the regulations were expanded, surely Krümmel was eventually authorized to wear a crimson top. The color of his collar patches was crimson as he was assigned to the OSAF.

Oberführer: (rank name was reintroduced)	Color according to district color for the collar patch	gold or silver, same as button	no piping	color as for district;
Gruppenstabsführer (division staff leader)	ibid	ibid	gold or silver according to button color	ibid;
Reichszeugmeister:	no colored top	gold	no piping	gold.[93]

1932

During the years 1932 through 1934 the continuing development of the SA essentially reached a final stage. Regulations were constantly modified and re-

[93] *Ibid.*

Chris Bruner

SA Gruppenführer Freiherr von Eberstein wears silver piping around the crown and flap. Note the flap piping extending along the vertical edge.

Below: SA cap for leaders with golden piping around the crown, as well as the flaps. The final pattern national emblem is positioned on this specimen. This indicates that this cap was worn by the ranks of Sturmbannführer and Obersturmbannführer from 1939. If an early eagle pattern was positioned, then the cap was authorized for wear by the rank of Obergruppenführer from November 1931 until May 1933. This form was also worn by the position of Adjutant des Führers.

Al Ex

Otto Spronk

Oberführer Manfred von Killinger from Dresden, the OSAF deputy of group "Mitte," is wearing a red colored top, silver crown and flap piping authorized for his position. When ranked as an Oberführer he would have worn a green top for his district of Thüringen, with golden piping and button. Note the wearing of the first pattern national emblem. His flap piping does not follow the curvature of the flap. Von Killinger became the prime minister of Saxony.

vised. In most of the districts, there was no unity in the colors of the two colored piping worn around the crown. Röhm had apparently given up on this, until July 1932. The SA grew much too fast and the uniform changes did not keep pace with this growth, as the boundary of districts was not yet final.[94] To give an impression of the many changes instituted, the list of September 1932 is provided, as this list gave detailed information on what areas existed within a district. (It must be noted that the list mainly gives information on the top colors worn and the two–color piping).

Districts were also newly classified: In July the "Nordmark" district evolved from the groups Nordmark and Hamburg. In September this was Schleswig, Ostholstein, Westholstein and Südholstein. The group Hamburg was now located in the "Nordsee" district. In the September list it must be noted that a part

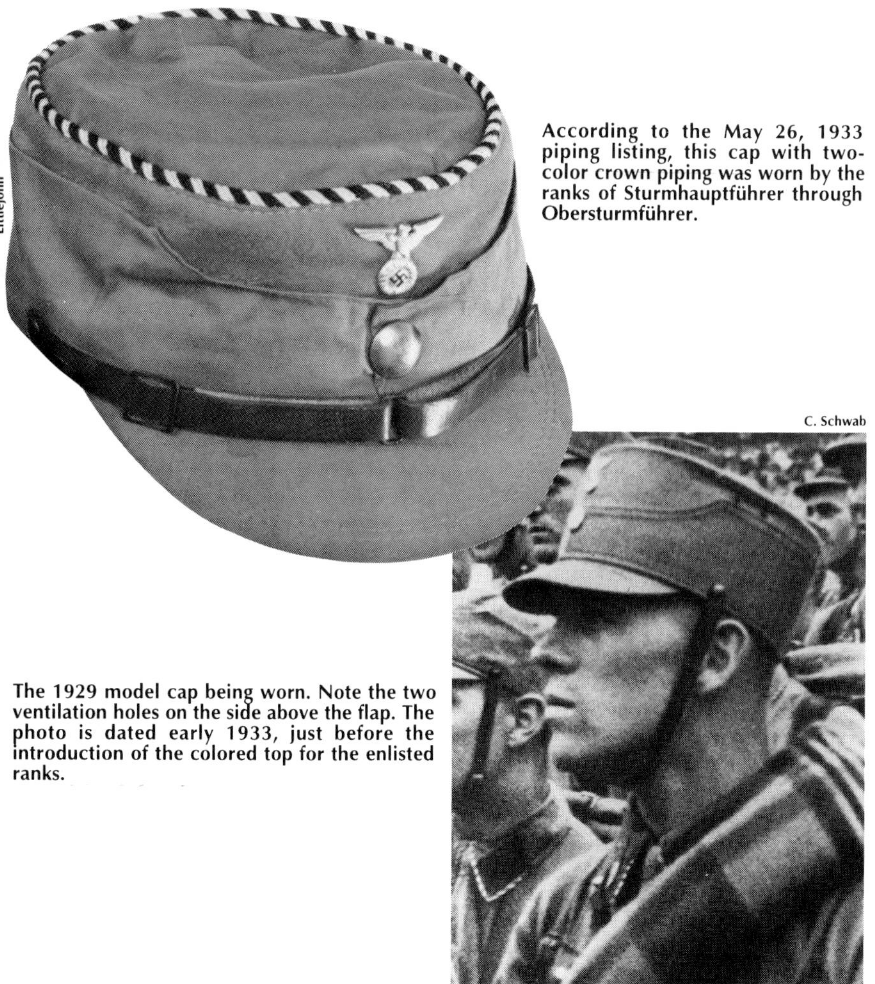

According to the May 26, 1933 piping listing, this cap with two-color crown piping was worn by the ranks of Sturmhauptführer through Obersturmführer.

C. Schwab

The 1929 model cap being worn. Note the two ventilation holes on the side above the flap. The photo is dated early 1933, just before the introduction of the colored top for the enlisted ranks.

94 *Ibid. München: July 7, 1932. Order Qu.Nr. 1543/32: Bekleidung. Once again the wearing of a colored top was a privilege only for SA leaders with the rank of Standartenführer and upwards who actually had command of a unit. A person holding Standartenführer rank, but who was not in command of a "Standarte," was not allowed to wear a colored top. (Vbl.d.OSAF, Nr. 8. August 8, 1932).*

Otto Spronk

A member of the staff of Obergruppe X (10) wearing the semi–stiff cap. Note the wear of a silver piping around the crown.

of the city of Hannover (Ost) was located in the Nordsee district: The city of Hannover was located in the Niedersachsen district. Hopefully this example gives the reader some idea of the intricacy of the systems used and may explain the reason for the various lists within this SA chapter. They may possibly help with photo identification.

Some ranks wore other piping or top colors. For example: members of a "Gruppenstab" (who since March wore a red crown piping) were ordered in September to wear a bi–colored bright red and silver piping. The function "Gruppenstabsführer" was ordered to wear a bright red top (and silver button). The function "Obergruppenstab" wore the top color as ordered for "Gruppenstab," being bright red, bright red/silver piping and silver button. A crimson/golden piping was ordered for the lower ranked members of the OSAF .

Even during preparations of the September list by the OSAF a change was ordered for the color of the button worn by two groups: for Hannover–Ost this was changed from gold to silver; for Weser–Ems this was changed from silver to gold. This correction had to be in force by October 1, 1932. The piping lists, dated April 22 and November 28, 1931 remained the same. In September 1932 a few additions were made.

List September 20, 1932 :

GROUP OR DISTRICT: (WITH UNTERGRUPPE)	TOP COLOR:	PIPING: (WHEN ALLOWED)	BUTTON:
Ostland	white	black/white	silver;

Ostsee			
Pommern–Ost:	green	green/yellow	gold;
Pommern–West:	ibid	ibid	ibid;
Mecklenburg:	blue	blue/yellow	ibid;
West			
Hessen–Darmstadt:	ibid	red/white	silver;
Hessen–Nassau–Süd:	ibid	blue/red	ibid;
Hessen–Nassau–Nord:	ibid	blue/yellow	ibid;
Koblenz–Trier:	ibid	blue/black	ibid;
Ostmark			
Grenzland:	white	white/black	ibid;
Lausitz:	ibid	white/red	ibid;
Independent Standarte 3: (Königsberg)	ibid	ibid	ibid;
Berlin–Brandenburg			
Berlin–Ost:	black	black/white	ibid:
Berlin–West:	ibid	ibid	ibid;
Brandenburg–Ost:	white	white/red	ibid;
Brandenburg–West:	ibid	ibid	ibid;
Nordmark			
Schleswig:	green	green/red	gold;
Ostholstein:	ibid	ibid	ibid;
Westholstein:	ibid	ibid	ibid;
Südholstein:	ibid	ibid	ibid;
Nordsee			
Weser–Ems:	brown	brown/yellow	silver;
Hannover–Ost:	black	black/yellow	gold;
Hamburg:	white	white/green	ibid;
Niedersachsen			
Hannover:	brown	brown/yellow	ibid;
Leine:	ibid	ibid	ibid;
Braunschweig:	ibid	ibid	ibid;
Göttingen:	ibid	ibid	ibid;
Westfalen			
Westfalen–Nord:	white	white/red	silver;
Westfalen–Süd	ibid	ibid	ibid;
Niederrhein			
Essen:	black	black/green	ibid;
Düsseldorf:	ibid	ibid	ibid;
Köln–Aachen:	blue	blue/black	ibid;
Südwest			
Württemberg:	black	black/red	ibid;
Baden:	yellow	yellow/red	gold;

Pfalzsaar:	black	black/blue	ibid;
Hochland			
Oberpfalz–Niederbayern:	blue	white/blue	silver;
München–Oberbayern:	ibid	ibid	ibid;
Schwaben:	ibid	ibid	ibid;
Franken			
Mittelfranken:	yellow	yellow/black	gold;
Unterfranken:	ibid	ibid	ibid
Oberfranken:	ibid	ibid	ibid;
Thüringen			
Thüringen–Ost:	green	green/black	ibid;
Thüringen–Mitte:	ibid	ibid	ibid;
Thüringen–Süd:	ibid	ibid	ibid;
Thüringen–West (this West were the Standarte numbers 71 and 95 resp. Sounderhausen area and Gotha):	ibid	ibid	ibid;
Sachsen			
Chemnitz:	ibid	white/green	silver;
Plauen:	ibid	ibid	ibid;
Leipzig:	ibid	ibid	ibid;
Dresden:	ibid	ibid	ibid;
Mitte			
Halle–Merseburg:	yellow	yellow/green	gold;
Magdeburg–Anhalt:	ibid	ibid	ibid;
Schlesien			
Oberschlesien:	ibid	yellow/white	silver;
Niederschlesien:	ibid	ibid	ibid;
Mittelschlesien–Süd:	ibid	ibid	ibid;
Mittelschlesien–Nord:	ibid	ibid	ibid;
Standarte 11 (this was the city of Breslau):	ibid	ibid	ibid;
Österreich			
Alpenland–West:	brown	brown/white	ibid;
Alpenland–Süd	ibid	ibid	ibid;
Wien:	ibid	ibid	ibid;
Niederösterreich:	ibid	ibid	ibid;
and the independent			
Standarte 10 (Amstetten)	ibid	ibid	ibid;
Standarte 84 (Baden b.Wien)	ibid	ibid	ibid.[95]

[95] *Ibid. München: September 20, 1932. Order I.Nr. 2462/32 the appendix. Note the remark in the text regarding the button color for Hannover–Ost and Weser–Ems.*

John McCoy

Early photograph of a Sturmführer wearing a cap without a colored top. The crown is piped according to regulations with two-colored piping.

Below: SA men with their flags awaiting orders to enter the stadium at Berlin–Lichterfelde, just before the arrival of Hitler. Various units are present, no colored top was authorized. The Sturmführer (in the foreground at right) is wearing a two-colored crown piping. Note the flowers on the flag tops. Officially, this was never authorized.

Otto Spronk

Bernd Wedeking

A Sturmbannführer is wearing his SA cap (as authorized for the brown shirt) with his tunic. In the case of the tunic, he officially had to wear the heavier manufactured cap. Note the correct wear of the crown piping and the Tyr-Rune, also known as the Kampfrune and first introduced in August 1931. It is certain that this person belongs to a staff and is wearing a bright red colored top.

The gilt piping worn by Stabschef Ernst Röhm in the early, thick form on his SA cap.

1933

The years 1933 and 1934 may be considered untidy years because of the numerous modifications of the systems. New specifications were authorized May 26, 1933, due to the reorganizing of the rank system for the SA and SS. The SA leaders of the SA high command had to constantly wear the ordered colored top:

The Chef des Stabes, Obergruppen–and Gruppenführer ranks and Obergruppen–and Gruppenstab wore the bright red top; the ranks Obergruppenführer and Gruppenführer of the OSAF Staff, as well as the position of Chef des Ausbildungswesens, General–Inspekteur, Reichsführerschule and those who were assigned to the OSAF (not having a command position) wore the crimson colored top. The position "Chef des Kraftfahrwesens" was ordered to wear the black top and the position "Chef des Sanitätswesens" the violet top.[96]

Piping list May 26, 1933 :

	TOP PIPING:	FLAP PIPING:	BUTTON:
Oberste SA–Führung: (SA High Command, later referred to as "höhere Führer," higher ranked leaders)			
Chef des Stabes:	gold	gold	gold;
Obergruppenführer:	ibid	ibid	silver;
Gruppenführer:	silver	silver	ibid;
Brigadeführer:	gold or silver according to button color	no piping	color according to district;
Oberführer:	ibid	ibid	ibid;
Standartenführer:	ibid	ibid	ibid;
Gruppe: (later referred to as "mittlere Führer," middle class ranked leaders)			
Obersturmbannführer	ibid	ibid	ibid;
Sturmbannführer	ibid	ibid	ibid;
Sturmhauptführer:	two color piping (see September 1932 list)	ibid	ibid;
Obersturmführer:	ibid	ibid	ibid;

---

[96] *Ibid. München: May 26, 1933, Order Nr. 1, Abt.I. Nr. 1228/33, appendixes I, II and III: Dienstgrade und Dienstgradabzeichen; Ibid, decree dated July 7, 1933, Ch.Nr. 1350/33: Neugliederung der SA (for detailed information about the top colors, consult the section for the enlisted ranks: July 7, 1933 list).*

Nia'l Malcolm

A semi–stiff SA cap without the colored top, as worn and permitted until September 1933 with the brown shirt. The crown is piped in thick gold, worn by the ranks Sturmbannführer through and including Brigadeführer (for districts having the golden front button). This form was also allowed for wear, for example, in 1931 by the Reichszeugmeister and the managers of those departments; the leader of the signals staff of the OSAF; OSAF officials and the adjutants of the chief of staff, the "Untergruppe" and/or "Standarte."

Jill Halcomb-Smith

The last chief of staff, Wilhelm Schepmann, in brown shirt and the pre–July 1933 SA leaders cap. Schepmann is seldom seen in photographs wearing this type of early uniform. In 1933, he was the police president of Dortmund and held that position until he succeeded Lutze, who had died.

Sturmführer:	ibid	ibid	ibid;
Standarte: (“untere Führer,” lower ranked cadre)			
Obertruppführer and below:	no piping	ibid	ibid.[97]

97 Ibid. The decree, dated July 7, 1933 specified the two–colored piping as ordered for the lower ranked OSAF staff members. Crimson/gold was worn by Sturmhauptführer through Sturmführer; the ranks Obertruppführer and below wore yellow/crimson. For lower ranked members of Obergruppen–and Gruppen staffs, it was specified as: bright red/silver worn by Sturmhauptführer through Sturmführer; the ranks Obertruppführer and below wore white/bright red. This was changed in 1934 with the introduction of the new SA dress regulations.

SA–Gruppenführer Hans–Georg Hofmann wearing his cap piped in silver around the crown, as well as the edge of the flap. Note that the flap piping does not follow the flap vertically as ordered. The top color is bright red. Hofmann was later appointed to the rank of SA–Obergruppenführer and became Parliamentary Undersecretary to the Reichsstatthalter in Bavaria.

Otto Spronk

A. Stam

Sturmführer Grunert, the chief of police from Mönchengladbach, during festivities on April 30, 1933. Grunert officially, should have worn the two–colored crown piping.

W.P.B.R. Saris

Oberführer Richter is wearing a golden crown piping, light blue/sulfur–yellow flap piping and a navy–blue colored top. Richter was the senator of the "internal government" for the city of Hamburg and chairman of the supervisory board for the airport for Hamburg when this photograph was taken.

The SA leaders from "Untergruppen" and "Standort" with the rank of Standartenführer and above, holding the command of an actual unit, had to wear the top color of the group, according to the collar tab color (see also note 94). The ranks Standartenführer, Oberführer and Brigadeführer, who were classified as members of a staff (but who did not have the command of a unit), were not allowed to wear the colored top. A Standartenführer commanding a Sturmbann was not allowed to wear the colored top.[98] The colored top custom was to distinguish between those who held an active command or a function of rank. Apparently these systems did not work and alterations to them were introduced shortly thereafter.

Five weeks later, on July 7, due to the reorganization of the SA districts and group systems, new specifications were published. Simultaneously, the colored top was ordered for wear by <u>all SA members</u>; high ranks, as well as enlisted ranks. For the first time a group or a district wore unified colors.[99] To avoid higher costs it was proposed, by the SA high command, that the districts would exchange cap buttons. The old systems were permitted to be worn until September 15, 1933. The ranks Standartenführer, Oberführer and Brigadeführer had to wear the regular authorized gold or silver crown piping, but were simultaneously ordered to wear the two colored flap piping.

---

98 *Ibid. München: May 26, 1933, Decree, Nr. 1. Abt.I. Nr. 1228/33: Dienstgrade und Dienstgradabzeichen.*

99 *Ibid. München: July 7, 1933, Order and decree Nr. 2, Ch.Nr. 1350/33: Neugliederung der SA with appendix. Note some districts had to wear other colored tops. Compare July 1933 list.*

Al Ex

An SA cap with two–colored crown piping as worn by the ranks of Sturmführer through and including Sturmhauptführer.

A. Stam

Standartenführer Hahn from Mönchen-Gladbach in conversation with Kreisleiter Pelzer, the mayor of Mönchen-Gladbach-Rheydt. The photograph is dated July 11, 1933. Hahn wears the black top and a golden button and crown piping, according to regulations.

Hans v. Diggelen

A Sturmführer wearing the two-colored crown piping and the colored top, according to the 1933 regulations. This photograph must be from approximately August 1933, as he is wearing the badge for the SA meeting held on August 5/6, 1933 in Berlin (at right upon his left breast pocket).

Staatskommissar Lippert, with SA–Standartenführer rank, wears his SA cap piped on the crown and with two–colored piping on his flaps, during the laying of the first stone for the "Kriegsopfersiedlung" (War Victims Shelter) at Berlin–Britz in 1933. Note the wear of the dark visored caps with an oakleaf on the cap band and an insigne in the center front of the top: These personnel are not members of the naval SA but members of the NSKOV, wearing their regular small NSKOV badge.

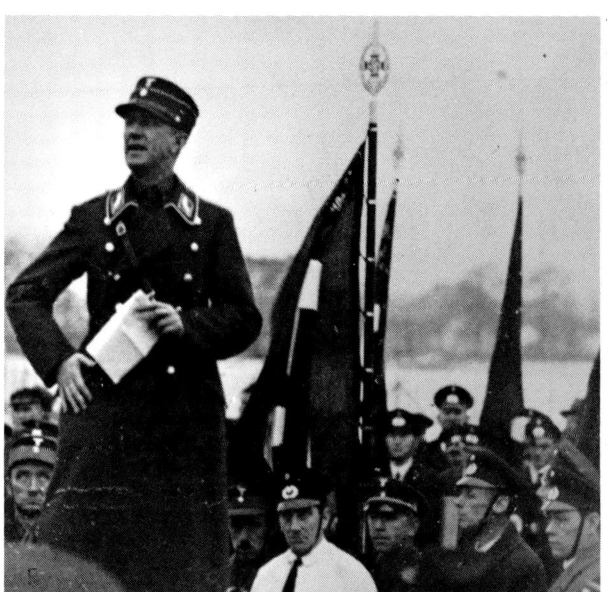

Otto Spronk

Standartenführer Hahn and his adjutant, photographed on July 11, 1933. As a commanding officer he was allowed to wear the colored top, but from four days earlier, others were also allowed to wear the colored top. His adjutant could have worn it also. Obviously, the adjutant did not have time to purchase one yet. Hahn is wearing the black top as ordered for the Niederrhein group

A. Stam

The top color for the chief of staff of motor vehicles sections was of black material since May 1933. This was changed in July to crimson. Other members of motorized units wore the color of the district to which they belonged. No evidence was found that indicated that velvet was introduced for members of the OSAF highest ranked leaders, as such an order was carried out for administrative leaders and doctors in July 1933 (consult the related sections). No headdress was worn with the newly introduced "Gesellschaftsanzug" (greater evening dress). For descriptions of piping, see the list May 26, 1933. Before the July 7 system was employed, the piping for one rank was corrected: the rank Obergruppenführer to be in gold, was changed to silver.[100]

W.P.B.R. Saris

Der Oberste SA-Führer München, den 26. Juli 1933

I Nr. 1228/33. II. Ang.

Verteilt gemäß Verteiler IV.

Betrifft: Dienstgradabzeichen.

Berichtigung des Erlasses Nr. 1 I Nr. 1228/33 v. 26. 5. 33:

In Anlage I des Erlasses Nr. 1 „Dienstgradabzeichen der SA und SS" ist beim Druck ein Fehler unterlaufen. Bei Obergruppenführer ist einzusetzen:

„**Silberschnur** um Kragen, Spiegel, Mützendeckel und Mützenaufschlag".

Goldschnur um Kragen, Spiegel, Mützendeckel und Mützenaufschlag bezieht sich nur auf den Chef des Stabes.

Der Chef des Stabes:

Röhm.

A copy of the OSAF order, dated July 26, 1933, which states that in the May 26 order a mistake had been made because of a printers error regarding the wear of the silver or gold cords on the cap crown and flap edge.

Although bright red is mentioned in the lists as the color used by the Stabschef and others we will define this color to avoid any possible confusion: in 1929 this red was named simply "rot" in various orders, decrees or regulations and no different color was given for the chief of staff (Stabschef) or the deputy's of the SA high command.

A distinction was made for the first time in April 1931. Bright red (Hochrot) was to be worn by the chief of staff and some other ranks, such as group staff members (Gruppenstab). Crimson (Karminrot) was to be worn by staff members of the OSAF (Stab der OSAF).[101] Through the years this "red" was always referred to, in spite of the fact that other names were also used, as "Karmesin," "Karmesinrot" or even "Karmin."

Between July 1932 and July 1933 the orders and regulations did not mention "hochrot," and for one year it was consequently referred to as "Scharlachrot" (scarlet red). It must be noted that during 1933 no other color was ordered for the top. No reason has been found which explains why after exactly one year the word "bright red" was once more used. At least three decrees mentioned the

[100] *Ibid. München: July 26, 1933, I.Nr. 1228/33. II.Ang.: Dienstgradabzeichen. Correction for the decree Nr. 1. It was specified that a printer's error was made.*

[101] *Ibid. München: April 22, 1931, Decree Ia. Nr. 1679/31.*

word "scarlet red."[102] This word was probably used by the originator of the regulations during the particular period mentioned above. "Karmesinrot" or "Karminrot" can best be described as "a red with a bluish shade," giving the red a more purple appearance.

National Archives

An SA–Gruppenführer wearing his cap with piping and 2cm wide Tresse. The zig–zag pattern of the Tresse is clearly visible. The top color is crimson.

Due to the introduction of the colored top for all SA members, the SA high command evidently was not satisfied. A very important modification was made, regarding the higher ranked leaders in command positions which were not sufficiently recognizable. With the date July 19, 1933, the chief of staff, Röhm, introduced the Tresse. It had to be worn by SA leaders commanding a unit in the size of a "Standarte." From fall 1933, this Tresse was normally worn.[103] The gold or silver Tresse (according to the button color) had to officially be positioned along the upper edge of the flap and ending in a vertical downward direction behind the button to where the visor joined the top.[104]

Deutsche Lufthansa

The Prince of Hessen, with SA–Oberführer rank, wearing his cap piped in gold only around the crown, according to early 1933 regulations.

RIOD, Amsterdam

Reichsparteitag at Nürnberg: Note the curve of the flaps on the caps of the SA leaders. None of these flaps are of the exact same style.

---

102 Ibid. July 7, 1932. Qu.Nr. 1543/32: Bekleidung; also September 20, 1932. I.Nr. 2462/32 and May 26, 1933, Abt.I.Nr. 1228/33. The decree dated July 7, 1933 (Ch.Nr. 1350/33) mentions bright red again in the appendix.

103 Ibid. München: July 19, 1933, Decree I.Nr. 1377/33: Sonderabzeichen der Führer grösserer SA–Einheiten.

104 Von Eelking, Freiheer. "Die Uniformen der Braunhemden" München: 1934, pp. 67–68.

Those SA leaders who did not have a command, but having the same rank, were never authorized to wear Tresse. The ranks up to Truppführer were not permitted to wear Tresse or a piping.[105] To avoid mistakes, we will point out once more that the wearing of any form of Tresse was authorized only for leaders commanding a unit or the chiefs of a department of the OSAF and was never meant as an indication of rank. The July 19, 1933 order specified the use of Tresse as:

1. Führer von Standarten:
   A two–colored piping around the flap edge, according to district colors,. Below this a 1cm wide gold or silver Tresse according to button color;
2. Führer von Brigaden:
   As above, but a 1.5cm Tresse instead;

W.P.B.R. Saris

Brigadeführer Heinrich Böhmcker wears a steel–green colored cap top with a golden crown piping and the black/white colored flap piping in this September 1933 photograph. Officially Böhmcker was already authorized to wear the 1.5cm Tresse, as he was a commanding officer at that time. The Tresse was introduced in July 1933.

Jeff Hanson

SA–Obergruppenführer Heinrich Knickmann, photographed just after his appointment as leader of the SA district on July 1, 1933. Knickmann is still wearing his old collar patches with Gruppenführer rank. This photograph must be dated at least towards the end of July, as the Tresse system was introduced on July 19.

National Archives

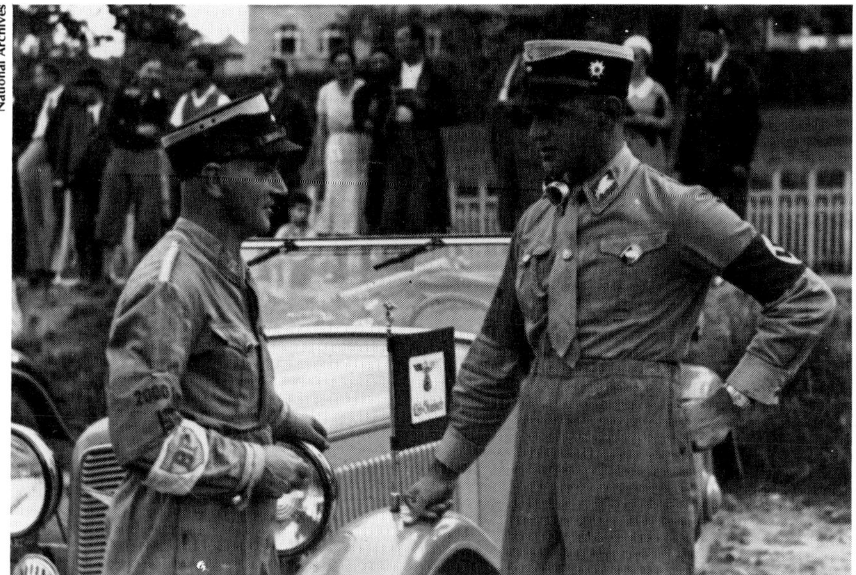

An SA–Oberführer of the Gruppe Hochland, wearing his cap crown probably piped in silver: the flap is edged in white/light blue. Note that no Tresse is installed and that the leader is wearing the loose type of cover (no ventilation holes are visible). The Tresse system was introduced on July 19, 1933 and this photograph was taken during the journey "2000 Kilometer durch Deutschland," which ended on July 24, 1933. The commanding officer was not yet able to put the Tresse on his cap: That he is a commanding officer is obvious because a command flag is mounted on his automobile.

Otto Spronk

SA–Oberführer Franz Schwede–Coburg shown wearing an apple–green top for Pomerania. His cap crown is piped in gold, the flaps being piped in black/white. Note that he is wearing his chin strap, probably secured with a golden button: This was not officially allowed. Note, also, that he does not wear the Tresse on his cap. The reason for this is simple: Schwede–Coburg was *not* a commanding officer of any unit when this photograph was taken.

---

105 "Vbl.d.OSAF," Nr. 41, November 12, 1934, p. 1. Nr. 3: Dienstgradabzeichen. Here it was especially noted that it was established that various lower ranked leaders, commanding a unit in the size of a "Sturm" or a "Sturmbann" wore unauthorized two–colored or gold as well as silver piping around the crown.

3. Führer von Gruppen und Obergruppen:
   A silver piping around the flap edge. Below this a 2cm wide silver Tresse was worn. This was also ordered for: OSAF department chiefs (Abteilungschefs der Obersten SA–Führung), chief of the motorized sections (Chef des Kraftfahrwesens), chief of the health department (Chef des Sanitätswesens), Generalinspekteur, chief of the training's department (Chef des Ausbildungswesens) and the leader of the Reich leader school (Führer der Reichsfühereschule);
4. Chef des Stabes:
   Same Tresse as for Gruppen–and Obergruppenführer, but 2cm gold.[106]

National Archives

The chief of staff, Viktor Lutze, boarding his personal plane, D–AZIS, from the Deutsche Lufthansa. This plane was known as the "Horst Wessel" and was partly painted in SA brown. For many years this plane was assigned to the "Regierungsstaffel." Note the wear of the front button by Lutze in a high position upon the flaps center. Through the years, Lutze always wore a bright red top color.

106 Der Oberste SA–Führer, I.Nr. 1377/33. Decree, dated July 19, 1933, Betrifft: Sonderabzeichen der Führer grösserer SA–Einheiten.

W.P.B.R. Saris

Der Oberste SA-Führer
I Nr. 1377/33.

München, den 19. Juli 1933.

Verteilt nach Verteiler IV.

Betrifft: Sonderabzeichen der Führer größerer SA-Einheiten.

Verfügung

Durch die gemäß Erlaß Nr. 2, Ziffer D, vom 7. 7. 33 erfolgte Einführung der farbigen Mützenbänder für die gesamte SA ergibt sich die Notwendigkeit, die Führer größerer SA-Einheiten besonders kenntlich zu machen.

Ich befehle daher, daß von jetzt ab alle Führer von SA-Einheiten von der Standarte an aufwärts, auch wenn sie nur mit der Führung beauftragt sind, durch Gold- oder Silbertressen (je nach der Farbe der Knöpfe) um den Mützenaufschlag in folgender Weise besonders gekennzeichnet werden:

1. **Die Führer von Standarten:** um den oberen Rand des Mützen a u f s c h l a g e s die Zweifarbenschnur in der für die Gruppe vorgeschriebenen Farbe, darunter anschließend eine 1 cm breite Gold- oder Silbertresse (je nach Knopffarbe).

2. **Die Führer von Brigaden:** um den oberen Rand des Mützen a u f s c h l a g e s die Zweifarbenschnur in der für die Gruppe vorgeschriebenen Farbe, darunter anschließend eine 1½ cm breite Gold- oder Silbertresse (je nach Knopffarbe).

3. **Führer von Gruppen und Obergruppen** sowie die Abteilungschefs der Obersten SA-Führung, Chef des Kraftfahrwesens, Chef des Sanitätswesens, Generalinspekteur, Chef des Ausbildungswesens, Führer der Reichsführerschule: um den obersten Rand des Mützen a u f s c h l a g e s unterhalb der für sie vorgeschriebenen Silberschnur anschließend eine 2 cm breite Silbertresse.

4. **Der Chef des Stabes:** trägt die gleiche Tresse wie die Gruppen- und Obergruppenführer in Gold

Muster dieser Tressen, sowie Zeichnungen über die Anbringung werden noch ausgegeben.

Der Chef des Stabes

Röhm.

A copy of the official OSAF order dated July 19, 1933 introducing the forms of Tresse with paragraphs 1, 2 and 3. Paragraph 4 pertains to the chief of staff Röhm, who was authorized to wear a 2cm Tresse in gold.

Franz Seldte, the leader of the NS. Deutscher Frontkämpferbund (Stahlhelm), with the rank of SA–Obergruppenführer on the OSAF staff. He wears his cap piped and with Tresse as authorized for his rank. Note the positioning of the flap piping. Seldte is shown wearing a crimson cap top, with piping in silver. Seldte was appointed to this rank in July 1933 by Röhm and given the same rights as Himmler, Göring, Hühnlein and the (then) eight SA leaders of the "Obergruppe."

Rudie Dolfin

A Brigadeführer, as a "Führer" of a Brigade wears two–colored flap piping and the 1.5cm Tresse in accordance with the 1933 regulations.

1934 – 1935

In January 1934 a new design for the SA leaders corps (SA–Führerkorps) was implemented. The following distinctions were noted:

1. Active SA–Führer:

    * To the active SA leaders corps belonged all SA leaders in active SA service, but also within the SS, SAR I and NSKK. They were ordered to wear the headdress form or rank distinction according to their rank or position;

    * Active SA leaders (with the rank Sturmbannführer and above), who were not assigned to a specific staff position were referred to as:

    z.b.V. = "zur besonderer Verwendung" (seconded for a special duty) and as such they were a staff–member. These "z.b.V" SA leaders wore the headdress of the unit or staff they were assigned to for this special duty. No Tresse was allowed;

    * Those who were assigned for a longer period to another "district" (or SS, SAR I or NSKK) are referred as: "kommandiert" (attached). These SA leaders wore the headdress of the unit he was originally assigned to. No Tresse was allowed.

    * SA leaders with an advisors function, seconded for a special duty (beratende SA Führer, z.b.V.) and assigned to the OSAF staff were authorized Tresse, positioned on the flap.

2. SA–Führer der SAR II:
    Consult the SAR section.

3. SA–Führer z.V:
   SA leaders who were not yet needed for active SA service were at the disposal of the OSAF, Reichsführer–SS, Obergruppe, Gruppe (or SS–Oberabschnitt) or Standarte. They were referred to as: z.V = "zur Verfügung" or "Verwendung." These SA leaders wore the regular headdress with colored top of their last assignment. No Tresse was allowed. One must note that by a decree dated, July 7, 1933, these SA leaders were allowed to wear a silver–grey top.[107] This colored top was abolished in the January 1934 order.
4. Ehrenführer:
   Consult the honorary members section.
5. Rangführer:
   Consult the honorary members section.[108]

The above order had to be implemented by February 15, 1934. With the March 1, 1934 SA dress regulations, "out of service" SA leaders (SA–Führer a.D.) also were mentioned. These SA leaders were allowed to wear the silver–grey (velvet) top, formerly worn by "SA–Führer z.V," with the authorized piping. The Tresse was however never allowed.[109] This "rank" was already abolished in mid–June 1934, so it is doubtful this was ever worn.

In early February 1934, the Tresse list was already supplemented. An order published in the Verordnungsblatt, dated February 1, specified a Tresse for the OSAF inspectors assigned to the districts east, south-east, mid and west (Inspekteure Ost, Südost, Mitte und West). They wore a silver 2cm wide Tresse as ordered for chiefs of a department. They were allowed to wear this form even if their rank was lower than Gruppenführer.[110]

Two weeks later on February 14, the Tresse system was totally implemented and new specifications were given. The old regulations were simultaneously abolished. This Tresse (Dienststellungsabzeichen) indicated without exception the position of the SA–leader and never his rank. The crimson top color was still used by all members of the OSAF staff ; the buttons, piping etc. were silver.[111]

Tresse list February 14, 1934 :

		TRESSE:	WIDTH:
I:	Stabschef: (The chief of staff wore a special pattern Tresse)	gold	2cm;

[107] *Ibid. München: July 7, 1933, Ch.Nr. 1350/33: Neugliedering der SA with appendixes.*

[108] *Ibid. München: January 27, 1934, Ch.II.Nr. 1134/34: this order concerns the reorganization of the SA leaders corps and gives specific detailed information for: 1) das aktive SA–Führerkorps; 2) das SA–Führerkorps der SAR II; 3) SA–Führerkorps z.V.; 4) das Ehrenführerkorps and 5) die Rangführer.*

[109] *"Anzugs–Ordnung für die SA," Teil I. Der Oberste SA–Führer. München: March 1, 1934. Section II: Anzugsarten–Sonderabzeichen, pp. 29–30; "Vbl.d.OSAF," Nr. 26, June 18, 1934, p. 3. Nr. 13: abolishing.*

[110] *"Vbl.d.OSAF," Nr. 17, February 1, 1934, p. 3. Nr. 10: Abzeichen der Inspekteure.*

[111] *Der Oberste SA–Führer. München: February, 14, 1934, I.Nr. 2729: Zugehörigkeits–Abzeichen, incl. appendix.*

SA–Standartenführer Friedrich Foerster, wearing his cap with an orange–yellow top, per regulations for the Südwest district. Foerster was the mayor of the city of Ulm. His cap crown is piped in silver and the button is silver. His cap flap is piped in black/orange–yellow. Note the position of the front button; which is not proper, as is the use of a single ventilation hole properly painted in the correct top color. Note the color difference between the Tresse and the button. He is probably wearing the old gold button that he was allowed to wear in accordance with the September 1932 regulations. His Tresse is also not positioned correctly, as it should run vertically downwards behind the button.

Clyde Davis

W.P.B.R. Saris

Hans von Tschammer–Osten, the Reichssportführer, in his rank of Gruppenführer, welcoming youth during sport matches at Nürnberg in 1934. Note the wearing of a totally different form of SA cap here and in the next photograph.

Niall Malcolm

Hans von Tschammer–Osten, with SA–Obergruppenführer rank, wearing his cap with piping and Tresse in silver, as per regulations for his rank and position. Note the taper of the cap top.

National Archives

Members of the SA from Berlin–Brandenburg wear various forms of piping and Tresse. This photograph clearly shows the dark (black) top as worn by the enlisted ranks and the lighter colored top, being bright red of the SA –Gruppenführer at left. SA–Obergruppenführer von Jagow is in the foreground with the collections box. Note the Tresse of the Gruppenführer: According to the regulations, he should be wearing the same width Tresse as von Jagow, but he is probably in a staff position. Such a person wore the narrower golden Tresse with the middle stripe in red.

A. Southard

SA–Gruppenführer Wilhelm Brückner, Hitler's SA adjutant, wearing silver Tresse and piping in this photograph dated October 1934. Earlier, Brückner had been allowed to wear golden piping.

II:	Führer höherer SA–Einheiten: (Leaders of a "higher" SA unit)		
a:	Führer der SA–Obergruppen (Leader of a higher SA corps):	silver	2cm
	Führer der SA–Gruppen (Leader of an SA corps):	ibid	ibid;
	vortragende Chefs im Stabe der OSAF (Reporting chiefs within the OSAF staff):	ibid	ibid;
	Generalinspekteur (Generalinspector):	ibid	ibid;
	Generalinspekteur des Sanitätswesens (Generalinspector of the health service):	silver	ibid;
	Inspekteure West, Ost, Mitte und Südost (Inspectors for west, east, mid and southeast):	ibid	ibid;
	Beratende SA–Führer im Stabe des Obersten SA–Führers (Advising leaders within the OSAF staff with the rank Obergruppen– and Gruppenführer):	ibid	ibid;
	Oberstlandesführer der SAR II (Highest SAR II district leader):	ibid	ibid;
b:	Führer der SA–Brigaden (Leaders of an SA Division):	ibid	1.5cm
	Kraftfahrinspekteure der Motor–SA (Inspectors of motor vehicles for the Motor–SA):	ibid	ibid;
	Gruppenstaffelführer der Motor–SA (Corps squadron leaders for the Motor–SA):	ibid	ibid;
	Beratende SA–Führer im Stabe des Obersten SA–Führers (Advising leaders within the OSAF staff with the rank Brigadeführer or Oberführer):	ibid	ibid;
	Führer der Landesverbände der SAR II (Leaders of a state formation for the SAR II):	ibid	ibid;
c:	Führer der SA–Standarten (Leaders of an SA regiment):	ibid	1cm
	Beratende SA–Führer im Stabe des Obersten SA–Führers (Advising leaders within the		

	OSAF staff with the rank Standarten–führer and below):	ibid	ibid;
	Führer der Kreisverbände und der Unterverbände der SAR II (Leaders of a district or a formation in the SAR II):	ibid	ibid;
III:	Stabsführer, usw : (Staff leaders, etc.)		
	Abteilungschefs im Stabe des Obersten SA–Führers (Department leaders within the OSAF staff):	gold with interwoven red	1cm
	Stabsführer im Stabe des Obersten SA–Führers (Staff leaders within the OSAF staff):	ibid	ibid;
	Stabsführer der SA–Obergruppen (Staff leaders of an SA higher or upper group):	ibid	ibid:
	Stabsführer der SA–Gruppen (Staff leaders of an SA group):	ibid	ibid:
	Stabsführer der SA–Brigaden (Staff leaders of an SA brigade):	ibid	ibid;
	Inspekteure beim Chef des Ausbil–dungswesens (Inspectors at the disposal of the chief for training and education):	ibid	ibid;
	Stabsführer des Oberstlandesführers und der Landesverbandsführer der SAR II (Staff leaders to the highest district leader or the state formation leaders for the SAR II).	ibid	ibid;[112]

Various patterns are known, however only one pattern was the official version. All other forms used were in fact not allowed. Any such variations had to be removed from the caps before February 23, 1934.[113] This order was never strictly adhered to and even during the late 1930's the old patterns of Tresse were still in use.

A person with the rank of Sturmbannführer who had not yet been promoted to Standartenführer, but who actually commanded a "Standarte," was allowed to

[112] *"Anzugs–Ordnung für die SA," Teil I. Der Oberste SA–Führer. München: March 1, 1934. Section IX: Übersicht der Dienstgradabzeichen, b) Dienststellungsabzeichen für Führer höherer SA–Einheiten und Stäbe, pp. 50–52.*

[113] *von Eelking, Freiherr."Die Uniformen der Braunhemden," München: 1934, pp. 101.*

National Archives

This photograph shows examples of the various coffee can caps worn: The stiff as well as the semi–stiff forms. In addition, a cap with the very high body is worn by the person standing second from the left. This photograph also shows the positioning of the different forms of Tresse, buttons and the closure of the flaps. Note the wear of the Pfeiffenschnur by the person standing in the middle background: His cap is *NOT* the regular SA coffee can style , but the SA forage cap for leaders, introduced in early 1937, but with the metal instead of a woven eagle emblem. Probably the person standing at his left is also wearing this leader's forage cap. Most often the difference is hardly noticeable from a distance. Only the material used and construction indicate its style.

National Archives

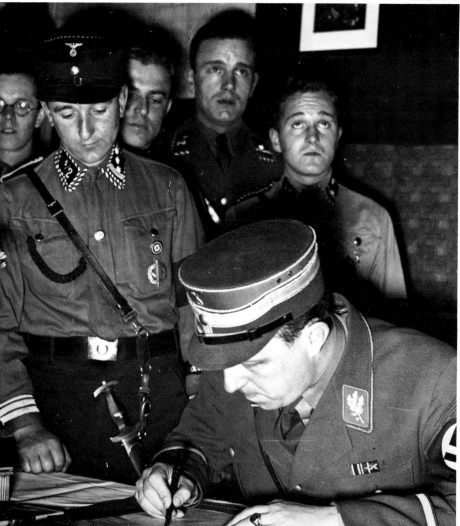

This photograph gives an excellent view of the positioning of the 3mm crown and flap piping, as well as the 2cm silver Tresse, worn by the SA–Gruppenführer. The Sturmhauptführer at his right is wearing the two–colored crown piping according to regulations in black/white for Berlin–Brandenburg as he is a member of Standarte 2 "Kuetemeyer."

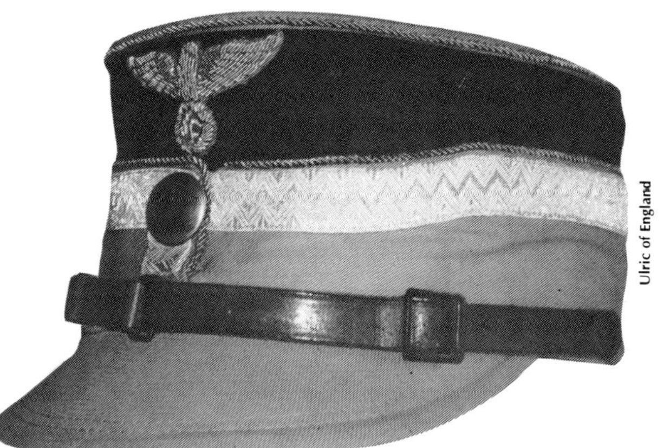

Ulric of England

An SA cap with Obergruppenführer form of Tresse, having a Westmark colored top, being dark brown and with a silver colored button. The reason for the dark brown top could indicate a person holding an honorary rank (zur Ehrendienstleistung) per early 1934 orders that permitted such persons to wear the standard top color of the district. This pracice was uncommon in the SA. The eagle style indicates an early form. Why an embroidered national emblem is used is however unknown and the use of Tresse denoting a person holding the rank of Obergruppenführer was not allowed for honorary ranks. The inside has an RZM tag with nr.104, being the firm of J.C. Kornacker of Hildesheim–Hannover. Note the beautiful golden logo on the inside of the top.

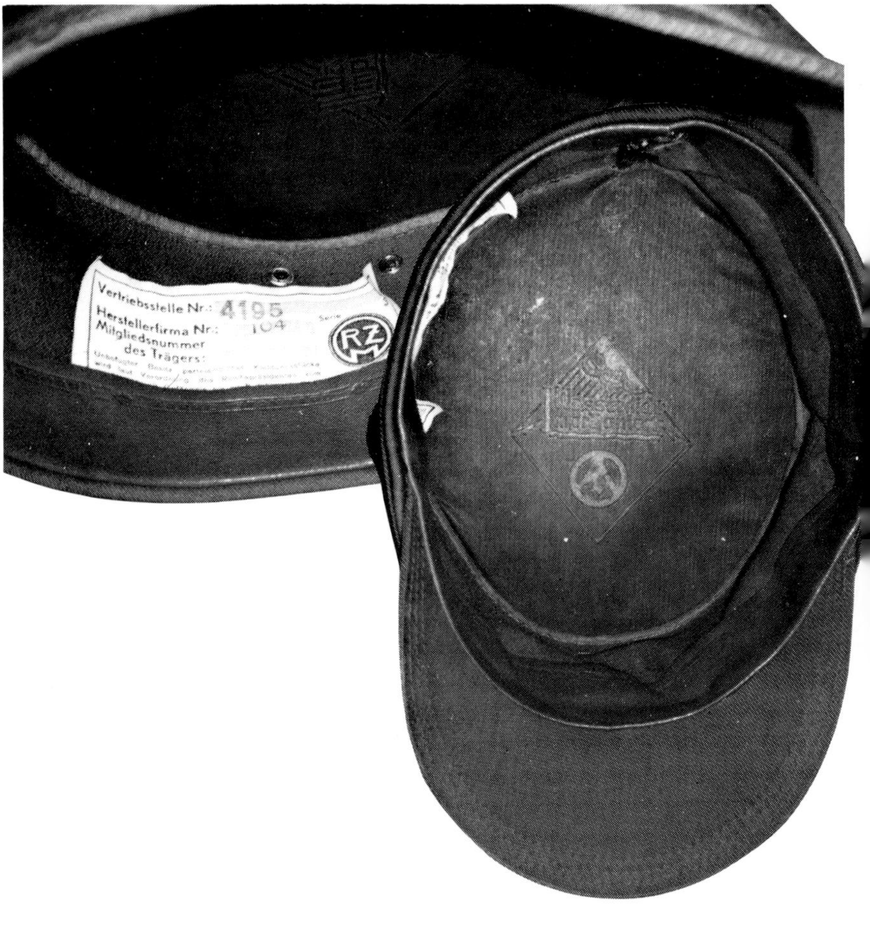

Jeff Hanson

Obergruppenführer Johann–Heinrich Böhmcker from the Nordsee district (Bremen) wearing his Tresse and piping according to his rank and position. His cap top is in the bright red color. Note the excellent detail of the stripe type of Tresse, the positioning of the piping, and the two ventilation holes. Note also the space between the Tresse and the piping on the edge of the flap.

Jeff Hanson

Gruppenführer Günther Gräntz, the SA leader of the Westmark district (Koblenz), wearing his piping and Tresse according to his rank and position. Gräntz was appointed as leader of the Westmark district on October 1, 1936.

Ed Stadnicki

A cap of an SA higher leader with a 2cm wide silver Tresse with an approximately 4mm wide red middle stripe. This red stripe is in the same color as the top. No regulation has been found describing this form of Tresse, but for a short period of only four weeks (between January 12th and February 14th 1934), an unknown Tresse form was worn experimentally by the positions of "Stabsführer," as well as "Referenten."

W. Walker

An SA cap meant for wear from February 1934 by SA staff leaders, serving as department leaders within the OSAF staff, staff leaders as such or staff leaders of an Obergruppe, Gruppe, Brigade and others, as specified in the text. The Tresse is gold and has two interwoven stripes (a pattern which was also worn as a chevron in the SA). The flaps for this cap are piped in crimson/gold. This two–colored form of piping was worn by lower ranked staff leaders of the OSAF in the ranks of Sturmführer through and including Sturmhauptführer. The color of the top was also crimson.

National Archives

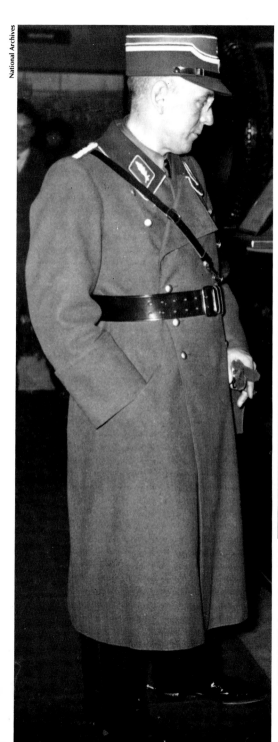

This photograph shows how the piping and Tresse should be worn. Note the space between the flap piping and the Tresse of this person holding SA–Standartenführer rank.

L. van Aerle

Standartenführer Hoffmann of Standarte 92, Braunschweig, wearing Tresse and piping according to his rank and position: The cap crown is piped in gold, his flap has the black/white piping and the Tresse is 1cm wide in silver in accordance with the 1934 regulations. Braunschweig is located in the Niedersachsen district, so the color of the top is dark brown and the front button is the golden version. Prior to February 1934, Hoffmann wore a 1cm wide golden Tresse.

Otto Spronk

Gruppenführer Heinrich Schoene, the leader of the Ostland district, wears his Tresse and piping according to rank and regulations. The top and flap are piped with a 3mm silver piping, the Tresse is 2cm silver. His top color is bright red. This photograph was taken just before his appointment to the rank of Obergruppenführer. It should be noted that both ranks wore the same form of Tresse. Schoene was promoted on February 1, 1934.

National Archives

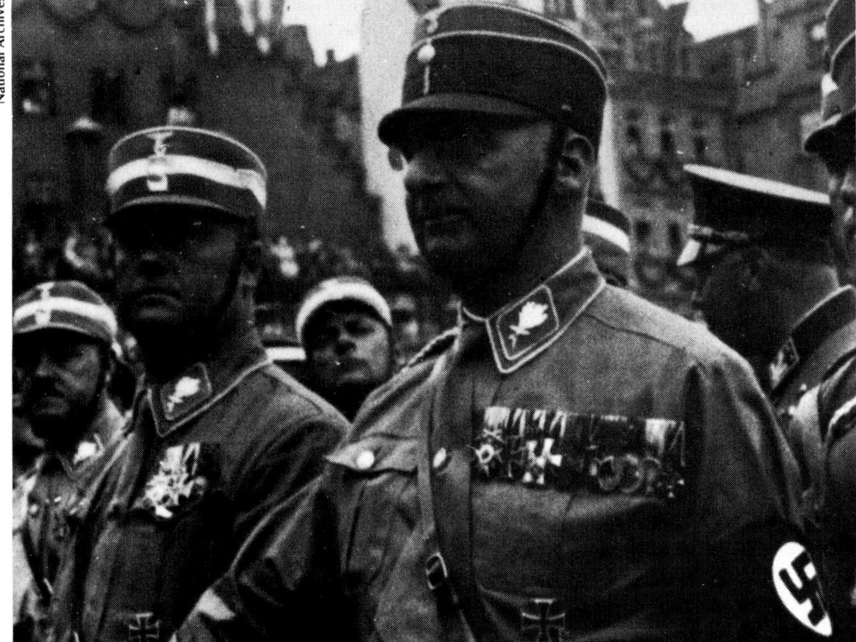

Two persons with Gruppenführer rank, wearing various forms of piping and Tresse. The person at right wears the simple piping, indicating that he was *not* a commanding officer. The person at his right is wearing the correct Tresse, indicating that he in fact was the commanding officer of a group.

Jeff Hanson

SA–Gruppenführer Joachim Meyer–Quade just before his promotion to SA–Obergruppenführer and leader of the Nordmark district in February 1934. From May 1934, Meyer–Quade was also the commissioner of police in Kiel. Note the wear of the correct zig–zag Tresse and his flap piping which is positioned directly above the Tresse.

SA–Gruppenführer Heinrich Georg Graf Finck von Finckenstein, wears Tresse in a striped form. Note the high position of the flap piping and Tresse, partly covering the lower portion of the national emblem. In August 1936, von Finckenstein was appointed as leader of the Schlesien district.

Willy Liebel, mayor of Nürnberg, wearing two-colored flap piping although he is wearing Gruppenführer collar patches. His flap piping should be in silver, not the two-colored type.

A. Southard

Below: Note the wearing of various forms of piping and Tresse, as well as two-colored piping, by these SA leaders. Standing in the foreground is Böhmcker, the Obergruppenführer of the Nordsee district. This photograph is dated between February and mid-October 1934 since the "old fighters" chevron is being worn.

National Archives

wear the Tresse as ordered for the regular Standartenführer position.[114] Those Standartenführer who commanded a unit in the size of a "Brigade," or Brigadeführer who commanded a unit in the size of a "Gruppe" were allowed to wear the Tresse according to these positions. Other ranks, took to wearing unauthorized systems: for example, a Truppführer commanding a "Sturm," or a Sturmführer commanding a "Sturmbann" started wearing the piping versions. This was officially prohibited in November 1934.[115] (It is known however that in later years lower ranking persons continued to wear forms of Tresse that they weren't authorized to use).

The wearing of the two–colored, 3mm piping was strictly restricted to the ranks Sturmführer, Obersturmführer and Sturmhauptführer and was to be worn only around the crown of the cap. Lower ranks were never allowed to wear this piping. The wearing of the two–colored piping around the edge of the flap was only permitted for the ranks Brigadeführer, Oberführer and Standartenführer until approximately 1940.

After Röhm was killed, Lutze took over the command of the SA as Stabchef, and a period of quiet and stabilization began.

Jess Lukens

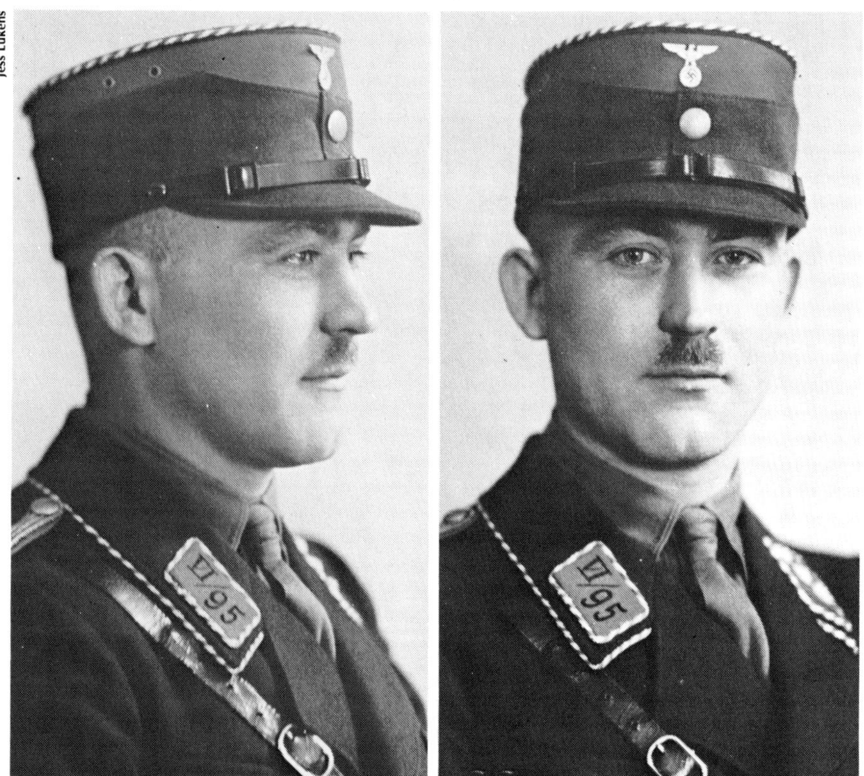

SA-Sturmführer Max Probst wears the two-colored, 3mm piping around the crown of his cap. Probst is wearing a light blue top as Standarte 95 is located at Coburg.

---

114 *"Organisationsbuch der NSDAP. " München: 1936, p. 387; "Vbl.d.OSAF," Nr. 12, August 17, 1936, p. 71. Nr. 223: Dienststellungs–und Dienstgradabzeichen.*

115 *"Vbl.d.OSAF," Nr. 41, November 12, 1934, p. 1. Nr. 3: Dienstgradabzeichen.*

A. Southard

SA–Sturmbannführer Lawnick wears a golden crown piping, two–colored flap piping and the 1cm silver Tresse. Due to the fact that he was not yet promoted to the rank of Standartenführer, but was actually commanding a Standarte, he was authorized to wear the piping and Tresse by orders dated August 1936. Note the ventilation holes are in the same color as the cap top and the vertical position of the two–colored flap piping behind the button.

A. Southard

SA–Standartenführer Melzer, a commanding officer on the staff of Standarte 18 of Parchim in the Hansa district, wearing his cap with golden button and crown piping, silver Tresse and a blue/sulfur–yellow flap piping. His Tresse is 1cm wide.

National Archives

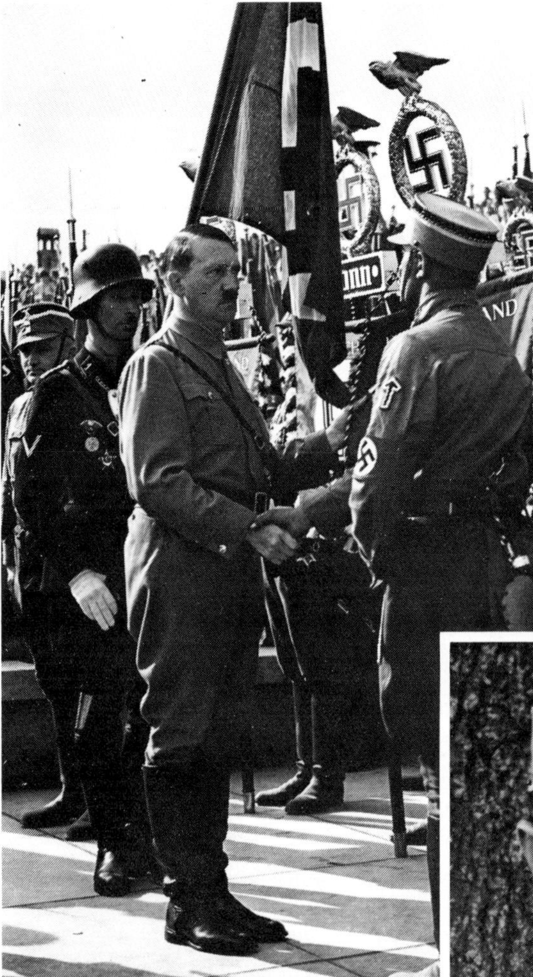

Hitler consecrates a SA standard during Party Day festivities. Note the piping and Tresse as worn by the person Hitler is shaking hands with, and also by the person standing behind Jakob Grimminger, who is holding the "Blood Flag."

A Sturmbannführer wearing his cap with incorrect piping. Officially he was only authorized to wear golden or silver crown piping. The introduction of a two-colored flap piping took place in July 1933, but at that time was restricted to the ranks of Standartenführer, Ober– and Brigadeführer. It is known that commanding leaders sometimes used unauthorized systems. Another possibility is that this person was expecting his promotion to Standartenführer and had already put on the authorized piping system.

Clyde Davis

Various patterns of unofficial forms of Tresse:

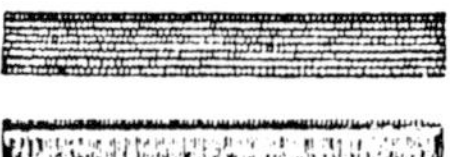

1cm "Bandtresse" or 1.1cm "Drahttresse":

1.5cm "Altertresse" with a silk middle stripe, also available in 0.9cm :

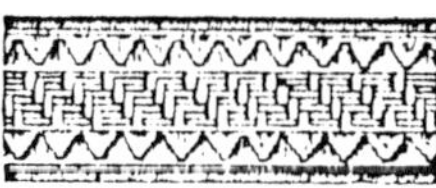

2cm "Drahttresse" with two "Balletten" and zig–zag pattern:

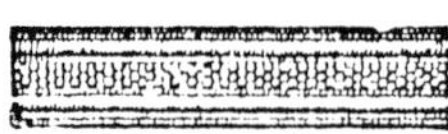

1.3cm "Drahttresse" or "Bandtresse" with two "Balletten":

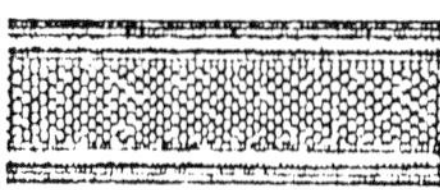

2cm "Drahttresse" or "Bandtresse" with two "Balletten":

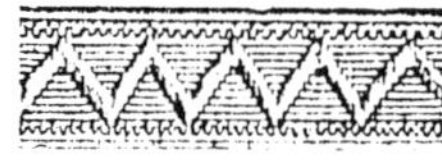

1.7cm "Zickzacktresse" in Husarenpattern:

1.3cm "Bandtresse" with or without "Balletten," also available in 2cm:

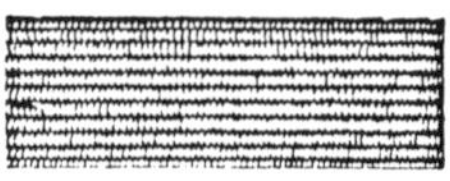

2cm "Bandtresse," also available in 1.6cm:

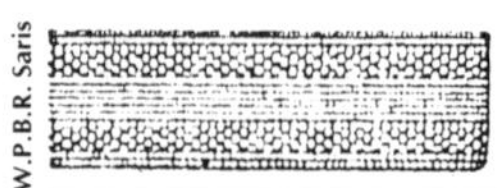

2cm "Bandtresse," also available in 1.6cm:

Ron Kwan

Obergruppenführer von Jagow of the SA district Berlin–Brandenburg, photographed at the Berlin Tempelhof airport. Note the wearing of the 3mm wide silver piping and the 2cm Tresse according to his rank and position.

W.P.B.R. Saris

W.P.B.R. Saris

Members of district Hochland, standing guard on November 8, 1935 in Munich during the memorial service at the Waldfriedhof prior to the transfer of the sixteen bodies of those killed during the 1923 putsch to their new resting place on the Königsplatz. All persons in the front line have the rank of SA–Sturmführer and wear the correct two–colored crown piping (white/light blue). The man at far right however is wearing a silver piping which was officially prohibited since November 1934. Note the wear of the Edelweiss flower and the light blue cap tops and that none of the caps have ventilation holes.

W.P.B.R. Saris

Several authorities are photographed during celebrations renaming Lessing Strasse as Lima Strasse at Berlin–Zehlendorf on January 19, 1935. Second from right is Dr. Lippert, the mayor of Berlin. He holds the rank of Standartenführer; his cap top is black. Close observation shows that his collar patches are much lighter. This photograph shows that the higher ranked persons did not always wear the Tresse but only the piping according to their rank. The Sturmhauptführer on the right of the SS–Rottenführer is wearing a black/white crown piping according to his rank for the Berlin–Brandenburg district.

1936 – 1945

During the years 1936 through 1945 little changed regarding the 3mm piping, or Tresse systems for the higher ranks with few exceptions. It was intended in 1936 to introduce cords for high ranking SA leaders, however, this plan was not implemented, but for a short while, some persons with SA rank were seen wearing them.

On June 22, 1936 the Tresse, as ordered in July 1933 and February 1934, for SA leaders "grösserer SA–Einheiten" were abolished and had to be removed. Simultaneously a new order (largely the same as the old orders, but simplified) was published; the pattern for the Tresse did not change:

a)	Stabschef:	2.0cm gold;
b)	Gruppen–, as well as Obergruppenführer:	2.0cm silver;
c)	Oberführer, as well as Brigadeführer:	1.5cm silver;
d)	Standartenführer:	1.0cm silver.[116]

The 2.0cm gold Tresse of the Stabschef rank consisted of golden-yellow cotton thread, covered by gilt nickel or gold wire. The 2.0cm form worn by other SA leaders consisted of silver cotton thread, covered by silvered or nickeled silver wire. The 1.5cm Tresse form consisted of iron, probably stainless steel wire and cotton thread, covered by glazed nickeled silver wire. The 1.0cm Tresse form was interwoven with red silk thread.[117] The red stripe was not mentioned in the OSAF order, but did not disappear. It was worn by staff members and chiefs of a department. However they mostly wore the Tresse according to their rank.

180. Betrifft: Dienststellungs- und Dienstgradabzeichen.
Ch. 13731.

1. Die mit Verfügung I Nr. 1377/33 vom 19. 7. 1933 (Verteiler IV) und I Nr. 2742 vom 14. 2. 1934 (Verteiler IV) für die Führer größerer SA-Einheiten und die Stabsführer eingeführten Dienststellungsabzeichen sind sofort abzulegen.

2. Mit sofortiger Wirkung tragen als Dienstgradabzeichen um den oberen Rand des Mützenaufschlages:

a) Der Stabschef: eine 2 cm breite Goldtresse,

b) Gruppen- und Obergruppenführer: eine 2 cm breite Silbertresse,

c) Oberführer und Brigadeführer: eine 1,5 cm breite Silbertresse,

d) Standartenführer: eine 1 cm breite Silbertresse.

Die Ausführung der Tressen bleibt wie mit Verfügung I Nr. 1377/33 vom 19. 7. 1933 angeordnet.

W.P.B.R. Saris

In June 1936, the Tresse system was simplified. The order was published in the Vbl.d.OSAF and gave specific details about the correct Tresse forms for wear by position or rank. The orders dated July 19, 1933 and February 14, 1934 were abolished. The last phrase states that the various forms of Tresse did not change.

Otto Spronk

Jill Halcomb Smith

Hermann Göring wears an SA cap with cords instead of the regulation leather chin strap. Note that these cords have knots as worn by political leaders. The wearing of cords was at no time officially authorized in the SA. Their introduction was probably intended for a short while as this was also planned for the NSKK during the summer of 1936. On most occasions, changes relating to the SA cap were not implemented while the SA high commanded continued the old traditions. Göring also wore the cords during the Party Day Rally at Nürnberg in 1934 and probably for a short period of time in 1938. It is thought that he wore the old form of SA uniform at this time.

---

116 *Ibid, Nr. 10, June 22, 1936, p. 55. Nr. 180: Dienststellungs–und Dienstgradabzeichen; "Mbl.d.RZM," Nr. 10, May 9, 1936, p. 187. Here it was described as: Führer von Standarten (1cm silver); Führer von Brigaden (1.5cm silver); Führer von Gruppen (2cm silver); Stabschef (2cm gold); Stabsführer der Gruppen und Abteilungschefs der OSAF (1cm gold with red middle stripe). The rule that this Tresse was only worn by persons having a position or function remained unchanged.*

117 *"RZM–Herstellungsvorschriften," 1936, pp. 141–142.*

Mützentressen

Goldschnur Silberschnur

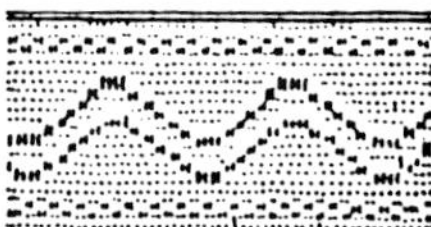

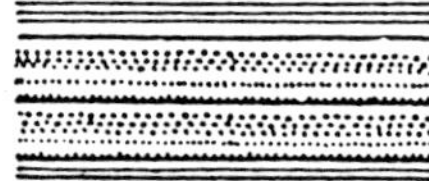

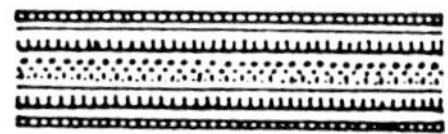

Gruppenführer und Obergruppenführer

Oberführer und Brigadeführer

Führer von Standarten und Standartenführer

The official forms of Tresse used by SA high ranking personnel and leaders in command positions, as published in the organization books.
From left to right: 2cm "Zickzacktresse," referred to as Husaren, for Gruppenführer and Obergruppenführer; 1.5cm Tresse with three so-called "Balletten" for Oberführer and Brigadeführer and the 1cm Tresse with two "Balletten" – the two somewhat upraised, horizontal stripes, as authorized for leaders of a "Standarte" or Standartenführer.

Otto Spronk

Prince August Wilhelm, with the rank of SA-Gruppenführer, photographed on January 1937. Note the view of the piping and Tresse. The Tresse should be in the zig-zag form. He is still wearing the early form of national emblem, as the new version had not yet been introduced.

The weave pattern, as published in the RZM manufacturing regulations of 1936, for the rank of Standartenführer, in silver, 10mm wide, Tresse. Note that the Stabsführer der Gruppen and Abteilungschefs der OSAF wore this Tresse in gold with a interwoven small red stripe.

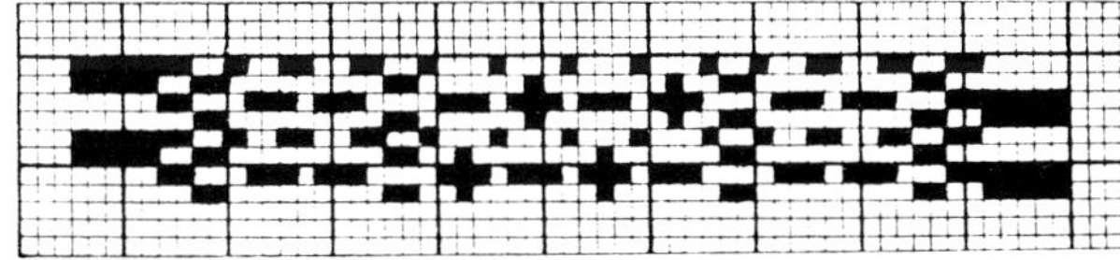

Patrone für die Mützentresse für Standartenführer

W.P.B.R. Saris

The weave pattern for the rank of Brigadeführer in silver, 15mm wide, Tresse.

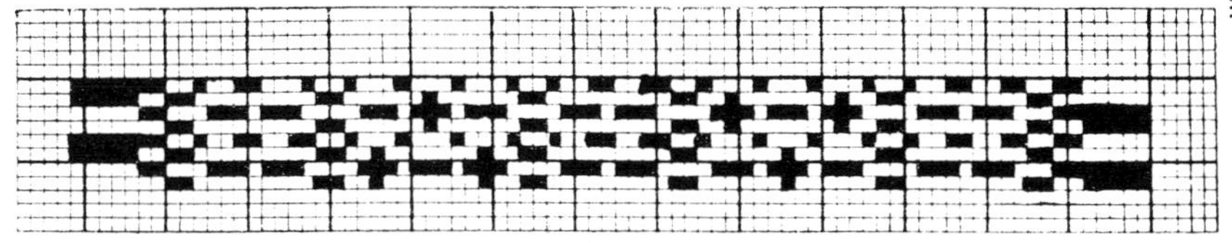

Patrone für die Mützentresse für Brigadeführer

The weave pattern for the rank of Stabschef and Gruppenführer, respectively in gold and silver, 20mm wide, Tresse. It is unknown if the Stabschef ever wore this special style introduced in 1934

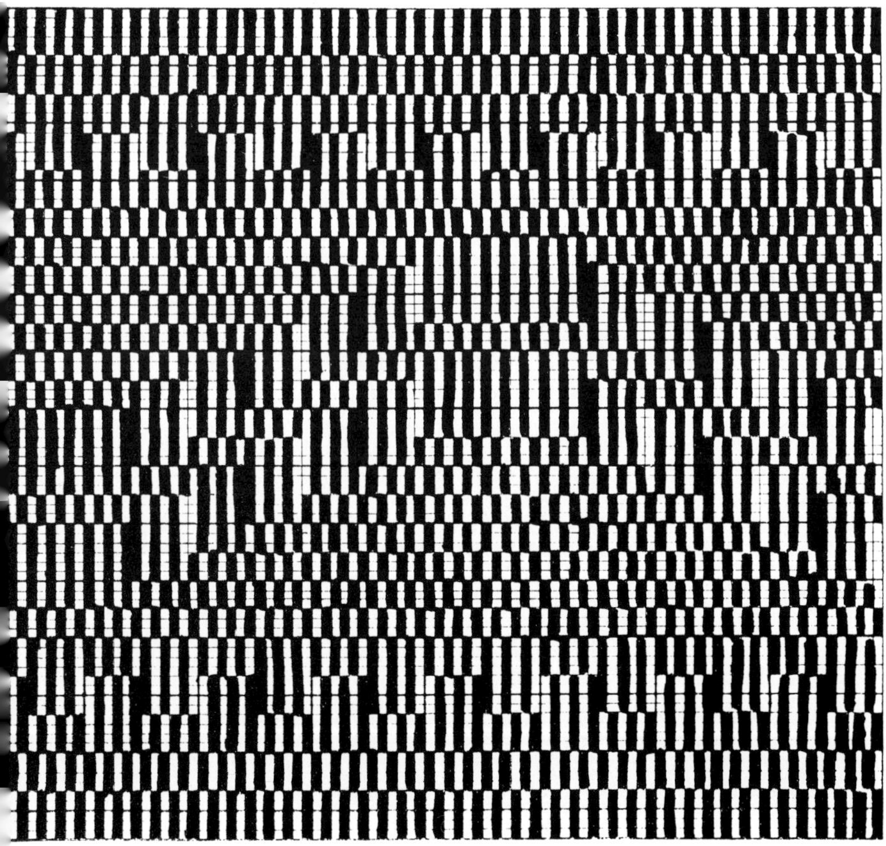

W.P.B.R. Saris

Patrone für die Mützentresse für Gruppenführer und Stabschef

SA leader's cap with the Tresse as ordered for Standartenführer, being 1.0cm with two "Balletten." Note that no ventilation grommets are visible on this orange-yellow top as used by the districts Mitte (in August 1942 renamed Elbe) and Südwest (also then renamed Neckar). A silver piping is installed along the edge of the flap, indicating a cap used since early war. Before then, the two-colored piping had to be worn by the Standartenführer rank or position.

Art Sylvie

SA leader'a cap with the Tresse as ordered specifically for Oberführer, being 1.5cm with three "Balletten." Since the summer of 1943 this rank was also allowed to carry a bright red top color. The ventilation grommets are the same color as the top. Note the flap piping does not run downwards, but uninterrupted along the edge of the flaps.

Otto Spronk

Members of the SA marching during festivities. The SA–Sturmhauptführer is wearing the Tresse. According to his rank, he was never officially allowed to do this. Probably due to the fact that he was a commanding leader of a "Standarte" and the highest in rank for that group the wear was probably permitted.

John Coy

This SA cap has the silver crown piping, indicating that it was worn by someone with the rank of either Sturmbannführer or Obersturmbannführer (from 1933 until 1938). This piping could be worn either in silver or in gold, depending on the button color. Note that the 1937 eagle emblem is positioned on this specimen. This indicates that this cap was actually worn in this form between July 1937 and early 1938.

In the fall of 1938 aluminum pattern piping and Tresse were introduced to replace the expensive silver wire woven material. This however did not affect the headdresses already worn: it was not necessary to replace the silver piping or the silver Tresse.

In July 1939 gold and silver/aluminum celleon (Cellophan) was introduced within the SA to replaced the golden or silver/aluminum wire piping. Celleon was a cheaper material to manufacture than the old forms.[118] It took until the fall of 1940 before celleon became an often used material. Officially the wear of the two–colored piping was discontinued. Even as late as spring 1941 many ignored orders that were issued to remove all obsolete forms of piping .

48. Betrifft: **Änderungsanzeige der RZM. Nr. 3/40.**

Nr.	Artikel	RM.
Neuzugänge:		
1410/18	Mützenumrandungsschnur, 3 mm, silberfarben, Cellophan	—.16
1410/21	Mützenumrandungsschnur, 3 mm, goldfarben, Cellophan	—.17

W.P.B.R. Saris

In 1940, a price list correction was made for the introduction of the material celleon (cellophan) to be used as cap piping.

This also occurred with an order in May 1941 that required the abolishment of "gold."[119] This order included the cap piping (the Tresse was not specifically mentioned). Many leaders continued to wear caps with banned sys-

[118] *"Uniformen–Markt, Nr. 13, July 1939, p. 196; "Vbl.d.OSAF," Nr. 8, July 1, 1939. Nr. 86: Änderung der Abzeichen. Section 3a mentions the celleon was to be worn by the ranks Sturmführer and above.*

[119] *"Vbl.d.OSAF," Nr. 2, May 20, 1941, p. 5. Nr. 11: "Vereinheitlichung des SA–Dienstanzuges." In this order the word "Mützenumrandungsschnüre" was used. It should be noted however that for the collar patches new piping–systems were introduced, including gold; "Mbl.d.RZM, Nr. 8, May 31, 1941, p. 45.*

tems, since the order stated that those caps which were already manufactured could be worn until stocks were exhausted. With newly manufactured caps however, the aluminum materials were to be used (in later regulations often the word silver was used. This however actually meant aluminum material[120]). At the same time the cap button worn in the center front of the cap flaps was to be silver, i.e. a gold button was no longer to be worn, despite the former group colors. This order did not effect the rank of Stabschef. He was allowed to wear his golden piping, Tresse and button.

In late summer 1943 the color of the cap top worn by SA leaders with the rank of Oberführer and above was bright red. Staff leaders of the SA high command retained the crimson cap top.[121]

During the war years (approximately 1940) some ranks were reclassified into other leader groups. For example the rank Standartenführer, earlier classified as "höhere Führer," was reclassified to the "mittleres SA–Führerkorps." Leaders, classified as the "unteres SA–Führerkorps" (lower cadre) being, Hauptsturmführer, Obersturmführer and Sturmführer were ordered to wear gold or silver crown piping, replacing the earlier worn two–colored forms of piping. SA leaders with the ranks Brigadeführer, Oberführer and Standartenführer also wore a gold or silver piping around the edge of the flap, instead of the two colored piping worn earlier.[122]

Otto Spronk

Stabschef Viktor Lutze (at right) and SA–Obergruppenführer Herzog, the Stabsführer at Grünwald near Munich. Herzog wears his cap piped in silver around the crown and edge of the flaps. He is wearing 2cm wide silver Tresse. Note the difference in color when compared with Lutze's piping, which is gold in color.

---

120 *"Schwert u. Spaten," Nr. 4. April, 1941, p. 50.*

121 *"Deutsche Uniformen–Zeitschrift," Nr. 7, October 15, 1943, p. 9; "Mbl.d.RZM," Nr. 6, September 9, 1943, p. 49.*

122 *"Organisationsbuch der NSDAP." Ausgabe 1938, 1940 and 1943, pp. 384–385. In the 1943 issue it is described that all SA leading ranks wore the silvered (aluminum) piping around crown and/or flap edge. The only exception being the rank of Stabschef. He was authorized to wear the golden colored piping and Tresse.*

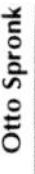

SA–Obergruppenführer Arthur Böckenhauer, appointed as leader of the Niedersachsen district on November 1, 1937. This photograph was taken due to this promotion: Note the rare tapering of his cap, having a bright red top and silver flap and crown piping.

SA–Gruppenführer Bernhard Hoffmann wears the 2cm wide silver Tresse and 3mm piping. Note the excellent detail of the zig–zag pattern and the ventilation holes.

Jill Halcomb Smith

Hitler's adjutant, Wilhelm Brückner wears his cap piped with Tresse according to regulations. Note the additional width of the national emblem. This eagle was probably embroidered upon a crimson backing in the form as worn upon the sleeve of members of the SA assigned to Hitler's headquarters after the start of the war.

Below: SA high leader's cap with the 2cm Tresse as introduced in July 1933 and worn by the ranks Gruppenführer and Obergruppenführer until the war's end. In 1937, the final form of national emblem was introduced and required to be worn. The color of the ventilation holes is correct and in the color of the cap top, which is bright red.

Ron Kwan

Detail of the 2cm Tresse and the piping worn along the edge of the flap of the above SA cap.

Otto Spronk

The poet, Otto Paust, with the rank of Standartenführer, wears his cap with cord crown piping and the two–colored piping on the flap; the Tresse is in silver and 1cm wide. The photograph was taken in 1938.

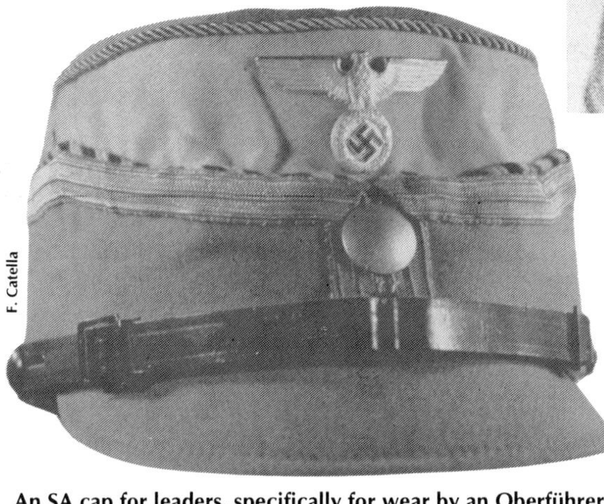

F. Catella

An SA cap for leaders, specifically for wear by an Oberführer or Brigadeführer, with crown piping and the 1.5cm wide Tresse. The two–colored piping is black/orange–yellow. The color of the top is also orange–yellow. This color was worn by the Südwest district, but in this case, the button should be silver and not the gold as with this example. The golden button and orange–yellow top were worn by the Mitte district, but if this was the case, then the two–colored piping should have been black/white.

SA cap for the rank of Brigadeführer in the Hansa district with the navy–blue top, as worn officially until the early war. The crown is piped in gold, the flap is piped in light blue/yellow and the Tresse is 1.5cm silver, as ordered from 1936. The final pattern national emblem is worn. Note the Tresse, being an unofficial form.

Robert Bernard

A. Stam

Authorities visiting a "flak" unit at Hardt, a part of Mönchen-Gladbach. Standing at left is a Standartenführer assigned to the staff of Standarte 97. Note the wear of the brassard at right.

Otto Spronk

The SA–Gruppenführer, second from left, wears his SA cap with piping and Tresse according to his rank; silver crown, flap piping and 2cm Tresse.

Jill Halcomb Smith

The chief of staff, Viktor Lutze, photographed on February 20, 1940 at the grave of Horst Wessel. To his left is SA–Obergruppenführer von Jagow wearing a navy uniform. Note the various forms of Tresse being worn by the other high ranked SA leaders. In the background, at left of the political leader, is standing Heinsius, the NSKK Brigadeführer from the NSKK motor group in Berlin.

W.P.B.R. Saris

Shown is the funeral in 1942 of Ludwig Siebert, the Bavarian prime minister, with his cap laying on the coffin. Note that it has the first pattern national emblem.

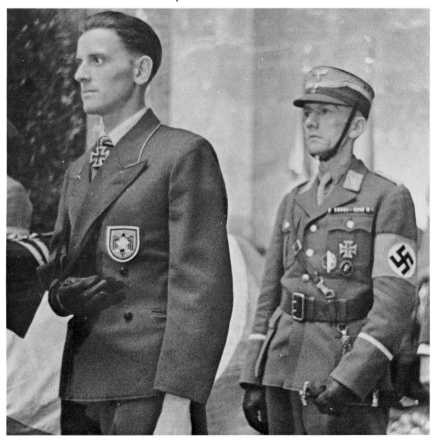

Honor guards at Reichssportführer von Tschammer und Osten's funeral on March 30, 1943. At left is Knight's Cross Holder Georg Müller and at right an unidentified SA-Oberführer.

Jill Halcomb-Smith

The chief of staff, Schepmann photographed in the fall of 1943 during a presentation of SA leaders. From left to right: Schepmann, Kicker, Wilcke, v. Hedemann (wearing his army uniform), Escher and Fritsch. Note the two caps at far right: The piping on Escher's for the crown and flap are in gold; Fritsch is wearing silver. The colored top of Escher's cap is very short compared to that worn by Fritsch.

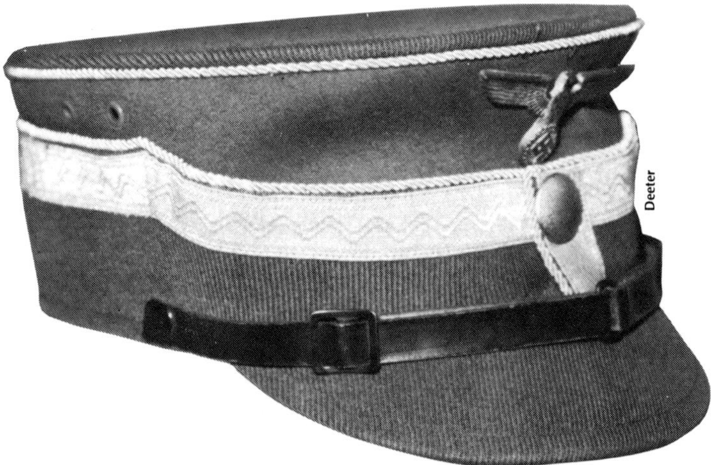

Deeter

An SA high leader's cap with the 2.0cm official pattern Tresse, as ordered for wear by persons holding the rank of Gruppenführer and Obergruppenführer, and who were authorized to wear Tresse from 1939 through 1945. The top of this cap is a variation shade of pinkish-red indicating a higher-ranked leader for the SA group of Ostmark. If a slightly different shade of top color was used it could indicate a member of the OSAF staff, or a high-ranked leader of the special SA unit "Feldherrnhalle."

Clyde Davis

SA–Brigadeführer Breitmeyer wear his cap properly piped with the 15mm Tresse during the summer of 1944. Note the wrinkled top which has apparently been damaged above the flap which is without any ventilation holes. Breitmeyer was the deputy Reichssportführer from March 1943, when Hans Tschammer von Osten passed away.

Hans v. Diggelen

An SA cap worn by a lower ranked member of a staff, particularly for the district Hessen–Nassau–Süd. The crown piping is in blue/red. The national emblem is aged, giving it a dark appearance.

Hoover

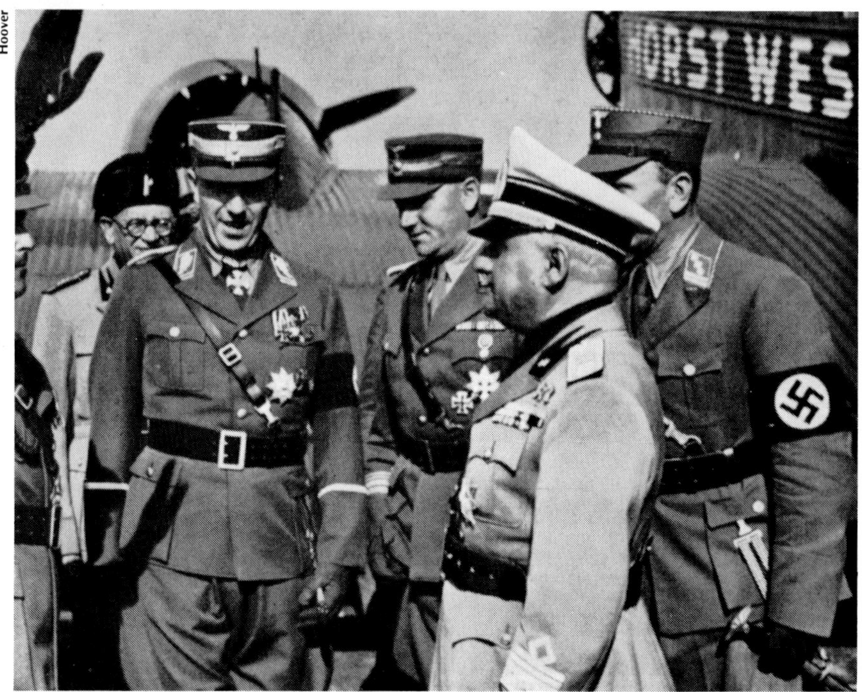

A SA-Hauptsturmführer of the Feldherrnhalle at right is wearing his crown piping according to regulations. It also appears that he is wearing the 1cm golden Tresse as used by staff leaders.

Ed Stadnicki

An SA cap manufactured in the heavier material, as ordered for wear with the tunic, with a 1937 pattern national emblem. A golden Tresse is positioned on this cap. For a short while, between July 1933 and February 1934, this was allowed for the rank of Standartenführer in districts with the golden button. However when used, the two–colored piping was to be positioned on the edge of the flap. If the cap was meant for wear by a staff member, then the golden Tresse should have the interwoven red stripe. The top of this cap is crimson, indicating service in the SA high command.

Right: Stabschef Lutze arrives at the Prague railway station in late October 1939. SA men of the Protectorate greet him.

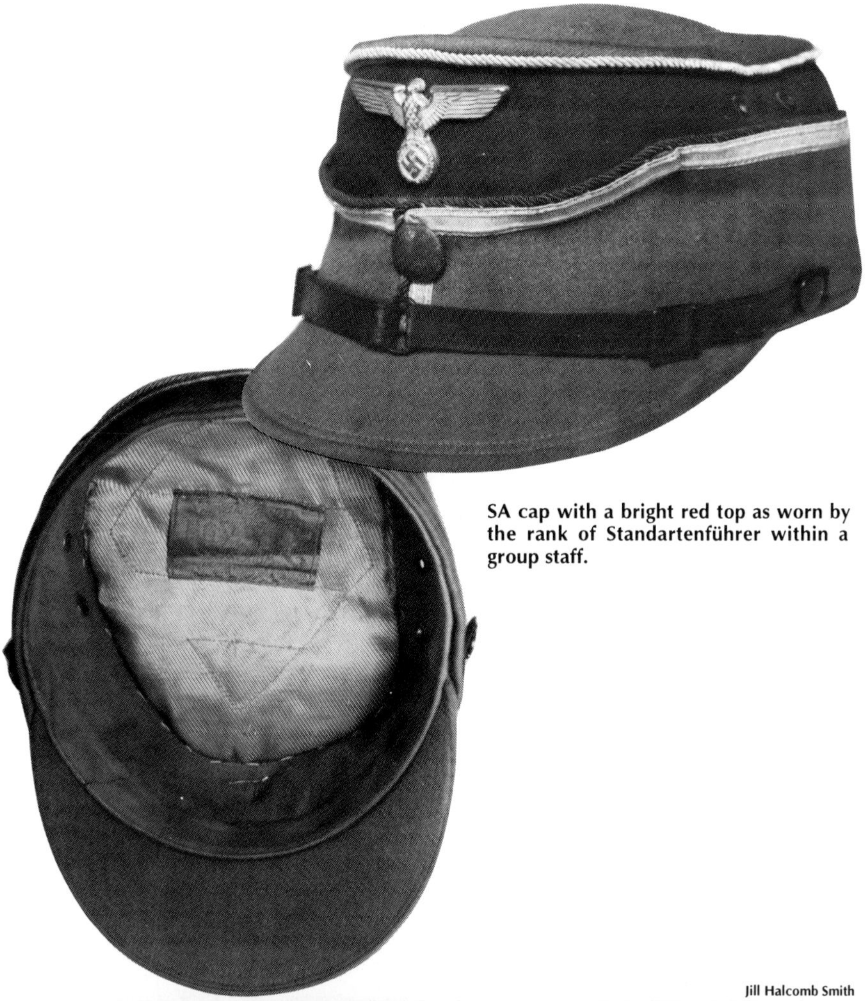

SA cap with a bright red top as worn by the rank of Standartenführer within a group staff.

Niall Malcolm

Jill Halcomb Smith

Stabschef Viktor Lutze wears his cap with golden piping and 2cm Tresse. Lutze was the only person allowed to wear this wide Tresse in the golden form, and in addition, the golden national emblem was allowed to be worn by him only within the SA until May 1938.

Lutze wears his SA cap with a single button on May 24, 1941. Note that he wears the embroidered pattern national emblem upon a cloth backing.

Stabschef Lutze's SA cap with golden buttons, piping and Tresse. Note the hand–embroidered national emblem on a bright red backing, as used for the top.

Viktor Lutze wears his final form of SA cap with the two front buttons and the embroidered national emblem during a visit to Pomerania in 1942.

Belgium Army Museum

Stabchef Lutze wears a subdued cap without Tresse during a tour of the Eastern front in August 1942.

Ed Stadnicki

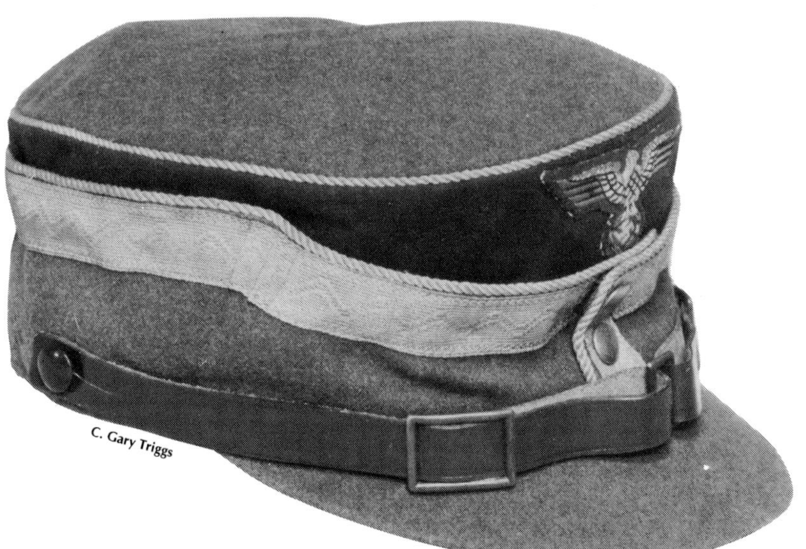
C. Gary Triggs

An SA cap often attributed to Stabschef Lutze, but this form was also worn by his successor, Wilhelm Schepmann. The piping, Tresse and the national emblem are in gilt colored rayon material, known as celleon (or cellophan). Note the two gilt pebbled buttons in front.

Niall Malcolm

Note the detail of the gold wire national emblem.

National Archives

Stabschef Schepmann wearing the single button version cap (as Lutze) but with a metal national emblem.

Honorary SA Leaders (Ehrenführerkorps) 1933 – 1945

In the spring of 1933 the first honorary ranks were created and introduced by Hitler. With a decree, May 26, an honorary rank for political leaders was first mentioned.[123] With a new order in early July these persons were authorized to wear a velvet silver–grey top.[124] With an order dated November 11, 1933 inactive leaders of the SA–Reserve I, who were granted an honorary rank, were also allowed to wear the silver–grey top.[125]

W.P.B.R. Saris

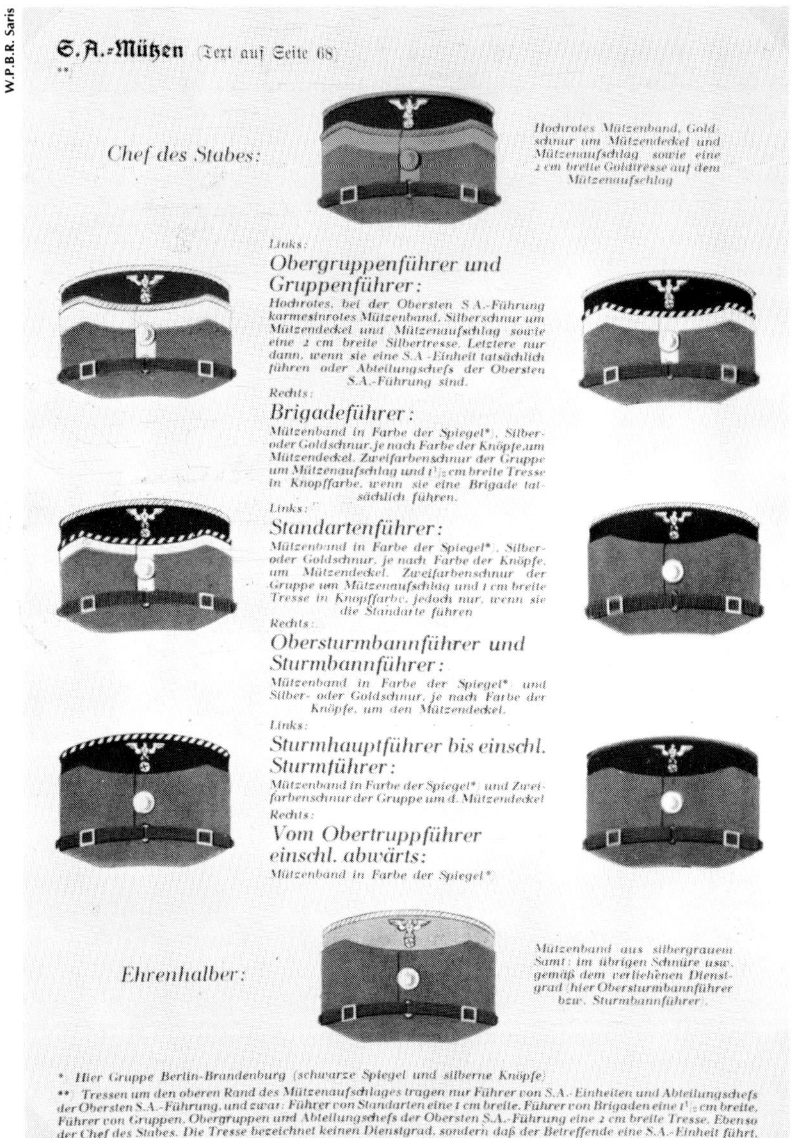

S.A.-Mützen (Text auf Seite 68) **)

Chef des Stabes:

Hochrotes Mützenband, Goldschnur um Mützendeckel und Mützenaufschlag sowie eine 2 cm breite Goldtresse auf dem Mützenaufschlag

Links:

Obergruppenführer und Gruppenführer:

Hochrotes, bei der Obersten S.A.-Führung karmesinrotes Mützenband, Silberschnur um Mützendeckel und Mützenaufschlag sowie eine 2 cm breite Silbertresse. Letztere nur dann, wenn sie eine S.A.-Einheit tatsächlich führen oder Abteilungschefs der Obersten S.A.-Führung sind.

Rechts:

Brigadeführer:

Mützenband in Farbe der Spiegel*), Silber- oder Goldschnur, je nach Farbe der Knöpfe, um Mützendeckel, Zweifarbenschnur der Gruppe um Mützenaufschlag und 1½ cm breite Tresse in Knopffarbe, wenn sie eine Brigade tatsächlich führen.

Links:

Standartenführer:

Mützenband in Farbe der Spiegel*), Silber- oder Goldschnur, je nach Farbe der Knöpfe, um Mützendeckel. Zweifarbenschnur der Gruppe um Mützenaufschlag und 1 cm breite Tresse in Knopffarbe, jedoch nur, wenn sie die Standarte führen

Rechts:

Obersturmbannführer und Sturmbannführer:

Mützenband in Farbe der Spiegel*) und Silber- oder Goldschnur, je nach Farbe der Knöpfe, um den Mützendeckel.

Links:

Sturmhauptführer bis einschl. Sturmführer:

Mützenband in Farbe der Spiegel*) und Zweifarbenschnur der Gruppe um d. Mützendeckel

Rechts:

Vom Obertruppführer einschl. abwärts:

Mützenband in Farbe der Spiegel*)

Ehrenhalber:

Mützenband aus silbergrauem Samt; im übrigen Schnüre usw. gemäß dem verliehenen Dienstgrad (hier Obersturmbannführer bzw. Sturmbannführer).

*) Hier Gruppe Berlin-Brandenburg (schwarze Spiegel und silberne Knöpfe)

**) Tressen um den oberen Rand des Mützenaufschlages tragen nur Führer von S.A.-Einheiten und Abteilungschefs der Obersten S.A.-Führung, und zwar: Führer von Standarten eine 1 cm breite, Führer von Brigaden eine 1½ cm breite, Führer von Gruppen, Obergruppen und Abteilungschefs der Obersten S.A.-Führung eine 2 cm breite Tresse. Ebenso der Chef des Stabes. Die Tresse bezeichnet keinen Dienstgrad, sondern daß der Betreffende eine S.A.-Einheit führt.

Page 67 of the book *Die Uniformen der Braunhemden* by Freiherr von Eelking, showing the official Tresse and piping systems of approximately 1934. Note the lowest cap for persons with honorary rank, being specified having a silver–grey velvet top.

Ehrenführer

In late January 1934 new specifications for honorary ranks (Ehrenführer) were published. An honorary rank was granted to such a person who had been meritorious to Hitler and the NSDAP party system, and who had especially served well in the SA. Only Hitler granted the honorary rank (on proposal of the SA chief of staff). These persons held the ranks of Obergruppenführer, Gruppenführer, Brigadeführer, Oberführer and Standartenführer and were assigned "zur Ehrendienstleistung" (abbreviated as "z.E.") for honorary rendered services to a "Standarte" or the staffs of a "Brigade" or "Gruppe."

Due to the above mentioned service such an honorary ranked person wore the standard color for the top, as worn for the district or staff they were associated with. They were authorized to wear the gold or silver piping, but were not allowed to wear the Tresse (this was also not allowed to those with an honorary rank in the health or administrative sections). This order took effect on February 15, 1934.[126]

In June 1934 a person with honorary rank, who served as a "Führer von Standarten" was authorized to wear the 1cm silver Tresse.[127]

Rangführer

SA leaders who were granted the rank Obersturmbannführer through Sturmführer were designated as "Rangführer" (simply translated, as a leader with a rank) and assigned to a "Sturmbann." These persons wore the regular standard ordered top and piping for the district. No Tresse was allowed.

Ehrenhöfe

Persons serving in those organs for law, order and discipline did not wear any special sign of recognition.[128]

No orders were found in later issues of the "Verordnungsblatt der OSAF" with corrections and changes for honorary ranked persons.

SA Administrative Officials and Medical Leaders (SA–Verwaltungs–und SA–Sanitätsführer) 1931 – 1934

Due to the enormous growth of the SA it became necessary in April 1931 to introduce special insignia of recognition for wear by administrative leaders and medical personnel, such as doctors, chemists, etc. Shortly thereafter, systems were introduced that included top and piping colors for the cap worn by these officials. Six months later the ranking system was expanded and a new list was authorized on November 28, 1931. For information relating to members of the so–called "Zeugmeisterei" see the section SA leaders.

---

123 *Der Oberste SA–Führer. Decree Nr. 1. from Adolf Hitler, dated May 5, 1933. Abt.I.Nr. 1228/33: Dienstgrade und Dienstgradabzeichen. Section F.*

124 *Ibid. München: July 7, 1933, Decree Nr. 2. Section G.*

125 *Ibid. München: November 11, 1933, Ch.Nr. 1634/33 II.Angel. Section 3.*

126 *Ibid. München: January 27, 1934, Ch.II. Nr. 1134/34. Sections 4 and 5; "Vbl.d.OSAF," Nr. 18, March 15, 1934, p. 8. Nr. 34.*

127 *"Vbl.d.OSAF," Nr. 26, June 18, 1934, p. 2. Nr. 4: Abzeichen für Ehrenführer.*

128 *Ehrenordnung für die SA der NSDAP. Der Oberste SA–Führer. München: December 12, 1933,*

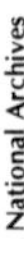

An SA–Sturmbannführer wearing the appropriate crown piping on his cap, which is without of ventilation holes.

Sanitätsführer

With an April 22, 1931 order only the person ranked as "Reichsarzt" was allowed to wear a colored top, being violet. He also wore golden crown and flap piping and button. Neither his deputy (Stellv.des Reichsarztes), nor the lower ranking doctors were allowed to wear the colored top. They were authorized to wear golden crown piping only.[129]

List: April 22, 1931

	TOP COLOR:	CROWN PIPING:	FLAP PIPING:	BUTTON:
Reichsarzt:	violet	gold	gold	gold;
Stellvertreter des Reichsarztes:	no colored top	ibid	no piping	ibid;
Untergruppenarzt:	ibid	ibid	ibid	ibid;
Standartenarzt:	ibid	ibid	ibid	ibid;
Sturmbannarzt:	ibid	ibid	ibid	ibid.[130]

Seven months later, on November 28, 1931, additional positions were established. Simultaneously the ranks for doctors and chemists were announced. The position of "Untergruppenarzt" was not included in this list.

List: November 28, 1931

	TOP COLOR:	CROWN PIPING:	FLAP PIPING:	BUTTON:
Reichsarzt (a doctor with Gruppenführer rank):	violet	gold	gold	gold;
Gruppenarzt and Oberarzt (a doctor with Oberführer rank):	no colored top	ibid	no piping	ibid;
Oberapotheker (a chemist with Oberführer rank):	ibid	ibid	ibid	ibid;
Standarten–und Sturm–bannarzt (most often both being doctors with Standartenführer rank):	ibid	ibid	ibid	ibid;
Apotheker (a chemist with Sturmbannführer rank):	ibid	ibid	ibid	ibid.[131]

---

[129] *Der Oberste SA–Führer. München: April 22, 1931, Decree, I.a.Nr. 1679/31: Dienststellungsabzeichen.*

[130] *Ibid. München: April 22, 1931, I.a.Nr. 1679/31: Dienststellungsabzeichen, section b: Ärzte.*

[131] *Ibid. Decree 4/5. München: November 28, 1931, I/II.a.Nr. 7162/31: Dienstgrad–und Dienststellungsabzeichen. Appendix 2.*

In early 1932, medical positions in motor units were first introduced. These personnel did not have separate regulations.[132] In September 1932, further additions were made: the rank Untergruppenarzt was reintroduced (in fact this was the Oberarzt position that was renamed); simultaneously the position of Untergruppenapotheker was introduced. Piping was like that worn by Gruppenarzt. Aids to the rank of Sturmbannarzt and Apotheker were allowed to wear a 3mm violet piping around the crown of the cap.[133]

Otto Spronk

The leader of the "Deutscher Apothekerstand," Standartenführer Apotheker Schmierer, from Freudenstadt (at left) and his deputy SS–Sturmführer Apotheker Kaufmann from Munich, during the first day of a meeting of chemists at Weimar in July 1934. Schmierer was authorized to wear a violet cap top until the spring of 1934. He is still wearing this, otherwise the orange/yellow colored top he should be wearing since March, would be in contrast. Note the wearing of the Tresse, and also the lettering of the SS cuff–title.

Otto Spronk

The chief of the SA health department, Obergruppenführer Brauneck, during an inspection of the Reichssanitätsschule at Tübingen. Braineck was assigned to the OSAF and was therefore authorized to wear the crimson top and due to his position, the 2cm wide silver Tresse.

With the reorganization of May 1933, the ranks or positions of medical personnel were adapted, changed or extended. For example, candidate doctors (Arzt), dentists (Zahnarzt), chemist or pharmacists (Apotheker) held the rank Obertruppführer. No piping was allowed to be worn. The highest rank medical personnel could hold was Obergruppenführer, wearing a violet top with golden crown and flap piping. The ranks Gruppen–, Brigade–, Ober–, Standarten–, Obersturmbann– and Sturmbannführer wore golden crown piping; the ranks Sturmhaupt–, Obersturm– and Sturmführer were ordered to wear two–colored piping in violet/gold around the crown.[134]

This SA–Obersturmführer doctor wears the regular style SA cap with the violet/golden crown piping and a colored top, probably according to district. This photo must be dated approximately in the summer of 1933, but he is wearing an unauthorized doctor's symbol to the rear of his collar tabs. The Obersturmführer and Sturmhauptführer ranks were introduced no earlier than May 26, 1933. Simultaneously, however the wearing of the above mentioned device was abolished for about one year and the doctors oval was introduced with the Askulap.

Wayne Milburn

National Archives

An SA Mann wearing the black colored top for Berlin–Brandenburg. This photograph must be dated between July 7, 1933 when the colored top was introduced and August 1 of the same year when the arm insigne using the red cross upon a white shield was introduced. The wear of this insigne means that the SA man is a Sanitätsführer, but has not yet passed the medical state examination. Note the wearing of the Rossbach brassard.

---

132 *"Vbl.d.OSAF," Nr. 6, January 26, 1932. p. 4. Nr. 9: SA–Ärzte für Motorverbänden.*

133 *"Dienstvorschrift für die SA der NSDAP," 1932, Heft 2, pp. 142–143: Übersicht der Dienstgradabzeichen.*

134 *Der Oberste SA–Führer. Decree Nr. 1. München: May 26, 1933, Abt.I.Nr. 1228/33: Dienstgrade und Dienstgradabzeichen. Appendix III.*

SA–Sanitäts–Sturmbannführer Hans–Friedrich Ahl wears his cap crown piped in gold. The color for his top is without any doubt violet, as this color was introduced on July 7, 1933. He is also wearing the doctor's oval introduced in May 1933, which was discontinued with the SA dress regulations of March 1934. The metal device behind the collar patch was reintroduced. The violet top was worn until approximately March 1934 when the regular district colors became required for wear.

July 7, 1933 a violet velvet top was introduced for wear by all medical personnel. A simple violet piping was used replacing the earlier ordered violet/ gold piping.[135] The ranks Brigadeführer, Oberführer and Standartenführer were ordered to wear a two–colored piping around the upper edge of the cap flap. The wearing of the violet velvet top was abolished from March 1934 and medical personnel was ordered to wear the top color of their assigned district or staff.[136] The SA headdress no longer bore any special sign of recognition for medical personnel. This remained as such until the end of the war.

No rank or position within the medical services was allowed to wear any form of Tresse until 1936. With an order published in August 1936, higher ranked personnel with the ranks Standartenführer and above were authorized to wear the Tresse form according to their position (for detailed rank and Tresse information, consult the June 22, 1936 order within the section SA leaders).[137]

No documentation concerning the abolishment of the violet piping has been found. It is assumed it was done away with about the same time that the blue piping for administrative personnel was abolished. It is not mentioned in later regulations. It is certain that SA caps with a violet top or piping are extremely rare.

---

[135] *Ibid. Decree, dated July 7, 1933, Ch.Nr. 1350/33. Also order Nr. 2: Neugliederung der SA. Appendix 1.*

[136] *"Anzugs–Ordnung für die SA," Teil I. Der Oberste SA–Führer. München: March 1, 1934, Section VIII: Zusammenstellung der Abzeichen usw., pp. 44–45.*

[137] *"Vbl.d.OSAF," Nr. 12, August 17, 1936, p. 71. Nr. 223: Dienststellungs–und Dienstgradabzeichen (F.3 h13731).*

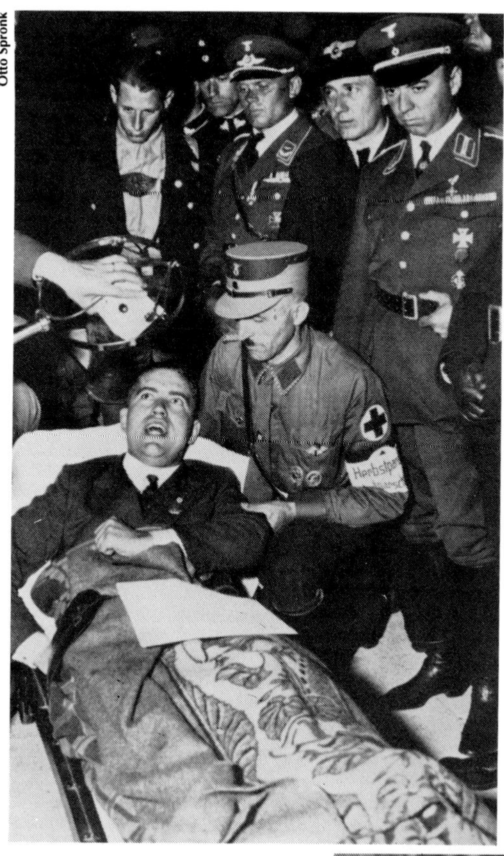

During the 1934 Party Day Rally, a member of SA medical unit gives a demonstration. He wears the regular form of SA kepi with the colored top of a district. Note that both collar patches are without any device. He wears a white brassard with the lettering "Herbstparade (autumn parade) Aufmarschstab" (advance staff) over his regular swastika brassard.

Adolf de Crousaz

SA medical personnel wear the regular SA cap during exercises in late 1935. The photograph shows persons from the Nordsee district wearing the steel–green colored top. Note the wearing of the white disc with red cross as introduced in August 1933.

Verwaltungsführer

Simultaneously with the introduction of special insignia of recognition for medical personnel, special orders were also introduced for administrative personnel. Administrative positions were not allowed to wear the colored top nor any flap piping, not even the person holding the highest position of "Gruppengeldverwalter."

List: April 22, 1931

	TOP COLOR:	CROWN PIPING:	FLAP PIPING:	BUTTON:
Gruppengeldverwalter:	no colored top	silver	no piping	silver;
Untergruppengeld–verwalter:	ibid	gold or silver according to district	ibid	gold or silver according to district;
Standartengeldver–walter:	ibid	ibid	ibid	ibid;
Sturmbanngeldver–walter:	ibid	two–colored piping according to district	ibid	ibid;
Sturmgeldverwalter:	ibid	ibid	ibid	ibid.[138]

With the November 28, 1931 order, ranks were given for most of the administrative positions. The Gruppen–, as well as Untergruppengeldverwalter were both positions authorized Standartenführer rank. The Standartengeldverwalter held Sturmbannführer rank; the Sturmbanngeldverwalter held Sturmführer rank and the Sturmgeldverwalter Truppführer rank.

In May 1933 the regulations for administrative positions were extended, modified and classified into three levels: Stabsverwaltungsführer (the ranks Ober–, Standarten– or Obersturmbannführer); Oberverwaltungsführer (the ranks Standarten–, Obersturmbann– or Sturmbannführer) and Verwaltungsführer (the ranks Obersturmbann–, Sturmbann– or Sturmhauptführer). New functions were introduced: in a "Gruppe," the position Stabsrechnungsführer (a Sturmhaupt– or Obersturmführer); in a "Brigade," the position Oberrechnungsführer (the rank Sturmhaupt–, Obersturm– or Sturmführer); in a "Standarte," the position Rechnungsführer (the rank Obersturm–, Sturm– or Obertruppführer); in a "Sturmbann," the position Obergeldverwalter (the rank Sturm–, Obertrupp– or Truppführer) and in a "Sturm" the position Geldverwalter (the rank Obertrupp–

[138] *Der Oberste SA–Führer. München: April 22, 1931, I.a.Nr. 1679/31: Dienststellungsabzeichen, section G: Geldverwalter.*

or Truppführer). The piping worn was silver for the rank Sturmbannführer and above, the highest rank being Oberführer.

The ranks authorized to wear the earlier two–colored piping now wore blue crown piping instead. Previously used rank or function names were abolished. A colored top was only allowed for the highest ranked persons, assigned to a staff (being red) or the OSAF (being crimson). The fact that Department IV within the OSAF was the "Verwaltungsabteilung" did not have any effect regarding wear of a colored top for lower ranked persons.[139] Soon an important change was made.

A. Stam

SA–Obergruppenführer Knickmann, the chief of police from Duisburg/Hamborn, photographed just before an SA parade on September 24, 1933. At left is Standartenführer Grunert of Standarte 97 of Mönchen-Gladbach. He wears the proper piping and Tresse for his position of command. Approximately five months earlier, Grunert held the rank of Sturmführer. In the middle, with his back to the photographer is Brigadeführer Fuchs from Düsseldorf; Knickmann is standing at right. Both are wearing the correct types of Tresse, as well as piping. Second from left in the background is a Verwaltungssturmbannführer, also known as an Oberverwaltungsführer.

On July 7, 1933, a light blue velvet top was introduced for wear by all administrative personnel. The ranks Brigadeführer, Oberführer and Standartenführer were ordered to use two–colored flap piping. The wearing of the light blue velvet top was abolished from March 1934 and administrative personnel were ordered to wear the top color of their assigned district or staff.[140] Simultaneously, the blue crown piping was also abolished and the headdress no longer bore any special sign of recognition.

---

139 *Der Oberste SA–Führer, Abt.I.Nr. 1228/33. Erlass Nr. 1. München: May 26, 1933, Betrifft: Dienstgrade und Dienstgradabzeichen. Appendixes I and II.*

140 *"Anzugs–Ordnung für die SA," Teil 1. Der Oberste SA–Führer. München: March 1, 1934, Section VIII: Zusammenstellung der Abzeichen usw., pp. 44–45.*

In July 1936 blue was reintroduced, but this effected only the collar tabs, and not the cap piping of the headdress.[141] These remained unchanged until the end of the war. As it is noted in the section on medical personnel: SA caps with a light blue top or piping are extremely rare.

No rank or position within the administrative section was allowed to wear Tresse on the cap until 1936. With an order published in August 1936 higher ranked personnel with the ranks of Standartenführer and above were authorized to wear the Tresse form according to their position (for detailed rank and Tresse information consult the June 22, 1936 order within the section on SA leaders).[142]

Otto Spronk

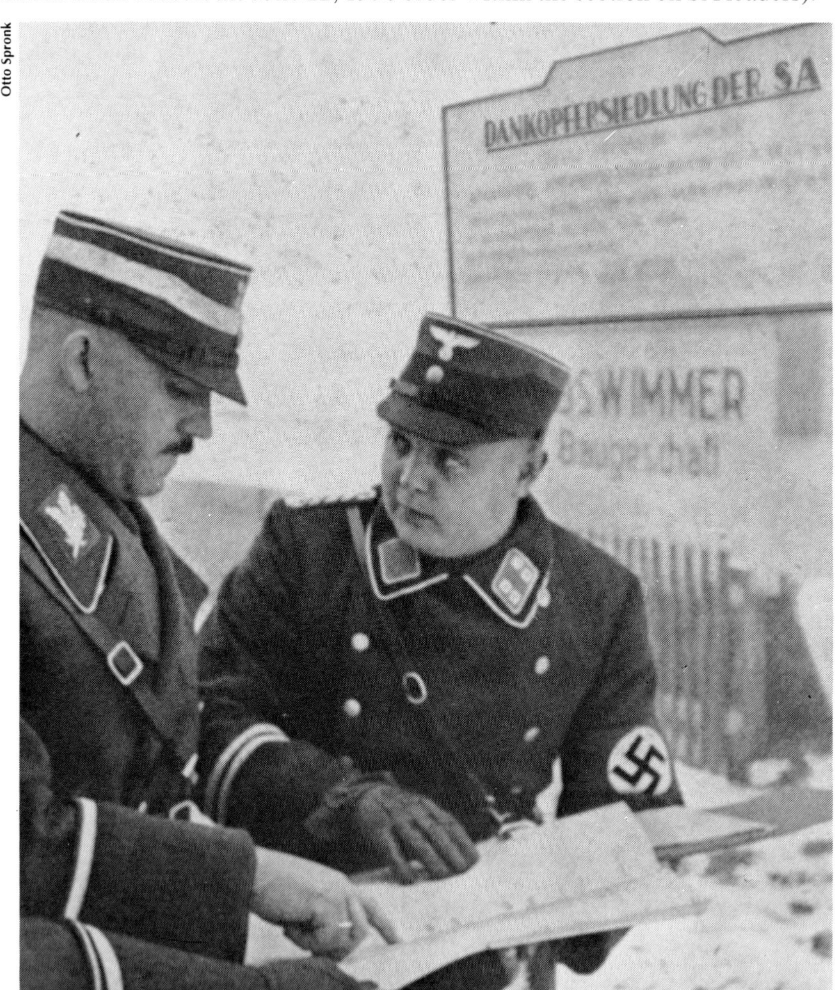

Gruppenführer Mappes, the chief of the Administration Main Office with his "Referent" (chief of a department), a Sturmbannführer. For the latter, the crown is piped in silver according to his rank and position.

---

141 *"Vbl.d.OSAF," Nr. 11, July 20, 1936, p. 64. Nr. 205: Abzeichen der SA–Verwaltung, bzw. des Verwaltungs–Führerkorps.*

142 *Ibid, Nr. 12, August 17, 1936, p. 71. Nr. 223: Dienststellungs–und Dienstgradabzeichen (F.3h 13731).*

Special SA units included Signal–SA (Nachrichten–SA, including the so–called "Hundewesen" – units serving with dogs), Cavalry SA (Reiter–SA, co–existing with the NSRK. [see also this chapter]), engineer SA (Pionier–SA), Medical SA (Sanitäts–SA, consult also the section "Sanitätsführer"), Foot SA (Fuss–SA), SA railway units (SA–Eisenbahnereinheiten: these units did not exist in Germany, but only in Austria in the early 1930's), patrol service (Streifendienst), Flying SA (Fliegerstürme der SA, for more information, consult Volume 2, pp.160–162, and SA music units (Musikeinheiten der SA)).

The standard forms of SA headdress were worn by members of all of the above units, having no special signs of recognition or insignia. It must be noted that members of the Marine–SA units, who joined the NSRK, wore the regular naval SA style headdress. Only the highest ranking personnel were occasionally allowed to wear a special cap top color (consult the section about SA leaders) and for a short period, members of the SA–Reserve were allowed to wear a special cap top color or headdress (consult also this section). This was abolished in 1935.

Other special units also existed, such as mountain troops (SA–Gebirgsjäger–Einheiten), Naval SA (Marine–SA, including "Seesportschulen"), Motorized SA and motor schools (Motorstürme der SA, as well as "Schulen der Motor–SA"), SA military police (SA–Feldjägerkorps), SA auxiliary police (SA–Hilfspolizei), etc. Some of these were allowed to wear special forms of headdress, top color or insignia. Consult the related sections for detailed information. Included in the SA chapter are also: Ausbildungswesen (schools), Techn.Lehrstürme, Stabswache and Feldherrnhalle, SA–Hilfswerklager, NS.Reiterkorps, Reichsautozug "Deutschland," SA–Wehrmannschaften, SA im Führerhauptquartier, Verstärkter Grenzschutz and the Auslandsorganisation der SA. These organizations are discussed in the respective sections. For information on the NSAK, consult the chapter on NSKK in the future volume IV of this series.

Guard Troops for the SA Staff (Stabswache) 1923/1932 – 1934

An elite unit, the "Stabswache München," was raised in March 1923. In May of the same year this unit was incorporated into the "Stosstrupp Adolf Hitler" (Hitler's personal shock troop. For more information consult the chapter: "Schutzstaffeln der NSDAP" in a coming volume). In the late 1920's guard duties were performed by Himmler and his SS.

Due to the growth of the SA, another elite guards unit, known as "Stabswache," was created to protect members of the SA high command (Stabswache der OSAF) at the same time as the SA reorganizations in 1932. Other SA special guards units were created at the same time as well, such as the "Stabswache Göring" and the "Stabswachen der Obergruppen und Gruppen."

The "Stabswache München" was in 1923 the first unit to wear the grey, ski–style cap with the death's head positioned on the front.[143] Klintzsch was one

[143] *Volz."Daten der Geschichte der NSDAP. " 11.Auflage. Berlin/Leipzig: 1943, p. 120.*

A member of the Reiter–SA of Standarte 72, from Wuppertal–Elberfeld, wears the regular form of SA cap with the colored top in black for the Niederrhein district. Note the wear of the early form of national emblem.

Richard Kindel

Otto Spronk

This photograph shows a member of the "SA–Verpflegung" (SA care) wearing the white cook's cap. On the front of the cap is embroidered (probably in red): "Reichsparteitag Verpflegung." It has no relationship to either the Hilfszug "Bayern" or Reichsautozug "Deutschland."

of its first members. As commander of this unit he probably wore a black cap.

During this research no variations in headgear was found, other than the steel helmet being worn. The members of these units wore the standard SA cap with the button in the district color. No colored top was worn until 1933. With the introduction of the colored top for all SA members in July 1933 the guards units also had to wear the color of the district they were assigned to. The special cuff title for these units was introduced in 1933 at the latest.[144]

144 *"Vbl.d.OSAF," Nr. 16, December 1, 1933, p. 2. Nr. 6: Angehörige von Stabswachen.*

Guards Regiment (Wachstandarte Feldherrnhalle) 1934 – 1945

On June 30, 1934 the new Chief of Staff, Viktor Lutze, announced future development plans for the SA. These new directives were announced on September 10th, and mentioned a new elite unit for the SA, the "Wachdienst," raised from the earlier Stabswachen.[145] In late October 1934 this guard regiment was reorganized and renamed as "Wachstandarte."

On September 11, 1936 these guard units were renamed as SA–Wachstandarte "Feldherrnhalle" and the next day its new members swore the oath of allegiance. On January 12, 1937, Hermann Göring in his rank of SA–Obergruppenführer, was appointed by Hitler to the position of chief of the Wachstandarte Feldherrnhalle.[146]

Peter Klubert

Willi Biller, a member of the Wachstandarte, wears the steel helmet with special decals in 1936. Note the "W" on the collar patch and the gorget, as ordered for members of a guard unit, the pattern later worn within the Feldherrnhalle units. The helmet shield is in the form and probably the colors of the OSAF command flag.

---

[145] *Ibid, Nr. 42, November 19, 1934, p. 2. Nr. 6: Wachdienst. Here it was specially noted that the new name was "Wachdienst." The use of the word "Stabswache" (a reminder of the Röhm period) was forbidden.*

[146] *Volz. "Daten der Geschichte der NSDAP. " 11.Auflage, Berlin/Leipzig: 1943, section VII: Die SA, SS und das NSKK (1921–1943), pp. 129–130.*

During 1935, six guard units were formed, known as "Sturmbanne" and stationed in the cities of Berlin, München, Hattingen (near the city of Bochum), Krefeld, Stettin and Stuttgart.[147] In the summer of 1938 another unit was formed at Wien.[148] During the war, a unit was stationed at Stahnsdorf.[149] This unit was known as the SA–Brigade Stahnsdorf, but was in fact a unit of the "Feldherrnhalle."

W.P.B.R. Saris

The units were meant to guard SA buildings and those of the Party and State. Their training was not exclusively political in nature, but they were also highly trained militarily. Soon these units were known as the best at the well–known Prussian "goose step." They were well equipped and were always ready for special duties, when ordered by the commander–in–chief of the Luftwaffe.[150] Service in the "Standarte Feldherrnhalle" was considered to be fulfilling one's military service obligation.

Members of the Wachstandarte often wore the steel helmet with special decals. In late 1935 it was ordered that all such guard units wear the same color top in crimson on the standard SA kepi. The cap button was silver. The service dress for wear in public or parades was the regular SA uniform with the Luftwaffe national emblem over the right tunic pocket from 1938. The SA kepi was

147 *"Organisationsbuch der NSDAP. " München: 1937 thru 1943, p. 364b.*

148 *"Handbuch der SA." Berlin: October 27, 1938, p. 26.*

149 *"Uniformen–Markt," Nr. 21, November 1, 1942, p. 166.*

150 *"Handbuch der SA." Berlin: October 27, 1938, p. 26.*

Hermann Göring inspects members of a "Feldherrnhalle" unit in the garden of the Reichsluftfahrtministerium. Göring is accompanied by SA chief of staff, Viktor Lutze (on his left) and the commander of the SA–Standarte "Feldherrnhalle," Erich Reimann (on his right). This photograph is dated January 12, 1937, Göring's 44th birthday. On this day, Lutze brought the message that Göring had been appointed as the chief of the Wachstandarte "Feldherrnhalle." Reimann, as well as the person behind him, already wear a larger national emblem. This is probably not the SA pattern, as this version was not introduced until June 1937.

This photograph of a member of the Standarte "Feldherrnhalle," standing guard, was often used in periodicals and newspapers during the years 1937 and 1938. He wears the crimson colored cap top, and in addition, the metal device upon his right collar patch, the "Feldherrnhalle" gorget and cuff title. The last item was officially introduced for wear in December 1936.

Otto Spronk

The crimson-topped kepi in wear by these Feldherrnhalle members.

Deeter/Odegard

A Standartenführer from the "Feldherrnhalle" waits during the consecrating of the Standarte "Feldherrnhalle" during the 1936 Party Day Rally at Nürnberg. He wears the crimson cap top, Tresse and piping which was ordered in 1935.

Otto Spronk

The heart of the SA, the Standarte "Feldherrnhalle," wearing the SA garrison cap during shooting exercises.

worn with this dress. The regular Luftwaffe uniform with the "Feldherrnhalle" cuff title and Luftwaffe field cap was worn during maneuvers and field service.

The brown SA garrison cap with the cloth crimson triangle was also worn with the SA uniform, mainly during marksmanship exercises, ground and reconnaissance activities and with disaster assistance.[151]

Otto Spronk

Two members of the SA-Feldherrnhalle wearing the kepi. Note the wear of the Luftwaffe breast eagle above the right pocket which was ordered in 1938.

151 *"Die SA." Sonderausgabe Völkischer Beobachter. München: 1938, pp. 46–47.*

Library of Congress

SA–Gruppenführer Erich Reimann, commander of the SA–Standarte "Feldherrnhalle," presents Göring the "Feldherrnhalle" dagger in honor of his birthday on January 12, 1938. Note the inside of the cap Reimann is holding as well as the cap of the Sturmbannführer. Reimann's cap differs in shape from the one worn in the January 12, 1937 photograph.

Otto Spronk

An SA leader of the Standarte "Feldherrnhalle" wears his cap with piping and Tresse for the rank of Gruppenführer. Note the wear of the "Feldherrnhalle" dagger.

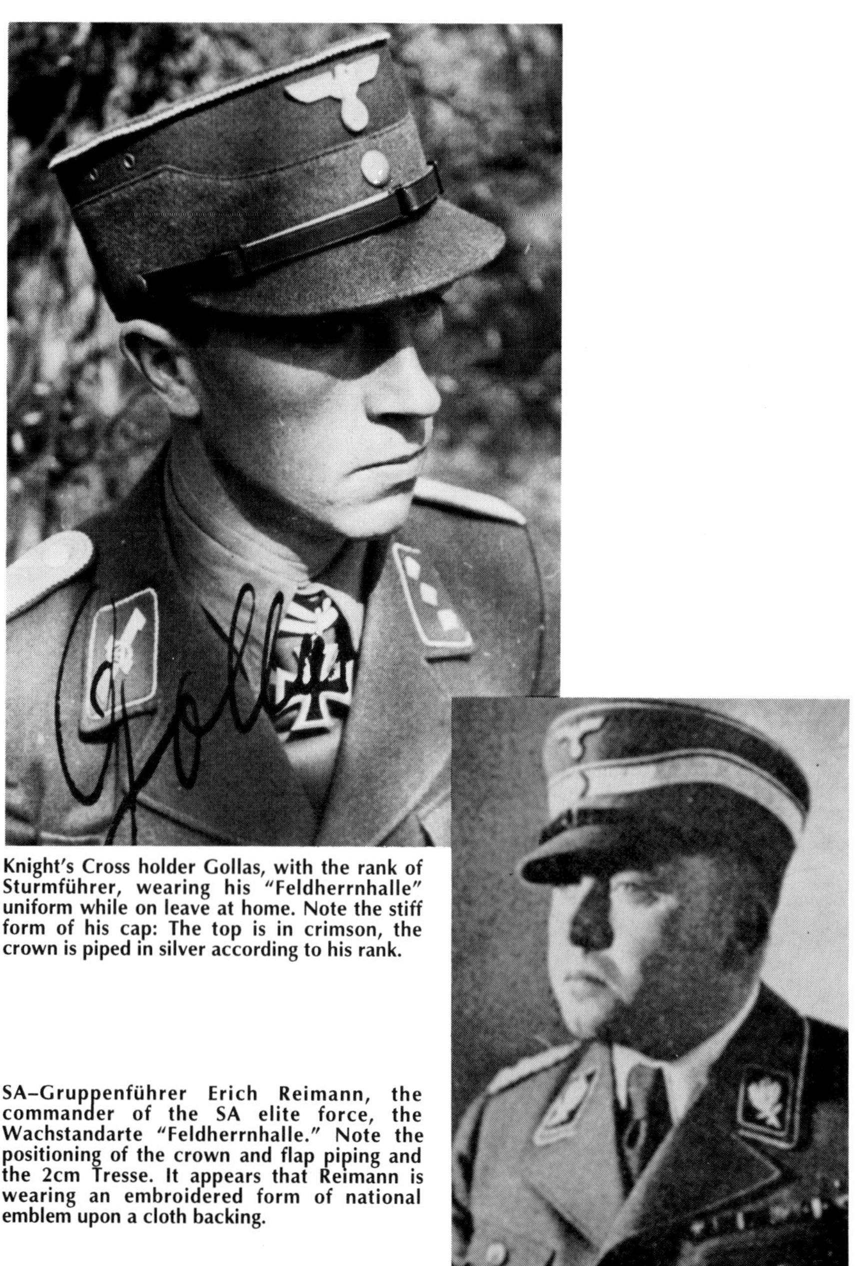

Knight's Cross holder Gollas, with the rank of Sturmführer, wearing his "Feldherrnhalle" uniform while on leave at home. Note the stiff form of his cap: The top is in crimson, the crown is piped in silver according to his rank.

SA–Gruppenführer Erich Reimann, the commander of the SA elite force, the Wachstandarte "Feldherrnhalle." Note the positioning of the crown and flap piping and the 2cm Tresse. It appears that Reimann is wearing an embroidered form of national emblem upon a cloth backing.

The SA-Standarte "Feldherrnhalle" was disolved on March 31, 1939. Its members were either dismissed or incorporated with the "Fallschirmtruppe" (I./ Fallschirm-Jäger-Regiment 2), the "General Göring" Regiment, its "Wachbataillon" or transferred to armed forces units.[152]

152 "Besondere Luftwaffen-Bestimmungen," Nr. 6, March 13, 1939. Pages 80-84, Nr. 189, Rückgliederung des Regiments "SA-Standarte Feldherrnhalle." O.K.W. orders dated January 25 and February 18, 1939.

W.P.B.R. Saris

The newly appointed Stabschef of the SA, Wilhelm Schepmann, visits wounded members of Wachbataillon Feldherrnhalle and members of the Infantry–Regiment Nr.271–"Feldherrnhalle" in the fall of 1943, in the city of Iserlohn. Note the wear of the (silver) piping by the two Sturmbannführer. The field–grey worn by the infantry must not be confused with the field–grey that was authorized for wear by the SA while with the "Führerhauptquartier," or in the "Operationsgebiet".

Otto Spronk

SA Guards Units (SA–Wachposten)

SA–Wachposten, guard units from regular SA units, wore their standard SA kepi with the top color according to their district (Gruppe). On some occasions it is known that the old form steel helmet, as worn by staff guards, was worn.

A member of the SA performing duty as a guard at the concentration camp at Oranienburg near Berlin, wears his regular SA uniform. This photograph is dated between February and July 1933: The KZ Oranienburg was formed in early 1933, shortly after the assumption of power by Hitler. The collar patches are still white.

J. Bornebroek

Members of a guard unit salute during the wedding of one of their comrades at Hannover in the Niedersachsen district. Note that they are not from a Feldherrnhalle unit as their uniform is without the special cuff title and they are not wearing the special gorget.

SA Reserve
1929 – 1945

A reserve–unit was created on March 28, 1929 for persons forty years old and above.[153] Due to the growth of these reserve units the members also had to wear the golden or silver cap button according to district standards. From September 1932 its wear was ordered. Piping according to rank was also authorized.[154] Upon the introduction of the top color for all SA members it was also worn by the members of the SA reserve according to the SA district color.

Otto Müller of the SA Reserve (note "R1/62" on collar patch) wears a cap top in the appropriate SA color for the Nordsee district with a gold button. This reserve unit was located in the Osnabrück area.

Hans v. Diggelen

---

[153] *Ibid, pp. 123 and 127.*

[154] *"Vbl.d.OSAF," Nr. 9, September 23, 1932, Nr. 5: Abzeichen der SA–Reserve.*

Richard Kindel

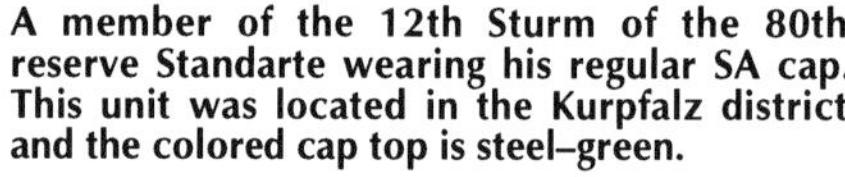

A member of the 12th Sturm of the 80th reserve Standarte wearing his regular SA cap. This unit was located in the Kurpfalz district and the colored cap top is steel–green.

W.P.B.R. Saris

A member of the SA reserve wears the semi–stiff form of SA cap with the dark brown colored top. He is a member of the 21st Sturm from the 68th Standarte, from the Westmark district. This Standarte was known as "Mittelrhein."

With a reorganization in November 1933, the SA–Reserve I (SAR I) and SA–Reserve II (SAR II) were created.[155] The SAR I consisted largely of members from "Der Stahlhelm," the veterans' organization. The SAR II also consisted of Stahlhelm members, the Kyffhäuserbund, as well as persons from other military traditions groups. From the SAR II grew the so–called "SA–Landsturm–Einheiten" (SA–L).

The SAR I (in fact a transitional organization) existed officially only for a few months. It was fused with the SA by orders dated January 25, 1934; the SAR II/SA–L existed until December 1935, to become again the SA reserve, existing in all SA districts throughout the war.

SAR I
1933 – 1934

Due to financial problems, the members of the NSDFB.St. were permitted to wear their Stahlhelm uniform with the regular Stahlhelm visored cap during the time while members of the SAR I (and even later when the SAR I was combined with the regular SA in the fall of 1935).[156] The January 1934 order

---

155 *Der Oberste SA–Führer. München: November 11, 1933, Ch.Nr. 1634/33. II.Angel.: Gliederung der SA–Reserve I.*

156 *"Vbl.d.OSAF," Nr. 18, March 15, 1934, p. 5. Nr. 23: SAR I–Dienstanzug.*

Bernd Wedeking

Members of the 4th Sturm from Standarte 17 of the reserve from Bochum. Note the age, most of whom are at least 45 years old. The colored top worn is wine–red, as Bochum was in the Westfalen district.

specified that at larger meetings, the service dress of the Stahlhelm with a brown shirt and the regular SA kepi had to be worn. It is known however that this order was largely disobeyed, even up to the disbanding of the NSDFB.St. The SAR I members kept wearing the regular Stahlhelm uniform with the Stahlhelm form of headdress.

Those members of the SA–Reserve I, that were equipped with the regular SA cap, wore the brown leather chin strap and the top color according to the district color system. It is known that members of the former Nat.Soz.Deutscher Frontkämpfer–Bund for a time, often wore the black leather chin strap as did members of the NSDFB.St. (For more information consult Volume 2, the chapter "Soldatenbünde," pp.216 through 226). SAR I leaders wore the regulation piping or occasionally the ordered forms of Tresse.[157]

SAR II
1933 – 1935

An order dated February 12, 1934 stated that only staff units of the SAR II existed and as yet, no (active) units had been created.[158] For the immediate future, basic units of the SAR II were planned utilizing persons who came from the SA and SAR I and were above the age of 45. As far as researched the first units were created not earlier than late spring 1934. Persons who formerly had not joined the SA or the SAR I were not allowed to join the SAR II.

It was planned that SAR II leaders (in fact practically all leaders of the SAR II formerly had leading positions within the Stahlhelm organization) would wear caps with the silver–grey top.[159] An order dated February 12, 1934 stated once more that in addition the lower ranks had to wear a silver–grey top. The button and piping color were as ordered for the district. Administrative and medi-

157 *"Anzugs–Ordnung für die SA." Teil I. Der Oberste SA–Führer. München: March 1, 1934, section II: Sonderabzeichen, p. 30.*

158 *Der Oberste SA–Führer. München: February 12, 1934, Ch.Nr. 2273: Organisation der SAR II.*

159 *Ibid. München: January 27, 1934 with appendixes. Ch.II.Nr. 1134/34, section II: SA–Führer der SAR II. This section also states that all others had to wear silver–grey cap tops.*

Otto Spronk

A group of SA members from the 3rd Sturm of Standarte 14, part of the SAR II, photographed January 28, 1934 in Hainberg. The leader of this unit was Sturmführer Grillenberger. Note that practically all of the people shown are wearing civilian cloths as these SAR II units were not active. The persons leading this group are wearing the sulfur–yellow colored top being in the Franken district. In later years, the color was changed to light blue when the district was changed to the Bayr.Ostmark district.

Otto Spronk

A member of the reserve Sturm from the Leibstandarte at Munich wears the silver–grey colored cap top in this early 1934 photograph. One year later, the light blue colored top of the Hochland district was ordered to be worn.

cal personnel within the SAR II also wore a silver–grey top with the regulation button or piping of the SA districts. Some functions were permitted to wear the authorized Tresse:

Oberstlandesführer (A proposed chief within the OSAF staff, therefore authorized for):	2.0cm silver;
Führer eines Landesverbandes (Equal to a "Führer der SA–Brigade"):	1.5cm silver;
Führer eines Kreisverbandes und Unterverbandes (Equal to a "Führer der SA–Standarte"):	1.0cm silver;
Stabsführer des Oberstlandesführers und der Landesverbände:	1.0cm gold with red stripe.[160]

Otto Spronk

A group of SA members of SAR II from Altona, in the Nordmark district. Note the variety of material used for the caps, having the emerald–green colored top. The photograph is dated early 1935. In the middle is the leader of this unit, a Sturmhauptführer, wearing the 1cm silver Tresse of a Führer eines Kreisverbandes und Unterverbandes.

In December 1934 it was ordered that members of the SAR II had to stop the purchase of caps with the silver–grey top. A reorganization was expected.[161] Approximately one year later, with an order dated November 22, 1935 the functions of Oberstlandesführer, Landesverbands– and Kreisverbandsführer, as well as Unterverbandsführer were abolished.[162] The SAR II was disbanded and the reserves were incorporated within the regular SA–Reserve,[163] wearing the regular top color of their district.

---

160 "Anzugs–Ordnung für die SA." Teil I. Der Oberste SA–Führer. München: March 1, 1934, Section II: Sonderabzeichen. p. 30.

161 Der Oberste SA–Führer. München: December 5, 1934, Führungsamt, F4.Nr. 36389: Abzeichen SAR II; "Mbl.d.RZM," Nr. 30, December 22, 1934, p. 2.

162 Ibid. München: November 22, 1935, Führungsamt: SA–L (The NSDFB.St., the old Stahlhelm was officially disbanded November 7, 1935).

163 "Vbl.d.OSAF," Nr. 37, December 20, 1935, p. 184. Nr. 464: SA–L (F.63140) and Nr. 466: Dienststempel für SA–L.

Mitteilungsblatt der Reichszeugmeisterei

der Nationalsozialistischen Deutschen Arbeiter-Partei

Herausgeber: Reichszeugmeister Richard Büchner; verantwortlich: Dr. Hubert Ulsamer. Druck: Münchner Buchgewerbehaus M. Müller & Sohn G.m.b.H., sämtliche in München. Bezug nur durch die Reichspost. Unmittelbare Bestellungen bei der RZM. können nicht angenommen werden. Erscheint wöchentlich. Preis vierteljährl. RM. 3.–. Nachdruck, auch auszugsweise, verboten.

Ausgabe 30 — München, 22. Dezember 1934 — Jahrgang 1

Abzeichen der SAR. II

Nach Mitteilung der Obersten SA.-Führung dürfen die grauen Kragenspiegel, Achselstücke und die Mützen mit grauem Gaustreifen, die für die Angehörigen der SAR. II bereits angeschafft wurden, bis zur endgültigen Regelung weitergetragen werden. Neuanschaffungen haben bis auf weiteres zu unterbleiben.

The announcement in the *Mbl.d.RZM* in reference to the purchased SA cap's with the grey top. Note that this top color is referred to as "Gaustreifen." This publication allows its official wear. For many years it was thought that its introduction for use by the SAR II was based on a wrong interpretation of the January and February 1934 orders, but it is obvious that its wear was only a matter of time.

SA Technical–Instruction (Technische Lehrstürme der SA)

Members of these units wore the standard SA kepi with the appropriate top color. As a sign of identification, a light blue diamond with a silver spoked cogwheel (eight spokes with 16 teeth) was worn on the lower left sleeve from approximately 1933.[164]

Motorized SA (Motorstürme der SA) :

On April 1, 1930 a motor corps was created within the SA; at the same time the NSAK (Nat.Soz.Automobil–Korps) was established to act as auxiliaries for the NSDAP. This unit was led for a short time by Franz von Pfeffer von Salomon.[165] From mid–December 1930 it was led by Adolf Hühnlein, the inspector for all motorized troops (Inspekteur der Motorstürme und–staffeln). Motorized units had existed previously in the late 1920's.

From early August 1933, the drivers from the Stahlhelm organization (Wehrstahlhelm–Kraftfahrer) were incorporated into the Motor–SA, adding to it approximately 35,000 new members.[166] The SA motor corps was detached from the SA on August 23, 1934 and simultaneously combined with the NSKK to become an independent Party organization.[167] The total consolidation of the Motor–SA into the NSKK became official in the spring of 1935.

The members of the Motor–SA wore the regular forms of SA headdress and also later the colored top according to the district color. The button color was gold or silver according to the group color. The regular early national emblem was worn on the front center of the top.

With the incorporation of the Stahlhelm drivers since August 1933, it was ordered that these members were permitted to wear their regular Stahlhelm uni-

[164] *Von Eelking,Freiherr."Die Uniformen der Braunhemden." München: 1934, p. 90.*

[165] *Volz."Daten der Geschichte der NSDAP" 11.Auflage. Berlin/Leipzig: 1943, p. 123.*

[166] *"Stahlhelm–Kraftfahr–Dienstvorschrift. Berlin: 1933, p. 11. (Transfer ended in early 1935.)*

[167] *Volz."Daten der Geschichte der NSDAP" 11.Auflage. Berlin/Leipzig: 1943, p. 128.*

form during SA service. The field–grey visored cap with field–grey band and piping (or with the black band and piping if having purchased this type), black chin strap and visor was worn. The first form NSDAP national emblem was worn between the two cockades[168] (for more information, also consult Volume 2, chapter "Soldatenbünde," pp.220–222 and 249–250). The old style Stahlhelm uniforms were officially permitted to be worn by leaders until early September 1933, while lower ranking members could wear them until December 1933. (It is known that on many occasion lower ranks wore the Stahlhelm uniform up until the disbanding of the NSDFB.St. in November 1935).

Otto Spronk

Members of a Motor–SA unit lined up during a meeting at Dessau in 1932. The headdress does not have a colored top, as this was not yet introduced. Note the wear of goggles.

Otto Spronk

Members of an SA–Motorsturm, photographed in late 1933: Note the wear of the colored cap tops and the various forms of goggles. The person chatting with the SA motorcyclist is a former member of the Stahlhelm–Motor–Brigade. As a member of the Wehrstahlhelm–Kraftfahrer, incorporated within the SA since August 1933, he was still allowed to wear his old Sta uniform for a while. In fact, this was permitted because there was a lack of the required SA uniforms.

---

168 Order for the "Wehrstahlhelm–Kraftfahrer." Berlin, August 8, 1933, Der Wehrstahlhelm–Reichsführer von Morozowirz, p. 3; Gliederungsbefehl für das Kraftfahrwesen. Der Bundeshauptmann von Stephani. Berlin, August 8, 1933,

Deutsche Lufthansa

The well known tenor Franz Baumann, a member of the Motor–SA, photographed in 1933, wearing his regular SA cap with the colored top of the district. Note he wears the drivers qualification diamond on his lower left sleeve. Baumann was photographed at the airfield of Berlin, shortly before departure on a new tour.

SA–Sturmführer Stilzebach, a commanding officer in the Motorstandarte 45 from Mühlhausen near Heilbronn in the Kurpfalz district, wears a rare combination of piping and Tresse. This photograph is dated before May 1935 as the pinkish–red colored top is being worn. According to his rank, Stilzebach was allowed to wear the two–colored piping on the crown only. As seen in this photograph, however, he is wearing the two–colored piping on the flap as well as the 1cm Tresse as authorized for the Führer der Motorstandarten und Abteilungen. The reason for this is unknown, but it could indicate that Stilzebach was already wearing the required piping and Tresse for his new rank. The two–colored crown piping, however, is still a question.

A. Southard

Adolf de Crousaz

The title page of a private photo album of a Motor–SA member, who later became a member of the NSKK. Note the artistic shaping of the swastika and a driver wearing the simple motor cap with the first pattern national emblem, on the front. The phrases mean: "Camouflaged and filthy, Agitated, but there is the orderly, From the brown-black Motor–SA!"

National Archives

This photograph gives an excellent view of the side of the crash helmet, as worn by a Motor–SA Standartenführer. Note the neck protection.

With special orders, members were allowed to wear the black leather crash helmet with the first form large, metal national emblem (for detailed information regarding the crash helmets and insignia worn by SA motor units, consult the chapter: Nat.Soz.Kraftfahr–Korps in the coming volume IV).

In the spring of 1935 it was ordered that members of the SA–Motorstürme wear the NSKK national emblem, in place of the standard first pattern Party eagle.[169] The colored top according to the district color remained for a while.

---

169 *"Mbl.d.RZM," Nr. 16, May 11, 1935, p. 154.*

A Motor-SA leather crash helmet with first form national emblem and Edelweiss (Hochland District).

After the consolidation and total incorporation into the NSKK, SA personnel of course continued to drive motorcycles for SA duties. These drivers were referred to as "Motorrad–Meldefahrer" (messengers). Through the years they wore the regular SA uniforms; with driving duties, most often the crash helmet (or occasionally the SA garrison cap) was worn. In spring 1939 new orders specified that these persons had to wear the brown steel helmet. On the right the SA decal and on the left the national emblem were worn. When not in service, the SA field cap was authorized.[170]

SA AUXILIARY POLICE (SA–HILFSPOLIZEI) MILITARY FIELD POLICE (SA–FELDJÄGERKORPS)

SA–Hilfspolizei 1933

To support the Schutzpolizei, especially in the larger cities, Hermann Göring ordered the institution of a new police force on February 22, 1933. This force was called the "Hilfspolizei," or auxiliary force and was for the most part raised from members of the SA, SS and Der Stahlhelm. They wore their regular uniforms with the addition of a white armband with "Hilfspolizei" upon it.

On special occasions, such as visits by foreign dignitaries to Germany, special detachments of SA members were called up through the years to act as auxiliary police, wearing the regular SA forms of headdress.[171]

SA–Hilfspolizei Berlin–Brandenburg :

In March 1933 the SA–Hilfspolizei from Berlin–Brandenburg was reconstituted as the "Feldpolizei der Gruppe Berlin–Brandenburg." This police unit was disbanded on August 8, 1933.

---

[170] *"Vbl.d.OSAF," Nr. 7, May 25, 1939. pp. 46–47. Nr. 60: Bekleidung für Motorrad–Meldefahrer (FO.2b.13708), section 2 from this order and general information about wearing of steel helmet and field cap.*

[171] *Ibid, Nr. 16, December 16, 1937, p. 132. Nr. 345: SA als Hilfspolizei (FO 1 Nr. 11109).*

An SA–Mann in 1933, serving as a member of the "Hilfspolizei." Note the wearing of the SA style cap in the early "soft" form, giving a very sloven impression.

Otto Spronk

Otto Spronk

SA–Hilfspolizei in 1933 together with regular police personnel. Note the police personnel are wearing the single cockade only on the cap band. The SA members are all wearing the soft version SA kepi.

This unit was allowed to wear the first form, regular silver colored, SA national emblem, on the front center of the cap top, in addition to a silver police star in the position of the button on the front center of the flaps (this badge was in fact the insigne worn by Prussian police on the sleeve of their uniforms). The regular SA–brown cap was worn, piped according to rank. The cap top was black from July 1933.

National Archives

The shako cover of the Schupo, being worn in this photograph. Note that one person is wearing his chin strap over the covered visor. At right, is a member of the SA from the Berlin–Brandenburg district, wearing his regular SA kepi with the black top.

National Archives

A member of the "Feldpolizei" Berlin–Brandenburg, wears his cap piped in silver around the crown; his flap is piped in black/white as used by the Berlin–Brandenburg district. The SA–Gruppenführer at right is Karl Ernst. He wears his cap piped around the crown and flap in accordance with the pre–July 19, 1933 regulations. Shortly thereafter, he would wear the Tresse.

Otto Spronk

Members of the Feldpolizei from the Berlin–Brandenburg district, the former SA–Hilfspolizei, during a funeral, wearing the SA kepi with the black colored top in addition to the national emblem and the silver Prussian police star. The wear of the black top indicates that this photograph is dated between July and August 1933, as this force was officially disbanded on August 8 and the black top was introduced on July 7.

National Archives

The Prussian police star worn by the "Feldpolizei" and "Feldjägerkorps": In silver for Feldpolizei and in gold for Feldjägerkorps.

Sturmbannführer Fritsch from the Feldpolizei at Berlin–Brandenburg. His cap is properly piped around the crown in silver. It should be noted that this photograph was taken before July 1933, as there is no colored top on the cap. Later, Fritsch wore a black top. Note the shape to this cap, and in addition, the rank insigne and the gorget of the unit with his personal number of 150.

SA–Feldjägerkorps (FJK)
1933 – 1935

With an order dated October 7, 1933,[172] these aforementioned police forces were reorganized into a new formation, the "Feldjägerkorps Preussen" (FJK). Orders for this formation came in the earliest stage from the Gestapo (Geheime Staatspolizei), and cooperated closely with the SA and police. Later in 1934, the Ministry of the Interior was given jurisdiction over this force. On April 1, 1935, this unit was incorporated into the Schupo (Schutzpolizei),[173] and was then known for a while as the Feldjäger–Bereitschaften. Smaller FJK sections were transferred to the "Kasernierte Polizei" (barracked police), replacing the Landespolizei (for more information, see the chapter discussing the German police organizations in a coming volume of this series).

From its institution, the FJK members wore an olive–brown SA style kepi, which had a white cap top. A gilt Prussian star was worn in the position normally occupied on standard SA caps by the silver or gilt button.[174] The diameter of the star was 37mm. In the front center the early form silvered national eagle emblem was worn (a golden form was not allowed). Above the cloth covered visor rested a brown leather chin strap with brown buckles. A piping system was also introduced.

SA–Feldjägerkorps kepi in olive–brown with the white colored top and the silver national emblem and gilt Prussian police star. One must consider the FJK caps as being extremely rare.

In the March 1934 SA regulations a full description for this ranking system was published;

a) The ranks Feldjäger through Feldjägerobertruppführer wore no piping;
b) Feldjägersturmführer through Feldjägerhauptsturmführer wore a black and white twisted cord around the crown of the cap;
c) Feldjägersturmbannführer and Feldjägerobersturmbannführer wore a gilt crown piping;
d) Führer des Feldjägerkorps (the leader for the FJK unit). This could be a person with the rank Sturmbann– or Obersturmbannführer. He wore a gilt crown piping, with an additional black and white twisted cord piping around

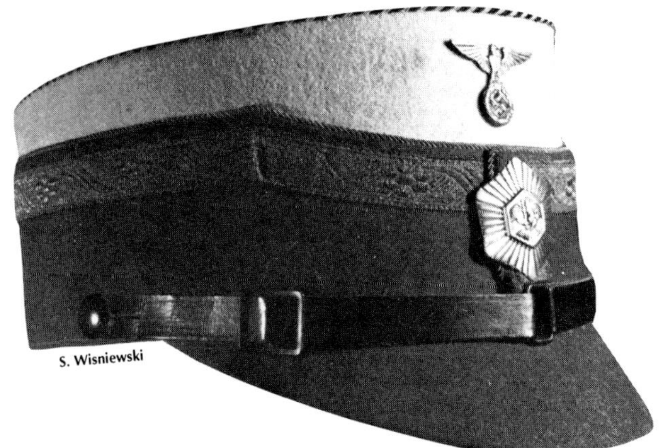

A rare example of a cap ordered for wear by the FJK leader. The crown on this sample has the black/white twisted cord; the flap has a golden piping above a 1.5cm wide golden Tresse. According to the regulations, this should be exactly the other way around: the golden cord around the crown and the two–colored piping around the edge of the flap. Probably this mistake was based upon a manufacturers error.

National Archives

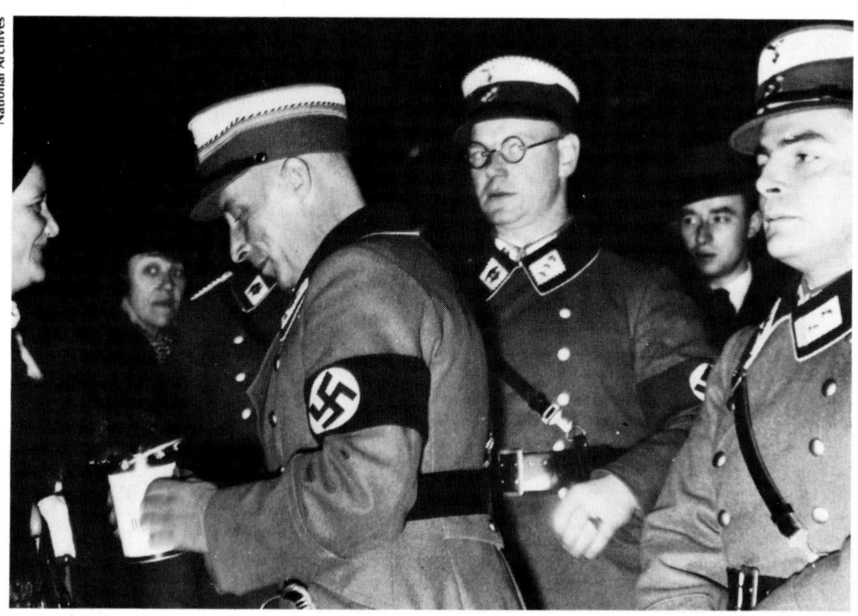

This photograph shows the kepis worn by the Feldjägerkorps. Center, the Führer of an FJK unit wearing the golden crown piping and the black/white twisted cord piping around the edge of the flap, above the 1.5cm golden Tresse. The Sturmführer directly at his right rear wears the black/white piping around the crown. One should note that at no time was a gilt national emblem allowed for wear by FJK units.

---

172 *Ibid, Nr. 16, December 1, 1933, Nr. 3: Feldjägerkorps in Preussen. By the German Public indicated as SA–Feldjägerkorps.*

173 *Ibid, Nr. 19, June 11, 1935, p. 87. Nr. 207: Feldjägerkorps; Decree from the Reichsinnenminister. II.S.Ia.Nr. 3/35, March 30, 1935,*

174 *Von Eelking,Freiherr."Die Uniformen der Braunhemden," München: 1934, p. 24. It is often said that olive–green was the FJK color; the regulations always describe it as: olive–brown. The actual color is however towards a greenish shade.*

Otto Spronk

Members of the FJK on parade. Note the black/white piping around the cap crown as worn by the man in the front with the rank Feldjägersturmführer. The leather chin straps are worn under the chin; the caps are in olive–brown material and the tops are white.

A member of the Feldjägerkorps accompanied by a member of the Schutzpolizei, during patrolling as the "motorisierte Landstrassenpolizei" in April 1935. In his rank as a Feldjägersturmführer, he wears the crown piped with the black/white twisted cord. Four weeks later, the visored caps were introduced with the first pattern police national emblem instead of the star shaped insigne. Note the white grommets on the white cloth: This is in accordance with the manufacturing regulations.

Otto Spronk

edge of the flap. Below this he was authorized to wear a 15mm wide Tresse in gold.[175]

The kepi was only worn within the Schutzpolizei for a short period, its use was discontinued in May 1935. The kepi was replaced by a visored cap (Klappmütze) in the style as worn by other police officers. Often these early form visored caps featured two ventilation grommets on each underside of the cap overlap. As far as researched, the FJK–model did not have these grommets. The cap top was made of olive–green cloth, the cap band was a white, felt–like material. The cap crown was piped in white, as were the upper and lower edges of the band. A black leather chin strap rested above the cap visor, being secured at each end by yellow metal, pebbled, buttons. Officers wore gold buttons and cap cords.[176]

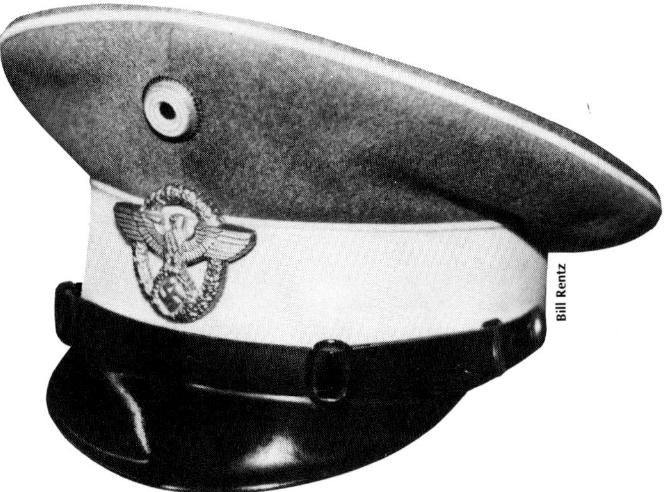

This form of visored cap replaced the kepi in May 1935. The cap top was olive-green with a white cap band and white piping.

The first pattern police national emblem, in gilt, was worn on the front center of the cap band. A black/white/red national cockade was worn on the front center of the cap top. After its introduction, the second pattern national emblem for the police, also in gilt, replaced the first pattern on this visored cap (for more information consult the chapter discussing the German police organizations in a coming volume of this series. Especially the section for "motorized street police"). No regulation indicated the wearing of a garrison style cap by members of the FJK.

---

[175] *"Anzugs–Ordnung für die SA." Teil 1. Der Oberste SA–Führer. München: March 1, 1934, p. 66. Section XIV: Bekleidung und Ausrüstung des Feldjägerkorps.*

[176] *Runderlass d.Ru.Pr.MdI. III M 6, Nr. 31/35 Fj. May 2, 1935, The golden insigne mentioned in this order is the golden police form and <u>not</u> the SA national emblem in gold.*

Nat.Soz.Reiterkorps (NSRK) 1936 – 1945

This equestrian corps was instituted by Hitler on March 10, 1936. Eighty percent of its membership consisted of the SA–Reiterei (SA horsemen).[177] Special training courses were begun, but during all activities the regular SA headdress was worn, primarily the kepi.

Those members of the NSRK who were not members of the SA or SS, had to be incorporated into an SA–Reitersturm. In areas where a Reitersturm did not exist, it was ordered that one had to be created.[178] Members of the Armed Forces, who often trained within such units, wore their regular headdress. Marine–SA members wore the regular ordered visored cap.

Otto Spronk

A member of the Reiter–SA wearing the regular SA kepi without the colored top. This would indicate that the photograph was taken before the summer of 1933. Note the "Schabracke" (saddle cloth) with the swastika symbol.

177 "Organisationsbuch der NSDAP. " München: 1935, p. 372; various newspaper articles, published in May and June 1936,

178 Order from the Reichsinspekteur für Reit–und Fahrausbildung, dated April 7, 1936 published in the German press.

National Archives

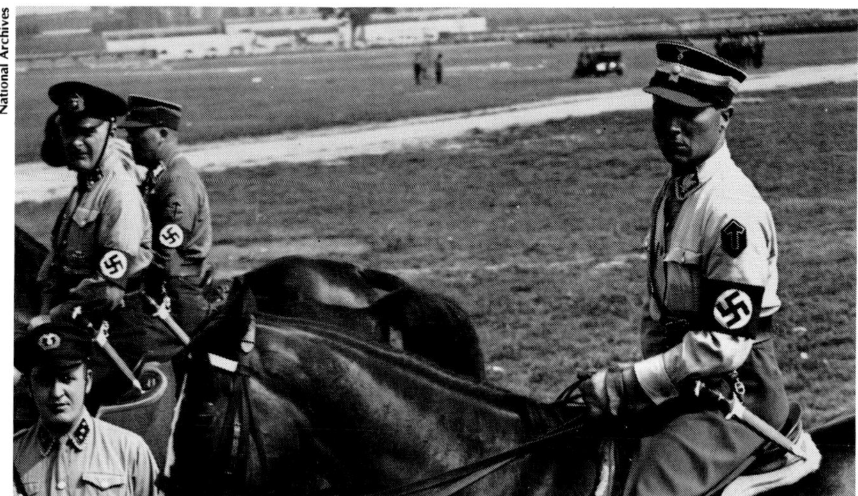

SA–Gruppenführer Karl Ernst, wearing his SA cap with Tresse and piping, according to his rank, during horse riding. Note the Tyr–rune above the brassard with the varying form of backing and the naval SA Sturmbannführer wearing his regular form of visored cap during this exercise.

In August 1937 the official dress for the "Reiter–SA" was published in various SA sources:

a) Greater service dress with the kepi with colored top, as ordered for the district;
b) Smaller service dress, ibid.[179] One must note that with both forms the SA garrison cap was never officially allowed for wear.

Otto Spronk

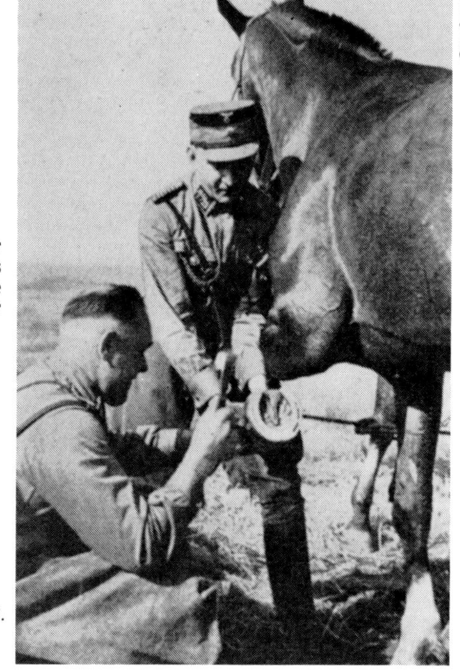

One of the duties of a Reiter–SA member was the shoeing of horses. At no time was the garrison cap allowed for wear with the regular SA uniform with either the greater service dress or the smaller service dress.

179 "Vbl.d.OSAF," Nr. 11, August 31,1937, p. 83. Nr. 239: Anzugsarten der Reiter–SA (F 2b Nr. 13704).

Otto Spronk

Members of the OSAF wear the regular SA uniform and headdress with piping and Tresse as members of the NSRK. Horse riding was a favorite pastime of many higher ranked SA leaders.

Otto Spronk

SA members from various districts lined up for inspection by the "Führer der Reichsführerschule," Brigadeführer Lehmann, during a course at this particular school at Zehlendorf. Note the wear of the so-called "SA-Übungsmütze" in olive-brown, as ordered for wear at schools or camps.

W.P.B.R. Saris

239. Betrifft: Anzugsarten der Reiter-SA.

F 2 b Nr. 13704.

Um bestehende Zweifel über die Anzugsarten der Reiter-SA. zu beheben, werden nachstehend die Anzugsarten für die Reiter-SA. aufgeführt:

I. Großer Dienstanzug:

1. Dienstmütze mit farbigem Band,
2. Braunhemd mit Binder,
3. Achselstück (nur auf rechter Schulter),
4. Kragenspiegel mit gekreuzten Lanzen,
5. Dienstgradabzeichen,
6. Dienststellungsabzeichen,
7. Halsbinde,
8. Parteiabzeichen (nur für Pg.),
9. Armbinde,
10. Reithose mit braunem Lederbesatz,
11. Reitstiefel (Sporen dürfen beim großen Dienstanzug nur beim Reiten angelegt werden),
12. Koppel mit doppeltem Schulterriemen,
13. Dolch mit Feststellriemen (zu Pferd wird kein Dolch getragen).

Soweit es der Bestand an Bekleidung gestattet, kann zum Reitdienst der kleine Dienstanzug getragen werden. Die Bekleidung innerhalb der Einheit muß jedoch einheitlich sein.

II. Kleiner Dienstanzug:

1. Dienstmütze mit farbigem Band,
2. Dienstrock (Reiterrock),
3. Achselstück (nur auf rechter Schulter),
4. Kragenspiegel mit gekreuzten Lanzen,
5. Dienstgradabzeichen,
6. Dienststellungsabzeichen,
7. Armbinde,
8. braunes Hemd mit Umlegekragen und Binder,
9. Reithose mit braunem Lederbesatz,
10. Reitstiefel mit Sporen,
11. Koppel mit doppeltem Schulterriemen,
12. Dolch mit Feststellriemen (zu Pferd wird kein Dolch getragen).

III. Sportanzug:
wie die übrige SA.

IV. Abendanzug:
wie die übrige SA. nur an Stelle des SA.-Dienstrockes den SA.-Reiterrock.

The publication shown is the order for the forms of service dress used by the SA, as published in the *Vbl.d.OSAF,* dated August 1937. SA members for the most part wore the standard SA–uniform with the exception of Nr.4, collar patches with lances; Nrs.10 & 11, riding breeches and riding boots and Nr.12, the double shoulder straps (cross–form). It is interesting to note that when riding, no dagger was officially worn. With the evening dress (IV), a special tunic was worn.

SA–Hilfswerklager (SA–HW)
1933 – 1938

Camps to provide employment for unemployed Party members were probably established in late 1933, and identified as SA–Hilfswerklager. With the reduction in unemployment, the size of these units was reduced in early summer 1937 and they were retitled as "SA–Umschulungslager"[180] which retrained unemployed persons.

During the earliest stages two camps existed: Lockstedt (operated by the SA Group Nordmark), and Falkenstein (operated by the SA Group Sachsen). Other camps were planned. It is said that due to economic prosperity in the nation these plans were postponed and all were disbanded in 1938. It is certain that in total at least ten camps existed throughout Germany by 1936, being: the two above mentioned and others at Frankfurt/Höchst (Hessen); Fichtenhain near Köln–Rhiel (Niederrhein); Breslau and Zülz (Schlesien); Dortmund–Eving and Witten (Westfalen); Koblenz–Asterstein (Westmark) and Magdeburg (Mitte).[181] No information was found indicating that the remaining retraining camps were ever disbanded.

Otto Spronk

The original title for this photograph reads: "The new ones are coming." SA members from various districts, arrive at the Umschulungslager at Falkenstein, operated by the SA district of Sachsen. In a period of about two years, a person was able to reach the status of a qualified skilled specialist.

The members of these so–called SA–Hilfswerklager (divided into "ständige Belegschaft," those being permanent personnel, as staff and supervisors and "wechselnde Belegschaft," those being rotating workers) had to wear their regular SA kepi with the district color for the top and button of their district of origin with the walking out uniform.[182] The "Lagermütze" cap was worn most often on other occasions. The leading staff was recognizable only by the wearing of a special collar tab, and from July 1937 all wore the special "Sch.L." collar tabs.

---

180 *"Organisationsbuch der NSDAP. " München: 1937, p. 364b; "Vbl.d.SA," Nr. 10, July 15, 1937, pp. 74–75. Nr. 212: Umbenennung der bisherigen SA–Hilfswerklager (F 2a Nr. 14001).*

181 *"Verordnungsblatt der NSKK–Korpsführung," Nr. 18, München: October 15, 1936, p. 119. Nr. 9: SA–Hilfswerklager (order I 4176/36, dated October 2, 1936).*

182 *Der Oberste SA–Führer. München: February 1, 1935, Order Abt.F4/F2 Nr. 5904, signed by Lutze: Dienstgradabzeichen in Hilfswerklager, stating the "ständige" and "wechselnde" Belegschaft in the order sections 1 and 2.*

An instructor of an SA–Umschulungslager gives a student instructions at the Lockstedter camp. This instructor wear the colored cap top as ordered for the Sachsen district, being emerald–green.

No indication mentioned the abolishment of these; no price–list mentions any cancellation of this article and so it is certain that at least one or two camps survived throughout the years.

Hilfswerk Nord–West (HW–NW)
1933 – 1938

This unit must not be confused with the above mentioned SA–Hilfswerklager. This unit was formed from Austrian SA members after the NSDAP was outlawed in that country in 1933. They transferred to Munich and were referred to as the "Österreichische Legion" (OL), which was divided into three divisions and eight regiments. The "OL" was renamed "Hilfswerk Nord–West" on August 4, 1934.[183] This unit was used chiefly for road construction in southern Germany (where they labored as workers, engineers and technicians while constructing the "Wallbergstrasse" at Tegernsee in September 1935 with 750 SA members).[184]

The cap top color of this group was reddish–brown, as it was also for Austria from spring of 1934 (formerly the Austrian SA used for a short while steel–

[183] *Volz."Daten der Geschichte der NSDAP" 11.Auflage. Berlin/Leipzig: 1943, section VII: Die NSDAP in Österreich von 1926 bis 1938, p. 113.*

[184] *"Die SA." Sonderausgabe Völkischer Beobachter. München: 1938, pp. 72–73.*

Otto Spronk

Members of the Austrian Legion wear the SA style headdress. This photograph is dated before July 1933, as no colored cap top is worn. This top would have extended over the khaki colored material used for these caps.

Navorsingsinstituut Brussel

Members of the Austrian Legion return from exile. Reschny is inspecting his men at Vienna on April 3, 1938. Note the wear of civilian clothes. Only one person in the line is wearing his SA style headdress with an Edelweiss flower on the left side. Reschny wears his regular high leader coffee can cap.

green as a top color during their stay in Germany).[185] The button was silver; the two–color piping was bright red and white.

After the "Anschluss" in March 1938, this unit was superfluous and was disbanded. The Austrian SA was in September 1938 divided into the SA groups Donau, Alpenland and Südmark (for the colors of these groups or special insignia, consult the section SA enlisted ranks, 1936–1945 and the section: Edelweiss for Austrian units). The special HW NW collar tabs were officially abolished in the spring of 1939.[186]

Reichsautozug Deutschland (RAZ) 1933-1945

This special formation was shrouded in mystery even during the Third Reich. It was a technically well-equipped force for propaganda purposes, and assisted by any means necessary during the larger meetings of the NSDAP and its sub-organizations, such as at the Party Day rallies from 1936 to 1938. Because of its significance, the RAZ will be covered in some depth to include its institution and specialty. Also, the unit known as Hilfszug "Bayern" (further known as HZB) will be covered superficially because both units occasionally worked together and were considered a "team" from 1936 onward. Both units were technical motor-columns or caravans. Because almost nothing is known about the RAZ, the following study is presented plus many unpublished photographs. The HZB is also photographically included in this SA chapter, but will be covered in more detail in Volume 4 (the NSKK chapter).

The first attempts to create a forerunner of the RAZ was by SA-Sturmführer Hermann Schäfer of the Niedersachsen district during the elections at Lippe, in January 1933.[187] In appreciation, Hitler appointed Schäfer to create a mobile loudspeaker unit later that year. In record time, Schäfer together with the staff leader from the sub-department for NSDAP propaganda, Hugo Fischer, raised a technical unit for propaganda purposes at Party events and rallies for the NSDAP and its sub-organizations.[187a] In early 1935, on the advice of the Party leadership and based on Hitler's wishes, the NSDAP Reichsleitung decided to develop plans to expand the 1933 "embryo" into a new, technical formation. This unit was equipped with technical equipment for loudspeaker transmission, electricity supply (for making films, recordings, transmitting by radio and signals, as well as illumination), building tribunes, galleries and decorations (such as flags, triumphal arches, etc.), and was also able to sweep streets, transport goods and sick or injured people when catastrophies occurred, plus office work. All of this was possible by means of specially constructed vehicles, manufactured mainly

---

185 "Anzugs–Ordnung für die SA." Teil 1. Der Oberste SA–Führer. München: March 1, 1934; "Organisationsbuch der NSDAP. " München: 1936, pp. 388–389.

186 "Vbl.d.OSAF," Nr. 7, May 25, 1939, p. 49. Nr. 69: Änderungsanzeige Nr. 2/39 der RZM (price list article numbers 5431 and 5432 were abolished).

187 "Die SA," Sonderausgabe Völkischer Beobachter. München: 1938, p. 84.

187a Ibid. Stabsleiter and Hauptamtsleiter Hugo Fischer led the Reichspropagandaleitung (RPL) sub-department "Rednervermittlung" (a form of Party oratorial agency), which existed within the main department (Hauptabteilung I, Propaganda) since the early 1930s. "Verordnungsblatt der Reichsleitung der NSDAP," from now on referred to as "Vbl.d.RL.d.NSDAP," Nr. 34, October 31, 1932, p. 76. Ibid. Nr. 40, January 31, 1933, p. 88.

by the C.D. Magirus factory of Ulm. 80 of these vehicles were planned and by the spring of 1937, 38 were available.[187b]

W.P.B.R. Saris

Der Reichsautozug „Deutschland"

verdankt seine Entstehung den Gedanken und Plänen der Reichspropagandaleitung der NSDAP. Er hat die Aufgabe, bei allen Großkundgebungen von Partei und Staat das Wort unseres Führers und seiner Mitarbeiter vielen hunderttausend Volksgenossen auf den Kundgebungsplätzen zu übermitteln. Dadurch schafft er die technischen Voraussetzungen und die Möglichkeit, Millionen Menschen in Deutschland und in der ganzen Welt die großen Nationalfeiertage des deutschen Volkes miterleben zu lassen.

Der Reichsautozug „Deutschland" wird nach seiner Vollendung aus mehr als 80 Fahrzeugen bestehen. Die Kolonnenlänge des fahrenden Zuges wird dementsprechend mehr als 3 Kilometer Fahrstrecke einnehmen. Durch zugweisen Einsatz ist es möglich, Einzelkundgebungen zu je 300000 Mann in verschiedenen Gauen des Deutschen Reiches zu gleicher Zeit durchzuführen.

Extract from a description of the RAZ mentioning its purposes, and also the plan for 80 vehicles which would be divided into sections called "zugweisen Einstaz."

187b "Völkischer Beobachter," Süddeutsche Ausgabe Nr. 130. München: May 10, 1935, front page. Ibid. Nr. 225. München: August 13, 1935, front page as well as page 2. "Zusammenstellungsplan" (plan of conception), approximately 1937, which shows about 40 vehicles for: I. Rundfunk-Fernmelde- u. Übertragungsanlagen (three vehicles); II. Tonfilm-Aufnahme u. Wiedergabe (2); III. Zentrale Kraftstation (2)' IV. Grossmontage u. Bauzug (7); V. Transportzug im Aufmarschgelände (1); VI. Material u. Personen-Transportzug (8); VII. Verpflegungs-Sanitäts- u. Reperaturzug (15). This last mentioned section was an idea taken from the plans for the HZB, which was created by Seidler, the Bavarian leader of the W.H.W. (Winterhilfswerk).

W.P.B.R. Saris/DB

Stadtarchiv München/W.P.B.R. Saris

On the afternoon of April 6, 1937 high-level visitors and the press are shown passing the lined-up HZB vehicles and equipment. The man wearing the light civilian hat is the American military attaché, Major Smith. To his left is the city commander of Munich, Oberstleutnant von Mann conversing with Reichsschatzmeister Schwarz. The political leader with his hands on his belt is the HZB leader, Artur Borchert. Other high-ranking officials in attendance were: Hauptdienststellenleiter Hans Saupert, the staff leader from the Reichsschatzmeister, and his staff, Hauptamtsleiter Dr. Dresler (who was in charge of the press) and SA-Oberführer Hermann Schäfer, the RAZ commander.

High level visitors at the "Reichsautobahnhof," the enormous RAZ garage, in late 1936. Next to Dr. Goebbels is Hugo Fischer who is pointing at a vehicle. He was the RPL staff leader. At Hitler's right is the RAZ leader, SA-Oberführer Hermann Schäfer, and at his right is the leader of the Hilfszug "Bayern." At far right is the adjutant to Goebbels, wearing a naval SA uniform. Note the RPL insigne on the side of the amplifier-loudspeaker vehicle, as well as the elevated footbridge for inspection.

An outstanding technically-equipped accomodation, which was referred to as the "Reichsautobahnhof," for the RAZ and HZB was built at the corner of the Soyerhofstrasse and Peter-Auzinger-Strasse in Munich, and was west of the Tegernseer Landstrasse and the new Reichszeugmeisterei complex. This garage was 184 meters long and could hold forty vehicles. The repair-workshop measured 62 x 85 meters, and was divided into three sections. There was also a yard for fueling and washing. Work on these facilities was started in the spring of 1935 and completed in late 1936.[187c]

The units official designation was the Reichsautozug "Deutschland" der Reichspropagandaleitung der NSDAP. Hermann Schäfer was appointed its commander on May 1, 1936. Simultaneously, he was promoted to the rank of SA-Brigadeführer. The RAZ was utilized for the first time at the opening of the Reichsautobahn between Köln and Düsseldorf (the Köln-Hilden section) on May

---

187c Ibid. Also, Norddeutsche Ausgabe on August 14, 1935. "Münchener Stadtanzeiger," Nr. 95 from April 7, 1937 and various information by Dr. Hans-Peter Rasp, author of "Eine Stadt für tausend Jahre." It is interesting to note that in April 1937 American President Roosevelt sent a mission to Germany which was led by the military attaché, Major Truman Smith. Various natural catastrophies had occured in the USA and apparently Roosevelt had heard of the RAZ and HZB. He intended to create a similar unit for use in his country. In Germany this was considered big news. On April 7 Major Smith visited the home garage and was impressed, especially when he saw the specially constructed HZB vehicles which were designed to aid victims by all means of aid, supply and food distribution ("Münchener Stadtanzeiger," April 7, 1937, and "Münchener Beobachter," a special supplement from the "Völkischer Beobachter" for the city of Munich, Nr. 97, also April 7, 1937, and various other newspapers.

W.P.B.R. Saris/DB

21, 1936. This portion of the roadway was officially opened by Dr. Goebbels, while Gauleiter Grohé and Dr. Todt were present.[188]

The RAZ was subordinated to the Party leadership and its accounting managed by Reichsschatzmeister Schwarz. The RAZ existed of four (possibly, later five) sections: The main section (Hauptzug) "München," and the sub-sections of "Donau," "Niedersachsen" and "Rheinland." It was possible to put every section into action at different locations, which would allow for even small meetings to be assisted.[188a]

From 1939 the unit was referred to as the "technische Sturm der Obersten SA-Führung, Reichsautozug Deutschland," and could be found anywhere that propaganda and technical equipment was required. One major event that they participated in was during the annexation of Austria. When Hitler visited Vienna on March 15, 1938, the RAZ was positioned near the "Heldenplatz" with twenty-

---

188 "Vbl.d.RL.d.NSDAP," Nr. 120, mid-May 1936, p. 400. "Broschure," approximately 1938 from the Humboldt-Deutzmotoren A.G., Magirus Werke at Ulm. "Organisationsbuch der NSDAP," München: 1936, Section Reichspropagandaleitung der NSDAP, pp. 295-297. Schäfer also held the political leader rank of "Hauptstellenleiter in der RPL." Through the years he continued to lead this unit, and his final rank was SA-Gruppenführer.

188a "Das Braune Haus," München: 1939, Section "Der Hilfszug Bayern und der Reichs-Autozug Deutschland," p. 55. Information provided to W.P.B.R. Saris by the Magirus auto manufacturer. In 1937/1938 the München secion had 21 vehicles, the other sections had six each. "Münchener Beobachter," Nr. 97, April 7, 1937, front page.

May 21, 1936: The first public appearance of the RAZ caravan during the opening of the Reichsautobahn section between Köln and Hilden. The driver who is hanging out of the vehicle window and chatting with a SA member, is wearing the garrison cap with the unique insigne. SA members are guarding the motorway. The crowd on the overpasses is mainly made up of political leaders with their Party flags.

five vehicles. The unit was also utilized in Sudetenland. It is not known when this unit ceased to exist, but by the mid-war years it had lost its importance. In 1942 it was directly assigned to Dr. Goebbels.

The HZB, which had been raised for the NS-Volkswohlfahrt in the fall of 1933 and based on the plans of SA-Sturmbannführer Seidler, was subordinated to the Party leadership on December 1, 1934. Schwarz required that the HZB and the RAZ work as a team as of early 1937. From the beginning of the war the HZB was subordinated and assigned to the Reichsschatzmeister and existed at the end of the war as a NSDAP Reichsleitung section.[189]

189"Vbl.d.RL.d.NSDAP," Nr. 88, mid-January 1935, p. 228. Section PRL: Order 1/35 signed by Goebbels. Also, "Das Archiv," a book of reference by Ernst Jaenicke and published by Ministerialrat Dr. Kurt Jahnke, Berlin: 1934, Volume 7-12, p. 1141. Notice in section Bo, dated January 1, 1934. The HZB (its full title being "Nationalsozialistische Deutsche Arbeiter-Partei, Reichsleitung - Reichspropagandaleitung Hilfszug 'Bayern'") was technically assigned to the RPL until the start of the war. The HZB was created within the SA but later transferred to the NSKK, probably in late 1934 or early 1935. The personnel were put into a specially created NSKK-Motorsturm 40/M86 from Munich. Throughout the years of 1933 to 1945 the HZB was led by Doppler, Borchert, Fischer, Strömsdörfer and Breitsameter. Not only were the HZB food supplies plundered by the German population in 1945, but also the stocks of the Reichszeugmeisterei.

The RAZ section "Rheinland" is ready for departure. The crew members are wearing the white overalls with garrison cap. Note that the car pennants have an early form national emblem with wings extending beyond the white central circle. A pennant in almost the same form, but with lettering, was carried by the HZB in about 1934.

National Archives

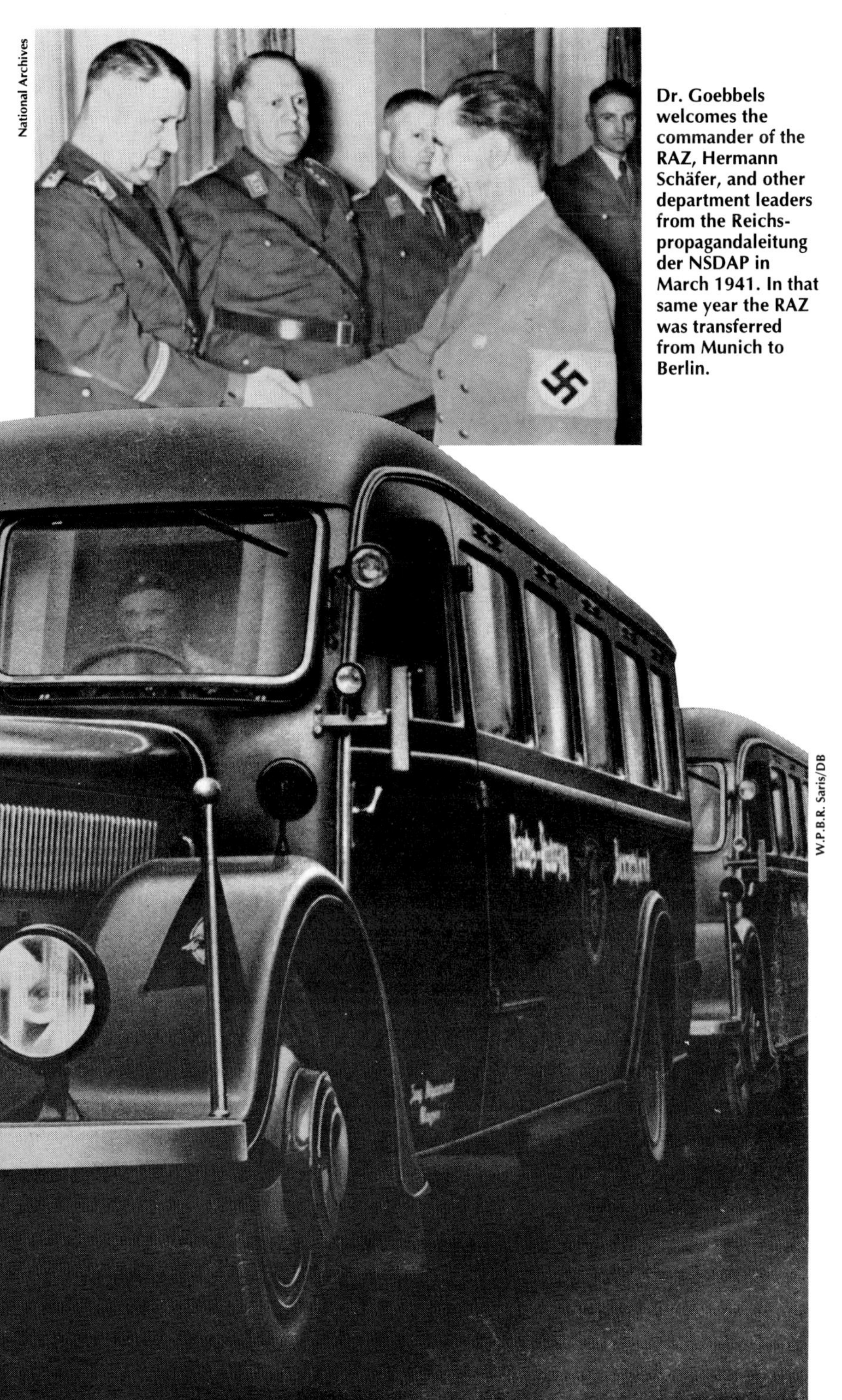

Dr. Goebbels welcomes the commander of the RAZ, Hermann Schäfer, and other department leaders from the Reichspropagandaleitung der NSDAP in March 1941. In that same year the RAZ was transferred from Munich to Berlin.

W.P.B.R. Saris/DB

Although the RAZ (called "Sturm Hilfszug Deutschland" by the German public) was part of the NSDAP Reichsleitung, its members were gathered together in a special unit called the SA-Sturm Reichsautozug "Deutschland." During the winter months the main portion of the membership was barracked on the grounds of the "home" garage.[190]

W.P.B.R. Saris

Der Führer

119. Betrifft: Namensverleihung.
F/Ch. Nr. 11 130.

Gruppe Hochland.

Ich verleihe der SA.-Standarte 2 der Gruppe Hochland den Namen

Michael Schmeidl.

*

Ich verleihe dem SA.-Sturm 1/16 L, Standort München, die Berechtigung in Erinnerung an den am 8 November 1939 dem ruchlosen Attentat im Bürgerbräukeller zu München zum Opfer gefallenen

Hauptsturmführer Franz Lutz

die Bezeichnung zu führen

SA.-Sturm 1/16 L — Franz Lutz.

*

Ich verleihe dem technischen Sturm der Obersten SA.-Führung, Reichsautozug Deutschland, die Berechtigung in Erinnerung an den am 8. November 1939 dem ruchlosen Attentat im Bürgerbräukeller zu München zum Opfer gefallenen

Obertruppführer Eugen Schachta

die Bezeichnung zu führen

SA.-Sturm Reichsautozug Deutschland
Eugen Schachta.

*

Ich verleihe dem technischen Sturm der Obersten SA.-Führung, Reichsautozug Deutschland, die Berechtigung in Erinnerung an den am 8. November 1939 dem ruchlosen Attentat im Bürgerbräukeller zu München zum Opfer gefallenen

Truppführer Wilhelm Weber

den Namen

Wilhelm Weber

an zweiter Stelle zu führen.

gez. Adolf Hitler.

Hitler's order, as published in the "Verordnungsblatt der Obersten SA-Führung," dated December 29, 1939, grants the use of two names on the Sturmfahne. The literal translation reads: "I (Adolf Hitler) do grant the technical Sturm of the OSAF, Reichsautozug Deutschland, in remembrance of the vile attack on November 8, 1939 at the Bürgerbräukeller at Munich, in which Obertruppführer Eugen Schachta fell a victim and was killed." The second portion is in the same form and additionally states: "The name Wilhelm Weber was to be carried in second position (Truppführer Wilhelm Weber was the second fallen member of the RAZ).

W.P.B.R. Saris

Ehrung für die Gefallenen des 8. November

München, 12. November

Der Führer hat auf Vorschlag des Stabschefs einem Sturm der Standarte 16 (List) den Namen „Franz Lutz" und dem Technischen Sturm der Obersten SA.-Führung Reichsautozug Deutschland den Namen „Eugen Schachta" verliehen.

Damit tragen zwei weitere Sturmfahnen der SA. die Namen von Blutzeugen der Bewegung, die ihr Leben gaben für Führer und Vaterland. Außerdem wird der NSKK.-Motorsturm 9/M 86 (München) fortan den Namen „Michael Wilhelm Kaiser" führen.

This announcement, published in a Munich newspaper dated November 12, 1939, mentions the first RAZ honor name, being "Eugen Schachta," granted by Hitler on Lutze's proposal. In the last paragraph, it is mentioned again that two flags will bear honor names (the other name mentioned was for the NSKK flag for Motorsturm 9/M96 from Munich, with the name "Michael Wilhelm Kaiser," who was one of the few wearers of the "Stosstrupp Adolf Hitler" cuffband.

190 "Die SA," Sonderausgabe "Völkischer Beobachter," München: 1938, p. 84. There is no doubt that this was a SA-Sturm. It stated: "Die ganze Besatzung vom SA-Sturm Reichsautozug Deutschland gestellt wird." The assertion that the RAZ members were from SS origins is baseless. For someone who has an understanding of the consecration of flags during the Third Reich, the proof is simple: At all times during the existence of the RAZ, the flag used was the SA-Sturmfahne. Various articles and orders confirm this. In November 1939 the RAZ (then designated as the technical unit for the Oberste SA-Führung) was granted the right by Hitler to carry a honor name with their flag. The name "Eugen Schachta" (an old comrade of the RAZ commander since about 1934) was the first honor name, later accompanied in second position was the name "Wilhelm Weber."

In Ausübung ihres Dienstes für Führer und Volk fielen am 8. November 1939 dem fluchwürdigen Attentat im Bürgerbräukeller zu München der

Haupteinsatzleiter des Reichsautozuges „Deutschland"
SA.-Obertruppführer

Parteigenosse Eugen Schachta

und der

Funktechniker des Reichsautozuges „Deutschland"
SA.-Truppführer

Parteigenosse Wilhelm Weber

zum Opfer. Wir werden diesen beiden Kämpfern der Bewegung ein treues Andenken bewahren.

München, den 9. November 1939

Dr. Goebbels
Reichspropagandaleiter der NSDAP.

Im kämpferischen Einsatz für Führer und Vaterland fielen dem ruchlosen Attentat im Bürgerbräukeller zu München mein langjähriger Mitarbeiter, unser getreuer Kamerad

SA.-Obertruppführer Eugen Schachta

und

SA.-Truppführer Wilhelm Weber

zum Opfer. Inmitten ihrer Arbeit schlug ihnen das Schicksal ihr Werkzeug aus der Hand. Die Männer des Reichsautozuges „Deutschland" ziehen den Sturmriemen fester, Eugen Schachta und Wilhelm Weber marschieren wie immer in unseren Reihen mit.

Der Führer und Kommandant
des Reichsautozuges „Deutschland"
Schäfer, SA.-Brigadeführer

Death announcements published on November 11, 1939, from Goebbels as the Reichspropagandaleiter and from RAZ commander, SA-Brigadeführer Hermann Schäfer. Note the rank for engineer Schachta, being a SA-Obertruppführer and assigned to the RAZ as a "Haupteinsatzleiter." Weber was an electro-mechanic and radio-technician with the rank of SA-Truppführer.

Both were SA and RAZ members, and were killed during the bomb explosion at the "Bürgerbräukeller" in Munich on November 8, 1939 ("Vbl.d.OSAF," Nr. 10, December 29, 1939, p. 67, Nr. 119: Namensverleihung, order F/Ch. Nr. 11130 for the Hochland district, "dem technischen Sturm der Obersten SA-Führung, Reichsautozug Deutschland"). For married RAZ members, as well as those from the HZB, houses were built near the home garade. Unmarried personnel were quartered in special buildings on the grounds of the garage. The buildings of the RZM and parts of the Reichsautobahnhof were confiscated by US forces after the war and became McGraw Barracks.

Hoheitszeichen:

On the beret, the first style small metal national emblem was worn occasionally, as was the white machine-embroidered cloth version on a brown backing. This national emblem was similar to that worn by the political leaders, but larger (possibly, approximately 7cm). Also, instead of a five-part wing section, the RAZ (and HZB) eagle had six. Available photos show the eagle's head facing to its right, indicating that the style had not yet been adapted to political standards (see explanation in the political leaders' section of this volume). It is almost a certainty that the eagle's head was changed to "its-left" facing form in mid-1937.

BEI LAUFENDEM MOTOR TORE ÖFFNEN
IA-50909

Stadtarchiv München/W.P.B.R. Saris

Members of the RAZ standing next to their vehicles inside the garage, known as the "Reichsautobahnhof" which was located on the grounds of the Reichszeugmeisterei. They are wearing the unique, dark beret during the visit by the American military attaché, Major Smith, on April 6, 1937. This form of headgear was probably worn for only a short time, and then only occasionally. It is interesting to note that when the RAZ uniforms were presented in Nürnberg in 1936, it was classified as a NSKK uniform. The newspapers and periodicals of the period described the uniform in August/September 1936 as practical and of a totally new design. Note the wear of the special aluminum wire RAZ cuffband with black lettering, which was for both the parade and service dress. Note also that the collars are without any rank insignia or designation. The size of the vehicles would indicate that each one would have at least two occupants, but when this photo was taken there were 30 crew members and 38 vehicles.

A unique insigne was worn on the garrison cap, and was styled after the attractive symbol of the Reichspropagandaleitung. This emblem was also painted on the sides of RAZ vehicles. The RAZ symbol consisted of a to-its-left facing eagle (army-style) with a wingspan of 9.6cm. The height of the eagle was 3.4cm. The round, bright red shield had a diameter of 5.1cm and the swastika on a black

The official symbol for the Reichspropagandaleitung as used on vehicles, as well as the cloth insigne for the garrison cap. The latter bears the word "Reichsautozug" instead of "Reichspropagandaleitung." Note the un-hyphenated word "Reichsautozug" and the straight wings of the national emblem.

field was .75cm. The backing was khaki-colored material. Above the eagle, within the circle, were the letters "N.S.D.A.P.," and on the lower portion of the circle the word "Reichsautozug" was positioned. The lettering, circle edge and eagle with elongated wings were in white. The contours of the eagle and wreath were of khaki-colored thread. This insigne was introduced in the spring of 1936.[190a]

An unused RAZ insigne. The backing is khaki-colored material. The lettering, circle edge and eagle (note the long wings) are done in white. The inner circle is bright red and the background of the swastika is black. The details of the eagle and wreath are in khaki-colored thread.

A rare photo of a RAZ member wearing a garrison cap with the unique RAZ insigne on the left side of the flap. Note that this cap has no front button. Note also the wearing of the 4.4cm wide black cuffband on the upper left arm as authorized for the working dress. This photo was taken a few days before the Schwarz visit on April 6, 1937 while the vehicles were being cleaned.

190a *The sign of the vehicles bears the word "Reichspropagandaleitung." It is also known that on occasions the word "Gaupropagandaleitung" was used instead.*

Iveco/Magirus

Shown is the "direction" and command car (Magirus type M50/5, six-cylinder with 110PS diesel motor), which was car Nr. 5 from the main München section. This photo of the RAZ vehicle with RPL emblem was taken just before its delivery from the factory (no license plates added yet). This vehicle was equipped with an amplifier plant and a telephone exchange.

W.P.B.R. Saris/DB

The same vehicle but with the observation structure raised. Unit commander Schäfer, wearing his standard SA uniform is standing on it with a control paddle. No photo has been found of him wearing any other form of uniform.

Sonderhilfszug Caps:

Before the official institution of the RAZ, personnel and drivers for the propaganda department were authorized to wear their regular uniforms with appropriate headgear...these could be from the SA, NSKK, SS or other NSDAP-related organizations.[191] A special uniform (Sonderhilfszuguniform) was designed for the RAZ between late 1935 and early 1936, and was to give the members a unique appearance during their official functions. This uniform was exhibited by the RZM at a show during the 1936 Party Days, in the "Zeichenschule am Gewerbemuseumsplatz" in Nürnberg.[191a]

The uniform included a large beret (Flachmütze) which was manufactured of a heavy, darker olive-brown wool. The crown was probably piped in silver (or even crimson). The beret was soft, seamless and flat with an approximate weight of 60-65 grams. The round top had an approximate diameter of 28-30cm (on a size 56 beret). The crown at the front top was approximately 7.2cm. On the inside edge a 1cm or 2.5cm wide piece of linen was sewn in. Overall, the inside was lined in Havana-brown silk. The 3cm wide sweat band was Havana-brown as well. The style of this beret was similar to that worn by NSFK members, which had been introduced in 1937. A silver metal or white embroidered cloth national emblem was positioned on the front center of the beret. Research indicates that this piece of headgear was meant only for wear at parades or inspections, and that it proved impractical and was rarely worn in the later years of the Third Reich. Instead, the standard SA kepi was normally worn with the regular SA service uniform. The cap top was crimson because the RAZ was the "technische Sturm der OSAF" at Munich.[192]

Stadtarchiv München/W.P.B.R. Saris

RAZ crews standing by their vehicles. They are wearing the "Sonderhilfszuguniform" with beret, which seems to have a light colored piping. Note the wear of the aluminum wire RAZ cuffband, and that the word "Reichs-Autozug" is hyphenated on the front of the driver's cab.

---

191 "Dienstanweisung für den Betrieb der reichseigenen Kraftwagen bei den Landesstellen des Reichsministeriums für Volksaufklärung und Propaganda," 1935. Anlage 3 (zu Ziff. 13): Bestimmungen über Dienst- und Schutzkleidung, a and b, pp. 19-20. Clothing provided by the ministry and authorities remained the property of the ministry. These orders were for those who served in the RAZ and HZB.

191a "Schwert und Spaten," Nr. 9, Berlin: September 28, 1936, p. 138. This uniform was not displayed with SA uniforms, but with those of the NSKK (the form of the breast pockets is NSKK origin). The color of the Sonderhilfszuguniform leans towards an olive-green or olive-brown shade (in spite of the color grey mentioned for the HZB in some articles). Also, "Uniformen-Markt," Nr. 15, September 15, 1936, p. 227, and "Völkischer Beobachter," München: September 9, 1936, p. 4. No additional details were given, other than this uniform was brand new. It is most probable that the members of the HZB were the first to receive this uniform, which varied slightly from the RAZ-Sonderhilfszuguniform. It should be remembered that they existed earlier as the official RAZ.

192 "Westarpscher Taschenkalender für die Luftwaffe," Grimmen, April 1, 1940 through March 31, 1941, p. 1261. It is not surprising that crimson was worn, since from the summer of 1939, and possibly earlier, the RAZ was assigned to the OSAF, whose color was crimson. "Vbl.d.OSAF," Nr. 10, December 29, 1939, p. 67, Nr. 199: Namensverleihung by Adolf Hitler. Ibid, Nr. 6, December 16, 1940, p. 24, Nr. 53: Ausschlüsse aus der SA. Available photographs show that the HZB beret was slightly lighter in color than that of the RAZ. And in most photos, the HZB personnel wear civilian clothing. The earliest photos, however, always show the wearing of standard SA or NSKK uniforms for the Hochland district.

Another view of the same event showing both the RAZ crew members and their vehicles.

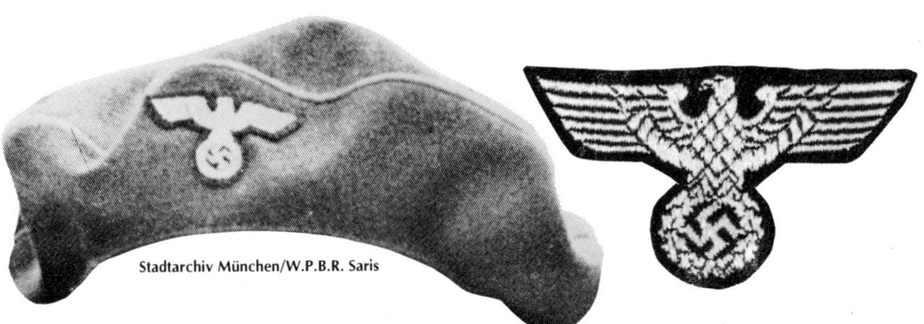

Enlargement of the beret with piping and its right-looking national emblem.

Another cap form was also worn by members of the RAZ. Its style was almost identical to the standard SA garrison cap, but was produced in a earth-brown color as used by the SS-Verfügungstruppen (SS-VT). What is unique, however, is that a regular RZM tag with "Feldmütze der SS" was positioned inside. To date, several such caps have been examined and all are the same. The curvature of the flap is slightly different from the standard SA garrison cap as it appears more elongated. A special woven RAZ emblem was positioned on the left side.[192a]

[192a]A series of photographs located in archives in Munich by W.P.B.R. Saris show the wear of the "Hausmütze," a garrison cap with the RAZ special insigne. These photos also show that the caps are of the same style as the standard SA garrison cap or the field cap worn by political leadiers during training courses. In early April 1937, just before the visit of Schwarz to the home garage, a number of photographs were taken. In them, practically all caps are without the front button, and at least seven are wearing the special RAZ insigne on the side of the cap and the black RAZ cuffband worn on the upper left arm of the overall. This is the position were the Party armband is normally worn. At least one photo shows the wear of the garrison cap with the special emblem on May 21, 1936. It should be noted that it is forbidden to use any of these photos which would have been credited to the Stadtarchiv München, Bayer. Staatsbibliothek, Iveco-Magirus or "DB" without special permission.

Derek Chapman

A SS tag on the inside of an earth-brown field cap which is attributed to the RAZ. Note the manufacturer's number "3."

Derek Chapman

The RAZ insigne is positioned on the left flap of the cap. The front button is pebbled silver.

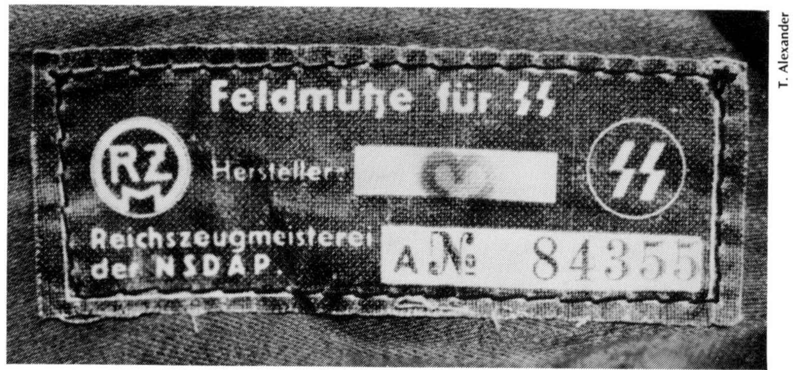

T. Alexander

The inside tag as illustrated before, but with the "3" positioned differently.

One wonders why SS field caps would have been worn by this organization? It should be noted that the RAZ had no connection with the SS (Note: Consult footnote 190...the only assignment of some members of the SS to the RAZ would have been as guards for the unit). In actuality, the size of the RAZ was relatively small: Statistics indicate the number was never greater than 80 persons (in the spring of 1937 the RAZ was only 30 persons strong). The unit possessed only one SA-Sturmfahne (otherwise, both awarded honor names would have been granted separate flags). With the above in mind, it is obvious that the cost to manufacture so few new unit caps was not economically feasible. And since the earth-brown SS field caps were no longer being used, but were still in stock (from 1936, field caps in other colors were worn by the SS-VT), this immediate supply was perfect for limited use. And additionally, the earth-brown color was a perfect match to the color of the overalls in use. It has been ascertained that at least from early 1937 the standard SA garrison cap (or a similar one) was also supplied.[192b]

A garrison cap was worn by RAZ members from at least May 1936, and worn officially only with the working dress (brownish and occasionally white overalls). This ensemble was worn at the "home garage" and on the grounds of the RZM complex, as well as when the RAZ was motoring through Germany and annexed countries.

W.P.B.R. Saris/DB

RAZ crew members and their vehicles. Note the wear of the garrison cap with overalls, and the various positions of the RPL emblem which is either on the side or door of the vehicle.

[192b]The number 30 was mentioned in articles from April 1937. All RAZ members were technically trained experts, in various grades. The members of the HZB consisted of approximately 100 persons at that time. Some photos show the wear of a field cap with two buttons (certainly NSKK) by members of the HZB, when this unit was in Flanders during the war. The emblem worn on the cap in some occasions was the SS eagle. It was not worn on the left flap, but just above the left flap. HZB vehicles also carried an RPL symbol on their sides from approximately 1937, but in varying forms. There is no lettering within the probably light grey colored shield, and the wings ar not straight, but pointed slightly downwards.

Hilfszug "Bayern" Photo Section

Stadtarchiv München/W.P.B.R. Saris

Above: HZB crew members waiting for their expected visitors on April 6, 1937. Note the old style HZB sign on the ambulance/medical vehicle.

Stadtarchiv München/W.P.B.R. Saris

HZB crew members lined up before their vehicles on the grounds of the "Reichsautobahnhof" during the visit of Reichsschatzmeister Schwarz and the American military attaché on April 6, 1937. Note the wear of the beret with piping, and that all are wearing a cloth national emblem except the third person from left who wears a metal version. They are all wearing collar patches without rank designation and the HZB aluminum cuffband as authorized by Schwarz.

Stadtarchiv München/W.P.B.R. Saris

Stadtarchiv München/W.P.B.R. Saris

Two HZB crew members wearing their "Sonderhilfszuguniform" with beret and national emblem. A close examination of the photos shows that the beret piping is the same color as the collar patches, but differs from the collar piping.

Alain Taugourdeau

The RPL symbol as used on the sides of HZB vehicles from late 1937. The driver is wearing a field cap with two front buttons.

W.P.B.R. Saris

The official design of the Hilfszug "Bayern" symbol. It was apparently intended for use on the vehicles, but then discarded. A variant was used instead. As far as is known, this insigne was never worn on the HZB field or garrison cap.

W.P.B.R. Saris/DB

Light grey HZB vehicles lined up with a uniformed guard. It is almost a certainty that the guard is not a regular HZB crew member as he is wearing a special light colored armband and an unidentified insigne on the left side of his field cap.

Naval SA (Marine–SA) 1930 – 1931

The first SA naval unit was formed in Hamburg during 1930. Its first members were probably Boschmann and Felsch from the steamer "Haparanda." Gauleiter Kaufmann from Hamburg approved the creation of a "Marinetrupp Hamburg," which was led by a former Free Corps member Wilhelm Boltz. The first collective meeting of this unit occurred on February 3, 1931 with approximately forty members present. After the reorganization of this group from Hamburg, it was recommissioned as the "Marinesturmbann–1 Hamburg" on June 15, 1931.[193] During the course of 1931 more naval units were raised in several districts all over Germany.

At the beginning of the war, many members joined the German Navy or the other armed forces; the importance of Naval SA units declined, but they remained in existence up until the end of the war.

Richard Kindel

Members of a Marine–SA unit, instructed by a merchant naval officer, wearing the early form of visored cap with the first pattern navy wreath with the national cockade in the center. Note that the cap is without an eagle, a common practice during the early thirties. Marine–SA units were often assigned, in larger harbors, to merchant navy ships that were using their particular city as home port.

National Emblem (Hoheitszeichen) 1931 – 1945

The early pattern silvered NSDAP national emblem was worn on the cap top center. By late 1931, this eagle with a 38mm wingspan was worn in the middle of the oakleaf wreath, upon the cap band center. (It is noted in photographs of the period that for a time a limited number of naval SA members at Kiel wore some sort of coat of arms in the center of the wreath in lieu of the national emblem. Coat of arms insigne were also worn in other districts).

With the December 1934 publication of the RZM manufacturing regulations for the Marine–SA visored cap, the position of the national emblem was

193 *"Militaria," Nr. 5, May 13, 1982, pp. 106–107.*

F. Catella

This national emblem and wreath combination is unique as both are fully hand-embroidered.

changed.[194] The eagle extended partially above the wreath. The swastika and its surrounding circle were positioned on the upper section of the wreath. This was probably not according to plans. In late May 1935, it was ordered that the early pattern national emblem once again had to be positioned in the center of the oakleaf wreath.[195]

Otto Spronk

Signal members of the 56th Marine–SA Standarte wearing the dark blue visored cap and its insigne, the wreath with in its center, the national emblem, as officially authorized until late 1934. Note the two different forms of wreath.

194 *"Mbl.d.RZM," Nr. 30, December 22, 1934, p. 3.*

195 *Ibid, Nr. 17, May 25, 1935, p. 169.*

A golden embroidered oakleaf wreath on a dark blue backing. The first form, metal silvered national emblem is positioned within the central open section, as ordered from late 1931 until 1934 and then from May 1935 until July 1937. In later years a higher version of the wreath was often used.

The gilt metal wreath of an early form on an oval of dark blue backing. Note that on this example, the metal national emblem extends partly above the wreath. The swastika and wreath of the national emblem is positioned on the highest part of the central open section. This form of insigne was authorized from late1934 through the spring of 1935.

By August 1937 the new SA version large, aluminum colored, national eagle emblem was also introduced for use by SA naval units, two months later than for the regular SA.[196] The orders specified its wear as: the lower wreath with swastika had to be positioned in the exact center of the gold colored wreath. (It must be noted that at *no time* before May 1938 was a gilt national emblem allowed for wear by Marine–SA units). This order would change approximately one year later.

The gilt metal SA national emblem was ordered for wear on May 23, 1938. This eagle was positioned on the front center of the cap top (consult for detailed information on sizes etc. also the beginning of this chapter).[197] Collectors may

---

[196] *"Vbl.d.OSAF," Nr. 11, August 31, 1937, p. 83. Nr. 240: Hoheitszeichen für Marine–SA.*

[197] *Ibid, Nr. 5. May 23, 1938, p. 44. Nr. 91: Abzeichen für Marine–SA–Dienstmützen (FO 2b Nr. 13704).*

A Marine–SA Oberführer from the Ostland district wears a naval style cap at the castle of Königsberg on June 16, 1938. Note the final pattern national emblem positioned over the large embroidered wreath.

240. Betrifft: **Hoheitsabzeichen für Marine SA.-Dienstmütze.** F 2 b Nr. 13736.

Das im Verordnungsblatt der Obersten SA.-Führung Nr. 9 Ziffer 176 vom 28. 6. 1937 angeführte Hoheitsabzeichen für die SA.-Dienstmütze wird auch zur Marine-SA.-Dienstmütze getragen. Das Abzeichen ist so anzubringen, daß der Kranz des Abzeichens genau in der Mitte des goldenen Eichenkranzes der Marine-SA.-Dienstmütze sitzt.

91. Betrifft: **Abzeichen für Marine-SA.-Dienstmützen.** FO 2b Nr. 13 704.

In Abänderung der Anzugsordnung für die SA., Teil 1, Absatz XII/6 und der Verfügung FO 2b Nr. 13 736 im Verordnungsblatt der Obersten SA.-Führung Nr. 11 vom 31. 8. 37 Ziffer 240, werden für die Marine-SA.-Dienstmützen mit sofortiger Wirkung folgende Abzeichen befohlen:

1. In der Mitte des oberen Mützenteiles wird das Hoheitsabzeichen in Gold, in der Mitte des Mützenbandes die SA.-Kokarde, umgeben von dem goldenen Eichenlaubkranz, getragen.
Die Abzeichen sind in Metall geprägt.

2. Vom Sturmführer aufwärts ist der Eichenlaubkranz in gestickter Ausführung zu tragen.

3. Die neuen Abzeichen sind bei der Reichszeugmeisterei und den zugelassenen Verkaufsstellen erhältlich.

W.P.B.R. Saris

Two publications from the *Vbl.d.OSAF.* With Number 240, published in August 1937, the standard new form of eagle was introduced for wear by the Marine–SA. The other publication, published in May 1938, gives in paragraph 1, specifications for the introduction of the golden national emblem for wear by the Marine–SA and its position. For the interest of the readers, these publications are shown, stating the exact introduction periods.

The golden, anodized, aluminum eagle with 64mm wingspan as worn by naval SA units.

thank the naval SA members for their disobedience. Various orders specified that old insignia (national eagle emblems, as well as the discontinued form of wreath) had to be returned for recycling.[198]

---

198 *Ibid, Nr. 11, October 30, 1938, p. 80. Nr. 193: Abzeichen für Marine–SA–Dienstmützen. Such an order had also been published in late September 1937,*

J. Floch

This Marine–SA unit marches in Vienna on June 3, 1938. Note the wear of the national emblem: It is positioned slightly above the wreath. This was officially allowed from 1934 through the spring of 1935. With the above mentioned date, the new national emblem was to be utilized but because of a lack of stock, caused by the entry of Austria into the Reich, the old form of eagle was used for a short period of time.

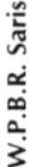

W.P.B.R. Saris

193. Betrifft: **Abzeichen für Marine-SA.-Dienstmützen.** VB 1 a — 44200.

Ich habe bereits im Verordnungsblatt Nr. 13 vom 30. 9. 1937, Ziffer 284, darauf hingewiesen, daß dafür Sorge zu tragen sei, daß abgelegte Metallabzeichen aller Art nicht weggeworfen, sondern gesammelt und an den nächsten arischen Rohproduktenhändler verkauft werden sollen. An diese Verfügung möchte ich heute nochmals erinnern. Gleichzeitig weise ich darauf hin, daß die Dienstmützen der SA.-Marine-Formationen neue Hoheitszeichen und Mützenkränze erhalten haben. Auch in diesem Fall verlange ich, daß die alten Hoheitszeichen und Mützenkränze nicht weggeworfen, sondern gesammelt und wie die übrigen Metallabzeichen verkauft werden. Auch diese Abzeichen sind vorher durch Hämmern unbrauchbar zu machen.

Im übrigen gilt das im Verordnungsblatt Nr. 13 Gesagte.

This publication instructs that the old national emblems must be destroyed by hammering. Collectors may thank SA members for not obeying the order. This order was not restricted to the SA only, but was meant for all Party organizations and the armed forces as well.

Oakleaf Wreath (Eichenlaubkranz)
1931 – 1945

The wearing of an oakleaf wreath with the Marine–SA visored cap became customary in 1932, the color of it being silver or gilt, depending upon the group or district color.[199] The wear of the silver wreath was abolished in the fall of 1933. Various forms of this wreath were used, like the models worn by members of army and navy.[200] (For more detailed information on these forms of oaklcaf wreaths, consult the chapter "Reichsheer/Heer," pp.–15 and 20, as well as the chapter "Reichsmarine/Kriegsmarine," p.131 – the coastal artillery version in Volume 1 of this series).

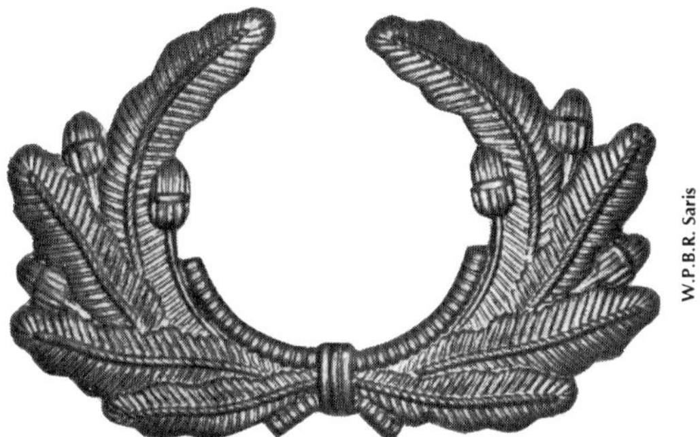

W.P.B.R. Saris

An early form of metal wreath in gilt, as taken from a sales catalogue and worn by the Marine–SA. This example differs from the earlier specimen shown with the eagle partly positioned above it. This example has a different position in respect to the leaves as well as the acorns.

James J. Boulton

Marine–SA gilt wire wreath, in the form formerly used by the Imperial navy. A silvered early pattern eagle emblem is positioned over the inner field of the cloth.

---

199 *Ruhl/Starke. "Adolf Hitler's Braunhemden" Leipzig: 1933, p. 12: Besonderheiten der Marine–Stürme.*

200 *Ibid.*

James J. Boulton

Imperial navy wreath. The same sample was used by the naval SA units, but without the national cockade and Prussian crown.

Metal as well as embroidered versions of the wreath were allowed. On most occasions, the metal wreath is shown in official publications; the embroidered wreath form was however often worn. Up until December 1934 this wreath was totally positioned upon the cap band; after this, the wreath was positioned with the lower leaves approximately upon the mid–center line of the ribbed mohair band. The early form wreath was worn until early 1938, when the second form navy style became available.[201]

W.P.B.R. Saris

Marine–SA members in a humorous moment. Note the wear of various forms of wreaths. Both persons, at right, wear the wreath in the position as ordered since December 1934, with the lower leaves on the mid–center line of the ribbed band. These old SA members come from the "Niederrhein" area. This was Düsseldorf and its outlying areas.

201 *"Vbl.d.OSAF," Nr. 3, March 31, 1938, p. 34. Nr. 63: Änderungsanzeige Nr. 1/38 der RZM, article–number 5081: Oakleaf wreath for Naval SA, new version; "Mbl.d.RZM," Nr. 3, January 29, 1938, p. 14.*

From the summer of 1937 an embroidered style oakleaf wreath, with a "high" top was on many occasions worn by leaders. With an order, dated May 23, 1938 the ranks Sturmführer and above were allowed to wear the embroidered version. This wreath was similar to the navy one. Various forms were observed. Some of the wreath forms used by naval SA leaders extended higher and had slender leaves, which pointed more upwards than regular naval wreaths. The large inner leaves extended higher as well, and the acorns were positioned differently. Surely these versions are nothing more than manufacturers variations. This wreath, having within its center the SA cockade, was sewn to the cap band with its lower leaves near to the lowest edge of the band. The official form was available from RZM sources no earlier than summer 1938.[202]

Bernd Wedeking

A Marine-SA member from Kiel, the "Holtenau" area, being in fact the Nordmark district, wears his dark blue visored cap with the new form national emblem and the first form wreath with the SA cockade in the middle, as authorized from May 1938. Note the wear of the brown shirt as well as the tunic with collar patches.

Enlisted ranks were simultaneously ordered to wear the second pattern army wreath in gilded metal with the SA monogram cockade in the center.[203] Nothing changed and the 1938 orders were maintained throughout the war.

---

202 *"Mbl.d.RZM," Nr. 17, August 13, 1938, p. 149. New article 5316, gold embroidered wreath.*

203 *Ibid, Nr. 12, June 4, 1938, p. 101. The last paragraph from the announcement states the abolishing of a golden colored wreath for the ranks Sturmführer and above; here it refers to the metal version.*

Final pattern Marine–SA wreath in gilt, in the standard final form for the army. The SA cockade is positioned in the center.

Naval–Youth Units (Marine–Jungstürme) 1932 – 1934

The first Naval SA youth units were probably formed in 1932. No unified uniform was yet determined, but simultaneously with the October 16, 1933 order for the Marine–SA, regulations were published for leaders and enlisted ranks for SA naval youth units and water–sport schools.[204]

Leaders wore the blue tunic and were ordered to wear the dark blue, navy style visored cap; a gold colored oakleaf wreath was worn with the early national emblem within its middle. The black chin strap was secured by gilt, anchor embossed buttons. These leaders were ordered to wear the black silk cap tally, as was authorized for enlisted ranks. However this tally was not to be worn with the headdress, but on the lower right sleeve in the manner of a cuff–title, 10cm above the cuff.[205]

Lower ranks wore the "Matrosenmütze," as worn by enlisted ranks in the German navy (for more detailed information regarding this form of headdress, consult the "Reichsmarine/Kriegsmarine" chapter in Volume 1 of this series, pp.160–162). A black silk tally was to be worn around the band of the cap. Golden, gothic lettering indicated their city of origin, for example, "S.A. Ortsname (city name) M.J.St." (tallies in this form have not been found and it is in fact unknown if they were ever manufactured). A first pattern silvered national emblem was worn on the front center of the cap top.[206] This cap was worn with the service, as well as the work dress.

These SA youth units were short–lived, being swallowed up in spring 1934 by the naval units of the Hitler–Jugend.[207]

---

204 Der Oberste SA–Führer. München: October 16, 1933, Order Ch.Nr. 1596/33: Bekleidung der Marine–SA und Marine–Jungstürme (with appendixes).

205 Ibid, p. 2. Section B: Bekleidung der Marine–Jungstürme, Nr. I.3.

206 von Eelking,Freiherr."Die Uniformen der Braunhemden" München: 1934, p. 51. It must be noted that the script for the tally is described as "deutsche Schrift." Often the Gothic script was used then, but it is known that tallies in Latin script were most often used in the early 1930's.

207 These "Marine–Jungstürme" were not included in the March 1, 1934 "Anzug–Ordnung" für die SA.

Water–Sport Schools (Wassersport–Schulen) 1932 – 1934

For training of the Marine–SA and the youth units, water–sport schools (often being a ship, located at a city) were established. Leaders, teachers (and auxiliaries) from such a school wore the October 1933 uniform ordered for leaders of the "Marine–Jungsturm," but instead of wearing the cuff title tally with the name of the city on their sleeve, they were authorized to wear a cuff title tally with for example: "SA–Wassersport–Schule Ortsname" (a city name).[208] During research tallies in this form have not been found and it is not known if this version was ever manufactured. Soon its form would change.

Students wore the regular Matrosenmütze. During the winter season a dark knitted sailing cap, called a "Pudelmütze," was worn. The early national emblem was worn with the Matrosenmütze; around the band the black silk tally with gold, gothic lettering as ordered for leaders and teachers had to be worn. One must note that students had to wear their regular Jungsturm tally when wearing the walking–out uniform.[209] The tallies for a water–sport school were only worn during courses at such a school or during courses with other districts. The permanent personnel for a school constantly wore the tally, as ordered.

A "Matrosenmütze" worn by members of a water or sea sport school of the SA. The light blue tally is woven in grey with the Gothic lettering, "SA–Seesportübungslager Heilbronn."

208 Der Oberste SA–Führer. München: October 16, 1933, Ch.Nr. 1596/33: Bekleidung und Ausrüstung der Marine–SA und Marine–Jungstürme. Section C: Bekleidung der Wassersport–Schulen, I1 and I2, also II.2.

209 Ibid, Section C, II.3.

Sea–Sport schools (SA–Seesport–Schulen) 1934 – 1940

In early 1934 the water–sport schools were renamed to seasport–schools and meant to be utilized for Naval SA training only. The uniforms worn and forms of headdress did not change, but with the March 1934 dress regulations the color of the tally as worn by leaders, teachers (and their auxiliaries), as well as the enlisted rank was changed from black to cornflower–blue.[210]

This tally was identified in the new orders as "Sportabzeichen der Marine–SA." The color of the lettering changed from gold into white gothic. The name indication was also changed, for example: S.A.–Seesportschule, Ortsname (city name). The tallies for a sea–sport school were only worn during courses at such a school. The permanent personnel of a school constantly wore the tally, as ordered. Students at such a school had to wear the standard SA uniform as the walking–out dress.

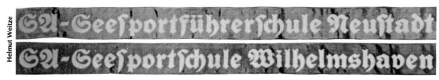

Helmut Weitze

Examples of light blue tallies with white or aluminum woven lettering as worn during courses for naval SA units.

A rare example of an early naval SA cap band tally with Latin lettering, yellow on black.

Carl Fromann

A black tally with golden, Gothic lettering unofficially worn by naval SA units. By regulation, these black, silk tallies carried the name of the school.

Instead of the Gothic lettering it has been mentioned that Latin script was also used. Occasionally black tallies are found with golden, Gothic lettering. In place of the lettering form used by the SA, the late 1938 lettering–form as used by the Marine–HJ was used. For example: 1/158 BIELEFELD 1/158. Just exactly when these tallies were introduced has not been determined. Research has not indicated if its wear was meant for the SA, but due to the late form this is probably out of the question.

The wearing of tallies by any Marine–SA unit or school was hardly practiced. It was also restricted to a very limited group of wearers. In general the tallies are 32mm wide and approximately 115mm long and made from artificial

210 *"Anzugs–Ordnung für die SA." Teil I. Der Oberste SA–Führer. München: March 1, 1934, pp. 64–65. Section XIII: Bekleidung der Seesportschulen.*

E.J. Bagale

Marine–SA personnel rowing during exercises, wearing the so–called Matrosenmütze with a tally. It is believed this tally reads "Hilfswerklager Lockstedt," but no reason has been found for such a tally. It is known that such a Hilfswerklager was operated by the SA group Nordmark, as Lockstedt exists in Holstein in the neighborhood of Elmshorn near the river Elbe. It is possible that the SA was trained at such a camp for merchant naval duties, and therefore, a tally was worn with the headdress.

silk. It is known that some tallies are manufactured in very small quantities; the lowest available stock was 12 samples.

The following tallies are known to have existed:

SA–SEESPORTÜBUNGSLAGER HEILBRONN;
SA–SEESPORTFÜHRERSCHULE NEUSTADT;
SA–SEESPORTSCHULE FRIEDRICHSORT;
SA–SEESPORTSCHULE SEEMOOS;

SA–SEESPORTSCHULE WILHELMSHAVEN;
MARINESTURM DER S.A. STANDARTE V.

It is almost certain that other forms were manufactured and we would like to hear of any other existing samples relating to the naval SA or photographs showing the wearing of any form, so that we are able to include these in a later addendum (for more information on HJ tallies, see the chapter on naval HJ–units in the future volume IV).

With the introduction of the garrison cap for naval units, the Matrosenmütze worn earlier slowly disappeared during the course of late 1936 and the SA tallies disappeared.

It is not known if these SA sea sport schools continued to exist. In later regulations these schools were not mentioned, but due to their training purposes their continuance is likely. With the commencement of the war it is almost certain that they were disbanded.

Otto Spronk

Members of the Marine–SA on the "Duhnen" during an inspection. The enlisted ranks wear the dark blue garrison caps with the triangular insigne, the leaders wear the visored caps with the wreath and national emblem still positioned in the center. This indicates that this photograph was taken before October 1937, as by then the larger, new form eagle was ordered.

From approximately 1937, members of the Marine–SA were trained at the Marine–SA–Schule "Düsternbrock" near Kiel. One ship was available, the Segelschulschff "Duhnen" (which earlier served in the Navy as the Segelschoner "Duhnen," before being taken out of service in November 1936). Other schools were no longer mentioned, neither in the handbook for the SA, nor in the organization books from 1938 on. It is known that at the "Duhnen" garrison caps in blue or white were mainly worn and the so–called "Matrosenmütze" with tallies was no longer used.[211]

A. Stam

Members of the Marine–SA from Mönchen-Gladbach, during festivities on May 1, 1935. Note that these SA members riding horses are wearing a coat of arms on the top center front of the visored cap and a cockade on the cap band. The mounted person at far left is adjusting his chin strap under his chin.

1932 – 1935

With the introduction of the SA–Dienstvorschrift in 1932, regulations were recorded, but it is known that prior to this, the "Elbsegler," a civilian form of naval cap, was worn with the first pattern NSDAP national emblem or an anchor insigne. From September 1931, Marine–SA members wore a dark blue, navy style visored cap with a black leather visor. A brown leather chin strap rested above this, secured by two small silver or gilt, anchor embossed buttons (their color depending on the district color).[212]

Marine–SA visored cap. This cap has two interesting features: The first being the thin, early pattern gilt metal wreath with a gilt national emblem. The other is the metal Edelweiss in the center of the cap top. Neither the Edelweiss or the gilt early eagle were officially allowed.

With an order, dated December 1, 1932 the brown chin strap was abolished and a black version had to be worn (the chin strap button now was to be in gold only).[213] A unified uniform (Dienstanzug) for Marine–SA units was implemented on October 16, 1933. The earlier worn form of headdress did not change; the aforementioned style wreath was worn on the front center of the cap band with the silver metal first pattern national emblem attached to its center. Piping was introduced, to be worn according to rank:

Sturmführer up to and including Sturmhauptführer the two–colored piping according to the SA–district colors around the crown;

Sturmbannführer up to and including Brigadeführer a golden piping around the crown;

Standartenführer up to and including Brigadeführer were also ordered to wear the two–colored piping around the upper edge of the cap band.[214]

---

211 *"Handbuch der SA," Berlin: 1939, Section: Sondereinheiten, a. Marine–SA, p. 22; also "Organisationsbuch der NSDAP. " München: 1938, Abschnitt 4: Die SA, p. 364b. This information was not yet included in the 1937 issue.*

212 *"Dienstvorschrift für die SA der NSDAP. " Heft 2. München: 1932. p. 33.*

213 *"Vbl.d.OSAF," Nr. 10, December 1, 1932, p. 2. Nr. 5: Bekleidung der Marinestürme (I Nr. 2085/32).*

214 *Der Oberste SA–Führer. München: October 16, 1933, Ch.Nr. 1596/33, section A: Bekleidung der Marine–SA. Nr. 5 describes the visored cap and piping systems. If this piping was indeed worn is not known, since little evidence was found in photographs to show that it was ever put into use.*

Bernd Wedeking

Two naval–minded brothers photographed in approximately 1935. The one at left is from the navy and wears the tally "Kreuzer Königsberg," while his brother on the right has joined the Marine–SA. He wears his dark blue visored cap with proper insigne according to the 1934 orders, with the lower wreath on the mid–line of the cap band.

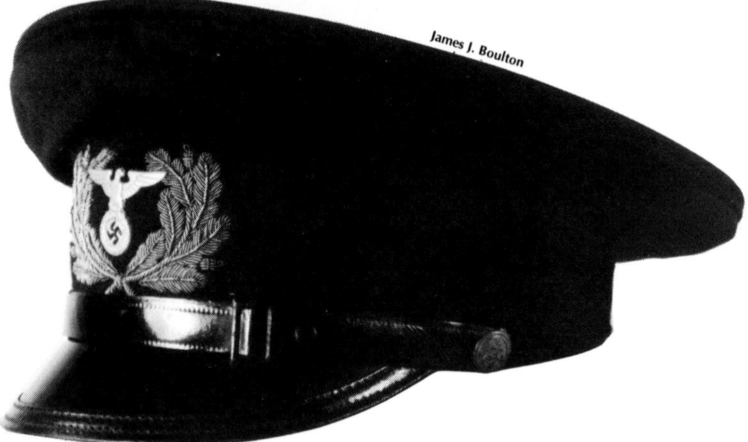

James J. Boulton

Early Marine–SA visored cap. The national emblem is worn in the center of the hand–embroidered wreath.

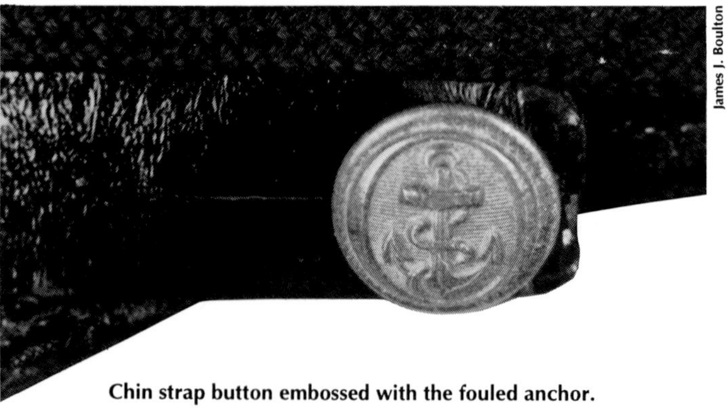

James J. Boulton

Chin strap button embossed with the fouled anchor.

National Archives

This Sturmbannführer from the Marine–SA wears his visored cap with a smooth cap band instead of the ribbed mohair type.

The visored cap was to be worn by all ranks with:

a) grosser Dienstanzug (the greater service–dress);

b) kleiner Dienstanzug (the regular service–dress). No headdress was worn when this uniform was ordered.

Not much changed with the March 1, 1934 regulations. The form of headdress for enlisted ranks and leaders of the regular naval–SA did not change. It was noted specifically that the band was of black mohair (ribbed, but without any adornment). In this order it was also specified that the chin strap buttons were of matte gold and pebbled. There was no mention of the embossed anchor.[215] Fourteen days later, an important change was announced in the

215 *"Anzugs–Ordnung für die SA." Teil I. Der Oberste SA–Führer. München: March 1, 1934, Section XII: Bekleidung der Marine–SA. With Nr. 6 it was noted as: "Knöpfe in mattgold gekörnt. Auch an der Dienstmütze für den Sturmriemen."*

W.P.B.R. Saris

28.) Betrifft: Bekleidung der Marine-SA.

In Abänderung der Verfügung I Nr. 1596 vom 16. 10. 33 wird angeordnet:

a) die Litze ist für die Dienstgrade Sturmmann, Rottenführer, Oberscharführer, Obertruppführer, Obersturmführer, Sturmhauptführer, Obersturmbannführer gelb mit dunkelblauem Längsfaden;

b) die Farbe der Nummern am Kragenspiegel der zuständigen SA-Einheit ist statt weiß gelb;

c) die Zweifarbenschnur bezw. Goldschnur um den Mützendeckel bezw. oberen Rand des Mützenbundes wird nicht mehr getragen.

Ch F Nr. 4477/34

This order, published May 1934, ordered the abolishment of the two–colored and gold piping for the crown and upper edge of the Marine–SA visored caps.

"Verordnungsblatt der OSAF": all piping, gold, as well as the two–colored form were abolished for wear on the Marine–SA visored cap.[216] In late December 1934 full descriptions for manufacturing the visored cap were published in the "Mitteilungsblatt der RZM"; the cap was classified as "Kapitänsmütze" (indicating the regularly worn German naval form, which also was worn by the merchant navy).

1936 – 1945

The years 1934 through 1936 hardly brought any important changes regarding the Marine–SA. In late October 1936 the garrison cap for the Naval SA units was introduced (consult the related section). The RZM once more published manufacturing regulations.

1936 Description for the Naval–SA Visored Cap (SA–Marine–Sturmmütze)

The visored cap was referred to as the "Tellermütze" in the "Klapp"-style and made of dark DAF cloth. The oval top (26.3 x 25cm) had a 2.5mm piping (stiffened on the inside by a 1.5 x 0.6mm iron, rust proof wire) from the same dark blue material as the top. This top, with its four under panels, measured in front 5.5cm, on both sides 4.7cm and 5cm at the back. The cap front was padded on the inside by wadding and gauze (20cm long and 6cm wide). The back was also reinforced by a 3cm wide piece of wadding. A linen covered stiffener retained the shape of the top.

The cap band was reinforced by a 0.5mm thick piece of black or natural colored, impregnated cardboard (known as "Friedensrandpappe"). It was approximately 5cm high, including the lower edge. Over this was sewn a black ribbed mohair band of standard navy style.

---

216 "Vbl.d.OSAF," Nr. 18, March 15, 1934, p. 6. Nr. 28: Bekleidung der Marine–SA (Ch/F Nr. 4474/34), Section C mentions the abolishment of piping. One must note that such an order was once more published, more than 3 1/2 years later. This order was then also published in the "Vbl.d.OSAF," Nr. 14 and dated October 30, 1937, p. 112. Nr. 300: Marine–SA Dienstmütze (order F 2b Nr. 13708 from the Führungsamt says : "with the immediate entry ranking nor function systems are to be worn with the naval–SA visored cap").

An excellent study of the Marine–SA uniform. Note the high, thick gilt wire wreath worn on the visored cap by this Obersturmbannführer from the Berlin staff.

National Archives

National Archives

A Marine–SA Standartenführer wearing the high styled wreath with the first pattern national emblem on its center in mid–November 1937. Officially, he should already be wearing the large eagle emblem as this emblem was authorized for wear since August of 1937. Note the silver eagle is in contrast with the gilt embroidered wreath. This person was assigned to the staff of Goebbels and appears with him in a number of the period photographs.

The cap was lined in medium–blue, black satin or cotton material. A celluloid sweat diamond, with the sizes 13.5 x 10cm, was sewn in the center of the inside top. On the left interior, a black RZM tag was sewn in, just behind the sweat band. This band, 4cm wide, was beige colored and made of sheepskin with perforations on the front section and closed at the back of the cap by stitches or a small piece of ribbon. Substitute materials could be used instead of sheepskin. A gummed pad was glued to the front underside of the band.

The black fiber visor (23cm long and 4.9cm wide in the center) was lacquered on the top. Muslin was glued on the underside and a 1cm wide piece of black muslin was sewn along the leading edge of the visor. Above this rested the two part black lacquered chin strap (in earlier regulations identified as the SS version), being 13mm wide and 1.5mm thick. A black rectangular buckle with rounded edges joined the two sections of the strap together. It could be extended by the two black, metal buckles and was secured to the cap by two gilt, prong type buttons, embossed with the anchor motif (the pebbled button version was discontinued and the old form returned). Dark blue, silk covered, buttons have also been observed, being worn.

The early insigne, being the golden early form Reichsheer oakleaf wreath with the early pattern silvered national emblem in its center, was worn on the cap band. The lower leaves touching the exact mid–center of the ribbed band.[217] This visored cap was ordered to be worn only with the greater service dress. An oakleaf pattern cap band (as used with DAF visored caps) was strictly forbidden.[218]

L. van Aerle

Marine–SA Obersturmbannführer Cabolet from Braunschweig's Marine–Standarte 35, located in the Niedersachsen district, wears a white–topped cap in the summer of 1937. Note the wearing of the high wreath.

In May 1938 the anchor style buttons were introduced in a metal that had a finish that gave a "golden" appearance. This type of button had no prongs, but instead an "eye," through which the buttons were sewn to the cap body. The anchor and the outside ring were polished.[219] The basic changes made in 1938 concerned the insignia. The SA monogram cockade was worn in the center of

---

217 *"RZM–Herstellungsvorschriften," 1936, p. 116.*

218 *"Organisationsbuch der NSDAP. " München: 1936, pp. 390–391.*

219 *"RZM–Herstellungsvorschriften," 1938, Section metal. p. 33.*

Final pattern Marine–SA visored cap with the gilt eagle emblem and the high–styled embroidered wreath and SA–style cockade. Note the cloth cap band instead of the ribbed pattern and the single ventilation hole.

Final pattern Marine–SA visored cap with golden cap cords. No regulation allowed the wearing of these golden cords, but it is known that higher ranked leaders occasionally wore them.

An SA–Sturmführer of the Marine–SA Sturm 4 of the Marinestandarte 9, as shown in the Organisationsbuch from 1943. Note he wears his visored cap with the final insigne with his smaller service dress. Marinestandarte 9 was located at Dortmund and was known as Standarte "Westfalen–Süd" from the Westfalen district.

Standard Marine–SA visored cap with the final form of wreath as worn by the army, and when in gilt, by the navy. The metal form of insigne was mainly used by the lower ranking Marine–SA members and the embroidered form by the higher ranking leaders. Note the SA monogram cockade.

the wreath, positioned upon the band. The national emblem was moved to the cap top.

In July 1939 the visored cap was officially altered into the style, as used by the German navy, with the larger round top. A white topped version visored cap was also authorized from spring 1939. This cap, with removable top, was ordered for the smaller service dress, or when the long dark blue trousers were worn.[220] Its wear was already condoned from the summer of 1937 and was then mainly worn by instructors of the sea–sport schools.

Brief Description: 1939 Dark Blue Visored Cap

The round top measured 28.0 x 28.0cm. The panels being 6.5cm in front, at the sides 5.5cm and at the back 6.0cm. The height for the cap band, including the edge, was 5.3cm. The reinforcement of the band was 0.8mm thick and 5.5cm wide. Artificial products were allowed for the chin strap; the diameter of the buttons was 12mm.

The mohair band was 5.2cm wide; the fiber visor being 26cm long and in the middle 5cm wide. Other manufacturing procedures were largely as before. It was noted that the upper leaves of the metal wreath touched the upper edge of the ribbed band.[221]

Brief Description: 1939 Visored Cap with White Top

The sizes were as for the dark blue version. The material used was white "cottondrell," according German navy orders. The use of white bleached gabar-

220 "Vbl.d.OSAF," Nr. 8, July 1, 1939, p. 54. Nr. 85: Marine–Mützen. Order FO 2b Nr. 13704 states that the old forms had to be worn out until May 31, 1940, Those Marine–SA units joining the planned RPT 1939 (which in fact did not take place due to the start of the war) were ordered to wear the new form (Section 2). The white top always had to be the removable version (Section 3) and was always ordered when a white tunic was worn. Photos, however, show otherwise.

221 "Mbl.d.RZM," Nr. 3, February 11, 1939, p. 57. Some late style Marine–SA visored caps found are in the form known as "Form 4." This form was never officially introduced for wear by the naval SA.

G. Rudloff

The permanent personnel of a Marine–SA seasport school or camp, photographed in approximately 1937, wearing the white–top visored cap. Note that the tally is worn on the lower right sleeve.

dine material was also allowed. The reinforcement of the band was 0.8mm thick, but higher than the blue version; 6.5cm wide. Artificial products were allowed for the chin straps. The buttons were also 12mm in diameter.

The dark blue covered cap body was manufactured differently due to the installation of the loose white cover. The upper edge of the reinforcement band was furnished with another 5mm wide specially constructed edge (with an iron wire for reinforcement on the inside) to hold the cover in its position. On the front center a white snap with a 7mm diameter was installed just above the ribbed mohair band, upon the special edge. This press button fitted into the other part that was sewn onto the cover. For extra reinforcement (to keep the cover in position) a 10cm long and 3cm wide stiffener, covered with white material, was sewn in on the inside front. On the inside the reinforcement was covered with a white silk lining. Officially these visored caps had a gauze, white lined top. Upon this the regular celluloid sweat shield diamond was sewn on and the regular beige sweatband was positioned on the inside of the body.

The crown piping for the loose cover was consolidated by a wire. In the front an approximately 10cm long and 4cm wide white tongue was positioned, in which fitted the stiffener of the body. An extra loose rustproof wire fitted in the crown of the inside of the cover.

The mohair band was 5.2cm wide; the fiber visor being 26cm long and in the middle 5cm wide. Other manufacturing procedures were largely as mentioned earlier. It was noted that the upper leaves of the metal wreath touched the upper edge of the ribbed band.[222] No further changes took place from this point until the end of the war.

---

[222] *Ibid, Nr. 3, February 11, 1933, p. 59.*

W.P.B.R. Saris

290. Betrifft: Lagermütze der Marine-SA.
F 3 h Nr. 13 706.

1. Mit sofortiger Wirkung wird für die Marine-SA eine Lagermütze eingeführt.

2. Die Marine-SA-Lagermütze ist im Schnitt der SA-Lagermütze, aus dunkelblauem Mützentuch. Das gleichseitige Dreieck an der linken Seite der Mütze ist aus kornblumenblauem Spiegeltuch, darauf das Hoheitsabzeichen in Silber. Vorne an der Mütze ein gekörnter Knopf in Gold.

3. a) Die Marine-SA-Lagermütze darf zum kleinen Dienstanzug in und außer Dienst getragen werden.
   b) Zum großen Dienstanzug darf die Lagermütze getragen werden:
      I) beim Aufenthalt in Lagern,
      II) beim Geländesport und Einsatzübungen,
      III) beim inneren Sturmdienst,
      IV) bei Gepäckmärschen und Übungsmärschen (nicht bei Propagandamärschen),
      V) von im Dienst einzeln auftretenden SA-Männern .
   c) Zum A r b e i t s a n z u g muß die Lagermütze getragen werden.

4. Die Marine-SA-Lagermütze ist ab 15. 10. 36 bei der Reichszeugmeisterei erhältlich.

291. Betrifft: Arbeitsanzug für Marine-SA.
F 3 h Nr. 13 706.

1. Mit sofortiger Wirkung wird für die Marine-SA ein Arbeitsanzug eingeführt. Der Arbeitsanzug kann von SA-Unterführern und -Männern zum Boots- und Signaldienst getragen werden, jedoch muß in den Abteilungen der Anzug einheitlich sein. Zum Arbeitsanzug werden k e i n e Dienstgradabzeichen getragen.

2. Der Arbeitsanzug besteht aus:
   a) Arbeitsbluse aus weißem (ungebleichtem) Moleskin im Schnitt der Kriegsmarine ohne Exerzierkragen,
   b) Hakenkreuzarmbinde,
   c) Arbeitshose aus weißem (ungebleichtem) Moleskin im Schnitt der Kriegsmarine,
   d) Lagermütze,
   e) leichte Schuhe.

3. Der Arbeitsanzug ist ab 15. 10. 36 bei der Reichszeugmeisterei erhältlich.

Two orders published in the *Vbl.d.OSAF* of October 1936 in reference to the Marine–SA "Lagermütze" and "Arbeitsanzug." Number 290 officially introduced the garrison cap. Paragraph 2 describes the cornflower–blue triangle with a *white* eagle emblem. Number 291 orders the introduction of a working dress. Paragraph 2a and b give white as its color. With d, the garrison cap, no specific color was given, meaning that dark blue was ordered. At no time, was an official correction authorizing white given.

Otto Spronk

An instructor shows how to tie a knot. Note that all Marine–SA members wear the dark garrison cap with the small pattern eagle emblem. Photographs show that most often this was the insigne used, instead of the new pattern, in later years. It is observed that almost all photos taken aboard a ship were taken on the "Duhnen" school ship.

The wear of the Edelweiss insigne was never officially sanctioned in any regulation for any form of headdress as worn by Marine–SA members. No photograph has been found showing it being worn. Cords were not introduced for wear with the naval SA visored cap at any time.

Naval SA Garrison Cap (Marine–SA Lagermütze) 1936 – 1945

In spite of the fact that the garrison cap had already been introduced for the regular SA in February 1934, it would take until the fall of 1936 before a similar cap would become available for Marine–SA personnel. With an order dated October 26, 1936 a garrison cap was officially introduced and immediately authorized for wear. Caps were in fact already available from RZM stocks from October 15.[223]

J.R. Angolia

Enlisted ranks from a Marine–SA unit wear the dark blue garrison cap. Note the variety of wreath forms worn by the instructors and leaders with the blue, as well as the white–top visored caps. One must note that the first garrison caps did not appear earlier than October 15, 1936 when they became available from RZM sources.

---

223 "Vbl.d.OSAF," Nr. 15, October 26, 1936, pp. 105–106. Nr. 290: Lagermütze der Marine–SA (F3h Nr. 13706) and Nr. 291: Arbeitsanzug für Marine–SA.

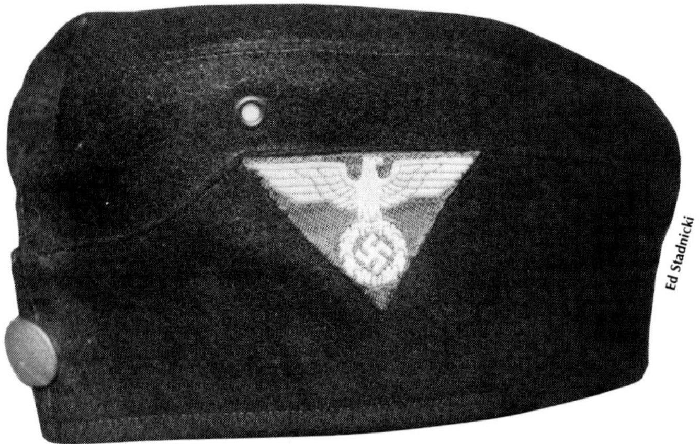

Naval SA garrison cap in dark blue with the gilt button. The aluminum wire, woven eagle always has a blue backing. One should note that officially, this cap was specified as the "Lagermütze." It is often described as the "Arbeitsmütze," but this term was never used in official documents or regulations. The dress, however, was described as the "Arbeitsanzug" and was always made of white cloth.

A stamp in the form often used on bolts of cloth, every two meters and in white paint.

The cap was made of dark blue cloth, mainly wool, The front button was gilt pebbled with an 18mm diameter. A cornflower–blue felt or cloth triangle was sewn to the left side of the flap. A silver metal early pattern national emblem was worn in its center.[224] Complete orders were published for wear:

a) The garrison cap was authorized for wear with the smaller service dress, during service, as well as when off duty;
b) With the greater service–dress it was allowed for wear during:
   I. Staying at a camp;
   II. With sports in the "field" (Geländesport) or preparedness exercise;
   III. With the so–called "inneren Sturmdienst," indoor service;
   IV. With marching with marching–kit or other marching exercises (the garrison cap was not allowed during marches of a propaganda nature);
   V. Within service, acting as individual.
c) The dark blue garrison cap was ordered with all occasions where the white working outfit was worn.[225]

224 *"RZM–Herstellungsvorschriften," 1936, pp. 212–213.*

225 *"Vbl.d.OSAF," Nr. 15, October 26, 1936, p. 106. Nr. 291: Arbeitsanzug für Marine–SA (F3h Nr. 13706). In this order white is the color given for the trousers and blouse; no further indication was given of any white garrison cap being introduced.*

The first pattern insigne for the garrison cap was a cloth triangle, officially in cornflower–blue, upon which was positioned the first form of national emblem. It is believed, but not officially stated, that sometime in 1938, a yellow or golden, woven larger national emblem was introduced, but was rarely worn.

In the "Mbl.d.RZM" the manufacturing procedures were published with the date September 26, 1936. The sizes were the same as the regular SA garrison cap. The material used was the regular DAF cloth. The inside lining was of black material or the blue as used by the DAF. The triangle for the insigne was equilateral, being 5cm and was positioned near the sharp curvature. The color of this triangle was described as being the blue as used for NSDAP courts. Just above the curvature, on both sides, one ventilation grommet was also installed. The button with prongs was pulled through a metal grommet, which was installed on the front of the flap center.[226]

It was not stated, but the woven version national emblem was also introduced for wear by the Marine–SA with the garrison cap in September 1937. In no regulation was the introduction of a white garrison cap ever mentioned in later years. Photographs show its wear, but it was surely no regularly authorized or standard item. Nothing was changed in the next years in relation to the form worn or insigne.

G. Innes

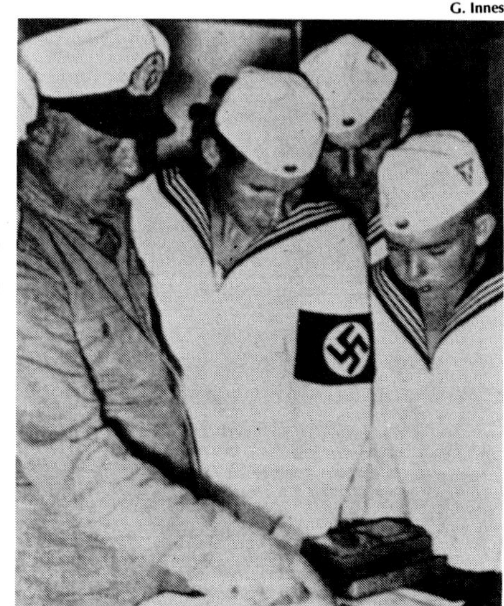

HJ members being trained at a Marine–SA camp, wear the rare white garrison cap with the early style eagle emblem on the triangle. The instructor is wearing the white–top visored cap with the large wreath and an early eagle emblem on the center.

226 *"Mbl.d.RZM, Nr. 20, September 26, 1936, p. 439; RZM–Herstellungsvorschriften, 1936, p. 235.*

Otto Spronk

During exercises, the naval SA members wear the dark and white cap simultaneously.

Education and Training Camps (SA–Schulen und Lagern des Ausbildungswesens) 1931 – 1945

It was in approximately 1931 that schools for educating SA leaders became a necessity. Advertisements were published during early summer 1931 by the Reichsführerschule (RFS – Reich Leaders School) at Munich to attract qualified teachers for this job.[227] The first course must have taken place during late fall. The number of courses was extended in the next few years and was later also opened to members of other NSDAP formations.[228] The main office of education (Erziehungshauptamt) was responsible for training, education and regulating the needs of the SA leader corps. For this purpose, in addition to the RFS, other schools were established for middle ranking SA leaders or for those with staff functions, for example the "Führerschule der OSAF," "Gruppenschulen" etc. At these schools the SA members were trained for sports (known as "Wehrsport"), but also to train examiners for the SA sports insigne. In later years training took place for positions as sports judges and sports trainers as well. Other training or forms of education were also established and specialized schools were formed, for example the Reichssanitätsschule and the Reichs–Reiterführerschule. These schools were attended by specially selected students.[229]

Personnel of these schools normally wore the standard SA cap (with in later years the colored top according to their district of origin color) with the service dress. An exception was the highest leader of the RFS. Since April 1931, he was ordered to wear a bright red top (consult the section for SA leaders for detailed information). From May 1933 this position, and also the "Chef des Ausbildungswesens" (and inspectors) were ordered to wear a crimson top. Staff personnel wore crimson/silver cap piping, as regularly ordered.

---

227 *"Vbl.d.OSAF," Nr. 2, June 10, 1931, Nr. 4: Reichsführerschule.*

228 *Ibid, Nr. 3, August 15, 1931, Nr. 2 and Nr. 3; Ibid, Nr. 12. April 1, 1933, Nr. 35.*

229 *"Die SA." Sonderausgabe Völkischer Beobachter. München: 1938, p. 30; "Handbuch der SA." Berlin: October 27, 1938, p. 128.*

A visored cap, in the style of the army field cap with cloth covered visor, was planned in 1933, but was probably never introduced, because it was not sanctioned by Röhm and Schneidhuber, the chief of education. In 1934 Schneidhuber was succeeded by Max Luyken. With the March 1934 dress regulations uniforms were specified and officially introduced for schools and education purposes. These uniforms will be discussed in order as published.

Otto Spronk

Gruppenführer Max Luyken, from early 1934 "Chef des Erziehungshauptamtes und des Ausbildungswesens," wears his cap piped according to his rank: 3mm silver piping around the cap crown and the edge of the flap. The photograph is dated before fall 1933 because then the Tresse was introduced: With his assignment as Chief of Education, Luyken was appointed Obergruppenführer and his cap top was crimson. Note the flap piping. It follows the curvature of the flap but does not extend down the front center as per regulations. Luyken succeeded Schneidhuber in early 1934.

Otto Spronk

SA–Obergruppenführer Luyken in the center, during an inspection with some of his chiefs from the department of education. Luyken wears a crimson cap top. His chiefs also wear this color due to their assignment to the OSAF.

Otto Spronk

Hitler congratulates some new SA leaders after they had finished their training at the Reichsführerschule at Munich. Note the wear of the two–colored crown piping by persons ranked as Sturmhauptführer and the bright colored piping, as worn by the Sturmbannführer.

Plenipotentiary (Beauftragte) assigned to "Obergruppe" or "Gruppe"

The service dress for this position or the SA leaders assigned to him was as ordered for the staff of the "Obergruppe" or "Gruppe" they were assigned to.

School or Camp Leaders, Teachers and Lower Ranked Administrative Officials (Führer der Schulen und Lager, Lehrer und Verwaltungspersonal)

During training or service within schools or camps, the newly introduced so–called "Übungsanzug" (training– and exercise dress) in the color olive–brown (having an olive–green shade), was ordered. With this dress introduced in 1933, a special form of cap, known as the "SA–Übungsmütze" (resembling a mountain cap) was ordered in the same color. The flap ran in one piece in the front and upon this a silvered pebbled button was positioned. No colored top was authorized, but piping forms were introduced being:

a) Students: the crown and edge of the flap were piped in brown;
b) Leaders, teachers and assistants: red/white or silver piping according to rank. Red/white was worn around the crown by Obertrupp–, Obersturm–, Sturmhaupt– and Obersturmbannführer; the ranks Sturmbannführer and above were ordered to wear a silver crown piping. It was not specified if ranks of Gruppenführer or above existed in the school or camp system, but if they did, they had to also wear a silver flap piping.[230]

In later years the color changed slightly to a more brown than green fabric and it is known that from 1936, the regular form of garrison cap with the trian-

230 "Anzugs–Ordnung für die SA." Teil I. Der Oberste SA–Führer. München: March 1, 1934, pp. 68–69. Section XV: Dienstanzug der Führer an Schulen und Lagern des Chefs des Ausbildungswesens. It was noted that administrative officials were ordered to wear the same headdress, without a colored top. No specifications in relation to a piping system were given. No Tresse was worn with the special headdress for the "Übungsanzug."

A cap used at the Gruppenschule Hochland, as indicated by the stamp inside. This cap of olive–brown fabric in the regular SA or mountain cap style, is probably an experimental sample as it differs from the officially worn form. The flap is interrupted and closed by a silvered, pebbled button. Note the dark brown chin strap and the special adoption of a lower curvature to fit this strap. Above all, this sample had the brown or red–brown cap top but this was removed. Small pieces of colored top cloth are still present in the crown seam, but it is mainly indicated by the brownish–red grommets on the sides.

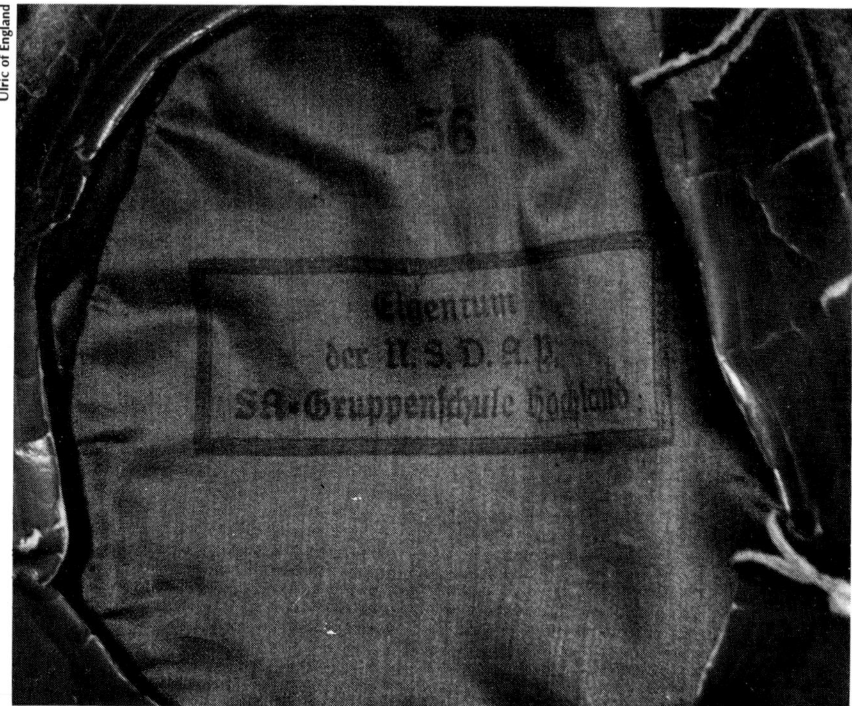

The stamp used in the aforementioned cap, reading: "Eigentum der NSDAP, SA–Gruppenschule Hochland." Translated this means: (Property of the NSDAP, SA–Group–School Hochland), for the Bavarian and Schwaben regions. Note the sweat band in Havana–brown.

gular insigne was often worn during courses or marches. The cap known as "Übungsmütze" lost its importance within the SA. From January 1938 the regularly ordered dress for "Wehrsport" (see related section) was worn.

Otto Spronk

Cadre and students from a school wear the special uniform for schools or camps in olive–brown with the brown collar and SA rank insigne, as officially introduced in spring 1934. Note the wear of the so–called Übungsmütze, the mountain style cap with the continuous flaps and silver colored button. These caps were without any colored top, but occasionally had a crown piping due to rank and position. The two Sturmführer wear the two–colored red/white crown piping.

Otto Spronk

Another photograph of the permanent cadre and students from a school. The instructors wear the ordered insigne for the collar in the form of stripes upon a patch. Officially, this ranking insigne had to be worn on both collars, directly on the cloth and not upon an extra patch. In the front row, second from right, is standing a Zugführer flanked by two Gruppenführer while at far left is a Hilfsgruppenführer. It should be noted that the same form of uniform was also worn by persons at the Reich- or motor schools at the same time and later within the NSKK.

Otto Spronk

The Oberscharführer ranked individuals wear brown crown piping.

Otto Spronk

Note the second person from the left wearing his stripe correctly upon the collar.

A school student wears the Übungsanzug with the mountain cap headdress piped along the edge of the flap and the crown. In other photographs of the same person, it is observed that his tunic buttons are painted brown. Also note his leg wrappings.

This Zugführer is apparently from the Ausbildungswesen and assigned as an instructor placed at disposal (zur Verfügung gestellter Ausbilder). He wears the SA-Übungsmütze with only crown piping. Note the wear of the dagger which was an uncommon practice.

SA-Sturm Reichsfinanzschule

Special schools (Reichsfinanzschule (RFS)) were instituted in August 1935 for training personnel from the Reichsfinanzverwaltung (RFV - Reich Finance Administration) and from customs. Veteran customs personnel were grouped together at these schools within the SA-Sturm Reichsfinanzschule, and the younger personnel were grouped together in special Hitler Youth units. The first

T. Knight

Lower ranking SA members, assigned to the department for education, wear the regular form of SA cap. Due to their assignment, it is possible that a crimson cap top was worn, but due to their low rank of Scharführer, no crown piping was allowed. Higher ranked persons wore the crimson/silver crown piping. This regular form of headdress was worn with the walking–out dress, but with the school or camp dress, (the so–called Übungsmütze,) the mountain cap style of headdress, was ordered. Note the wear of the extremely rare cuff title with the lettering "Chef AW." This means that these persons are assigned to the Chef Ausbildungswesen (chief of education).

SA-Sturm was instituted for the RFS at Herrsching (in Oberbayern) in July 1936. The SA-Sturm for this school was assigned to SA Group Hochland. At least eleven schools were established between July 1936 and December 1941. During the attendance of classes, the wearing of a SA uniform and garrison cap with colored triangle was ordered. The color of the triangle was for the SA group in which the school was located. The existence of these schools is almost unknown, even in today's Germany.

W.P.B.R. Saris/BFA

The SA-Sturm for the Reichsfinanzschule at Ilmenau in Thüringen is photographed in 1936 during one of the first courses given. Note the wearing of the regular SA uniform and garrison cap with triangle and small, early national emblem. The uniforms remained school property. Front row, second from left: The school leader, Oberregierungsrat Rogge; to his left is Landesfinanzamtpräsident Dr. Hillmer and Stellenleiter Pilatschick.

W.P.B.R. Saris/BFA

Above: Reichsfinanzminister Graf Schwerin von Krosigk and school leader Rogge inspecting SA-Sturm Ilmenau, October 1, 1937. All members of the SA-Sturm are wearing the SA uniform with garrison cap. Other photos show that the old style national emblem was still being worn.

Right: Reichsfinanzminister Graf Schwerin von Krosigk during his visit to the RFS school at Ilmenau, and school leader Rogge on October 1, 1937. Oberregierungsrat Rogge is wearing the garrison cap with the old style national emblem.

A garrison cap with the final form of woven triangle positioned on the left side. No regulation was found ordering the wear of the garrison cap at camps or schools. But with the introduction of this form of headdress, the cap known as Übungsmütze lost its importance and while indoors at camp's or school's, this new form of cap was worn. The brownish–red backing of the triangle indicates that schools all over Germany utilized this same color. Otherwise a triangle in light blue would have been positioned. This cap is attributed by stamps to the SA–Group–School Hochland. The use of stamps, does not of course, guarantee originality. At RFS-schools this form of headdress was also worn, but with appropriate district triangles.

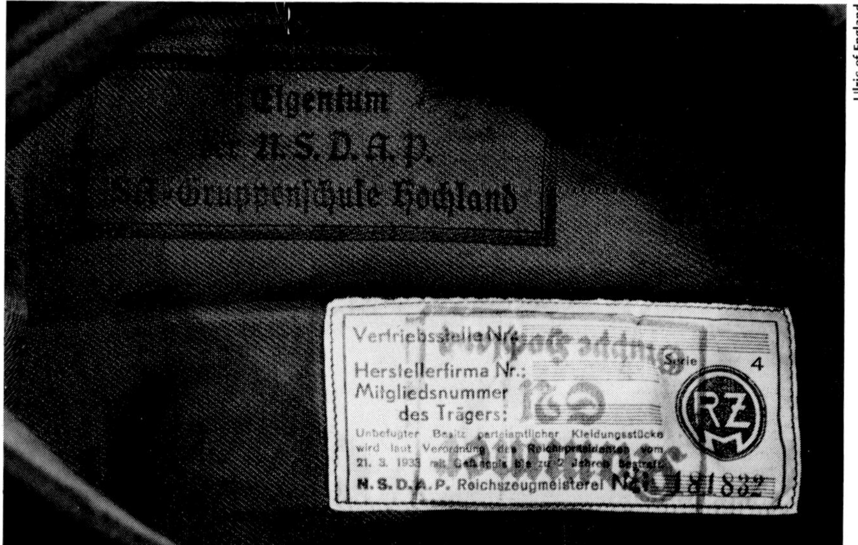

Ulric of England

The inside of the aforementioned garrison cap shows the RZM tag and two stamps, plus a size stamp. The upper stamp is of the same form as used in the earlier shown cap; the second stamp reads: "Kammer SA Gruppe Hochland." This means, (Stock–) room SA Group Hochland. Students were supplied with uniforms from existing stocks in the schools or camps.

Reich Schools for the Motor SA (Reichsschulen der Motor–SA)

During training or service at schools, the school leaders, teachers (in the ranks of Zug– and Gruppenführer), as well as administrative and domestic officials were also ordered to wear the "SA–Übungsanzug" in olive–brown and the above mentioned new style cap. No colored top was authorized, but piping forms were ordered, being:

Adolf de Crousaz

This photograph could easily be confusing as these are not students from a Motor–SA school, but students of the NSKK–Motorsportschule Pommern. The photograph was taken in April 1936 and the students and instructors are wearing the dress authorized in 1934 for use during driving instruction, being the Übungsanzug with the leather crash helmet. The occasion for this photograph was the visit of Hitler to Falkenburg during the official opening of the Ordensburg at Crössinsee. These students are lined up near the railway station in Falkenburg for inspection by Hitler, Hühnlein and other high ranked officials of the Party.

a) Leaders, teachers and assistants crimson/red or silver according to the regular SA regulations (note the earlier given ranks and piping positions);

b) Students: brown (as noted earlier, but it is known that caps existed with the crown piping only).[231]

During regular service or when wearing the walking–out dress the regular SA kepi with the colored top and/or piping according to rank within the OSAF were ordered for the leader of a school, the teachers and assistants; the students had to wear the regular SA uniform and headdress with the colored top according to their district of origin, when ordered or during arrival and departure.[232]

J.R. Angolia

Two instructors from the (motor) sport school at Hamm wear the special dress for schools. This photograph has some interesting details. According to the regulations, the Zugführer at right wears the brown collar patch. The Zugführer is ranked as a Truppführer. The collar patch with the A was officially allowed only for wear with the regular SA service dress. The person at left is a Gruppenführer, placed at the disposal of a school as an assistant instructor, "zur Verfügung gestelltes Ausbildungspersonal." As such, he is recognizable by the star directly positioned upon the collar tip. Another interesting fact is that both wear the cap piping incorrectly: A two–colored piping was never authorized for the flap edge.

Motor SA Schools for Groups (Motor–SA–Schulen der Gruppen)

Consult the orders for the Reich school, but one must note that the piping, as ordered for rank or the two–colored piping had to be worn as used by the district, where the school existed.[233]

---

231 *Ibid, pp. 70–71. Section XVI: Anzug auf den Reichs– und Gruppenschulen der Motor–SA, 1a and b.*

232 *Ibid, p. 71: 2a.*

233 *Ibid, pp. 71–72: 1a and 2.*

For driving duty the special brown dress, identified as "Sonderbekleidung," was ordered. In March 1934 it was ordered that with this dress the crash helmet, as regularly worn within the SA, had to be worn.[234] It is known that most often the earlier mentioned "SA–Übungsmütze" or the regular SA garrison caps were worn instead.

344. Betrifft: **Dienstanzug für Wehrsport.**
FD 2b Nr. 13704.

Der zum Reichsparteitag 1937 von der Obersten SA.-Führung für die NS.-Kampfspiele festgelegte Kampfsportanzug wird ab 1. Jan. 1938 der Reichszeugmeisterei mit der Bezeichnung

„Dienstanzug für Wehrsport"

zum Vertrieb freigegeben.

Der Dienstanzug für Wehrsport ist bei Wehrsportveranstaltungen anläßlich von Gruppen-, Brigaden-, Standarten-Sportveranstaltungen u. dergl. sowie bei Lehrgängen auf der Reichsführerschule, der Führerschule in Dresden und den Gruppenschulen zu tragen.

Das Auftreten im Dienstanzug für Wehrsport ist jedoch nur zulässig, wenn die Einheit geschlossen mit diesem Dienstanzug ausgerüstet ist:

Die Teile des Dienstanzuges für Wehrsport sind:

1. Mütze mit farbigem Band,
2. Wehrsport-Rock mit Armbinde,
3. Achselstück mit Lasche (nur auf rechter Schulter),
4. Kragenspiegel,
5. braunes Hemd mit festem Kragen aus Trikot und Binder,
6. Stiefelhose,
7. Schaftstiefel,

oder

6a Überfallhose,
7a Schnürschuhe,
8. Koppel mit Schulterriemen,
9. Dolch mit Dolchtragetasche.

Die Stiefelhose ist zum Marsch, die Überfallhose auf der Hindernisbahn zu tragen.

In den Einheiten werden zum Dienstanzug für Wehrsport Dienstgrad- und Dienststellungsabzeichen wie zum großen bezw. kleinen Dienstanzug angelegt. Für Schulen und Lager erfolgt jeweils Sonderregelung.

Ehrenzeichen und Orden, Plaketten usw. dürfen zum Dienstanzug für Wehrsport nicht getragen werden.

Beschaffungen haben bei der Reichszeugmeisterei a. d. D. über die Oberste SA.-Führung zu erfolgen.

The December 1937 order relating to the "service dress for sports." This order was also in force for all SA schools and orders the abolishment of the so–called "Übungsmütze." No other headdress was ordered and the regular SA cap with colored top was to be worn (see para. 1).

[234] *Ibid, p. 72: Sonderbekleidung.*

With the separation of the Motor–SA from the SA and the combining with NSKK in summer 1934 the uniforms for the above mentioned SA motor schools and Reich school for the Motor–SA were taken over by the NSKK schools (consult for a further development the related chapter NSKK in the coming volume IV).

"Defence" Sports (Wehrsport)

At the Reichsparteitag in 1937 during matches and contests, the standard SA coffee can cap in the heavier fabric was worn with the ordered "sports" battledress (Kampfsportanzug). This dress form delighted the SA high command so much that it was introduced in December 1937 and was designated as the service dress for "Wehrsport." As such, it became official on January 1, 1938. The regular SA kepi with the colored top was standard with this sports dress. This form of dress was ordered to be worn during official SA sporting events from districts (and lower ranked units events through "Standarten–Sportveranstaltungen,") courses at district schools or the Reich leaders school. The "Wehrsport" tunic, was not allowed for wear during regular SA service. The normal piping systems were used.[235] It is believed that this dress was not available until sometime before 1939 and was then used by the members of the SA–Wehrmannschaften.

Otto Spronk

SA members during sports exercises are wearing the garrison cap with the smaller eagle emblem. It is known that during the Party Day Rally in 1937, the coffee can cap was the regular form of headdress during these exercises and was later officially ordered as such.

A. Stam

Members of the SA from Mönchen-Gladbach wear the SA cap on the belt during "Wehrsport." The photograph is dated as late as July 1937, since the final pattern, large eagle emblem is being worn.

W.P.B.R. Saris

SA members wear the SA cap during the "SA–Wehrkampftage" at the stadium in Nürnberg in 1942. During these events, it was ordered from January 1938 that this form of headdress had to be worn in place of the garrison cap.

---

235 "Vbl.d.OSAF, Nr. 16, December 16, 1937, p. 132. Nr. 344: Dienstanzug für Wehrsport (order FO 2b Nr. 13704, indicated that this form of dress was only available through RZM sources, in agreement with the SA High Command).

Military Defense Training Groups (SA–Wehrmannschaften) 1939 – 1945

With a decree, dated January 19, 1939[236] Hitler charged the SA with the responsibility for pre– and post military training. The "Wehrmannschaften" (SA–W, or SA–JW– "SA–Jungwehrmannschaften," existing for younger SA members),[237] originally were units by which an SA member (but also persons from other organizations) could obtain the SA sports badge. The basis for these units were the earlier created "SA–Wehrsportgruppen." From early 1939 it included SA members who were suitable for this service and had been relieved from active military service.[238] Operational plans were still in preparation in late August 1939.

SA–Wehrmann in his service dress as published in the "Organisationsbuch der NSDAP" on plate 37.

W.P.B.R. Saris

The SA monogram cockade.

Gerhard Rudloff

The SA–Wehrmannschaft forage cap in wear.

236 Volz."Daten der Geschichte der NSDAP" 11.Auflage. Berlin/Leipzig: 1943, p. 121; "Vbl.d.OSAF," Nr. 5, April 1, 1939. On the front–page Hitler's order referring to the orders, dated February 15, 1935 and March 18, 1937 for obtaining the SA sports insigne was published. He renamed the sports badge the "SA–Wehrabzeichen." For this purpose units had to be raised from soldiers from the Armed Forces "on furlough" These units were called "Wehrmannschaften."

Otto Spronk

A member of an SA–Wehrmannschaft during exercises wears his forage cap. Note that the triangle on this cap is *not* positioned between the angle, but upon the flap on the left side.

With the beginning of the war, more training programs were started to control homeguard anti–aircraft (Heimatflak) units, auxiliary urban police (Stadtwacht), and auxiliary rural police (Landwacht). The "SA–W" acted to reinforce the civilian or state security forces, such as the Luftschutz–Warndienst and customs–VGAD. One must note that these "SA–W" did not only exist within the regular SA, but also within the Marine–SA and the NSKK.[239] They cooperated closely with the army, navy and air force during the later stages of the war.

In 1941 many units were trained into "Wehrschützenbereitschaften" (prepared readiness groups) for the protection of Steiermark, Sudetenland and the General Government of Poland and were as such, in April 1942 renamed "SA–Wehrbereitschaften," which was a continuation of the earlier "SA–W."[240]

The introduction of a new uniform was planned for July 1939, but it was not approved until August. It took until December 1939 before the uniform for SA–Wehrmannschaften was officially instituted. Due to the beginning of the war and associated manufacturing problems, it did not become standard until the spring of 1941.[241] Most often the uniform for "Wehrsport" introduced in 1938 was worn with the regular SA garrison cap.

The December 1939 regulations specified the color as olive–green (material as used for the greatcoat, (SA–Manteltuch III)[242] and its form was copied from the "Wehrsport" dress, since it proved to be a functional design. Simultaneously a new form of headdress (identified as the "Käppi," neue Form) was designed and introduced to give the uniform a distinctive appearance.

---

237 "Vbl.d.OSAF," Nr. 9, August 8, 1939. p. 61. Nr. 103: SA–Wehrabzeichen–Gemeinschaften (order FK.1 16000/83 mentions the SA–Jungwehrmannschaften).

238 "Das Gesicht der Partei." München: 1940, p. 18.

239 "Uniformen–Markt," Nr. 16, August 15, 1939, p. 243.

240 Volz."Daten der Geschichte der NSDAP" 11.Auflage. Berlin/Leipzig: 1943, p. 132.

241 "Schwert u.Spaten," Nr. 3, March 1941, p. 38.

242 "Uniformen–Markt," Nr. 11, June 1, 1940, p. 86.

A forage cap as worn by members of the SA–Wehrmannschaft from late 1939. The triangle indicates that the owner was from the Hochland or Bayerische Ostmark district.

The forage cap in the "Schiffchen" style was copied from an Italian form with a front turn up and side flaps (indicated as "herunterklappbaren Ohrenschutz") extending over the cap top (the right one closing over the left), which were meant to fold down over the wearer's ears during cold weather situations and in the cold mountain areas. This cap was probably developed in early 1932 and was then meant to be worn experimentally by some special SA units. The SA chief of staff, Röhm, however did not approve it, and the cap design was put away for many years.

The ordered insigne was positioned at the left side of the flap and was in the same style as for the regular SA garrison cap, a white woven national emblem on a triangle of the district color. It was placed between the front turn up and the extending flap, approximately 6mm beneath the "crown" seam. On the center of the front turn the SA monogram cockade (as used by the Marine–SA) had to be positioned. This aluminum cockade with a black fluted base had a red felt center under the monogram (it must be noted that this cockade form was at no time authorized to be worn with the SA kepi).

At left, a drawing of the SA symbol which was originally the idea of Hans Zöberlein and Obersturmbannführer Max Zankl of Munich. This symbol was without the hook bar which was added to the final SA symbol. It is often thought that the SA symbol was an early 1920's device, but it was, in fact, not designed earlier than 1929.

It may be of interest to know that the SA symbol was designed in 1929, as the result of a contest sponsored by the OSAF. The idea for this symbol and its further development came from Standartenführer Hans Zöberlein, the German poet. He designed it together with the later leader of Sturmbann II Obersturmbannführer Max Zankl (from the Standarte "List").[243] The symbol was the old

It was not earlier than December 1939 that the uniform regulations for the SA–Wehrmannschaften were published in the *Vbl.d.OSAF.* One should note paragraph I.1, which specified the color of the tunic and buttons and I.4, which specifies the new form of headdress called the "Käppi" in olive–green. Paragraph 4.d gives specific details for wearing the insigne on the left side of the forage cap upon a colored backing in the group color. Additionally, its position is specified as well as the SA monogram cockade and the wear of piping. The claim that the triangle backing should always be black was not stated in any document and it is doubtful. The underlined word indicates that the group color was ordered.

W.P.B.R. Saris

123. Betrifft: Dienstanzug der SA.-Wehrmannschaften.
FO 2 b Nr. 13 704.

Die SA.-Wehrmannschaften tragen folgenden Dienstanzug:

I.

1. Rock; Schnitt ähnlich dem SA.-Wehrsportrock.
Abknöpfbare Kragenbinde,
am linken Oberarm Hakenkreuzbinde,
Knöpfe einheitlich silber,
Material: olivgrünes SA.-Manteltuch III.
2. Überfallhose, für Reiter-Stiefelhose,
Material wie vor.
3. Koppel, dunkelbraun, ohne Schulterriemen,
Koppelschloß aus Leichtmetall, alu-farben.
4. Mütze (Käppi), olivgrün, neue Form.
5. Schnürschuhe, schwarz.
Form und Qualität nach Wehrmachtsvorschrift.

4. Sonderabzeichen:

d) Abzeichen auf der Mütze:
Auf der linken Seite der Mütze befindet sich das, für die bisherige Lagermütze vorgeschriebene Hoheitsabzeichen auf Dreiecksunterlage in Gruppenfarbe gewebt. Das Abzeichen ist zwischen Schild- und Kappenrand, 6 mm unterhalb der Rundnaht anzubringen. In der Mitte des vorderen Aufschlages ist die SA.-Kokarde (wie für Marine-SA.-Dienstmütze) angebracht.
Ab Dienstgrad Sturmführer ist an der oberen Rundnaht der Mütze eine silberfarbene Schnur anzubringen.
Die Mütze ist mit einem herunterklappbaren Ohrenschutz versehen.

Teutonic sign for lightning together with the so–called "Mannrune" (the symbol of a stern and unbending man with a flaming sword). Both symbols were combined with a ring, to combine both ideas into one insigne. Shortly thereafter both symbols were connected to each other by the hook bar of the "A."

The ranks Sturmführer and above had to wear the same form of headdress, but the crown seam was supplied with a silver (aluminum) piping.[244] If a golden piping was worn, it would have to been no later than May 1941, since at that time all gold piping had to be replaced by aluminum or silver ones for the ranks of Oberführer through Obergruppenführer. A two–colored piping was not included in the regulations and was never officially authorized.

The uniform and headdress was ordered exclusively for SA–W leaders from a "Schar" up through "Sturm" and the regular ranked members, indicated as "Wehrmann." Plans for higher ranked staff leaders did not yet exist. The first

---

243 "Uniformen–Markt," Nr. 6, May 1, 1936, p. 86.

244 "Vbl.d.OSAF," Nr. 10, December 29, 1939, pp. 68–70. Nr. 123: Dienstanzug der SA–Wehrmannschaften (order FO 2b Nr. 13704). Section I: Nr. 1. mentions the color; Nr. 4. the new form cap. Section II: Nr. 4d mentions the ordered insigne and position.

Another SAW forage cap, but this one has the Alpenland colored triangle, being in red–brown. The original owner was from the 2nd Sturm of Standarte 59 of the Gebirgsjäger from the Salzburg area. This example shows the stitched–through edges on the flaps and the line of the flap at the back.

manufacturing regulations for the uniforms of these staff functionaries were published in March 1940.

The first forage caps for enlisted ranks and lower ranked leaders were probably delivered not earlier than spring 1940. Further supply was carried out slowly in stages and intended then for wear by higher ranks as well. No photograph has been found showing the wear of this cap by SA–W leaders. It is certain that mountain areas were supplied first. Photographs from late 1940 most often show the training of SA–Wehrmannschaft groups in various districts in regular civil cloth.[245] During the war this cap was most often replaced by the less distinctive,

Members of the SA–Wehrmannschaft from Metz, photographed in September 1944, wearing the SAW forage cap. Metz was probably located in the Oberrhein district. For this reason, the colored backing of the triangle should be cornflower–blue.

245 "Die SA." Zeitschrift der Sturmabteilungen der NSDAP. Nr. 45. November 29, 1940, p. 18; Ibid, Nr. 46. December 6, 1940: article about the SA–Wehrmannschaften at Munich. A very limited group, existing of enlisted ranks only, wore the ordered uniform.

high topped pattern mountain cap (see for detailed information also the section for ski and mountain caps).

Cap in the form often worn by members of the SA-Wehrmannschaften during the war (this example has gold piping and button). The triangular national emblem is in cornflower-blue for the Warthe district, as well as for Oberrhein. In both cases the crown piping, as well as the button color, should be silvered or aluminum. Warthe was instituted on March 9, 1940 and Oberrhein on March 31, 1941. According to established procedures Oberrhein should have received authorization for gold piping and button. But an official publication, dated May 20, 1941, ordered the button to be silver. In a simultaneously published order concerning the simplification of insignia and uniform parts, all gold itmes were, in fact, abolished. To distinguish between Warthe and Oberrhein, however, the latter was authorized to wear yellow or "gold"-colored, celleon piping around the collar (depending on rank). It is possible that the manufacturer of this cap misunderstood the confusing orders, or that he had not seen the last mentioned order, as it had not yet been released to the press.

SA at Hitler's Headquarters (SA im Führerhauptquartier) 1939 – 1945

From the beginning of the war in 1939, a very limited group of SA men, mainly staff leaders, were seconded to Hitler's headquarters for special duty.[246] Another small group of SA leaders was seconded for duties in combat areas (SA–Führer im Operationsgebiet).

With a decree, dated November 9, 1939 a field–grey uniform, known as SA–Feldgrau, was introduced. The uniform was granted and only allowed for wearing by special permission of the OSAF. It was the same style as that worn by members of the Waffen–SS, with influences from political uniforms. Not much evidence has been found, but it has been observed in period photographs that a field–grey visored cap with three white pipings was worn. The cap band was probably black (or even dark green). A black chin strap rested on most occasions above the visor. A white, aluminum second pattern army wreath was worn on the front center of the cap band with the metal SA monogram cockade

246 *"Verfügung der OSAF," F.Nr. 13704. November 9, 1939.*

W.P.B.R. Saris

Verordnungsblatt
der Obersten SA-Führung

10. Jahrgang — München, den 5. Oktober 1940 — Nummer 5

49. Betrifft: Änderungsanzeige der RZM. Nr. 4/40.

Nr.	Artikel	RM.
Neuzugänge:		
1080/18	Führermütze, feldgrau, mit Mützenkordel, Hoheitsadler und Kokarde	6.65
31082	Feldmütze, Tuch, mit Abzeichen und Kokarde, zum Wehrmannsanzug	3.90

The issue of the *Vbl.d.OSAF* in which number 1080/18 introduced the "Führermütze" in field–grey, simultaneously with the previously introduced forage cap for SAW members. Note the masthead of the *Vbl.d.OSAF*.

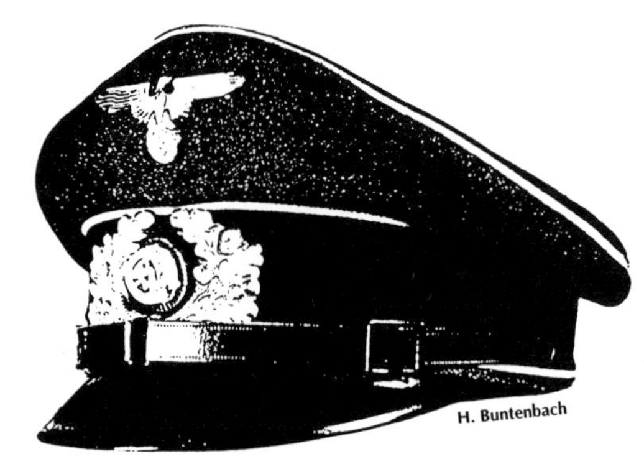

An example of the so–called "Führermütze" worn by the SA assigned to Hitler's headquarters. In November 1939, a field–grey uniform, known as SA–Feldgrau, was introduced.

in its middle. An SS national emblem was worn on the front center of the cap top, as were other eagle patterns.

It was thought that no cap cords were worn (not even by higher ranked persons), but in an official RZM price list from 1940 this visored cap was briefly mentioned. Information on the cap was also published in the "Verordnungsblatt der OSAF" in late 1940. It was described as a new entry with article number 1080/18: "Führermütze, feldgrau mit Mützenkordel, Hoheitsadler und Kokarde."[247] The field–grey SA uniform was still mentioned in later years.[248]

It has often been said that SA–Obergruppenführer Wilhelm Brückner was noted for his fondness in wearing non–regulation uniforms, but for a while (be-

SA–Obergruppenführer Wilhelm Brückner, Hitler's SA adjutant, wears the uniform in SA–Feldgrau as authorized in late 1939 for those persons assigned to Hitler's headquarters. Note the Waffen–SS style cap with bright piping, but with an army wreath and cockade. Above the black visor, rests the enlisted ranks chin strap. Also note the army style sleeve eagle, probably upon a crimson backing. The uniform in SA–Feldgrau was also worn for a short period by those who served in combat areas. In March 1940 this uniform was abolished for the latter. Therefore, it must be considered as the rarest of SA–uniforms.

A visored cap in the form authorized by the SA-Führerhauptquartier. It is without insignia and manufactured by Peter Küpper of Wuppertal-Rensdorf (RZM contract A1/1073).

247 *"Vbl.d.OSAF," Nr. 5, October 5, 1940, p. 22. Nr. 49: Änderungsanzeige der RZM Nr. 4/40.*

248 *"Mbl.d.RZM," Nr. 6, April 18, 1942, p. 28.*

An SA–Sturmführer probably assigned to the "Operationsgebiet" combat area. He is wearing the officer's old style field cap as used in the army, and his standard SA tunic with one shoulder board on his left shoulder.

tween late 1939 and mid–1940) he wore the above ordered field–grey uniform when he was assigned to the "Führerhauptquartier."

SA leaders assigned to combat areas wore this uniform in varying shades, while serving in those areas. After serious deliberation, SA–Stabschef Viktor Lutze, approved the wear of the field–grey instead of the regular SA brown, since brown was too visible and dangerous to wear at the Russian front.[249]

Officially the wearing of the field–grey uniform in combat areas was abolished by Hitler in March 1940,[250] and the wearing of it was restricted to his headquarters only. The field–grey SA uniform must be considered as one of the rarest forms of SA clothing.

---

249 In a book about General Andrei Wlassow, it stated: "I (Fröhlich, a liaison officer on the Wlassow staff) protested wearing brown, as this color was hated by the Russians. Imagine that I solely wore this brown between all the others who wore field–grey. I would have been the first to be shot by partisans. After long consideration Viktor Lutze, the SA chief of staff, gave me permission to wear the SA–Feldgrau. This color was worn in Germany by an extremely limited group of persons. During the entire war I only have seen one person wearing such a uniform. I wore dark–brown collar tabs and my visored cap did not have a death head insigne, but the regular national cockade with the SA monogram. No one knew what kind of uniform I was wearing. I wore the national emblem upon my arm and so it was thought that I held a very high Party–office." This statement by Fröhlich (who wore this uniform) indicates how rare the SA field–grey uniform was (from the book "General Wlassow," Russen und Deutsche Zwischen Hitler und Stalin. Köln: 1967 by Sergej Fröhlich).

250 Letter from the leader of the SA district Hansa at Hamburg, dated March 21, 1940, The order by Obergruppenführer Jüttner (Chef des Hauptamtes Führung) with regards to the wearing of field–grey and the OSAF order, dated March 11, 1940, were mentioned in this letter.

W.P.B.R. Saris

SA der N S D A P

Hamburg, den 21. März 1940

Der Führer der Gruppe Hansa

Abt.: F G.-

V e r t e i l e r : 3

Nr. 34

Betr.: Tragen der feldgrauen SA-Uniform.

Bezug: OSAF v.11.3.40.
F Nr., 13 704

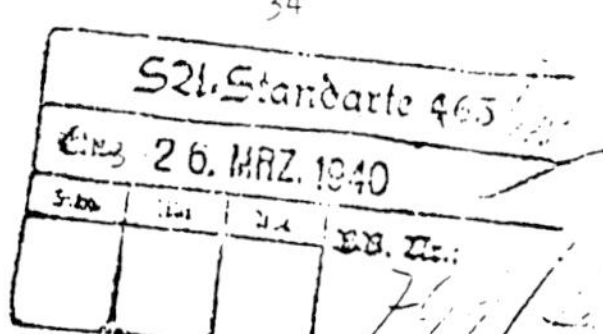

Gemäss einer Entscheidung des Führers bleibt künftig das Tragen der mit Verfügung F Nr. 13704 v. 9.11.39, Verteiler III/103, eingeführten feldgrauen SA-Uniform auf SA-Männer (Sammelbegriff) des Führer-Hauptquartiers beschränkt. Die Bestimmung gemäss Verfügung F Nr. 13 704 vom 9.11.39, dasz SA-Führer, die im Operationsgebiet tätig sind, die Genehmigung zum Tragen der feldgrauen SA-Uniform erhalten können, wird hiermit aufgehoben. Die bisher erteilten Genehmigungen werden von der Obersten SA-Führung in diesem Sinne überprüft. In Fällen, die den neuen Bestimmungen nicht mehr entsprechen, wird der bereits ausgehändigte Ausweis von der Obersten SA-Führung durch schriftliche Aufforderung eingezogen.

Es wird nochmals ausdrücklich darauf aufmerksam gemacht, dasz zum Tragen der feldgrauen SA-Uniform nur der von der Obersten SA-Führung ausgestellte Ausweis berechtigt. Die Anträge hierzu sind über die vorgesetzte Dienststelle bei der Obersten SA-Führung einzureichen. Die Dienststellen werden ermächtigt, Anträge, die den neuen Bestimmungen nicht entsprechen, unter Bezugnahme auf diese Verfügung abzulehnen.

Der Chef des Hauptamtes Führung.
gez.Jüttner
Obergruppenführer.

F.d.R.d.A.

Halting

Obersturmbannführer.

A copy of a letter giving the date of introduction of November 9, 1939 for the SA field–grey uniform and the discontinuance of its use by those serving in combat areas by an order of March 1940. The original document was issued by Obergruppenführer Jüttner, the chief of the "Hauptamt Führung."

Reinforced Border Surveillance (VGAD – Verstärkter Grenzaufsichtsdienst) 1938 – 1940

The SA-Division 6 from the Danzig area, led by Brigadeführer Hacker, started on June 20, 1939 preparing a unit to protect and patrol their borders.[251] This unit was known as the "SA–Grenzschutz"[252] During their first actions regular SA uniforms were worn. Later field–grey uniforms were worn. These uniforms were supplied by the German Army, who had ordered stocks to be kept since 1938, to be used also by VGAD–units.

Simultaneously another group was formed for use in border control, and titled as VGAD (the VGAD was in fact formed by the customs authorities). In September 1939, the Danzig VGAD group was incorporated within the "Danziger Landespolizei." The SA members, assigned to this unit, wore a mixture of regular SA uniforms. A "special" uniform was planned and it is noted that various tailors in Danzig started to manufacture it. With the SA dress the VGAD members wore a garrison cap, with on the front center of the lower part a standard cockade and on the front center of the top, a Danzig coat of arms. This coat of arms was from early October replaced by a national emblem.

W.P.B.R. Saris

A member of the VGAD from Danzig wearing a tunic (probably of the Wehrsport style) and cap, both of which are probably field-grey. The cap has the Danzig cockade on the lower front and the Danzig coat of arms on the upper front. Note the SA-monogram on the right collar patch, which is dark wine-red as used by members of the Ostland district in which Danzig was located. He is wearing an army pattern belt buckle and a SS style cuffband with the inscription "Grenzwache."

It is a misunderstanding that VGAD units were not raised earlier than August 1939. The first of these units was raised in March 1938 for the protection of the Austrian borders. In the same year, units were raised on the borders of the Sudetenland, Luxembourg, France, the "Südmährische" areas and the Saarland. Before the start of the war, VGAD units were raised during March 1939 for the Reichsprotektorat Böhmen u. Mähren. (Information supplied by Oberregierungsrat Dr. Walter Eulitz, the former adjutant of the Generalinspekteur des Zollgrenzschutzes Dr. Hossfeld.)

W.P.B.R. Saris

VGAD members from Danzig during the funeral of Johann Rusch (August 29, 1939), a comrade who was killed. They wear the special uniform with SA-monogram collar patch and "Grenzwache" cuffband. Note the cockade and coat of arms on the caps, and the flap piping worn by the Sturmführer. Note the Deutschland Erwache Standard "Weichsel" which had been consecrated before 1936.

In 1939 VGAD units were essentially created for use on all German borders to even include the Swiss. From May 1940 these "Landesschützen–Ersatzbataillonen" also patrolled along the borders with Italy. SA personnel, assigned to this VGAD, were identified as "Hilfsgrenzangestellten" (Higa) and most often wore the SA uniforms of their regions (being the mountain uniform and headdress), the standard SA garrison cap or the uniform as meant for the SA–Wehrmannschaften. Later the VGAD was purely concerned with customs.

Within the VGAD also existed the often mentioned "Küstenschutz" from Danzig, raised in August 1939 from Marine–SA members and customs personnel.

---

251 *"Die SA." Zeitschrift der Sturmabteilungen der NSDAP, Nr. 45, November 29, 1940, p. 18.*

252 *Volz."Daten der Geschichte der NSDAP" 11.Auflage. Berlin/Leipzig: 1943, p. 131.*

W.P.B.R. Saris

Grossadmiral Raeder and personnel from the Danzig "Küstenschutz." Raeder congratulates Marine-SA Sturmhauptführer Marckwardt from Marine-Sturmbann III/90 (Danzig) upon receiving his Iron Cross 2nd Class. Many Marine-SA members from Danzig served in the "Küstenschutz."

SA Flying Units (SA–Fliegerstürme)

See for detailed information Volume II: chapter 3, Air Organizations of Germany, section National Socialist Groups: Fliegerstürme der SA, pp.160–161, as well as NSFK pp.165–166.

The 1931 Nationalsoz.Fliegerkorps, was assigned to the SA high command, its "Korpsführer" was Standartenführer Günther Ziegler, who also was appointed as the inspector of these flying units. Hermann Göring was the NSFK president and this "union" was meant as a master organization for NS flying units from SA or SS.[253]

National Archives

Members of a SA Fliegersturm lined up during the awarding of a decoration. Note the distance between the two ventilation holes on the cap at far left, but also the excellent view of the crown and flap piping of the SA leader at right. Karl Ernst is at far right.

A notice from the "Verordnungsblatt der OSAF" must be mentioned. During inspections in mid–1933 it was established that during service SA members wore the visored cap as ordered for the "DLV Flieger–Ersatzstürme" (consult Volume II, pp.156–157) together with standard SA uniforms. This was of course forbidden. The wearing of an SA uniform with DLV service was allowed, but on such an occasion the standard SA headdress had to be worn.[254]

Foreign SA Groups (Auslandsorganisation der SA der NSDAP)

Not much evidence was found during this research pertaining to the cap top colors as worn by SA members in foreign countries. Authorized persons may have worn a (red–) brown color, like that worn by the Austrian SA. This is concluded from old orders of 1929 which stated that the leader of the Austrian SA, commander Reschny, wore the above color while commanding the Austrian, as well as the foreign units from Spain, Paraguay, Bolivia, Bohemia, Southwest Africa and Sweden.[255]

As stated in an unknown magazine of 1933: "...The SA outside the German Reich wear the uniform as authorized for the "Reichsdeutsche." Those belonging to special land groups are marked by the colors of the continent (Erdteilfarben)." Probably these colors conformed to the piping colors used on the crown of the Hitler Youth visored caps, which were introduced for wear in the summer of 1933 and ordered since 1934, being:

Europe (excluding Germany and Austria):	red
America:	yellow
Asia:	green
Africa:	blue
Australia:	white.[256]

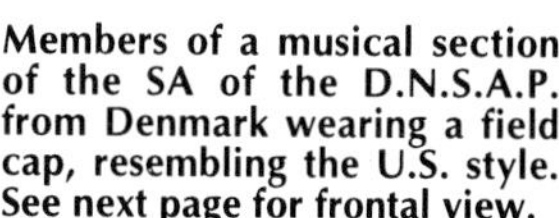
Members of a musical section of the SA of the D.N.S.A.P. from Denmark wearing a field cap, resembling the U.S. style. See next page for frontal view.

[253] "Vbl.d.OSAF," Nr. 5, November 30, 1931, Front page: NSFK with directives for creating this "union."

[254] Ibid, Nr. 14. August 1, 1933, p. 2 Nr. 7: Dienstanzug der Flieger–Ersatzstürme.

[255] Special order for the SA march at Nürnberg. August 4, 1929.

[256] "Uniformen der HJ, Vorschrift und Vorbild." Hamburg: 1934, Preface by Gebietsführer Willi–Botho Bicker, the leader of Department I of the RJF. Berlin: March 1, 1934,

Bendt Nielsen

In this chapter on SA we discussed the German organization. Likewise in various countries groups were formed, as for example in the Netherlands or Denmark. These groups did not adopt the typical SA coffee can cap, but utilized totally divergent forms. The Dutch NSNAP/SA wore visored caps with a light brown top and black cap band (consult the chapter: Pol.Leiter der NSDAP in this volume). Above the black visor rested a black chin strap. The crown was either piped with a two–color system (resembling the German SA style), silver or gold. Higher ranks wore an additional two–colored cord around the upper edge of the cap band.[257] Upon the front center of the band the NSNAP badge was worn.

In other countries field or forage caps were worn, but as these did not resemble the German styles we will not pursue the subject and would direct you to the series on "Foreign Legions of the Third Reich" by Mr. David Littlejohn and published by R.James Bender Publishing.

Note: All documentation, regulations, orders and other information used in the footnotes in this volume are in the possession of W.P.B.R. Saris. His efforts, especially on the RAZ, were of great importance.

257 *"Dienstvoorschrift voor de S.A. der N.S.N.AP. " Chef van den Staf (Afd.1.Nr. 14/33). The Hague: November 10, 1933, pp. 17–19 gives detailed information regarding ranks and systems for wear.*

Erik Rundkvist

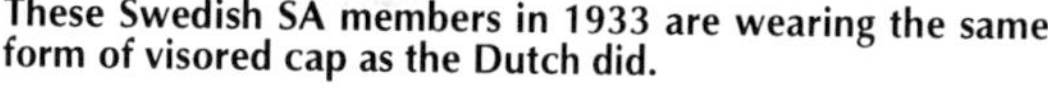

These Swedish SA members in 1933 are wearing the same form of visored cap as the Dutch did.

A member of the SA of the Danish D.N.S.A.P. wearing a dark topped visored cap with insignia.

David Littlejohn

Klaus D. Patzwall/B. Diroll

Members of the "Einsatz Mohrenberg" in Jugoslavia, 1941, which was a "Deutsche Volksgruppe" in the Banat and Batschka areas. Note the wear of the SA-style uniform with field cap.

Color Addendum

During the preparation of this book many collectors have requested that the various colors, especially those for the SA kepi top, be explained and printed in color. The best approach would be an accurate color chart from the period, but it has been determined that those available are not accurate in their tones. What has been done was to consult an *Amann* color chart to get as close as possible to the original tones. It should be noted that charts from the 1930 to 1945 time frame listed over 1,000 colors...today, this listing is just over 300.

Some of the old colors of the SA no longer exist and are no longer available on today's color charts. And even reproducing an old color chart does not insure accuracy due to discoloration caused by time and light. It should be noted that in approximately May 1935 the Reichszeugmeisterei made available their own official color chart to manufacturers who produced items for NSDAP organizations. But would the availability of such a color chart have given us the solution to our color questions?

We wish to stress that the colors from old and new charts will never match because of the lapse in time. The *Pantone* printers' ink company always supplies a warning with its *Color Formula Guide* which is used by printers when doing production work in color. They state that due to uncontrollable pigment fading, varnish discoloration, and paper aging (this also pertains to cloth materials), the colors in their guide will change tones in approximately one or two years. These color changes are more prominent in lighter colors. It is, therefore suggested that their guides and books with color plates be replaced regularly to maintain accurate color communication.

In various pre-1945 produced books, color plates showing uniforms, collar patches, etc., were illustrated, but in many cases the printed colors were not accurate or did not match the actual worn items. And to further complicate the situation, often the varying shades of the actual items worn were of different shades. One of the problems for this was in the manufacturing standards and procedures in place at that time. Not that there were many different manufacturers of the SA kepi tops or related piping...there were only a few. But not every "color or dye lot" was exactly the same as the one before. Normally, from a distance these slight variations were not noticeable, but in examining the material closely the differences were quite evident. It should be noted that a varying shade of 10% was allowed according to RZM specifications, resulting in a slight shade difference in practically all the colors used. This is combined with the fact that the photos supplied to us of headgear were not always photographed with the same exposure or under similar lighting conditions. Changes in color of the actual item can vary based on the use of artificial or natural light, what film was used, or in the development of the film. Also, one must consider the natural fading of a color which can take place after 60 years since original production.

One color which caused us many problems in the development of this addendum is the so-called "karmesin," which is translated as crimson. During our years of research we have observed that the color "red" (includes bright red, dark wine-red, carmine, pinkish-red and red-brown) has numerous variations. Pink is sometimes a soft pink, but occasionally is close to the color lilac with more blue, which may be confused with crimson. The Alpenland red-brown occasionally tends to be more red or closer to "Zinnoberrot," which was used by the Ausbildungswesen. Similar problems occur with the shades of green.

From research it has been concluded that two tones of crimson existed. One was used until 1934 and the second from 1934 to the end of the war. The first crimson was darker. With the introduction of colors for the SA in July 1933, and specifically dark wine-red which was to be worn by enlisted ranks, the similar OSAF color was discontinued shortly thereafter. This similarity was probably the reason another color shade was chosen, which would consequently be named as crimson (SA-Karmesin Nr. 4). This color leans more towards pink with a bluish-violett tone. The dark wine-red color was also changed shortly thereafter, now being more red.

It is interesting to note that upon close examination of cap colors by color experts, in a number of cases they cannot agree on the original designated color. This is due to the fading of the color from exposure to light, and to the type of cloth used...all resulting in tone variations to the original color. Original color charts used during these examinations created additional problems in identification. These charts, which were for artificial materials, silk, cotton or wool, and one for the so-called "Spiegeltuch," the material used for collar patches, piping and SA caps, had several variations of tones illustrated for the same color.

The piping colors for NSDAP political leaders and Werkscharen corresponded with SA colors. Note that one can immediately determine if the visored cap for political leaders from a Gauleitung is an early or late form. Bright red piping was worn until 1939 and should *never* have an oakleaf wreath positioned on the cap band. The dark wine-red piping was introduced in 1939. The Werkschar field caps should have a bright red piping, and *never* dark wine-red.

By early 1935 the final SA colors were more or less established, but the RZM standards of a shade variation of 10% was still permitted even to the end of the war. To show the extent of some variances the following samples are illustrated: (1) The second crimson color as used by the OSAF; (2) The apple-green color for Pommern and Thüringen; (3) Blue-grey for Sudetenland and Weichsel.

(1) (2) (3)

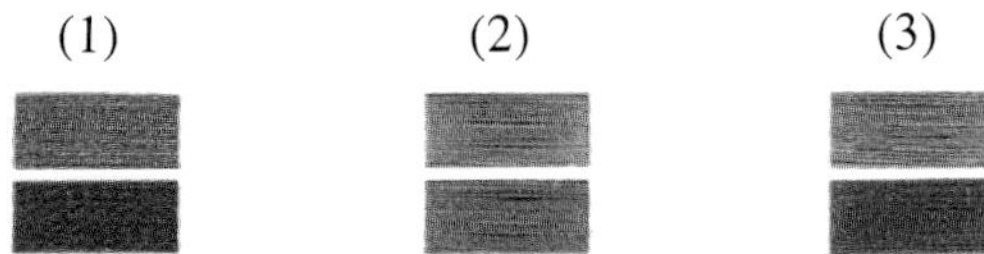

We have detailed the above color problems to explain the difficulties in determining exact coloring, and the numerous factors which create them. In presenting to you our findings, we must thank two sources for their active participation in explaining colors. We are most grateful to Mrs. Dirkse and Mr. Schöppner, as well as Amann in Amersfoort, Netherlands. It was with their help that we were able to construct a color chart which is close to the colors at the time of cap manufacture. Also, it was through the extensive negotiations of Wim Saris upon his contact with *Amann* and other color experts that this chart has been constructed. The illustrated colors are from the *Amann* chart for silk (Farbkarte Nr. 1 für Nähseide) which was quoted by the RZM in describing the colors used by the SA, NSDAP, political leaders and Werkschar on their headgear. It should be noted, however, that these will vary from actual worn colors and from other period color charts.

In this section we have duplicated the photos used previously in this volume, but in concentrated color for instant comparison. With the printing of this section we are also subject to all of the above problems listed, and will result in slight shade variances from our original reference works. But we believe that what we are presenting is the most accurate color representation done to date, and sincerely hope that it helps in identifying the color of your valued collectible.

Roger James Bender

Adolf Hitler

An early Hitler visored cap with heavy gold cord piping around the crown and white piping on the top and bottom of the cap band. The national emblem is silver wire, hand-embroidered on tan. The top is tan, the cap band is medium brown and the visor is dark-brown. The manufacturer was Holters of Berlin. (Credit: George Petersen)

Front view of the early Hitler visored cap.

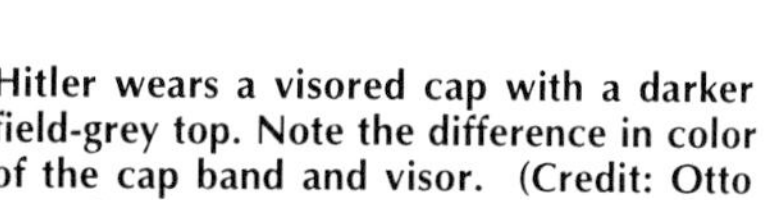

Hitler wears another form of visored cap. Note the gold color of the crown piping and insignia (eagle, wreath and cap cords), the regular national cockade, and the white piping of the cap band. Also note the reddish-brown cap band and the Havanna-brown visor. (Credit: Otto Spronk)

Hitler wears a visored cap with a darker field-grey top. Note the difference in color of the cap band and visor. (Credit: Otto Spronk)

NSDAP

A sample of the early "Hitlermütze" (Model 1923). The flaps have two small buttons and a national cockade is positioned on the front top. (Credit: Ulric of England)

Political Leaders

An early 1934-form visored cap for political leaders on Ortsgruppe-level. Note the top and cap band are of the same color material according to regulations. The 1934-form eagle is used, as well as the 1935 cockade with swastika and back-plate. The gold cords indicate Ortsgruppenleiter, and from 1935 were also worn by Stützpunktleiter. (Credit: John Coy)

An early Gau-level visored cap with red piping, rust-brown velvet cap band and early form national emblem. The gold cords indicate Gauleiter, but were also allowed for wear by his deputy. (Credit: Ulric of England)

A Model-1934 visored cap, piped in black for Kreis-level. Only the Kreisleiter was permitted to wear gold cords. (Credit: Ulric of England)

A Model-1936 visored cap with light blue piping and the 1934-form national emblem. Note that the cap band should be of the same material as the top. The cords are in silver. (Credit: John Coy)

An example of the Model-1936 (Form III) visored cap for Gauleitung (note the silver cap cords and national emblem) as worn by "Mitarbeiter" rank through "Hauptamtsleiter." (Credit: Len Champion)

A Model-1937 visored cap for Kreisleitung-level (black piping). Note the detail of the silver 1936 national emblem. This eagle faces to its right and was available in early 1936. On this level, only the Kreisleiter wore gold cords. (Credit: R. Bender)

A visored cap, as worn by political leaders on Reichsleitung-level. Note the brown velvet cap band and silver cords. A army national emblem is worn instead of the political leader's eagle. Silver cords were worn by the ranks "Mitarbeiter" through "Hauptstellenleiter." (Credit: Ed Stadnicki)

This form IV visored cap has the wreath embroidered directly onto the cap band. The piping is dark wine-red and used on Gauleitung-level. (Credit: John Coy)

A visored cap in the so-called "Tellermütze"-style with dark wine-red piping for Gauleitung-level. Note that the cap crown is lower than the Form IV. (Credit: Ron Kwan)

A Model-1939 (Form IV) visored cap with wreath in metal. The cap is piped in red for Gauleitung-level. (Credit: Ron Manion)

A 1939-form visored cap for Gau-level. The wreath is hand embroidered directly onto the velvet cap band; the gold eagle is the metal form. (Credit: Ulric of England)

A Model-1939, Kreisleitung-level visored cap with the gold wire wreath embroidered onto a separate piece of backed velvet and then sewn to the cap band. (Credit: Ulric of England)

A Kreisleitung-level visored cap with metal wreath. (Credit: W. Saris)

A Reichsleitung-level visored cap with yellow (Schwefelgelb) piping and metal wreath. The cords are of celleon material. (Credit: Ron Kwan)

A Model-1939, Reichsleitung-level visored cap in the "Klappmütze"-style. Note the ventilation grommets on the underside of the cap top. (Credit: John Coy)

A Reichsleitung-level visored cap with metal insignia. (Credit: Ulric of England)

Above: A visored cap for Reichsleitung in the form known as Wehrmachtschnitt IV. Note the wreath is embroidered directly onto the band and the light colored celleon cords. (Credit: Richard de Filippi)

Left: A golden-yellow piped visored cap with non-detachable white top. (Credit: Ulric of England)

A Model-1939, white top visored cap with cap band piped in black, indicating Kreis-level. Due to the new 1939 regulations, however, this was now to be in white. (Credit: Ulric of England)

The white top visored cap for Reich-level. The band is piped properly with gold piping, the top is correctly piped in white. (Credit: Ulric of England)

A field cap for political leaders on Gau-level. The flap and crown are piped. The swastika cockade is positioned on the front center of the flaps. (Credit: Ed Stadnicki)

A rare example of a visored cap, probably worn by officials of a court. The cap is piped in dark blue and the cap cords are woven alternating shades of light and dark gold. No regulations have been found which mention this alternating color. The regulations state "prescribed as for other political leaders." Normally, the cap band was in light brown velvet from the summer of 1935, but was then also worn by other Gau and Kreis court members. (Credit: Ulric of England)

Another court visored cap, but here with a velvet band. (Credit: Robert Velsir)

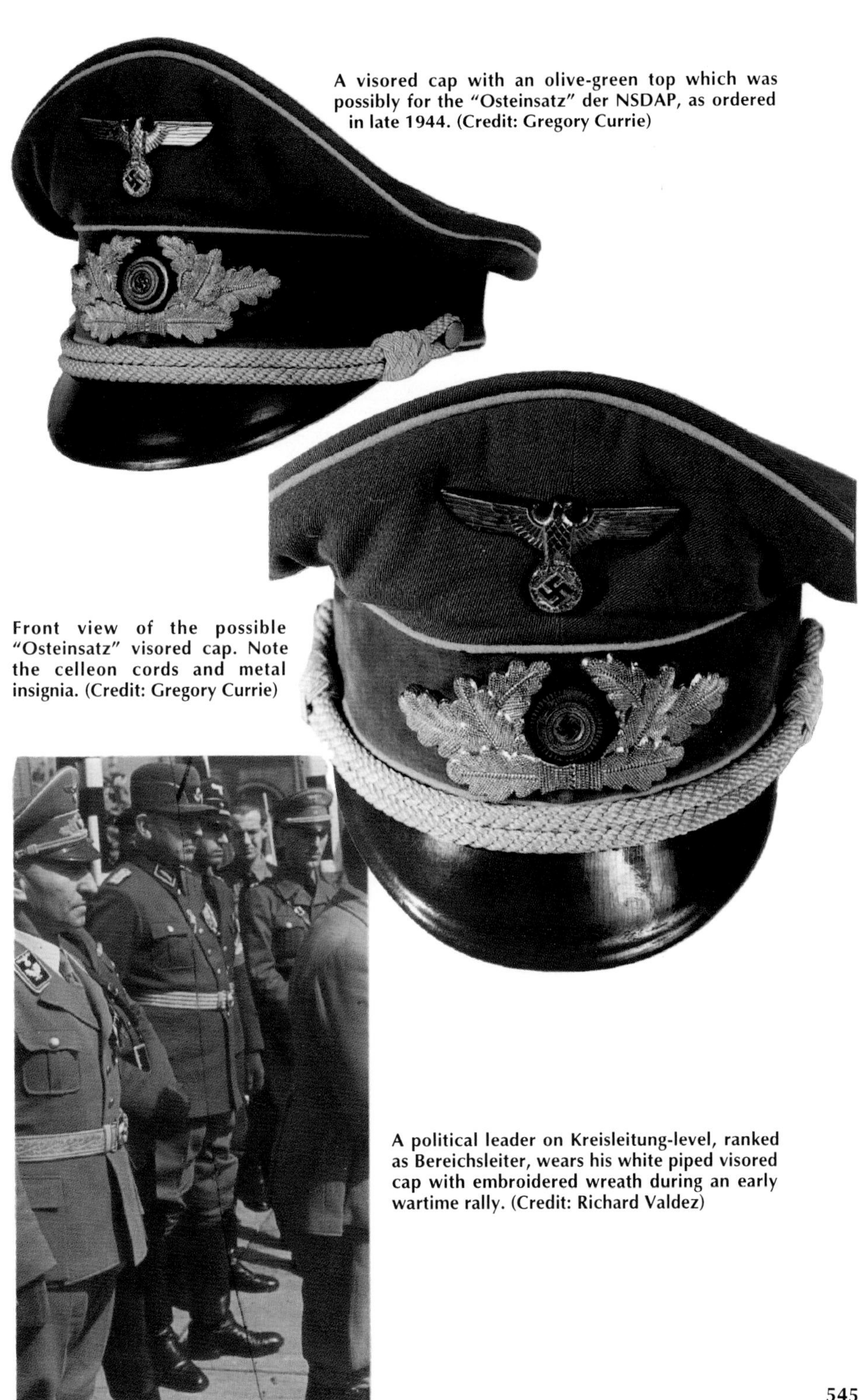

A visored cap with an olive-green top which was possibly for the "Osteinsatz" der NSDAP, as ordered in late 1944. (Credit: Gregory Currie)

Front view of the possible "Osteinsatz" visored cap. Note the celleon cords and metal insignia. (Credit: Gregory Currie)

A political leader on Kreisleitung-level, ranked as Bereichsleiter, wears his white piped visored cap with embroidered wreath during an early wartime rally. (Credit: Richard Valdez)

The field cap worn during courses at an Ordensburg. In the center of the flap's front is an embossed, silvered eagle-button; the machine-woven eagle faces to its right and is on a brown backing. (Credit: J.R. Angolia)

DAF

The DAF "Festival Cap." Note the oval cap insignia with gold colored swastika/cogwheel and oakleaf branches within the gold anodized outer ring; the visor with muslin edging, and the cap band with oakleaf pattern. (Credit: Len Champion)

A 1937-form field cap with improper piping and national emblem. The red and silver piping was never authorized. The national emblem is also incorrect as this version looks to its right. Werkschar field caps should have, officially, only a left-looking national emblem. (Credit: David Littlejohn)

A Werkschar Model-1937 field cap with gilt piping around the flap and crown, two gilt buttons, plus a silver national emblem looking to its left. (Credit: Jill Halcomb Smith)

A Model-1938 visored cap with silver metal insignia and silver cap cords. With metal insignia, officially, a leather chin strap should be worn. Note that the cap band is not ribbed and the oakleaves are of a somewhat larger and varying pattern. (Credit: Jill Halcomb Smith)

Illustrated are several examples of KdF cap tallies. For additional information see pages 244-251.

Summary of SA-Group Colors

	TOP/TRIANGLE COLOR	BUTTON COLOR		
Stabschef (Chief of Staff)	bright red	g		
Stab der OSAF (OSAF Staff)	crimson	s		
Gruppenstab	bright red	s		
Ostland (Tannenberg)	dark wine-red	g		
Westfalen	dark wine-red	s		
Niederrhein	black	g		
Berlin-Brandenburg	black	s		
Ostmark (Oder)	pinkish-red	g		
Südmark	pinkish-red	s		
Pommern	apple-green	g		
Thüringen	apple-green	s		
Westmark (Mittelrhein)	dark brown	s		*a
Niedersachsen	dark brown	g		
Sachsen	emerald-green	s		
Nordmark	emerald-green	g		
Mitte (Elbe)	orange-yellow	g		
Südwest (Neckar)	orange-yellow	s		
Schlesien	sulphur-yellow	s		
Franken	sulphur-yellow	g		
Hochland	light blue	s		*b
Bayer. Ostmark (Bayernwald)	light blue	g		
Nordsee	steel-green	g		
Kurpfalz	steel-green	s		
Hansa	navy-blue	g		*c
Hessen	navy-blue	s		
Donau	red-brown	g		
Alpenland	red-brown	s		
Sudeten	blue-grey	g		
Weichsel	blue-grey	s		
Warthe	cornflower-blue	s		
Oberrhein	cornflower-blue	g		
Generalgouvernement	light grey	s		

Summary of Special SA-Unit Colors

	TOP/TRIANGLE COLOR	BUTTON COLOR		
Ehrenhalber (Until 1934)	silver-grey	s or g		
Feldjägerkorps	white	g		
Führer ausser Dienst (Until 1934)	silver-grey	s or g		
Hilfswerk Nordwest (Until 1938)	red-brown	s		
Reichsautozug "Deutschland"	crimson	s		
Reichsführerschule (Note: Staff–bright red)	crimson	s		
Reichsnachrichtenschule	crimson	s		
Reichssanitätsschule	crimson	s		
Reichsschulen	crimson	s		
Sanitätsführer (Until 1934)	violett	g		
SA-Reserve II (Until 1935)	silver-grey	s or g		*d
Verwaltungsführer (Until 1934)	(bright) blue	s		
Wachstandarte (Felderrnhalle)	crimson	s		

Notes:

*a: In later years a somewhat darker shade was probably used.

*b: The grey tone disappeared and a somewhat brighter light blue tone was used.

*c: It is practically certain the navy-blue color was of a slightly lighter shade.

*d: The official color was lighter, in fact it was the grey later used by the Generalgouvernement. Surviving caps have a darker silver-grey.

In July 1939, new systems were introduced which included some changes to the wearing of silver or gold piping, according to the button color. The two-colored piping was now abolished.

The ranks of Sturmführer through Sturmhauptführer now wore a 3mm crown piping; the ranks of Sturmbannführer and Obersturmbannführer wore a 3mm crown and flap piping; and the rank Standartenführer wore a 3mm crown and flap piping and a 1cm Tresse (those who were not yet promoted as Standartenführer, but led a Standarte sized unit, were allowed to wear the

Tresse also); the ranks Oberführer and Brigadeführer wore both pipings and a 1.5cm Tresse; the ranks Gruppenführer and Obergruppenführer as above, but with the 2.0cm Tresse.

S.A.-Mützen (Text auf Seite 68)
**)

Chef des Stabes:

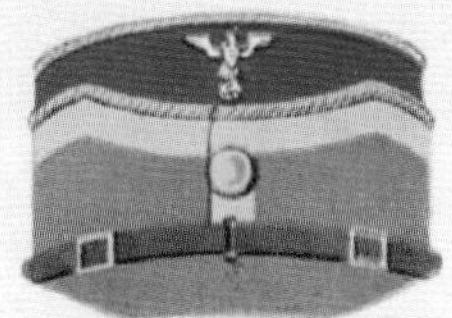

Hochrotes Mützenband, Goldschnur um Mützendeckel und Mützenaufschlag sowie eine 2 cm breite Goldtresse auf dem Mützenaufschlag

Links:

Obergruppenführer und Gruppenführer:

Hochrotes, bei der Obersten S.A.-Führung karmesinrotes Mützenband, Silberschnur um Mützendeckel und Mützenaufschlag sowie eine 2 cm breite Silbertresse. Letztere nur dann, wenn sie eine S.A.-Einheit tatsächlich führen oder Abteilungschefs der Obersten S.A.-Führung sind.

Rechts:

Brigadeführer:

Mützenband in Farbe der Spiegel*), Silber- oder Goldschnur, je nach Farbe der Knöpfe, um Mützendeckel. Zweifarbenschnur der Gruppe um Mützenaufschlag und 1½ cm breite Tresse in Knopffarbe, wenn sie eine Brigade tatsächlich führen.

Links:

Standartenführer:

Mützenband in Farbe der Spiegel*), Silber- oder Goldschnur, je nach Farbe der Knöpfe, um Mützendeckel. Zweifarbenschnur der Gruppe um Mützenaufschlag und 1 cm breite Tresse in Knopffarbe, jedoch nur, wenn sie die Standarte führen

Rechts:

Obersturmbannführer und Sturmbannführer:

Mützenband in Farbe der Spiegel*) und Silber- oder Goldschnur, je nach Farbe der Knöpfe, um den Mützendeckel.

Links:

Sturmhauptführer bis einschl. Sturmführer:

Mützenband in Farbe der Spiegel*) und Zweifarbenschnur der Gruppe um d. Mützendeckel

Rechts:

Vom Obertruppführer einschl. abwärts:

Mützenband in Farbe der Spiegel*)

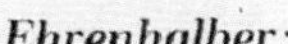

Ehrenhalber:

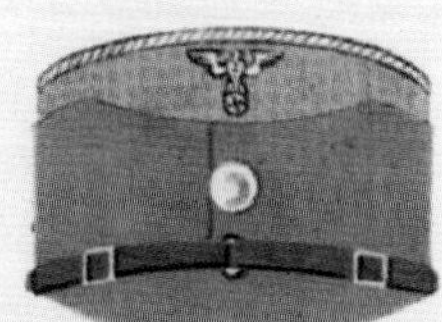

Mützenband aus silbergrauem Samt: im übrigen Schnüre usw. gemäß dem verliehenen Dienstgrad (hier Obersturmbannführer bzw. Sturmbannführer).

*) Hier Gruppe Berlin-Brandenburg (schwarze Spiegel und silberne Knöpfe)

**) Tressen um den oberen Rand des Mützenaufschlages tragen nur Führer von S.A.-Einheiten und Abteilungschefs der Obersten S.A.-Führung, und zwar: Führer von Standarten eine 1 cm breite, Führer von Brigaden eine 1½ cm breite, Führer von Gruppen, Obergruppen und Abteilungschefs der Obersten S.A.-Führung eine 2 cm breite Tresse. Ebenso der Chef des Stabes. Die Tresse bezeichnet keinen Dienstgrad, sondern daß der Betreffende eine S.A.-Einheit führt.

Plate 1

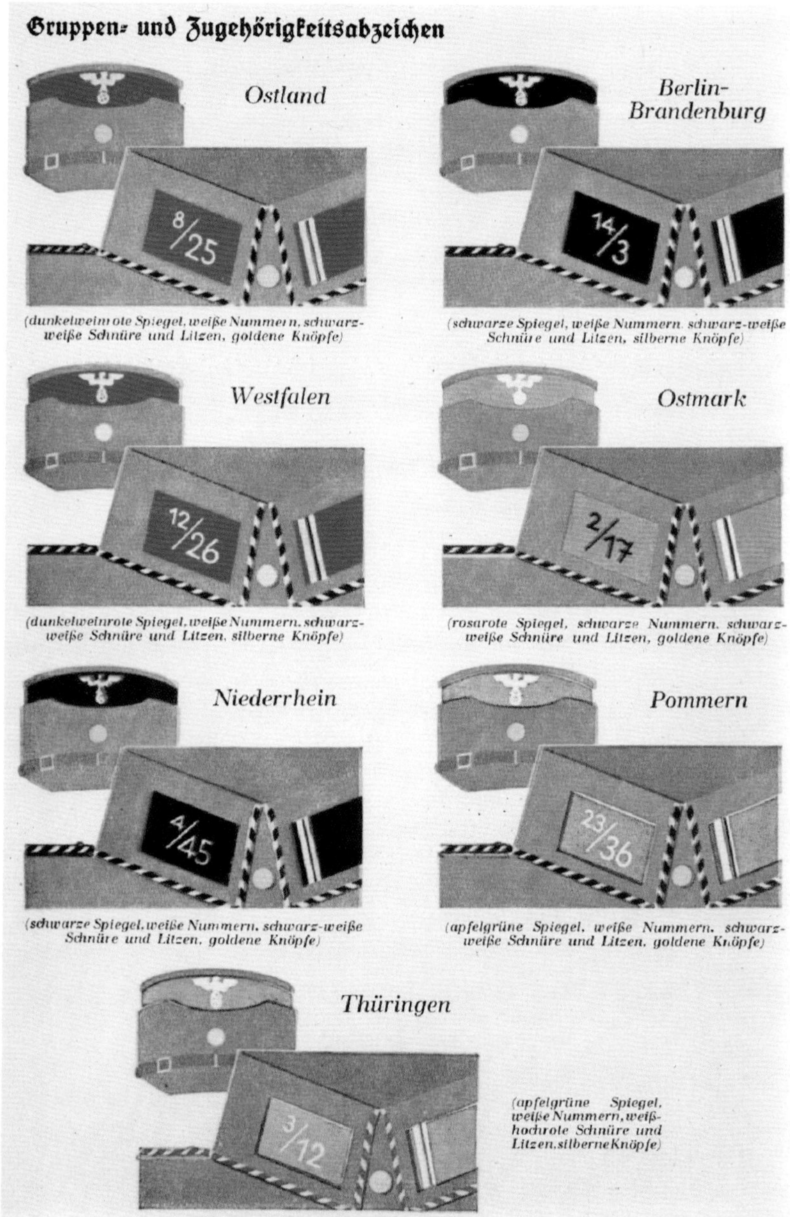

Gruppen- und Zugehörigkeitsabzeichen

Ostland

8/25

(dunkelweinrote Spiegel, weiße Nummern, schwarz-weiße Schnüre und Litzen, goldene Knöpfe)

Berlin-Brandenburg

14/3

(schwarze Spiegel, weiße Nummern, schwarz-weiße Schnüre und Litzen, silberne Knöpfe)

Westfalen

12/26

(dunkelweinrote Spiegel, weiße Nummern, schwarz-weiße Schnüre und Litzen, silberne Knöpfe)

Ostmark

2/17

(rosarote Spiegel, schwarze Nummern, schwarz-weiße Schnüre und Litzen, goldene Knöpfe)

Niederrhein

4/45

(schwarze Spiegel, weiße Nummern, schwarz-weiße Schnüre und Litzen, goldene Knöpfe)

Pommern

23/36

(apfelgrüne Spiegel, weiße Nummern, schwarz-weiße Schnüre und Litzen, goldene Knöpfe)

Thüringen

3/12

(apfelgrüne Spiegel, weiße Nummern, weiß-hochrote Schnüre und Litzen, silberne Knöpfe)

Four color plates from the well-known 1934 issue of von Eelking's "Die Uniformen der Braunhemden." Some of the colors shown are approximate colors, but others have a totally different shade. For example, the color for Ostland/Westfalen, which is close to the color used later by various Austrian groups. On plate 4 the first version of the crimson color is used. Note

Plate 2

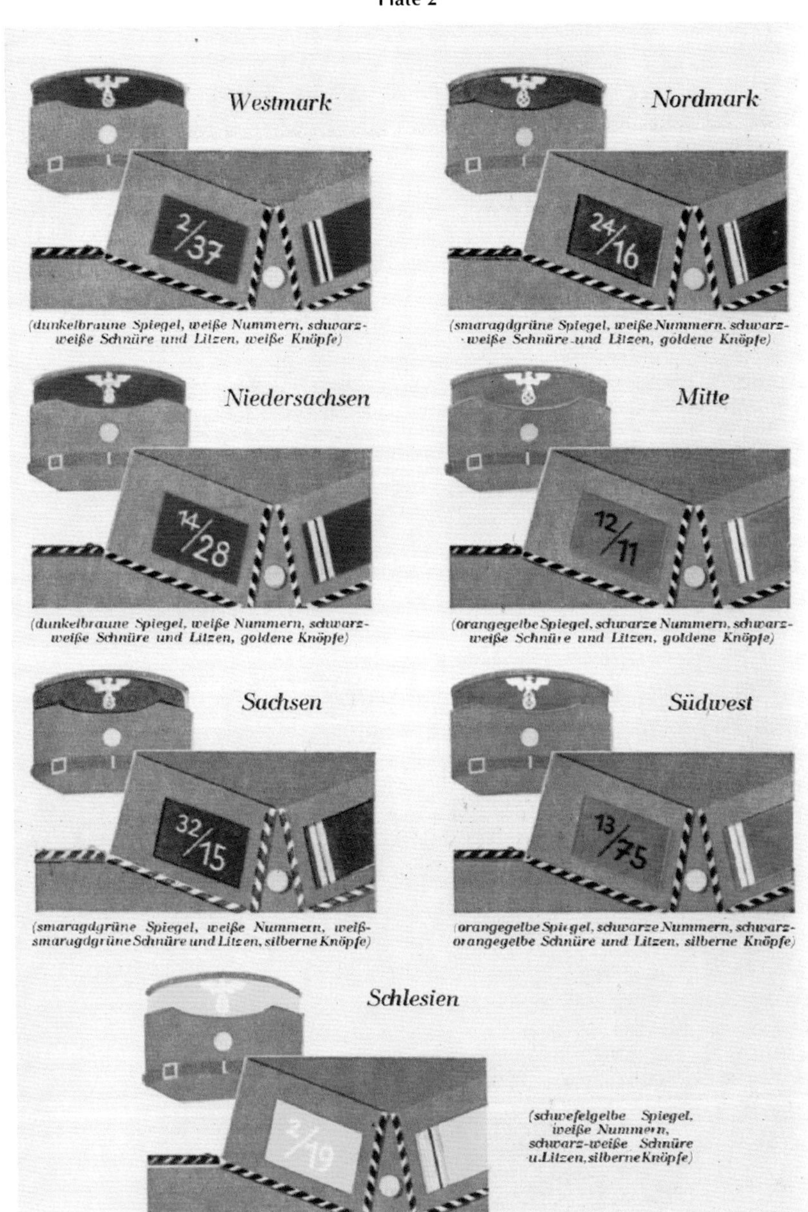

also that on plate 3 the group from Austria (Österreich) is shown, having the steel-green top. This color was changed shortly after the publication of this book in the summer of 1934 when Austrian members, living in Germany due to the NSDAP/SA ban in their homeland, were grouped into Hilfswerk Nordwest which wore the reddish-brown top. (Credit: W. Saris)

Plate 3

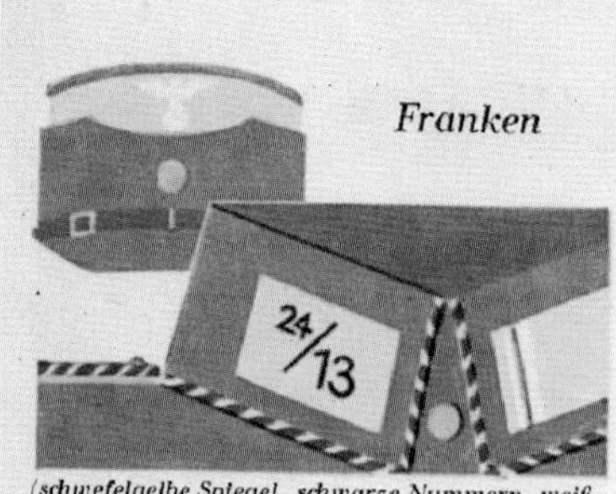

(schwefelgelbe Spiegel, schwarze Nummern, weiß-blaue Schnüre und Litzen, goldene Knöpfe)

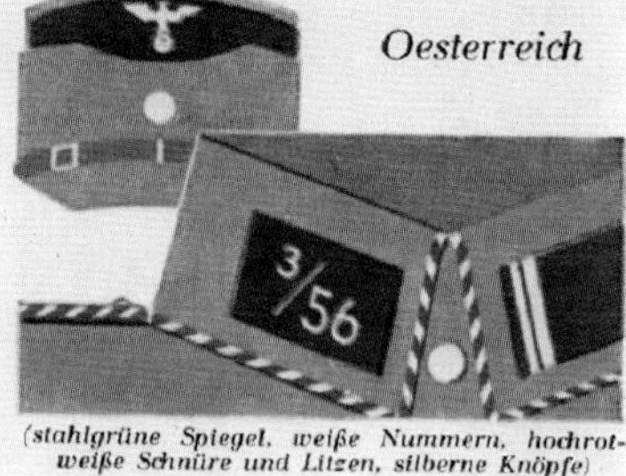

(stahlgrüne Spiegel, weiße Nummern, hochrot-weiße Schnüre und Litzen, silberne Knöpfe)

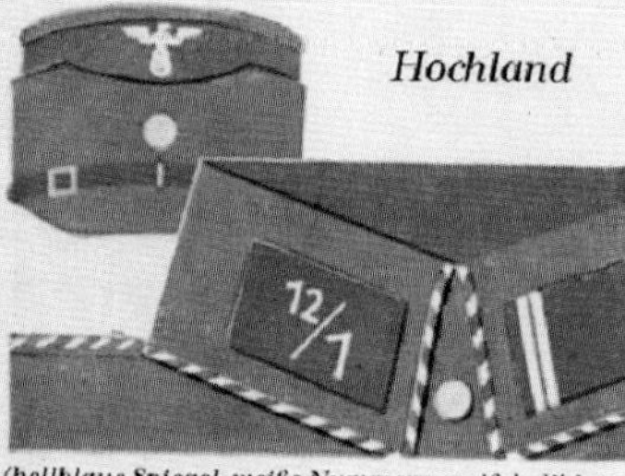

(hellblaue Spiegel, weiße Nummern, weiß-hellblaue Schnüre und Litzen, silberne Knöpfe)

(stahlgrüne Spiegel, weiße Nummern, schwarz-weiße Schnüre und Litzen, goldene Knöpfe)

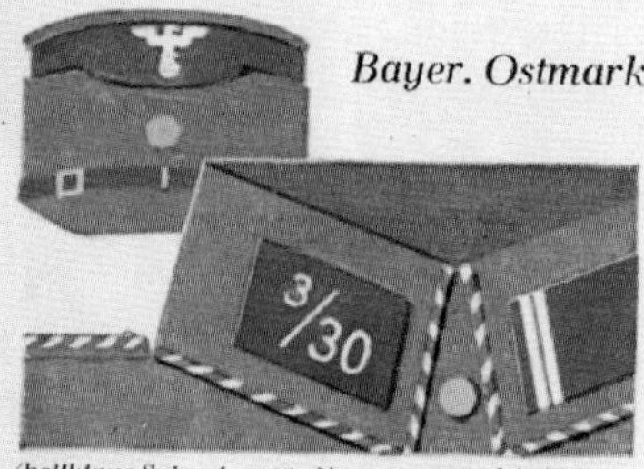

(hellblaue Spiegel, weiße Nummern, weiß-hellblaue Schnüre und Litzen, goldene Knöpfe)

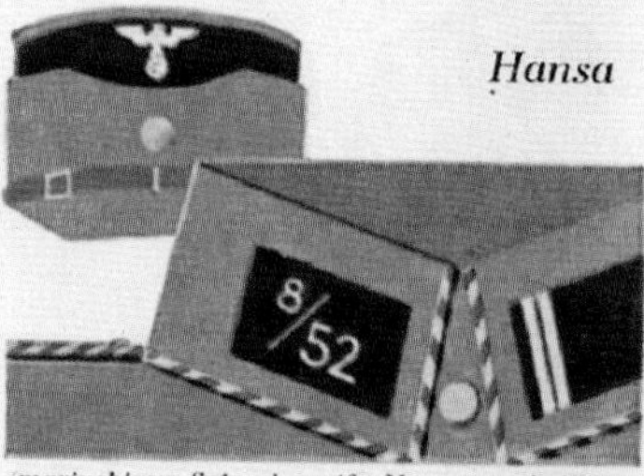

(marineblaue Spiegel, weiße Nummern, hellblau-schwefelgelbe Schnüre und Litzen, goldene Knöpfe)

(marineblaue Spiegel, weiße Nummern, hellblau-hochrote Schnüre und Litzen, silberne Knöpfe)

Plate 4

Chef des Stabes

(hochrote Spiegel, goldene Schnüre und Knöpfe)

Stab der Obersten S.A.-Führung, Chef des Kraftfahrwesens, des Ausbildungswesens, General-Inspekteur, Reichsführerschule

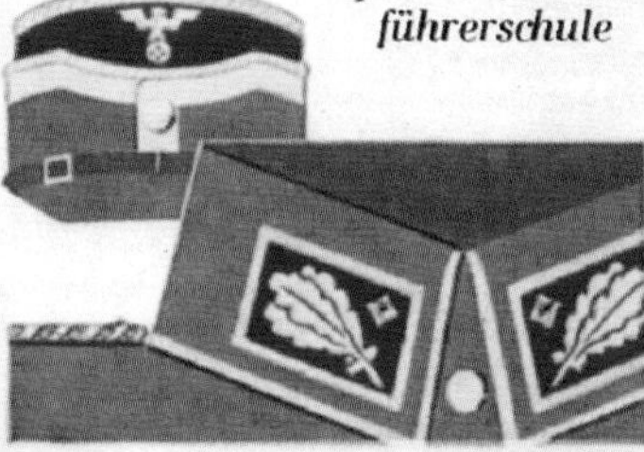

(karmesinrote Spiegel, karmesin-goldene [v. Obertruppführer einschl. abwärts karmesin-orangegelbe] Schnüre und Litzen, goldene [Gruppenführer und Obergruppenführer silberne] Knöpfe) *)

Obergruppenstäbe und Gruppenstäbe

(hochrote Spiegel, hochrot-silberne, vom Obertruppführer einschl. abwärts hochrot-weiße Schnüre und Litzen, silberne Knöpfe) *)

S.A.-Sanitätsführer

(violette Samtspiegel; bis einschl. San.-Sturmhauptführer violette, ab San.-Sturmbannführer goldene Schnüre; gelb-violette Litzen, gold. Knöpfe u. Dienstgradabzeichen, Mützenkopf in Gruppenfarbe) *)

S.A.-Verwaltungsführer

(hellblaue Samtspiegel; bis einschl. Sturmhauptführer blaue, ab Sturmbannführer silberne Schnüre; weiß-blaue Litzen, silberne Knöpfe und Dienstgradabzeichen, Mützenkopf in Gruppenfarbe) *)

*) bezüglich genauer Dienstgradabzeichen siehe die Tafeln auf S. 20/21

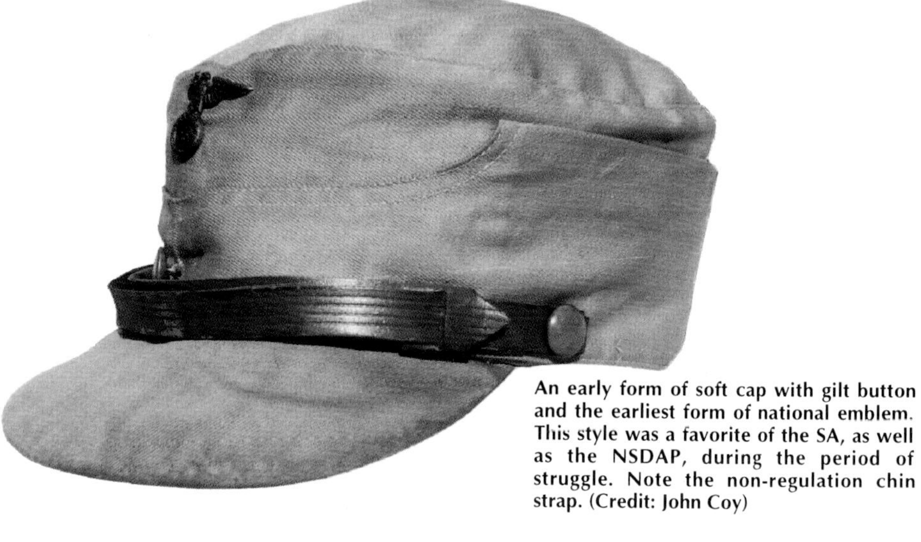

An early form of soft cap with gilt button and the earliest form of national emblem. This style was a favorite of the SA, as well as the NSDAP, during the period of struggle. Note the non-regulation chin strap. (Credit: John Coy)

Early SA cap with gilt button to be worn with the Greater Service Dress until July 1933 with early national emblem—which should be positioned higher on the front of the top. Note the rare tapering of the flap, and that no grommets or colored top are incorporated. (Credit: John Coy)

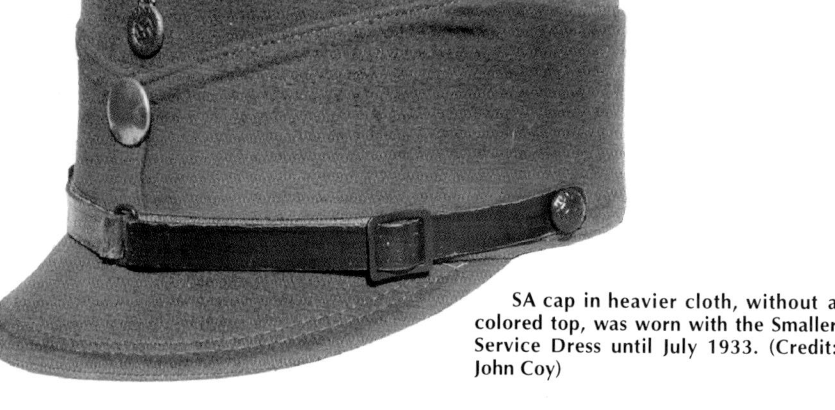

SA cap in heavier cloth, without a colored top, was worn with the Smaller Service Dress until July 1933. (Credit: John Coy)

This visored cap is thought to have been experimental and worn during the years 1932 through 1934 by smaller units such as the NSKK and Berlin-Brandenburg. (Credit: Ed Stadnicki)

SA "Dienstmütze" in the cloth for the Greater Service Dress with silver button and dark wine-red top, which indicates the SA group of Westfalen. A gold button would indicate the SA group Ostland. The grommets match the color of the top. (Credit: Philippe Gillain)

Another SA cap for Westfalen, but in the heavier cloth for the Smaller Service dress. The final form national emblem is worn on the cap. Note: The first color grommets were used with this cap. (Credit: Niall Malcolm)

SA cap for the Berlin-Brandenburg district with a black top and silver button. Note the black/white piping around the edge of the flaps. Officially, this piping should be installed at the crown. When a silver piping was installed at the crown, the position of the black/white piping would have been correct. (Credit: H.v. Diggelen)

SA district Berlin-Brandenburg cap with the earliest form of national emblem. The top is black and the button is silver. The chin strap is fastened by brown buttons. Niederrhein had the black top with gold button. (Credit: John Coy)

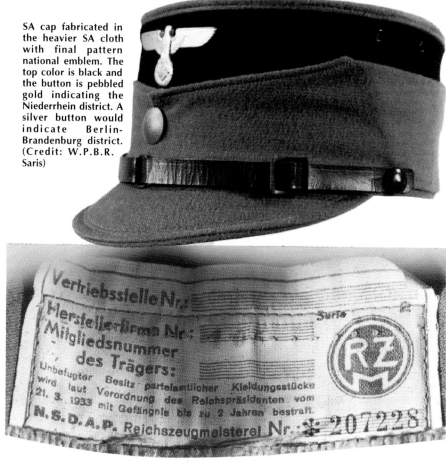

SA cap fabricated in the heavier SA cloth with final pattern national emblem. The top color is black and the button is pebbled gold indicating the Niederrhein district. A silver button would indicate Berlin-Brandenburg district. (Credit: W.P.B.R. Saris)

The RZM label positioned on the inside of the above SA cap. This form of tag was officially forbidden in January 1935, but was still being illustrated in the RZM magazine in 1936. (Credit: W.P.B.R. Saris)

This SA cap with black top has silver crown piping indicating that it was worn by someone with the rank of Sturmbannführer or Obersturmbannführer (from 1933 until 1938). This piping could be worn in silver or gold depending on the button color. Note the 1937 eagle emblem is positioned on this specimen, which indicates that this cap was actually worn between July 1937 and early 1938. (Credit: John Coy)

SA cap with black top and silver button indicating the Berlin-Brandenburg district. Note the curvature of the flap which is practically straight down to the front. (Credit: Niall Malcolm)

SA cap for Berlin-Brandenburg in the heavier cloth. Note the closure of the flaps. (Credit: Al Ex)

Right: Detailed photograph providing an excellent view at the fine workmanship of this cap. (Credit: Al Ex)

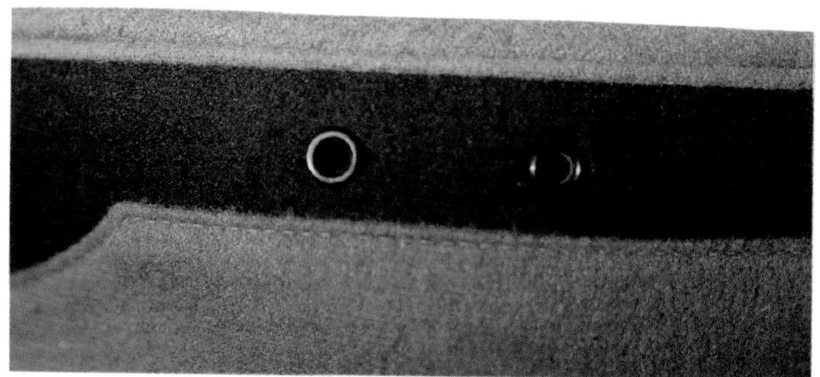

Same cap, but photographed from the side. The flaps are stitched to the body of the cap. The grommets are correctly installed in black to the black top. (Credit: Al Ex)

SA cap for the Ostmark district, with silver button. This cap was probably worn by a person who was transferred from another area to this SA group, thus, a new colored top was employed. No grommets are visible. (Credit: John Coy)

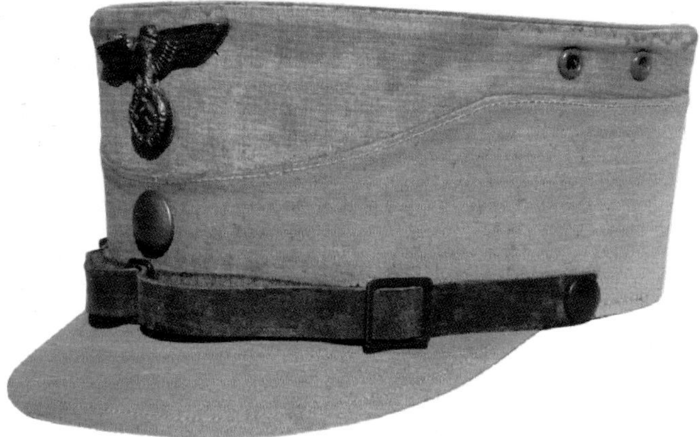

As above, but with a gilt button. Note the rare shade of the pinkish-red, which was probably caused by fading. The color of the grommets indicates the original color was probably dark wine-red. (Credit: John Coy)

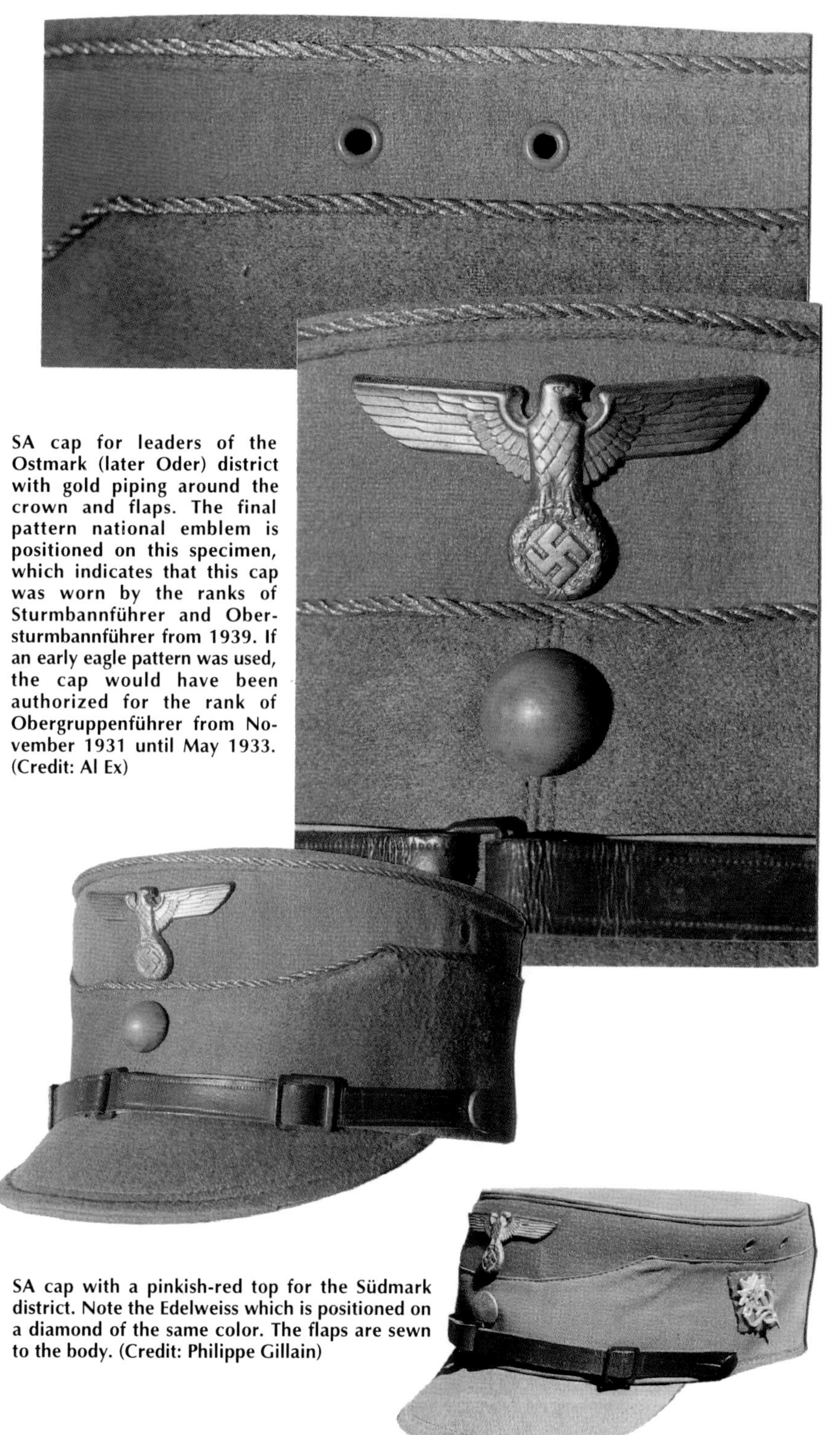

SA cap for leaders of the Ostmark (later Oder) district with gold piping around the crown and flaps. The final pattern national emblem is positioned on this specimen, which indicates that this cap was worn by the ranks of Sturmbannführer and Obersturmbannführer from 1939. If an early eagle pattern was used, the cap would have been authorized for the rank of Obergruppenführer from November 1931 until May 1933. (Credit: Al Ex)

SA cap with a pinkish-red top for the Südmark district. Note the Edelweiss which is positioned on a diamond of the same color. The flaps are sewn to the body. (Credit: Philippe Gillain)

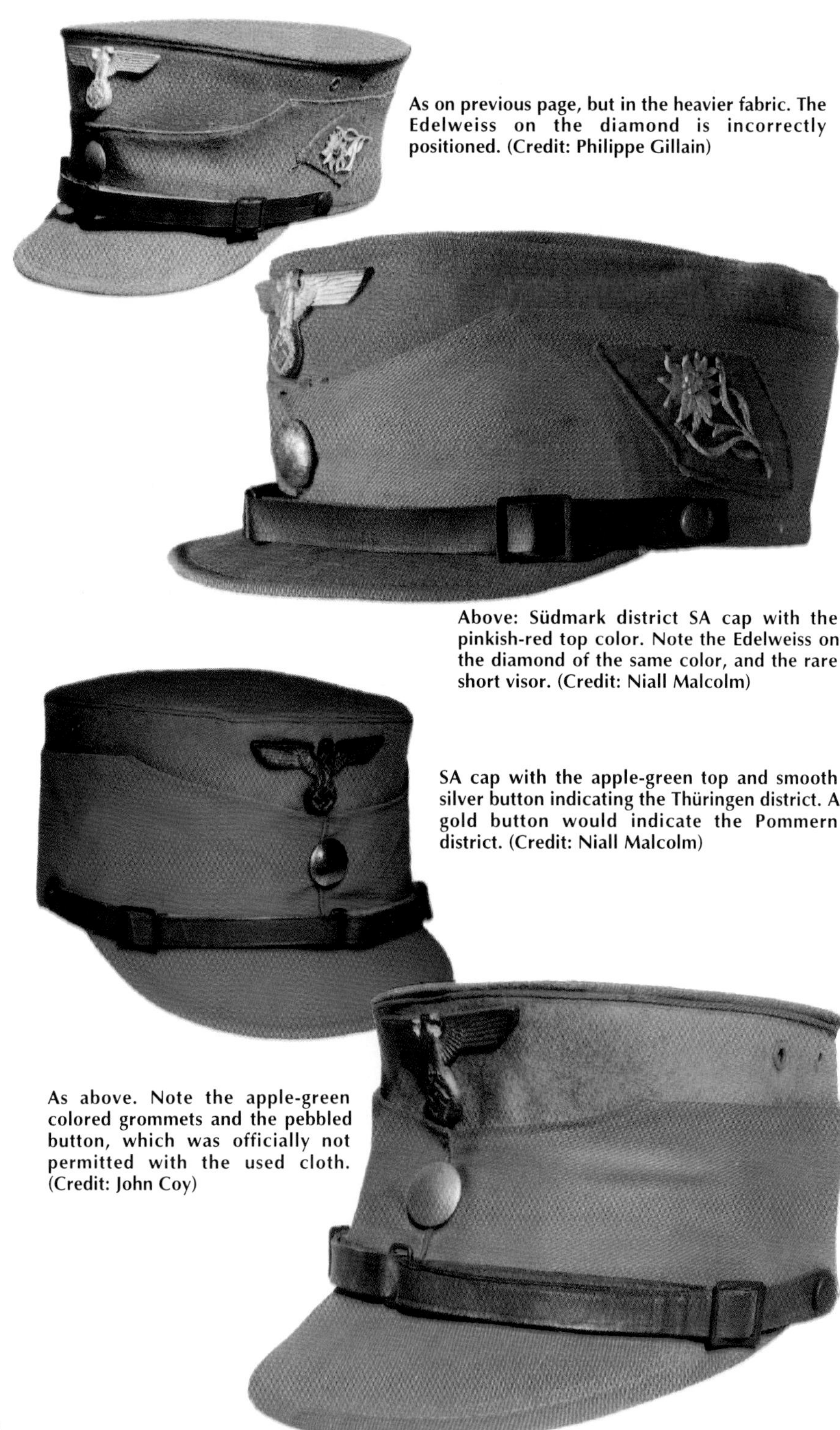

As on previous page, but in the heavier fabric. The Edelweiss on the diamond is incorrectly positioned. (Credit: Philippe Gillain)

Above: Südmark district SA cap with the pinkish-red top color. Note the Edelweiss on the diamond of the same color, and the rare short visor. (Credit: Niall Malcolm)

SA cap with the apple-green top and smooth silver button indicating the Thüringen district. A gold button would indicate the Pommern district. (Credit: Niall Malcolm)

As above. Note the apple-green colored grommets and the pebbled button, which was officially not permitted with the used cloth. (Credit: John Coy)

SA kepi for the Pommern district with apple-green top and gold button. Note the black/white piping, indicating this cap was worn in this form since July 1933. Earlier, the Ostsee district in which Pommern-east and west were located, had either a green/yellow or blue/yellow (Mecklenburg) crown piping . The apple-green top was allowed for wear then by only a few persons. (Credit: Len Champion)

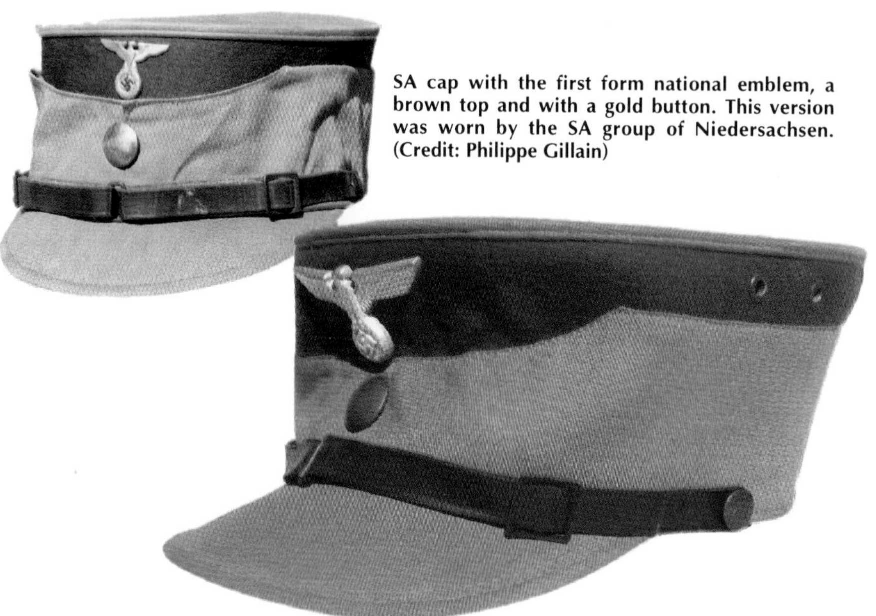

SA cap with the first form national emblem, a brown top and with a gold button. This version was worn by the SA group of Niedersachsen. (Credit: Philippe Gillain)

As above, but with a somewhat darker brown top and a gilt button. This form cap was manufactured according to October 1937 manufacturing regulations. The panels are sewn directly to the top. (Credit: John Coy)

An SA cap with Obergruppenführer Tresse, having a Westmark colored top, being dark brown, and a silver colored button. The reason for the dark brown top could indicate a person holding a honorary rank per early 1934 orders which permitted such persons to wear the standard color of the district. This practice was uncommon in the SA. The eagle style indicates an early form. It is unknown why an embroidered national emblem is used, and the use of Tresse denoting the rank of Obergruppenführer was not allowed for honorary ranks. The inside has a RZM tag with Nr. 104, being manufactured by J.C. Kornacker of Hildesheim-Hannover. (Credit: Ulric of England)

Above: Enlisted ranks SA cap for the Nordmark district with emerald-green top and gilt button. Note the wear of the final form national emblem, as introduced in July 1937. Caps with the same color top, but with a silver button, were worn in the Sachsen district. (Credit: Len Champion)

Right: SA cap with emerald-green top and a silver button, as worn by the SA group of Sachsen. (Credit: Philippe Gillain)

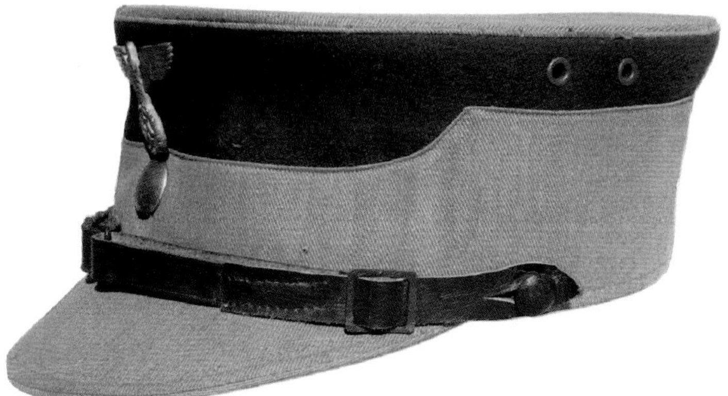

SA cap, according to the 1937 regulations with emerald green top and silver button, as used by the group of Sachsen. (Credit: John Coy)

Early form SA cap for a lower-ranked SA leader with a green top, early national emblem, and silver button. The color green was also worn by Austrian units until 1934, but in such a case a red/white piping was to be installed. In 1934 the green was changed into red-brown. Note the positioning of an embroidered, second form Edelweiss insignia on the same colored backing. The wearing of this insignia was unofficial. (Credit: John Coy)

SA cap for a Nordmark district leader with silver crown piping as well as black/white flap piping worn, with the early form national emblem. Note that instead of green, brown grommets are used. (Credit: Niall Malcolm)

SA cap with orange-yellow colored top and silver button for the Südwest district. Note the matching colored grommets and the cut of the flap, which is uncommon. (Credit: John Coy)

As above, but in the form according to 1937 manufacturing regulations. (Credit: John Coy)

SA cap with orange-yellow top, but for the Elbe district, having a gold colored button. Note that only one grommet is used. (Credit: Niall Malcolm)

SA leaders cap with the Tresse as ordered for Standartenführer, being 1.0cm with two "Balletten." Note that no ventilation grommets are visible on this orange-yellow top used by the districts Mitte (in August 1942 renamed Elbe) and Südwest (renamed Neckar at the same time). A silver piping is added to the edge of the flap indicating a cap used since the early war years. Before then, the two-colored piping was worn by the Standartenführer rank of position. (Credit: Art Sylvie)

A SA cap for Oberführer or Brigadeführer, with a crown piping and the 1.5cm wide Tresse. The two-colored piping is black/orange-yellow. The color of the top is also orange-yellow. This color was worn by the Südwest district, but in this case, the button should be silver and not gold. The gold button and orange-yellow top were worn by the Mitte district, but if this was the case, then the two-colored piping should have been black/white. (Credit: Francis Catella Collection)

SA cap worn by district Franken, denoted by the gold button. Officially, it was unauthorized to position a gold national emblem with the kepi. With the heavier cloth the smooth button is also incorrect. (Credit: Niall Malcolm)

SA cap for a lower-ranked SA leader from the Schlesien district, indicated by the silver button and the black/white crown piping. The grommets should be in the same yellow color as the top. (Credit: Philippe Gillain)

A SA cap with a two-colored crown piping worn by ranks of Sturmführer through and including Sturmhauptführer. The top is sulfur-yellow; the piping has a golden/white shade. This form of piping was worn until July 1933 by the Schlesien district, when it was changed to black/white. It is, therefore, probable that this cap was worn until late 1933. (Credit: Al Ex)

SA kepi with a sulfur-yellow top and blue/white crown piping, as worn by a lower-ranked leader from the Franken district. (Credit: Jerry Drake)

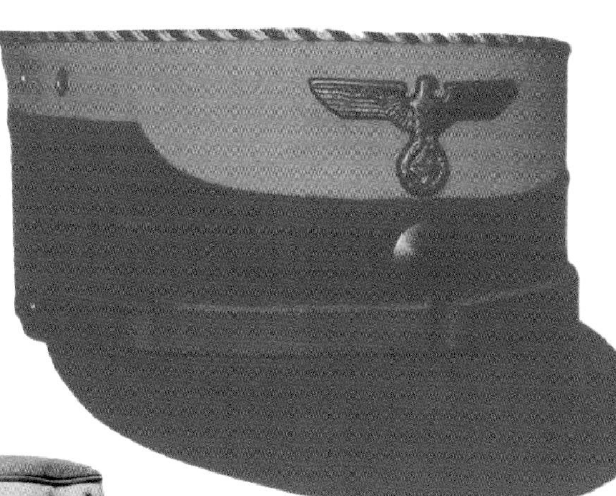

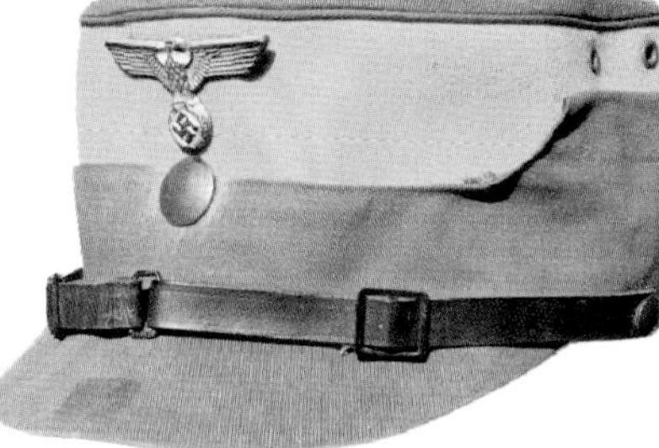

A SA cap with a sulfer-yellow top, gold button, and a late style national emblem. (Credit: Philippe Gillain)

Members of the SA from the district Hochland lined up during an early wartime celebration. Note the wearing of a light blue top and the various heights for these caps. (Credit: Richard Valdez)

SA kepi from group Hochland with light blue top and silver button. The body is light brown khaki. Note the curvature of the flap and the use of brown grommets. (Credit: Niall Malcolm)

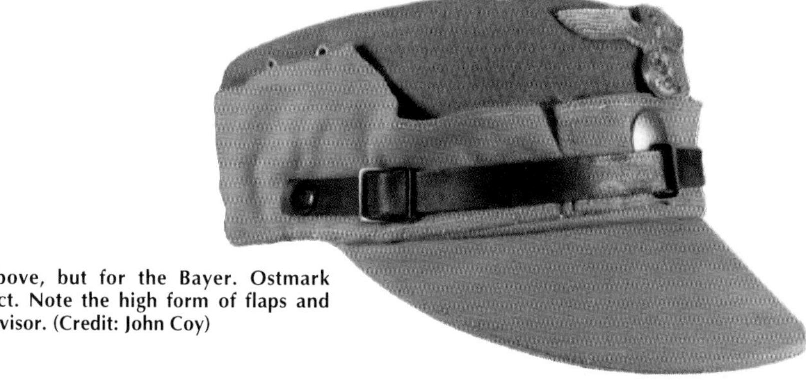

As above, but for the Bayer. Ostmark district. Note the high form of flaps and large visor. (Credit: John Coy)

SA-Gruppe Hochland SA cap. Note that the position of the Edelweiss is too high. According to regulations it was to be attached on the flap. The top color is light blue, but due to aging has faded to a greyish tone. (Credit: John Coy)

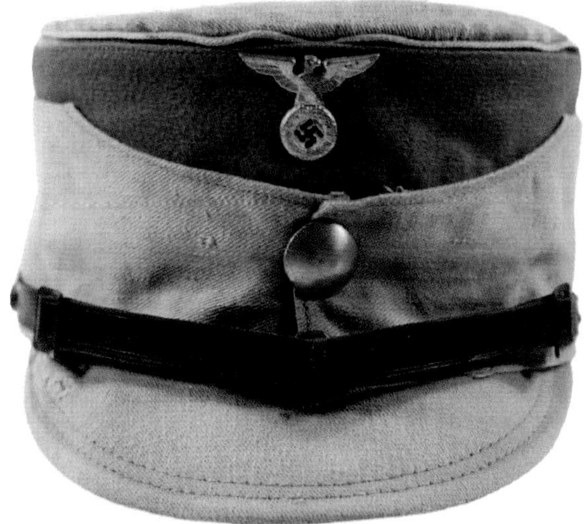

SA cap with blue top and gold button for the Bayer. Ostmark district. This district was later renamed Bayernwald. (Credit: H.v. Diggelen)

Interior of cap. Some areas of Franken were shifted to the BO district. The earlier sulfur-yellow top was removed. Simultaneously, the grommets were also removed so the new top color would fit better. (Credit: H.v. Diggelen)

SA cap in heavier material with a light blue top and silver button. In this form, the cap should have been worn within the Hochland district, but no Edelweiss is present. Note also that brown grommets are used and that the blue is much too bright. The eagle is a first army version. (Credit: Philippe Gillain)

SA cap in heavier cloth for the Smaller Service Dress according to the 1937 manufacturing regulations, with a steel-green top and silver button, indicating the Kurpfalz district. (Credit: Niall Malcolm)

SA cap with steel-green top as worn by the districts Nordsee and Kurpfalz. Instead of the regular button, the SA cockade is positioned. Officially this was never permitted on this form of cap. (Credit: Niall Malcolm)

SA cap with steel-green top and silver button for the Kurpfalz district. Note the green color of the grommets, but the incorrect positioning. They should have been installed horizontally in a single line. (Credit: John Coy)

Rare example of a SA cap, referred to as a garrison cap for SA leaders, with the steel-green top, gold button, and gold piping for the Nordsee district. Until September 1937 the metal, first national eagle emblem was worn and was replaced by the woven triangular emblem. The cap body is soft with no framework, and the visor is easy to fold. On this specimen, the flaps are not directly sewn to the body. Note there is practically no curvature to the flaps. (Credit: H.v. Diggelen)

SA cap with navy-blue top and silver button as used by the SA district of Hessen. If the button was gilt the cap would have been used in the Hansa district. No grommets are visible. (Credit: John Coy)

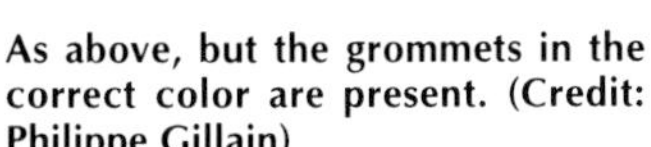

As above, but the grommets in the correct color are present. (Credit: Philippe Gillain)

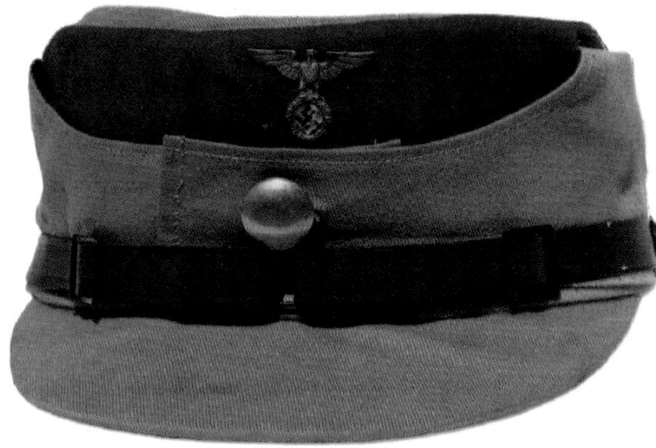

SA cap possibly used by the Hilfswerk Nordwest units between August 1934 and the summer of 1938. The top color is a reddish-brown, the button is silver. The Hilfswerk Nordwest units were SA members from Austria, living in "exile" in the south of Germany. (Credit: Nigel Cox)

SA cap in heavier cloth with a blue-grey top and gold button, as used by the SA groups from Sudeten. (Credit: John Coy)

SA cap manufactured according to the 1937 regulations. The flaps are sewn directly to the body of this Sudeten kepi with gilt button and final form national emblem. (Credit: Philippe Gillain)

SA cap with cornflower-blue top and grommets. This color was used by the districts Warthe and Oberrhein. The first used silver and the second SA group the gilt button. Officially, with this color, a first form national emblem could never be worn, since the color for Warthe was introduced in March 1940, and for Oberrhein in March 1941. The second form eagle is the correct form. (Credit: Niall Malcolm)

A SA higher leader's cap worn by Oberführer and Brigadeführer. This rare example has a bright grey colored top which was used by the unit from the Generalgouvernement (Poland, the area between Warsaw, Cracow, and Lemberg). Bright grey was introduced on September 1, 1942 and worn for about two years. The Tresse is an unofficial form. Its usage is not unique because of stock shortages during the war. (Credit: R. Kindel)

SA cap with a light blue-grey colored top and golden button. It is believed this cap was worn by SAR II or Generalgouvernement units. Note the tapering of the top. The eagle, used by state organizations, is an incorrect form. (Credit: Philippe Gillain)

SA mountain cap for leaders having the diamond and Edelweiss insigne for Austrian units, specifically the Südmark as the top is pinkish-red. The two buttons for the flap are pebbled silver. (Credit: Wolfe-Hardin)

Cap as above, but for enlisted ranks. This cap is officially designated as "Dienstmütze für Jägereinheiten" for the Südmark district, due to the pinkish-red top and the Edelweiss flower on the same colored diamond. Often this type of cap is incorrectly referred to as the "Einheitsfeldmütze 43." (Credit: Ed Stadnicki)

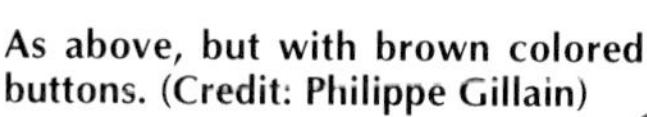

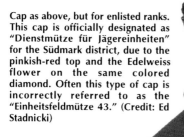

As above, but with brown colored buttons. (Credit: Philippe Gillain)

A semi-stiff SA cap without colored top as worn and authorized with the brown shirt until September 1933. The crown is piped in gold and worn by Sturmbannführer through Brigadeführer (for districts having the gold front button). This form was also allowed for wear in 1931 by the Reichszeugmeister and the managers of departments, the leader of the signals staff of the OSAF, OSAF officials and the adjutants of the chief of staff, the "Untergruppe" and/or "Standarte." (Credit: Niall Malcolm)

SA kepi in the material ordered for the Greater Service Dress, beautifully shaped with a bright red top, early national emblem and a silver button. The color for the top is for members of a staff. In this case, a lower-ranked SA person was possibly assigned to a staff. (Credit: Len Champion)

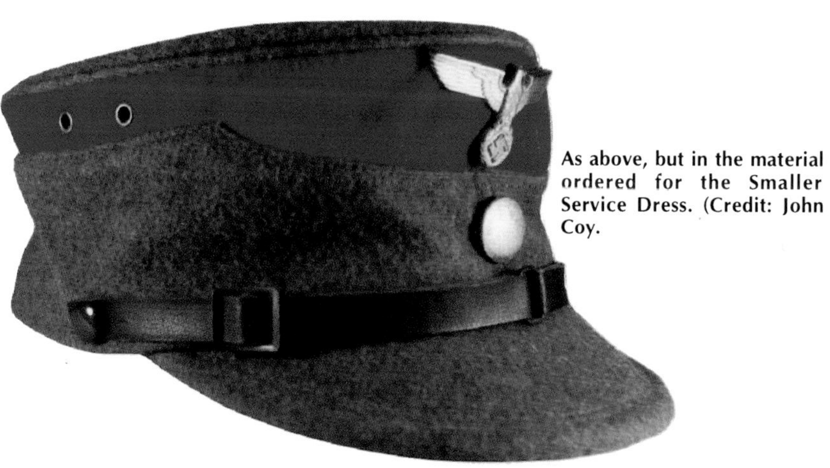

As above, but in the material ordered for the Smaller Service Dress. (Credit: John Coy.

A SA cap in gabardine material worn by a lower-ranked member of a staff in the district Hessen-Nassau-Süd until approximately 1940. The crown piping is blue/red. The national emblem is aged, giving it a dark appearance. (Credit: H.v. Diggelen)

SA cap manufactured according to the 1937 regulations for a staff member. Due to wartime regulations, the silver crown piping was to be worn by the "unteres Führerkorps," being Hauptsturmführer, Obersturmführer and Sturmführer, with a silver button. (Credit: Niall Malcolm)

SA cap for wear by a mid-level leader according to the 1940 regulations for the staff of the Südmark district, and the regions Steiermark and Kärnten. Probably due to a promotion, the flap piping was installed by hand. The ventilation holes are in a contrasting light pink color. With this cap, the Edelweiss and the final form national emblem had to be worn. (Credit: Ed Stadnicki)

SA cap with a bright red top as worn by the rank of Standartenführer within a group staff. The two-colored piping may indicate the staff for Nordmark. (Credit: Niall Malcolm)

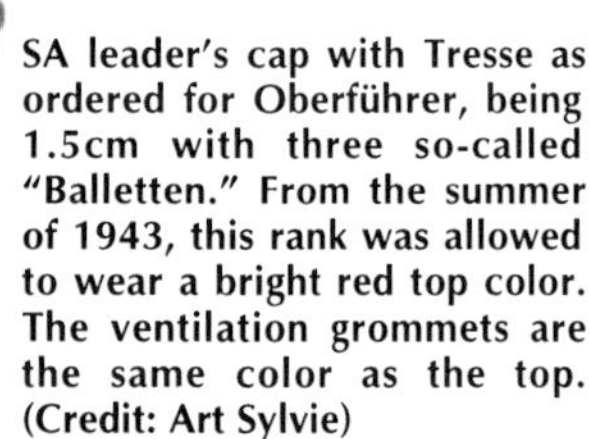

SA leader's cap with Tresse as ordered for Oberführer, being 1.5cm with three so-called "Balletten." From the summer of 1943, this rank was allowed to wear a bright red top color. The ventilation grommets are the same color as the top. (Credit: Art Sylvie)

A high leader's cap with a 2cm variation Tresse, as introduced in 1933 for Gruppenführer and Obergruppenführer until the war's end. In 1937, the final form national eagle emblem was introduced and required for wear The color of the ventilation grommets is the correct bright red color of the cap top. (Credit: Ron Kwan)

Detail of the 2cm Tresse and piping worn along the edge of the flap of the SA staff leader's cap at lower left. (Credit: Ron Kwan)

SA staff leader's cap, but with the official 1936 Tresse. (Credit: Philippe Gillain)

A SA higher leader's cap with a 2cm silver Tresse and an approximately 4mm wide red middle stripe. This red stripe is the exact same color as the top. No regulation has been found describing this rare form of Tresse, but for a short period of four weeks (between January 12th and February 14th 1934), an unknown Tresse form was worn experimentally by the positions of "Stabsführer," as well as "Referenten." (Credit: Ed Stadnicki)

Detail of the Tresse shown above. The pattern for the red middle stripe has vertical ribbing. (Credit: Ed Stadnicki)

A SA cap in the heavier material ordered for wear with the tunic with a 1937 pattern national emblem. A gold Tresse is positioned on this cap. For a short period, between July 1933 and February 1934, this was permitted for the rank of Standartenführer in districts with a gold button. However, when used, the two-colored piping was to be positioned on the edge of the flap. If the cap was meant for wear by staff members then the gold Tresse should have interwoven red. The top of this cap is crimson indicating service in the SA high command. It must be noted that from June 1936 this form of gold Tresse was abolished. (Credit: Ed Stadnicki)

An extremely rare SA cap with a crimson colored top for wear from February 1934 by SA staff leaders serving as department leaders within the OSAF staff, staff leaders for an Obergruppe, Gruppe, Brigade and others as specified in the text. The Tresse is gold and has two interwoven stripes in a pattern which was also worn as a chevron for long service in the SA. The flaps for this cap are piped in crimson/gold. This two-colored piping was worn around the crown by lower-ranked staff leaders of the OSAF in the ranks of Sturmführer through and including Sturmhauptführer. The color of the top was also crimson. (Credit: Ed Stadnicki)

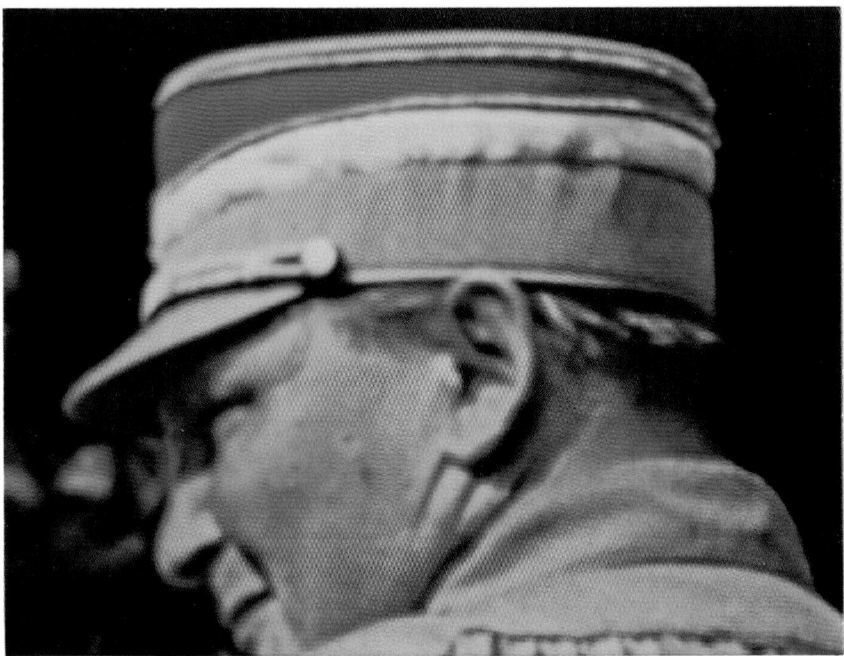

Hermann Göring wears a SA cap with cords instead of the regulation leather chin strap. Note that these cords have knots as worn by political leaders. The wearing of cords was at no time officially authorized in the SA. Their introduction was probably intended for a short time as this was also planned for the NSKK in the summer of 1936. On most occasions, changes relating to the SA cap were not implemented while the SA high command continued the old traditions. Göring also wore the cords during the Party Day Rally at Nürnberg in 1934 and probably for a short period of time in 1938. It is believed that he wore the old form of SA uniform at this time. (Credit: Jill Halcomb Smith)

Stabschef Lutze's SA cap with gold buttons, pipings and special Tresse as authorized for this position. Note the hand-embroidered national emblem on the same bright red backing as on the top. (Credit: Wolfe-Hardin)

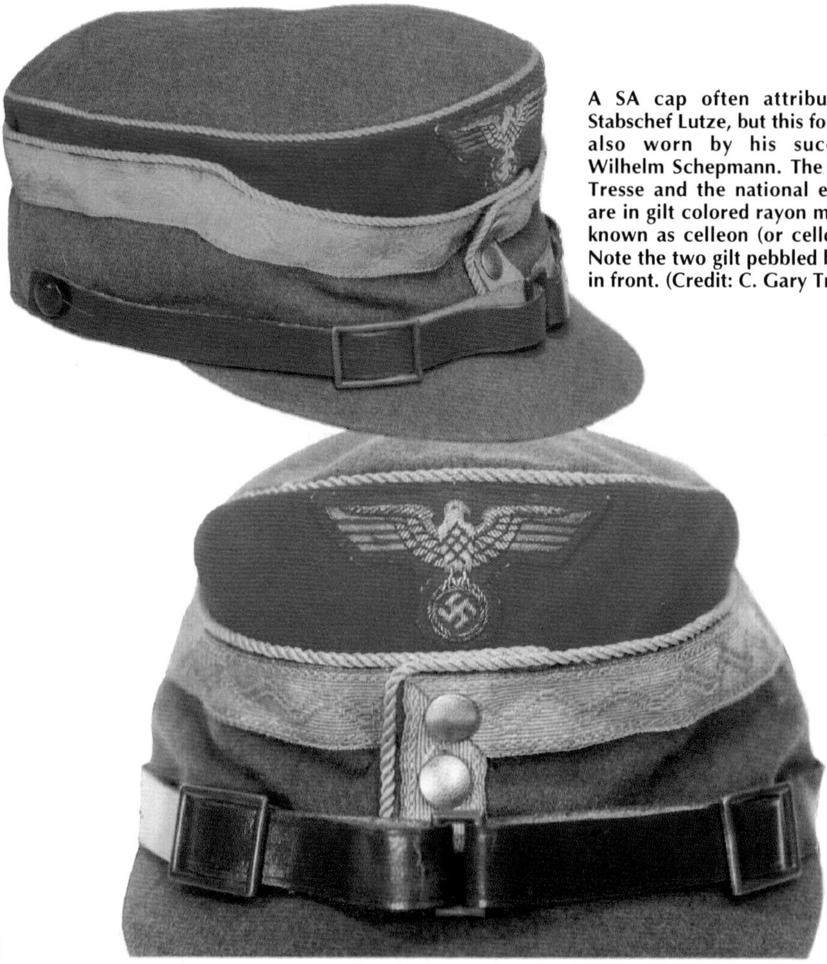

A SA cap often attributed to Stabschef Lutze, but this form was also worn by his successor, Wilhelm Schepmann. The piping, Tresse and the national emblem are in gilt colored rayon material, known as celleon (or cellophan). Note the two gilt pebbled buttons in front. (Credit: C. Gary Triggs)

Headgear for Special SA-Formations

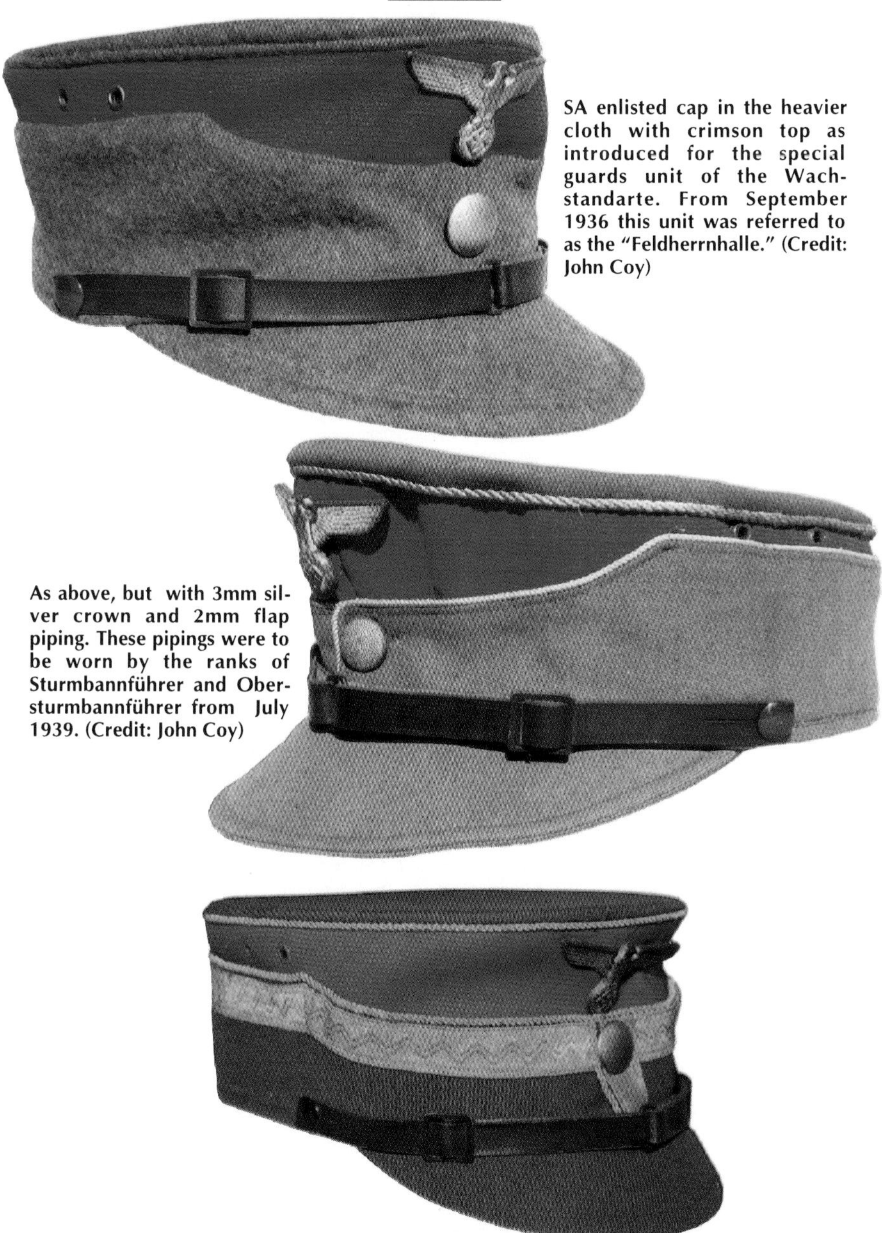

SA enlisted cap in the heavier cloth with crimson top as introduced for the special guards unit of the Wachstandarte. From September 1936 this unit was referred to as the "Feldherrnhalle." (Credit: John Coy)

As above, but with 3mm silver crown and 2mm flap piping. These pipings were to be worn by the ranks of Sturmbannführer and Obersturmbannführer from July 1939. (Credit: John Coy)

A SA high leader's cap with 2cm official pattern Tresse as ordered for persons with the rank of Gruppenführer and Obergruppenführer from 1939 through 1945. The top of this cap is a variation shade of the pinkish-red indicating a higher ranked leader for the SA group of Ostmark. If a slightly wrong top color was used, it could also be for a member of the OSAF staff or a high-ranked leader of the special SA unit "Feldherrnhalle." (Credit: Dick Deeter)

This form of visored cap replaced the kepi for the SA-Feldjägerkorps in May 1935 when this unit was incorporated into the Schutzpolizei. The cap top is olive-green with a white cap band and white pipings. Note the gilt police pattern national emblem. (Credit: Bill Rentz)

SA Lagermütze: Prior to the introduction of the woven silver wire national emblem, a metal national emblem in the early form was worn upon a colored felt triangle. This example has a brown backing indicating SA district Niedersachsen, as the button is gilt. If the button was in silver the district would be Westmark. (Credit: Jill Halcomb Smith)

Unique SA Lagermütze for the SA district of Hochland with unofficial light blue/white piping around the crown of the cap. On the garrison cap, no pipings were allowed. Note the 1937 style national emblem on a light blue triangle with white machine-woven eagle. A metal Edelweiss is positioned behind the triangle. (Credit: Edwin Johnson)

A SA Lagermütze in brown SA fabric with the second pattern insigne. The silver wire, machine-woven national emblem on a black triangle and a matte, gilt, pebbled front button indicate the Niederrhein district. Note the single grommet.

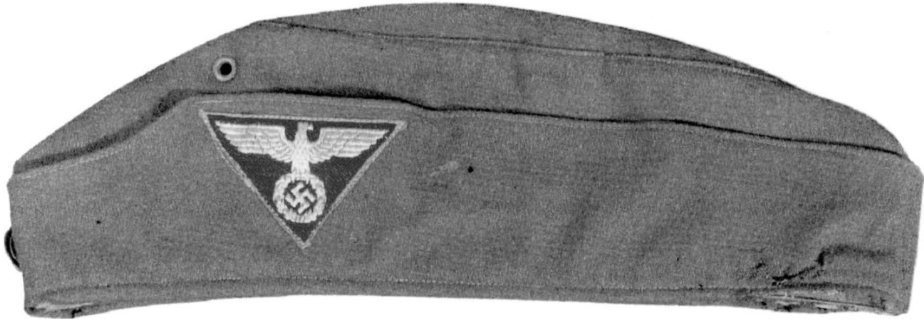

A garrison cap with the final form of woven triangle positioned on the left side. No regulation was found ordering the wear of the garrison cap at camps or schools. But with the introduction of this form of headdress, the cap known as Übungsmütze lost its importance and the new form of cap was worn. The brownish-red backing of the triangle indicates that schools all over Germany may have utilized this same color. Otherwise, a triangle in light blue would have been worn. This cap is attributed by markings to SA-Group-School Hochland. At RFS schools this form of headdress was also worn, but with the appropriate district triangle. The color red-brown was also used by districts Donau and Alpenland, and approaches the color as used with this triangle. (Credit: Ulric of England)

SA garrison cap in a greenish color with a light blue triangle and gilt button indicating the Bayer. Ostmark district. SA members serving in VGAD units along German borders wore this form of cap with insignia. It is believed that a VGAD unit at the borders of Sudetenland wore this form of headdress with regular insignia in 1938. (Credit: Ed Stadnicki)

A cap in the form often worn by members of SA-Wehrmannschaft units during the war. This cap is referred to as "Dienstmütze für Jägereinheiten." The triangle is in cornflower-blue, as ordered for the districts Warthe (March 1940) and Oberrhein (March 1941). In both cases, the crown piping, as well as the button color, should be either aluminum or silver. The district Oberrhein was later instituted as the Warthe district. According to standard procedures Oberrhein would have received the authorization for a gold crown piping and buttons. But with an official publication in May 1941, the button was already ordered, which was to be in silver, to simplify insignia and uniform parts. Gold items were then, in fact, abolished. To show a difference between Warthe and Oberrhein, a yellow or "gold"-colored celleon piping was ordered as a distinction around the collar (depending on rank). It is possible that the manufacturer of this cap may have misunderstood the confusing orders. The last mentioned order had not yet been released to the press. (Credit: Ed Stadnicki)

Triangle for the garrison cap and other forms of headgear. The white machine-woven national emblem is positioned on a wine-red backing, indicating the districts Ostland, the later Tannenberg (with gilt button) and Westfalen (with silver button). (Credit: Jill Halcomb Smith)

The woven national emblem for the garrison cap which was introduced in 1937. The apple-green triangle is 60mm wide and in the color for SA district Thüringen (with silver button) and Pommern (with gilt button). (Credit: H.v. Diggelen)

The first pattern insigne for the naval garrison cap was a cloth triangle, officially in cornflower-blue, upon which was positioned the first form national emblem. It is believed, but not officially stated in any regulation or document, that sometime in 1938, a yellow or golden, woven later form national emblem was authorized, but rarely worn. (Credit: Otto Spronk)

SA white woven national emblem on a wine-red triangle. The backing is in the same red. (Credit: Otto Spronk)

An unused RAZ insigne. The backing is khaki-colored material. The lettering, circle edge and eagle (note the long wings) are white. The inner circle is bright red and the background of the swastika is black. The details of the eagle and wreath are in khaki-colored thread. (Credit: Otto Spronk)

The RAZ cloth insigne positioned on the left flap, at the corner of the curvature. Note that the official RAZ symbol had the wording Reichspropagandaleitung while the insigne for the headdress reads Reichsautozug. (Credit: Derek Chapman)

A "Matrozenmütze" worn by members of a water or sea sport school of the SA. The light blue tally is woven in grey with the Gothic lettering: "SA-Seesportübungslager Heilbronn." (Credit: Ulric of England)

Early Marine-SA visored cap with a gilt wire wreath, in the form formerly used by the Imperial navy, and a silvered early pattern of national emblem. (Credit: James J. Boulton)

Marine-SA visored cap with the final form of wreath in gilt. Note the gilt eagle, indicating the cap was worn after May 1938. Between August 1937 and May 1938 the silver version was officially ordered. Note that there are no grommets in the top. (Credit: John Coy)

Marine-SA visored cap with gold cap cords. No regulation allowed the wear of these cords, but it is known that higher-ranked leaders occasionally wore them. Probably, this was caused by NSKK orders. In late 1941 leaders of NSKK motorboat units were ordered to wear cords instead of the leather chin strap. (Credit: Ulric of England)

Final pattern Marine-SA visored cap with gilt eagle emblem, high-styled embroidered wreath, and SA-style cockade. Note the cloth cap band instead of the ribbed pattern, the single ventilation hole, and the black chin strap button. (Credit: Jay Jeandron)

The SA-Führer Lagermütze, which is most often a camp or school form of headdress. This form does not have a framework, making it easy to fold. The manufacturing is according to the late 1937 standards. The flaps are sewn directly to the body. The color for the top, which is crimson, as well as the same colored cloth triangle with national emblem, and matching grommets, was officially ordered for this type of cap. It is believed this cap was worn at the Reichsführerschule or any other SA school on Reich level. In September 1937 extensive wearing regulations were published. (Credit: John Coy)

A SA cap, in accordance with 1937 manufacturing guidelines, often used by staff members of a camp or school. In this case, for Austria: The bright red triangle with national emblem in cloth is worn, as well as a diamond backing in the same color for the Edelweiss. Note the matching grommets, being bright red as well. (Credit: John Coy)

A SA cap, in accordance with early 1937 manufacturing procedures, has a woven white national emblem on a bright red top. This cap is not the standard SA kepi, but a SA garrison cap for leaders introduced in early 1937. The bright red top indicates group staff members. It is often difficult to identify a cap in this style in photographs. (Credit: David Littlejohn)

A cap used at Gruppenschule Hochland, as indicated by the stamp inside. This cap of olive-brown fabric in the regular SA or mountain cap style, is probably an experimental sample as it differs from the official form. The flap is closed by a silver pebbled button. Note the dark brown chin strap and the special adoption of a lower curvature to fit this strap. This sample had the brown or red-brown cap top for Ausbildungswesen, but this was removed. Small pieces of colored top cloth are still present in the crown seam, but it is mainly indicated by the brownish-red grommets on the sides. (Credit: Ulric of England)